Oracle High Availability, Disaster Recovery, and Cloud Services

Explore RAC, Data Guard, and Cloud Technology

Y V Ravi Kumar
Nassyam Basha
Krishna Kumar K M
Bal Mukund Sharma
Konstantin Kerekovski

Apress®

Oracle High Availability, Disaster Recovery, and Cloud Services

Y V Ravi Kumar
Chennai, Tamil Nadu, India

Bal Mukund Sharma
Belmont, CA, USA

Nassyam Basha
Riyadh, Saudi Arabia

Konstantin Kerekovski
Pinellas Park, FL, USA

Krishna Kumar K M
Bangalore, Karnataka, India

ISBN-13 (pbk): 978-1-4842-4350-3
https://doi.org/10.1007/978-1-4842-4351-0

ISBN-13 (electronic): 978-1-4842-4351-0

Managing Director, Apress Media LLC: Welmoed Spahr
Acquisitions Editor: Celestin Suresh John
Development Editor: Matthew Moodie
Coordinating Editor: Aditee Mirashi

Cover designed by eStudioCalamar

Cover image designed by Freepik (www.freepik.com)

Distributed to the book trade worldwide by Springer Science+Business Media New York, 233 Spring Street, 6th Floor, New York, NY 10013. Phone 1-800-SPRINGER, fax (201) 348-4505, e-mail orders-ny@springer-sbm.com, or visit www.springeronline.com. Apress Media, LLC is a California LLC and the sole member (owner) is Springer Science + Business Media Finance Inc (SSBM Finance Inc). SSBM Finance Inc is a **Delaware** corporation.

For information on translations, please e-mail rights@apress.com, or visit www.apress.com/rights-permissions.

Apress titles may be purchased in bulk for academic, corporate, or promotional use. eBook versions and licenses are also available for most titles. For more information, reference our Print and eBook Bulk Sales web page at www.apress.com/bulk-sales.

Any source code or other supplementary material referenced by the author in this book is available to readers on GitHub via the book's product page, located at www.apress.com/978-1-4842-4350-3. For more detailed information, please visit www.apress.com/source-code.

Printed on acid-free paper

Table of Contents

About the Authors

Yenugula Venkata Ravi Kumar (YVR) is an Oracle ACE Director and Oracle Certified Master (OCM) with 21+ years of experience in the banking, financial services, and insurance (BFSI) verticals. He has played various roles such as vice president (DBA), senior database architect, and senior specialist production DBA. He is also an OCP in Oracle 8i to 12c and Oracle certified in GoldenGate, RAC, performance tuning, and Oracle engineered systems (Exadata and ODA).

He has written 100+ articles for the Oracle Technology Network (in Spanish, Portuguese, and English), OraWorld, UKOUG, OTech Magazine, and Redgate. He is an Oracle speaker at @OOW, @IOUG, @NYOUG, @OTN, @AIOUG, @Sangam, and @SOUG. He designed, architected, and implemented the core banking system (CBS) database for the central banks of two countries, India and Mahe, Seychelles. He also coauthored *Oracle Database Upgrade and Migration Methods*, published by Apress.

Nassyam Basha is a technology expert with 11 years of Oracle Database experience. He holds a master's degree in computer science. In 2014 he became an Oracle Database 11g Certified Master. Nassyam was honored with the title of Oracle ACE Director in 2015 based on his extraordinary contributions to the Oracle community. He was the second Oracle ACE Director in India in the area of database management. He is board member of the Oracle RACSIG team. He actively participates in Oracle-related forums, such as OTN, Oracle Lists (with the status of Super Hero), and Oracle Support (with the title of Guru), and acts as an OTN moderator. He has deep knowledge in the business fields of finance, retail, health, manufacturing, and consulting.

He started his career with dBase and FoxPro, and participated in several projects with FoxPro and Oracle Database from Oracle 7. He currently works as a database expert with eProseed. Nassyam co-wrote his first book on Oracle Data Guard 11gR2 in 2013 and co-wrote *Oracle Database Upgrade and Migration Methods* in 2017. He has written more than 50 articles and published in OTN, IOUG, Oracle Scene, and various other portals on technologies such as Data Guard, EM 13c, RAC, Oracle Cloud, 12c DB, GDS/GSM and sharding technologies.

In 2012 Nassyam started presenting at various user group conferences, such as OTN Yathra, AIOUG Tech Days, and SANGAM, and appeared at international conferences such as OOW, TROUG, and OUGF. Nassyam maintains an Oracle technology blog (`www.oracle-ckpt.com`). Feel free to contact him at `nassyambasha@gmail.com`.

K M Krishna Kumar is a database administrator with 14 years of experience with Oracle Database (8i to 18c). He has a master's degree in business administration from Anna University. He started his career in 2004 as an Oracle database administrator and has been working with Oracle Corporation for the last eight years. He has expertise in Oracle Database installation, patching, upgrades, migration, Data Guard, RMAN, RAC, backup, and recovery. He is also proficient in Oracle public, private, and hybrid cloud environments. He is an Oracle 11g and 12c certified professional on an Oracle Cloud infrastructure. He has delivered presentations to customers through various channels. He actively participates in Oracle-related forums such as OTN communities. He is a Oracle speaker at @Oracle Open World, @OTN, @AIOUG, and @Sangam. He coauthored the book *Oracle Database Upgrade and Migration Methods*, published by Apress. He is reachable at `kmkittu2005@gmail.com`.

Bal Sharma works for Oracle America as a product manager of Oracle Cloud infrastructure. He is an Oracle Certified Professional (OCP) with 14 years of experience across various industries such as telecom, healthcare, financial services, and insurance; he has played various roles such as database manager, technical lead DBA, and content architect. He holds several certifications across the Oracle Cloud infrastructure and Oracle 10g/11g/12c, is certified in RAC and Oracle Exadata, and has a deep understanding of information technology and public cloud services. In his recent role, he advises customers on the adoption of cloud platforms, digital transformation, and database technologies such as high availability and engineered systems on the Oracle Cloud infrastructure. He is also setting up a database and infrastructure strategy for the largest banks and telcos in India and the United States and has led various complex implementations at top banks and telcos in India.

Bal is an avid technologist and believes customer satisfaction is of prime importance. His work with customers such as the State Bank of India, HDFC, Idea Cellular, and the Reliance Group is a testimonial for this.

Besides this, Bal enjoys cooking for friends and family.

Konstantin Kerekovski is an Oracle professional with more than six years of experience in the financial services industry. He is a member of the Independent Oracle User Group, Suncoast Oracle User Group, and New York Oracle User Group. He has worked as a senior and lead database administrator with production support duties in the financial services industry. He was a speaker at the OOW 17/18 IOUG 17/18, SOUG, and NYOUG meetings. He is an expert at Oracle Real Application Cluster technologies, ASM, GoldenGate, and Oracle 11g and 12c.

About the Technical Reviewer

Arup Nanda has been working in database management for 25 years and counting. With 6 books, more than 700 published articles, and 500 presentations in 22 countries, he is well known in the database area in general and Oracle technologies in particular. Today he is the chief data officer of Priceline.com in the New York area. He blogs at `arup.blogspot.com`.

Acknowledgments

I am grateful to God who gave us all the strength, courage, perseverance, and patience in this sincere and honest attempt of knowledge sharing. This second book of mine would not have been possible without the following people:

Shri Yenugula Venkata Pathi and Smt. Yenugula Krishna Kumari, my parents, instilled in me good thoughts and values. My uncle Shri K L Janardhan Rao (Tallapudi, AP) always encouraged me to work hard and be a step ahead in learning new things.

B. Suresh Kamath (founder of LaserSoft and Patterns), my mentor, my guru, my strength, and my guide, has inspired me for the last 21 years. He is an immensely talented and technically sound individual. He taught me how to be well-read with no compromises. He led by example in being content yet hungry of knowledge. He motivated me to go that extra mile in attempting and experimenting with newer technologies/environments and in being regularly out of my comfort zone.

Anitha Ravi Kumar, my wife, was immensely tolerant with me. "Behind every successful man, there is a good woman," as they say. I believe she is the embodiment of this well-known belief. Special thanks to my daughter, Sai Hansika, and my son, Sai Theeraz, for giving me time to write a second book.

I would like to thank Arup Nanda for accepting to be the technical reviewer for this book.

I would like to thank two people (Sateesh Prabakaran, SVP, and Puneet Dham, VP) from Raymond James Financial Inc. who extended their support in giving me expertise on the production side of Oracle engineered systems (Oracle Exadata, ODA, and ZFS systems).

Thanks to Mariami Kupatadze (senior solutions architect at FlashGrid Inc.) for excellent support when writing the Oracle sharding chapter.

Special thanks to two people, Jonathan Gennick (assistant editorial director) and Celestin Suresh John (senior manager, editorial acquisition), at Apress for giving me an opportunity to write a second book.

Thank you to the reader for picking up this book. We have attempted to be as simple and straightforward as possible when sharing this knowledge, and we truly believe that it will help you to steadily deep dive into various interesting concepts and procedures.

ACKNOWLEDGMENTS

I would also like to express my gratitude to the Oracle professionals Murali Vallath, Binay Rath, Mohit Singh (my RAC guru), Nassyam Basha, Krishna Kumar, Konstantin Kerekovski, Jennifer Nicholson (OTN), Bal Sharma, Archana Durai, and all of my LaserSoft colleagues.

—Y V Ravi Kumar

I would like to acknowledge all the people who have helped me write this book, both directly and indirectly.

First, I would like to thank my mother and father, Snejana and Roman Kerekovski, for their love, support, and constant encouragement.

Many thanks to Miladin Modrakovic for introducing me to Oracle and teaching me the trade from the time that I was a junior Oracle DBA. I would also like to thank Maryann Marnell for her professional guidance throughout my career.

Lastly, I would like to thank attorney Leonardo B. Perez III for protecting my legal interests.

—Konstantin Kerekovski

I would like to thank the Apress team who worked patiently until the end to produce an excellent book. This book is the result of continuous hours of work, and I hope you will find it extremely helpful. I thank the entire team for making it possible.

I would like to express my gratitude to Arup Nanda for the technical review of the entire book.

I would like to convey my sincere thanks to Jaikishan Tada and Vikash Palisetti for their great support, and special thanks to my management team for their support and encouragement.

Above all, I want to thank my wife, Swetha Ramesh, for standing beside me throughout my career and helping to complete this book. Her support and feedback helped me a lot to complete this book. I also want to thank my parents, Mohanram and Lalitha, and the rest of my family members, especially my brother, Ramkumar, who supported and heartened me to complete this book.

Also, I want to thank my friend Koushik Suresh who has been my motivation for continuing to improve my knowledge and move my career forward. I would like to thank my friend Velu Natarajan for his guidance in my DBA carrier.

Finally, last but not least, this book is dedicated to the Oracle database administrators around the world who work 24/7 in production environments.

All kinds of feedback, comments, and ideas are warmly welcomed. Any suggestions regarding the improvement of this book will be acknowledged.

—**Krishna Kumar**

I would like to thank the Apress team, my coauthors, and the technical reviewers for their great support and patience throughout the writing process. I must start by acknowledging the many IT professionals I have had the privilege of working alongside.

To start, to the team at Oracle USA, I would like to convey my sincere thanks to Oracle product manager and my mentor Rohit Rahi for technical guidance and enablement and to the Oracle Technology Sales Consulting Management group (Riz Mithani, Rich Hua, Steve Richardson, Carl Griffin, Tim Cowan, and Prasuj Loganathan) for encouraging me. To the team at Oracle India, thanks to Sandesh Naik and Dinesh Parekh for driving me to be better in life.

I would take a moment to thank my co-captain in life, my wife, my best friend, Suchitra, for standing beside me. Without her I would not have found my voice! I also want to thank my kids, Ishaanvi and Viransh; my parents; my brothers, Abhishek Kumar Suman and Rajesh Kumar Suman; and the rest of my family members.

Throughout my carrier I have been surrounded by an amazing set of mentors and colleagues. All have contributed in a big way, and this list would not be complete without Rashmi Ranjan Panda, Amit Kumar, and Kripa Sindhu. Thank you for being my friends as well as great colleagues.

—**Bal Sharma**

Above and beyond all others, I thank the Almighty and my parents, N.Abdul Aleem and Rahimunnisa.

Without their support, I wouldn't have been able to be what I am today. A special thanks to my family: my wife, Ayesha, and my daughter and my lucky charm, Yashfeen Fathima. I would also like to thank my brother, Nawaz Basha who has supported me all the time. Thanks to my family members Zaheer Ahmed, Farhana, Riyana, Aiman Fathima, Yaseen, Saad, and Maaz.

I would also like to express my gratitude to the Oracle Professionals Chinar Aliyev, Syed Jaffar, my first mentor Shahbaz sir, Emre Baransel, Michale Seberg, Franciso Munez Alvarez, Bjoern Rost, Andy Klock, Simon Pane, Javid Ur Rehman, Asif Momen, Syed Zaheer, and Monowar Mukul, and all the Oracle Community contributors across the world.

I thank my clients and colleagues who provided me with invaluable opportunities to expand my knowledge and shape my career.

ACKNOWLEDGMENTS

My heartfelt appreciation goes to the technical reviewer of this book, Arup Nanda, for the time he spent reviewing this book. I would like to thank the Apress team for giving us the opportunity to write this book and their support throughout. Last but not least, I would like to give a big thanks to my friends and coauthors for their contribution to the team and great direction.

—**Nassyam Basha**

CHAPTER 1

Introduction to High Availability and Disaster Recovery with Cloud Technology

Welcome to the world of high availability and disaster recovery. It is high time for us to learn about database software high availability concepts. Software has become an essential element in today's world. Almost all businesses in every industry have started using software to complete their business tasks more efficiently. In fact, some professions are completely dependent on software; they get all of their tasks done using software. On the other hand, there are some industries such as the manufacturing sector that use software for only a portion of their life cycle. But anyhow all businesses should be trying to utilize software to automate their work as much as possible.

Consider how the banking system has improved using software. In the past we had to visit a bank in person and conduct a transaction with the help of bank staff members. It took a lot of manual effort and time to conduct a transaction. Now, the banking system has been completely reformed and automated with most of its functions being done using software. Their tasks are automated with automatic teller machines (ATMs), which in turn has helped to build high-quality banking products. All banks now have websites that work 24/7, and customers are able to complete banking transactions without the involvement of bank staff members. All this has become possible because of the evolution of software.

© Y V Ravi Kumar, Nassyam Basha, Krishna Kumar K M, Bal Mukund Sharma, Konstantin Kerekovski 2019
Y V Ravi Kumar et al., *Oracle High Availability, Disaster Recovery, and Cloud Services*,
https://doi.org/10.1007/978-1-4842-4351-0_1

Another example is the manufacturing industry where human attention is mandatory at each phase of production work, but the industry uses software for data analysis, management, auditing, and wherever else it is possible.

Now we know about the influence of software in almost all businesses, but software runs on hardware. So, how much can an industry trust the availability of the software it is using? If something goes wrong with the hardware and that affects the software, then how will the business survive? If something happens to the environment where the software and hardware are hosted, then what will happen to the application? These questions insist on the necessity of Hardware & software's *high availability* and *disaster recovery*. With the booming software influence, Achieving high availability and disaster recovery is mandatory for any industry. Having high availability and disaster recovery denotes the capability of running a business continuously without any disruption or irrespective of any damages or planned maintenance in the environment.

Let's discuss an example explaining the necessity of high availability and disaster recovery. Suppose a bank needs to migrate its data to a new data center. We know that migration may require downtime, but the bank cannot afford downtime; that will affect its business a lot. This is not only for banks. In this competitive world, none of the industry can afford downtime to its business. Customers look for vendors that are capable of providing continuous service around the clock. So, the bank has to look for options to do migrations without any downtime.

Along with maintenance tasks, there could be a chance of other, unpredicted disruptions that may affect the software's availability. Natural disasters like earthquakes may affect the site where the hardware is located, and the building that has the physical server in it may collapse. This might be rare, but we cannot completely ignore this factor. When a disaster happens, we will not be able to access the physical servers; hence, the Application is not accessible, and the business cannot continue. That is unacceptable! Our environment design should be robust to handle these kind of situations. To be proactive, we need to set up alternate plans to be able to overcome the impact of an earthquake or any fire or server crash that affects your physical servers located in the data center. Remember when the World Trade Center in the United States was bombed in 2001. The companies located on that campus lost their physical servers, but that did not stop them from running their businesses. They came online and started serving customers within a couple of hours. How was that possible? What did they do to overcome such a situation? We can get answers to all these questions in this book. We will be discussing Oracle Database and its high availability concepts.

In addition, we will find many best practices that can be followed in our industry to make our data safe. This book also covers the Oracle public cloud. Enjoy reading!!!

Why High Availability?

Before proceeding into high availability, let's discuss what we are trying to achieve with high availability. Businesses in all industries rely on data, be it the software, medical, or insurance industry. Take, for example, a hospital. A patient's record is precious data. In the past, the data was seen just as a record, and it was used for querying purposes and to derive an annual progress report. Now data is not seen like that; it undergoes a data mining process, and many manipulations are done using the mining results. *Data mining* refers to extracting and discovering knowledge from large amounts of data stored in a database. For a hospital, data is required not only to calculate an annual financial sheet but to analyze how it has performed in the past and to predict how it will be doing in the future. This analysis can proactively find out whether any existing policy requires changes to make a better future. In fact, many industries mine their historical data and generate statistics using various algorithms to predict future business opportunities.

Another good example is the telecommunications industry, which mines its historical data and finds out customers' favorite phone plan, customers' calling behavior, ways to improve the quality of the service, and ways to achieve better customer retention and satisfaction. You probably have noticed many phone providers have introduced wallets recently to avail of their service. This is one of the promotions they invented after mining their historical data.

Another best example is e-commerce sites. When we purchase or review any item on a web site, it records the details in the background, and the next time we log into that site, we see items related to our past searches. Customers' favorites are the data.

Having discussed the importance of the data, now we know why the data has to be secured. That means the data has to be highly available in any circumstance.

Let's discuss the high availability options one by one. At first when industry required high availability option, they started looking at backup and restore strategies for their data. If they lose data, they can restore it from a backup. They had invested in creating remote backup storage, creating network connectivity for backup storage, taking backups of data regularly to the storage, and then periodically validating the stored backups. See Figure 1-1.

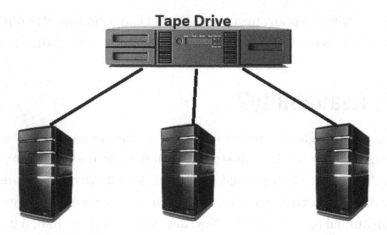

Figure 1-1. *Data backup to tape drive*

Low-cost media tape devices are commonly used as remote storage to store backups for restoring. In addition to being used for restore purposes, the backup is used in the development or preproduction environment for testing purposes.

Even now the backup/restore method is a standard practice that is used across many industries for securing data. But there are some challenges while dealing with backup/restore. Suppose there is a hardware failure or disaster and the current system crashes, then the data is not available, so a backup needs to be restored on the same or different system or in a different data center, based on the conditions. If you choose a different system, then an additional set of storage, memory, and other resources needs to be purchased, and then backup can be restored there. But it will take time to configure the environment. We need to install all the dependent operating system packages for our databases and then restore the backup. Also, the new environment should have access to the backup storage. Here the main concern is the time required for restoring the backup. Restoration will take time based on the volume of the data. But practically any organization cannot afford downtime to restore a backup while it is undergoing a disaster. Consider any international bank—their business cannot afford a single minute of downtime to customers. So, they need an alternate solution. In addition to downtime, there are many challenges while dealing with backups.

- Suppose your database size is huge. Then the backup size will also be huge. It will take more time to restore that big database.

- If there is a failure with the restoration process, then you need to start it again from the beginning, which will increase the restoration time.

- The restoration process performance should be appropriate.

- There is a chance that a backup piece might have gotten corrupted physically, which means we don't have valid backup.

- When our backup storage is at a remote location and network bandwidth with the remote location is poor, then the restore will take a long time to transfer.

- To access the backup storage, we may need help from storage administrators and system administrators along with database administrators.

In addition, at regular intervals, we should perform restore and recovery testing to ensure the integrity of the backup else we might end up in trouble. What if you don't validate your backup and it doesn't restore properly when we need it. In other words, the backup is not fulfilling its purpose. Another issue with backups is storage media failure. Suppose the site with the backup has met a disaster. Then we don't have any backup for our database, which is an unsafe position.

The next challenging point with backups is determining a retention period. How much backup can we store for your database? Suppose we have the need to restore data up to one week before, as an undesirable change has been made a week ago, and we need to restore the backup to get your database to that point. In that case, we should have backups from a week ago. Remember, the database size will keep increasing every day, so the backup size increases daily. So, we need to do a thorough study about the environment and make a proper judgment about the backup retention period. Having a high retention period will increase the need for more storage.

In addition, we have to choose the right backup media. Storing the backup on disk is expensive. We need to look for low-cost storage like an SBT tape. Currently many customers have started moving backups to cloud object storage.

This discussion shows that we cannot fully trust a backup. We need something beyond the backup to confirm that our environment is safe. Here comes the high availability (HA) and disaster recovery (DR) concepts as our savior. In this method, a similar environment as production/live will be maintained at a remote location, and it will play a role if a disaster strikes. This means we will have a copy of the data at another location, and any changes made in production will get replicated to that secondary site. When there is a disaster situation, we don't need to perform a restore/recovery from backup; instead, we can connect the replicated environment and starting working on that.

By having a replicated high availability environment, we will get the following benefits:

- The secondary environment can be switched to the live environment at any time. The replicate environment is similar to production from a hardware and software configuration perspective. So, it can serve the same workload as production was serving. See Figure 1-2.

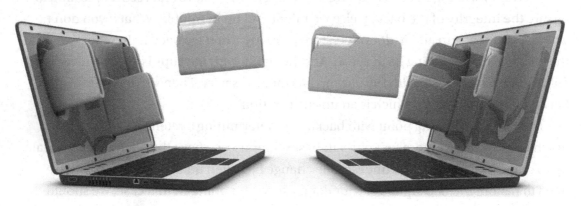

Figure 1-2. *Data replication*

- During a nondisaster period, the replicate environment can contribute as a reporting database as it has live data within it. This reduces the workload for the production database.

- Suppose we have planned to implement a change in the primary production database and are not sure how the environment will behave after the change. Generally these changes will be tested in a preproduction environment. But the preproduction environment may not have the same hardware or volume of data. So, the testing results may not be exactly the same as the production environment in all perspectives. Database administrator will always face this difficulty while implementing changes in production. With a high availability setup, we can implement the changes in the replicate environment first and perform all testing there. Once we have verified and are happy with the results, we can roll back the changes in the replicate environment to get back to the original position.

- Suppose we have some maintenance tasks scheduled at the production database center that require downtime to the production database. What do we do now? No worries. We have the replicate environment. Redirect all our database connections to the replicate environment. It will take seconds to do that. It is like switching our active connections to our available database. Hardly any customers will know about this switch.

Best Practices for a High Availability Environment

Let's start by listing some best practices.

- The replicate environment should have a similar infrastructure from a hardware perspective. The memory, CPU, and any other configuration should be the same as production.

- The distance between the primary and standby databases should be optimum. We cannot have both of them too close, which doesn't make sense. Also, they cannot be too far from each other, which would take time to transfer data to the replicate site.

- The network connectivity with the primary/production environment should be perfect.

So far we have seen the importance of data and how to make it highly available by using another server. We have secured only the data at this stage. However, this is not enough for achieving high availability; the database instance needs to be secured. The database includes the memory and background processes, which are called *instances*. We access the database's physical file using the instance. From a database perspective, we could say the physical data files and the database instance should be available for the active database. When we connect to the database, a new session will get created to the instance in the database, and this session should be active until we disconnect it. At no point in time should the session be disconnected.

For example, while we book a flight ticket on a vendor's web site, we expect that our connectivity to the site will continue until we complete the booking. This means that the web site's web server connection and database connection for the session should be alive until we complete the transaction. If the instance gets terminated in the middle of flight booking, then the session will be lost, and the whole booking effort was useless. So now we understand why we need to have high availability for database instances as well as the database.

To achieve a high availability solution, we can configure multiple instances connected to the same database, and these instances will run from different hardware/nodes. If one instance fails because of a hardware failure or any other failure, it won't be an issue. The other instances will start serving on behalf of the failed instance. The session of the failed instance will get transferred to the active instances running on other nodes.

Oracle has provided Real Application Cluster for high availability at the instance level, as shown in Figure 1-3, and has provided Data Guard for high availability at the database level, as shown in Figure 1-4. Let's learn about these concepts in detail.

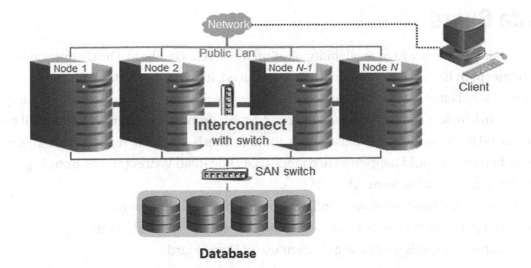

Figure 1-3. *Database instance high availability*

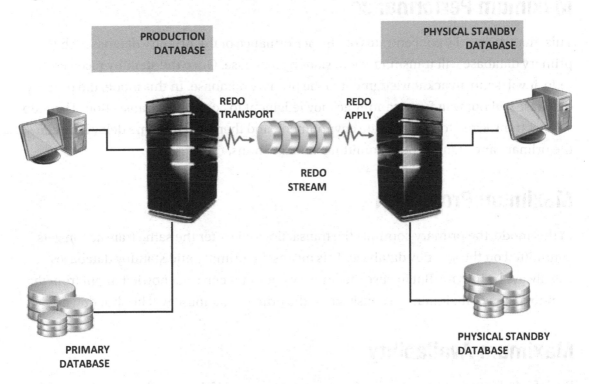

Figure 1-4. *Oracle Data Guard high availability*

9

Data Guard

Data Guard is Oracle's high availability solution for Oracle Database. Oracle introduced this concept in its 9i version. When it was introduced, it had only a data replication feature. Later Data Guard was enhanced and now provides more features such as Active Data Guard, logical standby, and so on. The redo data from the primary database will be transferred to the standby database and is applied. This is how data replication happens. The redo transfer could happen in two modes, i.e., Log Read Writer (LGWR from 10g) or archived logs (available from 9i).

Oracle Data Guard has three configuration methods: maximum protection, maximum performance, maximum availability. We should know about these configuration methods for making efficient use of Data Guard.

Maximum Performance

This mode primarily concentrates on the performance of the primary database. The primary database will transmit redo to standby database. Once the standby receives the redo, it will send an acknowledgment to the primary database. In this mode, the primary database will not wait for a standby acknowledgment to commit its transaction. The redo will get transferred to the replicate environment, and there will be some delay between the primary and standby on committing the same transaction.

Maximum Protection

In this mode, the primary commits the transaction only after the same transaction gets committed on the standby database. This means the primary and standby databases will always be in sync. But in case the primary doesn't receive acknowledgment from the standby, then to maintain the consistency, the primary database will be shut down.

Maximum Availability

By default this mode provides maximum protection, and if the standby is not in sync with the primary, then it automatically switches to maximum performance mode.

Importance of HA and DR

We have learned about high availability and disaster recovery. Both of them need to be used together for the environment to have high availability at the instance and database levels, as shown in Figure 1-5. That makes the environment complete in terms of high availability. A disaster may happen to the physical server or to the storage device. If the physical server gets affected, then the instances holding a customer's session will get terminated. This is considered as downtime to the customer. If the disaster affects storage, then the data gets affected. That also causes downtime to customers.

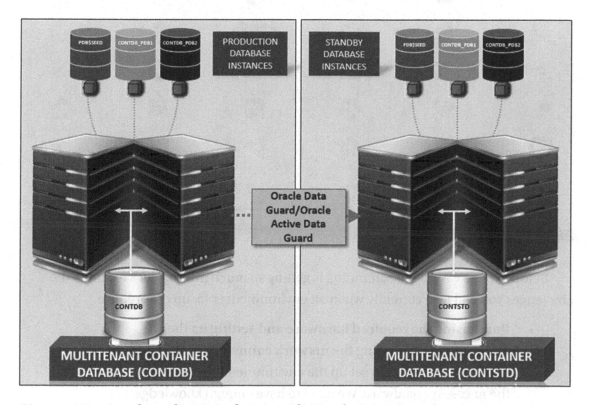

Figure 1-5. *Oracle replication cluster with Oracle Data Guard*

Evolution of Cloud Technologies

Cloud! Cloud! Cloud! This has become the most prevalent buzzword of the software industry these days. Cloud computing is a booming technology. It is an Internet-based technology that provides hardware and software services to customers.
Knowingly or unknowingly, you use cloud technology in your day-to-day environment.

11

Google products are a simple example as shown in Figure 1-6. You might use Google Drive (providing storage), `developer.google.com` (a platform for developing applications), or Gmail (an application).

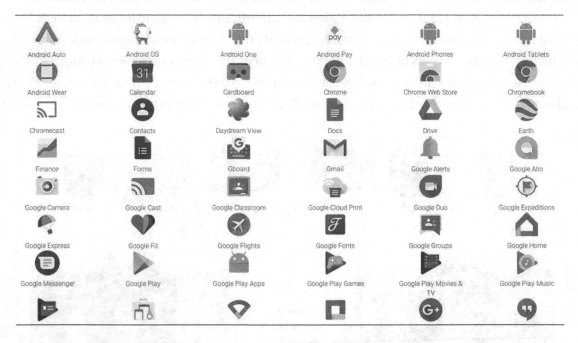

Figure 1-6. *Google products*

Before we see why cloud computing is getting so much priority, let's examine the challenges you will face currently when an environment is set up on-premise.

- **Purchasing the required hardware and setting up the environment, including the network connectivity, firewall setup, and load balancer**: To set up the environment, we need to purchase the necessary hardware. We need to have enough knowledge and money to purchase the right hardware according to your requirements.

- **Managing all the hardware and software license information**: Each purchased hardware and software will have its own licensing terms. You should be aware of those licensing affiliations. Also, we should know what type of license each software has and its expiry details. This is an additional duty for the administrator.

- **Appointing the right experts for the hardware and software support and also a backup for those engineers in case they are absent**: We will require hardware and software administrators to manage the environment. If the environment is set up for 24/7 access, then we need to have administrators on multiple shifts, and backups for those engineers are also required.

- **Creating disaster recovery setup**: We discussed the necessity of high availability and disaster availability. If we need to set up high availability in the existing environment, then we have to do all the tasks to replicate the environment that we have done for production including hardware setup, software installation, and also licensing.

- **Taking care of all maintenance tasks and scheduling them with the right timing**: All the maintenance tasks of the hardware and software have to be taken care of manually. Specifically, backup, patching, high availability, and all other tasks have to be taken care of by the administrator on-site.

- **Handling scalability requests for memory and storage**: There could be a need to upgrade the environment. For an on-premise environment, we need proper planning and the right timing. Lots of manual tasks need to be deployed to achieve this task.

- **Needing additional resources for a short span of time**: The environment may require additional resources only for a short span of time. For example, when there is a big sale, the number of connections and database load will be high. Once the sale is over, the number of connection will be normal. So, you require additional resources such as CPU and memory only for that short duration. But for an on-premise environment, you don't have a provision to own the resource for a short duration. Once you have purchased the resources, you become responsible for it.

- **Paying a large amount of money even though the resource is underutilized**: Consider that we purchased high-performance hardware to boost the performance of our application. We have gotten the expected performance, and we are happy with that. But the application is more active during the daytime. In off-shift hours, your application is not active, so the purchased costly resources are not utilized. This means we are not utilizing the resources though we have paid so much to configure them.

- **Optimizing the resource usage**: Consider a business that runs only from 9 a.m. to 6 p.m. The system requires being up only during that time. During off-shift times, the resource is unused. It can be set free and can be utilized by someone who is in need of resources. Creating such a kind of setup on-premise is a tough one.

- **Changing the environment style**: In on-premise, we have only one style of working. We will take care of everything on that premise, even if there is a need to change locations; all the responsibility falls to the owner.

In the 1990s, we got virtualization technology. All the resources are gathered in a pool, and the instance gets created from the pool of resources. When the instance is not active, the resources of that instance will be made available to the resource pool so that they will be used by another required instance.

Cloud computing uses this virtualization technology to create instances, and the services are offered via the Internet. The services could be either hardware or software.

A new startup company doesn't need to purchase and place hardware on-premise. Instead, it can contact a cloud vendor and explain the expected design of the environment. The startup can mention the specifications of the required hardware and software and get the cloud provider to run the business.

Currently there are three modes of service provided by a cloud vendor.

- **Infrastructure as a Service (IaaS)**: This is the basic level of service in the cloud. A cloud vendor offers hardware services through the Internet. We can purchase all the hardware services like memory, storage, firewalls, VPNs, and load balancers via the Internet.

- **Platform as a Service (PaaS)**: This is the next level of service. Along with the hardware, the platform will be provided. The platform may be a database or Java or a blockchain or a combination of multiple services. The service differs between the vendors. Using this type of platform service, we can develop applications. For example, we get Database as a Service (DBaaS) in PaaS. We can use this database for our application, and the application can be on-premise.

- **Software as a Service (SaaS)**: This is the top level of service. Along with IaaS and PaaS, we will get software with this service. We can immediately start using this application. The application is bundled with the platform and the infrastructure. For example, when we purchase software, we are indirectly purchasing a platform like a database and hardware to host the software and its dependents.

Advantages of Having a Cloud Environment

Let's look at the advantages of cloud environments.

Centralized Location

A cloud environment is located at some centralized data center. This means your data or application is located at a centralized location and it is available to access from anywhere in the world via the Internet.

Setup Cost

The initial setup cost is less on the cloud compared to on-premise. Here the cost indicates physical money for creating the setup. Suppose we are going to create a setup for a new startup; we need a set of physical servers, network switches, load balancers, and firewalls. After purchasing the hardware, we need to install the operating system, prerequisite operating libraries, database, web server, and all the other required software. We also need to configure everything. The process will start from purchasing the appropriate cost-effective hardware and then recruiting professionals to configure the hardware and network setup and then creating the database. We can imagine how much physical cost would be involved in this process. Consider the same setup in the cloud. The cloud vendor has everything in place already; we just need to specify our requirements, and the cloud vendor will create the setup. In this case, we don't need to contact the hardware vendor, and we don't require professionals to configure the hardware and database at the initial phase.

We can utilize the Cost Estimator, as shown in Figure 1-7, provided by Oracle to estimate the fee for having an environment in the cloud.

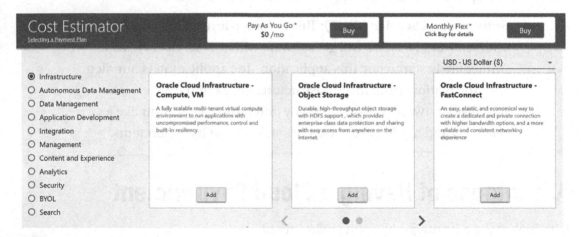

Figure 1-7. *Oracle Cloud Cost Estimator*

Oracle also has an autonomous database flavor. Most of the DBA tasks are automated in this model. The price estimation for the autonomous database environment can be done at `https://valuenavigator.oracle.com/benefitcalculator`.

Operational Cost

Operating costs involve the day-to-day expenses such as electricity, wages/salary for the engineers, maintenance cost, and license renewal. In the cloud, the charges will be based on usage. It is like a "pay-as-you-go" model. You pay only for your usage. You don't need to worry about maintenance costs.

Duration to Create the Setup

The time required to create the setup is minimal compared to the on-premise setup. Let's consider we want to create a setup with firewalls, load balancers, virtual private networks, and so on. On top of the hardware, we need to install all the required software, operating system libraries, and so on. Performing all these tasks on-premise may take months to complete. We need to start with the design and then purchase the appropriate hardware and then install all the necessary software. In the cloud, everything is in place already. We need to just communicate to the cloud vendor about our design and requirements. They can get us the system in a couple of hours. The initial setup creation is much more efficient in a cloud setup. That's one of the reasons why startup companies prefer the cloud for their environments.

Scalability

Scalability is one of the positive attributes of a cloud environment. In an on-premise environment, when we require additional CPU or memory, we need to purchase it and then merge it into the existing environment in the scheduled maintenance window. This will require manual effort, starting from purchase until the implementation. The same is applicable when we need to remove CPU or memory. But in the cloud, it is easy. The cloud vendor does this task for us. They will collect the required quantity from us and add it to the instance automatically with a little bit of service maintenance.

Optimization and Modification

Our environment may face resource shortages for a short span of time or require additional resources only for a small period. For an example, e-commerce sites advertise big sales for particular days. They are aware that the number of customer hits will be high on those days. They will require additional resources only for that duration. The resources could be additional CPU, memory, or database/application instances. After the sale, they won't require these resources. In the on-premise model, once we purchase the resource, we would own it. Just to satisfy the requirement of a small period, we need to spend a lot.

In the cloud, this difficulty has been overcome. We can scale up and scale down at any time. The CPU, memory, and storage can be increased and decreased at any point in time. The cost will be based on the time we use that resource. In our example, the e-commerce site owner can scale up with additional resources on the big sale day and return them once the sale is over. They will be charged only for the duration that they utilized the resources.

Ease of Handling

Though the cloud environment is handled by the cloud vendor, it has all the necessary elements for us to handle the environment easily. The cloud vendor provides user-friendly tools to manage the environment easily and efficiently.

The Oracle Cloud provides tools to handle each instance and also tools to manage the database. Database tasks such as taking backups and patching are made easy in the Oracle Cloud.

Migration

We may need to migrate our environment to the cloud. It may be a database or application. The cloud vendor provides tools to migrate data with minimum downtime. The Oracle Cloud has many ways to migrate data to the cloud, including logical backup, traditional hot backup, RMAN backup, PDB cloning, transient logical standby, and GoldenGate migration.

Security

Since the data is located remotely and someone else is managing it, obviously we may have doubts about database security in the cloud. But the cloud vendor takes much effort to ensure the security. First they choose the best location for having a data center. The location should be safe and less vulnerable for natural disasters. Then they control it at the access level. They create multiple security-level checks before letting someone touch the environment. Trained professionals do all the security checks. It is not easy to steal data from a cloud data center.

Also, mostly the transaction to the cloud will happen via an encrypted channel. All the data will be encrypted before storing it into the cloud. Also, the cloud vendor provides an option to define who can access the environment. We can create a filter so that only authorized people can communicate with the cloud environment.

Variety of Applications

In the cloud environment, we get a variety of applications. Oracle Cloud provides a wide range of applications under SaaS. We could choose the application based on our needs. The environment such as the operating system, database, and all related schemas will be set up according to our chosen application.

Free from Operations Headaches: Licensing Expiration

A major advantage of moving to the cloud is to be free from maintenance tasks. We don't need to worry about licensing. With an on-premise setup, we need to know the license we are using and when it's due to expire. If we miss the chance to renew, we may be in a position to miss the bug fixes. In a cloud environment, we don't need to worry about licensing. It will be taken care of by the cloud vendor.

Differences Between On-Premises, IaaS, PaaS, and SaaS

Table 1-1 shows the differences between on-premise, IaaS, PaaS, and SaaS.

Table 1-1. *Differences Between On-Premise and Cloud Services*

On-Premise	IAAS	PAAS	SAAS
Applications	Applications	Applications	**APPLICATIONS**
Data	Data	**DATA**	**DATA**
Runtime	Runtime	**RUNTIME**	**RUNTIME**
Middleware	Middleware	**MIDDLEWARE**	**MIDDLEWARE**
Operating System	Operating System	**OPERATING SYSTEM**	**OPERATING SYSTEM**
Virtualization	**VIRTUALIZATION**	**VIRTUALIZATION**	**VIRTUALIZATION**
Servers	**SERVERS**	**SERVERS**	**SERVERS**
Storage	**STORAGE**	**STORAGE**	**STORAGE**
Networking	**NETWORKING**	**NETWORKING**	**NETWORKING**

On-Premise

On-premise is the traditional way of maintaining an environment. All the tasks in the environment will be taken care of by on-site engineers.

IaaS

In the IaaS model, the cloud vendor hosts the hardware, including servers, storage hardware, and networking hardware, in the data center. The cloud vendor will take care of all the virtualization. The cloud vendor will provide hardware as a service. The customer can deploy their platform and application on top of the hardware.

PaaS

In the PaaS model, the cloud vendor will provide the hardware and the platform to deploy your application. The platform could be a database or Java or any platform to deploy the applications. For the database, the software installation and database configuration will be taken care of by the cloud vendor. PaaS makes application development, testing, and deployment of applications simple, quick, and cost effective.

SaaS

In the SaaS model, the cloud vendor provides everything from the hardware to the software and applications. Customers can start accessing their applications from day 1. They just need to input their data and start using the application.

We will be discussing more about the cloud in upcoming chapters.

Summary

This chapter gave an overview of high availability and disaster recovery and explored their importance. Moreover, we discussed the cloud revolution, the challenges you can face with an on-premise environment, and the advantages you can get with a cloud environment. We also covered cloud service models and the differences between them.

CHAPTER 2

Oracle Active Data Guard with Cloud Services

In Chapter 1, we were introduced to the concepts of high availability and disaster recovery. In this chapter, we will move on to the specifics of disaster recovery, which is handled with Oracle Data Guard (DG). This chapter will give more insight into Oracle Data Guard and its configuration and protection levels, cover the concepts of switchover and failover, and talk about configuring DG in a public Oracle Cloud environment.

In general, *guard* means protection; here, Data Guard denotes data safety. The traditional way of protecting a database is through a data backup. If something happens and we lose your data, we can restore it using the backup. However, there are some challenges with this method, as discussed in Chapter 1. To overcome those challenges, Oracle has provided a better high availability option via Data Guard. Specifically, data is protected by having a duplicate copy at a remote location. The changes happening in production and on the primary database will be copied to the remote/secondary database. You could say the production database has a constantly updated backup in terms of the replicated database. If any disaster affects the production database, then it can be recovered using the remote copy. It is highly recommended to have the remote copy at a faraway location, maybe in a different region, so that the remote environment will not be affected by the same disaster as the primary. The remote database is called the *disaster recovery* database or *standby* database.

Initially, the disaster recovery (DR) database, or replicated database, was considered to be for high availability purposes only. Later it was enhanced to serve data as a reporting database. Regardless, the remote database has the same data as the primary; hence, reports can query the DR database directly instead of the primary, which reduces the burden of the primary database.

© Y V Ravi Kumar, Nassyam Basha, Krishna Kumar K M, Bal Mukund Sharma, Konstantin Kerekovski 2019
Y V Ravi Kumar et al., *Oracle High Availability, Disaster Recovery, and Cloud Services*,
https://doi.org/10.1007/978-1-4842-4351-0_2

Types of DR Databases

There are two kind of DR databases: physical standby databases and logical standby databases.

Physical Standby Databases

This type of replicated database is an exact copy of the production database. You could say that both databases are similar in each database block. The standby receives a transaction of the production database through redo log entries and applies them to the DR database. The physical standby database will always be read-only (see Figure 2-1).

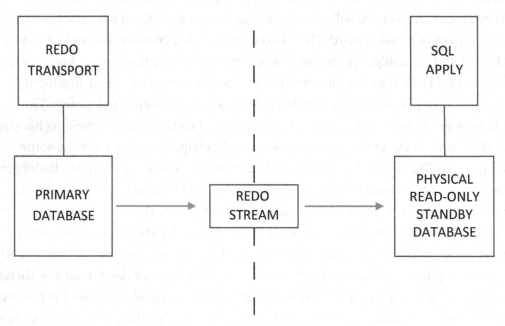

Figure 2-1. *Physical standby database*

Logical Standby Databases

The logical standby database is also a replicated database and is updated with transactions of the production database. Unlike the physical standby database, it is a read-write database; it mines the redo log entries received from the primary database into SQL statements and applies them to the replicated database. That means this database will be generating its own redo entries and also applying redo entries of the production database. Though it is a read-write database, we are not able to modify the objects that are part of the replication procedure; in other words, you cannot update the tables, which are supposed to be updated only by production database's redo log entries. See Figure 2-2.

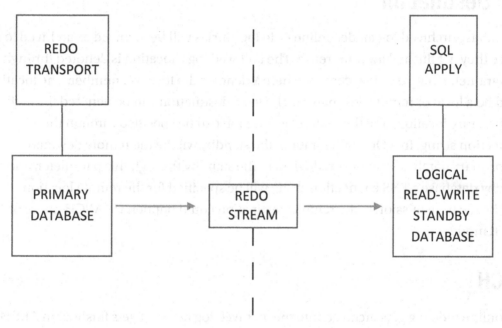

Figure 2-2. *Logical standby database*

We could have more than one DR database to achieve more high availability. When we have multiple DR databases, if one DR database fails, the others are available for recovery. Many industries will have multiple DR databases in different regions. These databases will be connected through a network to the primary database. Through this network, redo entries are transmitted from the primary to the DR databases. Remember that this is one-way communication; it means redo entries always flow from the primary to the standby databases or from the standby to the other standby databases. The network plays a crucial part in this DR activity. If the network is poor, the replication will be affected. If the network fails to communicate, then the databases will not be in sync.

DR Activity Attributes

Before discussing the activities involved with the DR database further, let's discuss the attributes involved in the DR activity.

Log Destination

In database archived log mode, online redo log entries will be archived as archived logs before they get flushed away for reuse. The archived logs' location is denoted through the parameter `log_archive_dest_N`, where N denotes the location number. The location could be a local or remote destination. The local destination can be denoted through the directory location, and the remote destination can be specified through the TNS connection string. In a DG configuration, the standby will be the remote destination. The primary database transfers redo data to the standby through this parameter, and the standby database's TNS connection string will be specified for the remote location.

The log transmission to the remote destination could happen via ARCH mode or LGWR mode.

ARCH

The online redo log gets archived into the archived log before it gets flushed. In ARCH mode, the archived log is created at the local destination and the remote destination, which is the standby in DG setup. The archived logs will be transferred to the standby, and the media recovery process (MRP) reads the archived logs and applies the transactions.

Log Writer Process

In log writer (LGWR) mode, the redo log entries will be transferred from the primary database server to the standby database servers, and the transferred entries will be written to the standby redo logs. This means in real time the redo data travels from the primary to the standby database server and gets stored in the standby redo log. The MRP will be reading the contents from the standby redo logs and applying them to the database. The MRP will not wait until the standby's archived logs get filled and archived. Two Data Guard processes, log network server (LNS) and remote file server (RFS), play role in LGWR mode.

LNS

The LNS process reads the redo data from the log buffer in the shared global area (SGA) and transmits it to the standby via Oracle Net services. It can transfer the redo to multiple destinations as defined by the `log_archive_dest_N` parameter.

RFS

The RFS process receives the redo data from the LNS process and writes it to a sequential file called the *standby redo logs*. The MRP reads the standby redo logs to apply transactions to the database. See Figure 2-3.

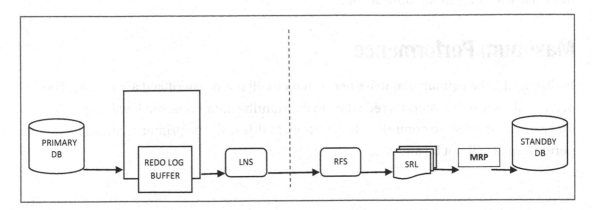

Figure 2-3. *LNS, RFS, SRL, and MRP*

Behavior of the DR Activity

DG has three modes of redo transportation. The mode denotes the behavior of the DR activity. The modes are maximum availability, maximum protection, and maximum performance.

Maximum Protection

In this mode, the primary database will not commit the transactions unless it receives an acknowledgment from the standby database that the transaction has been committed at the standby database. If the standby takes time to acknowledge, the primary database will be in a waiting state until it reaches the threshold period, and then it will be shut down. This gives the highest level of data protection so there is no data loss between the primary and standby databases.

Maximum Availability

In this mode, the primary database will transmit the transaction to the standby databases via redo log entries and commit the transaction once it receives acknowledgment from one of its standby databases. It differs from protection mode because it will not wait until the standby database commits the transaction. Once the redo entries are written to the standby redo logs of the standby database, the primary database will commit the transaction.

Maximum Performance

In this mode, the primary database performance will not be sacrificed at any cost. The primary database transfers its redo data to the standby databases, but it will not wait for acknowledgment to commit its transaction. In this way, the primary database's performance will not be affected.

Differences Between Modes

Table 2-1 compares the modes.

Table 2-1. *Differences Between Data Guard Modes*

	Maximum Performance	Maximum Availability	Maximum Protection
Possibility of data loss	Possible	Not guaranteed. In normal operation, it will provide zero data loss.	Zero data loss
Type of standby database	Physical and logical standby databases	Physical and logical standby database.	Physical standby database
Necessity of standby redo logs	Required only when LGWR transfer mode is chosen	Required for physical standby databases.	Required
Redo archival process	ARCH or LWGR	LGWR.	LGWR

Switchover

A switchover means flipping the roles of the primary and standby databases. We know that both databases have the same contents, and the primary is in read-write mode and allows modification to the data, whereas the standby will be used as the replicated database and is used for reporting purposes. When we need to do some maintenance tasks to the primary database that affect its availability, then we can perform the switchover activity. The standby database will take the primary role after switchover, and it opens its database to read-write mode. Application sessions can connect to the current primary database. Switchover is usually preferred when the primary database has maintenance activity such as patching or upgrading or hardware change/maintenance. In this way, the database will be available for applications, though maintenance activities are being carried out.

As soon as the switchover activity is started, end of redo (EOR) will be generated and attached to the current redo transmission. Once the standby receives the EOR, it understands that the switchover is happening at the primary database, and it will start converting the standby database role to the primary database. Note that before performing the switchover, the primary and standby databases should be in sync, or the switchover will not happen.

Here are the steps:

1) Verify that the standby database recovery has been started with real-time apply.

    The standby database recovery with real-time apply will enable the recovery to happen from the standby redo logs instead of the archived logs. It means the recovery will be faster.

    Real-time apply on the standby can be started using the following command:

```
Sql> Alter database recover managed standby database using current logfile
disconnect;
```

2) Check that the primary and standby databases are in sync.

    Before the standby becomes the primary, it should have received all the transactions of the primary database. This will make sure that there is no data loss between the primary and standby databases.

    The sync can be verified using the following command on the standby database:

```
select a.thrd "thread", almax "last seq received", lhmax "last seq applied"
from (select thread# thrd, max(sequence#) almax from v$archived_log where
resetlogs_change#=(select resetlogs_change# from v$database) group by
thread#) a, (select thread# thrd, max(sequence#) lhmax from v$log_history
where resetlogs_change#=(select resetlogs_change# from v$database) group by
thread#) l where a.thrd = l.thrd;
```

3) Clear the online redo logs of the standby database.

During the switchover activity, the standby will clear its online redo logs as it is going to use them after it becomes the primary. Clearing those logs before switchover will reduce the total time of the switchover.

```
Sql> alter database clear logfile group <group_number> ;
```

4) Make sure the primary database is free from user sessions.

During the switchover, the primary database will be shut down. User sessions will be disconnected from the database, hence making sure no important transactions are going on in the current primary database.

5) Check the switchover_status value from v$database.

If everything is fine, the switchover_status column of v$database in the primary database will have a value of TO STANDBY, which denotes that the primary database is ready for the switchover.

```
Sql> select switchover_status from v$database;
```

6) Invoke the switchover command on the primary database.

Start the switchover activity from the primary database first. Convert it to the standby database. You may wonder if you do this step, then there won't be any primary database. Yes, that's true. In DG, the main priority is no database loss. Considering that fact at any time, you should have the active standby database even though the primary database is not there.

```
SQL> Alter database commit to switchover to standby with session shutdown;
```

At this stage, the primary database will generate the EOR, and that will get transferred to the standby along with the redo data.

7) Invoke switchover commands at the standby database. If there are multiple standby databases, then choose the database that has to become the primary.

Verify the `switchover_status` column of the standby database.

```
Sql> select switchover_status from v$database;
```

It should have a value of TO PRIMARY.

```
Sql> alter database commit to switchover to primary;
```

This command will convert the control file type to the primary and clear the online redo logs. The database will still be in mount status. Open the database in read-write mode.

```
Sql> Alter database open;
```

The same steps can be followed for switching back to the old primary database.

Failover

The switchover activity is usually carried out because of maintenance tasks. In general it is a preplanned task, so everyone will be aware about the activity. However, there are circumstances where the primary database will be terminated because of unexpected failures, such as a hardware failure or network failure. In those conditions, the standby needs to be activated, and it should take the primary's role and serve application connections. This standby to the primary role conversion should happen even though the standby is not in sync with the primary database. It means the failover might come with data loss.

Here are the steps:

1. Register the archived logs, which are transferred to the standby and yet to be applied.

```
Sql> Alter database register logfile '<logfile>';
```

2. Cancel the media recovery and perform the failover.

```
Sql> Alter database recover managed standby database finish force;
Sql> Alter database commit to switchover to primary;
Sql> Alter database open;
```

If there is an unresolvable gap then

```
Sql> Alter database activate standby database; Sql> Alter database open;
```

Data Guard Broker

Data Guard Broker is an Oracle tool to manage the Data Guard environment. It monitors the primary and standby databases and reports whether there is any inconsistency in their states. It performs many Data Guard activities automatically. Data Guard Broker has a configuration file that has the centralized information about the Data Guard setup. dgmgrl is the Data Guard Broker command-line interface.

Here are some of the tasks performed by Data Guard Broker:

1) **Monitoring the primary and standby databases**: The databases, which are configured with Data Guard Broker, will be monitored. If one is disconnected, it will be reported immediately.

```
DGMGRL> show configuration;
```

The previous command lists the details of the primary and standby databases. If there are any issues with any of the databases, that will be listed here.

```
DGMGRL> show database verbose <DB_Name>;
```

The previous command will list the details of the database.

2) **Switchover and failover**: The switchover and failover operations will be done with a single command. It will perform role changes and restart the primary database. It performs switchover/failover operations for the RAC database as well.

```
DGMGRL> switchover to '<Standby database name>';
```

It will exchange the roles between the primary and standby databases.

3) **Snapshot standby database**: The read-only physical standby database can be converted to a read-write snapshot standby database through Broker in a single command.

```
DGMGRL> Convert database '<standby database name>' to Snapshot standby;
```

4) **Protection mode change**: The protection mode of Data Guard configuration can be changed easily through Data Guard Broker.

```
DGMGRL> Edit configuration set protection mode as <Protection Mode>;
```

5) **Fast-start failover**: Data Guard Broker will automatically activate the standby database when the primary goes down. The observer will be doing this task. When the observer and standby are not able to reach the primary database, then the observer will activate standby database once the threshold limit is reached. This feature is desirable for a critical production environment.

```
DGMGRL> start observer;
DGMGRL> Enable Fast_start failover;
```

6) **Reinstating a failed primary database**: After failover, the old primary database has to be reinstated as the standby database to become part of the Data Guard configuration.

```
DGMGRL > Reinstate database '<Old Primary Database Name>';
```

7) **Changing properties**: Data Guard properties can be changed via Data Guard Broker. Properties such Apply, Net Timeout Limit, and Transport Destination can be changed.

8) **Removing the standby database**: The standby database (physical, logical, or snapshot standby) can be removed and added to the Data Guard configuration.

```
DGMGRL> remove database '<database Name>';
```

9) **Pluggable database migration**: Since version 12-2, Broker has the provision to migrate the pluggable database to another container database.

10) **Enterprise Manager interface**: Enterprise Manager can perform high availability operations through Data Guard Broker.

DG Setup in the Cloud

Oracle Cloud DBaaS (which stands for Database as a Service) provides a provision to create Data Guard instances. The Data Guard feature is available with Cloud DBaaS Enterprise Edition, Enterprise Edition High Performance, and Enterprise Edition Extreme Performance. In a cloud environment, Data Guard creates the primary and standby databases at different data centers, thus providing isolation at the infrastructure level and geographical separation to support high availability. In the cloud, the Data Guard functionalists are the same as on-premise. In addition, the Oracle Cloud also provides tools to manage the Data Guard instances.

Let's first discuss the command-line utilities provided by Oracle to manage the Data Guard environment in the cloud; then we'll discuss the available GUI options.

dbaascli is the utility provided in the cloud environment to manage the databases in a DBaaS environment. This utility will do database patching, database and listener start/stop, TDE setup, and so on. It also helps to manage the Data Guard environment. When we do management through this utility, we don't need to connect via Data Guard Broker. Just invoke the dbaascli command as the root user. It knows the database roles and invokes the Data Guard operations in the background.

Oracle releases new DBaaS tool versions often that will have bug fixes and new features. So, always first update DBaaS tool before performing any activity through it.

DBaaS Tool Update

Find the existing DBaaS tool version.

```
[root@APDB-dg01 opc]# rpm -qa | grep dbaastools
dbaastools-1.0-1+18.1.4.0.0_180123.1336.x86_64
```

This shows that the DBaaS tool version is 18.1.4 and that it was released in January 2018 (180123).

Let's verify whether there is any other version available for upgrade.

Here's the command to verify the latest version:

```
/var/opt/oracle/patch/dbpatchmsm -list_tools
```

```
[root@APDB-dg01 opc]#  /var/opt/oracle/patch/dbpatchmsm -list_tools
INFO: non async case
INFO: cmd is: /var/opt/oracle/patch/dbpatchm -list_tools
```

Here's how to start DBPATCHM:

```
Logfile is /var/opt/oracle/log/dbpatchm/dbpatchm_2018-09-02_06:54:43.log
Config file is /var/opt/oracle/patch/dbpatchm.cfg
INFO: cdb is set to : yes
INFO: dbversion detected : 12201
INFO: patching type : psu

INFO: oss_container_url is not given, using the default
INFO: tools images available for patching
$VAR1 = {
          'last_async_precheck_txn_id' => ' ',
          'last_async_apply_txn_id' => ' ',
          'errmsg' => '',
          'err' => '',
          'current_version' => '18.1.4.0.180123',
          'last_async_precheck_patch_id' => ' ',
          'current_patch' => '180123',
          'last_async_apply_patch_id' => ' ',
          'patches' => [
                       {
                         'patchid' => '18.1.4.1.0_180309.0546',
                         'last_precheck_txnid' => '',
                         'description' => 'DBAAS Tools for Oracle Public
                         Cloud'
                       },
                       {
                         'patchid' => '18.1.4.1.0_180312.1800',
                         'last_precheck_txnid' => '',
                         'description' => 'DBAAS Tools for Oracle Public
                         Cloud'
                       },
          .
          .

                                 .
```

```
            {
    'patchid' => '18.3.1.1.0_180829.0000',
    'last_precheck_txnid' => '',
    'description' => 'DBAAS Tools for Oracle Public
    Cloud'
            }
        ]
};
```

The output shows there were many more recent DBaaS releases after our version. DBaaS updates are cumulative, so you can update the tool to the latest version, which is 18.3.1.1.0_180829.0000.

Here's the command to apply the update:

```
/var/opt/oracle/patch/dbpatchm -toolsinst_async -rpmversion=<patchrpmid>
[root@APDB-dg01 opc]#  /var/opt/oracle/patch/dbpatchm -toolsinst_async
-rpmversion=18.3.1.1.0_180829.0000
```

Here's how to start DBPATCHM:

```
Logfile is /var/opt/oracle/log/dbpatchm/dbpatchm_2018-09-02_06:57:23.log
Config file is /var/opt/oracle/patch/dbpatchm.cfg
INFO: cdb is set to : yes
INFO: dbversion detected : 12201
INFO: patching type : psu

INFO: oss_container_url is not given, using the default
INFO: existing dbaastools version - dbaastools-1.0-1+18.1.4.0.0_180123.1336.x86_64
Use of uninitialized value in concatenation (.) or string at /var/opt/
oracle/patch/dbpatchm line 4737.
INFO: updated dbaastools rpm to - dbaastools-1.0-1+18.3.1.1.0_180829.0000.x86_64
[root@APDB-dg02 opc]# rpm -qa | grep dbaastools
dbaastools-1.0-1+18.3.1.1.0_180829.0000.x86_64
```

dbaascli Commands to Data Guard

Invoke the DBaaS utility as shown here:

```
[root@APDB-dg01 opc]# dbaascli
DBAAS CLI version 1.0.0
DBAAS> list
```

This will list all the available commands with dbaascli.

The available commands for Data Guard in dbaascli can be found with the following:

```
DBAAS>dataguard
Executing command dataguard
Valid Subcommands:
    switchover
    status
    failover
    reinstate
```

The Data Guard status can be checked, a switchover/failover can be done, and reinstating the old primary also can be done.

Note   All the activities are done through dbaascli. It knows the database's role.

Here is how to check the dbaacli Data Guard status:

```
DBAAS>dataguard status
Executing command dataguard status
SUCCESS : Dataguard is up and running

DETAILS:
 Connected as SYSDG.
Configuration - fsc
  Protection Mode: MaxPerformance
  Members:
  hadb_01 - Primary database
```

```
    hadb_02 - Physical standby database
  Properties:
    FastStartFailoverThreshold         = '30'
    OperationTimeout                   = '120'
    TraceLevel                         = 'USER'
    FastStartFailoverLagLimit          = '30'
    CommunicationTimeout               = '180'
    ObserverReconnect                  = '0'
    FastStartFailoverAutoReinstate     = 'TRUE'
    FastStartFailoverPmyShutdown       = 'TRUE'
    BystandersFollowRoleChange         = 'ALL'
    ObserverOverride                   = 'FALSE'
    ExternalDestination1               = ''
    ExternalDestination2               = ''
    PrimaryLostWriteAction             = 'CONTINUE'
    ConfigurationWideServiceName       = 'hadb_CFG'

Fast-Start Failover: DISABLED
Configuration Status:
SUCCESS
```

We can see that the output is almost similar to Data Guard Broker.

To get more details about the status, we could add a details option with the previous command.

```
[root@APDB-dg01 .ssh]#  dbaascli dataguard status—details yes
DBAAS CLI version 18.3.1.1.0
Executing command dataguard status—details yes
SUCCESS: Dataguard is up and running
{
    "instances" : [
      {
        "PROTECTION_LEVEL" : "MAXIMUM PERFORMANCE",
        "ADDITIONAL_MESSAGES" : "",
        "APPLY_LAG" : "00 days 00 hrs 00 min 00 sec",
        "DATABASE_NAME" : "hadb_01",
```

```
        "APPROXIMATE_ROLE_TRANSITION_TIME" : "00 days 00 hrs 00 min 00 sec
        + 30 sec",
        "ACTIVE_SESSIONS" : "3",
        "HOST_NAME" : "APDB-dg01",
        "TRANSPORT_LAG" : "00 days 00 hrs 00 min 00 sec last computed 0
        days 0 hrs 0 min 12 sec before",
        "PROTECTION_MODE" : "MAXIMUM PERFORMANCE",
        "DATABASE_TYPE" : "PHYSICAL STANDBY",
        "OPEN_MODE" : "MOUNTED"
    },
    {

        "PROTECTION_LEVEL" : "MAXIMUM PERFORMANCE",
        "ADDITIONAL_MESSAGES" : "",
        "DATABASE_NAME" : "hadb_02",
        "ACTIVE_SESSIONS" : "2",
        "HOST_NAME" : "APDB-dg02",
        "DATABASE_TYPE" : "PRIMARY",
        "PROTECTION_MODE" : "MAXIMUM PERFORMANCE",
        "PENDING_APPLY_LOG_CNT" : 0,
        "OPEN_MODE" : "READ WRITE"
    }
  ]
}
```

dbaascli Data Guard Switchover

Let's try a switchover through dbaascli.

```
DBAAS>dataguard switchover
Executing command dataguard switchover

DBAAS>dataguard switchover
Executing command dataguard switchover
Connected as SYSDBA.
Performing switchover NOW, please wait...
New primary database "hadb_02" is opening...
```

```
Operation requires start up of instance "hadb" on database "hadb_01"
Starting instance "hadb"...
ORACLE instance started.
Database mounted.
Connected to "hadb_01"
Switchover succeeded, new primary is "hadb_02"
SUCCESS : Switchover to Standby operation completed successfully
```

Here are some of the points to note from the alert log:

```
Old Primary:
SWITCHOVER VERIFY: Send VERIFY request to switchover target hadb_02
SWITCHOVER VERIFY WARNING: switchover target has no standby database
defined in LOG_ARCHIVE_DEST_n parameter. If the switchover target is
converted to a primary database, the new primary database will not be
protected.
Data Guard Broker: Switchover processing will set LOG_ARCHIVE_DEST_n
parameter. Continuing switchover
2018-09-02T07:35:37.963328+00:00
SWITCHOVER VERIFY: Send VERIFY request to switchover target hadb_02
SWITCHOVER VERIFY COMPLETE: READY FOR SWITCHOVER
2018-09-02T07:35:39.715380+00:00
ALTER DATABASE SWITCHOVER TO 'hadb_02'
```

The previous entries denote that dbaascli has invoked Data Guard Broker to perform the switchover activity.

```
[root@APDB-dg01 .ssh]# dbaascli dataguard status
DBAAS CLI version 18.3.1.1.0
Executing command dataguard status
SUCCESS : Dataguard is up and running

DETAILS:
 Connected as SYSDG.
Configuration - fsc
  Protection Mode: MaxPerformance
  Members:
  hadb_02 - Primary database
```

```
     hadb_01 - Physical standby database
  Properties:
    FastStartFailoverThreshold      = '30'
    OperationTimeout                = '120'
    TraceLevel                      = 'USER'
    FastStartFailoverLagLimit       = '30'
    CommunicationTimeout            = '180'
    ObserverReconnect               = '0'
    FastStartFailoverAutoReinstate  = 'TRUE'
    FastStartFailoverPmyShutdown    = 'TRUE'
    BystandersFollowRoleChange      = 'ALL'
    ObserverOverride                = 'FALSE'
    ExternalDestination1            = "
    ExternalDestination2            = "
    PrimaryLostWriteAction          = 'CONTINUE'
    ConfigurationWideServiceName    = 'hadb_CFG'

Fast-Start Failover: DISABLED
Configuration Status:
SUCCESS
```

dbaascli Data Guard Failover

Let's try a failover through the dbaascli command interface.

```
[oracle@APDB-dg01 ~]$ dbaascli dataguard status-details yes
DBAAS CLI version 1.0.0
Executing command dataguard status-details yes
SUCCESS: Dataguard is up and running
{
   "instances" : [
     {
        "PROTECTION_LEVEL" : "MAXIMUM PERFORMANCE",
        "ADDITIONAL_MESSAGES" : "",
        "APPLY_LAG" : "00 days 00 hrs 00 min 00 sec",
        "DATABASE_NAME" : "hadb_01",
```

```
        "APPROXIMATE_ROLE_TRANSITION_TIME" : "00 days 00 hrs 00 min 00 sec
        + 30 sec",
        "ACTIVE_SESSIONS" : "3",
        "HOST_NAME" : "APDB-dg01",
        "TRANSPORT_LAG" : "00 days 00 hrs 00 min 00 sec last computed 0
        days 0 hrs 0 min 1 sec before",
        "PROTECTION_MODE" : "MAXIMUM PERFORMANCE",
        "DATABASE_TYPE" : "PHYSICAL STANDBY",
        "OPEN_MODE" : "MOUNTED"
    },
    {
        "PROTECTION_LEVEL" : "MAXIMUM PERFORMANCE",
        "ADDITIONAL_MESSAGES" : "",
        "DATABASE_NAME" : "hadb_02",
        "ACTIVE_SESSIONS" : "2",
        "HOST_NAME" : "APDB-dg02",
        "DATABASE_TYPE" : "PRIMARY",
        "PROTECTION_MODE" : "MAXIMUM PERFORMANCE",
        "PENDING_APPLY_LOG_CNT" : 0,
        "OPEN_MODE" : "READ WRITE"
    }
  ]
}[oracle@APDB-dg01 ~]$ dbaascli dataguard failover
DBAAS CLI version 1.0.0
Executing command dataguard failover
Connected as SYSDBA.
Performing failover NOW, please wait...
Failover succeeded, new primary is "hadb_01"
SUCCESS : Successfully failed over to Standby
[oracle@APDB-dg01 ~]$ dbaascli dataguard status-details yes
DBAAS CLI version 1.0.0
Executing command dataguard status-details yes
ERROR: Dataguard not up and running
{
    "instances" : [
```

```
    {
        "DATABASE_TYPE" : "PRIMARY",
        "PROTECTION_MODE" : "MAXIMUM PERFORMANCE",
        "PROTECTION_LEVEL" : "MAXIMUM PERFORMANCE",
        "ADDITIONAL_MESSAGES" : "",
        "DATABASE_NAME" : "hadb_01",
        "PENDING_APPLY_LOG_CNT" : 0,
        "ACTIVE_SESSIONS" : "2",
        "HOST_NAME" : "APDB-dg01",
        "OPEN_MODE" : "READ WRITE"
    },
    {

        "DATABASE_TYPE" : "REINSTATE",
        "PROTECTION_MODE" : "UNKNOWN",
        "PROTECTION_LEVEL" : "UNKNOWN",
        "ADDITIONAL_MESSAGES" : "ORA-16661: the standby database needs to
         be reinstated",
        "DATABASE_NAME" : "hadb_02",
        "HOST_NAME" : "APDB-dg02",
        "OPEN_MODE" : "DOWN"
    }
  ]
}[oracle@APDB-dg01 ~]$

}
```

The status reports an error since the standby has to be reinstated.

dbaascli Data Guard Reinstate

Let's reinstate the old primary database to the standby database.

```
[oracle@APDB-dg01 ~]$ dbaascli dataguard reinstate
DBAAS CLI version 1.0.0
Executing command dataguard reinstate
Successfully reinstated dataguard instances
Detail : Successfully reinstated database : hadb_02
```

```
[oracle@APDB-dg01 ~]$ dbaascli dataguard status-details yes
DBAAS CLI version 1.0.0
Executing command dataguard status-details yes
SUCCESS: Dataguard is up and running
{
    "instances" : [
        {
            "DATABASE_TYPE" : "PRIMARY",
            "PROTECTION_MODE" : "MAXIMUM PERFORMANCE",
            "PROTECTION_LEVEL" : "MAXIMUM PERFORMANCE",
            "ADDITIONAL_MESSAGES" : "",
            "DATABASE_NAME" : "hadb_01",
            "PENDING_APPLY_LOG_CNT" : 0,
            "ACTIVE_SESSIONS" : "2",
            "HOST_NAME" : "APDB-dg01",
            "OPEN_MODE" : "READ WRITE"
        },
        {
            "PROTECTION_LEVEL" : "MAXIMUM PERFORMANCE",
            "ADDITIONAL_MESSAGES" : "",
            "APPLY_LAG" : "00 days 00 hrs 00 min 00 sec",
            "DATABASE_NAME" : "hadb_02",
            "APPROXIMATE_ROLE_TRANSITION_TIME" : "00 days 00 hrs 00 min 00 sec
            + 30 sec",
            "ACTIVE_SESSIONS" : "3",
            "HOST_NAME" : "APDB-dg02",
            "TRANSPORT_LAG" : "00 days 00 hrs 00 min 00 sec last computed 0
            days 0 hrs 0 min 1 sec before",
            "PROTECTION_MODE" : "MAXIMUM PERFORMANCE",
            "DATABASE_TYPE" : "PHYSICAL STANDBY",
            "OPEN_MODE" : "MOUNTED"
        }
    ]
}
```

Data Guard Switchover Through the GUI

Data Guard switchover and failover operations can be done in GUI mode via the cloud portal. We'll do a switchover first.

Log into the cloud portal and go to the database instances, as shown in Figure 2-4 and Figure 2-5.

Figure 2-4. *Database instances*

We should see in the Resource section the primary and standby database details. The Public IP, SID, Database Role, OCPU, Memory, and Storage fields are displayed.

It also provides Data Guard metrics details. The apply lag, transport lag, standby active sessions, and last updated time for details are also shown in the portal, as shown in Figure 2-5.

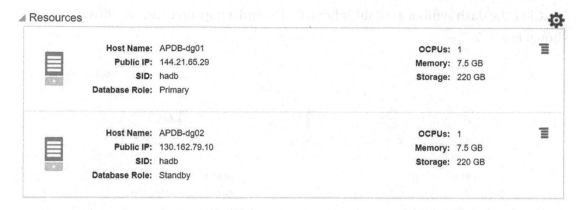

Data Guard Metrics

Apply Lag:	00 days 00 hrs 00 min 01 sec
Transport Lag:	00 days 00 hrs 00 min 00 sec last computed 0 days 0 hrs 0 min 0 sec before
Standby Active Sessions:	3
Last Updated Time:	2018-04-14T12:39:47.941+0000

Figure 2-5. *Data Guard metrics*

The Data Guard status is shown in Figure 2-6.

Figure 2-6. *Data Guard status*

Click the dash symbol available after OCUPS, and a pop-up window will appear, as shown Figure 2-7.

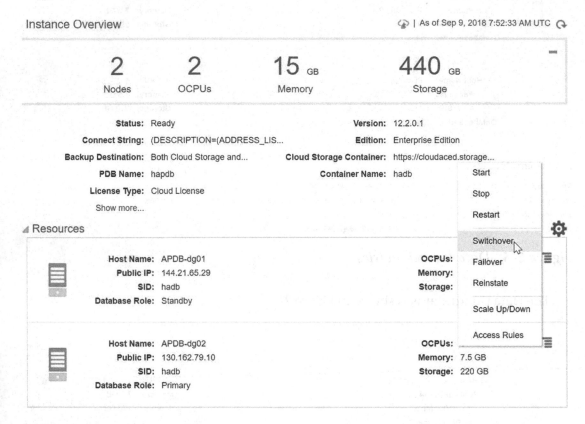

Figure 2-7. *Switchover option*

Choose the switchover option; it will ask for confirmation, as shown in Figure 2-8.

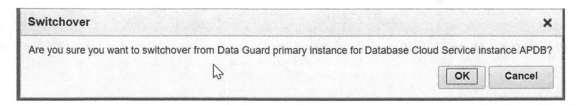

Figure 2-8. *Switchover confirmation*

Click the OK button. It will start the switchover and provide confirmation, as shown in Figure 2-9.

Figure 2-9. *Switchover accepted*

During the switchover operation, the instance will move to the Service Maintenance mode. Most of the options such as backup will not be available during the maintenance mode.

As shown Figure 2-10, the instance status moves to Service Maintenance mode. We can monitor the switchover operation through alert log entries. Refresh the status in the portal. Once the switchover is completed, the database role will be reflected in the cloud portal, as shown in Figure 2-11.

Figure 2-10. *Service maintenance*

Figure 2-11. *Database role after switchover*

Data Guard Failover Through the GUI

We have seen the switchover through the GUI. Similarly, the failover operation also can be done through the GUI. See Figure 2-12.

Figure 2-12. *Data Guard setting before failover*

From the cloud portal, click the dash icon available after OCPUs, as shown in Figure 2-13.

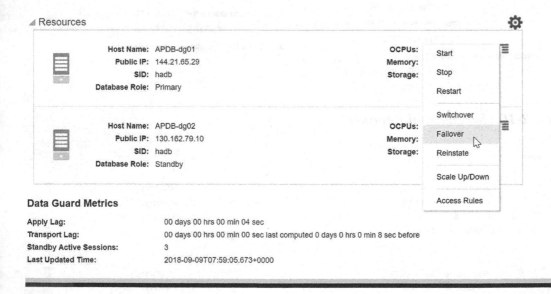

Figure 2-13. *Data Guard Failover option*

Choose the Failover option, and you will be asked for confirmation, as shown in Figure 2-14.

Figure 2-14. *Data Guard failover confirmation*

Click OK; this will start the failover and provide confirmation, as shown in Figure 2-15.

Figure 2-15. *Data Guard failover accepted*

After failover, the status will be updated in the cloud portal, as shown in Figure 2-16.

Notice in Figure 2-16 that after failover, the primary database moves to a reinstate status. It needs to be reinstated as a standby database. We can also see the Data Guard metrics in Figure 2-16. To reinstate the former primary database, click the dash icon located near OCUPs, as shown in Figure 2-17.

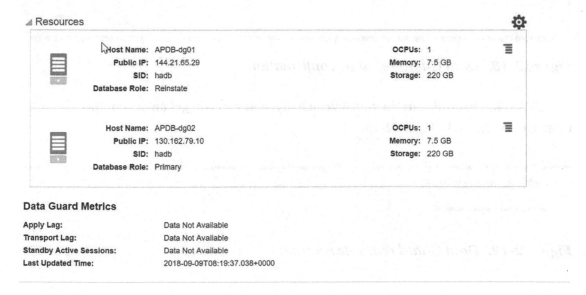

Figure 2-16. *Data Guard status after failover*

51

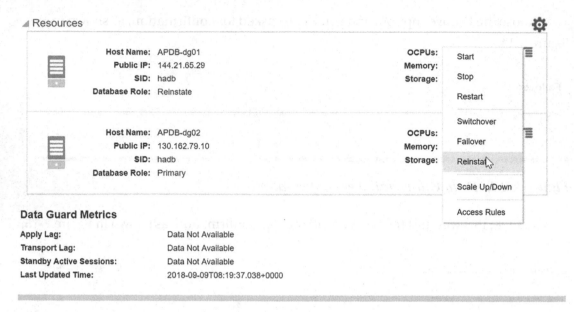

Figure 2-17. *Data Guard's Reinstate option*

After choosing the Reinstate option, we will be asked for confirmation, as shown in Figure 2-18.

Figure 2-18. *Data Guard reinstate confirmation*

Click OK. This will start the reinstate activity, and you will get an acceptance message, as shown in Figure 2-19.

Figure 2-19. *Data Guard reinstate acceptance*

Once the reinstate activity is completed, the former primary database role is changed to standby, as shown in Figure 2-20.

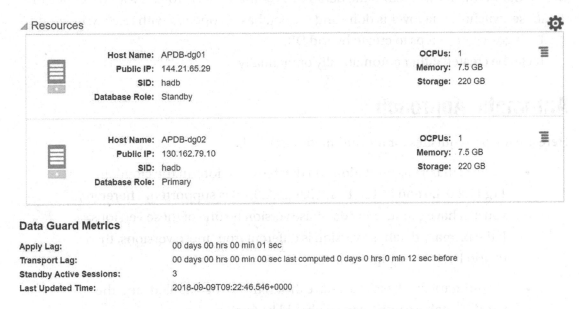

Data Guard Metrics

Apply Lag:	00 days 00 hrs 00 min 01 sec
Transport Lag:	00 days 00 hrs 00 min 00 sec last computed 0 days 0 hrs 0 min 12 sec before
Standby Active Sessions:	3
Last Updated Time:	2018-09-09T09:22:46.546+0000

Figure 2-20. *Data Guard status after reinstate*

We can also see Data Guard metrics after the reinstate in Figure 2-20. We could also do the switchover activity here to get the former primary database back.

Hybrid DR

Hybrid DR will have only the standby database in the cloud and leave the primary database at the on-premise environment. This requirement is sometimes feasible when you want to have one instance in the cloud. In addition, this method can be used for migration. Suppose you have planned to migrate to the cloud, but it has to be done with very little downtime. Then hybrid is the best choice. First create a standby in the cloud for the on-premise database and then do the switchover or failover at a convenient time. Only the switchover or failover activity time is considered as downtime. If the best practices mentioned for the switchover/failover are followed, then we can reduce the required downtime. Note that the primary database is not necessarily only on-premise; it could be located in another cloud like AWS or Google Cloud, or it could be in the Oracle Cloud but not managed by DBaaS.

The hybrid database will be in read-only mode. So, some of the `dbaascli` features will not work for a hybrid DR setup. Patching and backup utilities provided by the Oracle Cloud will not work until the database is in the standby role. It will work once the database switchover/failover is done and the database is opened with read-write mode.

Let's go over the steps to create hybrid DR.

It can be created either automatically or manually.

Automatic Approach

Here are the prerequisites for the automatic approach:

- Oracle DBaaS has limitations on database versions in the cloud. In 11g 11.2.0.4.0 and in 12c 12.1.0.2.0, 12.2.0.1.0 is supported. Therefore, you can have the standby database version be one of these versions. If the primary database version is different from these versions, then hybrid DR is not supported.

- The primary database must have the archived log enabled, and the Oracle Database home owner should be Oracle.

- By default Oracle tablespaces inside the Oracle Cloud are encrypted. Hence, the on-premise database should have all the tablespaces encrypted using Transparent Data Encryption (TDE), for which the Oracle Advanced Security option should have been purchased.

- If you are creating a hybrid database for a version higher than 12c, then the on-premise database should be a multitenant database. Oracle will not support nonmultitenant 12c databases in the cloud.

- In 12c, all pluggable databases should be in an open state.

- Currently hybrid DR doesn't support RAC databases, and also ASM is not supported.

- Enable force logging mode at the on-premise primary database to avoid any data loss when a statement is executed with the NOLOGGING class.

- The primary database should not be part of another Data Guard configuration.

- You should have a valid storage service account. You will be using cloud storage to keep the primary database backed up.

Here are the steps:

1. Hybrid DR needs to be created from the primary database backup.
    So, first you need to place the on-premise primary database
    backup in the cloud. For that, create a container in the storage
    cloud service and place the backup there.

    The storage container can be created through the cloud portal.

    From the dashboard, select ➤ Storage classic ➤ Create container.
    The dialog shown in Figure 2-21 will appear.

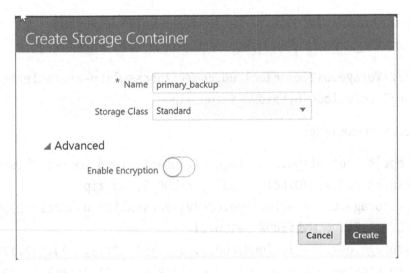

Figure 2-21. Storage container creation

Enter the name and storage class. The storage class could be
either Standard or Archive. Advanced denotes encryption at the
server level, which is not required in this case.

The storage creation can be done at the command level using the
curl command also.

```
curl -v -s -X PUT -U '<username>:<Password> <Storage End point>/<New
container name>
```

Here's an example:

```
curl -v -s -X PUT -u '****:********'   https://***.storage.oraclecloud.com/
v1/Storage-****/Primary_backup
> Host: **.storage.oraclecloud.com
> Accept: /
>
< HTTP/1.1 201 Created
< X-Trans-Id: tx83624605c6a94228bdab4-005b8bea1dga
```

The HTTP response shows the container has been created.

2. On the on-premise database server, download OracleCloud_
    HybridDR_Setup.zip from the Oracle Storage Cloud Service.

```
wget https://storage.us2.oraclecloud.com/v1/dbcsswlibp-usoracle29538/hdg/
DBCS_version/OracleCloud_HybridDR_Setup.zip
```

Here's an example:

```
[root@KKDB opc]# wget https://storage.us2.oraclecloud.com/v1/dbcsswlibp-
usoracle29538/hdg/18.2.3/OracleCloud_HybridDR_Setup.zip
--  https://storage.us2.oraclecloud.com/v1/dbcsswlibp-usoracle29538/
hdg/18.2.3/OracleCloud_HybridDR_Setup.zip
Resolving storage.us2.oraclecloud.com... 129.152.172.3, 129.152.172.4
Connecting to storage.us2.oraclecloud.com|129.152.172.3|:443... connected.
HTTP request sent, awaiting response... 200 OK
Length: 138247232 (132M) [application/zip]
Saving to: "OracleCloud_HybridDR_Setup.zip"

100%[=======================================================================
=============================================>] 138,247,232 18.6M/s    in
9.9s
(13.3 MB/s) - "OracleCloud_HybridDR_Setup.zip" saved [138247232/138247232]
```

In this example, 18.2.3 is the DBCS version. You can also get the
available DBCS versions by executing https://storage.us2.
oraclecloud.com/v1/dbcsswlibp-usoracle29538/hdg in the
web browser.

3. Unzip OracleCloud_HybridDR_Setup.zip.

```
-r-xr-xr-x. 1 root              98508 Apr  3  2014 perl-JSON-2.15-5.el6.noarch.rpm
-r-xr-xr-x. 1 root               2718 Nov 29  2017 README
-rw-rw-r--. 1 root          109740116 Jan 20  2018 dbaastools.rpm
```

4. As the root user, perform the next steps. Install the perl RPM and then the dbaastools RPM.

```
# rpm -Uvh perl-JSON-2.15-5.el6.noarch.rpm
# mkdir -p /home/oracle ; if the dir does not exist.
# rpm -Uvh dbaastools.rpm
# cd /var/opt
```

5. As the Oracle user, edit the config file /var/opt/oracle/hdg/
    setupdg.cfg. This file was created while performing the previous
    RPM installation.

```
cloud_ipaddr=<cloud Instance Public check>
oss_url=<Storage end point URL along with Container name>
onprem_ipaddr=<On-premise server IP address>
tde=Y
dbname=<Database Name>
wallet_passwd= <Wallet Password>
sys_passwd=<DB SYS user password>
oss_passwd=<Cloud login password>
cloud_shost=<service name on Oracle Public Cloud>
oss_user=<cloud login username>
firewall_acl=Y
```

6. Perform a DG readiness check. This is to check whether the
    on-premise database is ready to become part of Data Guard and
    meets all the prerequisites discussed earlier.

```
[oracle@goldengate hdg]$ ./setupdg.py
```

DG-readiness check

OK: On-premises Firewall ACLs configured
OK: Will use TDE to encrypt the standby database in cloud environment
OK: sys & system passwords are identical
OK: supported java version
OK: supported db
OK: supported database edition for Data Guard
OK: supported os
WARNING: Installed APEX version : 4.2.5.00.08; Recommended minimum apex
version : 5.0.0.00.31
OK: socket_size ok
OK: Data Vault is not enabled
OK: Flashback mode of the database is enabled
OK: The log mode is Archive Mode and the archive destination is /u01/app/
oracle/fast_recovery_...
OK: Database DB12cs is not part of an existing DG configuration
OK: DBID of DB12cs database is 1395628293
OK: Size of DB12cs database

data(MB)	temp(MB)	redo(MB)	archive(MB)	control(MB)	total(MB)
1561	60	30	107	10	1768

OK: sqlnet.ora has the following information
    SQLNET.ENCRYPTION_SERVER = requested
    SQLNET.ENCRYPTION_TYPES_SERVER = (RC4_256, AES256)
    SQLNET.ENCRYPTION_CLIENT = requested
    SQLNET.ENCRYPTION_TYPES_CLIENT = (RC4_256, AES256)
OK: Oracle Net Listener Configuration file listener.ora is present
OK: perl-JSON rpm is installed
OK: netcat (nc) rpm is installed
OK: /etc/hosts entries are verified fine
OK: Domain information available for goldengate
    All checks passed. Database backup can be performed

New set of priv/pub ssh keypair is created for oracle user. The keypair
is under /home/oracle/.ssh, please use this to access this VM. Backup of
original /home/oracle/.ssh is saved as /home/oracle/.ssh.bak
    Created hdgonpreminfo.tgz. Uploaded to OSS

DG-readiness check completed
---

7. Once the prerequisite checks are successful, invoke the backup
    operation to take the on-premise database back to the cloud.
    The backup command will again check the prerequisites. If there
    are any prerequisite failures, then the backup command will
    terminate. So, invoke the backup command only after having
    successful prerequisite checks.

./setupdg.py -b is the command to take backup of on-premise primary
database backup to cloud.
[oracle@goldengate hdg]$ ./setupdg.py -b

DG-readiness check

OK: On-premises Firewall ACLs configured
OK: Will use TDE to encrypt the standby database in cloud environment
OK: sys & system passwords are identical
OK: supported java version
OK: supported db
OK: supported database edition for Data Guard
OK: supported os
WARNING: Installed APEX version : 4.2.5.00.08; Recommended minimum apex
version : 5.0.0.00.31
OK: socket_size ok
OK: Data Vault is not enabled
OK: Flashback mode of the database is enabled
OK: The log mode is Archive Mode and the archive destination is /u01/app/
oracle/fast_recovery_...
OK: Database DB12cs is not part of an existing DG configuration

OK: DBID of DB12cs database is 1395628293

OK: Size of DB12cs database

data(MB)	temp(MB)	redo(MB)	archive(MB)	control(MB)	total(MB)
1561	60	30	117	10	1778

OK: sqlnet.ora has the following information

    SQLNET.ENCRYPTION_SERVER = requested

    SQLNET.ENCRYPTION_TYPES_SERVER = (RC4_256, AES256)

    SQLNET.ENCRYPTION_CLIENT = requested

    SQLNET.ENCRYPTION_TYPES_CLIENT = (RC4_256, AES256)

OK: Oracle Net Listener Configuration file listener.ora is present

OK: perl-JSON rpm is installed

OK: netcat (nc) rpm is installed

OK: /etc/hosts entries are verified fine

OK: Domain information available for goldengate

    All checks passed. Database backup can be performed

100% of checks completed successfully

running opc installer

creating config file for rman backup

generating rman.bkup

initiating backup

backup in progress. Takes a while

....

database backup to oss complete.

New set of priv/pub ssh keypair is created for oracle user. The keypair
is under /home/oracle/.ssh, please use this to access this VM. Backup of
original /home/oracle/.ssh is saved as /home/oracle/.ssh.bak

    Created hdgonpreminfo.tgz. Uploaded to OSS

 DG-readiness check completed

8. As the next step, create the database instance in the cloud through the GUI portal and set the type to Data Guard Standby for Hybrid DR, as shown in Figure 2-22.

Instance
Provide basic service instance information.

* Instance Name	DG-DB	* Service Level	Oracle Database Cloud Service
Description		* Metering Frequency	Monthly
Notification Email	cloudaced@gmail.com	* Software Release	Oracle Database 12c Release 1
Region	No Preference	* Software Edition	Enterprise Edition
Tags		* Database Type	Single Instance

Single Instance
Database Clustering with RAC
Single Instance with Data Guard Standby
Data Guard Standby for Hybrid DR
Database Clustering with RAC and Data Guard Standby

Figure 2-22. *Hybrid DR instance creation*

9. The next page will ask about the backup details. You need to give information about where the backup is stored, as shown in Figure 2-23.

* Cloud Storage Container   https://cloudaced.storage.oracle

* Username   Username

* Password   Password

Figure 2-23. *Storage container specification*

10. The page will ask you to confirm the details. Once you confirm, the hybrid instance will get created.

Manual Approach

In the previous section, we discussed how to create hybrid DR in the cloud using the utility provided by Oracle. It performed all the prerequisite checks and also took an RMAN backup of the on-premise database to the cloud automatically. But note that the automatic method performs a full database restoration of the on-premise database in the cloud and converts it to standby. In this section, we will discuss how to create hybrid DR manually.

The prerequisite section is the same for the automatic and manual methods. So, all the prerequisites discussed in the automatic method are applicable here as well.

Once the prerequisites are met, you need to take an on-premise database backup and put it in the cloud. In the automated method, the `/var/opt/oracle/hdg/setupdg.py` script did this task.

Here are the steps to do it manually:

1. Create a storage container in the Oracle cloud. You are going to take on-premise database backup of this storage container.

2. Download the Oracle Cloud Backup Module from the Oracle Technology Network web site (see Figure 2-24).

`http://www.oracle.com/technetwork/database/availability/oracle-cloud-backup-2162729.html`

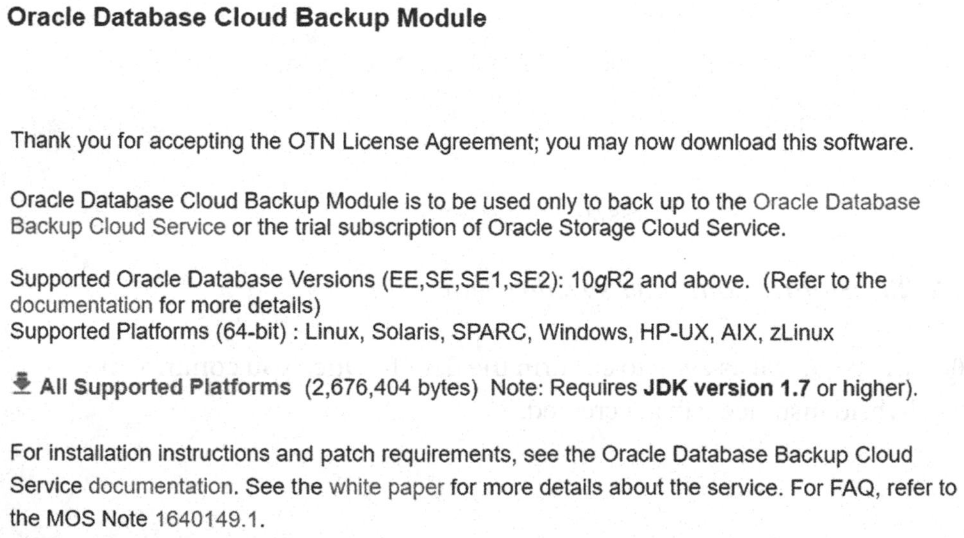

Oracle Database Cloud Backup Module

Thank you for accepting the OTN License Agreement; you may now download this software.

Oracle Database Cloud Backup Module is to be used only to back up to the Oracle Database Backup Cloud Service or the trial subscription of Oracle Storage Cloud Service.

Supported Oracle Database Versions (EE,SE,SE1,SE2): 10gR2 and above. (Refer to the documentation for more details)
Supported Platforms (64-bit) : Linux, Solaris, SPARC, Windows, HP-UX, AIX, zLinux

⬇ **All Supported Platforms** (2,676,404 bytes) Note: Requires **JDK version 1.7** or higher).

For installation instructions and patch requirements, see the Oracle Database Backup Cloud Service documentation. See the white paper for more details about the service. For FAQ, refer to the MOS Note 1640149.1.

Figure 2-24. *Oracle Cloud Backup Module download page*

The downloaded zip file will be opc_installer.zip.

Extract the opc_installer.zip file. You will get opc_install.jar and opc_readme.txt.

This JAR file will perform the backup module installation using Java. You will be passing the necessary arguments including your cloud login credentials to opc_install.jar. It will connect to the Oracle repository to validate the cloud login credentials and then download the Oracle Cloud Library to the local machine. Here is how to use it:

```
Usage: java -jar opc_install.jar
-opcId:              The userid for the Oracle Public Cloud account
-opcPass:            The password for the Oracle Public Cloud account
-host:               Host name for the Oracle Public Cloud account.
-walletDir:          Directory to store wallet
-configFile:         File name of config file
-libDir:             Directory to store library
-libPlatform:        The desired platform for the library
-proxyHost:          HTTP proxy server
-proxyPort:          HTTP proxy server port
-proxyID:            HTTP proxy server username
-proxyPass:          HTTP proxy server password
-container:          OPC container to store backups
-container class     OPC container Storage class
-containerLTP:       file name of lifecycle tiering policy (LTP)
-trustedCerts:       SSL certificates to be imported
-argFile:            File name of arguments file
-help:               Print this usage information and exit
-import-all-trustcerts:  Import all certificates from Java truststore
```

- **opcId**: This is the cloud login username.

- **opcPass**: This is the cloud login password.

- **host**: This is the host name for the Oracle public cloud account.

- **walletDir**: This is the directory at which the wallet gets created. This wallet will have the login credentials of the cloud. Note that this wallet is different from the database wallet. This wallet is only for login purposes.

- **libDir**: This is the location at which the cloud library will be downloaded from the Oracle repository. This parameter is optional. If this parameter is omitted, then the library will not be downloaded. This parameter will be omitted when only a wallet needs to be created, like the cloud login password expiry. After the password expiry, you will specify a new password, and the wallet will be re-created using a new password. You don't need to download a library for this task.

- **libPlatform**: `opc_install.jar` will automatically detect the operating system. If it is not able to detect the operating system, the `libPlatform` parameter is required to be specified. The supported values for the parameter are:

  - `linux64`, `windows64`, `solaris_sparc64`, `solaris_x64`, `zlinux64`, `hpux_ia64`, `aix_ppc64`

- **Container**: This is the OPC storage container to store the backups. It could be the existing container or any new container name that will get created in cloud storage.

- **Container Storage Class**: This is the storage class for the container. It could be either Standard or Tiering. Standard is the default container class for storing backups. Tiering is for long-lived data that is accessed infrequently.

- **Container LTP**: This is the file name of the OPC container lifecycle tiering policy (LTP). The file must be a JSON document specifying the time after which objects in the OPC container will be moved to the archive tier and specifying the type of objects that can be excluded from being archived.

- **-argFile**: This reads the remainder of the command-line arguments from the specified file. Specify the file name as - to read arguments from standard input.

- **-import-all-trustcerts**: This imports all X.509 certificates from the Java trust store.

  The JDK version should be 1.7 or higher, and `ORACLE_SID` should be set before executing `opc_installer`. Otherwise, an error will be thrown. This value is required to create the `opc` parameter file in the `$ORACLE_HOME dbs` folder.

  Here's an installation example:

```
$ java -jar opc_install.jar -host https://abc.storage.oraclecloud.com/v1/
Storage-IDD/container1 -opcId 'John@abc.com' -opcPass 'WelcOme' -walletDir
//home/oracle/opc/wallet/ -libdir /home/oracle/opc/lib/
Oracle Database Cloud Backup Module Install Tool, build 2016-10-07
Oracle Database Cloud Backup Module credentials are valid.
Oracle Database Cloud Backup Module wallet created in directory /u01/app/
oracle/opc/wallet.
Oracle Database Cloud Backup Module initialization file /u01/app/oracle/
product/12.1.0/dbhome_1/dbs/opcDB121.ora created.
Downloading Oracle Database Cloud Backup Module Software Library from file
opc_linux64.zip.
Downloaded 26528348 bytes in 4 seconds. Transfer rate was 6632087 bytes/second.
Download complete.
```

You can see that the files are created as part of the execution.

- Wallet file at **/u01/app/oracle/opc/wallet**

- Parameter file `opcDB121.ora` at **/u01/app/oracle/product/12.1.0/ dbhome_1/dbs**

  `ORACLE_SID` was set to DB121; hence, the `opc` parameter file was created as `opcDB121.ora`.

  The content of the parameter file is as follows:

```
OPC_HOST=https://abc.storage.oraclecloud.com/v1/Storage-IDD OPC_
WALLET='LOCATION=file: /home/oracle/opc/wallet/ CREDENTIAL_ALIAS=alias_opc'
OPC_CONTAINER=container1
```

- The library file `libopc.dll` at /home/oracle/opc/lib/.

  This parameter file and library will be specified with RMAN SBT channel configuration.

  Here's an example:

```
CONFIGURE CHANNEL DEVICE TYPE 'SBT_TAPE' PARMS  'SBT_LIBRARY=/home/oracle/
opc/lib/libopc.so,SBT_PARMS=(OPC_PFILE=/u01/app/oracle/product/12.1.0.2.0/
dbs/opcDB12c.ora)';
```

  The RMAN backups should be encrypted while storing a backup to Oracle Cloud storage. RMAN supports three methods of encryption: password-based encryption, TDE, and both.

  In password-based encryption, RMAN backups will be encrypted with the password. The same password will be required during decryption. If the password is forgotten, then the backup piece cannot be decrypted and restored.

```
RMAN> set encryption on identified by "<Password>" only;
```

  In the TDE encryption, the backup piece will be encrypted using the wallet. The same wallet should be available during restore. Without the same wallet, the backup piece cannot be decrypted and restored.

```
RMAN> set encryption on;
```

  Another model includes both TDE and the password. At the time of restore, you need a password plus a wallet.

```
RMAN> set encryption on identified by "<password>";
```

  The only word is the only difference between password-based encryption and password plus TDE encryption.

  Here's an example:

```
RMAN> set encryption on identified by "oracle" only;
executing command: SET encryption
RMAN> run
```

```
{
allocate channel c1 type sbt parms='SBT_LIBRARY=/u01/app/oracle/opc/lib/
libopc.so,SBT_PARMS=(OPC_PFILE=/u01/app/oracle/product/12.1.0/dbhome_1/dbs/
opcCDB121.ora)';
backup current controlfile;
}
```

At this stage, a backup is stored in cloud storage and ready for restore. The next step is creating a hybrid standby database. From here you can follow the automatic creation method. In the GUI cloud portal, choose Data Guard Standby for Hybrid DR, as shown in Figure 2-25.

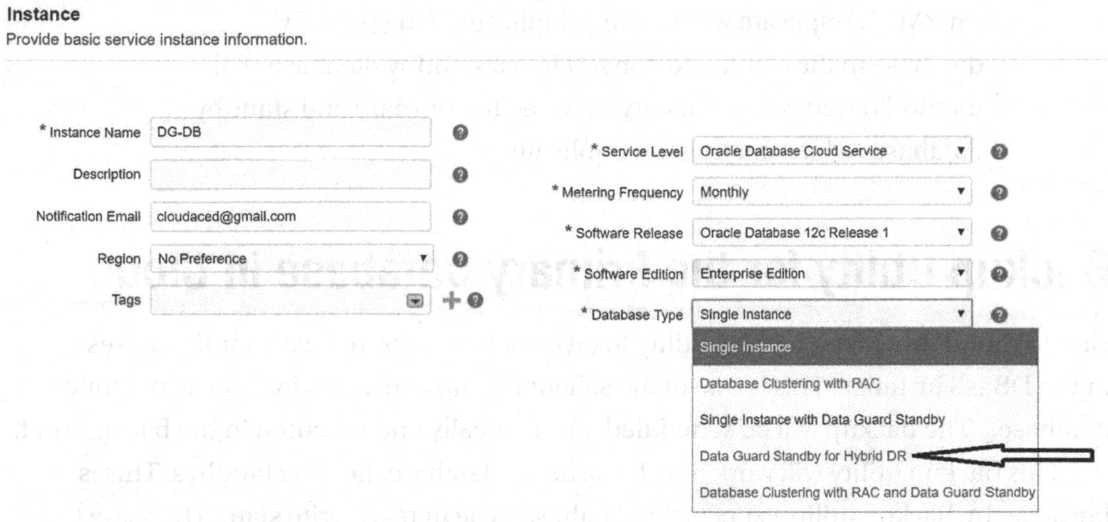

Instance
Provide basic service instance information.

* Instance Name	DG-DB		* Service Level	Oracle Database Cloud Service ▾
Description			* Metering Frequency	Monthly ▾
Notification Email	cloudaced@gmail.com		* Software Release	Oracle Database 12c Release 1 ▾
Region	No Preference ▾		* Software Edition	Enterprise Edition ▾
Tags	▾ ➕		* Database Type	Single Instance ▾

Single Instance
Database Clustering with RAC
Single Instance with Data Guard Standby
Data Guard Standby for Hybrid DR ⟵
Database Clustering with RAC and Data Guard Standby

Figure 2-25. *Hybrid DR instance creation*

It will ask for a storage container where the backup is stored, as shown in Figure 2-26.

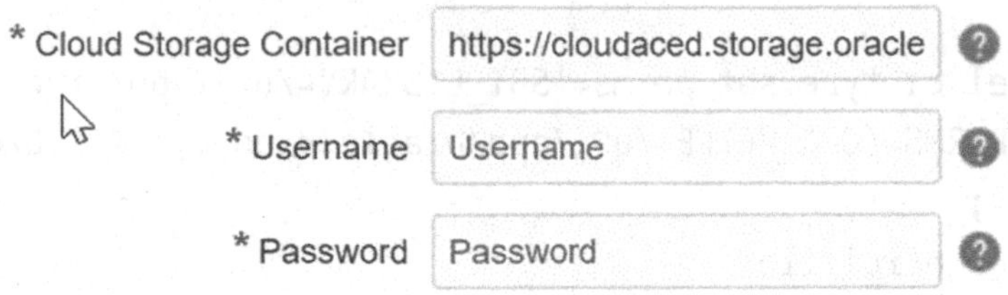

* Cloud Storage Container   https://cloudaced.storage.oracle   ❓

* Username   Username   ❓

* Password   Password   ❓

Figure 2-26. *Cloud storage container creation*

We can provide the container name where your on-premise primary database backup is stored.

We can also create a standby in the cloud using traditional methods like RMAN Duplicate or RMAN Active Duplicate.

An RMAN duplicate will create a duplicate of the primary database in the cloud and convert it to a standby database. This method requires connectivity between the primary and standby databases while creating the duplicate.

Backup Utility for the Primary Database in Cloud

Oracle Cloud provides a backup utility to take backups automatically for databases in the DBasS instance. This is one of the salient features provided by Oracle for cloud databases. The backup will be scheduled automatically and executed in the background.

This backup utility will work only for primary database, not for standbys. This is because the backup utility expects the database to be in read-write state. There are two types of backup models.

Backing Up to Cloud Storage

Backups will be taken to the cloud storage container. It will take incremental level 0 backups on the weekend and level 1 backup on other days. The backup will be executed at night. You can find the backup scheduling time in /etc/crontab. The backup retention by default will be 30 days. The obsolete backups will be deleted automatically. An archived logs backup will be taken every 30 minutes, and the backed-up archived logs will be deleted automatically to maintain the space. In the DG environment, it works as follows:

1. A level 0 backup of the primary database will be taken on the cloud on the first day.

2. An incremental 1 backup will be taken from day 2.

3. On the weekend, again a level 0 backup will be taken.

4. The backup retention is 30 days by default. This is a maximum limit.

5. During every backup, obsolete backups (older than 30 days) will be deleted automatically.

Backing Up to Disk and Cloud Storage

A backup will be taken at both destinations, disk and cloud. This method uses the RMAN recovery image copy method. A disk image copy of it will be stored in FRA, and every day an incremental backup will be taken and applied to the image copy.

In the DG environment, it works as follows:

1. The primary database data files will be copied to the FRA location on the first backup attempt.

2. The incremental backup will be taken starting on day 2, and that incremental backup will be applied to the image copy stored in FRA based on the disk retention you have defined. By default the disk has seven days of retention. This means the incremental backup will get applied to the image copy after seven days. The image copy always is seven days older; hence, you can recover the database anytime within the past seven days.

3. The incremental backup of the last seven days will be stored in the disk, and older backups will get deleted.

4. The archived logs are backed up to the cloud every 30 minutes, and the backed-up archived logs will be deleted based on retention policy.

5. Image copies stored in the FRA will be backed up as the backup set to the cloud.

6. Backups that are older than 30 days will be deleted from the cloud.

7. Along with the database backup, the OS and Oracle database
    configuration files will be backed up.

The primary database backup can be taken either to the disk and cloud or to the
cloud alone through the backup utility.

We can find out details of the current backup configuration using the dbaascli tool.
As discussed earlier, first check for any dbaascli tool updates. If so, first update it first.
As the root user in a DBaaS environment, execute the following command:

```
/var/opt/oracle/bkup_api/bkup_api get config [--file=filename] --dbname=dbname
```

Here, filename denotes the output file with the collected configuration details.
dbname is required if there are multiple databases configured in the instance.
Here's an example:

```
/var/opt/oracle/bkup_api/bkup_api get config–file=/tmp/bkup.cfg–dbname=ORCL
DBaaS Backup API V1.5 @2016 Multi-Oracle home
-> Action : get_config
-> logfile: /var/opt/oracle/bkup_api/log/bkup_api.log
File /tmp/bkup.cfg created
```

File /tmp/bkup.cfg will have the current backup configuration details.
Here's an example:

```
#Enable automatic backup. Can be set yes/no
bkup_cron_entry=yes

#Enable backup of config files. Can be yes/no
bkup_cfg_files=yes

# Time of the daily incremental backup. The format must be hh:mm. It
denotes at what time the backup has to be executed.
bkup_daily_time=0:59
#### Disk Configuration Parameters ####
#Enable backup to disk. Can be yes/no. If no then only Cloud backup will be taken.
bkup_disk=yes
#Recovery window of disk. Must be between 1 and 14
bkup_disk_recovery_window=7
```

CHAPTER 2   ORACLE ACTIVE DATA GUARD WITH CLOUD SERVICES

```
#### OSS Configuration Parameters ####
# Enable backup to oss container. Can be set yes/no. It denotes Cloud Backup.
bkup_oss=yes
## Below parameter are only applicable when bkup_oss is set to yes
# OSS Day of Level 0 Backup. Available options are: mon, tue, wed, thu,
fri, sat, sun. The day at which Full backup has to be taken
bkup_oss_l0_day=Sun
# Recovery window of oss. Must be between 1 and 30.
bkup_oss_recovery_window=30
# OSS url. Example:  https://storage.oraclecorp.com/v1/Storage-test/test
bkup_oss_url=<Storage End Point>
# OSS username
bkup_oss_user=<Cloud login username>

# OSS password. Uncomment the below line and introduce a password for
reconfiguration.
#bkup_oss_passwd= <Cloud login password>
```

If we want to change the backup configuration such as changing the retention period or changing the cloud login password, then specify those changes in the configuration file like /tmp/bkup.cfg and execute the following command:

```
/var/opt/oracle/bkup_api/bkup_api set config-file=filename-dbname=dbname
```

- Filename: File with the configuration details

- Dbname: Database to which the configuration to be set

Managing DR Instances Through DBaaS Monitor/Oracle SQL Developer Web

We saw how to use the command utility dbaascli to manage the database environment. Oracle DBaaS has also provided a GUI utility to perform DBA tasks to cloud database instances called Oracle SQL Developer Web. (An earlier tool was the DBaaS Monitor.)

You can access this utility after logging into the instance; click the dash symbol available at the top, as shown in Figure 2-27.

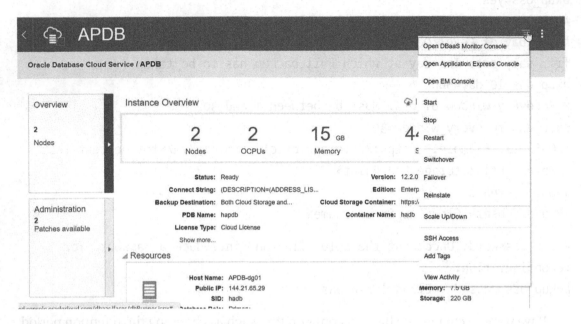

Figure 2-27. *DBaaS Monitor option*

Click Open DBaaS Monitor Console, as shown in Figure 2-28.

Figure 2-28. *DBaaS Monitor console*

You will see a page with the GUI tools, as shown in Figure 2-29.

Figure 2-29. *SQL Developer Web*

The page has the options Application Express, SQL Developer Web, Documentation, and Oracle Cloud Service.

Enable the Login Schema

SQL Developer Web is a web interface, which needs database schema details. It is a schema-based authentication utility.

Using this too, the primary database can be monitored and managed. You need to enable the schema to log into SQL Developer Web.

This can be done by executing the Oracle Rest Data Services (ORDS) function.

```
enable_schema_sdw( $password, $pdb_name, $schema_name, [$is_dba] )
```

Here are the parameters:

- password: The password of the schema to be connected to

- schema_name: The name of the schema that is going to be enabled for sdw

- is_dba: Whether you are going to give grants as a DBA to the schema

Log into the DBaaS machine as the opc user and switch to root.

```
#sudo -s
```

Create a text file and enter the password in the file.

```
[root@APDB-dg02 opc]#  touch /u01/app/oracle/system_password.txt
[root@APDB-dg02 opc]# vi /u01/app/oracle/system_password.txt
[root@APDB-dg02 opc]# cat /u01/app/oracle/system_password.txt
Welcome#1
```

Change the permission of the text file to 600.

```
[root@APDB-dg02 opc]# chmod 600 /u01/app/oracle/system_password.txt
```

Move to the present directory, **/var/opt/oracle/ocde/assistants/ords**.

```
[root@APDB-dg02 opc]# cd /var/opt/oracle/ocde/assistants/ords
```

Invoke the ords command for the function enable_schema_for_sdw. We will be passing the values required for the arguments of the function.

```
./ords -ords_action="enable_schema_for_sdw" \
-ords_sdw_schema="schema-name" \
-ords_sdw_schema_password="<File Containing Password>" \
-ords_sdw_schema_enable_dba="dba-boolean"
```

If we are enabling a schema that is located inside the pluggable database, then do the following:

```
./ords -ords_action="enable_schema_for_sdw" \
-ords_sdw_schema="schema-name" \
-ords_sdw_schema_password="<File Containing Password>" \
-ords_sdw_schema_container="pdb-name" \
-ords_sdw_schema_enable_dba="dba-boolean"
```

- schema-name is the name of the schema you want to enable. If it doesn't exist, it will be created.

- dba-boolean is TRUE or FALSE. If you enter TRUE, the schema will be enabled to support the database administrator features of SQL Developer Web.

- pdb-name is the name of the pluggable database (PDB) containing the schema you want to enable.

Here's an example:

```
[root@APDB-dg02 ords]# ./ords -ords_action="enable_schema_for_sdw" \
> -ords_sdw_schema="system" \
> -ords_sdw_schema_password="/u01/app/oracle/system_password.txt" \
> -ords_sdw_schema_enable_dba="TRUE"
sStarting ORDS
Logfile is /var/opt/oracle/log/ords/ords_2018-09-09_07:34:30.log
Config file is /var/opt/oracle/ocde/assistants/ords/ords.cfg
INFO: Starting environment summary checks...
INFO: Database version : 12201
INFO: Database CDB : yes
INFO: Original DBaaS Tools RPM installed : dbaastools-1.0-1+18.1.4.0.0_
180123.1336.x86_64
INFO: Actual DBaaS Tools RPM installed : dbaastools-1.0-1+18.3.1.1.0_
180829.0000.x86_64
INFO: DBTools JDK RPM installed : dbtools_jdk-1.8.0-2.74.el6.x86_64
INFO: DBTools JDK RPM "/var/opt/oracle/rpms/dbtools/dbtools_jdk-1.8.0-2.74.
el6.x86_64.rpm" MD5 : 48f13bb401677bfc7cf0748eb1a6990d
INFO: DBTools ORDS Standalone RPM installed : dbtools_ords_standalone-
3.0.9.348.07.16-5.el6.x86_64
INFO: DBTools ORDS Standalone RPM "/var/opt/oracle/rpms/dbtools/
dbtools_ords_standalone-18.1.0.11.22.15-1.el6.x86_64.rpm" MD5 :
480355ac3ce0f357d5741c2c2f688901
INFO: DBTools DBaaS Monitor RPM installed : dbtools_dbaas_monitor-
4.1.10-1.el6.x86_64
INFO: DBTools DBaaS Landing Page RPM installed : dbtools_dbaas_landing_page-
1.0.1-4.el6.x86_64
INFO: DBTools DBaaS Landing Page RPM "/var/opt/oracle/rpms/
dbtools/dbtools_dbaas_landing_page-2.0.0-1.el6.x86_64.rpm" MD5 :
af79e128a56b38de1c3406cfcec966db
INFO: Environment summary completed...
INFO: Action mode is "full"
INFO: Database Role is "PRIMARY"
INFO: Enabling "system" schema in "CDB$ROOT" container for SQL Developer Web...
```

```
SQL*Plus: Release 12.2.0.1.0 Production on Sun Sep 9 07:34:46 2018
Copyright © 1982, 2016, Oracle.  All rights reserved.

Connected to:
Oracle Database 12c Enterprise Edition Release 12.2.0.1.0 - 64bit
Production
SQL> SQL> SQL> SQL> SQL> SQL> SQL> SQL Developer Web user enable
starting...
Enabling "SYSTEM" user for SQL Developer Web...
PL/SQL procedure successfully completed.
PL/SQL procedure successfully completed.
PL/SQL procedure successfully completed.
PL/SQL procedure successfully completed.
PL/SQL procedure successfully completed.
Call completed.
Commit complete.
PL/SQL procedure successfully completed.
Session altered.
PL/SQL procedure successfully completed.
PL/SQL procedure successfully completed.
"SYSTEM" user enabled successfully. The schema to access SQL Developer Web is
"system"...
PL/SQL procedure successfully completed.
SQL Developer Web user enable finished...
Disconnected from Oracle Database 12c Enterprise Edition Release
12.2.0.1.0 - 64bit Production
INFO:  To access SQL Developer Web through DBaaS Landing Page, the schema
"system" needs to be provided...
INFO: "SYSTEM" schema in the "CDB$ROOT" container for SQL Developer Web was
enabled successfully...
[root@APDB-dg02 ords]#
```

The function will evaluate the DBaaS tool version and all related OS RPMs. It will log into the database and perform SQL operations to enable a schema for SQL Developer Web.

Using the Schema

Give the schema a name, as shown in Figure 2-30.

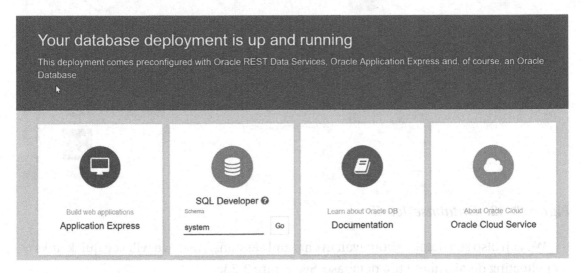

Figure 2-30. *Schema for SQL Developer Web*

Click the Go button; it will ask for a password, as shown in Figure 2-31. The username should be in capital letters.

Figure 2-31. *Login details for SQL Developer Web*

Using the GUI

After successfully logging in, we should see the details of the primary database. As shown in Figure 2-32 and Figure 2-33, we should see the status, number of alert errors, how many are related to the primary database, and how much storage has been used.

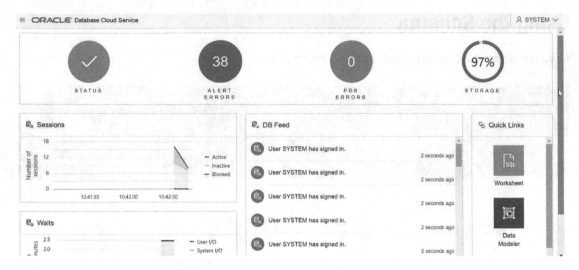

Figure 2-32. *Database details*

We can also see details about wait events and sessions. Also, we will see quick links for collecting details about the database. See Figure 2-33.

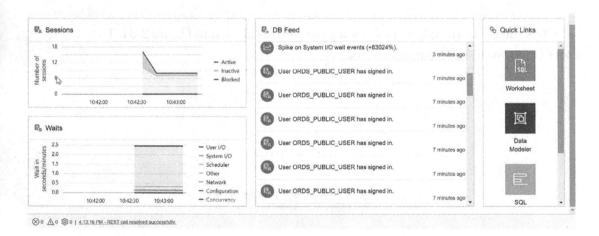

Figure 2-33. *Database details*

SQL Developer Web has five menus: Home, Worksheet, DBA, OS Tasks, and Data Modeler.

- **Home (Figure 2-34)**: This will provide details of recently modified objects, invalid database objects, and table details such as number of rows, blocks, and when the table was last analyzed.

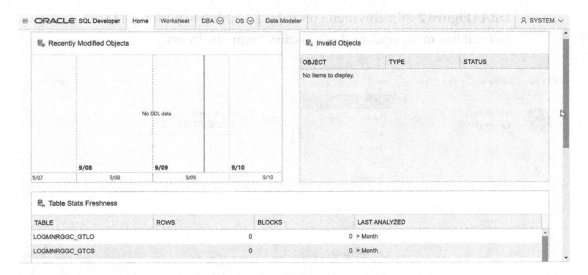

Figure 2-34. Oracle SQL Developer Web, Home

- **Worksheet (Figure 2-35):** This is the place where you execute SQL commands. It is a kind of SQL editor. This sheet is useful to execute and tune queries. It has Explain Plan and Auto Trace tabs.

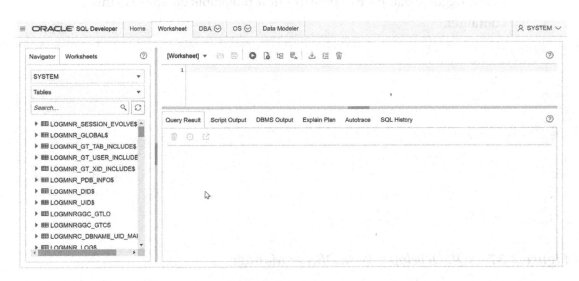

Figure 2-35. SQL Developer Web, Worksheet

- **DBA (Figure 2-36):** This menu provides an option to perform all DBA tasks. It has many options. Let's discuss them one by one.

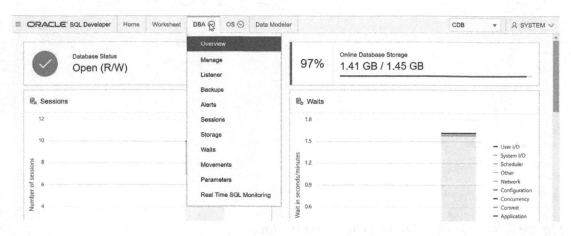

Figure 2-36. *SQL Developer Web, DBA*

- **DBA tasks, Manage (Figure 2-37):** This shows the root database and the pluggable database's Open status. It has an option to create a new pluggable database or plug in a new pluggable database to this container.

Figure 2-37. *SQL Developer Web, DBA ➤ Manage*

Create PDB will collect details such as the pluggable database's name, admin username and password, file name conversion (primary database file name location; Figure 2-39), storage limitations on data files, new or reused temp file for the primary database, database encryption, and key to do encryption. It has also a provision to show the SQL statement (Figure 2-40) used to create the pluggable database, as shown in Figure 2-38.

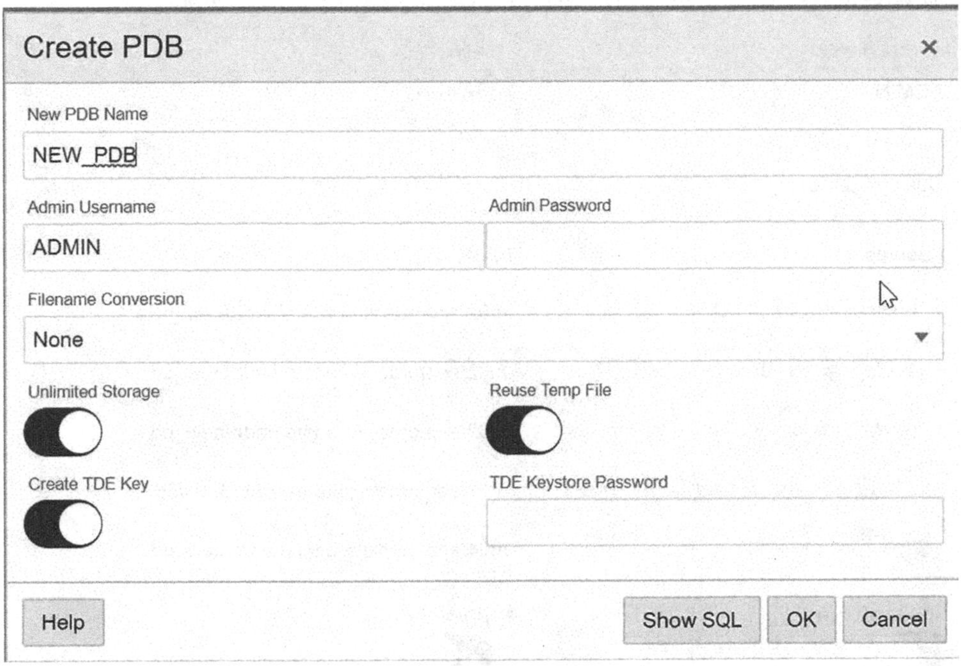

Figure 2-38. *SQL Developer Web, DBA ➤ Manage ➤ Pluggable database creation*

Create PDB   ✕

New PDB Name

NEW_PDB

Admin Username   Admin Password

ADMIN   ··········

Filename Conversion

Custom Names   ▼

Source	Target
/u02/app/oracle/oradata/hadb/pdbseec	/u02/app/oracle/oradata/hadb/new_pd
/u02/app/oracle/oradata/hadb/pdbseec	/u02/app/oracle/oradata/hadb/new_pd
/u02/app/oracle/oradata/hadb/pdbseec	/u02/app/oracle/oradata/hadb/new_pd
/u02/app/oracle/oradata/HADB_01/5FI	/u02/app/oracle/oradata/HADB_01/5FI
/u04/app/oracle/oradata/temp/pdbseec	/u04/app/oracle/oradata/temp/new_pd

Unlimited Storage   Reuse Temp File

Create TDE Key   TDE Keystore Password

Figure 2-39. *SQL Developer Web, DBA ➤ Manage ➤ Pluggable database creation*
➤ Customize PDB file location

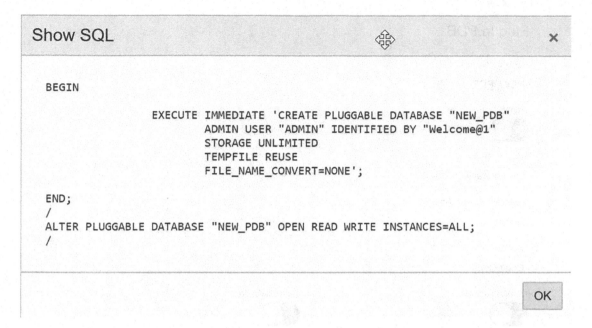

```
Show SQL                                            ⊕                    ✕


    BEGIN

                EXECUTE IMMEDIATE 'CREATE PLUGGABLE DATABASE "NEW_PDB"
                        ADMIN USER "ADMIN" IDENTIFIED BY "Welcome@1"
                        STORAGE UNLIMITED
                        TEMPFILE REUSE
                        FILE_NAME_CONVERT=NONE';

    END;
    /
    ALTER PLUGGABLE DATABASE "NEW_PDB" OPEN READ WRITE INSTANCES=ALL;
    /


                                                                     OK
```

Figure 2-40. *SQL Developer Web, DBA* ➤ *Manage* ➤ *Pluggable database creation* ➤ *Show SQL statement*

The plugin option is to plug a new pluggable database into the current container. It will ask for the primary database name, XML file name with primary database metadata, any file name conversion for the new primary database, whether you need to copy the primary database to a different location as part of this plug-in, and details about storage, temp, and encryption, as shown in Figure 2-41.

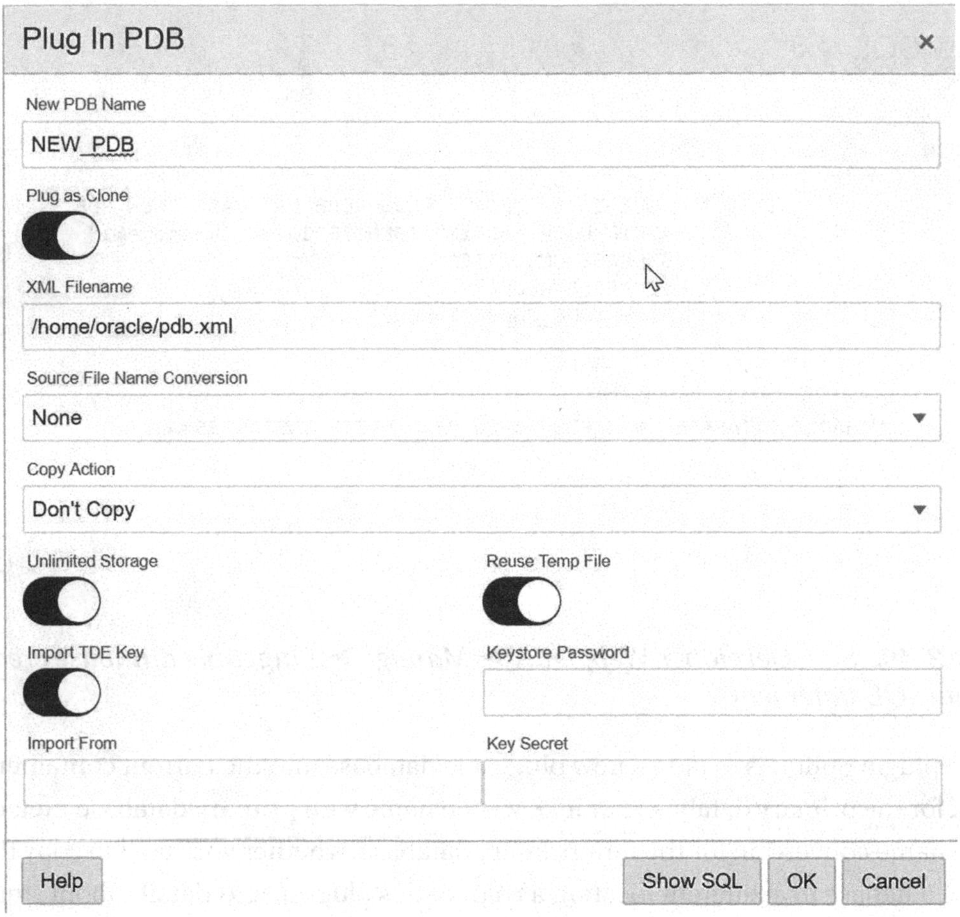

Figure 2-41. *SQL Developer Web, DBA ➤ Manage ➤ Plug in PDB*

We now have seen all the details about the Manage option, so let's move to next option, Listener.

- **Listener**: This is the current listener status, as shown in Figure 2-42.

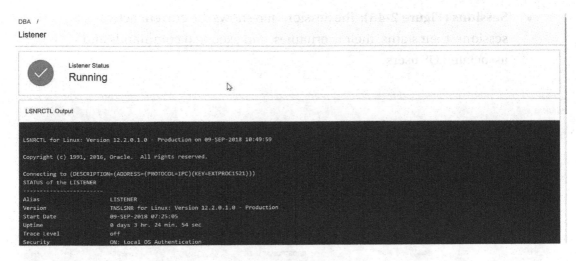

Figure 2-42. *SQL Developer Web, DBA ➤ Listener*

- **Backups (Figure 2-43):** The Backup tab shows details of the backup status, the start and end times, and a message. If the backup has failed, the Message column will have the reason for the failure.

DBA /

Backups

	STATUS	START_TIME	END_TIME	PROCESS_ID	MESSAGE
1	✕ Failed	2018-09-09T09:34:28.859Z	2018-09-09T09:35:47.374Z	13938	Unable to complete backup process. Please check obkup.lo

Figure 2-43. *SQL Developer Web, DBA ➤ Backup*

- **Alert (Figure 2-44):** The Alerts tab will have database alerts, their timestamps, and messages with alert details.

DBA /

Alerts

Column		Operator		Value			⟳
TYPE	▼	equals	▼			🔍	

	TYPE	TIMESTAMP	HOST	MESSAGE_TEXT
1	Message	2018-09-09T10:48:14.07Z	APDB-dg01 (10.28.193.150)	Pluggable database NEW_PDB opened read write
2	Message	2018-09-09T10:48:14.07Z	APDB-dg01 (10.28.193.150)	Completed: ALTER PLUGGABLE DATABASE "NEW_PDB" OPEN READ WRITE INSTAN
3	Message	2018-09-09T10:48:10.651Z	APDB-dg01 (10.28.193.150)	**
4	Message	2018-09-09T10:48:10.65Z	APDB-dg01 (10.28.193.150)	**

Figure 2-44. *SQL Developer Web, DBA ➤ Alerts*

- **Sessions (Figure 2-45):** The Sessions tab shows the current active sessions, their status, their usernames, and executed commands and associated OS users.

DBA /
Sessions

	CON_ID	SID	SERIAL	SQL_ID	USERNAME	COMMAND	OS_USER	
1	1	273	16134	dqhaxxggpcbra	SYSTEM	SELECT	oracle	active
2	1	35	60735	(null)	ORDS_PUBLIC_USER	(null)	oracle	inactiv
3	1	39	48778	(null)	ORDS_PUBLIC_USER	(null)	oracle	inactiv
4	1	251	60781	(null)	ORDS_PUBLIC_USER	(null)	oracle	inactiv
5	1	252	24450	(null)	ORDS_PUBLIC_USER	(null)	oracle	inactiv
6	1	253	46468	(null)	ORDS_PUBLIC_USER	(null)	oracle	inactiv
7	1	28	26499	(null)	PUBLIC	(null)	oracle	inactiv
8	1	41	16337	(null)	ORDS_PUBLIC_USER	(null)	oracle	inactiv

Column: SID   Operator: equals   Value: 0

Figure 2-45. *SQL Developer Web, DBA ➤ Sessions*

- **Storage (Figure 2-46):** This tab talks about the storage occupied by each tablespace and its free space.

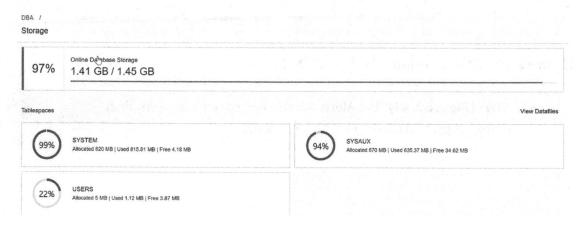

DBA /
Storage

97%   Online Database Storage
1.41 GB / 1.45 GB

Tablespaces   View Datafiles

99%   SYSTEM
Allocated 820 MB | Used 815.81 MB | Free 4.18 MB

94%   SYSAUX
Allocated 670 MB | Used 635.37 MB | Free 34.62 MB

22%   USERS
Allocated 5 MB | Used 1.12 MB | Free 3.87 MB

Figure 2-46. *SQL Developer Web, DBA ➤ Storage*

- **Waits (Figure 2-47)**: This tab is helpful to diagnose performance issues. It has all the required details related to wait events.

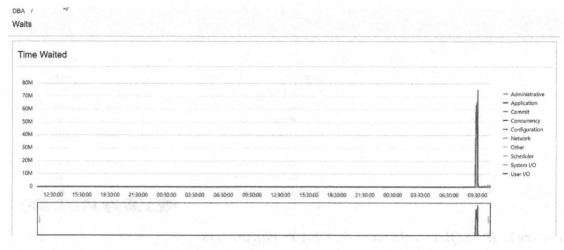

Figure 2-47. *SQL Developer Web, DBA* ➤ *Waits*

- **Movements (Figure 2-48)**: If there is data movement like a transfer of data through an insert/update operation, then this page will get updated. If not, this page will be empty.

DBA /

Movements

No movement logs found.

Figure 2-48. *SQL Developer Web, DBA* ➤ *Movements*

- **Parameters (Figure 2-49)**: This lists all the database init parameters, including their values, types, and descriptions.

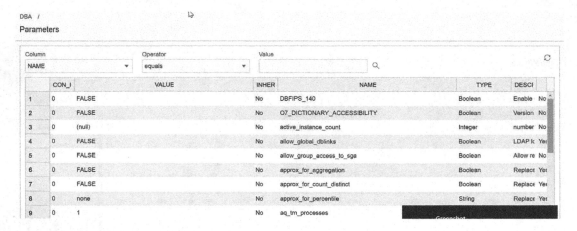

Figure 2-49. *SQL Developer Web, DBA ➤ Parameters*

- **OS**: This lists OS details such as the current memory utilization (Figure 2-50), current CPU status (Figure 2-51), and OS process details (Figure 2-52).

OS /
Memory

	Used RAM							
75%	5.52 GB / 7.3 GB							

	USER	PR	NI	VIRT	RES	SHR	S	%CPU
1	oracle	20	0	4478m	1.1g	16m	S	0.0
2	oracle	20	0	3104m	134m	98m	S	0.0
3	oracle	20	0	3102m	129m	106m	S	0.0

Figure 2-50. *SQL Developer Web, OS ➤ Memory*

OS /
CPU

	10:55:02	AM	CPU	%USR	%NICE	%SYS	%IOWAIT	%IRQ	%SOFT	%STEAL	%GUEST	%IDLE
1	10:55:03	AM	all	0.00	0.00	0.00	1.04	0.00	0.00	0.00	0.00	98.96
2	10:55:03	AM	0	0.00	0.00	1.06	0.00	0.00	0.00	0.00	0.00	98.94
3	10:55:03	AM	1	0.00	0.00	0.00	2.02	0.00	0.00	0.00	0.00	97.98

Figure 2-51. *SQL Developer Web, OS ➤ CPU*

OS /

Processes

	USER	PID	%CPU	%MEM	VSZ	RSS	TTY	STAT	START	TIME	COMM
1	oracle	8989	4.2	0.7	3142132	56704	?	Ss	09:21	4:03	ora_vktm_hadb
2	oracle	14093	1.1	14.6	4586108	1118724	?	Sl	09:34	0:55	/u01/app/oracle/product/j
3	oracle	6823	1.0	0.0	110368	2396	?	R	10:56	0:00	/bin/ps aux --sort=-pcpu
4	oracle	314	0.3	1.4	3165360	108584	?	Ss	10:35	0:04	oraclehadb (LOCAL=NO
5	root	4981	0.3	1.6	2470404	126348	?	Sl	07:27	0:42	/var/opt/oracle/tfa/apdb-c

Figure 2-52. *SQL Developer Web, OS ➤ CPU*

- Finally, on the Data Modeler tab (Figure 2-53) you can draw a diagram to show dependencies between the tables.

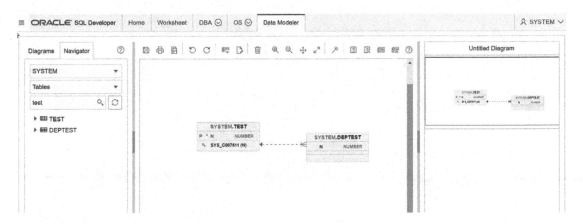

Figure 2-53. *Data Modeler tab*

Summary

In this chapter, we first discussed Data Guard concepts. Then we explored the switchover and failover concepts. Later we learned about setting up Data Guard in an Oracle public cloud environment and the utilities available to manage databases in the cloud.

CHAPTER 3

High Availability for Cloud Control 13c

In previous chapters, you learned about the importance of high availability (HA). Now, you will learn about what it takes to configure a completely fault-tolerant and bulletproof Oracle Enterprise Management installation. In-depth setup instructions will be provided for configuring all aspects of Oracle Enterprise Manager for high availability and disaster recovery. High availability configurations will be explained for the agent, database, and OMS stacks. Oracle Enterprise Manager (OEM) Cloud Control is an important tool that allows a business to manage and monitor its most mission-critical Oracle and non-Oracle assets; therefore, it is important to remove as many single points of failure in an OEM installation as possible.

OEM Agent High Availability Setup

OEM monitors and manages targets via the OEM Agent, which is a piece of software that is installed on each managed host. Through the OEM Agent, OEM can monitor critical metrics and also run OS commands. If the OEM Agent processes are not running, the Oracle Management Server (OMS) becomes blind to the status of important targets such as Oracle Databases and host metrics, such as CPU utilization, memory utilization, and so on.

Directory Structures and Their Purpose

Oracle introduced a concept called *shared agents* in OEM 13c. This required a rework of the agent installation directory structures and is used regardless of the usage of shared agents. In this new shared architecture, the files in a given Agent Home can be shared

© Y V Ravi Kumar, Nassyam Basha, Krishna Kumar K M, Bal Mukund Sharma, Konstantin Kerekovski 2019
Y V Ravi Kumar et al., *Oracle High Availability, Disaster Recovery, and Cloud Services*,
https://doi.org/10.1007/978-1-4842-4351-0_3

across multiple hosts, which each store their host agent's state-specific files in the Agent Instance directory. In this way, storage costs can be cut by sharing core agent software. In the examples throughout this chapter, the agent software will be installed in the locations indicated by Table 3-1.

Table 3-1. *Agent Directory Structure*

Directory Name	Directory Path	Function
Agent Base	/u01/software/em13c/agentbasedir	Houses both Agent Home and Agent Instance
Agent Home	/u01/software/em13c/ agentbasedir/agent_13.2.0.0.0	Contains the agent binaries (can be shared across hosts on NFS)
Agent Instance	/u01/software/em13c/ agentbasedir/agent_inst	Contains host-specific instance of an agent installation

By default, the OEM Agent is configured to be restartable. The restarting of the OEM Agent is controlled by a watchdog process that watches the running agent process. In OEM Agent version 13.2.0.0.0, which ships with OEM 13.2, the watchdog process is a Perl script, emwd.pl. This Perl script can be found at $AGENT_HOME/bin/emwd.pl.

Once the watchdog determines that the agent is down, it will attempt to restart the agent at a configurable interval and number of attempts. This behavior can be configured by exporting environment variables and restarting the OEM Agent. The following are the environment variables:

- EM_MAX_RETRIES, the default value of which is 3, controls how many times the watchdog emwd.pl tries to restart the agent.

- EM_RETRY_WINDOW, the default value of which is 600 in terms of seconds, controls how long emwd.pl waits between OEM Agent restart attempts.

Checking the Current Agent High Availability Configuration

On a running watchdog process, the values for EM_MAX_RETRIES and EM_RETRY_WINDOW can be determined by examining the /proc/<PID>/environ file for the watchdog process, emwd.pl.

By default, these values will not be set and will use the default values.

```
[oracle@rac101 bin]$ ps -ef|grep emwd.pl |grep -v grep
oracle    3987    1  0 Feb15 ?        00:00:06
/u01/software/em13c/agentbasedir/agent_13.2.0.0.0/perl/bin/perl
```
/u01/software/em13c/agentbasedir/agent_13.2.0.0.0/bin/emwd.pl agent
```
/u01/software/em13c/agentbasedir/agent_inst/sysman/log/emagent.nohup
```

If you examine the environment variables via /proc/3987/environ, you will find that there are no values for EM_MAX_RETRIES and EM_RETRY_WINDOW.

```
[oracle@rac101 bin]$ cat /proc/3987/environ  |tr '\0' '\n' |grep EM_
EM_OC4J_HOME=#EM_OC4J_HOME#
EM_STANDALONE=NOSTANDALONE
EM_SECURE_HOSTNAME=rac101.localdomain
EM_SECURE_PORT=3872
EM_LISTEN_ON_ALL_NICS=true
```

Changing the Agent's High Availability Configuration

The current configuration uses the defaults, as shown here:

```
[oracle@rac101 bin]$ ps -ef|grep emwd.pl |grep -v grep
oracle    3987    1  0 Feb15 ?        00:00:06
/u01/software/em13c/agentbasedir/agent_13.2.0.0.0/perl/bin/perl
/u01/software/em13c/agentbasedir/agent_13.2.0.0.0/bin/emwd.pl agent
/u01/software/em13c/agentbasedir/agent_inst/sysman/log/emagent.nohup

[oracle@rac101 bin]$ cat /proc/3987/environ  |tr '\0' '\n' |grep EM_
EM_OC4J_HOME=#EM_OC4J_HOME#
EM_STANDALONE=NOSTANDALONE
EM_SECURE_HOSTNAME=rac101.localdomain
EM_SECURE_PORT=3872
EM_LISTEN_ON_ALL_NICS=true
```

In this example, you will see how to change the retry count to 10 and set the retry delay between retries to 5 minutes.

```
[oracle@rac101 bin]$ export EM_MAX_RETRIES=10
[oracle@rac101 bin]$ export EM_RETRY_WINDOW=300
```

Then you can restart the agent.

```
[oracle@rac101 ~]$ /u01/software/em13c/agentbasedir/agent_inst/bin/emctl
stop agent
Oracle Enterprise Manager Cloud Control 13c Release 2
Copyright (c) 1996, 2016 Oracle Corporation.  All rights reserved.
Stopping agent ... stopped.
```

```
[oracle@rac101 ~]$ /u01/software/em13c/agentbasedir/agent_inst/bin/emctl
start agent
Oracle Enterprise Manager Cloud Control 13c Release 2
Copyright (c) 1996, 2016 Oracle Corporation.  All rights reserved.
Starting agent ................... started.
```

After the agent is restarted, you can confirm that the settings were picked up by the new emwd.pl process, which is spawned through the emctl start agent command.

```
[oracle@rac101 ~]$ ps -ef|grep emwd.pl |grep -v grep
oracle    31773     1  0 02:18 pts/0    00:00:00
/u01/software/em13c/agentbasedir/agent_13.2.0.0.0/perl/bin/perl
/u01/software/em13c/agentbasedir/agent_13.2.0.0.0/bin/emwd.pl agent
/u01/software/em13c/agentbasedir//agent_inst/sysman/log/emagent.nohup
```

```
[oracle@rac101 ~]$ cat /proc/31773/environ  |tr '\0' '\n' |grep EM_
EM_MAX_RETRIES=10
EM_RETRY_WINDOW=300
EM_OC4J_HOME=#EM_OC4J_HOME#
EM_STANDALONE=NOSTANDALONE
EM_SECURE_HOSTNAME=rac101.localdomain
EM_SECURE_PORT=3872
EM_LISTEN_ON_ALL_NICS=true
```

HA and MAA Best Practices for the OEM 13c Repository Database

It is recommended that the OEM repository be created as a pluggable database in a RAC database with no fewer than two instances. This is to ensure that the OEM repository can take advantage of all of the benefits of the multitenant architecture and be tolerant to hardware faults that can take down a stand-alone Oracle Database.

Creating the Repository in a 12.2 Primary Database on a RAC Database

In version 12.2.0.1.0 of the RDBMS software, creating a pluggable database is essentially the same whether on RAC or on a stand-alone database. In this example, you will see how to create the pluggable database OEMREPO in the container database ORCLCDB.

```
SQL> select db_unique_name from v$database;

DB_UNIQUE_NAME
--------------------------------
orclcdb
```

The OEM repository primary database can be created with the CREATE PLUGGABLE DATABASE command. In this example, you can see how to create a pluggable database that is a clone of the PDB$SEED database.

```
SQL> CREATE PLUGGABLE DATABASE OEMREPO ADMIN USER PDBADMIN IDENTIFIED BY
"database_123" ROLES=(CONNECT) file_name_convert=NONE  STORAGE ( MAXSIZE
UNLIMITED MAX_SHARED_TEMP_SIZE UNLIMITED);

Pluggable database created.
```

Once the database has been created, it will be in a mounted state and must be opened for read-write operations. Since we are working in a RAC cluster, specifying instances=all will ensure that the primary database is opened on all available instances. It is also recommended that you save the preferred state for the primary database as READ WRITE. This is accomplished by opening the database in the desired mode and saving that state as the preferred state. This will ensure that the primary database is opened in the appropriate state when the container database instance is restarted.

```
SQL> alter pluggable database OEMREPO open READ WRITE instances=all;
```

Pluggable database altered.

```
SQL> alter pluggable database OEMREPO save state instances=all;
```

Pluggable database altered.

As an optional step, you can create a USERS default tablespace, as shown here:

```
SQL> alter session set container=OEMREPO;
```

Session altered.

```
SQL> CREATE SMALLFILE TABLESPACE USERS LOGGING  DATAFILE  SIZE 5M
AUTOEXTEND ON NEXT  1280K MAXSIZE UNLIMITED  EXTENT MANAGEMENT
LOCAL  SEGMENT SPACE MANAGEMENT  AUTO;
```

Tablespace created.

```
SQL> ALTER DATABASE DEFAULT TABLESPACE USERS;
```

Database altered.

Setting Recommended Parameters for the Primary Database

It is recommended by the Oracle Universal Installer that you set the following parameters for the OEM repository:

```
SQL> alter system set "_allow_insert_with_update_check"=TRUE scope=BOTH
sid='*';
```

System altered.

```
SQL> alter system set processes=700 scope=SPFILE sid='*';
```

System altered.

Creating a Data Guard Standby of the OEMREPO Database with OEM 13.2 Cloud Control

In this section of the chapter, you will see how to create a Data Guard physical standby for the OEM repository. This will ensure that the OEM installation can survive a site failover. After all, having a working OEM installation is crucial to successfully recovering from a datacenter failure.

To showcase OEM 13.2's utility, follow these steps to use OEM to create a standby for itself:

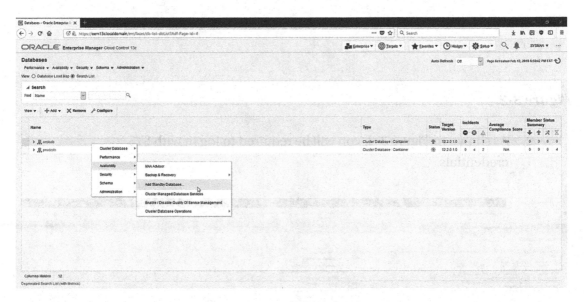

Figure 3-1.

1. Navigate to the list of database targets, right-click the OEM primary database, in this example `ORCLCDB`, and add a standby through the Availability drop-down menu, as shown in Figure 3-1.

Figure 3-2.

2. As shown in Figure 3-2, you will be required to log in with SYS
    credentials.

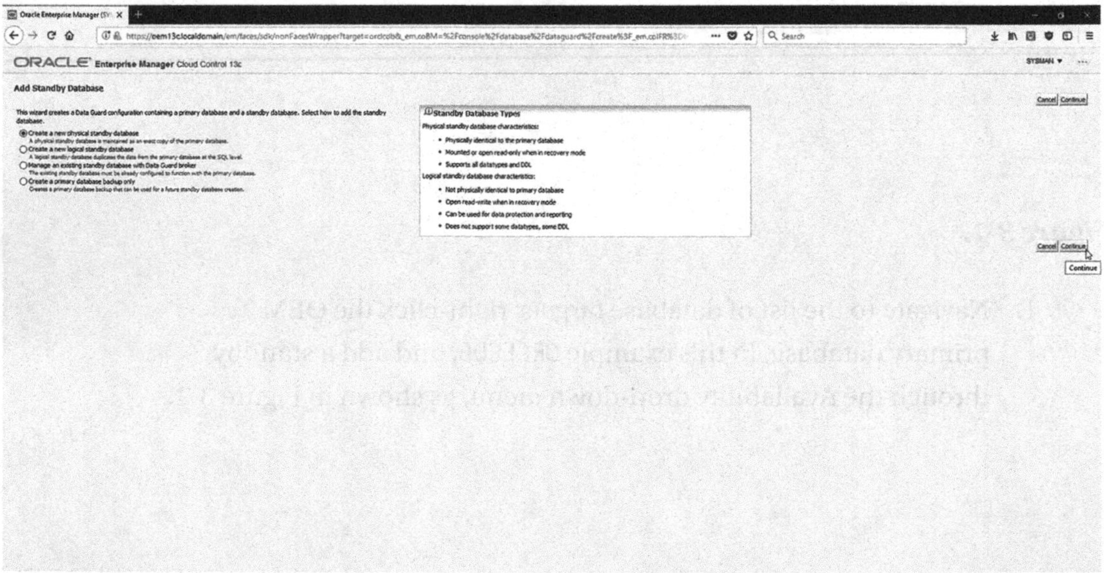

Figure 3-3.

3. Once authenticated, you are presented with a wizard that will
    guide you through logical and physical Data Guard setups. Choose
    the "Create a new physical standby database" option, as shown in
    Figure 3-3.

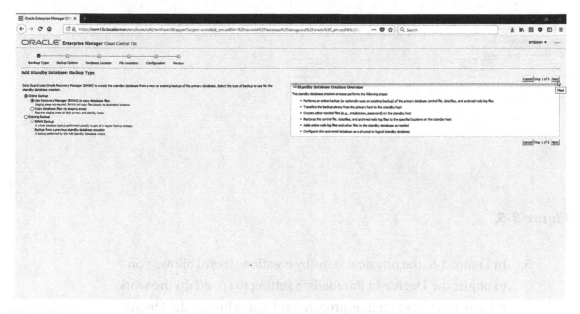

Figure 3-4.

4. As shown in Figure 3-4, the physical standby database can be
    created either by using an existing backup of the primary database
    or by performing an online backup. Click the radio button Online
    Backup, which performs an `RMAN DUPLICATE DATABASE FROM
    ACTIVE DATABASE` operation.

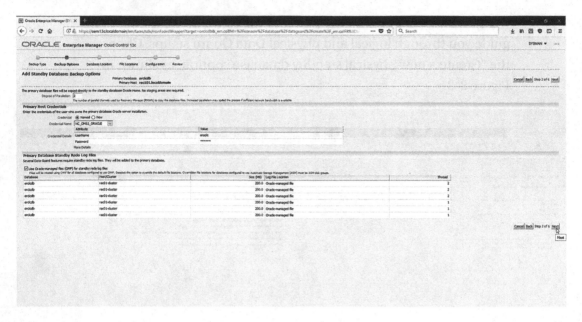

Figure 3-5.

5. In Figure 3-5, the physical standby creation wizard allows you
    to adjust the Degree of Parallelism setting to speed up the work.
    Be sure not to use an inappropriately high value for the Degree
    of Parallelism setting so that the Data Guard creation does not
    monopolize all the available resources on the primary host.

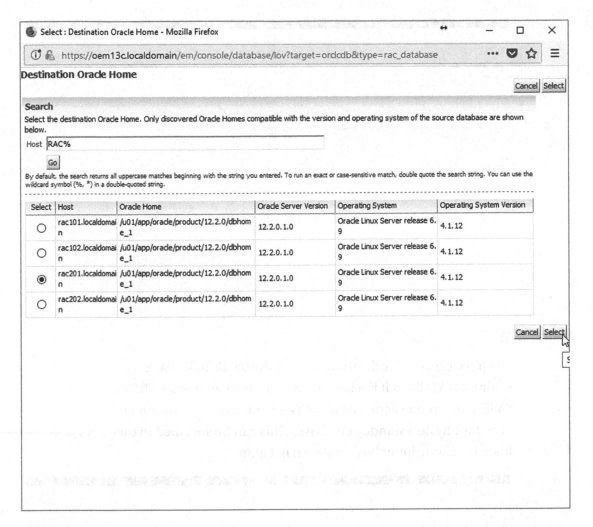

Figure 3-6.

6. In Figure 3-6, we picked the server `rac201` as the destination host for the physical standby database.

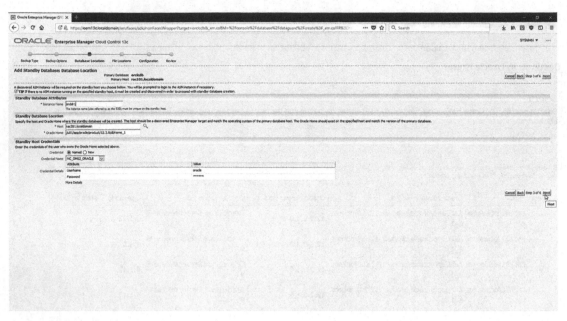

Figure 3-7.

7. The physical standby database will use the DB_UNIQUE_NAME setting of ORCLDR as it is a best practice for the value of DB_UNIQUE_ NAME to be unique across all databases in an Oracle environment, even for physical standby databases. This can be specified in the Instance Name input box, as shown in Figure 3-7.

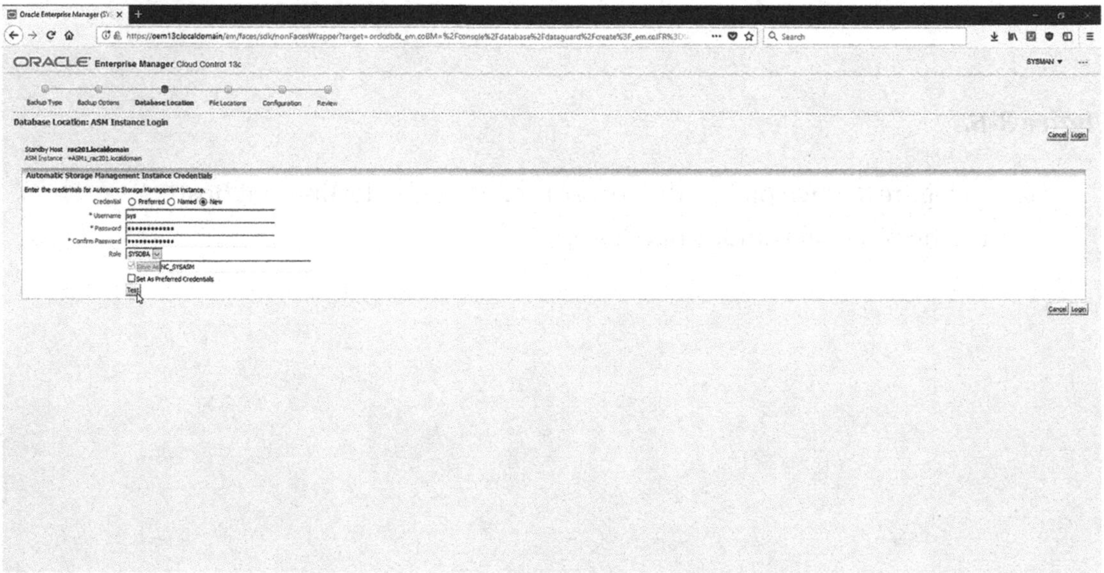

Figure 3-8.

8.   Since ASM is being used, SYSASM credentials will need to be
     provided to complete certain operations during the Create Data
     Guard process, as shown in Figure 3-8.

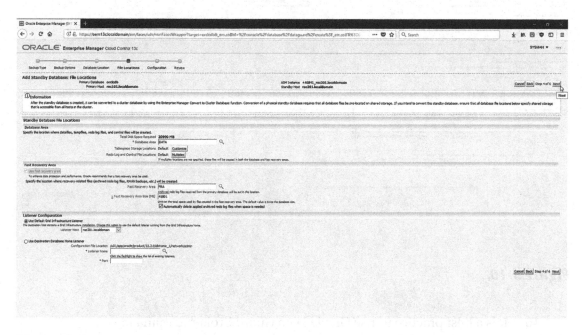

Figure 3-9.

9.   Store the data files in the disk group DATA and then set the FRA
     disk group to FRA.

Note   The prefix + in the disk group names is not being supplied as it is
unnecessary in this dialog box.

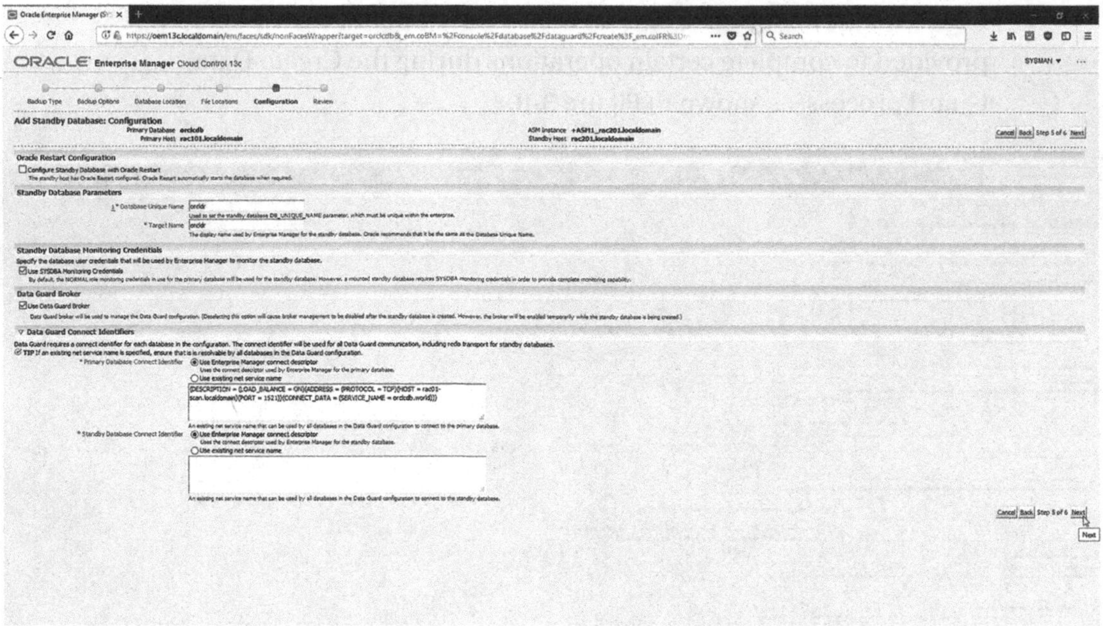

Figure 3-10.

10.   It is a best practice to use Oracle Data Guard Broker to manage standby databases. This will significantly reduce the amount of work needed during switchover and failover scenarios and serve as a central interface to manage the standby configuration at the command line. Figure 3-10 shows how to ensure that OEM creates a broker configuration for the database.

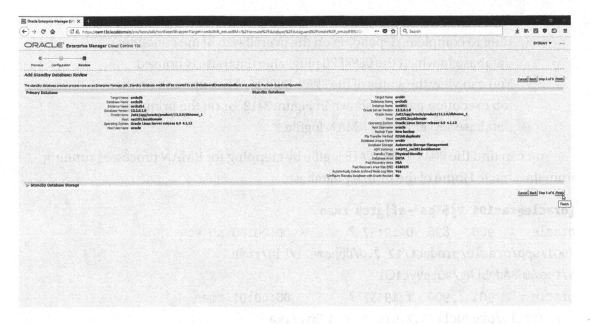

Figure 3-11.

11. The physical standby creation wizard allows you to review all the options specified prior to kicking off the standby creation process, as shown in Figure 3-11. Ensure that no mistakes or typographical errors were made prior to starting the creation process.

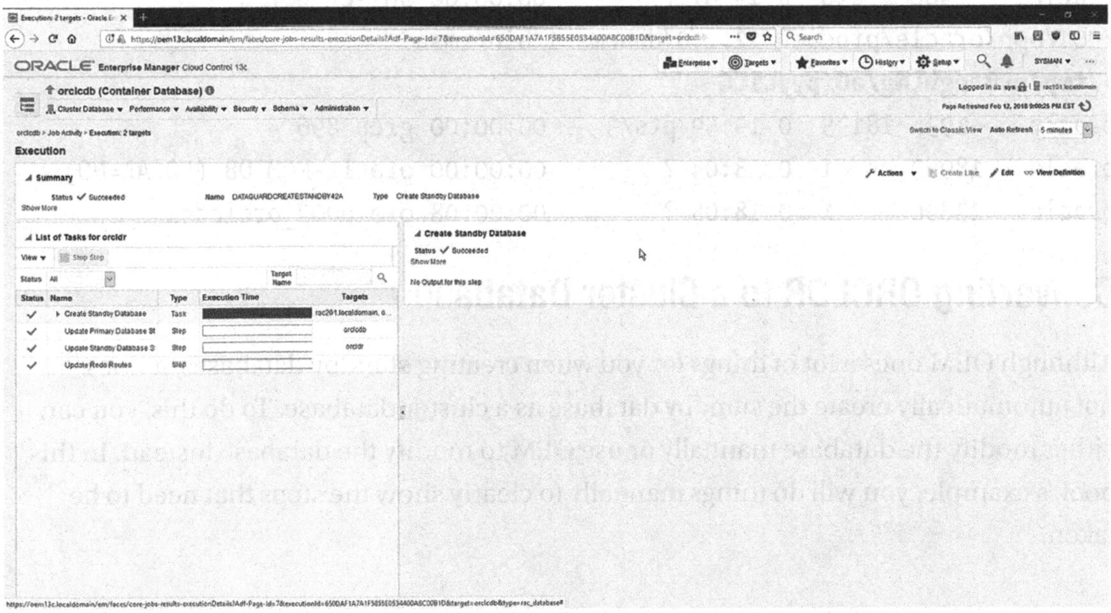

Figure 3-12.

12. Once the OEM job is started, it can take a variable amount of
time to complete, depending on the overall size of the container
database in which the OEMREPO pluggable database is housed.
You can view the status of the RMAN DUPLICATE command on the
job execution page, as shown in Figure 3-12, or on the primary
database server via the RMAN logfile.

You can find the RMAN DUPLICATE logfile by grepping for RMAN processes running
from the Oracle Home of the primary database.

```
[oracle@rac101 ~]$ ps -ef|grep rman
oracle    900    896  0 19:57 ?          00:00:00 sh -c
/u01/app/oracle/product/12.2.0/dbhome_1/bin/rman
>/tmp/mHBAdgbLNg/aQrpyyL1CG
oracle    901    900  1 19:57 ?          00:00:01 rman
app/oracle/product/12.2.0/dbhome_1/bin/rman
oracle   1837  18135  0 19:59 pts/3      00:00:00 grep rman
 [oracle@rac101 ~]$ ps -ef|grep 896
oracle    896    894  0 19:57 ?          00:00:00
/u01/software/em13c/agentbasedir/agent_13.2.0.0.0/perl/bin/perl -
STANDBY_NO_RECOVERY N
oracle    900    896  0 19:57 ?          00:00:00 sh -c
/u01/app/oracle/product/12.2.0/dbhome_1/bin/rman
>/tmp/mHBAdgbLNg/aQrpyyL1CG
oracle   1931  18135  0 19:59 pts/3      00:00:00 grep 896
oracle  18963      1  0 18:04 ?          00:00:00 oracle-MGMTDB (LOCAL=NO)
oracle  23896      1  0 18:08 ?          00:00:08 ora_p007_orclcdb1
```

Converting ORCLDR to a Cluster Database

Although OEM does a lot of things for you when creating standby databases, it does
not automatically create the standby database as a cluster database. To do this, you can
either modify the database manually or use OEM to modify the database instead. In this
book's example, you will do things manually to clearly show the steps that need to be
taken.

First you will have to the remove the Oracle database cluster resource for the ORCLDR standby database. This step is needed because once a database resource is created with –dbtype SINGLE, it cannot be modified to a RAC database type.

```
[oracle@rac201 ~]$ srvctl remove database -d orcldr -y
```

It is important that the DR databases use a password file on shared storage. The recommended way to do this in RDBMS version 12.2.0.1.0 is to place the password file in ASM. You can copy the file from the primary node, secure-copy it, and then place it in ASM on the standby cluster using asmcmd.

```
[oracle@rac101 ~]$ asmcmd cp +DATA/orclcdb/orapworclcdb /tmp/orapworclcdb
copying +DATA/orclcdb/orapworclcdb -> /tmp/orapworclcdb

[oracle@rac101 ~]$ scp /tmp/orapworclcdb rac201:/tmp/orapworclcdb
The authenticity of host 'rac201 (192.168.0.94)' can't be established.
RSA key fingerprint is 4e:e4:18:c1:6e:87:87:70:43:34:df:a3:8a:f8:b2:a5.
Are you sure you want to continue connecting (yes/no)? yes
Warning: Permanently added 'rac201,192.168.0.94' (RSA) to the list of known hosts.
oracle@rac201's password:
orapworclcdb
100% 3584      3.5KB/s    00:00

[oracle@rac201 ~]$ . oraenv
ORACLE_SID = [+ASM1] ? +ASM1
The Oracle base remains unchanged with value /u01/app/oracle

[oracle@rac201 ~]$ asmcmd cp /tmp/orapworclcdb +DATA/orcldr/orapworcldr
copying /tmp/orapworclcdb -> +DATA/orcldr/orapworcldr
```

Once the password file is in place, you can add the database to clusterware.

```
[oracle@rac201 ~]$ srvctl add database -db orcldr -oraclehome /u01/
app/oracle/product/12.2.0/dbhome_1 -dbtype RAC -spfile +DATA/orcldr/
spfileorcldr1.ora_42 -pwfile +DATA/orcldr/orapworcldr -role PHYSICAL_
STANDBY -startoption "READ ONLY" -diskgroup DATA,FRA

[oracle@rac201 ~]$ srvctl add instance -d orcldr -i orcldr1 -n rac201

[oracle@rac201 ~]$ srvctl add instance -d orcldr -i orcldr2 -n rac202
```

Add a database resource with a dbtype value of RAC does not automatically make the database a clustered database. A few parameter changes are necessary to complete the process. In RAC, a few database parameters are needed.

- **THREAD**: Each RAC instance must have a separate redo thread.

- **UNDO_TABLESPACE**: Each RAC instance must use a separate UNDO tablespace.

- **INSTANCE_NUMBER**: Each RAC instance needs to have a separate instance number.

- **CLUSTER_DATABASE**: All RAC instances need to set CLUSTER_DATABASE=TRUE. This will change the database behavior to mount the controlfiles in a SHARED mode instead of the default EXCLUSIVE mode.

[oracle@rac201 ~]$. oraenv
```
ORACLE_SID = [+ASM1] ? orcldr1
The Oracle base remains unchanged with value /u01/app/oracle
```

[oracle@rac201 ~]$ sqlplus / as sysdba

```
SQL*Plus: Release 12.2.0.1.0 Production

Copyright (c) 1982, 2016, Oracle.  All rights reserved.

Connected to:
Oracle Database 12c Enterprise Edition Release 12.2.0.1.0 - 64bit Production
```

SQL> show spparameter undo

SID	NAME	TYPE	VALUE
*	temp_undo_enabled	boolean	
*	undo_management	string	
*	undo_retention	integer	
*	undo_tablespace	string	UNDOTBS1

SQL> show spparameter thread

SID	NAME	TYPE	VALUE
*	ofs_threads	integer	
*	parallel_threads_per_cpu	integer	
*	thread	integer	
*	threaded_execution	Boolean	

SQL> show spparameter instance_number

SID	NAME	TYPE	VALUE
*	instance_number	integer	

SQL> show spparameter CLUSTER_DATABASE

SID	NAME	TYPE	VALUE
*	cluster_database	boolean	
*	cluster_database_instances	integer	

SQL> alter system set thread=1 scope=SPFILE sid='orcldr1';

System altered.

SQL> alter system set thread=2 scope=SPFILE sid='orcldr2';

System altered.

Note   Notice that UNDO_TABLESPACE is being reset to SID='*'. This is done because SID='*' values take precedence over parameter values set at specific instance levels and you do not want both instances to use the default value for UNDO_TABLESPACE.

SQL> alter system set undo_tablespace='UNDOTBS1' scope=SPFILE sid='orcldr1';

System altered.

SQL> alter system set undo_tablespace='UNDOTBS2' scope=SPFILE sid='orcldr2';

System altered.

SQL> alter system reset undo_tablespace scope=SPFILE sid='*';

System altered.

SQL> alter system set instance_number=1 scope=SPFILE sid='orcldr1';

System altered.

SQL> alter system set instance_number=2 scope=SPFILE sid='orcldr2';

System altered.

SQL> alter system set cluster_database=TRUE scope=SPFILE sid='*';

System altered.

You can validate that the parameter values are properly stored in the spfile with the show spparameter command.

SQL> show spparameter undo_tablespace

```
SID       NAME                            TYPE          VALUE
--------  ------------------------------  -----------   ------------------------
orcldr1   undo_tablespace                 string        UNDOTBS1
orcldr2   undo_tablespace                 string        UNDOTBS2
```

SQL> show spparameter instance_number

```
SID       NAME                            TYPE          VALUE
--------  ------------------------------  -----------   ------------------------
orcldr1   instance_number                 integer       1
orcldr2   instance_number                 integer       2
```

SQL> show spparameter thread

```
SID        NAME                          TYPE         VALUE
--------   ----------------------------  -----------  ----------------------------
*          ofs_threads                   integer
*          parallel_threads_per_cpu      integer
orcldr1    thread                        integer      1
orcldr2    thread                        integer      2
*          threaded_execution            Boolean
```

SQL> show spparameter CLUSTER_DATABASE

```
SID        NAME                          TYPE         VALUE
--------   ----------------------------  -----------  ----------------------------
*          cluster_database              boolean      TRUE
*          cluster_database_instances    integer
```

The database needs to be restarted for the new parameter values to be used.

[oracle@rac201 ~]$ srvctl stop database -d orcldr
[oracle@rac201 ~]$ srvctl start database -d orcldr
[oracle@rac201 ~]$ srvctl status database -d orcldr
```
Instance orcldr1 is running on node rac201
Instance orcldr2 is running on node rac202
```

[oracle@rac201 ~]$ sqlplus / as sysdba

```
SQL*Plus: Release 12.2.0.1.0 Production

Copyright (c) 1982, 2016, Oracle.  All rights reserved.

Connected to:
Oracle Database 12c Enterprise Edition Release 12.2.0.1.0 - 64bit Production
```

SQL> select inst_id, open_mode from gv$database;

```
   INST_ID OPEN_MODE
---------- --------------------
         1 READ ONLY
         2 READ ONLY
```

Flashback Database

It is recommended that you enable flashback for both the primary database and the standby database. This will ensure that failed primary reinstantiations can be performed, in the case of a Data Guard failover scenario. With flashback enabled, guaranteed restore points can be used in the case of OEM plug-in deployment failures to reduce the recovery time in case of plug-in deployment rollbacks.

To enable flashback on the standby, Media Recovery will have to be stopped. It is recommended to stop Media Recovery via the Data Guard Broker.

SQL> select db_unique_name,flashback_on from v$database;

```
DB_UNIQUE_NAME                  FLASHBACK_ON
------------------------------- -------------------
orcldr                          NO
```

SQL> alter database flashback on;
```
alter database flashback on
*
ERROR at line 1:
ORA-01153: an incompatible media recovery is active
```

DGMGRL> edit database orcldr set state=apply-off;
```
Succeeded.
```

SQL> alter database flashback on;

```
Database altered.
```

SQL> select db_unique_name,flashback_on from v$database;

```
DB_UNIQUE_NAME                  FLASHBACK_ON
------------------------------- -------------------
orcldr                          YES
```

No special prerequisites are required to enable flashback on the primary database.

```
SQL> select db_unique_name,flashback_on from v$database;

DB_UNIQUE_NAME                      FLASHBACK_ON
---------------------------------   ------------------
orclcdb                             NO
```

```
SQL> alter database flashback on;
```

```
Database altered.
```

```
SQL> show parameter db_flashback_retention_target
```

```
NAME                                TYPE        VALUE
-----------------------------------  ----------  ----------------------------
db_flashback_retention_target       integer     1440
```

```
SQL> select db_unique_name,flashback_on from v$database;
```

```
DB_UNIQUE_NAME                      FLASHBACK_ON
---------------------------------   ------------------
orclcdb                             YES
```

The amount of flashback logs in terms of minutes is configurable. The parameter DB_FLASHBACK_RETENTION_TARGET has a default value of 1440, or 24 hours. For some installations, the value may need to be adjusted.

```
SQL> show parameter db_flashback_retention_target
```

```
NAME                                TYPE        VALUE
-----------------------------------  ----------  ----------------------------
db_flashback_retention_target       integer     1440
```

```
SQL> select (1440/60) as hours from dual;
     HOURS
----------
        24
```

Configuring Logfile and Datafile Name Conversion

Because the DB_UNIQUE_NAME parameters are different between the primary and the standby, the Oracle Managed File datafiles and logfiles have different names, and each database must be able to convert the datafile/logfile paths to the appropriate directory structure.

Because the same disk group names are being used in the primary site and in the standby site but DB_UNIQUE_NAME is different, two parameters must be set.

- **DB_FILE_NAME_CONVERT**: Replaces the first string in the datafile path with the second string

- **LOG_FILE_NAME_CONVERT**: Replaces the first string in the logfile path with the second string

The DB_FILE_NAME_CONVERT and LOG_FILE_NAME_CONVERT parameters must be modified by their respective database properties, DbFileNameConvert and LogFileNameConvert, as the Broker configuration must be consistent with the spfile. Furthermore, the databases need to be restarted so that the parameter changes can take effect.

```
DGMGRL for Linux: Release 12.2.0.1.0 - Production

Copyright (c) 1982, 2017, Oracle and/or its affiliates.  All rights reserved.

Welcome to DGMGRL, type "help" for information.
Connected to "orcldr"
Connected as SYSDG.
```

DGMGRL> edit database orcldr set property DbFileNameConvert='orclcdb,orcldr, ORCLCDB,ORCLDR';

```
Warning: ORA-16675: database instance restart required for property value
modification to take effect

Property "dbfilenameconvert" updated
```

DGMGRL> edit database orcldr set property LogFileNameConvert='orclcdb,orcldr, ORCLCDB,ORCLDR';

```
Warning: ORA-16675: database instance restart required for property value
modification to take effect

Property "logfilenameconvert" updated
```

DGMGRL> edit database orclcdb set property DbFileNameConvert='orcldr,orclcd b,ORCLDR,ORCLCDB';

Warning: ORA-16675: database instance restart required for property value modification to take effect

Property "dbfilenameconvert" updated

DGMGRL> edit database orclcdb set property LogFileNameConvert='orcldr, orclcdb,ORCLDR,ORCLCDB';

Warning: ORA-16675: database instance restart required for property value modification to take effect

Property "logfilenameconvert" updated

[oracle@rac201 ~]$ srvctl stop database -d orcldr; srvctl start database -d orcldr -o 'READ ONLY'

SQL> show parameter convert

NAME	TYPE	VALUE
db_file_name_convert	string	orclcdb, orcldr, ORCLCDB, ORCL DR
log_file_name_convert	string	orclcdb, orcldr, ORCLCDB, ORCL DR
pdb_file_name_convert	string	

[oracle@rac101 ~]$ srvctl stop database -d orclcdb; srvctl start database -d orclcdb

SQL> show parameter convert

NAME	TYPE	VALUE
db_file_name_convert	string	orcldr, orclcdb, ORCLDR, ORCLC DB
log_file_name_co	string	orcldr, orclcdb, ORCLDR, ORCLC DB
pdb_file_name_convert	string	

115

Static Listener Entries

To perform seamless switchover and failover operations, the StaticConnectIdentifier property for each database instance in the Data Guard configuration must refer to a Static Listener entry that is always being listened on regardless of whether the Oracle instance is actually started. In this way, Data Guard Broker can perform remote SYSDBA operations such as starting stopped instances, and so on.

By default, the StaticConnectIdentifier property expects a service to exist with the name pattern <DB_UNIQUE_NAME>_DGMGRL.<DB_DOMAIN>.

DGMGRL> show instance verbose orcldr1

```
Instance 'orcldr1' of database 'orcldr'

  Host Name: rac201.localdomain
  PFILE:
  Properties:
    StaticConnectIdentifier         = '(DESCRIPTION=(ADDRESS=(PROTOCOL=TCP)
(HOST=rac201.localdomain)(PORT=1521))(CONNECT_DATA=(SERVICE_NAME=orcldr_
DGMGRL.world)(INSTANCE_NAME=orcldr1)(SERVER=DEDICATED)))'
    StandbyArchiveLocation          = 'USE_DB_RECOVERY_FILE_DEST'
    AlternateLocation               = ''
    LogArchiveTrace                 = '0'
    LogArchiveFormat                = '%t_%s_%r.dbf'
    TopWaitEvents                   = '(monitor)'

  Log file locations:
    Alert log             : /u01/app/oracle/diag/rdbms/orcldr/orcldr1/
                            trace/alert_orcldr1.log
    Data Guard Broker log : /u01/app/oracle/diag/rdbms/orcldr/orcldr1/
                            trace/drcorcldr1.log

Instance Status:
SUCCESS
```

However, this service must be created by editing the appropriate listener.ora file because it is not created by default. In an Oracle RAC environment, the listener.ora file in the Grid Infrastructure home must be modified, rather than the listener.ora file in the database installation home. Additionally, a static listener entry needs to be created on all database hosts that run the database.

For Grid Infrastructure installations, the file exists in the $GI_HOME/network/admin directory.

The service is defined with the SID_LIST_LISTENER entry.

[oracle@rac201 admin]$ grep -A7 "SID_LIST_LISTENER"
```
/u01/app/12.2.0/grid/network/admin/listener.ora
SID_LIST_LISTENER=
    (SID_LIST=
        (SID_DESC=
        (SID_NAME=orcldr1)(GLOBAL_DBNAME=orcldr_DGMGRL.world)
        (ORACLE_HOME=/u01/app/oracle/product/12.2.0/dbhome_1)
        )
    )
```

Once the entry has been placed in the listener.ora file, the listener configuration can be reloaded with the LSNRCTL binary.

[oracle@rac201 admin]$ lsnrctl reload

```
LSNRCTL for Linux: Version 12.2.0.1.0 - Production

Copyright (c) 1991, 2016, Oracle.  All rights reserved.

Connecting to (DESCRIPTION=(ADDRESS=(PROTOCOL=IPC)(KEY=LISTENER)))
The command completed successfully
[oracle@rac201 admin]$ lsnrctl status

LSNRCTL for Linux: Version 12.2.0.1.0 - Production

Copyright (c) 1991, 2016, Oracle.  All rights reserved.

Connecting to (DESCRIPTION=(ADDRESS=(PROTOCOL=IPC)(KEY=LISTENER)))
STATUS of the LISTENER
------------------------
Alias                   LISTENER
Version                 TNSLSNR for Linux: Version 12.2.0.1.0 - Production
Start Date              12-FEB-2018 17:59:57
```

```
Uptime                      0 days 13 hr. 11 min. 8 sec
Trace Level                 off
Security                    ON: Local OS Authentication
SNMP                        OFF
Listener Parameter File     /u01/app/12.2.0/grid/network/admin/listener.ora
Listener Log File           /u01/app/oracle/diag/tnslsnr/rac201/listener/
alert/log.xml
Listening Endpoints Summary...
  (DESCRIPTION=(ADDRESS=(PROTOCOL=ipc)(KEY=LISTENER)))
Services Summary...
Service "orcldr_DGMGRL.world" has 1 instance(s).
  Instance "orcldr1", status UNKNOWN, has 1 handler(s) for this service...
The command completed successfully
```

The availability of the service can be tested by attempting to directly connect to it.

[oracle@rac201 admin]$ sqlplus sys/database_123@'(DESCRIPTION=(ADDRESS= (PROTOCOL=TCP)(HOST=rac201.localdomain)(PORT=1521))(CONNECT_DATA=(SERVICE_ NAME=orcldr_DGMGRL.world)(INSTANCE_NAME=orcldr1)(SERVER=DEDICATED)))' as sysdba

```
SQL*Plus: Release 12.2.0.1.0 Production

Copyright (c) 1982, 2016, Oracle.  All rights reserved.

Connected to:
Oracle Database 12c Enterprise Edition Release 12.2.0.1.0 - 64bit
Production
```

SQL> select host_name from v$instance;

```
HOST_NAME
------------------------------------------------------------------
rac201.localdomain
```

SQL> exit

In our example installation, the StaticConnectIdentifier property was incorrectly pointing to the wrong node for the instance ORCLDR2.

DGMGRL> show instance verbose orcldr2

Instance 'orcldr2' of database 'orcldr'

  Host Name: rac202.localdomain
  PFILE:
  Properties:
    StaticConnectIdentifier   = '(DESCRIPTION=(ADDRESS=(PROTOCOL=TCP)
(HOST=**rac201.localdomain**)(PORT=1521))(CONNECT_DATA=(SERVICE_NAME=orcldr_
DGMGRL.world)(INSTANCE_NAME=**orcldr2**)(SERVER=DEDICATED)))'
    StandbyArchiveLocation   = 'USE_DB_RECOVERY_FILE_DEST'
    AlternateLocation   = ''
    LogArchiveTrace   = '0'
    LogArchiveFormat   = '%t_%s_%r.dbf'
    TopWaitEvents   = '(monitor)'

  Log file locations:
    (Failed to retrieve log file locations.)

Instance Status:
SUCCESS

The property must be changed to point to the appropriate node, rac202.

DGMGRL> edit instance orcldr2 set property StaticConnectIdentifier='
(DESCRIPTION=(ADDRESS=(PROTOCOL=TCP)(HOST=rac202.localdomain)(PORT=1521))
(CONNECT_DATA=(SERVICE_NAME=orcldr_DGMGRL.world)(INSTANCE_NAME=orcldr2)
(SERVER=DEDICATED)))';

Much like with the host rac201, you must add the static listener entry to rac202.

[oracle@rac202 ~]$ grep -A7 "SID_LIST_LISTENER" /u01/app/12.2.0/grid/
network/admin/listener.ora
SID_LIST_LISTENER=
      (SID_LIST=
          (SID_DESC=
(SID_NAME=orcldr2)(GLOBAL_DBNAME=orcldr_DGMGRL.world)(ORACLE_HOME=/u01/app/
oracle/product/12.2.0/dbhome_1)
)
)

[oracle@rac202 ~]$ lsnrctl status

LSNRCTL for Linux: Version 12.2.0.1.0 - Production

Copyright (c) 1991, 2016, Oracle. All rights reserved.

Connecting to (DESCRIPTION=(ADDRESS=(PROTOCOL=IPC)(KEY=LISTENER)))
STATUS of the LISTENER

Alias   LISTENER
Version   TNSLSNR for Linux: Version 12.2.0.1.0 -
Production
Start Date   12-FEB-2018 17:58:45
Uptime   0 days 13 hr. 14 min. 42 sec
Trace Level   off
Security   ON: Local OS Authentication
SNMP   OFF
Listener Parameter File   /u01/app/12.2.0/grid/network/admin/listener.ora
Listener Log File   /u01/app/oracle/diag/tnslsnr/rac202/listener/
alert/log.xml
Listening Endpoints Summary...
  (DESCRIPTION=(ADDRESS=(PROTOCOL=ipc)(KEY=LISTENER)))
Services Summary...
Service "orcldr_DGMGRL.world" has 1 instance(s).
  Instance "orcldr2", status UNKNOWN, has 1 handler(s) for this service...
The command completed successfully

[oracle@rac202 ~]$ sqlplus sys/database_123@'(DESCRIPTION=(ADDRESS=(PROTOCOL= TCP)(HOST=rac202.localdomain)(PORT=1521))(CONNECT_DATA=(SERVICE_NAME=orcldr_ DGMGRL.world)(INSTANCE_NAME=orcldr2)(SERVER=DEDICATED)))' as sysdba

SQL*Plus: Release 12.2.0.1.0 Production

Copyright (c) 1982, 2016, Oracle. All rights reserved.

Connected to:
Oracle Database 12c Enterprise Edition Release 12.2.0.1.0 - 64bit Production

SQL> select host_name from v$instance;

```
HOST_NAME
----------------------------------------------------------------
rac202.localdomain
```

The same thing must be done on the primary database hosts, in the case of a switchover or failover.

DGMGRL> edit instance orclcdb1 set property StaticConnectIdentifier=
'(DESCRIPTION=(ADDRESS=(PROTOCOL=TCP)(HOST=rac101.localdomain)(PORT=1521))
(CONNECT_DATA=(SERVICE_NAME=orclcdb_DGMGRL.world)(INSTANCE_NAME=orclcdb1)
(SERVER=DEDICATED)))';

[oracle@rac101 admin]$ grep -A7 SID_LIST_LISTENER /u01/app/12.2.0/grid/
network/admin/listener.ora
```
SID_LIST_LISTENER=
        (SID_LIST=
                (SID_DESC=

                (SID_NAME=orclcdb1)(GLOBAL_DBNAME=orclcdb_DGMGRL.world)
                (ORACLE_HOME=/u01/app/oracle/product/12.2.0/dbhome_1)
                )

        )
```

[oracle@rac101 admin]$ lsnrctl reload

```
LSNRCTL for Linux: Version 12.2.0.1.0 - Production

Copyright (c) 1991, 2016, Oracle.  All rights reserved.

Connecting to (DESCRIPTION=(ADDRESS=(PROTOCOL=IPC)(KEY=LISTENER)))
The command completed successfully
[oracle@rac101 admin]$ lsnrctl status

LSNRCTL for Linux: Version 12.2.0.1.0 - Production

Copyright (c) 1991, 2016, Oracle.  All rights reserved.

Connecting to (DESCRIPTION=(ADDRESS=(PROTOCOL=IPC)(KEY=LISTENER)))
STATUS of the LISTENER
------------------------
Alias                     LISTENER
```

Version   TNSLSNR for Linux: Version 12.2.0.1.0 -
Production
Start Date   12-FEB-2018 18:02:00
Uptime   0 days 13 hr. 32 min. 7 sec
Trace Level   off
Security   ON: Local OS Authentication
SNMP   OFF
Listener Parameter File   /u01/app/12.2.0/grid/network/admin/listener.ora
Listener Log File   /u01/app/oracle/diag/tnslsnr/rac101/listener/
alert/log.xml
Listening Endpoints Summary...
  (DESCRIPTION=(ADDRESS=(PROTOCOL=ipc)(KEY=LISTENER)))
Services Summary...
Service "orclcdb_DGMGRL.world" has 1 instance(s).
  Instance "orclcdb1", status UNKNOWN, has 1 handler(s) for this service...
The command completed successfully

[oracle@rac202 ~]$ sqlplus sys/database_123@'(DESCRIPTION=(ADDRESS=(PROTOCOL=
TCP)(HOST=rac101.localdomain)(PORT=1521))(CONNECT_DATA=(SERVICE_NAME=
orclcdb_DGMGRL.world)(INSTANCE_NAME=orclcdb1)(SERVER=DEDICATED)))' as sysdba

SQL*Plus: Release 12.2.0.1.0 Production

Copyright (c) 1982, 2016, Oracle. All rights reserved.

Connected to:
Oracle Database 12c Enterprise Edition Release 12.2.0.1.0 - 64bit Production

SQL> select host_name from v$instance;

HOST_NAME
----
rac101.localdomain

[oracle@rac102 admin]$ grep -A7 SID_LIST_LISTENER listener.ora
SID_LIST_LISTENER=
        (SID_LIST=
                (SID_DESC=

```
(SID_NAME=orclcdb2)(GLOBAL_DBNAME=orclcdb_DGMGRL.world)(ORACLE_HOME=/u01/
app/oracle/product/12.2.0/dbhome_1)
                )
        )
```

[oracle@rac102 admin]$ lsnrctl reload

LSNRCTL for Linux: Version 12.2.0.1.0 - Production

Copyright (c) 1991, 2016, Oracle. All rights reserved.

Connecting to (DESCRIPTION=(ADDRESS=(PROTOCOL=IPC)(KEY=LISTENER)))
The command completed successfully
[oracle@rac102 admin]$ lsnrctl status

LSNRCTL for Linux: Version 12.2.0.1.0 - Production

Copyright (c) 1991, 2016, Oracle. All rights reserved.

Connecting to (DESCRIPTION=(ADDRESS=(PROTOCOL=IPC)(KEY=LISTENER)))
STATUS of the LISTENER

```
Alias                     LISTENER
Version                   TNSLSNR for Linux: Version 12.2.0.1.0 -
Production
Start Date                13-FEB-2018 07:54:38
Uptime                    0 days 1 hr. 22 min. 5 sec
Trace Level               off
Security                  ON: Local OS Authentication
SNMP                      OFF
Listener Parameter File   /u01/app/12.2.0/grid/network/admin/listener.ora
Listener Log File         /u01/app/oracle/diag/tnslsnr/rac102/listener/
alert/log.xml
```
Listening Endpoints Summary...
  (DESCRIPTION=(ADDRESS=(PROTOCOL=ipc)(KEY=LISTENER)))
Services Summary...
Service "orclcdb_DGMGRL.world" has 1 instance(s).
  Instance "orclcdb2", status UNKNOWN, has 1 handler(s) for this service...
The command completed successfully

DGMGRL> edit instance orclcdb2 set property StaticConnectIdentifier=
'(DESCRIPTION=(ADDRESS=(PROTOCOL=TCP)(HOST=rac102.localdomain)(PORT=1521))
(CONNECT_DATA=(SERVICE_NAME=orclcdb_DGMGRL.world)(INSTANCE_NAME=orclcdb2)
(SERVER=DEDICATED)))';

Property "staticconnectidentifier" updated

DGMGRL> show instance verbose orclcdb2

Instance 'orclcdb2' of database 'orclcdb'

  Host Name: rac102.localdomain
  PFILE:
  Properties:
    StaticConnectIdentifier   = '(DESCRIPTION=(ADDRESS=(PROTOCOL=TCP)
(HOST=rac102.localdomain)(PORT=1521))(CONNECT_DATA=(SERVICE_NAME=orclcdb_
DGMGRL.world)(INSTANCE_NAME=orclcdb2)(SERVER=DEDICATED)))'
    StandbyArchiveLocation   = 'USE_DB_RECOVERY_FILE_DEST'
    AlternateLocation   = ''
    LogArchiveTrace   = '0'
    LogArchiveFormat   = '%t_%s_%r.dbf'
    TopWaitEvents   = '(monitor)'

  Log file locations:
    Alert log   : /u01/app/oracle/diag/rdbms/orclcdb/orclcdb2/
trace/alert_orclcdb2.log
    Data Guard Broker log   : /u01/app/oracle/diag/rdbms/orclcdb/orclcdb2/
trace/drcorclcdb2.log

Instance Status:
SUCCESS

[oracle@rac102 admin]$ sqlplus sys/database_123@'(DESCRIPTION=(ADDRESS=
(PROTOCOL=TCP)(HOST=rac102.localdomain)(PORT=1521))(CONNECT_DATA=(SERVICE_
NAME=orclcdb_DGMGRL.world)(INSTANCE_NAME=orclcdb2)(SERVER=DEDICATED)))' as
sysdba

SQL*Plus: Release 12.2.0.1.0 Production

Copyright (c) 1982, 2016, Oracle. All rights reserved.

```
Connected to:
Oracle Database 12c Enterprise Edition Release 12.2.0.1.0 - 64bit Production
SQL> select host_name from v$instance;

HOST_NAME
---------------------------------------------------------------
rac102.localdomain
```

DGConnectIdentifier for Databases

Ensure that the DGConnectIdentifier property for each database is using the scan address so that the broker configuration does not experience problems in connectivity when individual nodes are shut down.

```
DGMGRL> show database verbose orcldr

Database - orcldr

  Role:                 PHYSICAL STANDBY
  Intended State:       APPLY-ON
  Transport Lag:        0 seconds (computed 0 seconds ago)
  Apply Lag:            0 seconds (computed 0 seconds ago)
  Average Apply Rate:   25.00 KByte/s
  Active Apply Rate:    484.00 KByte/s
  Maximum Apply Rate:   552.00 KByte/s
  Real Time Query:      ON
  Instance(s):
    orcldr1 (apply instance)
    orcldr2

  Properties:
    DGConnectIdentifier             = '(DESCRIPTION=(ADDRESS=(PROTOCOL=TCP)
(HOST=rac201.localdomain)(PORT=1521))(CONNECT_DATA=(SERVICE_NAME=orcldr.
world)(SERVER=DEDICATED)))'
    ObserverConnectIdentifier       = ''
    LogXptMode                      = 'ASYNC'
    RedoRoutes                      = ''
    DelayMins                       = '0'
```

```
Binding                         = 'optional'
MaxFailure                      = '0'
MaxConnections                  = '1'
ReopenSecs                      = '300'
NetTimeout                      = '30'
RedoCompression                 = 'DISABLE'
LogShipping                     = 'ON'
PreferredApplyInstance          = 'orcldr1'
ApplyInstanceTimeout            = '0'
ApplyLagThreshold               = '30'
TransportLagThreshold           = '30'
TransportDisconnectedThreshold  = '30'
ApplyParallel                   = 'AUTO'
ApplyInstances                  = '0'
StandbyFileManagement           = 'AUTO'
ArchiveLagTarget                = '0'
LogArchiveMaxProcesses          = '4'
LogArchiveMinSucceedDest        = '1'
DataGuardSyncLatency            = '0'
DbFileNameConvert               = ''
LogFileNameConvert              = 'null, null'
FastStartFailoverTarget         = ''
InconsistentProperties          = '(monitor)'
InconsistentLogXptProps         = '(monitor)'
SendQEntries                    = '(monitor)'
LogXptStatus                    = '(monitor)'
RecvQEntries                    = '(monitor)'
PreferredObserverHosts          = ''
StaticConnectIdentifier(*)
StandbyArchiveLocation(*)
AlternateLocation(*)
LogArchiveTrace(*)
LogArchiveFormat(*)
TopWaitEvents(*)
(*) - Please check specific instance for the property value
```

```
Log file locations(*):
  (*) - Check specific instance for log file locations.
```

Database Status:
SUCCESS

DGMGRL> edit database orcldr set property DGConnectIdentifier='(DESCRIPTION =(ADDRESS=(PROTOCOL=TCP)(HOST=rac02-scan.localdomain)(PORT=1521))(CONNECT_ DATA=(SERVICE_NAME=orcldr.world)(SERVER=DEDICATED)))';
Property "dgconnectidentifier" updated

DGMGRL> show database verbose orclcdb

Database - orclcdb

```
  Role:               PRIMARY
  Intended State:     TRANSPORT-ON
  Instance(s):
    orclcdb1
    orclcdb2

  Properties:
    DGConnectIdentifier              = '(DESCRIPTION = (LOAD_BALANCE = ON)
(ADDRESS = (PROTOCOL = TCP)(HOST = rac01-scan.localdomain)(PORT = 1521))
(CONNECT_DATA = (SERVICE_NAME = orclcdb.world)))'
    ObserverConnectIdentifier        = "
    LogXptMode                       = 'ASYNC'
    RedoRoutes                       = "
    DelayMins                        = '0'
    Binding                          = 'optional'
    MaxFailure                       = '0'
    MaxConnections                   = '1'
    ReopenSecs                       = '300'
    NetTimeout                       = '30'
    RedoCompression                  = 'DISABLE'
    LogShipping                      = 'ON'
    PreferredApplyInstance           = "
    ApplyInstanceTimeout             = '0'
```

```
    ApplyLagThreshold                = '30'
    TransportLagThreshold            = '30'
    TransportDisconnectedThreshold   = '30'
    ApplyParallel                    = 'AUTO'
    ApplyInstances                   = '0'
    StandbyFileManagement            = 'AUTO'
    ArchiveLagTarget                 = '0'
    LogArchiveMaxProcesses           = '4'
    LogArchiveMinSucceedDest         = '1'
    DataGuardSyncLatency             = '0'
    DbFileNameConvert                = "
    LogFileNameConvert               = "
    FastStartFailoverTarget          = "
    InconsistentProperties           = '(monitor)'
    InconsistentLogXptProps          = '(monitor)'
    SendQEntries                     = '(monitor)'
    LogXptStatus                     = '(monitor)'
    RecvQEntries                     = '(monitor)'
    PreferredObserverHosts           = "
    StaticConnectIdentifier(*)
    StandbyArchiveLocation(*)
    AlternateLocation(*)
    LogArchiveTrace(*)
    LogArchiveFormat(*)
    TopWaitEvents(*)
    (*) - Please check specific instance for the property value

  Log file locations(*):
    (*) - Check specific instance for log file locations.

Database Status:
SUCCESS
```

OMS High Availability Setup

Thus far, we have covered the topic of high availability for the OMS repository database. Now we will move on to the topic of high availability of the OMS. It is important to have fault tolerance at the application level as well as the database level. This can be achieved by adding at least one extra Oracle Management Server and configuring a software load balancer. To take things a step further, this chapter will cover disaster recovery scenarios.

The end state of the configuration within the primary datacenter will look something like Figure 3-13.

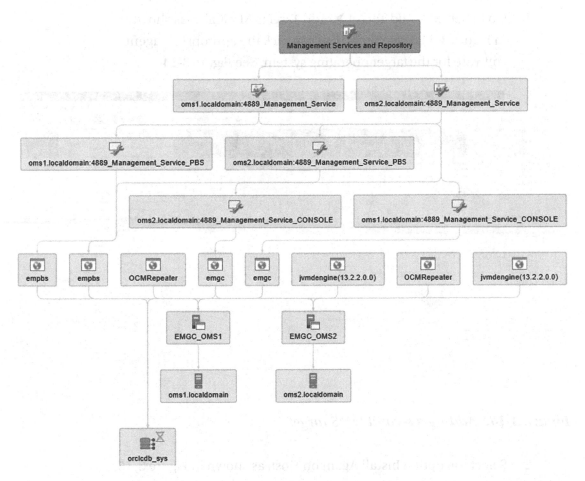

Figure 3-13. *OMS HA topology*

Adding a Second OMS Server

The first step toward high availability will be to add a second OMS server. This will entail discovering a second candidate OMS server, installing agents, mounting shared storage, and configuring a load balancer, among other things. In this book, the SLB software will be HAProxy.

Adding a Second OMS Server as a Managed Target

Adding a second OMS target is a simple matter. Follow these steps:

1. Go to Setup ➤ Add Target ➤ Add Targets Manually, as shown in Figure 3-14. Once there, you can pick the appropriate agent software for the target operating system. See Figure 3-14.

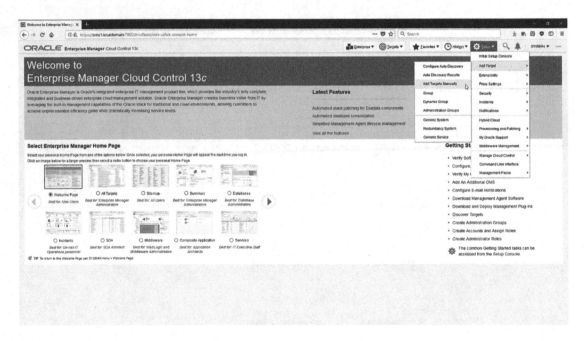

Figure 3-14. *Adding a second OMS target*

2. Select the option Install Agent on Host, as shown in Figure 3-15.

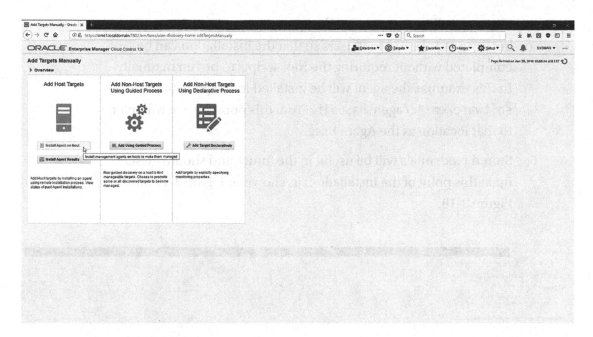

Figure 3-15. *Adding a second OMS target*

3. The second OMS host will be a 64-bit Linux host like the first OMS host. Ensure that the fully qualified domain name of the host is specified, as shown in Figure 3-16.

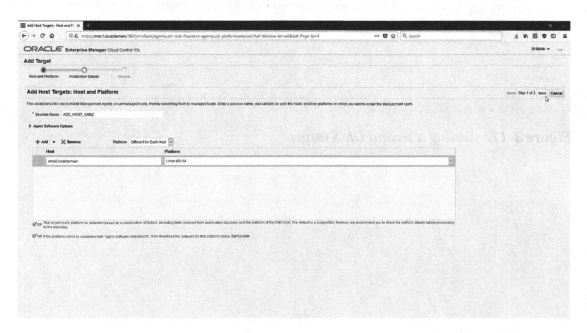

Figure 3-16. *Adding a second OMS target*

4. The user will be prompted to set up named credentials for both the `oracle` and root users so that the installation can be completed without requiring the root scripts to be run manually. In this example, the agent will be installed in the path `/u01/software/em13c/agentbasedir`. From this point on, we will refer to that location as the Agent Base.

5. Stored credentials will be useful in the future and should be set up at this point of the installation, as shown in Figure 3-17 and Figure 3-18.

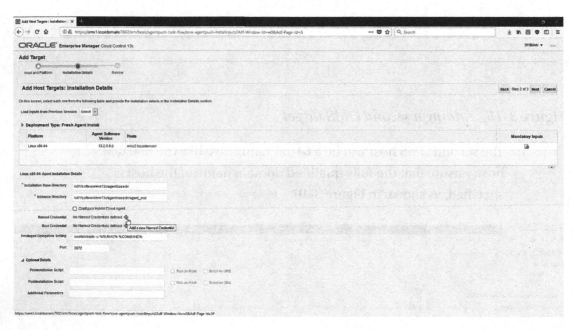

Figure 3-17. *Adding a second OMS target*

Figure 3-18. *Adding a second OMS target*

6. Stored credentials for the Oracle user are necessary because the Oracle user will be running the agent processes.

7. Ensure that an appropriate installation base directory and instance directory have been specified, as shown in Figure 3-19.

Figure 3-19. *Adding a second OMS target*

8. Create a root stored credential to automate all the root post-install actions, as shown in Figure 3-20.

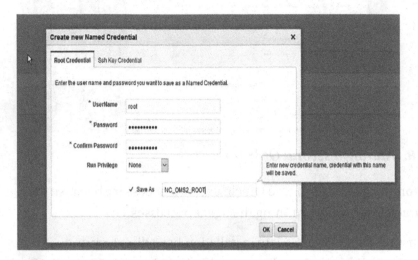

Figure 3-20. *Adding a second OMS target*

9. Click the Next button on the right side of the page to get to the review screen, as shown in Figure 3-21.

Figure 3-21. *Adding a second OMS target*

10. The agent is installed on the target OMS host through an OEM job
whose execution status can be viewed like any regular OEM job.
Review the information supplied and click Deploy Agent to start
the installation, as shown in Figure 3-22.

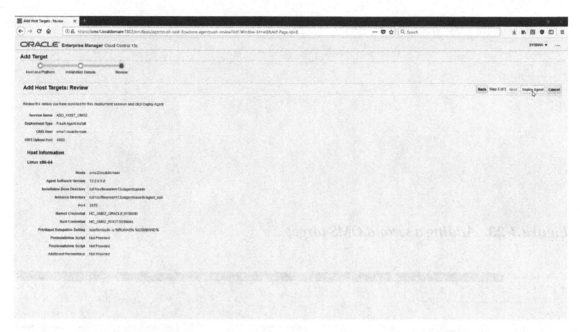

Figure 3-22. *Adding a second OMS target*

11. Figure 3-23 through Figure 3-27 show the output that you should
expect from a successful installation.

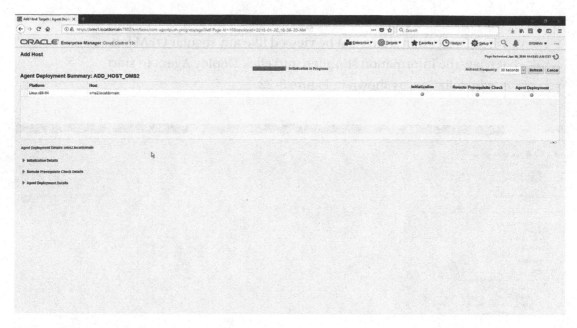

Figure 3-23. *Adding a second OMS target*

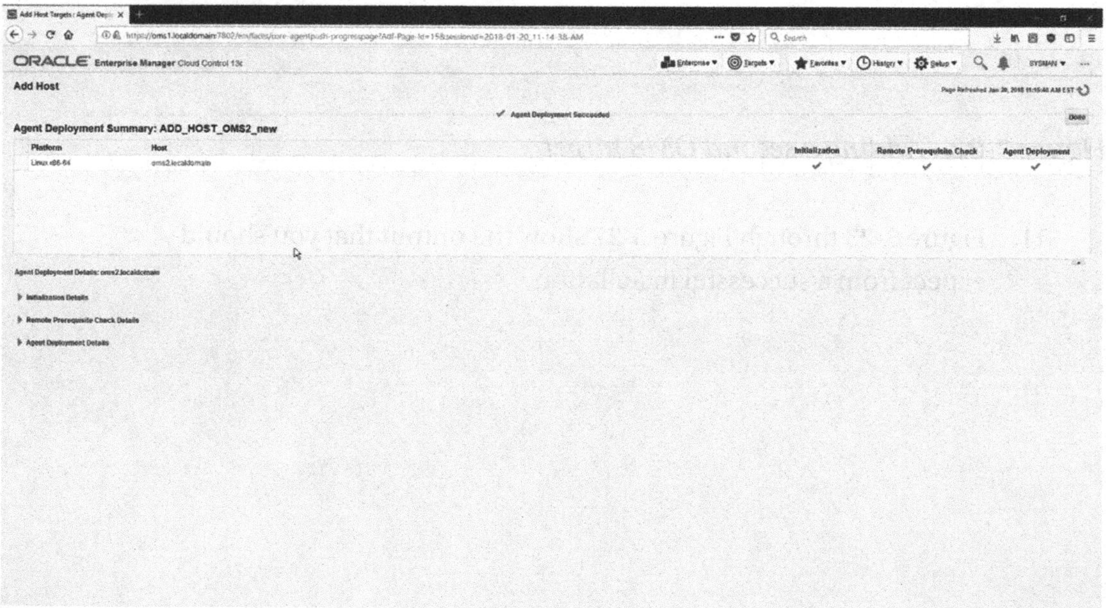

Figure 3-24. *Adding a second OMS target*

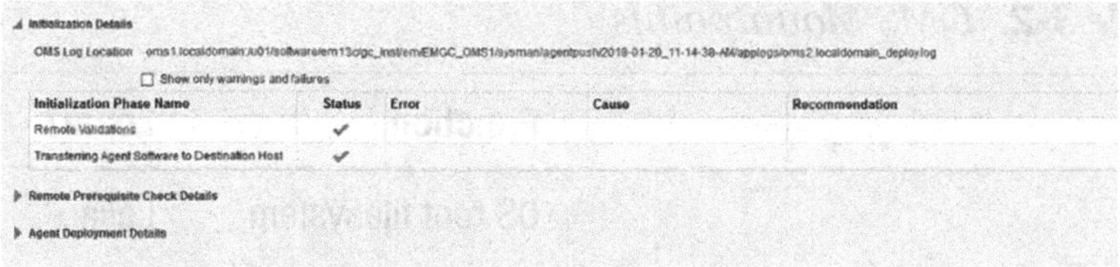

Figure 3-25. *Adding a second OMS target*

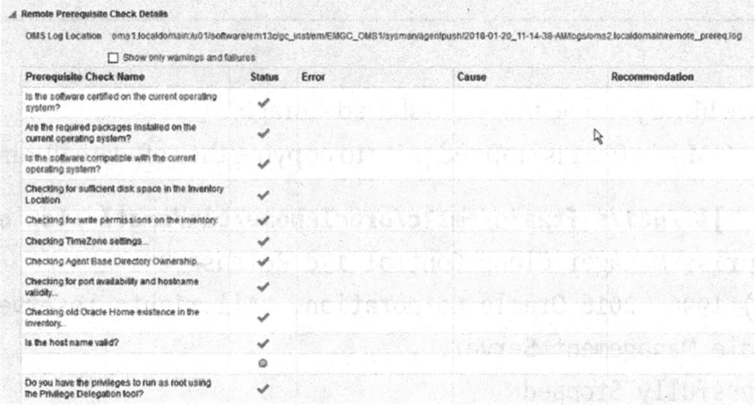

Figure 3-26. *Adding a second OMS target*

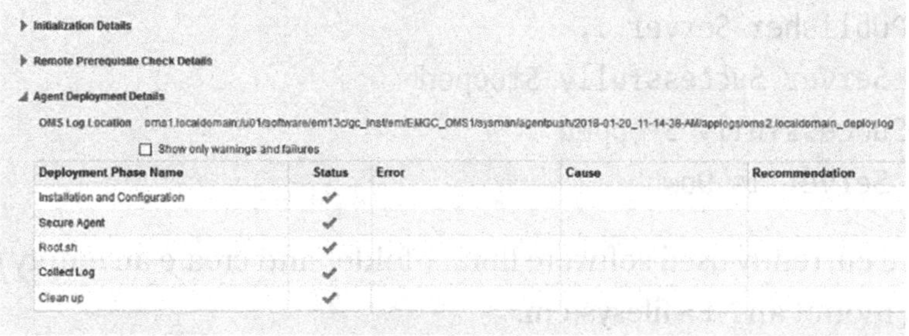

Figure 3-27. *Adding a second OMS target*

Moving the Software Library Location

If the OMS installation was initially sized for a small datacenter, the software library may have been installed on local storage. For multiple OMS servers to work properly, the software library will need to be on shared storage. Please refer to Table 3-2 for the mountpoints on the OMS server oms1.localdomain.

Table 3-2. *OMS Mountpoints*

Path	Function	Local?
/	OS root filesystem	Local
/boot	OS boot partition	Local
/u01/oms_shared	Shared BI storage	NFS
/u01/software/em13c/swlib	Software library	Local

The software library will be moved to shared storage.

Ensure that OMS on OMS1 is stopped prior to copying the software library.

[oracle@oms1 ~]$ /u01/software/em13c/oraclehome/bin/emctl stop oms -all
```
Oracle Enterprise Manager Cloud Control 13c Release 2
Copyright (c) 1996, 2016 Oracle Corporation.  All rights reserved.
Stopping Oracle Management Server...
WebTier Successfully Stopped
Oracle Management Server Successfully Stopped
Oracle Management Server is Down
JVMD Engine is Down
Stopping BI Publisher Server...
BI Publisher Server Successfully Stopped
AdminServer Successfully Stopped
BI Publisher Server is Down
```

Rename the currently used software library folder and create an empty directory on which you can mount an NFS filesystem.

[oracle@oms1 em13c]$ mv swlib/ swlib_bak

For NFS mounts to persist on OS reboots, the filesystem should be placed in the /etc/fstab configuration file. Here we are using an NFS filesystem exported by NFS server nas.localdomain.

[root@oms1 ~]# cat /etc/fstab
```
#
# /etc/fstab
```

```
# Created by anaconda on Thu Jul 20 22:33:14 2017
#
# Accessible filesystems, by reference, are maintained und'r '/dev/d'sk'
# See man pages fstab(5), findfs(8), mount(8) and/or blkid(8) for more info
#
/dev/mapper/vg_oms1-lv_root /                    ext4    defaults          1 1
UUID=60f0cf75-512e-4a4d-a7fa-52f1051b8781 /boot  ext4    defaults          1 2
/dev/mapper/vg_oms1-lv_swap swap                 swap    defaults          0 0
tmpfs                    /dev/shm                tmpfs   defaults          0 0
devpts                   /dev/pts                devpts  gid=5,mode=620    0 0
sysfs                    /sys                    sysfs   defaults          0 0
proc                     /proc                   proc    defaults          0 0
nas.localdomain:/data_pool/oms_shared_
storage /u01/oms_shared                          nfs     defaults          0 0
nas.localdomain:/data_pool/swlib /u01/software/
em13c/swlib                                      nfs     defaults          0 0
```

The filesystem will be mounted with the mount command.

```
[root@oms1 ~]# mount -a
[root@oms1 ~]# df -h
Filesystem              Size  Used Avail Use% Mounted on
/dev/mapper/vg_oms1-lv_root
                         95G   50G   41G  55% /
tmpfs                   5.8G     0  5.8G   0% /dev/shm
/dev/sda1               477M  161M  287M  36% /boot
192.168.0.59:/data_pool/oms_shared_storage
                         90G  533M   90G   1% /u01/oms_shared
192.168.0.59:/data_pool/swlib
                         90G     0   90G   0% /u01/software/em13c/swlib
```

Once the filesystem is available, the software library contents should be copied to the NFS filesystem.

```
[oracle@oms1 em13c]$ cp -r swlib_bak/* swlib/
```

SLB HAProxy Configuration

To provide a consistent URL for agents and web console end users, a software load balancer should be configured to route traffic to the appropriate OMS server. A software load balancer will carry out these two important functions:

- The SLB will balance web traffic across multiple OMS hosts to distribute load.

- The SLB will monitor the different components of the OMS stack to ensure that requests are being sent only to functioning OMS servers.

A good high-level analogy is that the SLB is to the OMS as the scan listener is to the RAC database. In this chapter, we will go over how HAProxy, which is open source SLB software, can be installed on an Ubuntu 16.04.1 LTS installation. This process can more or less be followed on any Linux distribution, although the location of important configuration files may be different on Linux distributions that are not Debian based.

Installing HAProxy

You can install the software through the `apt-get` command, which is the package manager command-line utility for Ubuntu.

```
root@nas:~# apt-get update && apt-get install haproxy -y
```

HAProxy is easily configurable and has two important files that should be known to the administrator. Please refer to Table 3-3 for those file details.

Table 3-3. *HAProxy Files*

File	Function
/etc/haproxy/haproxy.cfg	HAProxy configuration file
/var/log/haproxy.log	HAProxy logfile

SLB Virtual IP Configuration

It is recommended that a virtual IP be assigned to an interface on the appropriate public-facing subnet for the purpose of load balancing connections. This can be accomplished via the ifconfig command. The output has been abbreviated to show only the interfaces relevant to HAProxy.

```
root@nas:~# ifconfig enp0s10:0 192.168.0.93
root@nas:~# ifconfig enp0s10:0 up
root@nas:~# ifconfig
enp0s10    Link encap:Ethernet  HWaddr 08:00:27:c1:f5:89
           inet addr:192.168.0.59  Bcast:192.168.0.255  Mask:255.255.255.0
           inet6 addr: fe80::a00:27ff:fec1:f589/64 Scope:Link
           inet6 addr: ::a00:27ff:fec1:f589/64 Scope:Global
           UP BROADCAST RUNNING MULTICAST  MTU:1500  Metric:1
           RX packets:108917 errors:0 dropped:0 overruns:0 frame:0
           TX packets:91685 errors:0 dropped:0 overruns:0 carrier:0
           collisions:0 txqueuelen:1000
           RX bytes:10899013 (10.8 MB)  TX bytes:37323219 (37.3 MB)

enp0s10:0 Link encap:Ethernet  HWaddr 08:00:27:c1:f5:89
           inet addr:192.168.0.93  Bcast:192.168.0.255  Mask:255.255.255.0
           UP BROADCAST RUNNING MULTICAST  MTU:1500  Metric:1
```

The virtual interface enp0s10:0 will not persist through a host reboot, so it must be defined in the /etc/network/interface file, which holds the network configuration of the Ubuntu server.

```
root@nas:~# cat /etc/network/interfaces
# This file describes the network interfaces available on your system
# and how to activate them. For more information, see interfaces(5).

source /etc/network/interfaces.d/*

# The loopback network interface
auto lo
iface lo inet loopback

# The primary network interface
```

```
auto enp0s10
iface enp0s10 inet static
        address 192.168.0.59
        netmask 255.255.255.0
        gateway 192.168.0.1

auto enp0s10:0
iface enp0s10:0 inet static
address 192.168.0.93
netmask 255.255.255.0
broadcast 192.168.0.1
```

Creating SSL Certificates

It is important to properly configure OMS with web certificates so that communications between web console users and browsers and the OEM Agent and OMS servers are encrypted using SSL. This is needed for compliance reasons as well as for basic security.

In this section of the chapter, an example of a self-signed certificate that can be used by with an OMS will be created and configured for use.

First a directory will need to be created to house the public and private keys.

```
root@nas:~# cd /root/ha_proxy_certs
root@nas:~/ha_proxy_certs#
```

A private key can be generated via the `openssl genrsa` command.

```
root@nas:~/ha_proxy_certs# openssl genrsa -out
/root/ha_proxy_certs/oem13c.localdomain.ca 2048

Generating RSA private key, 2048 bit long modulus
....................................................+++
...........................................+++
e is 65537 (0x10001)
```

Once a private key exists, it can be used to create a certificate signing request (CSR). You will be prompted for details that will be stored with the certificate. User input is written in bold to help you differentiate output from the `openssl` command with the input required from the user to complete a certificate signing request.

```
root@nas:~/ha_proxy_certs# openssl req -new -key /root/ha_proxy_certs/
oem13c.localdomain.ca \
> -out /root/ha_proxy_certs/oem13c.localdomain.csr
```

You are about to be asked to enter information that will be incorporated
into your certificate request.
What you are about to enter is what is called a Distinguished Name or a DN.
There are quite a few fields but you can leave some blank
For some fields there will be a default value,
If you enter '.', the field will be left blank.

Country Name (2 letter code) [AU]:**US**
State or Province Name (full name) [Some-State]:**FL**
Locality Name (eg, city) []:**Tampa**
Organization Name (eg, company) [Internet Widgits Pty Ltd]:
Organizational Unit Name (eg, section) []:
Common Name (e.g. server FQDN or YOUR name) []:**oem13c.localdomain**
Email Address []:

Please enter the following 'extra' attributes
to be sent with your certificate request
A challenge password []:
An optional company name []:

The certificate can be signed for a configurable number of days with the –days flag. This controls how long a certificate can be used before it is rejected for being stale.

```
root@nas:~/ha_proxy_certs# openssl x509 -req -days 365 -in /root/ha_
proxy_certs/oem13c.localdomain.csr -signkey /root/ha_proxy_certs/oem13c.
localdomain.ca -out /root/ha_proxy_certs/oem13c.localdomain.csr
```

```
Signature ok
subject=/C=US/ST=FL/L=Tampa/O=Internet Widgits Pty Ltd/CN=oem13c.localdomain
Getting Private key
```

The certificate signing request and the private key must be placed in a PEM format file. This step is important and if not done correctly will result in SSL-related communication issues. The PEM formatted file is a Base64-encoded version of the keys.

Because the private key, which was used to sign the certificate request, is stored in the PEM file, this is considered a *self-signed* certificate and should be used only for proof-of-concept implementations and not in production systems. The private key must follow the certificate signing request.

root@nas:~/ha_proxy_certs# cat /root/ha_proxy_certs/oem13c.localdomain. csr /root/ha_proxy_certs/oem13c.localdomain.ca |tee /root/ha_proxy_certs/ oem13c.localdomain.pem

```
-----BEGIN CERTIFICATE-----
MIIDUDCCAjgCCQDIqy6f5u5RhDANBgkqhkiG9w0BAQsFADBqMQswCQYDVQQGEwJV
UzELMAkGA1UECAwCRkwxDjAMBgNVBAcMBVRhbXBhMSEwHwYDVQQKDBhJbnRlcm5l
dCBXaWRnaXRzIFB0eSBMdGQxGzAZBgNVBAMMEm9lbTEzYy5sb2NhbGRvbWFpbjAe
Fw0x0DAxMjAyMDMyMTNaFw0x0TAxMjAyMDMyMTNaMGoxCzAJBgNVBAYTAlVTMQsw
CQYDVQQIDAJGTDEOMAwGA1UEBwwFVGFtcGExITAfBgNVBAoMGEludGVybmV0IFdp
ZGdpdHMgUHR5IEx0ZDEbMBkGA1UEAwwSb2VtMTNjLmxvY2FsZG9tYWluMIIBIjAN
BgkqhkiG9w0BAQEFAAOCAQ8AMIIBCgKCAQEAweiy47f0E2fanyrOu62HeB98a07O
Sg5Dcw08FYgiTFPo2e+81JjuuVFG1zeFZA4G6NvCpIz+ULK+YOvDWNXsjtwJTg+Y
t9sDbDihVv39rUL6ZiBDLGHnOHO3F/CFexsc39bnafHWemIWm6qqVtuxOwNN48uV
wQU07AFARxqDGYUMft/9QXoqa8Vc1rxUw5i59gdIJ9x30ZWrEpMY1N1KMr+IwGFU
cm/G3eYpiahjr86/TMYE95SUtBluTIn2ZB8ZjZmjmNtSR81VS7+9VbpIHNwBfuRN
urFzzqhLbEmkh5M1En6k4q3YfCbAnNCH3QdhImunzqFtZvmoCXjx4OxmKQIDAQAB
MAOGCSqGSIb3DQEBCwUAA4IBAQBSbvRGmZQp4x681fjgBHdOi/HCQ7XM2pZvEeiO
ZaJ18dzwLfyw1QQ3Ls9+/uW7/DjdP9S4KFF+nxeruJLuuHNu+Qg/vqAROFWWVh2H
o5F/b9Md5aHdWd7FMNXCHG/O+tZLu9Wne/mbOyuvTyDizMXGbTOQS5i2YNPcfb9h
u5XxE3HvKDAULwEKJu4cWDf2EjamIvNhJDckojpMdFSP3fytEEEmJTkciRqrlWw6
6Ac0tD2FlZmgx1oBPU3ayCLajdfYPMPKzxZs4GiLLg5ffsLoleRcN4VBDHtBy2pn
HHNdqOXfc0IBZhV2ZWo+CNX4625zE65jNjq6u1150kdO9FxR
-----END CERTIFICATE-----
-----BEGIN RSA PRIVATE KEY-----
MIIEpQIBAAKCAQEAweiy47f0E2fanyrOu62HeB98a07OSg5Dcw08FYgiTFPo2e+8
1JjuuVFG1zeFZA4G6NvCpIz+ULK+YOvDWNXsjtwJTg+Yt9sDbDihVv39rUL6ZiBD
LGHnOHO3F/CFexsc39bnafHWemIWm6qqVtuxOwNN48uVwQU07AFARxqDGYUMft/9
QXoqa8Vc1rxUw5i59gdIJ9x30ZWrEpMY1N1KMr+IwGFUcm/G3eYpiahjr86/TMYE
95SUtBluTIn2ZB8ZjZmjmNtSR81VS7+9VbpIHNwBfuRNurFzzqhLbEmkh5M1En6k
4q3YfCbAnNCH3QdhImunzqFtZvmoCXjx4OxmKQIDAQABAoIBAQCMmQwOnyoDdBcJ
t8FERbNnPvU43Xu1wpfXcS4yso2j6Gd6tiClyem2Rx9lZ2V5wc3yw31jULQJkUEH
```

```
B4uR+zLV9udsSVTDYrMdogYiDHIGUf07VYM/SBGeVhDY89XlCCisiKcso2SPQlYA
MwPljNBoHwo39GK2HO9dfB6+L5QFSLQobD2dG7WLl9uuYpwmKrC7B2UUTlvqo/QJ
yanQ36Vu9Pp1+b9Bz8/TEh3eVrkqM3Q8pbIfgbuTCZORCbq8oHy17LpLmvIdVfpW
9o5W/3dsj1QXqyuO4q8gMCVMXsA4xy1HdfNKOQWbSPpeYuTvp9t4UdEnL88WWzLO
W3fWjy+9AoGBAP+/r8FtbPDTYv/NGZwpRmORAPeFc8OmZyLe4l1gSihhfi9SukJ5
FeFHgJhfaJOIf36yQzxn5mYHms94utVsocMbZTOMo+cTJjqoS7UgKOiQrvR5kKO6
8VDVdQPsxO3DX33bWLrDHWHXY1/ZKfcFLSD1rMA6ef0qrhUzk9pewLljAoGBAMIZ
dhikUXqR8FbfjF8jBpTg1dmej1iu9uBZwj5ATfJNqvRmctrlfj3b/Y3uIPwYniLy
IW4xeoBXZq5qO3KKJFkfE344T3VgGzq96TMAzNSvE4yWTwuzc1W+hSn2SXdl3i+x
qO4Zs4LVXUupAOjN6f9EdYr+A9vtWRADJDmMnv4DAoGBALZla1+OPwHygKSXDjDF
byILhHkDgHdLcDr6Ys7doYXzIh92DMjjuqsUZ65EPUPhj6w4TqOCJluWCN7256jW
9PdFToPZRfvDOHyVEol3CjXzGhPZr0kcxIY19mJ6Nmir8iq8iSeJiCcDiigNpVQ7
KNhc3nuqON5J1iXgxw3yjdipAoGBAKtzli/aJebhNq1mNjZrWAr2N7BNMU4i7wvp
/XzDjJa2KIZOYLIe+c5mnqhaamSEOlsICqOtrQnlKlxyliRtBgJ7QtrBnt6NkD/p
NS7KTCSqqdgLhbNORli9PB9+4BJJt2PlyNTZewncstZ8aMM78LB9pl6qVnpUQ9Gz
FLKJFoBFAoGAdnaLB/QfWLQcgrWrsUKxJd5/T+PGr/vxMYhFb8kGJsjpmSoB3NRW
EPi4TIifUqvegRamSnNSepOO+rudH5VJX12p8wqGbZt4pBpchv6ZVPWp8Lp1VTU/
o6qgyE5JAzmib7JwbC7Ycgr9Pw9hoYbehzMzgLYfToQOyK/XhhssftY=
-----END RSA PRIVATE KEY-----
```

```
root@nas:~/ha_proxy_certs# ll
total 20
drwxr-xr-x 2 root root 4096 Jan 20 15:32 ./
drwx------ 8 root root 4096 Jan 20 15:26 ../
-rw-r--r-- 1 root root 1679 Jan 20 15:29 oem13c.localdomain.ca
-rw-r--r-- 1 root root 1208 Jan 20 15:32 oem13c.localdomain.csr
-rw-r--r-- 1 root root 2887 Jan 20 15:32 oem13c.localdomain.pem
```

The certificate files must then be placed in a secure location and be guarded by strict OS file privileges. In this example, only the user haproxy, which runs the load balancing software, will have permissions to the files.

```
root@nas:~/ha_proxy_certs# cp * /ha_proxy_certs/
root@nas:~/ha_proxy_certs# chown -R haproxy:haproxy /ha_proxy_certs/
root@nas:~/ha_proxy_certs# chmod -R 700 /ha_proxy_certs/
root@nas:~/ha_proxy_certs# ll -la /ha_proxy_certs/
total 20
```

```
drwx------   2 haproxy haproxy 4096 Jan 20 15:06 ./
drwxr-xr-x 25 root     root    4096 Jan 20 15:06 ../
-rwx------   1 haproxy haproxy  887 Jan 20 15:06 oem13c.localdomain.ca*
-rwx------   1 haproxy haproxy  631 Jan 20 15:06 oem13c.localdomain.csr*
-rwx------   1 haproxy haproxy 1518 Jan 20 15:06 oem13c.localdomain.pem*
```

OEM-Specific HAProxy Configuration

Per the relevant documentation on SLB setup for OEM, you will need to configure HAProxy to route traffic to several endpoints. See the following:

https://docs.oracle.com/cd/E91266_01/EMADV/GUID-F45A2F2E-FE04-414E-A4F0-A33518157F82.htm#EMADV14386

For this configuration, static IP addresses will be used to help insulate the HAProxy configuration from DNS resolution errors.

Hostname	IP	Function
oms1.localdomain	192.168.0.89	First OMS server
oms2.localdomain	192.168.0.92	Second OMS Server
oem13c.localdomain	192.168.0.93	SLB hostname for OMS

The following configuration file entries show how HAProxy can be configured route traffic to oms1.localdomain and the future oms2.localdomain.

Add the following entries into /etc/haproxy/haproxy.cfg:

```
### ORACLE
backend secureuploadpool
      balance leastconn
      mode tcp
      server oms1 192.168.0.89:4903 check ssl verify none
      server oms2 192.168.0.92:4903 check ssl verify none

backend agentregistrationpool
    balance leastconn
      mode tcp
      cookie SERVERID insert indirect nocache
```

```
        server oms1 192.168.0.89:4889 check cookie
        server oms2 192.168.0.92:4889 check cookie

backend secureconsolepool
    balance leastconn
        mode tcp
    stick-table type ip size 1m
    stick on src
        server oms1 192.168.0.89:7802 check ssl verify none
        server oms2 192.168.0.92:7802 check ssl verify none

backend unsecureconsolepool
    balance leastconn
    mode tcp
    stick-table type ip size 1m
    stick on src
    server oms1 192.168.0.89:7788 check
    server oms1 192.168.0.92:7788 check

frontend secureuploadvirtualserver
  bind 192.168.0.93:1159 ssl crt /ha_proxy_certs/oem13c.localdomain.pem
  mode tcp
  default_backend secureuploadpool

frontend agentvirtualserver
  bind 192.168.0.93:4889
  mode tcp
  default_backend agentregistrationpool

frontend secureconsolevirtualserver
  bind 192.168.0.93:443 ssl crt /ha_proxy_certs/oem13c.localdomain.pem
  mode tcp
  default_backend secureconsolepool

frontend unsecureuploadvirtualserver
  bind 192.168.0.93:80
  mode tcp
  default_backend unsecureconsolepool
```

Once the configuration file has been set up, the HAProxy service can be restarted with the service command.

root@nas:~# service haproxy restart

Resecuring the OMS and Agents

The OMS server will need to be resecured with the certificate using the oem13c. localdomain fully qualified domain name.

[oracle@oms1 ~]$ /u01/software/em13c/oraclehome/bin/emctl secure oms -host oem13c.localdomain -secure_port 4903 -slb_port 1159 -slb_console_port 443 -console -trust_certs_loc /tmp/oem13c.localdomain.csr -slb_jvmd_https_port 7301
```
Oracle Enterprise Manager Cloud Control 13c Release 2
Copyright (c) 1996, 2016 Oracle Corporation.  All rights reserved.
Securing OMS... Started.
Enter Enterprise Manager Root (SYSMAN) Password :
Enter Agent Registration Password :
Securing OMS... Successful
Restart OMS
```

In an unpatched version of the OMS software, you may experience the following issue. Ensure that you follow the directions outlined in the metalink note.

EM 13c: "emctl secure oms" Command Fails with Error: Either of -slb_jvmd_http_port or -slb_jvmd_https_port must be specified (Doc ID 2120008.1)

Once OMS has been resecured, ensure that the proper output is displayed by the emctl status oms command. The pertinent information is in bold. This will show that OMS is configured to use software load balancing and will use the virtual hostname oem13c.localdomain instead of the physical hostname of the OMS server.

[oracle@oms1 ~]$ /u01/software/em13c/oraclehome/bin/emctl status oms -details
```
Oracle Enterprise Manager Cloud Control 13c Release 2
Copyright (c) 1996, 2016 Oracle Corporation.  All rights reserved.
Enter Enterprise Manager Root (SYSMAN) Password :
Console Server Host        : oms1.localdomain
HTTP Console Port          : 7788
HTTPS Console Port         : 7802
```

```
HTTP Upload Port            : 4889
HTTPS Upload Port           : 4903
EM Instance Home            : /u01/software/em13c/gc_inst/em/EMGC_OMS1
OMS Log Directory Location : /u01/software/em13c/gc_inst/em/EMGC_OMS1/
sysman/log
SLB or virtual hostname: oem13c.localdomain
HTTPS SLB Upload Port : 1159
HTTPS SLB Console Port : 443
HTTPS SLB JVMD Port : 7301
Agent Upload is locked.
OMS Console is locked.
Active CA ID: 1
Console URL: https://oem13c.localdomain:443/em
Upload URL: https://oem13c.localdomain:1159/empbs/upload

WLS Domain Information
Domain Name             : GCDomain
Admin Server Host       : oms1.localdomain
Admin Server HTTPS Port: 7102
Admin Server is RUNNING

Oracle Management Server Information
Managed Server Instance Name: EMGC_OMS1
Oracle Management Server Instance Host: oms1.localdomain
WebTier is Up
Oracle Management Server is Up
JVMD Engine is Up

BI Publisher Server Information
BI Publisher Managed Server Name: BIP
BI Publisher Server is Up

BI Publisher HTTP Managed Server Port   : 9701
BI Publisher HTTPS Managed Server Port  : 9803
BI Publisher HTTP OHS Port              : 9788
BI Publisher HTTPS OHS Port             : 9851
BI Publisher HTTPS SLB Port             : Not Set
```

BI Publisher is locked.

BI Publisher Server named 'BIP' running at URL: https://oem13c. localdomain:9851/xmlpserver

BI Publisher Server Logs: /u01/software/em13c/gc_inst/user_projects/ domains/GCDomain/servers/BIP/logs/

BI Publisher Log   : /u01/software/em13c/gc_inst/user_projects/ domains/GCDomain/servers/BIP/logs/bipublisher/bipublisher.log

For the changes to be fully implemented, the OMS server will need to be restarted.

```
[oracle@oms1 ~]$ /u01/software/em13c/oraclehome/bin/emctl stop oms -all
Oracle Enterprise Manager Cloud Control 13c Release 2
Copyright (c) 1996, 2016 Oracle Corporation.  All rights reserved.
Stopping Oracle Management Server...
WebTier Successfully Stopped
Oracle Management Server Successfully Stopped
Oracle Management Server is Down
JVMD Engine is Down
Stopping BI Publisher Server...
BI Publisher Server Successfully Stopped
AdminServer Successfully Stopped
BI Publisher Server is Down
[oracle@oms1 ~]$ /u01/software/em13c/oraclehome/bin/emctl start oms
Oracle Enterprise Manager Cloud Control 13c Release 2
Copyright (c) 1996, 2016 Oracle Corporation.  All rights reserved.
Starting Oracle Management Server...
WebTier Successfully Started
Oracle Management Server Successfully Started
Oracle Management Server is Up
JVMD Engine is Up
Starting BI Publisher Server ...
BI Publisher Server Successfully Started
BI Publisher Server is Up
[oracle@oms1 ~]$ /u01/software/em13c/oraclehome/bin/emctl status oms -details
Oracle Enterprise Manager Cloud Control 13c Release 2
Copyright (c) 1996, 2016 Oracle Corporation.  All rights reserved.
```

```
Enter Enterprise Manager Root (SYSMAN) Password :
Console Server Host        : oms1.localdomain
HTTP Console Port          : 7788
HTTPS Console Port         : 7802
HTTP Upload Port           : 4889
HTTPS Upload Port          : 4903
EM Instance Home           : /u01/software/em13c/gc_inst/em/EMGC_OMS1
OMS Log Directory Location : /u01/software/em13c/gc_inst/em/EMGC_OMS1/
sysman/log
SLB or virtual hostname: oem13c.localdomain
HTTPS SLB Upload Port : 1159
HTTPS SLB Console Port : 443
HTTPS SLB JVMD Port : 7301
Agent Upload is locked.
OMS Console is locked.
Active CA ID: 1
Console URL: https://oem13c.localdomain:443/em
Upload URL: https://oem13c.localdomain:1159/empbs/upload

WLS Domain Information
Domain Name            : GCDomain
Admin Server Host      : oms1.localdomain
Admin Server HTTPS Port: 7102
Admin Server is RUNNING

Oracle Management Server Information
Managed Server Instance Name: EMGC_OMS1
Oracle Management Server Instance Host: oms1.localdomain
WebTier is Up
Oracle Management Server is Up
JVMD Engine is Up

BI Publisher Server Information
BI Publisher Managed Server Name: BIP
BI Publisher Server is Up

BI Publisher HTTP Managed Server Port    : 9701
BI Publisher HTTPS Managed Server Port   : 9803
```

```
BI Publisher HTTP OHS Port                : 9788
BI Publisher HTTPS OHS Port               : 9851
BI Publisher HTTPS SLB Port               : Not Set
BI Publisher is locked.
BI Publisher Server named 'BIP' running at URL:
https://oem13c.localdomain:9851/xmlpserver
BI Publisher Server Logs: /u01/software/em13c/gc_inst/user_projects/
domains/GCDomain/servers/BIP/logs/
BI Publisher Log          : /u01/software/em13c/gc_inst/user_projects/
domains/GCDomain/servers/BIP/logs/bipublisher/bipublisher.log
```

Before continuing with any further setup, all OEM Agent instances must be secured against the new SLB virtual hostname. This will cause the OEM Agent to upload metric collection data to oem13c.localdomain instead of the physical hostname of the OMS server. In a multi-OMS environment, this will ensure that the unavailability of any one OMS server does not halt metric collection.

[oracle@oms1 ~]$ /u01/software/em13c/agentbasedir/agent_inst/bin/emctl secure agent database_123 -emdWalletSrcUrl https://oem13c.localdomain:1159/em
```
Oracle Enterprise Manager Cloud Control 13c Release 2
Copyright (c) 1996, 2016 Oracle Corporation.  All rights reserved.
Agent successfully stopped...   Done.
Securing agent...    Started.
Agent successfully restarted...    Done.
Securing agent...    Successful.
[oracle@oms1 ~]$ /u01/software/em13c/agentbasedir/agent_inst/bin/emctl
status agent
Oracle Enterprise Manager Cloud Control 13c Release 2
Copyright (c) 1996, 2016 Oracle Corporation.  All rights reserved.
---------------------------------------------------------------

Agent Version           : 13.2.0.0.0
OMS Version             : 13.2.0.0.0
Protocol Version        : 12.1.0.1.0
Agent Home              : /u01/software/em13c/agentbasedir/agent_inst
Agent Log Directory     : /u01/software/em13c/agentbasedir/agent_inst/
                          sysman/log
```

```
Agent Binaries          : /u01/software/em13c/agentbasedir/agent_13.2.0.0.0
Core JAR Location       : /u01/software/em13c/agentbasedir/agent_13.2.0.0.0/
                          jlib
Agent Process ID        : 11460
Parent Process ID       : 11398
Agent URL               : https://oms1.localdomain:3872/emd/main/
Local Agent URL in NAT  : https://oms1.localdomain:3872/emd/main/
Repository URL          : https://oem13c.localdomain:1159/empbs/upload
Started at              : 2018-01-20 16:52:22
Started by user         : oracle
Operating System        : Linux version 4.1.12-94.3.9.el6uek.x86_64 (amd64)
Number of Targets       : 34
Last Reload             : (none)
Last successful upload                       : 2018-01-20 16:52:45
Last attempted upload                        : 2018-01-20 16:52:45
Total Megabytes of XML files uploaded so far : 0.14
Number of XML files pending upload           : 0
Size of XML files pending upload(MB)         : 0
Available disk space on upload filesystem    : 47.89%
Collection Status                            : Collections enabled
Heartbeat Status                             : Ok
Last attempted heartbeat to OMS              : 2018-01-20 16:52:31
Last successful heartbeat to OMS             : 2018-01-20 16:52:31
Next scheduled heartbeat to OMS              : 2018-01-20 16:53:34

---------------------------------------------------------------
Agent is Running and Ready
[oracle@oms1 ~]$ /u01/software/em13c/agentbasedir/agent_inst/bin/emctl
upload agent
Oracle Enterprise Manager Cloud Control 13c Release 2
Copyright (c) 1996, 2016 Oracle Corporation.  All rights reserved.
---------------------------------------------------------------
EMD upload completed successfully
```

**[oracle@oms1 ~]$ /u01/software/em13c/agentbasedir/agent_inst/bin/emctl
status agent**

```
Oracle Enterprise Manager Cloud Control 13c Release 2
Copyright (c) 1996, 2016 Oracle Corporation.  All rights reserved.
----------------------------------------------------------------
Agent Version          : 13.2.0.0.0
OMS Version            : 13.2.0.0.0
Protocol Version       : 12.1.0.1.0
Agent Home             : /u01/software/em13c/agentbasedir/agent_inst
Agent Log Directory    : /u01/software/em13c/agentbasedir/agent_inst/
sysman/log
Agent Binaries         : /u01/software/em13c/agentbasedir/agent_13.2.0.0.0
Core JAR Location      : /u01/software/em13c/agentbasedir/agent_13.2.0.0.0/
jlib
Agent Process ID       : 11460
Parent Process ID      : 11398
Agent URL              : https://oms1.localdomain:3872/emd/main/
Local Agent URL in NAT : https://oms1.localdomain:3872/emd/main/
Repository URL         : https://oem13c.localdomain:1159/empbs/upload
Started at             : 2018-01-20 16:52:22
Started by user        : oracle
Operating System       : Linux version 4.1.12-94.3.9.el6uek.x86_64 (amd64)
Number of Targets      : 34
Last Reload            : (none)
Last successful upload                       : 2018-01-20 16:53:06
Last attempted upload                        : 2018-01-20 16:53:06
Total Megabytes of XML files uploaded so far : 0.16
Number of XML files pending upload           : 0
Size of XML files pending upload(MB)         : 0
Available disk space on upload filesystem    : 47.89%
Collection Status                            : Collections enabled
Heartbeat Status                             : Ok
Last attempted heartbeat to OMS              : 2018-01-20 16:52:31
Last successful heartbeat to OMS             : 2018-01-20 16:52:31
Next scheduled heartbeat to OMS              : 2018-01-20 16:53:34

----------------------------------------------------------------
Agent is Running and Ready
```

Although there are no managed targets other than the host on oms2.localdomain, this agent will need to be resecured against the SLB virtual hostname to allow for a smooth OMS addition.

```
[oracle@oms2 ~]$ /u01/software/em13c/agentbasedir/agent_inst/bin/emctl
secure agent database_123 -emdWalletSrcUrl
https://oem13c.localdomain:1159/em
Oracle Enterprise Manager Cloud Control 13c Release 2
Copyright (c) 1996, 2016 Oracle Corporation.  All rights reserved.
Agent successfully stopped...   Done.
Securing agent...   Started.
Agent successfully restarted...   Done.
Securing agent...   Successful.

[oracle@oms2 ~]$ /u01/software/em13c/agentbasedir/agent_inst/bin/emctl
upload agent
Oracle Enterprise Manager Cloud Control 13c Release 2
Copyright (c) 1996, 2016 Oracle Corporation.  All rights reserved.
---------------------------------------------------------------
EMD upload completed successfully
[oracle@oms2 ~]$ /u01/software/em13c/agentbasedir/agent_inst/bin/emctl
status agent
Oracle Enterprise Manager Cloud Control 13c Release 2
Copyright (c) 1996, 2016 Oracle Corporation.  All rights reserved.
---------------------------------------------------------------
Agent Version        : 13.2.0.0.0
OMS Version          : 13.2.0.0.0
Protocol Version     : 12.1.0.1.0
Agent Home           : /u01/software/em13c/agentbasedir//agent_inst
Agent Log Directory  : /u01/software/em13c/agentbasedir//agent_inst/
sysman/log
Agent Binaries       : /u01/software/em13c/agentbasedir/agent_13.2.0.0.0
Core JAR Location    : /u01/software/em13c/agentbasedir/agent_13.2.0.0.0/
jlib
Agent Process ID     : 16320
Parent Process ID    : 16283
```

```
Agent URL                : https://oms2.localdomain:3872/emd/main/
Local Agent URL in NAT : https://oms2.localdomain:3872/emd/main/
Repository URL           : https://oem13c.localdomain:1159/empbs/upload
Started at               : 2018-01-20 16:55:45
Started by user          : oracle
Operating System         : Linux version 4.1.12-112.14.11.el6uek.x86_64
(amd64)
Number of Targets        : 5
Last Reload              : (none)
Last successful upload                      : 2018-01-20 16:56:34
Last attempted upload                       : 2018-01-20 16:56:34
Total Megabytes of XML files uploaded so far : 0.05
Number of XML files pending upload          : 0
Size of XML files pending upload(MB)        : 0
Available disk space on upload filesystem   : 90.80%
Collection Status                           : Collections enabled
Heartbeat Status                            : Ok
Last attempted heartbeat to OMS             : 2018-01-20 16:55:49
Last successful heartbeat to OMS            : 2018-01-20 16:55:49
Next scheduled heartbeat to OMS             : 2018-01-20 16:56:51

---------------------------------------------------------------
Agent is Running and Ready
```

Creating the Second OMS Through the Web Console

You can add OMS servers in an OEM-guided process through the secure portal
accessible in the initial setup console. Log in as a user with Super Administrator
privileges, as shown in Figure 3-28.

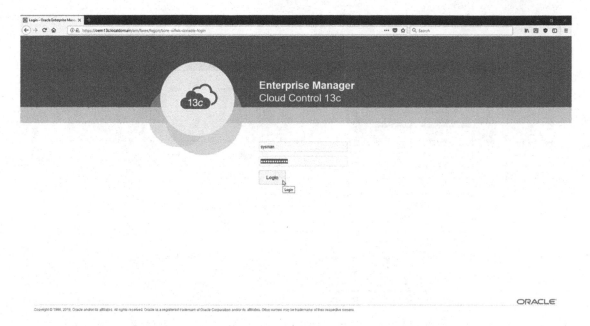

Figure 3-28. *Adding a second OMS*

The initial setup console can be reached by clicking Setup and then Initial Setup Console, as shown in Figure 3-29.

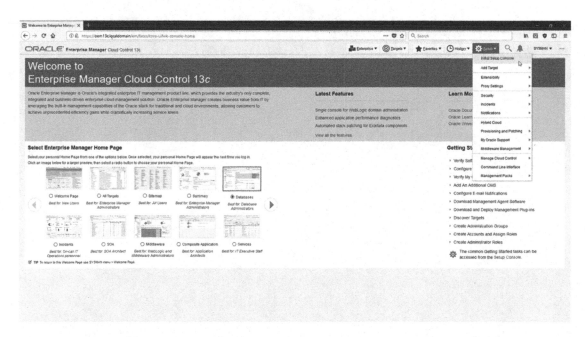

Figure 3-29. *Adding a second OMS*

Figure 3-30 shows the prerequisites that must be met to add a second OMS.

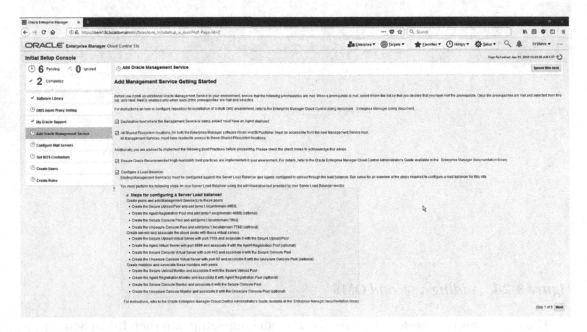

Figure 3-30. *Adding a second OMS*

Navigate to the Management Servers screen. This can be done from any page by using the Setup drop-down, as shown in Figure 3-31.

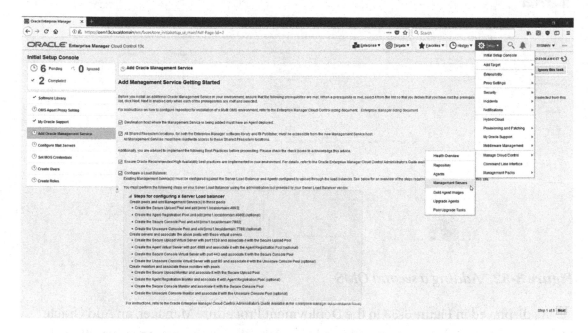

Figure 3-31. *Adding a second OMS*

Once at the Management Servers screen, you can add a second OMS by selecting Add Oracle Management Service, as shown in Figure 3-32.

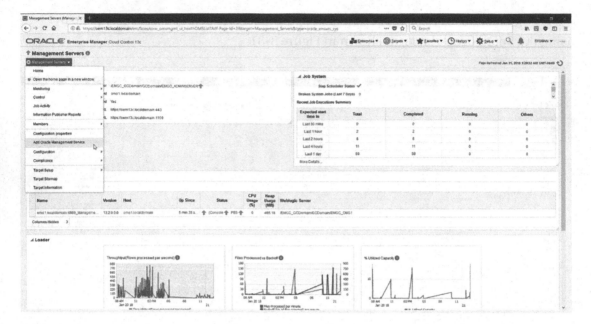

Figure 3-32. *Adding a second OMS*

As displayed in Figure 3-33 in the Deployment Procedure Manager, an Add Oracle Management Service procedure will need to be launched from the procedure library.

Figure 3-33. *Adding a second OMS*

As shown in Figure 3-34, the Getting Started page of the Add Oracle Management Service procedure will show all the prerequisites necessary for adding a second OMS. All of these prerequisites have been met by following the steps in this section. The administrator can simply go to this page by hitting the Next button on the right side of the page.

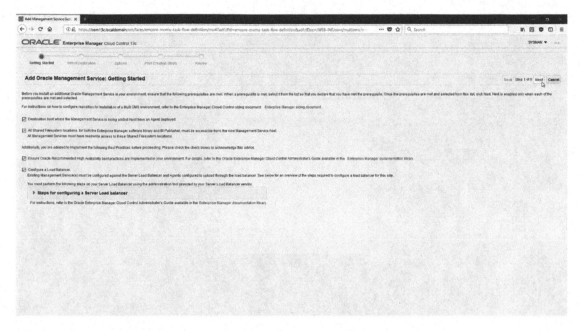

Figure 3-34. *Adding a second OMS*

The host on which the Oracle Management Service will be installed must be picked via the drop-down of available discovered host targets, as shown in Figure 3-35 and Figure 3-36. This is why it is important to first discover the host and install an OEM Agent prior to starting this install.

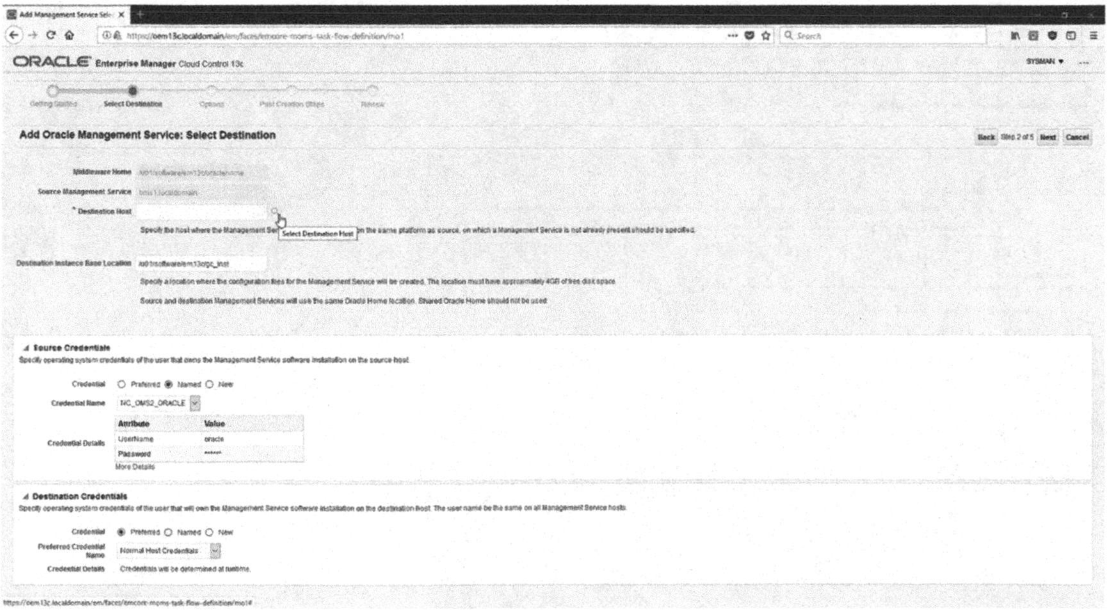

Figure 3-35. *Adding a second OMS*

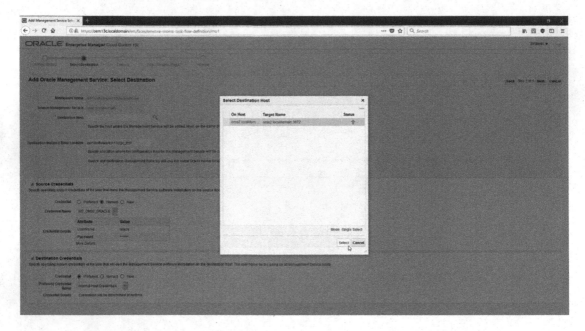

Figure 3-36. *Adding a second OMS*

If the credentials are not saved for the original OMS server, take the time to create a named credential and test it to avoid any issues during the installation process, as shown in Figure 3-37.

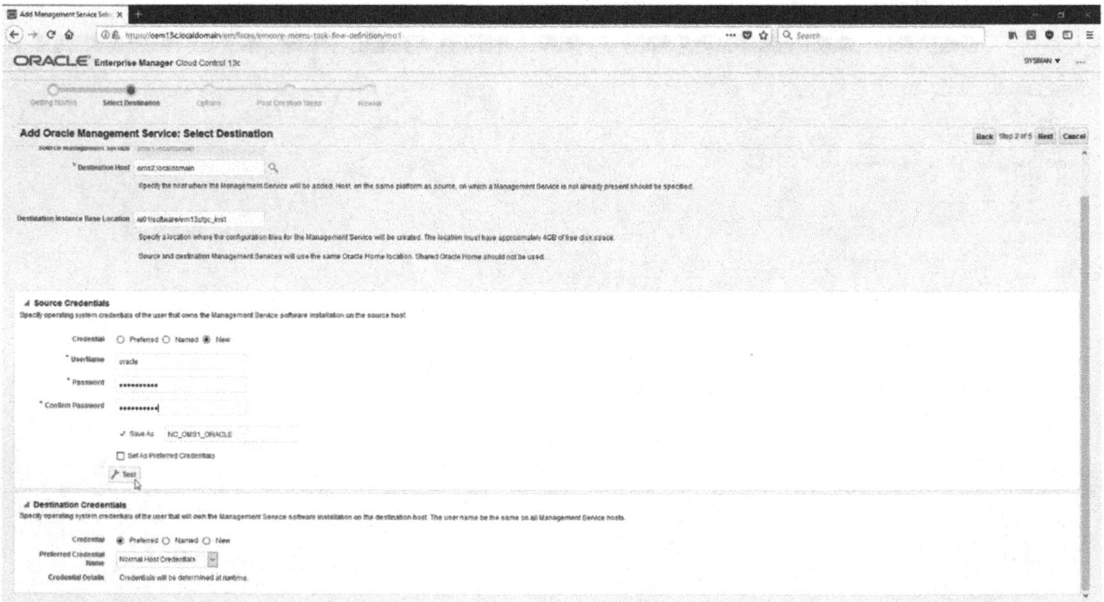

Figure 3-37. *Adding a second OMS*

It is prudent to test the credentials being stored, as shown in Figure 3-38. Testing the credentials ahead of time will help you to avoid any install-time issues with credentials.

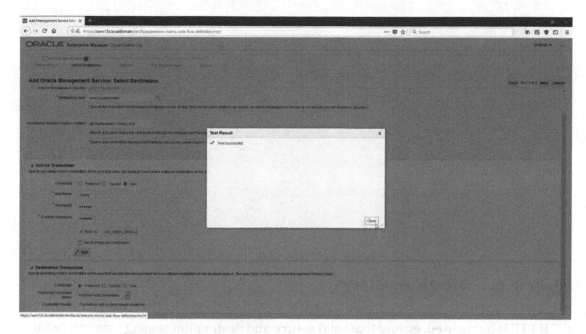

Figure 3-38. *Adding a second OMS*

Per Figure 3-39, ensure that stored credentials are also entered for the destination server, which is the target of the second Oracle Management Service installation. The stored credentials options for the destination is at the bottom of the Select Destination page, as shown in Figure 3-39.

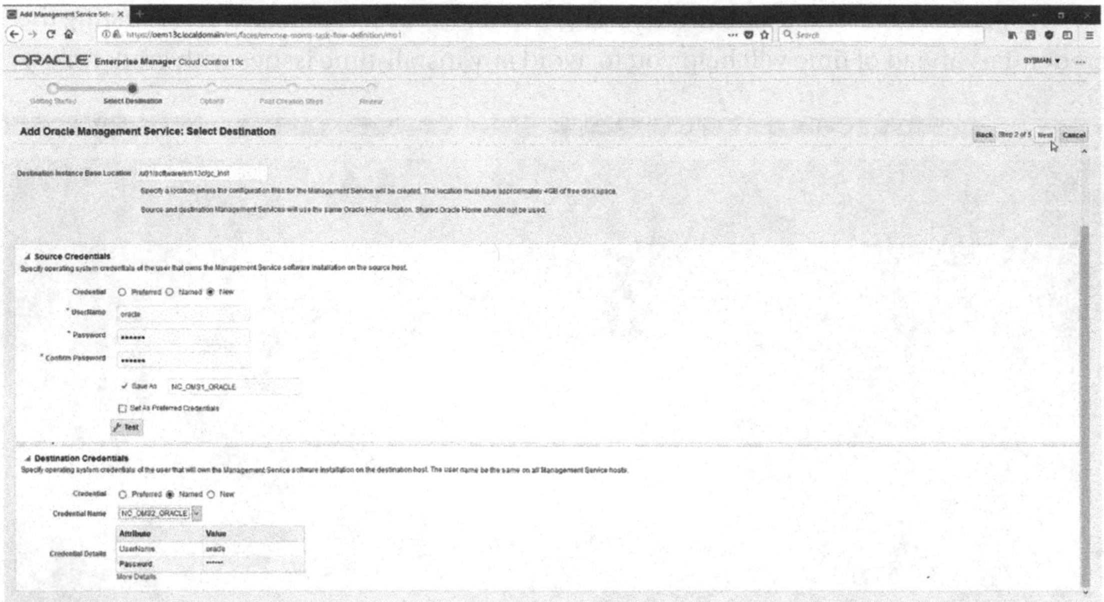

Figure 3-39. *Adding a second OMS*

If FTP is being used, ensure that valid source and destination staging locations with enough free space are specified. Regardless of the Transfer Mode setting, ensure that the ports used by OMS are not being used by other software on the host. Figure 3-40 shows how the Transfer Mode setting can be picked as well as the range of ports that the OMS will be configured with. You can check the ports by clicking the Check Ports button on the bottom left of the page, as shown in Figure 3-40.

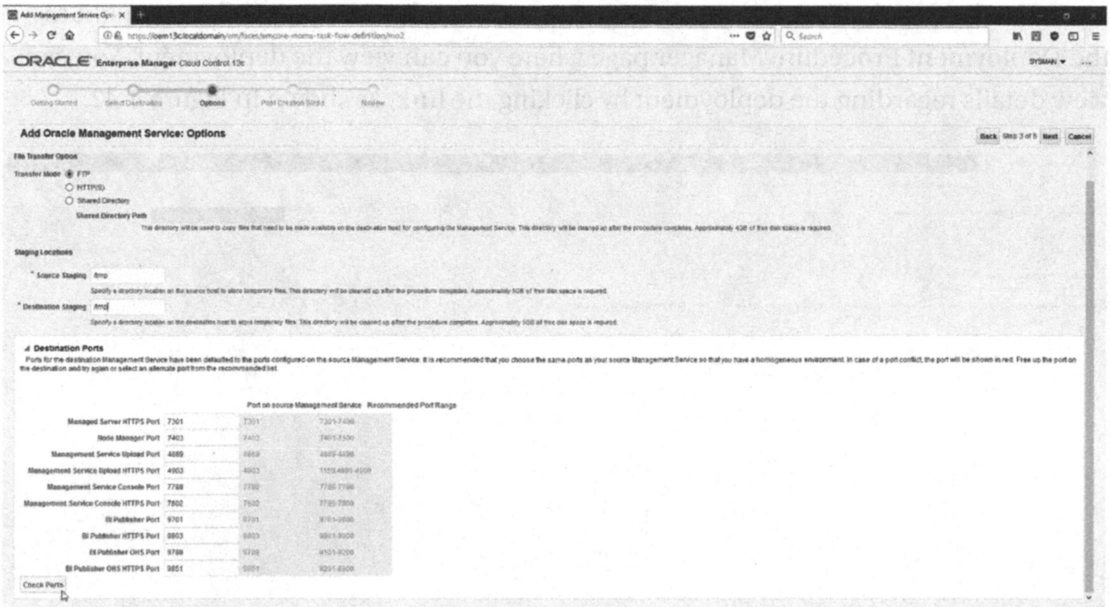

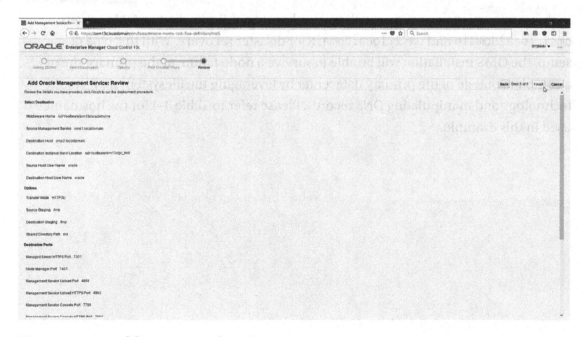

Figure 3-40. *Adding a second OMS*

As in most web-based installation wizards, the configuration can be reviewed, as shown in Figure 3-41. The installation can be started by clicking the Finish button on the top right of the page.

Figure 3-41. *Adding a second OMS*

After clicking the Finish button in Figure 3-41, the administrator will be brought to the Deployment Procedure Manager page where you can view the deployment. You can view details regarding the deployment by clicking the link, as shown in Figure 3-42.

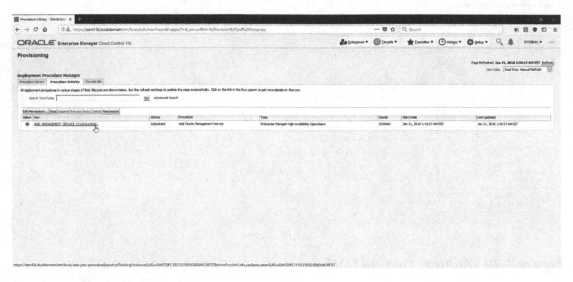

Figure 3-42. *Adding a second OMS*

Configuring the Application Servers for Disaster Recovery

In this section of the chapter, we will go over how to configure the two OMS servers `oms1.localdomain` and `oms2.localdomain` for disaster recovery. With this type of setup, the OMS installation will be able to survive a node failure at the primary site or a complete outage of the primary datacenter by leveraging the filesystem replication technology and manipulating DNS records. Please refer to Table 3-4 for the hostnames used in this example.

Table 3-4. OMS DNS Details

Hostname	IP	Function
oms1.localdomain	192.168.0.89	First OMS server (primary)
oms2.localdomain	192.168.0.92	Second OMS Server (primary)
oem13c.localdomain	192.168.0.93	SLB hostname for OMS (primary)
oms1-standby.localdomain	192.168.0.103	First OMS server (standby)
oms2-standby.localdomain	192.168.0.102	Second OMS Server (standby)
oem13c-standby.localdomain	192.168.0.104	SLB hostname for OMS (standby)

Some directories will need to be replicated from the primary OMS site to the standby OMS site. Please refer to Table 3-5 for the specifics on the directories and how they will be replicated.

Table 3-5. Filesystem Replication

Software Directory	Function	Replication Method
/u01/software/em13c/agentbasedir	Agent Base	rsync
/u01/software/em13c/gc_inst	OMS Instance	rsync
/u01/software/em13c/oraclehome	OMS Base	rsync
/u01/software/em13c/swlib	Software Library	NAS replication
/u01/app/oraInventory	Oracle Inventory	rsync

In this example, the primary and standby servers both use the same subnet mask for ease of configuration but are geographically separated in different datacenters.

The **oracle** user will need to be created on the oms1-standby server with the same UID and GID values to ensure that file ownership and permissions do not cause issues on the standby site.

```
[root@oms1-standby tmp]# useradd oracle
[root@oms1-standby tmp]# id oracle
uid=500(oracle) gid=500(oracle) groups=500(oracle)
[root@oms1-standby tmp]# groupadd oinstall
```

```
[root@oms1-standby tmp]# usermod -G oinstall oracle
[root@oms1-standby tmp]# id oracle
uid=500(oracle) gid=500(oracle) groups=500(oracle),501(oinstall)
```

The software location will need to be owned by the `oracle` user.

```
[root@oms1-standby tmp]# mkdir -p /u01/software/em13c
[root@oms1-standby tmp]# chown -R oracle:oinstall /u01/
```

An important step in the DR setup is to ensure that identical YUM packages are installed on the standby and primary sites. The currently installed packaged can be dumped to a text file with the following command. This will dump both the package name and the version number so that the two sites can operate under the same package versions.

```
[root@oms1 ~]# rpm -qa > /u01/software/em13c/rpm_list.txt
```

The majority of the software will be replicated to the standby OMS servers via the `rsync` utility. This will ensure that fast incremental file transfers are made and will reduce infrastructural cost and complexity by removing the need for using replicated network-attached storage for OMS software.

After this initial load, most incremental changes will consist of logfiles and plug-in deployments, which when compared to the overall OMS installation are small.

Note   The `swlib` directory is being excluded as it already exists on shared storage and will be replicated with the existing NAS infrastructure.

```
[oracle@oms1 ~]$ rsync --exclude 'swlib' --delete --progress -avzhe ssh /
u01/software/em13c/ oracle@oms1-standby:/u01/software/em13c
```

```
[oracle@oms1 ~]$ rsync --delete --progress -avzhe ssh /u01/app/
oraInventory/ oracle@oms1-standby:/u01/app/oraInventory
```

The `rpm_list.txt` file will be replicated to the standby site along with the software and can be used to install the necessary YUM packages.

```
[root@oms1-standby em13c]# yum -y install $(cat /u01/software/em13c/
rpm_list.txt)
```

The same steps must be followed for servers oms2.localdomain and oms2-standby. localdomain.

Once all servers are at the same software level, it is recommended that they all be updated and upgraded to ensure that security patches are installed. This can be done with the yum update/upgrade commands.

[root@oms1 ~]# yum update -y

[root@oms1 ~]# yum upgrade -y

[root@oms1 ~]# init 6

It is necessary that the domain name resolution is configured properly so that the standby hosts refer to themselves by their primary hostname equivalents. This will ensure that no configuration files need to be modified during a failover/switchover scenario and will shorten site recovery times.

This can be accomplished by modifying the /etc/hosts file on the standby OMS servers. On Red Hat distributions, the /etc/hosts contents take precedence over a configured name server. Thus, the standby hosts will always use the primary hostname equivalents.

[root@oms1-standby ~]# cat /etc/hosts
```
127.0.0.1    localhost localhost.localdomain localhost4 localhost4.localdomain4
::1          localhost localhost.localdomain localhost6 localhost6.localdomain6

#MAP IP of STANDBY OMS to hostname of PRIMARY OMS
192.168.0.102    oms2.localdomain oms2
192.168.0.103    oms1.localdomain oms1
```
[root@oms2-standby ~]# cat /etc/hosts
```
127.0.0.1    localhost localhost.localdomain localhost4 localhost4.localdomain4
::1          localhost localhost.localdomain localhost6 localhost6.localdomain6

#MAP IP of STANDBY OMS to hostname of PRIMARY OMS
192.168.0.102    oms2.localdomain oms2
192.168.0.103    oms1.localdomain oms1
```

This can be validated by pinging one packet to each hostname to ensure that the correct IP is resolved.

```
[root@oms1-standby em13c]# ping -c 1 oms1
PING oms1.localdomain (192.168.0.103) 56(84) bytes of data.
64 bytes from oms1.localdomain (192.168.0.103): icmp_seq=1 ttl=64 time=0.014 ms

--- oms1.localdomain ping statistics ---
1 packets transmitted, 1 received, 0% packet loss, time 0ms
rtt min/avg/max/mdev = 0.014/0.014/0.014/0.000 ms
```

```
[root@oms1-standby em13c]# ping -c 1 oms1-standby
PING oms1-standby.localdomain (192.168.0.103) 56(84) bytes of data.
64 bytes from oms1.localdomain (192.168.0.103): icmp_seq=1 ttl=64 time=0.017 ms

--- oms1-standby.localdomain ping statistics ---
1 packets transmitted, 1 received, 0% packet loss, time 0ms
rtt min/avg/max/mdev = 0.017/0.017/0.017/0.000 ms
```

```
[root@oms1-standby em13c]# ping -c 1 oms2
PING oms2.localdomain (192.168.0.102) 56(84) bytes of data.
64 bytes from oms2.localdomain (192.168.0.102): icmp_seq=1 ttl=64 time=2.72 ms

--- oms2.localdomain ping statistics ---
1 packets transmitted, 1 received, 0% packet loss, time 2ms
rtt min/avg/max/mdev = 2.725/2.725/2.725/0.000 ms
```

```
[root@oms1-standby em13c]# ping -c 1 oms2-standby
PING oms2-standby.localdomain (192.168.0.102) 56(84) bytes of data.
64 bytes from oms2.localdomain (192.168.0.102): icmp_seq=1 ttl=64 time=1.44 ms

--- oms2-standby.localdomain ping statistics ---
1 packets transmitted, 1 received, 0% packet loss, time 1ms
rtt min/avg/max/mdev = 1.444/1.444/1.444/0.000 ms
```

The shared storage for the BI publisher files and the software library will need to be configured on the standby OMS hosts as well.

```
[oracle@oms1-standby ~]$ mkdir -p /u01/oms_shared
[oracle@oms1-standby ~]$ mkdir -p /u01/software/em13c/swlib
```

```
[oracle@oms2-standby ~]$ mkdir -p /u01/oms_shared
[oracle@oms2-standby ~]$ mkdir -p /u01/software/em13c/swlib
```

/etc/fstab entries will need to be set up on the standby hosts to reference the standby NAS server and NFS exported filesystems.

```
[root@oms1-standby ~]# cat /etc/fstab |grep nas
nas-standby.localdomain:/data_pool/oms_shared_storage /u01/oms_
shared      nfs      defaults 0 0
nas-standby.localdomain:/data_pool/swlib /u01/software/em13c/swlib
nfs      defaults 0 0
```

```
[root@oms2-standby ~]#  cat /etc/fstab |grep nas
nas-standby.localdomain:/data_pool/oms_shared_storage /u01/oms_
shared      nfs      defaults 0 0
nas-standby.localdomain:/data_pool/swlib /u01/software/em13c/swlib
nfs      defaults 0 0
```

Once the /etc/fstab entries are set up, the NFS mounts can be mounted with the mount command.

```
[root@oms1-standby ~]# mount -a
```

```
[root@oms2-standby ~]# mount -a
```

Configuring Time Interval–Based Software Replication

Configuring NAS storage replication is out of scope for this chapter; however, an example of how to replicate the OMS software, agent software, and Oracle inventories will be shown.

This can configured via rsync and cron. This will require that the oracle user on oms1.localdomain has SSH equivalency configured for passwordless access to oms1-standby.localdomain. The reverse should also be configured in the case of a failover/switchover scenario.

```
[oracle@oms1 ~]$ crontab -l |grep rsync
*/5 * * * * rsync --exclude 'swlib' --delete -aze ssh /u01/software/em13c/
oracle@oms1-standby:/u01/software/em13c
```

```
*/5 * * * * rsync --delete -aze ssh /u01/app/oraInventory/ oracle@oms1-
standby:/u01/app/oraInventory

[oracle@oms2 ~]$ crontab -l |grep rsync
*/5 * * * * rsync --exclude 'swlib' --delete -aze ssh /u01/software/em13c/
oracle@oms2-standby:/u01/software/em13c
*/5 * * * * rsync --delete -aze ssh /u01/app/oraInventory/ oracle@oms2-
standby:/u01/app/oraInventory
```

Monitoring Standby OMS Hosts

It is a best practice to monitor all hosts in the Oracle environment as OEM managed
hosts. This requires that even the standby OMS servers have working OMS agents
for metric collection. These standby OMS agents will need to use a secondary Oracle
Inventory as configuring them to use the default Oracle Inventory location will cause
issues because of the filesystem replication setup.

The secondary inventory location is configured by creating a root-owned but world-
readable Oracle Inventory pointer in the /etc directory. This must be done on both
standby OMS hosts.

[root@oms1-standby etc]# cat /etc/oraInventory_standby.loc
```
inventory_loc=/u01/oraInventory_standby
inst_group=oinstall
```

[oracle@oms1-standby ~]$ mkdir -p /u01/app/oraInventory_standby

[oracle@oms2-standby ~]$ cat /etc/oraInventory_standby.loc
```
inventory_loc=/u01/app/oraInventory_standby
inst_group=oinstall
```

[oracle@oms2-standby ~]$ mkdir -p /u01/app/oraInventory_standby

After the secondary Oracle Inventory location has been configured, the standby OMS
agents can be installed via the Add Target Wizard, which can be accessed by clicking the
appropriate drop-down menu option, as shown in Figure 3-43, to add the target hosts
manually.

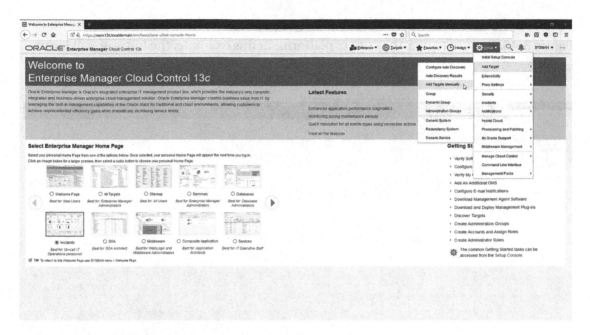

Figure 3-43. *OMS standby agent install*

Because the standby hosts need to be added as a target, choose the Install Agent on Host option, as shown in Figure 3-44.

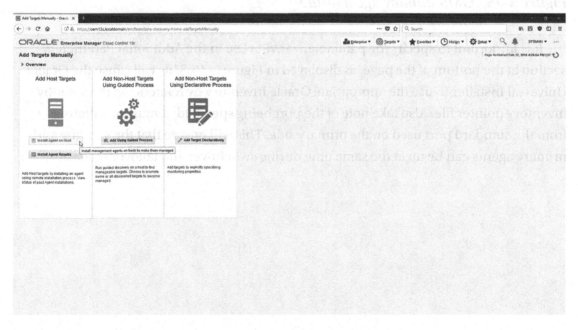

Figure 3-44. *OMS standby agent install*

Multiple hosts can be added at once by specifying all of the hostnames, as shown in Figure 3-45. Be sure to pick the correct platform; in this example, the hosts are all Linux x86-64.

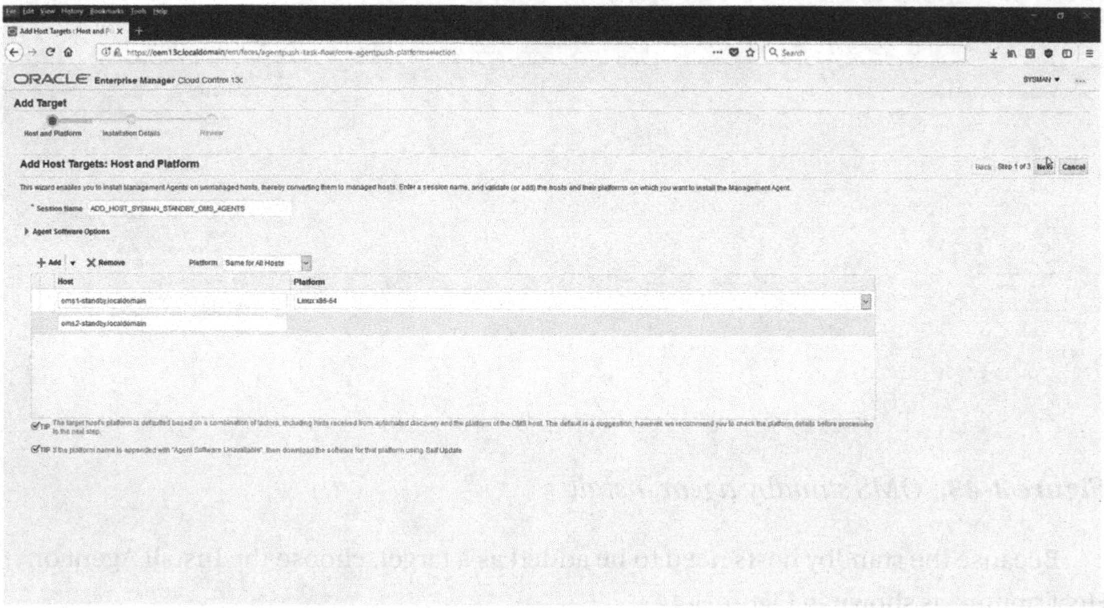

Figure 3-45. *OMS standby agent install*

It is important to specify the parameter `-invPtrLoc` in the Additional Parameters section at the bottom of the page, as displayed in Figure 3-46. This will cause the Oracle Universal Installer to use the appropriate Oracle Inventory by referencing the standby inventory pointer file. Also take note of the port being specified; it must be different from the standard port used on the primary side. This will ensure that the standby and primary agents can be up at the same time during switchover and failover scenarios.

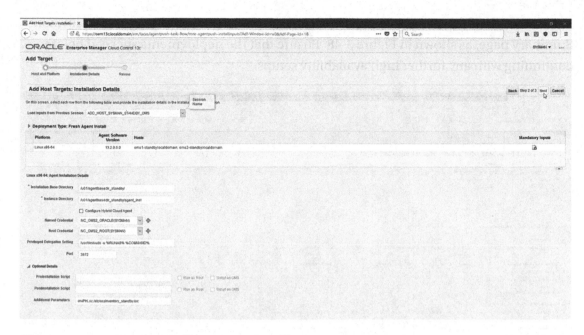

Figure 3-46. *OMS standby agent install*

Always double-check the installation options specified and pay close attention to the additional parameters, which are required for the standby OMS Agents, as shown in Figure 3-47.

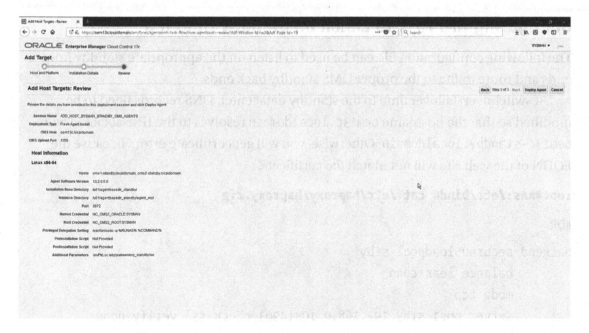

Figure 3-47. *OMS standby agent install*

The status of the standby agent installation can be viewed on the Agent Deployment Summary page, as shown in Figure 3-48. Ensure that the deployments succeed before continuing with any further high availability setups.

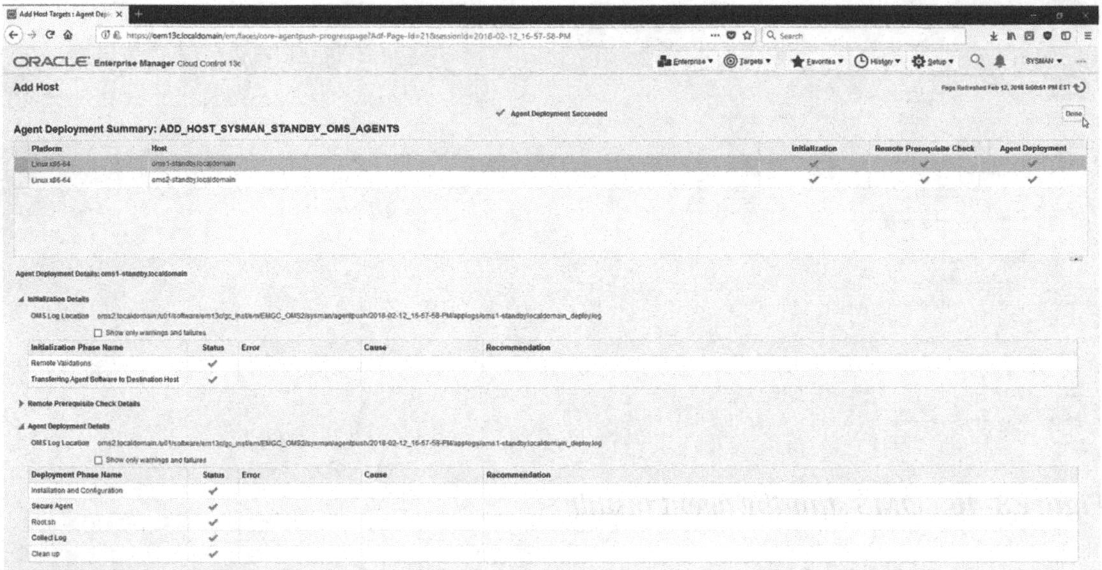

Figure 3-48. *OMS standby agent install*

Configuring HAProxy to Listen on Standby OMS IPs

The following configuration file can be used to listen on the appropriate standby front ends and route traffic to the proper OMS standby back ends.

At switchover/failover time to the standby datacenter, DNS records need to be modified so that the hostname oem13c.localdomain resolves to the IP associated with oem13c-standby.localdomain. Otherwise, you will get certificate errors because the FQDN of the web site will not match the certificate.

root@nas:/etc/bind# cat /etc/haproxy/haproxy.cfg

```
#DR
backend secureuploadpool_stby
        balance leastconn
        mode tcp
        server oms1_stby 192.168.0.103:4903 check ssl verify none
        server oms2_stby 192.168.0.102:4903 check ssl verify none
```

```
backend agentregistrationpool_stby
    balance leastconn
        mode tcp
        cookie SERVERID insert indirect nocache
        server oms1_stby 192.168.0.103:4889 check cookie
        server oms2_stby 192.168.0.102:4889 check cookie

backend secureconsolepool_stby
    balance leastconn
        mode tcp
    stick-table type ip size 1m
    stick on src
        server oms1_stby 192.168.0.103:7802 check ssl verify none
        server oms2_stby 192.168.0.102:7802 check ssl verify none

backend unsecureconsolepool_stby
    balance leastconn
    mode tcp
    stick-table type ip size 1m
    stick on src
    server oms1_stby 192.168.0.103:7788 check
    server oms1_stby 192.168.0.102:7788 check

frontend secureuploadvirtualserver_stby
  bind 192.168.0.104:1159 ssl crt /ha_proxy_certs/oem13c.localdomain.pem
  mode tcp
  default_backend secureuploadpool_stby

frontend agentvirtualserver_stby
  bind 192.168.0.104:4889
  mode tcp
  default_backend agentregistrationpool_stby

frontend secureconsolevirtualserver_stby
  bind 192.168.0.104:443 ssl crt /ha_proxy_certs/oem13c.localdomain.pem
  mode tcp
  default_backend secureconsolepool_stby
```

```
frontend unsecureuploadvirtualserver_stby
  bind 192.168.0.104:80
  mode tcp
  default_backend unsecureconsolepool_stby
```

OEM Always-On Monitoring

OEM always-on monitoring (AOM) ensures that downtime notifications are sent to the appropriate parties even while the OMS servers are down for patching or other major infrastructural work. AOM uses its own repository database, which must be manually synced with the OEM repository any time there are target additions or downtime notification changes.

Configuring AOM

It is recommended that the AOM repository be created in a separate database from the OEM repository if possible. In this chapter, the AOM database will be created as a pluggable database in the container ORCLCDB to show how AOM is configured.

```
[oracle@rac101 ~]$ sqlplus / as sysdba

SQL*Plus: Release 12.2.0.1.0 Production

Copyright (c) 1982, 2016, Oracle.  All rights reserved.


Connected to:
Oracle Database 12c Enterprise Edition Release 12.2.0.1.0 - 64bit
Production

SQL> select db_unique_name from v$database;

DB_UNIQUE_NAME
--------------------------------
orclcdb

SQL> CREATE PLUGGABLE DATABASE AOMPDB ADMIN USER PDBADMIN IDENTIFIED BY
"database_123" ROLES=(CONNECT)  file_name_convert=NONE  STORAGE ( MAXSIZE
UNLIMITED MAX_SHARED_TEMP_SIZE UNLIMITED);
```

Pluggable database created.

SQL> alter pluggable database AOMPDB open READ WRITE instances=all;

Pluggable database altered.

SQL> alter pluggable database AOMPDB save state instances=all;

Pluggable database altered.

SQL> alter session set container=AOMPDB;

Session altered.

SQL> show con_name

CON_NAME

AOMPDB

**SQL> CREATE SMALLFILE TABLESPACE USERS LOGGING DATAFILE   SIZE 5M
AUTOEXTEND ON NEXT   1280K MAXSIZE UNLIMITED   EXTENT MANAGEMENT
LOCAL   SEGMENT SPACE MANAGEMENT   AUTO;**

Tablespace created.

SQL> ALTER DATABASE DEFAULT TABLESPACE USERS;

Database altered.

The AOM database will need to be accessed via a user called EMS. The user will be granted the least amount of privileges possible to perform its function.

**[oracle@rac101 aom]$ sqlplus sys/database_123@//rac01-scan:1521/aompdb.
world as sysdba**

SQL*Plus: Release 12.2.0.1.0 Production

Copyright (c) 1982, 2016, Oracle.   All rights reserved.

Connected to:
Oracle Database 12c Enterprise Edition Release 12.2.0.1.0 - 64bit Production

SQL> create user ems identified by "database_123";

User created.

```
SQL> grant CREATE SESSION,
  2         ALTER SESSION,
  3         CREATE DATABASE LINK,
  4         CREATE MATERIALIZED VIEW,
  5         CREATE PROCEDURE,
  6         CREATE PUBLIC SYNONYM,
  7         CREATE ROLE,
  8         CREATE SEQUENCE,
  9         CREATE SYNONYM,
 10         CREATE TABLE,
 11         CREATE TRIGGER,
 12         CREATE TYPE,
 13         CREATE VIEW,
 14         UNLIMITED TABLESPACE,
 15         SELECT ANY DICTIONARY to ems;
```

Grant succeeded.

```
SQL> grant EXECUTE ON SYS.DBMS_CRYPTO to ems;
```

Grant succeeded.

```
SQL> grant EXECUTE ON SYS.DBMS_AQADM to ems;
```

Grant succeeded.

```
SQL> grant EXECUTE ON SYS.DBMS_AQ to ems;
```

Grant succeeded.

```
SQL> grant EXECUTE ON SYS.DBMS_AQIN to ems;
```

Grant succeeded.

```
SQL> grant EXECUTE on SYS.DBMS_LOCK to ems;
```

Grant succeeded.

```
SQL> grant EXECUTE ON SYS.DBMS_SCHEDULER to ems;
```

Grant succeeded.

SQL> grant create job to ems;

Grant succeeded.

SQL>

Once the user is created, the AOM installation can be set up. AOM ships with the base Oracle Enterprise Manager software.

```
[oracle@oms1 ems]$ pwd
/u01/software/em13c/oraclehome/sysman/ems
[oracle@oms1 ems]$ ll
total 89932
-rw-r----- 1 oracle oracle 92087822 Sep 30  2016 ems_13.2.0.0.0.zip
[oracle@oms1 ems]$

[oracle@oms1 ems]$ unzip -d /u01/aom ems_13.2.0.0.0.zip
```

AOM requires that Java 1.7 or newer is used and that the JAVA_HOME environment variable is exported. The JAVA_HOME value can be determined by following the symbolic links to the Java installation path.

[oracle@oms1 ~]$ /u01/aom/ems/scripts/emsca
```
Either JAVA_HOME environment variable is not set or an incorrect Java
version is used. To run emsca, use Java 1.7
```

[oracle@oms1 ~]$ which java
```
/usr/bin/java
```

[oracle@oms1 ~]$ java -version
```
java version "1.7.0_161"

OpenJDK Runtime Environment (rhel-2.6.12.0.0.1.el6_9-x86_64 u161-b00)
OpenJDK 64-Bit Server VM (build 24.161-b00, mixed mode)
```

[oracle@oms1 ~]$ ll /usr/bin/java
```
lrwxrwxrwx 1 root root 22 Feb 11 22:39 /usr/bin/java -> /etc/alternatives/
java
```

[oracle@oms1 ~]$ ll /etc/alternatives/java

```
lrwxrwxrwx 1 root root 46 Feb 11 22:39 /etc/alternatives/java -> /usr/lib/
jvm/jre-1.7.0-openjdk.x86_64/bin/java
```

[oracle@oms1 ~]$ ll /usr/lib/jvm/jre-1.7.0-openjdk.x86_64/bin/java

```
-rwxr-xr-x 1 root root 9928 Dec  6 09:02 /usr/lib/jvm/jre-1.7.0-openjdk.
x86_64/bin/java
```

Once the location has been found, it can be exported for the current shell and for all future shells by modifying the .bash_profile file.

```
[oracle@oms1 ~]$ export JAVA_HOME=/usr/lib/jvm/jre-1.7.0-openjdk.x86_64
```

[oracle@oms1 ~]$ echo "export JAVA_HOME=**/usr/lib/jvm/jre-1.7.0-openjdk.x86_64**" >> ~/.bash_profile

During setup, AOM requires that the Enterprise Manager key be stored in the repository database. This allows AOM to properly read the SMTP configurations and the downtime notification contacts from the OEM repository.

[oracle@oms1 ~]$ emctl config emkey -copy_to_repos
```
Oracle Enterprise Manager Cloud Control 13c Release 2
Copyright (c) 1996, 2016 Oracle Corporation.  All rights reserved.
Enter Enterprise Manager Root (SYSMAN) Password :
The EMKey has been copied to the Management Repository. This operation will
cause the EMKey to become unsecure.
After the required operation has been completed, secure the EMKey by
running "emctl config emkey -remove_from_repos".
```

AOM is configured by using the emsca utility.

[oracle@oms1 ~]$ /u01/aom/ems/scripts/emsca
```
Oracle Enterprise Manager Cloud Control 13c Release 2
Copyright (c) 2015, 2016, Oracle Corporation.  All rights reserved.
----------------------------------------------------------------
 Always-On Monitoring Repository Connection String : (DESCRIPTION=(ADDRESS_
LIST=(ADDRESS=(PROTOCOL=TCP)(HOST=rac01-scan.localdomain)(PORT=1521)))
(LOAD_BALANCE=ON)(CONNECT_DATA=(SERVICE_NAME=aompdb.world)))
 Always-On Monitoring Repository Username [ems] : ems
 Always-On Monitoring Repository Password [ems] :
```

Always-On Monitoring Repository user "ems" has already been created
 Enterprise Manager Repository Connection String : **(DESCRIPTION=(ADDRESS_
LIST=(ADDRESS=(PROTOCOL=TCP)(HOST=rac01-scan.localdomain)(PORT=1521)))
(LOAD_BALANCE=ON)(CONNECT_DATA=(SERVICE_NAME=oemrepo.world)))**
 Enterprise Manager Repository Username : **sysman**
 Enterprise Manager Repository Password :
 Agent Registration Password :
 Keystore for host oms1.localdomain created successfully.
 Connecting to Always-On Monitoring Repository.
 Creating Always-On Monitoring Repository schema
 Creating repository storage for Targets data.
 Creating repository storage for Alerts and Availability data.
 Creating repository storage for Notification Metadata data.
 Creating repository storage for Target Metric Metadata data.
 Registering Always-On Monitoring instance
 Always-On Monitoring Upload URL: https://oms1.localdomain:8081/upload

Once AOM has been successfully configured, remove the EM key from the repository. Leaving it there poses a security risk because it can be used to decrypt sensitive OEM information.

[oracle@oms1 ~]$ emctl config emkey -remove_from_repos
Oracle Enterprise Manager Cloud Control 13c Release 2
Copyright (c) 1996, 2016 Oracle Corporation. All rights reserved.
Enter Enterprise Manager Root (SYSMAN) Password :
The EMKey has been removed from the Management Repository.

To ease configuration, a global downtime contact can be configured. This contact will be the recipient of AOM downtime notifications.

**[oracle@oms1 ~]$ /home/oracle/emcli/emcli set_oms_property -property_
name='oracle.sysman.core.events.ems.downtimeContact' -property_value='john.
smith@example.com'**

Property "oracle.sysman.core.events.ems.downtimeContact" has been
successfully set to value "john.smith@example.com" on all Management Servers.
Server restart is not required for the property change to get reflected

Before AOM can be used, it must first sync up its data with the OEM repository. This is accomplished via the emsctl sync command.

```
[oracle@oms1 ~]$ /u01/aom/ems/scripts/emsctl sync
Oracle Enterprise Manager Cloud Control 13c Release 2
Copyright (c) 2015, 2016, Oracle Corporation.  All rights reserved.
-----------------------------------------------------------------
 Connecting to Always-On Monitoring Repository.
Starting synchronization with Enterprise Manager.
Synchronizing with Enterprise Manager repository: sysman@
(DESCRIPTION=(ADDRESS_LIST=(ADDRESS=(PROTOCOL=TCP)(HOST=rac01-scan.
localdomain)(PORT=1521)))(LOAD_BALANCE=ON)(CONNECT_DATA=(SERVICE_
NAME=oemrepo.world)))
Synchronizing Targets data.
Synchronizing Alerts and Availability data.
Synchronizing Notification Metadata data.
Synchronizing Target Metric Metadata data.
Synchronization complete at : Fri Feb 16 14:44:05 EST 2018
```

The OEM Agent needs to be configured to upload to the AOM installation; this step will need to be performed for each management agent. Additionally, firewall rules may need to be set up so that the agent can upload to the appropriate port on the AOM installation server.

```
[oracle@oms1 ~]$ emctl set property -name "oracle.sysman.core.events.ems.
emsURL" -value "https://oms1.localdomain:8081/upload"

Oracle Enterprise Manager Cloud Control 13c Release 2
Copyright (c) 1996, 2016 Oracle Corporation.  All rights reserved.
SYSMAN password:
Property oracle.sysman.core.events.ems.emsURL has been set to value
https://oms1.localdomain:8081/upload for all Management Servers
OMS restart is not required to reflect the new property value
```

Starting AOM

The AOM can be started with emsctl. However, the base release shipped with OEM 13.2 has a bug that needs to be patched prior to being able to start AOM.

```
[oracle@oms1 25132376]$ /u01/aom/ems/scripts/emsctl start
Oracle Enterprise Manager Cloud Control 13c Release 2
Copyright (c) 2015, 2016, Oracle Corporation.  All rights reserved.
-----------------------------------------------------------------
Starting Always-On Monitoring.
Waiting for process to start
Retrying...
Notifications Enabled                    : false
Total Downtime Contacts Configured       : 1
Always-On Monitoring is up.
```

Bug 25132376

> *EM 13c: Starting Always on Monitoring Fails with Message: Error starting*
> *EMS: Unable to start the HTTP Server: null (Doc ID 2266243.1)*

You will need to patch AOM so that it can start. The base release has a bug that does not allow you to start EMS. The patch consists of replacing a .jar file in the AOM install location. Although the bug references AIX operating systems, it is a generic Java archive file replacement that works for all architectures.

```
[oracle@oms1 ~]$ /u01/aom/ems/scripts/emsctl start
Oracle Enterprise Manager Cloud Control 13c Release 2
Copyright (c) 2015, 2016, Oracle Corporation.  All rights reserved.
-----------------------------------------------------------------
Starting Always-On Monitoring.
Waiting for process to start
Retrying...
Retrying...
Retrying...
Retrying...
Error starting EMS: Unable to start the HTTP Server: null
```

Enabling Notifications

By default, AOM will not send any notifications. If there is a planned OMS outage, AOM can be directed to start sending notifications via the emsctl enable_notification command. This will perform an implicit AOM repository sync with the OEM repository if it is available.

```
[oracle@oms1 ~]$ /u01/aom/ems/scripts/emsctl enable_notification
Oracle Enterprise Manager Cloud Control 13c Release 2
Copyright (c) 2015, 2016, Oracle Corporation.  All rights reserved.
---------------------------------------------------------------------
Notifications have been enabled.  There are downtime contacts configured.
 Connecting to Always-On Monitoring Repository.
Starting synchronization with Enterprise Manager.
Synchronizing with Enterprise Manager repository: sysman@
(DESCRIPTION=(ADDRESS_LIST=(ADDRESS=(PROTOCOL=TCP)(HOST=rac01-scan.
localdomain)(PORT=1521)))(LOAD_BALANCE=ON)(CONNECT_DATA=(SERVICE_
NAME=oemrepo.world)))
Synchronizing Targets data.
Synchronizing Alerts and Availability data.
Synchronizing Notification Metadata data.
Synchronizing Target Metric Metadata data.
```

Summary

With the configuration steps outlinesd in this chapter, you learned how to modify OEM Agent restart settings, configure Oracle Data Guard for the OEM repository database, install multiple OMS servers, configure software load balancers for host fault tolerance, set up standby OMS servers at geographically disparate locations, and configure downtime notifications even during planned OMS outages.

CHAPTER 4

GI and RAC Options

In this chapter, we will go over new and enhanced Grid Infrastructure concepts in Grid Infrastructure Oracle 12c R2 (12.2). Each feature covered in this chapter will be explained via technical examples and explanations. The purpose of this chapter is to showcase important features available in Oracle 12c R2 (12.2).

ASM Filter Driver

The ASM Filter Driver is a kernel module that is now installed by default during a Oracle 12c R2 (12.2) Grid Infrastructure setup (although you can opt out of installing the ASM Filter Driver by unchecking a box in the installation wizard during the install). The purposes of the ASM Filter Driver are to simplify ASM disk management and to be the last line of defense against accidental disk overwrites, for example by a system administrator accidentally pointing the dd command at a block device belonging to an ASM disk. The ASM Filter Driver is not compatible with ASMLIB and is meant to be a replacement for it. As such, ASMLIB must be deconfigured prior to configuring the ASM Filter Driver.

If the ASM Filter Driver was not in use prior to a 12.1.0.2 to 12.2.0.1 GI upgrade, the upgrade process, unlike the regular install process, will not assume that the ASM Filter Driver should be configured. If the graphical wizard is being used to upgrade GI, the option for configuring the ASM Filter Driver will not be shown.

You can check the state of the ASM Filter Driver by running the following command as the GI owner:

```
[oracle@stpldb101 ~]$ asmcmd afd_state
ASMCMD-9530: The AFD state is 'NOT INSTALLED'
```

© Y V Ravi Kumar, Nassyam Basha, Krishna Kumar K M, Bal Mukund Sharma, Konstantin Kerekovski 2019
Y V Ravi Kumar et al., *Oracle High Availability, Disaster Recovery, and Cloud Services*,
https://doi.org/10.1007/978-1-4842-4351-0_4

Configuring the ASM Filter Driver

The ASM Filter Driver can be configured either at the time of a 12.2.0.1 GI installation or manually. As stated in the introduction of the chapter, the ASM Filter Driver cannot co-exist with ASMLIB, so you must remove ASMLIB prior to configuring the ASM Filter Driver.

Figure 4-1 shows the screen with the option to configure the ASM Filter Driver during an install of the GI software.

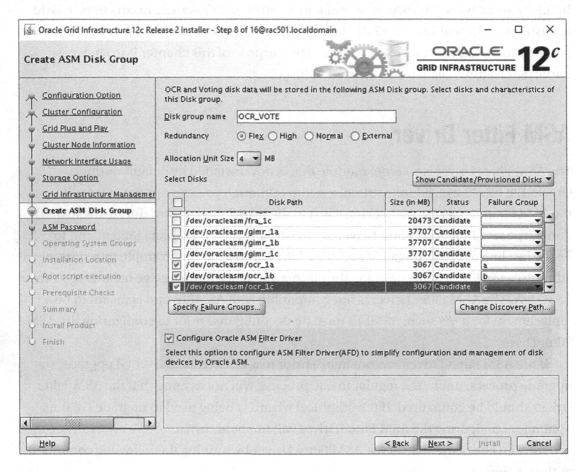

Figure 4-1.

Manual Configuration of the ASM Filter Driver

In the following hands-on example, you will see how to work on a two-node Oracle RAC cluster with the nodes stpldb101 and stpldb102 that do not have the ASM Filter Driver configured.

The ASM Filter Driver can be configured manually after a GI install or upgrade.

1. First, it is important to check the state of the ASM Filter Driver on all nodes.

```
[oracle@stpldb101 ~]$ asmcmd afd_state
ASMCMD-9530: The AFD state is 'NOT INSTALLED'

[oracle@stpldb102 ~]$ asmcmd afd_state
ASMCMD-9530: The AFD state is 'NOT INSTALLED'
```

2. Add the ASM Filter Driver (AFD) paths to the ASM disk string from any node.

The ASM_DISKSTRING parameter needs to be set so that ASM can find the disks labeled by the ASM Filter Driver as well as the previously used location. This is important because Oracle Clusterware should be able to fall back on the old paths for the disks in case there is an issue with AFD.

In this hands-on example, the two-node RAC is using static UDEV rules to uniquely identify ASM disks.

```
[oracle@stpldb101 ~]$ ll /dev/oracleasm/*
lrwxrwxrwx 1 root root 7 Jul  9 19:07 /dev/oracleasm/data_1a -> ../sdk1
lrwxrwxrwx 1 root root 7 Jul  9 19:07 /dev/oracleasm/data_1b -> ../sdl1
lrwxrwxrwx 1 root root 7 Jul  9 20:10 /dev/oracleasm/data_1c -> ../sdm1
lrwxrwxrwx 1 root root 7 Jul  9 19:07 /dev/oracleasm/fra_1a -> ../sdn1
lrwxrwxrwx 1 root root 7 Jul  9 20:10 /dev/oracleasm/fra_1b -> ../sdo1
lrwxrwxrwx 1 root root 7 Jul  9 20:10 /dev/oracleasm/fra_1c -> ../sdp1
lrwxrwxrwx 1 root root 7 Jul  9 19:07 /dev/oracleasm/gimr_1a -> ../sdb1
lrwxrwxrwx 1 root root 7 Jul  9 20:10 /dev/oracleasm/gimr_1b -> ../sde1
lrwxrwxrwx 1 root root 7 Jul  9 19:07 /dev/oracleasm/gimr_1c -> ../sdh1
lrwxrwxrwx 1 root root 7 Jul  9 20:10 /dev/oracleasm/gimr_2a -> ../sdc1
lrwxrwxrwx 1 root root 7 Jul  9 20:10 /dev/oracleasm/gimr_2b -> ../sdf1
lrwxrwxrwx 1 root root 7 Jul  9 19:07 /dev/oracleasm/gimr_2c -> ../sdi1
```

```
lrwxrwxrwx 1 root root 7 Jul  9 20:10 /dev/oracleasm/gimr_3a -> ../sdd1
lrwxrwxrwx 1 root root 7 Jul  9 20:10 /dev/oracleasm/gimr_3b -> ../sdg1
lrwxrwxrwx 1 root root 7 Jul  9 19:07 /dev/oracleasm/gimr_3c -> ../sdj1
lrwxrwxrwx 1 root root 7 Jul  9 20:10 /dev/oracleasm/ocr_1a -> ../sdq1
lrwxrwxrwx 1 root root 7 Jul  9 20:10 /dev/oracleasm/ocr_1b -> ../sdr1
lrwxrwxrwx 1 root root 7 Jul  9 20:10 /dev/oracleasm/ocr_1c -> ../sds1

[oracle@stpldb101 ~]$ asmcmd dsget
parameter:/dev/oracleasm/*
profile:/dev/oracleasm/*

[oracle@stpldb101 ~]$ asmcmd dsset '/dev/oracleasm/*,AFD:*'

[oracle@stpldb101 ~]$ asmcmd dsget
parameter:/dev/oracleasm/*, AFD:*
profile:/dev/oracleasm/*,AFD:*
```

3. As the root user, Clusterware needs to be stopped on all nodes.

```
[root@stpldb101 ~]# crsctl stop crs -f
[root@stpldb102 ~]# crsctl stop crs -f
```

4. Configure the ASM Filter Driver as the root on all nodes.

```
[root@stpldb101 ~]# asmcmd afd_configure
AFD-636: Installing requested AFD software.
AFD-637: Loading installed AFD drivers.
AFD-9321: Creating udev for AFD.
AFD-9323: Creating module dependencies - this may take some time.
AFD-9154: Loading 'oracleafd.ko' driver.
AFD-649: Verifying AFD devices.
AFD-9156: Detecting control device '/dev/oracleafd/admin'.
AFD-638: AFD installation correctness verified.
Modifying resource dependencies - this may take some time.

[root@stpldb102 ~]# asmcmd afd_state
ASMCMD-9526: The AFD state is 'LOADED' and filtering is 'ENABLED' on host
'stpldb102.localdomain'

[root@stpldb102 ~]# asmcmd afd_configure
AFD-636: Installing requested AFD software.
```

AFD-637: Loading installed AFD drivers.

AFD-9321: Creating udev for AFD.

AFD-9323: Creating module dependencies - this may take some time.

AFD-9154: Loading 'oracleafd.ko' driver.

AFD-649: Verifying AFD devices.

AFD-9156: Detecting control device '/dev/oracleafd/admin'.

AFD-638: AFD installation correctness verified.

Modifying resource dependencies - this may take some time.

```
[root@stpldb101 ~]# asmcmd afd_state
ASMCMD-9526: The AFD state is 'LOADED' and filtering is 'ENABLED' on host
'stpldb101.localdomain'
```

5. Label all the disks with the ASM Filter Driver labels on all nodes.

The following is an example of the commands that would be
required to label all the disks on this example two-node RAC. The
--migrate command-line option is required because the disks are
currently part of an ASM disk group.

```
asmcmd afd_label data_1a /dev/oracleasm/data_1a --migrate
asmcmd afd_label data_1b /dev/oracleasm/data_1b --migrate
asmcmd afd_label data_1c /dev/oracleasm/data_1c --migrate
asmcmd afd_label fra_1a /dev/oracleasm/fra_1a --migrate
asmcmd afd_label fra_1b /dev/oracleasm/fra_1b --migrate
asmcmd afd_label fra_1c /dev/oracleasm/fra_1c --migrate
asmcmd afd_label gimr_1a /dev/oracleasm/gimr_1a --migrate
asmcmd afd_label gimr_1b /dev/oracleasm/gimr_1b --migrate
asmcmd afd_label gimr_1c /dev/oracleasm/gimr_1c --migrate
asmcmd afd_label gimr_2a /dev/oracleasm/gimr_2a --migrate
asmcmd afd_label gimr_2b /dev/oracleasm/gimr_2b --migrate
asmcmd afd_label gimr_2c /dev/oracleasm/gimr_2c --migrate
asmcmd afd_label gimr_3a /dev/oracleasm/gimr_3a --migrate
asmcmd afd_label gimr_3b /dev/oracleasm/gimr_3b --migrate
asmcmd afd_label gimr_3c /dev/oracleasm/gimr_3c --migrate
asmcmd afd_label ocr_1a /dev/oracleasm/ocr_1a --migrate
asmcmd afd_label ocr_1b /dev/oracleasm/ocr_1b --migrate
asmcmd afd_label ocr_1c /dev/oracleasm/ocr_1c --migrate
```

6. Start Clusterware on all nodes.

The -wait flag used in this example is handy for debugging issues with Clusterware startup. It will display output regarding each cluster-managed service as it starts up and will return the prompt only once Clusterware has started or failed to start as a whole.

```
[root@stpldb101 ~]# crsctl start crs -wait
[root@stpldb102 ~]# crsctl start crs -wait
```

7. Once Clusterware has started on all nodes, check the header status of the disks.

Notice that the non-AFD disks are ignored by ASM. In the presence of the ASM Filter Driver, the ASM instance will ignore non-AFD disks.

```
SQL> select path, header_status, mount_status from v$asm_disk where header_
status = 'MEMBER';
```

PATH	HEADER_STATU	MOUNT_S
/dev/oracleasm/gimr_3a	MEMBER	IGNORED
/dev/oracleasm/data_1a	MEMBER	IGNORED
/dev/oracleasm/gimr_3c	MEMBER	IGNORED
/dev/oracleasm/data_1b	MEMBER	IGNORED
/dev/oracleasm/gimr_2b	MEMBER	IGNORED
/dev/oracleasm/fra_1a	MEMBER	IGNORED
/dev/oracleasm/gimr_1b	MEMBER	IGNORED
/dev/oracleasm/gimr_1c	MEMBER	IGNORED
/dev/oracleasm/gimr_2a	MEMBER	IGNORED
/dev/oracleasm/data_1c	MEMBER	IGNORED
/dev/oracleasm/gimr_3b	MEMBER	IGNORED
/dev/oracleasm/gimr_2c	MEMBER	IGNORED
/dev/oracleasm/fra_1b	MEMBER	IGNORED
/dev/oracleasm/gimr_1a	MEMBER	IGNORED
/dev/oracleasm/fra_1c	MEMBER	IGNORED
AFD:DATA_1A	MEMBER	CACHED
AFD:DATA_1B	MEMBER	CACHED

```
AFD:DATA_1C                    MEMBER        CACHED
AFD:FRA_1A                     MEMBER        CACHED
AFD:FRA_1B                     MEMBER        CACHED
AFD:FRA_1C                     MEMBER        CACHED
AFD:GIMR_1A                    MEMBER        CACHED
AFD:GIMR_1B                    MEMBER        CACHED
AFD:GIMR_1C                    MEMBER        CACHED
AFD:GIMR_2A                    MEMBER        CACHED
AFD:GIMR_2B                    MEMBER        CACHED
AFD:GIMR_2C                    MEMBER        CACHED
AFD:GIMR_3A                    MEMBER        CACHED
AFD:GIMR_3B                    MEMBER        CACHED
AFD:GIMR_3C                    MEMBER        CACHED
```

8. Reset the `ASM_DISKSTRING` parameter.

Once it has been established that ASM is using the ASM Filter Driver to access the disks, you can modify the `ASM_DISKSTRING` parameter using `asmcmd` to only look at ASM Filter Driver disks.

```
[oracle@stpldb101 ~]$ asmcmd dsset 'AFD:*'
[oracle@stpldb101 ~]$ sqlplus / as sysdba

SQL> select path from v$asm_disk;

PATH
---------------
AFD:OCR_1C
AFD:OCR_1A
AFD:OCR_1B
AFD:DATA_1A
AFD:DATA_1B
AFD:DATA_1C
AFD:FRA_1A
AFD:FRA_1B
AFD:FRA_1C
AFD:GIMR_1A
```

```
AFD:GIMR_1B
AFD:GIMR_1C
AFD:GIMR_2A
AFD:GIMR_2B
AFD:GIMR_2C
AFD:GIMR_3A
AFD:GIMR_3B
AFD:GIMR_3C

18 rows selected.
```

ACFS Snapshot Replication

Starting with 12.2, the method used to replicate ACFS has changed dramatically. The new method of replication is snapshot based, and data is transmitted over the Secure Shell (SSH) protocol. This new methodology gives the ASM administrator more granular control over replication.

This example will show how to create an ACFS filesystem, configure snapshot-based replication over SSH, and monitor replication. Replication will be configured between two separate two-node RACs. The source filesystem will be in a cluster named dscrac01 with the nodes dscrac101 and dscrac102. The destination filesystem will be in a cluster named stpldb01 with the nodes stpldb101 and stpldb102.

ACFS Creation on the Source Cluster

First, a volume needs to be created. ACFS filesystems are created on ASM dynamic volumes.

1.   Create a volume on cluster dscrac01.

This can be done via SQLPlus through any +ASM instance.

```
SQL> ALTER DISKGROUP GIMR ADD VOLUME replvol SIZE 5242880K UNPROTECTED
STRIPE_WIDTH 1M STRIPE_COLUMNS 8;
```

2.   Enable the volume.

```
[oracle@dscrac101 oracle]$ asmcmd volenable -G GIMR REPLVOL
[oracle@dscrac101 oracle]$ asmcmd volinfo -G GIMR REPLVOL

Diskgroup Name: GIMR
        Volume Name: REPLVOL
        Volume Device: /dev/asm/replvol-439
        State: ENABLED
        Size (MB): 5120
        Resize Unit (MB): 512
        Redundancy: UNPROT
        Stripe Columns: 8
        Stripe Width (K): 1024
        Usage:
        Mountpath:
```

3.   Create an ACFS filesystem directly on the volume. This can be done as the GI owner.

```
[oracle@dscrac101 oracle]$ /sbin/mkfs -t acfs /dev/asm/replvol-439
mkfs.acfs: version              = 12.2.0.1.0
mkfs.acfs: on-disk version      = 46.0
mkfs.acfs: volume               = /dev/asm/replvol-439
mkfs.acfs: volume size          = 5368709120  (   5.00 GB )
mkfs.acfs: Format complete.
```

4.   Create the mountpoint location on all nodes of the dscrac01 cluster.

```
[oracle@dscrac101 oracle]$ ssh dscrac102 mkdir /u01/app/oracle/acfs_repl_
example/
[oracle@dscrac101 oracle]$ mkdir -p /u01/app/oracle/acfs_repl_example/
```

5. As root, the filesystem needs to be added to Clusterware and "chowned" for the appropriate user.

```
[root@dscrac101 ~]# /u01/app/12.2.0/grid/bin/srvctl add filesystem -d /
dev/asm/replvol-439 -m /u01/app/oracle/acfs_repl_example -fstype ACFS
-autostart ALWAYS

[root@dscrac101 ~]# /u01/app/12.2.0/grid/bin/srvctl start filesystem -d /
dev/asm/replvol-439

[root@dscrac101 ~]# chown oracle:oinstall /u01/app/oracle/acfs_repl_example
[root@dscrac101 ~]# chmod 775 /u01/app/oracle/acfs_repl_example
```

6. The status of the filesystem can be confirmed using crsctl.

```
[oracle@dscrac101 oracle]$ crsctl stat res -t -w "NAME = ora.gimr.replvol.
acfs"
--------------------------------------------------------------------------
Name            Target  State          Server               State details
--------------------------------------------------------------------------
Local Resources
--------------------------------------------------------------------------
ora.gimr.replvol.acfs

ONLINE  ONLINE           dscrac101              mounted on /u01/app/
oracle/acfs_repl_example,STABLE

ONLINE  ONLINE           dscrac102              mounted on /u01/app/
oracle/acfs_repl_example,STABLE
```

ACFS Creation on the Standby

An empty filesystem will need to be created on the standby for replication.

1. First, create a volume on cluster stpldb01.

```
SQL>  ALTER DISKGROUP DATA ADD VOLUME replvol SIZE 5242880K;
Diskgroup altered.
```

2.   Enable the volume.

```
[oracle@stpldb101 ~]$ asmcmd volinfo -G data replvol
Diskgroup Name: DATA

        Volume Name: REPLVOL
        Volume Device: /dev/asm/replvol-122
        State: ENABLED
        Size (MB): 5120
        Resize Unit (MB): 512
        Redundancy: HIGH
        Stripe Columns: 8
        Stripe Width (K): 1024
        Usage:
        Mountpath:
```

If the volume is not enabled, it can be enabled with the following command:

```
[oracle@stpldb101 ~]$ asmcmd volenable -G data replvol
```

3.   Create an empty ACFS filesystem as the GI home owner.

```
[oracle@stpldb101 ~]$ /sbin/mkfs -t acfs /dev/asm/replvol-122
mkfs.acfs: version                = 12.2.0.1.0
mkfs.acfs: on-disk version        = 39.0
mkfs.acfs: volume                 = /dev/asm/replvol-122
mkfs.acfs: volume size            = 5368709120 (   5.00 GB )
mkfs.acfs: Format complete.
```

4.   Create the mountpoint directory on each node.

```
[oracle@stpldb101 ~]$ mkdir -p /u01/app/oracle/acfs_repl_example/
[oracle@stpldb101 ~]$ ssh stpldb102 "mkdir -p /u01/app/oracle/acfs_repl_
example/"
```

5.   Add the filesystem as a Clusterware resource.

```
[root@stpldb101 ~]# srvctl add filesystem -d /dev/asm/replvol-122 -m /u01/
app/oracle/acfs_repl_example -fstype ACFS -autostart ALWAYS
```

```
[root@stpldb101 ~]# srvctl start filesystem -d /dev/asm/replvol-122
[root@stpldb101 ~]# chown oracle:oinstall /u01/app/oracle/acfs_repl_example
[root@stpldb101 ~]# chmod 775 /u01/app/oracle/acfs_repl_example
```

6. Ensure that the Clusterware resource shows the proper output.

```
[root@stpldb101 ~]# crsctl stat res -t -w "NAME = ora.data.replvol.acfs"
--------------------------------------------------------------------------
Name             Target  State         Server                State details
--------------------------------------------------------------------------
Local Resources
--------------------------------------------------------------------------
ora.data.replvol.acfs
ONLINE  ONLINE         stpldb101                   mounted on /u01/app/
oracle/acfs_repl_example,STABLE

ONLINE  ONLINE         stpldb102                   mounted on /u01/app/
oracle/acfs_repl_example,STABLE
--------------------------------------------------------------------------
```

Public Keys

Because ACFS snapshot-based replication uses SSH for communications between the
primary and standby clusters, it is necessary to set up SSH public keys. The root user on
all nodes of the primary cluster (dscrac01) must be able to connect to the oracle user
on the standby cluster (stpldb01).

1. First, public keys will need to be generated for the root user on
    each primary node.

```
[root@dscrac101 .ssh]# ssh-keygen -t rsa
Generating public/private rsa key pair.
Enter file in which to save the key (/root/.ssh/id_rsa):
Enter passphrase (empty for no passphrase):
Enter same passphrase again:
Your identification has been saved in /root/.ssh/id_rsa.
Your public key has been saved in /root/.ssh/id_rsa.pub.
The key fingerprint is:
```

d5:18:98:48:00:a6:d1:89:7b:e5:35:10:23:7a:07:07 root@dscrac101.localdomain
The key's randomart image is:

```
+--[ RSA 2048]----+
|.oE+*=.. o.      |
|.=o+..+ o  +     |
|o..o.. .  o .    |
|.....    .       |
| .    S          |
|                 |
|                 |
|                 |
|                 |
+-----------------+
```

```
[root@dscrac101 .ssh]# cat id_rsa.pub
ssh-rsa
AAAAB3NzaC1yc2EAAAABIwAAAQEAvfCXoj2r5USaoEqYoFXKVL2UsLSdmDiBFYezEZ+jsSfO
dXHxd6DPMFbb5M9BaoGEaEzQmswb4idbLFT4je6ivbKbdr9kBEPRRIflevZvgvZ1+AyuDnF67
FgpV+WNOQELvUMag7PpGQukioSYY6n1OO2BLIqbVq6RrFyHegghMJ6nCaUFJT6J7zEpjWZfC
rLhVjTX4X2b8qWGUtFRZDM8LCiuzJpXWloXx+vN356GNgdSmM2M2CxveILvhBVhXxX4ForAwFAP
ZZjQ95QV3dZk4mcO46PYELgDf+WeoqMSo7TbNqC1hjk4BA4aGECovdN6OI8m8WnTvfMQ9HShnS
70rw== root@dscrac101.localdomain
```

[root@dscrac102 ~]# ssh-keygen -t rsa
Generating public/private rsa key pair.
Enter file in which to save the key (/root/.ssh/id_rsa):
Enter passphrase (empty for no passphrase):
Enter same passphrase again:
Your identification has been saved in /root/.ssh/id_rsa.
Your public key has been saved in /root/.ssh/id_rsa.pub.
The key fingerprint is:
09:8e:19:ed:59:63:72:b2:92:3f:e6:4a:03:56:a1:55 root@dscrac102.localdomain
The key's randomart image is:

```
+--[ RSA 2048]----+
|   o.E           |
|  o o            |
| . o - -         |
```

```
|   . B X o         |
|   o = = S         |
|   . . o           |
|     o +           |
|   . + .           |
|     ...           |
+-----------------+
```

[root@dscrac102 ~]# cat .ssh/id_rsa.pub
ssh-rsa AAAAB3NzaC1yc2EAAAABIwAAAQEAnXL6vSGOONHtzIr4j1nmRSZt31jOF9UIW6YIX
6KgtJkobORnTa1tAmM2pQ3GvB/BNgLPzHDbJqJCT6J8h3TsJiztkStnHHpbI4tAadl/3Rcf6rVO
XMqVEW/CN6Qc17gjR5wuqX5a2CxoV3jBDhssQvkAQ3PTw3o+ebrxsnNqLz44mJqpqnS59u8fNMV
2zLw9cHHLosq20YcOVdoMtpkhm+/DeLsoZO50xsANV+GV3kWQOFSbZNLWk42ZRqza5o1egpVB2e
/dlt1C9+/rKwiv7lWkY9t4ECELOlmDYXx7bzqru56OJUwJeqUlLv2YGSLbk7llx1/6sgJWOqhFR
G5P2Q== root@dscrac102.localdomain

> 2. The oracle user on each standby node will need to have the
>   public keys for the root user.

[oracle@stpldb101 ~]$ cat ~/.ssh/authorized_keys
ssh-rsa AAAAB3NzaC1yc2EAAAABIwAAAQEAsGHOV8SriFJH3KievgB74sad9dS7RVWs3+3HzqA
ISYD1eMk/lLpDyjy4tPEN6xfk/EGjg+ObKFQIh/4kn22GFQO38ilKbd5r+Bh+hsjd+S7edQ7XFZ
SKf7KENU5Nk9fcJIhXjOt+Z2B68SbCYlaleR2pLfEJTwO7pknSOdIf/R7Pb3LRIBg7OIv98VW+
E6uA6LeDoKcHwbY6NITYELUF3GNKHfRNewvJQQj9sPurj7d+LUYDt49h3af/SxbigYOgAWQ+WU/
U7C90VVJNDCMXF+7XCggHacB+SU+ff9FX2aoQ851T7vNEpMmrxtv7wdGyUZxE/VMjouSDf+P/
SK/PCQ== oracle@stpldb101.localdomain
ssh-rsa AAAAB3NzaC1yc2EAAAABIwAAAQEAyVnMtg5wFIe6KaKqTvTer/W+/p6GJrO/JwNCUn
xmWRZmMms8pqD4Eklyz7yiLf7TbKRv91jUQWNM254Hc941N4jOMWaLHBeDBrUN+sapToMH6DZ79
dAHskOLY87pztPQNLEWKQ7GolHbk//9qzrYZLNsKfgRNt3KqdE2DWhM5IRsh6MP35m+rVkB4Wy
VyOnOTMN63+xA/aHqYZrvyLGOFCs/rqoSGgBzzHL9z4K+ZfmYFB6kPdWmHmEOGhfAMg1MRZi8o+
bTCorXrsE1Pb/sjul5Y12ofwRIGFwpshO3ioJqgGJUGPywpYk+Q9qC2MCSP6URXfydYajep9p+
/6Hvpw== oracle@stpldb102.localdomain
ssh-rsa AAAAB3NzaC1yc2EAAAABIwAAAQEAvfCXoj2r5USaoEqYoFXKVL2UsLSdmDiBFYezEZ+
jsSfOdXHxd6DPMFbb5M9BaOGEaEzQmswb4idbLFT4je6ivbKbdr9kBEPRRIflevZvgvZ1+AyuDn
F67FgpV+WNOQELvUMag7PpGQukioSYY6n1OO2BLIqbVq6RrFyHegghMJ6nCaUFJT6J7zEpjWZfC
rLhVjTX4X2b8qWGUtFRZDM8LCiuzJpXWloXx+vN356GNgdSmM2M2CxveILvhBVhXxX4ForAwFAP

ZZjQ95QV3dZk4mcO46PYELgDf+WeoqMSo7TbNqC1hjk4BA4aGECovdN6OI8m8WnTvfMQ9HShnS7
Orw== root@dscrac101.localdomain
ssh-rsa AAAAB3NzaC1yc2EAAAABIwAAAQEAnXL6vSGOONHtzIr4j1nmRSZt31jOF9UIW6YIX
6KgtJkobORnTa1tAmM2pQ3GvB/BNgLPzHDbJqJCT6J8h3TsJiztkStnHHpbI4tAadl/3Rcf6rVO
XMqVEW/CN6Qc17gjR5wuqX5a2CxoV3jBDhssQvkAQ3PTw3o+ebrxsnNqLz44mJqpqnS59u8fNMV
2zLw9cHHLosq2oYcOVdoMtpkhm+/DeLsoZO5OxsANV+GV3kWQOFSbZNLWk42ZRqza5o1egpVB2e
/dlt1C9+/rKwiv7lWkY9t4ECELOlmDYXx7bzqru56OJUwJeqUlLv2YGSLbk7llx1/6sgJWOqhFR
G5P2Q== root@dscrac102.localdomain

3.   Validate the SSH connectivity from the primary to the standby.

[root@dscrac101 ~]# /sbin/acfsutil repl info -c -v -u oracle stpldb101.
localdomain /u01/app/oracle/acfs_repl_example/
A valid 'ssh' connection was detected for standby node stpldb101.
localdomain as user oracle.

[root@dscrac101 ~]# /sbin/acfsutil repl info -c -v -u oracle stpldb102.
localdomain /u01/app/oracle/acfs_repl_example/
A valid 'ssh' connection was detected for standby node stpldb102.
localdomain as user oracle.

[root@dscrac102 ~]# /sbin/acfsutil repl info -c -v -u oracle stpldb101.
localdomain /u01/app/oracle/acfs_repl_example/
A valid 'ssh' connection was detected for standby node stpldb101.
localdomain as user oracle.

[root@dscrac102 ~]# /sbin/acfsutil repl info -c -v -u oracle stpldb102.
localdomain /u01/app/oracle/acfs_repl_example/
A valid 'ssh' connection was detected for standby node stpldb102.
localdomain as user oracle.

Initiating Replication on the Standby

ACFS replication must be initiated on the standby node as the root user. Note that the
ADVM compatibility attribute for the disk group must be at least 12.2.0.0.0 and that the
filesystem needs to be mounted on one node only.

The ACFS filesystem can be initiated for replication using the following command:

```
[root@stpldb101 ~]# /sbin/acfsutil repl init standby -u oracle /u01/app/
oracle/acfs_repl_example/
```

ADVM Compatibility Attributes

If your ADVM compatibility attribute is not high enough, the acfsutil repl init command will return an error.

```
[root@stpldb101 ~]# /sbin/acfsutil repl init standby -u oracle /u01/app/
oracle/acfs_repl_example/
acfsutil repl init: ACFS-03322: The ADVM compatibility attribute for the
diskgroup is below the required version (12.2.0.0.0) for the 'acfsutil
repl' commands.
```

ADVM compatibility attributes cannot be higher than ASM compatibility attributes for a disk group. As such, you will need to increase the ASM compatibility attributes for the disk group if they are too low as well.

```
SQL> select name, compatibility from v$asm_diskgroup where name = 'DATA';


NAME        COMPATIBILITY
----------  -------------
DATA        12.1.0.0.0

SQL> alter diskgroup data set attribute 'COMPATIBLE.ADVM' = '12.2.0.0.0';
alter diskgroup data set attribute 'COMPATIBLE.ADVM' = '12.2.0.0.0'
*
ERROR at line 1:
ORA-15032: not all alterations performed
ORA-15242: could not set attribute compatible.advm
ORA-15493: target ADVM compatibility (12.2.0.0.0) exceeds ASM compatibility
(12.1.0.0.0)
```

Therefore, if your COMPATIBLE.ASM attribute is lower than 12.2.0.0.0, you can increase both the ASM and ADVM compatibility attributes using the following two commands while connected as SYSASM in an +ASM instance; it is not necessary to take the disk group offline or mount it in EXCLUSIVE mode.

```
SQL> alter diskgroup data set attribute 'COMPATIBLE.ASM' = '12.2.0.0.0';
Diskgroup altered.

SQL> alter diskgroup data set attribute 'COMPATIBLE.ADVM' = '12.2.0.0.0';
Diskgroup altered.

SQL> select name, compatibility from v$asm_diskgroup where name = 'DATA';

NAME        COMPATIBILITY
----------  ---------------
DATA        12.2.0.0.0
```

Mounting ACFS Standby Filesystems

ACFS standby filesystems may be mounted on only one node at a time. As such, ensure
that it is not mounted on the second node of the cluster; otherwise, you will receive the
following error when attempting to initialize the filesystem for replication:

```
[root@stpldb101 ~]# /sbin/acfsutil repl init standby -u oracle /u01/app/
oracle/acfs_repl_example/
acfsutil repl init: ACFS-05054: standby replication file system is mounted
on more than one cluster node

[root@stpldb101 ~]# srvctl config filesystem -d /dev/asm/replvol-122
Volume device: /dev/asm/replvol-122
Diskgroup name: data
Volume name: replvol
Canonical volume device: /dev/asm/replvol-122
Accelerator volume devices:
Mountpoint path: /u01/app/oracle/acfs_repl_example
Mount point owner:
Mount users:
Type: ACFS
Mount options:
Description:
ACFS file system is enabled
```

```
ACFS file system is individually enabled on nodes:
ACFS file system is individually disabled on nodes:

[root@stpldb101 ~]# srvctl stop filesystem -d /dev/asm/replvol-122 -n
stpldb102
```

Initiating Replication on the Primary

Replication will need to be initiated on the primary. You can choose to either have continuous replication or replicate at specific second, minute, hour, day, or week intervals. In the following example, continuous replication is chosen, denoted by the -C option:

```
[root@dscrac101 ~]# /sbin/acfsutil repl init primary -C -s oracle@stpldb101
-m /u01/app/oracle/acfs_repl_example/ /u01/app/oracle/acfs_repl_example/

[root@dscrac101 ~]# /sbin/acfsutil repl info -v /u01/app/oracle/acfs_repl_
example/
Events Log: /u01/app/oracle/acfs_repl_example/.ACFS/repl/logs/
ReplicationEventsLog

Time: Tue Dec 10 05:44:07 2017
Transfer completed at:          Tue Dec 10 05:44:07 2017
Transfer status:                0

Time: Tue Dec 10 05:44:07 2017
Event: Clone created
Session started at:             Tue Dec 10 05:44:07 2017
Session ended at:               Tue Dec 10 05:44:07 2017
Number of bytes transmitted:    20759

Time: Tue Dec 10 05:44:07 2017
Create completed at:            Tue Dec 10 05:44:07 2017
Create status:                  0

Time: Tue Dec 10 05:44:07 2017
Event: Replication Initialization Started
Initialization Start Time: Tue Dec 10 05:44:07 2017
```

```
Time: Tue Dec 10 05:44:07 2017
Create started at:                    Tue Dec 10 05:44:07 2017

Time: Tue Dec 10 05:44:07 2017
Transfer started at:                  Tue Dec 10 05:44:07 2017

Number of Events: 6
```

Testing the Replication

Let's test it:

1. Create a file on the primary ACFS filesystem.

```
[oracle@dscrac101 ~]$ echo "Test replication" > /u01/app/oracle/acfs_repl_
example/replication_testing.txt
```

2. Use the repl info command to check whether any bytes were
   sent.

```
[root@dscrac101 ~]# /sbin/acfsutil repl info -v /u01/app/oracle/acfs_repl_
example/
Events Log: /u01/app/oracle/acfs_repl_example/.ACFS/repl/logs/
ReplicationEventsLog

Time: Tue Dec 10 05:44:07 2017
Transfer completed at:                Tue Dec 10 05:44:07 2017
Transfer status:                      0

Time: Tue Dec 10 05:44:07 2017
Event: Clone created
Session started at:                   Tue Dec 10 05:44:07 2017
Session ended at:                     Tue Dec 10 05:44:07 2017
Number of bytes transmitted:          20759

Time: Tue Dec 10 05:44:07 2017
Create completed at:                  Tue Dec 10 05:44:07 2017
Create status:                        0
```

Time: Tue Dec 10 05:44:07 2017
Event: Replication Initialization Started
Initialization Start Time: Tue Dec 10 05:44:07 2017

Time: Tue Dec 10 05:44:07 2017
Create started at: Tue Dec 10 05:44:07 2017

Time: Tue Dec 10 05:44:07 2017
Transfer started at: Tue Dec 10 05:44:07 2017[oracle@
dscrac101 ~]$ /sbin/acfsutil repl info -v /u01/app/oracle/acfs_repl_
example/
Events Log: /u01/app/oracle/acfs_repl_example/.ACFS/repl/logs/
ReplicationEventsLog

Time: Tue Dec 10 05:49:08 2017
Transfer completed at: Tue Dec 10 05:49:08 2017
Transfer status: 0

Time: Tue Dec 10 05:49:08 2017
Event: Clone created
Session started at: Tue Dec 10 05:49:08 2017
Session ended at: Tue Dec 10 05:49:08 2017
Number of bytes transmitted: 22094

Time: Tue Dec 10 05:49:08 2017
Create completed at: Tue Dec 10 05:49:08 2017
Create status: 0

Time: Tue Dec 10 05:49:08 2017
Create started at: Tue Dec 10 05:49:08 2017

Time: Tue Dec 10 05:49:08 2017
Transfer started at: Tue Dec 10 05:49:08 2017

Time: Tue Dec 10 05:44:07 2017
Transfer completed at: Tue Dec 10 05:44:07 2017
Transfer status: 0

3. Check whether the file was replicated to the standby site.

```
[oracle@stpldb101 ~]$ cat /u01/app/oracle/acfs_repl_example/replication_
testing.txt
Test replication
```

HANFS Filesystems (NFS v3)

Starting with Oracle 12c R2 (12.2), Oracle Grid Infrastructure allows for what is called a *high availability network file system* (HANFS). In essence, this is an ACFS filesystem that is exposed to external clients via the NFS v3/v4 protocols. In this example, an implementation of HANFS with NFSv3 will be examined.

In the hands-on example in this chapter, we will be using a two-node RAC cluster named `rac01` with the nodes `rac101` and `rac102` and an application server with the hostname `appserver1`. The `rac01` cluster will have a highly available ACFS filesystem complete with all the protections and availabilities that ASM and GI offer, such as high availability across all cluster nodes, ASM mirroring and striping, ACFS snapshots, and ACFS snapshot-based replication.

ACFS systems will be made available by way of the HAVIP cluster resource and an `exportfs` cluster resource, which will work in tandem to provide access to the NFS filesystem. The HAVIP resource will run with a cardinality of 1, meaning that it will run on one node only and fail over to surviving cluster nodes in the case of a node eviction or local ASM/ACFS failure that makes the filesystem unavailable. The `exportfs` resource will run on all nodes and will contain information regarding the export options of each exported filesystem such as `READ WRITE`, `READ ONLY`, or allowed NFS clients.

HANFS (NFS v3) Server-Side Setup

Now you need to set up the server side.

Start with an ACFS Filesystem

In this example, we will start with an ACFS filesystem on the `rac01` cluster, which is mounted on the mountpoint `/u01/acfs_mnts/app_data`. This is a standard ACFS filesystem.

[oracle@rac101 ~]$ srvctl config filesystem -d /dev/asm/acfs_vol-160

```
Volume device: /dev/asm/acfs_vol-160
Diskgroup name: data
Volume name: acfs_vol
Canonical volume device: /dev/asm/acfs_vol-160
Accelerator volume devices:
Mountpoint path: /u01/acfs_mnts/app_data
Mount point owner: oracle
Mount users:
Type: ACFS
Mount options:
Description:
ACFS file system is enabled
ACFS file system is individually enabled on nodes:
ACFS file system is individually disabled on nodes:
```

Make a DNS Entry for a High Availability VIP

To ensure that exported filesystems maintain availability in the case of a failure on any given node of the ACFS, a consistent hostname must be available to all nodes. In this example, we will use the hostname acfsexport, which will be resolvable to the IP of the HAVIP resource.

```
[oracle@rac101 ~]$ nslookup acfsexport
Server:         192.168.0.59
Address:        192.168.0.59#53

Name:    acfsexport.localdomain
Address: 192.168.0.101
```

Create an HAVIP and Associate It with the DNS Hostname

As the root user, you can create a high availability VIP and associate it with your chosen hostname/IP.

```
[root@rac101 ~]# srvctl add havip -id acfs_export -address acfsexport.
localdomain -description "HANFS VIP"
```

The new resource can be found via crsctl stat res -t as ora.acfs_export.havip.

```
[root@rac101 ~]# crsctl stat res -t
--------------------------------------------------------------------------------
Name           Target  State      Server                 State details
--------------------------------------------------------------------------------
Local Resources
--------------------------------------------------------------------------------
ora.ASMNET1LSNR_ASM.lsnr
               ONLINE  ONLINE     rac101                 STABLE
               ONLINE  ONLINE     rac102                 STABLE
ora.ASMNET2LSNR_ASM.lsnr
               ONLINE  ONLINE     rac101                 STABLE
               ONLINE  ONLINE     rac102                 STABLE
ora.DATA.ACFS_VOL.advm
               ONLINE  ONLINE     rac101                 STABLE
               ONLINE  ONLINE     rac102                 STABLE
ora.DATA.dg
               ONLINE  ONLINE     rac101                 STABLE
               ONLINE  ONLINE     rac102                 STABLE
ora.FRA.dg
               ONLINE  ONLINE     rac101                 STABLE
               ONLINE  ONLINE     rac102                 STABLE
ora.LISTENER.lsnr
               ONLINE  ONLINE     rac101                 STABLE
               ONLINE  ONLINE     rac102                 STABLE
ora.MGMT.dg
               ONLINE  ONLINE     rac101                 STABLE
               ONLINE  ONLINE     rac102                 STABLE
ora.OCR_VOTE.dg
               ONLINE  ONLINE     rac101                 STABLE
               ONLINE  ONLINE     rac102                 STABLE
ora.chad
               ONLINE  ONLINE     rac101                 STABLE
               ONLINE  ONLINE     rac102                 STABLE
```

```
ora.data.acfs_vol.acfs
                ONLINE    ONLINE        rac101                         mounted on /
u01/acfs_mnts/app_data,STABLE
                ONLINE    ONLINE        rac102                         mounted on /
u01/acfs_mnts/app_data,STABLE
ora.net1.network
                ONLINE    ONLINE        rac101                         STABLE
                ONLINE    ONLINE        rac102                         STABLE
ora.ons
                ONLINE    ONLINE        rac101                         STABLE
                ONLINE    ONLINE        rac102                         STABLE
ora.proxy_advm
                ONLINE    ONLINE        rac101                         STABLE
                ONLINE    ONLINE        rac102                         STABLE
--------------------------------------------------------------------------------
Cluster Resources
--------------------------------------------------------------------------------
ora.LISTENER_SCAN1.lsnr
      1       ONLINE    ONLINE        rac102                         STABLE
ora.LISTENER_SCAN2.lsnr
      1       ONLINE    ONLINE        rac101                         STABLE
ora.LISTENER_SCAN3.lsnr
      1       ONLINE    ONLINE        rac101                         STABLE
ora.MGMTLSNR
      1       ONLINE    ONLINE        rac101                         169.254.37.195
                                                                     192.168.10.63
                                                                     192.168.11.63,
STABLE
ora.acfs_export.havip
      1       OFFLINE OFFLINE                                        STABLE
ora.asm
      1       ONLINE    ONLINE        rac101                         Started,STABLE
      2       ONLINE    ONLINE        rac102                         Started,STABLE
      3       OFFLINE OFFLINE                                        STABLE
```

```
ora.cvu
    1         ONLINE  ONLINE        rac101                    STABLE
ora.mgmtdb
    1         ONLINE  ONLINE        rac101                    Open,STABLE
ora.orclcdb.db
    1         ONLINE  ONLINE        rac101                    Open,HOME=/
u01/app/oracle/product/12.2.0

                                                                      /
dbhome_1,STABLE
    2         ONLINE  ONLINE        rac102                    Open,HOME=/
u01/app/oracle/product/12.2.0

                                                                      /
dbhome_1,STABLE
ora.qosmserver
    1         ONLINE  ONLINE        rac101                    STABLE
ora.rac101.vip
    1         ONLINE  ONLINE        rac101                    STABLE
ora.rac102.vip
    1         ONLINE  ONLINE        rac102                    STABLE
ora.scan1.vip
    1         ONLINE  ONLINE        rac102                    STABLE
ora.scan2.vip
    1         ONLINE  ONLINE        rac101                    STABLE
ora.scan3.vip
    1         ONLINE  ONLINE        rac101                    STABLE
```

[root@rac101 ~]# srvctl config havip -id acfs_export
HAVIP exists: /acfs_export/192.168.0.101, network number 1
Description: HANFS VIP
Home Node:
HAVIP is enabled.
HAVIP is individually enabled on nodes:
HAVIP is individually disabled on nodes:

Associate an ACFS Export with the HAVIP

Once the HAVIP has been created, you can create an exportfs cluster resource and associate it with the HAVIP. The association is accomplished via the -id flag, which is the unique ID of the HAVIP. The exportfs cluster resource is valid for only one mountpoint at a time. As such, an exportfs cluster resource needs to be created for each filesystem in the case of multiple filesystems.

Starting the Exported Filesystem

The HAVIP can be controlled via the srvctl start command and will automatically start the exportfs cluster resource on its node if the resource is down.

```
[root@rac101 ~]# srvctl start havip -id acfs_export
[root@rac101 ~]# srvctl status havip -id acfs_export
HAVIP ora.acfs_export.havip is enabled
HAVIP ora.acfs_export.havip is running on nodes rac102

[root@rac101 ~]# srvctl config exportfs -name app_data
export file system app_data is configured
Exported path: /u01/acfs_mnts/app_data
Export Options:
Configured Clients: 192.168.0.0/24
Export Type: NFS
Export file system is enabled.
Export file system is individually enabled on nodes:
Export file system is individually disabled on nodes:
```

Changing the Export Options for Filesystems

By default, the exportfs cluster resource exports filesystems with the following options. Take special note of the ro option, which marks the exported filesystem as read-only.

```
ro,wdelay,root_squash,no_subtree_check,fsid=627694234,sec=sys,ro,
root_squash,no_all_squash
```

In most use cases, NFS filesystems need to be writable to clients, which can be achieved by modifying the exportfs resource for the given filesystem and restarting the HAVIP and exportfs resources.

```
[root@rac102 app_data]# srvctl status exportfs -name app_data
export file system app_data is enabled
export file system app_data is exported on node rac102
[root@rac102 app_data]# exportfs -v
/u01/acfs_mnts/app_data

192.168.0.0/24(ro,wdelay,root_squash,no_subtree_check,fsid=627694234,sec=
sys,ro,root_squash,no_all_squash)
```

Modifying the Filesystem to Be Read-Write

Follow these steps:

1. First, the exportfs resource needs to be modified with the srvctl
   modify command with the desired options.

```
[root@rac102 app_data]# srvctl modify exportfs -name app_data -options rw
```

2. The change in the resource's configs can be checked with the
   srvctl confg command.

```
[root@rac102 app_data]# srvctl config exportfs -name app_data
export file system app_data is configured
Exported path: /u01/acfs_mnts/app_data
Export Options: rw
Configured Clients: 192.168.0.0/24
Export Type: NFS
Export file system is enabled.
Export file system is individually enabled on nodes:
Export file system is individually disabled on nodes:
```

Restarting the exportfs Resource

In an NFS v3 configuration for HANFS, the exportfs resources do not follow the state
of their respective HAVIP resources. Because of this, when an HAVIP is restarted, its
associated exportfs resources will not restart themselves and thus will not reflect any
changes made to the export options.

In the following example, you can see that despite there having been made a change to the export options to allow for rw as opposed to ro access, the change is not reflected in the exports -v output.

```
[root@rac102 app_data]# srvctl stop havip -id acfs_export
[root@rac102 app_data]# srvctl start havip -id acfs_export
[root@rac102 app_data]# srvctl status havip -id acfs_export
HAVIP ora.acfs_export.havip is enabled
HAVIP ora.acfs_export.havip is running on nodes rac102
[root@rac102 app_data]# exportfs -v
/u01/acfs_mnts/app_data
                192.168.0.0/24(ro,wdelay,root_squash,no_subtree_check,fsid=
627694234,sec=sys,ro,root_squash,no_all_squash)
/u01/test_export
                <world>(rw,wdelay,root_squash,no_subtree_
check,sec=sys,rw,root_squash,no_all_squash)
```

Additionally, exportfs resources have a Clusterware dependency on their respective HAVIP. To restart the exportfs resource, its HAVIP must be stopped as well.

```
[root@rac102 app_data]# srvctl stop exportfs -name app_data
PRCR-1065 : Failed to stop resource ora.app_data.export
CRS-2974: unable to act on resource 'ora.app_data.export' on server
'rac102' because that would require stopping or relocating resource 'ora.
acfs_export.havip' but the -force option was not specified

[root@rac102 app_data]# srvctl stop havip -id acfs_export
[root@rac102 app_data]# srvctl status exportfs -name app_data
export file system app_data is enabled
export file system app_data is exported on node rac102

[root@rac102 app_data]# srvctl stop exportfs -name app_data
[root@rac102 app_data]# srvctl start havip -id acfs_export
[root@rac102 app_data]# srvctl status exportfs -name app_data
export file system app_data is enabled
export file system app_data is exported on node rac102
```

Once the `exportfs` resource has been stopped and started successfully, the change in the resource configuration can be shown to be reflected in the `exportfs -v` output. Take special note of the `rw` export option, which was previously `ro`.

```
[root@rac102 app_data]# exportfs -v
/u01/acfs_mnts/app_data
                192.168.0.0/24(rw,wdelay,root_squash,no_subtree_check,fsid=
627694234,sec=sys,rw,root_squash,no_all_squash)
```

HANFS (NFS v3) Client-Side Setup

It is best practice to ensure that an environment has consistent UID and GID values for users and groups, respectively. However, if this is not the case, HANFS can still be configured to work properly.

In this example, we are showing an example where the app server has a UID:GID for the `oracle:oinstall` group as 500:501 and the Oracle Cluster (`rac01`) that is serving up the filesystem has a different set of values for `oracle:oinstall`, for example, 54321:54321.

1. You can check the UID:GID for a user by using the `id` command.

```
[oracle@rac101 ~]$ id
uid=54321(oracle) gid=54321(oinstall) groups=54321(oinstall),54322(dba),543
23(oper),54324(backupdba),54325(dgdba),54326(kmdba),54330(racdba)
```

```
[oracle@appserver1 ~]# id
uid=500(oracle) gid=500(oracle) groups=500(oracle),501(oinstall)
```

In the case of differing IDs, an exported file or entire mountpoint can be "chowned" with reference to the UID:GID, as opposed to the friendly name for the user and group. Do note that this can be done even the group or user does not exist on the NFS server (each node on cluster `rac01`).

```
[root@rac102 app_data]# cd /u01/acfs_mnts/app_data
[root@rac102 app_data]# mkdir appserver_storage
[root@rac102 app_data]# chown 500:501 appserver_storage/
```

2.   Mount the filesystem on the client.

The HANFS filesystem can be mounted on any client within the allowed client subnet either manually via the mount command or via the fstab.

```
[root@appserver ~]# mount -v -t nfs acfsexport.localdomain:/u01/acfs_mnts/
app_data /u01/acfs_storage/
mount.nfs: timeout set for Sat Feb 10 18:15:29 2018
mount.nfs: trying text-based options 'vers=4,addr=192.168.0.101,clientad
dr=192.168.0.89'
acfsexport.localdomain:/u01/acfs_mnts/app_data on /u01/acfs_storage type
nfs (rw)
[root@appserver ~]# df -h
Filesystem           Size  Used Avail Use% Mounted on
/dev/mapper/vg_appserver-lv_root
                      95G   32G   60G  35% /
tmpfs                3.8G    0  3.8G   0% /dev/shm
/dev/sda1            477M  161M  287M  36% /boot
acfsexport.localdomain:/u01/acfs_mnts/app_data
                      10G  504M  9.6G   5% /u01/acfs_storage
```

Once mounted, it is good practice to test that the filesystem can be written to and read from.

```
[oracle@appserver1 ~]$ ll /u01/acfs_storage/appserver_storage/
total 0
[oracle@appserver1 ~]$ echo "test" > /u01/acfs_storage/appserver_storage/
testfile.txt
[oracle@appserver1 ~]$ cat /u01/acfs_storage/appserver_storage/testfile.txt
Test
```

Oracle Flex Clusters

In Oracle 12c R1 (12.1), Oracle Flex Clusters were an option; however, starting with 12.2.0.1, GI will automatically configure the cluster for Flex clustering. This type of cluster has a number of exciting features associated with it.

With Oracle Flex Clusters, there are hub nodes and leaf nodes, as shown in Table 4-1.

Table 4-1. *Hub and Leaf Nodes*

Type	Description
HUB	• Hosts ASM Instance: Yes • Read-Only RDBMS Instances: Yes • Read-Write RDBMS Instances: Yes • Requires Direct Access to ASM Disks: Yes
LEAF	• Hosts ASM Instance: No • Read-Only RDBMS Instances: Yes (requires direct access to ASM disks) • Read-Write RDBMS Instances: No • Requires Direct Access to ASM Disks: No

Leaf nodes can be added either during the initial GI install or after the fact using rapid home provisioning or by cloning the GI home using addnode.sh. See Figure 4-2.

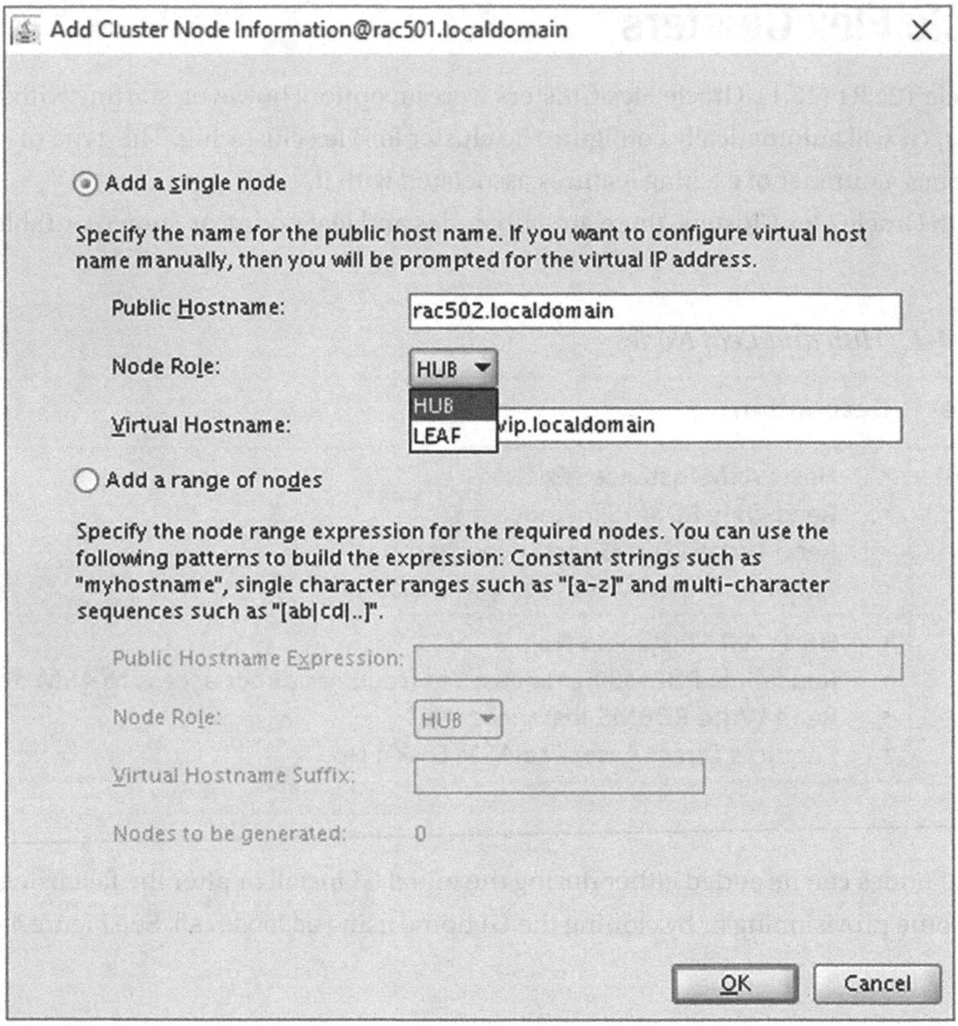

Figure 4-2.

In the case of a cluster that was upgraded from 12.1 to 12.2 GI, the cluster will have the option of enabling Flex clustering and adding leaf nodes, but all preexisting cluster nodes will initially be hub nodes.

The *role* of each node in the cluster can be checked with the crsctl get node role command.

```
[oracle@stpldb101 ~]$  /u01/app/12.2.0.1/grid/bin/crsctl get node role
status -all
Node 'stpldb101' active role is 'hub'
Node 'stpldb102' active role is 'hub'
```

Adding a Leaf Node to a Freshly Installed Cluster

In this example, I will show how a leaf node can be added to a freshly installed cluster
that does not use GNS. In this example, the cluster starts out as a two-node cluster with
the hub nodes rac501 and rac502 and will have a third node added as a leaf node. In
this example, we will assume a standard install where the owner of the Grid software is
oracle and the OINSTALL group is oinstall.

Installing Required Binaries

Follow these steps:

1. First, the cvuqdisk RPM needs to be installed on the node being
   added.

The cvuqdisk RPM file can be found on any 12.2 Grid home in the $ORACLE_
HOME/cv/rpm directory.

```
[oracle@rac501 ~]$ find /u01/app/12.2.0.1/grid/cv/rpm -name "cvuqdisk*.rpm"
/u01/app/12.2.0.1/grid/cv/rpm/cvuqdisk-1.0.10-1.rpm
```

The standard rpm command can be used to install the RPM on a Red Hat
variant system.

```
[root@rac503 ~]# rpm -Uvh /home/oracle/cvuqdisk-1.0.10-1.rpm
Preparing...                       ###########################################
[100%]
Using default group oinstall to install package
   1:cvuqdisk                      ###########################################
[100%]
```

2. Create the /u01 mountpoint and ensure it is writable by
   oracle:oinstall on the leaf node.

```
[root@rac503 ~]# mkdir /u01
[root@rac503 ~]# chown oracle:oinstall /u01
```

Performing Preinstall Checks

It is best practice to perform a check using the cluvfy utility prior to attempting to install nodes. Some failures can be ignored, such as swap space.

[oracle@rac501 ~]$ cluvfy stage -pre nodeadd -flex -leaf rac503

```
Verifying Physical Memory ...PASSED
Verifying Available Physical Memory ...PASSED
Verifying Swap Size ...FAILED (PRVF-7573)
Verifying Free Space: rac503:/usr,rac503:/var,rac503:/etc,rac503:/u01/
app/12.2.0.1/grid,rac503:/sbin,rac503:/tmp ...PASSED
Verifying Free Space: rac501:/usr,rac501:/var,rac501:/etc,rac501:/u01/
app/12.2.0.1/grid,rac501:/sbin,rac501:/tmp ...PASSED
Verifying User Existence: oracle ...
  Verifying Users With Same UID: 54321 ...PASSED
Verifying User Existence: oracle ...PASSED
Verifying User Existence: root ...
  Verifying Users With Same UID: 0 ...PASSED
Verifying User Existence: root ...PASSED
Verifying Group Existence: dba ...PASSED
Verifying Group Existence: oinstall ...PASSED
Verifying Group Membership: oinstall ...PASSED
Verifying Group Membership: dba ...PASSED
Verifying Run Level ...PASSED
Verifying Hard Limit: maximum open file descriptors ...PASSED
Verifying Soft Limit: maximum open file descriptors ...PASSED
Verifying Hard Limit: maximum user processes ...PASSED
Verifying Soft Limit: maximum user processes ...PASSED
Verifying Soft Limit: maximum stack size ...PASSED
Verifying Architecture ...PASSED
Verifying OS Kernel Version ...PASSED
Verifying OS Kernel Parameter: semmsl ...PASSED
Verifying OS Kernel Parameter: semmns ...PASSED
Verifying OS Kernel Parameter: semopm ...PASSED
Verifying OS Kernel Parameter: semmni ...PASSED
Verifying OS Kernel Parameter: shmmax ...PASSED
```

```
Verifying OS Kernel Parameter: shmmni ...PASSED
Verifying OS Kernel Parameter: shmall ...PASSED
Verifying OS Kernel Parameter: file-max ...PASSED
Verifying OS Kernel Parameter: ip_local_port_range ...PASSED
Verifying OS Kernel Parameter: rmem_default ...PASSED
Verifying OS Kernel Parameter: rmem_max ...PASSED
Verifying OS Kernel Parameter: wmem_default ...PASSED
Verifying OS Kernel Parameter: wmem_max ...PASSED
Verifying OS Kernel Parameter: aio-max-nr ...PASSED
Verifying OS Kernel Parameter: panic_on_oops ...PASSED
Verifying Package: binutils-2.20.51.0.2 ...PASSED
Verifying Package: compat-libcap1-1.10 ...PASSED
Verifying Package: compat-libstdc++-33-3.2.3 (x86_64) ...PASSED
Verifying Package: libgcc-4.4.7 (x86_64) ...PASSED
Verifying Package: libstdc++-4.4.7 (x86_64) ...PASSED
Verifying Package: libstdc++-devel-4.4.7 (x86_64) ...PASSED
Verifying Package: sysstat-9.0.4 ...PASSED
Verifying Package: ksh ...PASSED
Verifying Package: make-3.81 ...PASSED
Verifying Package: glibc-2.12 (x86_64) ...PASSED
Verifying Package: glibc-devel-2.12 (x86_64) ...PASSED
Verifying Package: libaio-0.3.107 (x86_64) ...PASSED
Verifying Package: libaio-devel-0.3.107 (x86_64) ...PASSED
Verifying Package: nfs-utils-1.2.3-15 ...PASSED
Verifying Package: e2fsprogs-1.42.8 ...PASSED
Verifying Package: e2fsprogs-libs-1.42.8 (x86_64) ...PASSED
Verifying Package: smartmontools-5.43-1 ...PASSED
Verifying Package: net-tools-1.60-110 ...PASSED
Verifying Users With Same UID: 0 ...PASSED
Verifying Current Group ID ...PASSED
Verifying Root user consistency ...PASSED
Verifying Package: cvuqdisk-1.0.10-1 ...PASSED
Verifying Node Addition ...
Verifying CRS Integrity ...PASSED
Verifying Clusterware Version Consistency ...PASSED
```

```
Verifying '/u01/app/12.2.0.1/grid' ...PASSED
Verifying Node Addition ...PASSED
Verifying Node Connectivity ...
Verifying Hosts File ...PASSED
Verifying Check that maximum (MTU) size packet goes through subnet
...PASSED
Verifying subnet mask consistency for subnet "192.168.57.0" ...PASSED
Verifying subnet mask consistency for subnet "192.168.56.0" ...PASSED
Verifying subnet mask consistency for subnet "192.168.58.0" ...PASSED
Verifying Node Connectivity ...PASSED
Verifying Multicast check ...PASSED
Verifying Device Checks for ASM ...
Verifying ASM device sharedness check ...
Verifying Package: cvuqdisk-1.0.10-1 ...PASSED
Verifying Shared Storage Accessibility:/dev/oracleasm/data_1a,/dev/
oracleasm/data_1b,/dev/oracleasm/data_1c,/dev/oracleasm/fra_1a,/dev/
oracleasm/fra_1b,/dev/oracleasm/fra_1c ...PASSED
Verifying ASM device sharedness check ...PASSED
Verifying Access Control List check ...PASSED
Verifying Device Checks for ASM ...PASSED
Verifying OCR Integrity ...PASSED
Verifying Time zone consistency ...PASSED
Verifying Network Time Protocol (NTP) ...
Verifying '/etc/ntp.conf' ...PASSED
Verifying '/var/run/ntpd.pid' ...PASSED
Verifying Daemon 'ntpd' ...PASSED
Verifying NTP daemon or service using UDP port 123 ...PASSED
Verifying NTP daemon is synchronized with at least one external time source
...PASSED
Verifying Network Time Protocol (NTP) ...PASSED
Verifying User Not In Group "root": oracle ...PASSED
Verifying resolv.conf Integrity ...
Verifying (Linux) resolv.conf Integrity ...PASSED
Verifying resolv.conf Integrity ...PASSED
Verifying DNS/NIS name service ...PASSED
```

```
Verifying User Equivalence ...PASSED
Verifying /dev/shm mounted as temporary file system ...PASSED
Verifying /boot mount ...PASSED
Verifying zeroconf check ...PASSED

Pre-check for node addition was unsuccessful.
Checks did not pass for the following nodes:
        rac501

Failures were encountered during execution of CVU verification request
"stage -pre nodeadd".


Verifying Swap Size ...FAILED
rac501: PRVF-7573 : Sufficient swap size is not available on node "rac501"
        [Required = 9.7639GB (1.023822E7KB) ; Found = 4.8984GB (5136380.0KB)]

CVU operation performed:      stage -pre nodeadd
CVU home:                     /u01/app/12.2.0.1/grid/
User:                         oracle
```

GNS and Flex Clustering

Initially, Flex clustering will be enabled but will not allow leaf nodes to be added because of a lack of GNS. The current state of the cluster can be checked by using asmcmd. You will see errors from the cluvfy utility and will not be able to perform preinstall checks.

```
[oracle@rac501 ~]$ asmcmd showclustermode
ASM cluster : Flex mode enabled
```

```
[oracle@rac501 ~]$ cluvfy stage -pre nodeadd -flex -leaf rac503
PRVG-11410 : illegal specification of nodes with leaf role for a non-Flex
Cluster
```

Flex clustering can be enabled only if the GNS resource is running because of dependencies. Even if the cluster currently uses static IPs defined in a DNS server, a GNS VIP must exist and be enabled for proper Flex ASM clustering.

A GNS VIP can be added as a cluster resource using srvctl as root. You do not have to necessarily use GNS for hostname resolution at this stage.

```
[root@rac501 ~]# . oraenv
ORACLE_SID = [root] ? +ASM1
The Oracle base has been set to /u01/app/oracle
[root@rac501 ~]# srvctl add gns -vip gns-rac5 -verbose
GNS was successfully added.
```

Add the Node

Here's how to add the node:

[oracle@rac501 ~]$. oraenv
```
ORACLE_SID = [+ASM1] ? +ASM1
The Oracle base remains unchanged with value /u01/app/oracle
[oracle@rac501 ~]$ cd $ORACLE_HOME/addnode
```

[oracle@rac501 addnode]$ ll
```
total 36
-rw-r--r-- 1 oracle oinstall  2098 Jan 26  2017 addnode_oraparam.ini
-rw-r----- 1 oracle oinstall  2106 Jan 26  2017 addnode_oraparam.ini.sbs
-rw-r----- 1 oracle oinstall  2106 Jan 26  2017 addnode_oraparam.ini.sbs.ouibak
-rw-r----- 1 oracle oinstall 12836 Aug  5  2016 addnode.pl
-rwxr-x--- 1 oracle oinstall  3714 Jun 30 00:42 addnode.sh
-rw-r----- 1 oracle oinstall  3729 Jan 26  2017 addnode.sh.ouibak
```

[oracle@rac501 addnode]$ ./addnode.sh -silent "CLUSTER_NEW_NODES={rac503}"
"CLUSTER_NEW_VIRTUAL_HOSTNAMES={rac503-vip}" "CLUSTER_NEW_NODE_
ROLES={leaf}"

[oracle@rac501 addnode]$ ./addnode.sh -silent "CLUSTER_NEW_NODES={rac503}"
"CLUSTER_NEW_VIRTUAL_HOSTNAMES={rac503-vip}" "CLUSTER_NEW_NODE_
ROLES={leaf}"
```
[WARNING] [INS-13014] Target environment does not meet some optional
requirements.
```

CAUSE: Some of the optional prerequisites are not met. See logs for details. /u01/app/oraInventory/logs/addNodeActions2017-07-01_10-59-04-PM.log

ACTION: Identify the list of failed prerequisite checks from the log: /u01/app/oraInventory/logs/addNodeActions2017-07-01_10-59-04-PM.log. Then either from the log file or from installation manual find the appropriate configuration to meet the prerequisites and fix it manually.

```
Prepare Configuration in progress.
Prepare Configuration successful.
................................................. 7% Done.
Copy Files to Remote Nodes in progress.
................................................. 12% Done.
................................................. 17% Done.
.............................................
Copy Files to Remote Nodes successful.
You can find the log of this install session at:
 /u01/app/oraInventory/logs/addNodeActions2017-07-01_10-59-04-PM.log

Instantiate files in progress.
Instantiate files successful.
................................................. 49% Done.

Saving cluster inventory in progress.
................................................. 83% Done.

Saving cluster inventory successful.
The Cluster Node Addition of /u01/app/12.2.0.1/grid was successful.
Please check '/u01/app/12.2.0.1/grid/inventory/silentInstall2017-07-01_10-
59-04-PM.log' for more details.

Setup Oracle Base in progress.
Setup Oracle Base successful.
................................................. 90% Done.

Update Inventory in progress.
Update Inventory successful.
................................................. 97% Done.
```

As a root user, execute the following script(s):
        1. /u01/app/oraInventory/orainstRoot.sh
        2. /u01/app/12.2.0.1/grid/root.sh

Execute /u01/app/oraInventory/orainstRoot.sh on the following nodes:
[rac503]
Execute /u01/app/12.2.0.1/grid/root.sh on the following nodes:
[rac503]
The scripts can be executed in parallel on all the nodes.

.... 100% Done.
Successfully Setup Software.

Run Root Scripts

Now run the root scripts.

[root@rac503 ~]# /u01/app/oraInventory/orainstRoot.sh
Changing permissions of /u01/app/oraInventory.
Adding read,write permissions for group.
Removing read,write,execute permissions for world.

Changing groupname of /u01/app/oraInventory to oinstall.
The execution of the script is complete.

[root@rac503 ~]# /u01/app/12.2.0.1/grid/root.sh
Performing root user operation.

The following environment variables are set as:
    ORACLE_OWNER= oracle
    ORACLE_HOME= /u01/app/12.2.0.1/grid
   Copying dbhome to /usr/local/bin ...
   Copying oraenv to /usr/local/bin ...
   Copying coraenv to /usr/local/bin ...

Creating /etc/oratab file...
Entries will be added to the /etc/oratab file as needed by
Database Configuration Assistant when a database is created
Finished running generic part of root script.
Now product-specific root actions will be performed.

226

Relinking oracle with rac_on option
Using configuration parameter file: /u01/app/12.2.0.1/grid/crs/install/
crsconfig_params
The log of current session can be found at:
  /u01/app/oracle/crsdata/rac503/crsconfig/rootcrs_rac503_2017-07-01_11-04-
59PM.log
2017/07/01 23:05:00 CLSRSC-594: Executing installation step 1 of 19:
'SetupTFA'.
2017/07/01 23:05:00 CLSRSC-4001: Installing Oracle Trace File Analyzer
(TFA) Collector.
2017/07/01 23:05:24 CLSRSC-4002: Successfully installed Oracle Trace File
Analyzer (TFA) Collector.
2017/07/01 23:05:24 CLSRSC-594: Executing installation step 2 of 19:
'ValidateEnv'.
2017/07/01 23:05:26 CLSRSC-363: User ignored prerequisites during
installation
2017/07/01 23:05:26 CLSRSC-594: Executing installation step 3 of 19:
'CheckFirstNode'.
2017/07/01 23:05:27 CLSRSC-594: Executing installation step 4 of 19:
'GenSiteGUIDs'.
2017/07/01 23:05:27 CLSRSC-594: Executing installation step 5 of 19:
'SaveParamFile'.
2017/07/01 23:05:29 CLSRSC-594: Executing installation step 6 of 19:
'SetupOSD'.
2017/07/01 23:05:31 CLSRSC-594: Executing installation step 7 of 19:
'CheckCRSConfig'.
2017/07/01 23:05:32 CLSRSC-594: Executing installation step 8 of 19:
'SetupLocalGPNP'.
2017/07/01 23:05:33 CLSRSC-594: Executing installation step 9 of 19:
'ConfigOLR'.
2017/07/01 23:05:35 CLSRSC-594: Executing installation step 10 of 19:
'ConfigCHMOS'.
2017/07/01 23:05:35 CLSRSC-594: Executing installation step 11 of 19:
'CreateOHASD'.

2017/07/01 23:05:36 CLSRSC-594: Executing installation step 12 of 19: 'ConfigOHASD'.

2017/07/01 23:05:52 CLSRSC-330: Adding Clusterware entries to file 'oracle-ohasd.conf'

2017/07/01 23:06:08 CLSRSC-594: Executing installation step 13 of 19: 'InstallAFD'.

2017/07/01 23:06:31 CLSRSC-594: Executing installation step 14 of 19: 'InstallACFS'.

CRS-2791: Starting shutdown of Oracle High Availability Services-managed resources on 'rac503'

CRS-2793: Shutdown of Oracle High Availability Services-managed resources on 'rac503' has completed

CRS-4133: Oracle High Availability Services has been stopped.

CRS-4123: Oracle High Availability Services has been started.

2017/07/01 23:06:58 CLSRSC-594: Executing installation step 15 of 19: 'InstallKA'.

2017/07/01 23:06:59 CLSRSC-594: Executing installation step 16 of 19: 'InitConfig'.

CRS-2791: Starting shutdown of Oracle High Availability Services-managed resources on 'rac503'

CRS-2793: Shutdown of Oracle High Availability Services-managed resources on 'rac503' has completed

CRS-4133: Oracle High Availability Services has been stopped.

CRS-4123: Oracle High Availability Services has been started.

CRS-2791: Starting shutdown of Oracle High Availability Services-managed resources on 'rac503'

CRS-2673: Attempting to stop 'ora.drivers.acfs' on 'rac503'

CRS-2677: Stop of 'ora.drivers.acfs' on 'rac503' succeeded

CRS-2793: Shutdown of Oracle High Availability Services-managed resources on 'rac503' has completed

CRS-4133: Oracle High Availability Services has been stopped.

2017/07/01 23:07:16 CLSRSC-594: Executing installation step 17 of 19: 'StartCluster'.

CRS-4123: Starting Oracle High Availability Services-managed resources

CRS-2672: Attempting to start 'ora.mdnsd' on 'rac503'

CRS-2672: Attempting to start 'ora.evmd' on 'rac503'
CRS-2676: Start of 'ora.mdnsd' on 'rac503' succeeded
CRS-2676: Start of 'ora.evmd' on 'rac503' succeeded
CRS-2672: Attempting to start 'ora.gpnpd' on 'rac503'
CRS-2676: Start of 'ora.gpnpd' on 'rac503' succeeded
CRS-2672: Attempting to start 'ora.gipcd' on 'rac503'
CRS-2676: Start of 'ora.gipcd' on 'rac503' succeeded
CRS-2672: Attempting to start 'ora.cssdmonitor' on 'rac503'
CRS-2676: Start of 'ora.cssdmonitor' on 'rac503' succeeded
CRS-2672: Attempting to start 'ora.cssd' on 'rac503'
CRS-2672: Attempting to start 'ora.diskmon' on 'rac503'
CRS-2676: Start of 'ora.diskmon' on 'rac503' succeeded
CRS-2676: Start of 'ora.cssd' on 'rac503' succeeded
CRS-2672: Attempting to start 'ora.cluster_interconnect.haip' on 'rac503'
CRS-2672: Attempting to start 'ora.ctssd' on 'rac503'
CRS-2676: Start of 'ora.ctssd' on 'rac503' succeeded
CRS-2672: Attempting to start 'ora.crf' on 'rac503'
CRS-2676: Start of 'ora.crf' on 'rac503' succeeded
CRS-2672: Attempting to start 'ora.crsd' on 'rac503'
CRS-2676: Start of 'ora.crsd' on 'rac503' succeeded
CRS-2676: Start of 'ora.cluster_interconnect.haip' on 'rac503' succeeded
CRS-6017: Processing resource auto-start for servers: rac503
CRS-2672: Attempting to start 'ora.chad' on 'rac503'
CRS-2676: Start of 'ora.chad' on 'rac503' succeeded
CRS-6016: Resource auto-start has completed for server rac503
CRS-6024: Completed start of Oracle Cluster Ready Services-managed
resources
CRS-4123: Oracle High Availability Services has been started.
2017/07/01 23:20:58 CLSRSC-343: Successfully started Oracle Clusterware
stack
2017/07/01 23:20:58 CLSRSC-594: Executing installation step 18 of 19:
'ConfigNode'.
Successfully accumulated necessary OCR keys.
Creating OCR keys for user 'root', privgrp 'root'..
Operation successful.

```
2017/07/01 23:21:01 CLSRSC-594: Executing installation step 19 of 19:
'PostConfig'.
2017/07/01 23:21:07 CLSRSC-325: Configure Oracle Grid Infrastructure for a
Cluster ... succeeded
[root@rac503 ~]#
```

Extend the RDBMS Home to the Leaf Node

Here is the next step:

```
[oracle@rac501 addnode]$ cd /u01/app/oracle/product/12.2.0.1/dbhome_1/
addnode/
[oracle@rac501 addnode]$ ./addnode.sh -silent "CLUSTER_NEW_NODES={rac503}"
Starting Oracle Universal Installer...

Checking Temp space: must be greater than 120 MB.    Actual 23036 MB
Passed
Checking swap space: must be greater than 150 MB.    Actual 5015 MB
Passed
[WARNING] [INS-13014] Target environment does not meet some optional
requirements.
   CAUSE: Some of the optional prerequisites are not met. See logs for
details. /u01/app/oraInventory/logs/addNodeActions2017-07-01_11-26-35PM.log
   ACTION: Identify the list of failed prerequisite checks from the log: /
u01/app/oraInventory/logs/addNodeActions2017-07-01_11-26-35PM.log. Then
either from the log file or from installation manual find the appropriate
configuration to meet the prerequisites and fix it manually.

Prepare Configuration in progress.
Prepare Configuration successful.
..................................................   7% Done.

Copy Files to Remote Nodes in progress.
..................................................   12% Done.
..................................................   18% Done.
.............................
Copy Files to Remote Nodes successful.
```

You can find the log of this install session at:
 /u01/app/oraInventory/logs/installActions2017-07-01_11-26-35PM.log

Instantiate files in progress.
Instantiate files successful.
.... 52% Done.

Saving cluster inventory in progress.
.... 89% Done.

Saving cluster inventory successful.
The Cluster Node Addition of /u01/app/oracle/product/12.2.0.1/dbhome_1 was
successful.
Please check '/tmp/silentInstall2017-07-01_11-26-36-PM.log' for more
details.

Setup Oracle Base in progress.
Setup Oracle Base successful.
.... 96% Done.

As a root user, execute the following script(s):
        1. /u01/app/oracle/product/12.2.0.1/dbhome_1/root.sh

Execute /u01/app/oracle/product/12.2.0.1/dbhome_1/root.sh on the following
nodes:
[rac503]

.... 100% Done.
Successfully Setup Software.

Run the Root Script for the RDBMS Home on the Leaf Node

Here's the root script:

[root@rac503 ~]# /u01/app/oracle/product/12.2.0.1/dbhome_1/root.sh

Extend the RDBMS Home to the Leaf Node

Finally, extend the RDBS home to the leaf node, as shown here:

```
[oracle@rac503 ~]$ /u01/app/12.2.0.1/grid/bin/crsctl get node role status
-all
Node 'rac501' active role is 'hub'
Node 'rac502' active role is 'hub'
Node 'rac503' active role is 'leaf'
Start the LISTENER_LEAF listener on the leaf node
[oracle@rac501 ~]$ srvctl status listener -l LISTENER_LEAF
Listener LISTENER_LEAF is enabled
Listener LISTENER_LEAF is not running
[oracle@rac501 ~]$ srvctl start listener -l LISTENER_LEAF
[oracle@rac501 ~]$ srvctl status listener -l LISTENER_LEAF
Listener LISTENER_LEAF is enabled
Listener LISTENER_LEAF is running on node(s): rac503
```

Flex Redundancy Disk groups

With Oracle 12c R2 (12.2), ASM supports a new type of disk group redundancy, Flex redundancy. Flex redundancy disk groups allow ASM administrators to manage files in a database-oriented way and allow an administrator to determine space quotas on a per database level for each disk group by way of two new management concepts called *filegroups* and *quotas*.

Creating a Flex Disk group

A flex disk group requires a minimum of three failure groups but should have five or more if at all possible because if a flex disk group has fewer than five failure groups, it can tolerate only one failure. This section will show two ways to create a flex redundancy disk group.

- You can do it at the command line, as shown here:

```
SQL> CREATE DISKGROUP DATA FLEX REDUNDANCY
 FAILGROUP A  DISK 'AFD:DATA1' SIZE 15358M
 FAILGROUP B  DISK 'AFD:DATA2' SIZE 15358M
 FAILGROUP C  DISK 'AFD:DATA3' SIZE 15358M
 ATTRIBUTE 'compatible.asm'='12.2.0.1','compatible.advm'='12.2.0.1','au_
size'='4M'
```

- You can do it with the ASM Configuration Assistant, as shown in Figure 4-3.

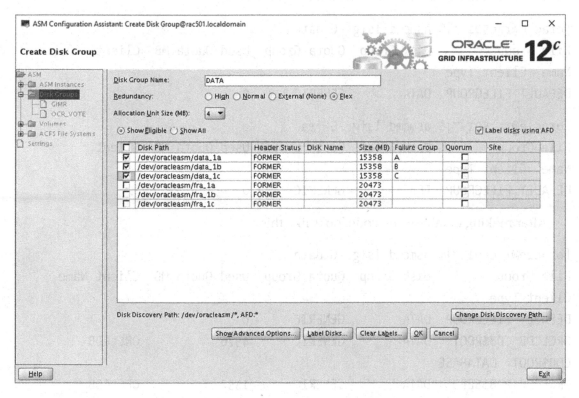

Figure 4-3.

Filegroup

One of the main new concepts introduced with Flex disk groups is the filegroup. A *filegroup* is a logical entity that refers to all of the files that a particular database uses within a disk group. When a database is first created, a filegroup with the same name as the database (and all of its PDBs) is created in each disk group that the database stores its files. There is a filegroup called DEFAULT_FILEGROUP that exists in all Flex disk groups. Each filegroup in turn belongs to a particular quota group, which can be modified to limit the amount of space a database can consume within a disk group.

The following is an example of a Flex disk group named DATA, which has no files. Before making database, the code looks like this:

```
[oracle@rac501 ~]$ asmcmd lsfg -G data
File Group         Disk Group  Quota Group  Used Quota MB  Client
Name  Client Type
DEFAULT_FILEGROUP  DATA        GENERIC      0

[oracle@rac501 ~]$ asmcmd lsfg -G fra
File Group         Disk Group  Quota Group  Used Quota MB  Client
Name  Client Type
DEFAULT_FILEGROUP  FRA         GENERIC      0
```

After making database, the code looks like this:

```
[oracle@rac501 ~]$ asmcmd lsfg -G data
File Group         Disk Group  Quota Group  Used Quota MB  Client Name
Client Type
DEFAULT_FILEGROUP  DATA        GENERIC      0
ORCLCDB_CDB$ROOT   DATA        GENERIC      4576           ORCLCDB_
CDB$ROOT  DATABASE
ORCLCDB_PDB$SEED   DATA        GENERIC      1552           ORCLCDB_
PDB$SEED  DATABASE
SOMEPDB            DATA        GENERIC      1776           SOMEPDB
DATABASE

[oracle@rac501 ~]$ asmcmd lsfg -G fra
File Group         Disk Group  Quota Group  Used Quota MB  Client Name
Client Type
```

```
DEFAULT_FILEGROUP   FRA         GENERIC     0
ORCLCDB_CDB$ROOT    FRA         GENERIC     1728              ORCLCDB_
CDB$ROOT   DATABASE
```

Querying Filegroup Properties

Filegroup properties can be queried directly from an +ASM instance.

The following example shows all the filegroup properties for a filegroup named SOMEPDB in a disk group named DATA. From the following output, it can be seen that every type of ASM file has its own individual settings within a filegroup for redundancy and striping. This allows for far greater granularity over how files are managed in ASM at the database level.

```
SQL> select
  2   fg.name as FILEGROUP_NAME,
  3   fgp.name as PROPERTY_NAME,
  4   fgp.value as VALUE,
  5   fgp.FILE_TYPE as FILE_TYPE
  6   from
  7   v$asm_diskgroup dg,
  8   v$asm_filegroup fg,
  9   v$asm_filegroup_property fgp
 10   where dg.GROUP_NUMBER = fg.GROUP_NUMBER
 11   and fg.GROUP_NUMBER = fgp.GROUP_NUMBER
 12   and fg.FILEGROUP_NUMBER = fgp.FILEGROUP_NUMBER
 13   and dg.name = '&DG_NAME'
 14   and fg.name = '&FG_NAME'
 15* order by FILE_TYPE
SQL> /
Enter value for dg_name: DATA
old  13: and dg.name = '&DG_NAME'
new  13: and dg.name = 'DATA'
Enter value for fg_name: SOMEPDB
old  14: and fg.name = '&FG_NAME'
new  14: and fg.name = 'SOMEPDB'
```

FILEGROUP_NAME	PROPERTY_NAME	VALUE	FILE_TYPE
SOMEPDB	STRIPING	COARSE	ARCHIVELOG
SOMEPDB	REDUNDANCY	MIRROR	ARCHIVELOG
SOMEPDB	STRIPING	COARSE	ASMVDRL
SOMEPDB	REDUNDANCY	MIRROR	ASMVDRL
SOMEPDB	REDUNDANCY	MIRROR	ASMVOL
SOMEPDB	STRIPING	COARSE	ASMVOL
SOMEPDB	REDUNDANCY	MIRROR	AUDIT_SPILLFILES
SOMEPDB	STRIPING	COARSE	AUDIT_SPILLFILES
SOMEPDB	STRIPING	COARSE	AUTOBACKUP
SOMEPDB	REDUNDANCY	MIRROR	AUTOBACKUP
SOMEPDB	STRIPING	COARSE	AUTOLOGIN_KEY_STORE
SOMEPDB	REDUNDANCY	MIRROR	AUTOLOGIN_KEY_STORE
SOMEPDB	STRIPING	COARSE	BACKUPSET
SOMEPDB	REDUNDANCY	MIRROR	BACKUPSET
SOMEPDB	REDUNDANCY	MIRROR	CHANGETRACKING
SOMEPDB	STRIPING	COARSE	CHANGETRACKING
SOMEPDB	REDUNDANCY	MIRROR	CONTAINER
SOMEPDB	STRIPING	COARSE	CONTAINER
SOMEPDB	REDUNDANCY	HIGH	CONTROLFILE
SOMEPDB	STRIPING	FINE	CONTROLFILE
SOMEPDB	STRIPING	COARSE	DATAFILE
SOMEPDB	REDUNDANCY	MIRROR	DATAFILE
SOMEPDB	STRIPING	COARSE	DATAGUARDCONFIG
SOMEPDB	REDUNDANCY	MIRROR	DATAGUARDCONFIG
SOMEPDB	REDUNDANCY	MIRROR	DUMPSET
SOMEPDB	STRIPING	COARSE	DUMPSET
SOMEPDB	STRIPING	COARSE	FLASHBACK
SOMEPDB	REDUNDANCY	MIRROR	FLASHBACK
SOMEPDB	STRIPING	COARSE	FLASHFILE
SOMEPDB	REDUNDANCY	MIRROR	FLASHFILE
SOMEPDB	REDUNDANCY	MIRROR	INCR XTRANSPORT
BACKUPSET			

SOMEPDB	STRIPING	COARSE	INCR XTRANSPORT BACKUPSET
SOMEPDB	REDUNDANCY	MIRROR	KEY_STORE
SOMEPDB	STRIPING	COARSE	KEY_STORE
SOMEPDB	REDUNDANCY	MIRROR	OCRBACKUP
SOMEPDB	STRIPING	COARSE	OCRBACKUP
SOMEPDB	REDUNDANCY	MIRROR	OCRFILE
SOMEPDB	STRIPING	COARSE	OCRFILE
SOMEPDB	REDUNDANCY	MIRROR	ONLINELOG
SOMEPDB	STRIPING	COARSE	ONLINELOG
SOMEPDB	REDUNDANCY	MIRROR	PARAMETERFILE
SOMEPDB	STRIPING	COARSE	PARAMETERFILE
SOMEPDB	STRIPING	COARSE	TEMPFILE
SOMEPDB	REDUNDANCY	MIRROR	TEMPFILE
SOMEPDB	STRIPING	COARSE	VOTINGFILE
SOMEPDB	REDUNDANCY	MIRROR	VOTINGFILE
SOMEPDB	STRIPING	COARSE	XTRANSPORT BACKUPSET
SOMEPDB	REDUNDANCY	MIRROR	XTRANSPORT BACKUPSET
SOMEPDB	PRIORITY	MEDIUM	

Modifying Filegroup Properties

Filegroup properties can be modified by logging into +ASM as SYSASM with ALTER DISKGROUP commands. In the following example, we are modifying the redundancy of ONLINELOG files to HIGH:

```
SQL> ALTER DISKGROUP DATA MODIFY FILEGROUP SOMEPDB SET 'ONLINELOG.
REDUNDANCY' = 'HIGH';
Diskgroup altered.
```

Note Filegroup properties can be modified using ASMCMD, but the syntax requires writing XML, so it is being omitted for brevity. For more details, run asmcmd help chfg from the Grid Home.

Quota Groups

Each filegroup within a disk group belongs to one quota group. By default, system-generated filegroups belong to the GENERIC filegroup, but the quota limit and quota name can be changed.

```
[oracle@rac501 ~]$ asmcmd lsfg -G fra
File Group          Disk Group  Quota Group  Used Quota MB  Client Name
Client Type
DEFAULT_FILEGROUP   FRA         GENERIC      0
ORCLCDB_CDB$ROOT    FRA         GENERIC      5320                         ORCLCDB_
CDB$ROOT   DATABASE
```

Listing Quota Groups

Although quota groups can be listed via ASMCMD, the output is not user-friendly unless an ASM administrator has memorized GROUP_NUMBERS for their databases.

```
[oracle@rac501 ~]$ asmcmd lsqg
Group_Num  Quotagroup_Num  Quotagroup_Name  Incarnation  Used_Quota_MB
Quota_Limit_MB
1          1               GENERIC          1            11832          0
2          1               GENERIC          1            5320           0
3          1               GENERIC          1            67968          0
4          1               GENERIC          1            320            0
```

A more human-readable approach is to query the v$asm_quotagroup and join it with v$asm_diskgroup.

```
SQL> select
  2   dg.name as DG_NAME,
  3   qg.name as QG_NAME,
  4   qg.USED_QUOTA_MB,
  5   qg.QUOTA_LIMIT_MB
  6   from
  7   v$asm_diskgroup dg, v$asm_quotagroup qg
  8   where qg.group_number = dg.group_number
```

```
  9* and dg.name ='&DG_NAME'
SQL> /
Enter value for dg_name: FRA
old     9: and dg.name ='&DG_NAME'
new     9: and dg.name ='FRA'


DG_NAME     QG_NAME                  USED_QUOTA_MB QUOTA_LIMIT_MB
---------- -------------------- -------------- --------------

FRA         GENERIC                           5320              0
```

Making a New Quota Group

A quota group can be created and have a filegroup associated with it using the ALTER DISKGROUP command as SYSASM in the +ASM instance.

```
SQL> ALTER DISKGROUP FRA ADD QUOTAGROUP SOMEPDB_FRA_QUOTA SET quota =
6000m;
Diskgroup altered.

SQL> alter diskgroup FRA modify filegroup ORCLCDB_CDB$ROOT set 'quota_
group' = 'SOMEPDB_FRA_QUOTA';
Diskgroup altered.
```

You can validate that the changes to the filegroup and quota have occurred with the asmcmd lsfg command and by querying ASM views.

```
[oracle@rac501 ~]$ asmcmd lsfg -G fra
File Group          Disk Group  Quota Group          Used Quota MB  Client
Name        Client Type
DEFAULT_FILEGROUP  FRA          GENERIC              0
ORCLCDB_CDB$ROOT   FRA          SOMEPDB_FRA_QUOTA 5648               ORCLCDB_
CDB$ROOT   DATABASE

SQL> select
  2  dg.name as DG_NAME,
  3  qg.name as QG_NAME,
  4  qg.USED_QUOTA_MB,
  5  qg.QUOTA_LIMIT_MB
```

```
  6   from
  7   v$asm_diskgroup dg, v$asm_quotagroup qg
  8   where qg.group_number = dg.group_number
  9   and dg.name ='&DG_NAME'
 10*
SQL> /
Enter value for dg_name: FRA
old   9: and dg.name ='&DG_NAME'
new   9: and dg.name ='FRA'
```

DG_NAME	QG_NAME	USED_QUOTA_MB	QUOTA_LIMIT_MB
FRA	GENERIC	0	0
FRA	SOMEPDB_FRA_QUOTA	5648	6000

Rapid Home Provisioning

Rapid Home Provisioning is a feature of the Oracle Grid Infrastructure that allows for provisioning, patching, upgrading, and scaling up and down Oracle software across a data center. Rapid Home Provisioning is a key tool in managing large environments and for simplifying maintenance activities associated with all sorts of Oracle RDBMS homes ranging from 11.2.0.4 up to 12.2.0.1. Rapid Home Provisioning also allows an administrator to provision and configure RAC clusters with just one command.

RHP works by creating *golden images* of Oracle software and storing them on the RHP server. RHP can then provision these software homes onto servers in the data center, which are referred to as *RHP clients*. Additionally, the RHP server can be used to configure databases and Grid Infrastructure installations.

In the following example, we will go through the steps necessary to provision a stand-alone 12.2 Oracle cluster and create a database instance, all through Rapid Home Provisioning, to showcase the utility of this feature. Rapid Home Provisioning will be set up on a two-node RAC cluster called rac05 with the nodes rac501 and rac502. Once the RHP server is set up, it will be used to provision and create a stand-alone cluster and database on a server named mongoose.

Configuring the RHP Server Resource

Now let's configure the RHP server resource.

Create an ACFS Filesystem to House RHP Data

All of the golden images that will be used for this RHP server will be housed in an ACFS filesystem, which will be mounted on a mountpoint on all servers. Ensure that the disk group chosen for the RHP data has at least 50GB of free space as it will be storing Oracle software, which can take some space.

```
[oracle@rac501 ~]$ mkdir -p /u01/app/oracle/rhp
[oracle@rac501 ~]$ ssh rac502 "mkdir -p /u01/app/oracle/rhp"
```

Once the mountpoint is created, add the rhpserver resources and ensure rhpserver is started.

```
[root@rac501 ~]# srvctl add rhpserver -storage /u01/app/oracle/rhp
-diskgroup RHP_DATA -verbose
rac501.localdomain: Creating a new volume...
rac501.localdomain: Checking for the existence of file system...
rac501.localdomain: Creating a new ACFS file system...
rac501.localdomain: Starting the ACFS file system...
rac501.localdomain: Creating authentication keys...
[root@rac501 ~]# srvctl config rhpserver
Storage base path: /u01/app/oracle/rhp
Disk Groups: RHP_DATA
Port number: 23795
Rapid Home Provisioning Server is enabled
Rapid Home Provisioning Server is individually enabled on nodes:
Rapid Home Provisioning Server is individually disabled on nodes:
Email address:
Mail server address:
Mail server port:

[root@rac501 ~]# srvctl status rhpserver
Rapid Home Provisioning Server is enabled
Rapid Home Provisioning Server is not running
```

Once created, rhpserver can be started with the GI home owner.

```
[oracle@rac501 ~]$ srvctl start rhpserver
[oracle@rac501 ~]$ srvctl status rhpserver
Rapid Home Provisioning Server is enabled
Rapid Home Provisioning Server is running on node rac501
```

Create a High Availability VIP Resource on the RHP Server

You will not be able to start this HAVIP resource, but it is needed internally by the RHP server for creating temporary HANFS filesystems for presenting working copies to RHP clients.

```
[root@rac501 ~]# srvctl add havip -id rhp_havip -address rhp-havip.
localdomain -description "HAVIP for RHP"
```

Ensure that NFS daemons are started and restart on node reboots. NFS daemons are necessary as RHP will utilize HANFS functionality to initially present working copies to RHP clients.

```
[root@rac502 ~]# service rpcbind start
[root@rac502 ~]# service nfs start
Starting NFS services:                                    [  OK  ]
Starting NFS quotas:                                      [  OK  ]
Starting NFS mountd:                                      [  OK  ]
Starting NFS daemon:                                      [  OK  ]
[root@rac502 ~]# chkconfig nfs on
[root@rac502 ~]# chkconfig rpcbind on

[root@rac501 ~]# service rpcbind start
[root@rac501 ~]# service nfs start
Starting NFS services:                                    [  OK  ]
Starting NFS quotas:                                      [  OK  ]
Starting NFS mountd:                                      [  OK  ]
Starting NFS daemon:                                      [  OK  ]
```

```
[root@rac501 ~]# chkconfig rpcbind on
[root@rac501 ~]# chkconfig nfs on
```

Using the Existing RDBMS and GI Installations on the RHP Server as Golden Images

The RDBMS and GI installations already present on the RHP server cluster can be imported as golden images so that they can be provisioned as *working copies* to RHP clients.

```
[oracle@rac501 ~]$ rhpctl import image -image gi_12201 -path /u01/
app/12.2.0.1/grid -imagetype ORACLEGISOFTWARE
rac501.localdomain: Creating a new ACFS file system for image "gi_12201"
...
rac501.localdomain: Copying files...
rac501.localdomain: Copying home contents...
rac501.localdomain: Changing the home ownership to user oracle...
rac501.localdomain: Changing the home ownership to user oracle...

[oracle@rac501 ~]$ rhpctl import image -image rdbms_12201 -path /u01/app/
oracle/product/12.2.0.1/dbhome_1 -imagetype ORACLEDBSOFTWARE
rac501.localdomain: Creating a new ACFS file system for image "rdbms_12201"
...
rac501.localdomain: Copying files...
rac501.localdomain: Copying home contents...
rac501.localdomain: Changing the home ownership to user oracle...
rac501.localdomain: Changing the home ownership to user oracle...

[oracle@rac501 ~]$ rhpctl query image
Image name: rdbms_12201
Image name: gi_12201
[oracle@rac501 ~]$
```

Provisioning a Working Copy of the GI Home

First it is important to ensure that all prerequisite RPMs are installed on the target server.

```
[root@mongoose ~]# rpm -qa |egrep "cvu|oracle-database-server"
oracle-database-server-12cR2-preinstall-1.0-3.el6.x86_64
cvuqdisk-1.0.10-1.x86_64
```

A GI home can be provisioned with rhpctl. The following is an example of the output expected from a successful rhpctl deploy. You may receive an error at the end, which can normally be attributed to a CVU requirement check failure at the end of the GI installation.

```
[oracle@rac501 ~]$ rhpctl add workingcopy -workingcopy mongoose_gi_12201
-image gi_12201 -ignoreprereq -responsefile /home/oracle/rhp_response_
files/grid_install_single_node_rac.rsp -sudouser oracle  -sudopath /usr/
bin/sudo
Enter user "oracle" password:
rac501.localdomain: Storing metadata in repository for working copy
"mongoose_gi_12201" ...
rac501.localdomain: Creating snapshot "tmpgi_12201mongoose_gi_12201" ...
rac501.localdomain: Changing the home ownership to user oracle...
rac501.localdomain: Mounting file system...
rac501.localdomain: Copying software contents to Local File System ...
rac501.localdomain: Starting clone operation...
rac501.localdomain: Using inventory file /etc/oraInst.loc to clone ...
mongoose1.localdomain: Starting Oracle Universal Installer...
mongoose1.localdomain:
mongoose1.localdomain: Checking Temp space: must be greater than 500
MB.   Actual 57564 MB     Passed
mongoose1.localdomain: Checking swap space: must be greater than 500
MB.   Actual 15311 MB     Passed
mongoose1.localdomain: Preparing to launch Oracle Universal Installer from
/tmp/OraInstall2017-07-11_02-28-59PM. Please wait ...You can find the log
of this install session at:
mongoose1.localdomain:  /u01/app/oraInventory/logs/cloneActions2017-07-
11_02-28-59PM.log
```

```
mongoose1.localdomain: ........................................... 5% Done.
mongoose1.localdomain: ........................................... 10% Done.
mongoose1.localdomain: ........................................... 15% Done.
mongoose1.localdomain: ........................................... 20% Done.
mongoose1.localdomain: ........................................... 25% Done.
mongoose1.localdomain: ........................................... 30% Done.
mongoose1.localdomain: ........................................... 35% Done.
mongoose1.localdomain: ........................................... 40% Done.
mongoose1.localdomain: ........................................... 45% Done.
mongoose1.localdomain: ........................................... 50% Done.
mongoose1.localdomain: ........................................... 55% Done.
mongoose1.localdomain: ........................................... 60% Done.
mongoose1.localdomain: ........................................... 65% Done.
mongoose1.localdomain: ........................................... 70% Done.
mongoose1.localdomain: ........................................... 75% Done.
mongoose1.localdomain: ........................................... 80% Done.
mongoose1.localdomain: ........................................... 85% Done.
mongoose1.localdomain: .........
mongoose1.localdomain: Copy files in progress.
mongoose1.localdomain:
mongoose1.localdomain: Copy files successful.
mongoose1.localdomain:
mongoose1.localdomain: Link binaries in progress.
mongoose1.localdomain:
mongoose1.localdomain: Link binaries successful.
mongoose1.localdomain:
mongoose1.localdomain: Setup files in progress.
mongoose1.localdomain:
mongoose1.localdomain: Setup files successful.
mongoose1.localdomain:
mongoose1.localdomain: Setup Inventory in progress.
mongoose1.localdomain:
mongoose1.localdomain: Setup Inventory successful.
mongoose1.localdomain:
mongoose1.localdomain: Finish Setup successful.
```

mongoose1.localdomain: The cloning of mongoose_gi_12201 was successful.
mongoose1.localdomain: Please check '/u01/app/oraInventory/logs/
cloneActions2017-07-11_02-28-59PM.log' for more details.
mongoose1.localdomain:
mongoose1.localdomain: Setup Oracle Base in progress.
mongoose1.localdomain:
mongoose1.localdomain: Setup Oracle Base successful.
mongoose1.localdomain: .... 95% Done.
mongoose1.localdomain:
mongoose1.localdomain: As a root user, execute the following script(s):
mongoose1.localdomain: 1. /u01/oracle/12.2.0.1/grid/root.sh
mongoose1.localdomain:
mongoose1.localdomain: Execute /u01/oracle/12.2.0.1/grid/root.sh on the
following nodes:
mongoose1.localdomain: [mongoose1.localdomain]
mongoose1.localdomain:
mongoose1.localdomain:
mongoose1.localdomain: .... 100% Done.
rac501.localdomain: Successfully executed clone operation.
rac501.localdomain: Executing root script on nodes [mongoose1.localdomain].
mongoose1.localdomain: Changing permissions of /u01/app/oraInventory.
mongoose1.localdomain: Adding read,write permissions for group.
mongoose1.localdomain: Removing read,write,execute permissions for world.
mongoose1.localdomain:
mongoose1.localdomain: Changing groupname of /u01/app/oraInventory to
oinstall.
mongoose1.localdomain: The execution of the script is complete.
rac501.localdomain: Successfully executed root script on nodes [mongoose1.
localdomain].
rac501.localdomain: Executing configuration script on nodes [mongoose1.
localdomain]
rac501.localdomain: Successfully executed configuration script on nodes
[mongoose1.localdomain]
rac501.localdomain: Executing root script on nodes [mongoose1.localdomain].

mongoose1.localdomain: Check /u01/oracle/12.2.0.1/grid/install/root_
mongoose1.localdomain_2017-07-11_14-30-19-119194196.log for the output of
root script
rac501.localdomain: Successfully executed root script on nodes [mongoose1.
localdomain].
rac501.localdomain: Executing post configuration script on nodes
[mongoose1.localdomain]
PRGH-1062 : failure while executing the Oracle Grid Infrastructure
configuration tool
PRCZ-2010 : Failed to execute command "/u01/oracle/12.2.0.1/grid/
cfgtoollogs/configToolAllCommands" using 'sudo' from location "/usr/
bin/sudo" as user "oracle" within 4,000 seconds on nodes "mongoose1.
localdomain"
PRCZ-2103 : Failed to execute command "/u01/oracle/12.2.0.1/grid/
cfgtoollogs/configToolAllCommands" on node "mongoose1.localdomain" as user
"oracle". Detailed error:
Setting the invPtrLoc to /u01/oracle/12.2.0.1/grid/oraInst.loc
perform - mode is starting for action: configure
perform - mode finished for action: configure

You can see the log file: /u01/oracle/12.2.0.1/grid/cfgtoollogs/oui/
configActions2017-07-11_02-39-46-PM.log

If you encounter an error during the "post-configuration script" phase, check the
logfile. If the errors are due to the Cluster Verification Utility and the issues are ignorable,
it is safe to proceed.

[oracle@mongoose1 u01]# grep -i fail /u01/oracle/12.2.0.1/grid/cfgtoollogs/
oui/configActions2017-07-11_02-39-46-PM.log

The plug-in Oracle Cluster Verification Utility has failed its perform
method
The action configuration has failed its perform method

If CVU errors are ignored in this manner, you may have to manually unmount the
HANFS directory on the target cluster.

[root@mongoose1 ~]$ df -h

```
Filesystem              Size  Used Avail Use% Mounted on
/dev/mapper/vg_goldencopy-lv_root
                        84G   25G   55G  31% /
tmpfs                   4.9G  641M  4.3G  13% /dev/shm
/dev/sda1               477M  153M  295M  35% /boot
192.168.58.31:/u01/app/oracle/rhp/images/igi_12201599479/.ACFS/snaps/
tmpgi_12201mongoose_gi_12201/swhome
                        34G   16G   19G  46% /mnt/mongoose_gi_12201
```

[root@mongoose1 ~]# umount /mnt/mongoose_gi_12201

Additionally, the ACFS snapshot for the temporary working copy of the software home should be removed from the RHP server.

[root@rac501 ~]# acfsutil snap info /u01/app/oracle/rhp/images/
igi_12201599479

```
snapshot name:              tmpgi_12201mongoose_gi_12201
snapshot location:          /u01/app/oracle/rhp/images/igi_12201599479/.
ACFS/snaps/tmpgi_12201mongoose_gi_12201
RO snapshot or RW snapshot: RW
parent name:                /u01/app/oracle/rhp/images/igi_12201599479
snapshot creation time:     Wed Jul 11 14:02:55 2018
storage added to snapshot:  217833472   ( 207.74 MB )

number of snapshots:  1
snapshot space usage: 217837568  ( 207.75 MB )
```

[root@rac501 ~]# acfsutil snap delete tmpgi_12201mongoose_gi_12201 /u01/
app/oracle/rhp/images/igi_12201599479
acfsutil snap delete: Snapshot operation is complete.

ORACLE_HOME for 12.2 GI Provisioning

By default, a response file generated by gridSetup.sh during the graphical install of a GI home does not contain an ORACLE_HOME parameter. Ensure that you add an ORACLE_HOME parameter that points to the intended installation location of GI. If it is missing, you will see the following error:

```
[oracle@rac501 rhp_response_files]$ rhpctl add workingcopy -workingcopy
mongoose_gi_12201 -image gi_12201 -ignoreprereq -responsefile /home/oracle/
rhp_response_files/grid_install_single_node_rac.rsp -root
Enter user "root" password:
PRGO-1381 : Parameter "ORACLE_HOME" is empty.
```

At a minimum, you must also provide the ASMNMP and SYSASM passwords in the response file.

```
[oracle@rac501 rhp_response_files]$ cat grid_install_single_node_rac.rsp
|grep -v "^#" |grep -i pass
oracle.install.crs.config.ipmi.bmcPassword=
oracle.install.asm.SYSASMPassword=database_123
oracle.install.asm.monitorPassword=database_123
oracle.install.config.emAdminPassword=
```

If the ASMSNMP and SYSASM passwords are not provided, you will get errors during the install.

```
rac501.localdomain: Executing configuration script on nodes [mongoose1.
localdomain]
PRGH-1030 : The environments on nodes '[mongoose1.localdomain]' do not
satisfy some of the prerequisite checks.
PRCZ-2105 : failed to execute command "/u01/oracle/12.2.0.1/grid/gridSetup.
sh" as user "oracle" using root credentials within 4,000 seconds on nodes
"mongoose1.localdomain"
PRCZ-2103 : Failed to execute command "/u01/oracle/12.2.0.1/grid/gridSetup.
sh" on node "mongoose1.localdomain" as user "oracle". Detailed error:
Launching Oracle Grid Infrastructure Setup Wizard...
```

[FATAL] [INS-30001] The SYS password is empty.
  CAUSE: The SYS password should not be empty.
  ACTION: Provide a non-empty password.
[FATAL] [INS-30001] The ASMSNMP password is empty.
  CAUSE: The ASMSNMP password should not be empty.
  ACTION: Provide a non-empty password.

If the previous issue occurs, the response file being used for the configuration can be found on the server in question at the following location:

```
$ORACLE_HOME/crs/install/rhpdata/grid_install_single_node_rac.rsp
```

Ensure that passwordless sudo is set up for the Grid home user and choose the SUDO option for the install in the response file.

```
[oracle@rac501 rhp_response_files]$ cat grid_install_single_node_rac.rsp
|grep -i sudo |grep -v "^#"
oracle.install.crs.rootconfig.configMethod=SUDO
oracle.install.crs.rootconfig.sudoPath=/usr/bin/sudo
oracle.install.crs.rootconfig.sudoUserName=oracle
```

Converting the Target Cluster into an RHP Cluster

First, an XML file describing the client will need to be created on the RHP server and copied to the client.

```
[oracle@rac501 ~]$ rhpctl add client -client mongoose -toclientdata /home/
oracle/
rac501.localdomain: Creating client data ...
rac501.localdomain: Client data created for client "mongoose".
[oracle@rac501 ~]$ ll /home/oracle/mongoose.xml
-rw-r--r-- 1 oracle oinstall 3640 Jul 11 15:17 /home/oracle/mongoose.xml

[oracle@rac501 ~]$ scp /home/oracle/mongoose.xml oracle@mongoose:/home/
oracle/
```

As the root user, create an RHPCLIENT cluster resource and start it.

```
[root@mongoose1 ~]# srvctl add rhpclient -clientdata /home/oracle/mongoose.xml
[root@mongoose1 ~]# srvctl status rhpclient
Rapid Home Provisioning Client is enabled
Rapid Home Provisioning Client is not running
[root@mongoose1 ~]# srvctl start rhpclient
[root@mongoose1 ~]# srvctl status rhpclient
```

Rapid Home Provisioning Client is enabled
Rapid Home Provisioning Client is running on node mongoose1

Provisioning a Working Copy of the RDBMS Home

Next you need a working copy:

```
[oracle@rac501 ~]$ rhpctl add workingcopy -image rdbms_12201 -path /u01/
app/oracle/product/12.2.0.1/dbhome_1 -client mongoose -oraclebase /u01/app/
oracle -workingcopy mongoose_rdbms_12201
rac501.localdomain: Option storagetype is set to the following default
value: LOCAL.
rac501.localdomain: Adding storage for working copy ...
rac501.localdomain: Storing metadata in repository for working copy
"mongoose_rdbms_12201" ...
rac501.localdomain: Connecting to RHPC...
rac501.localdomain: Starting client-side action for 'add workingcopy'...
mongoose1.localdomain: Making a local copy ...
mongoose1.localdomain: Provisioning Oracle home...
mongoose1.localdomain: Starting clone operation...
==========================================
mongoose1.localdomain:
Starting Oracle Universal Installer...

Checking Temp space: must be greater than 500 MB.    Actual 47395 MB     Passed
Checking swap space: must be greater than 500 MB.    Actual 15311 MB     Passed
Preparing to launch Oracle Universal Installer from /tmp/OraInstall2017-07-
11_03-31-27PM. Please wait ...You can find the log of this install session at:
 /u01/app/oraInventory/logs/cloneActions2017-07-11_03-31-27PM.log
.............................................. 5% Done.
.............................................. 10% Done.
.............................................. 15% Done.
.............................................. 20% Done.
.............................................. 25% Done.
```

```
..............................................  30% Done.
..............................................  35% Done.
..............................................  40% Done.
..............................................  45% Done.
..............................................  50% Done.
..............................................  55% Done.
..............................................  60% Done.
..............................................  65% Done.
..............................................  70% Done.
..............................................  75% Done.
..............................................  80% Done.
..............................................  85% Done.
Copy files in progress.
Copy files successful.
Link binaries in progress.
Link binaries successful.
Setup files in progress.
Setup files successful.
Setup Inventory in progress.
Setup Inventory successful.
Finish Setup successful.
The cloning of mongoose_rdbms_12201 was successful.
Please check '/u01/app/oraInventory/logs/cloneActions2017-07-11_03-31-27PM.
log' for more details.

Setup Oracle Base in progress.
Setup Oracle Base successful.
..........................................  95% Done.
As a root user, execute the following script(s):
        1. /u01/app/oracle/product/12.2.0.1/dbhome_1/root.sh
Execute /u01/app/oracle/product/12.2.0.1/dbhome_1/root.sh on the following nodes:
[mongoose1]
..........................................  100% Done.
```

```
mongoose1.localdomain: Successfully executed clone operation.
mongoose1.localdomain: Executing root script on nodes mongoose1.
mongoose1.localdomain: Successfully executed root script on nodes mongoose1.
mongoose1.localdomain: Working copy creation completed.
mongoose1.localdomain: Oracle home provisioned.
rac501.localdomain: Client-side action completed.
```

Provisioning a Database on the Client Cluster

Create a disk group to store all the database data on the client server. This can be done via SQLPlus on an existing provisioned disk while connected to an +ASM instance as SYSASM.

```
SQL> CREATE DISKGROUP DATA EXTERNAL REDUNDANCY  DISK 'AFD:DATA1'
SIZE 30718M
ATTRIBUTE 'compatible.asm'='12.2.0.1','compatible.advm'='12.2.0.1','au_
size'='4M';
```

Once a disk group has been created, the database can be created with rhpctl from the RHP server.

```
[oracle@rac501 ~]$ rhpctl add database -workingcopy mongoose_rdbms_12201
-dbname orclcdb -dbtype RAC -datafileDestination DATA -cdb -node mongoose1
mongoose1.localdomain: Starting database creation on node mongoose1 ...
==================================================================
mongoose1.localdomain:
SYS_PASSWORD_PROMPT
*********
SYSTEM_PASSWORD_PROMPT
********

Copying database files
1% complete
2% complete
15% complete
27% complete
Creating and starting Oracle instance
29% complete
```

```
32% complete
33% complete
34% complete
38% complete
42% complete
43% complete
45% complete
Creating cluster database views
47% complete
63% complete
Completing Database Creation
64% complete
65% complete
68% complete
71% complete
72% complete
Executing Post Configuration Actions
100% complete
Look at the log file "/u01/app/oracle/cfgtoollogs/dbca/orclcdb/orclcdb.log"
for further details.
```

Once the database is provisioned, it can be seen running on the RHP client cluster.

```
[oracle@mongoose1 ~]$ srvctl status database -d orclcdb
Instance orclcdb1 is running on node mongoose1

[oracle@mongoose1 ~]$ srvctl config database -d orclcdb
Database unique name: orclcdb
Database name: orclcdb
Oracle home: /u01/app/oracle/product/12.2.0.1/dbhome_1
Oracle user: oracle
Spfile: +DATA/ORCLCDB/PARAMETERFILE/spfile.270.981215317
Password file: +DATA/ORCLCDB/PASSWORD/pwdorclcdb.256.981214881
Domain:
Start options: open
Stop options: immediate
Database role: PRIMARY
```

```
Management policy: AUTOMATIC
Server pools:
Disk Groups: DATA
Mount point paths:
Services:
Type: RAC
Start concurrency:
Stop concurrency:
OSDBA group: dba
OSOPER group: oper
Database instances: orclcdb1
Configured nodes: mongoose1
CSS critical: no
CPU count: 0
Memory target: 0
Maximum memory: 0
Default network number for database services:
Database is administrator managed
```

Database SYS/SYSTEM Passwords

RHP creates randomized passwords in a provisioned database. A good next step after database provisioning would be to create a new password for those users, set an FRA, and enable archive logging.

Summary

In this chapter, we discussed the ASM Filter Driver, ACFS features such as snapshot-based replication and HANFS, Flex Clusters, Flex redundancy ASM disk groups, and Rapid Home Provisioning. We provided detailed examples of how to implement these features along with caveats that should be observed in order to avoid issues in production environments. Armed with this knowledge, you should feel confident in implementing and testing these important GI features.

CHAPTER 5

Troubleshooting and Conducting Health Checks for High Availability

The goal of this chapter is to introduce you to the various health check utilities, both new in 12.2 and from previous versions, that can greatly ease management and troubleshooting efforts for High Availability and DR solutions. This chapter will focus mostly on features that are not necessarily Exadata specific but that can and should be used in Exadata and other engineered environments. The chapter will highlight important and often hidden aspects of the different features and software that can be used for health checks as well as cover a few of the new features available in the 12.2 GI and RDBMS software.

Cluster Verification Utility

The Cluster Verification Utility (CVU) is an extremely important component of the Grid Infrastructure installation. This tool can be used to perform a variety of health checks on an Oracle Real Application Cluster, regardless of whether the Real Application Cluster is on commodity hardware or an engineered system. This tool is essential in the installation of Grid Infrastructure as well as in the Database Creation Assistant (DBCA). However, there are several great and often underutilized one-off use cases for the tool, which this chapter will go over. The Cluster Verification Utility is available in $GRID_HOME. You will need to set your environment to +ASM to be able to successfully launch CVU.

© Y V Ravi Kumar, Nassyam Basha, Krishna Kumar K M, Bal Mukund Sharma, Konstantin Kerekovski 2019
Y V Ravi Kumar et al., *Oracle High Availability, Disaster Recovery, and Cloud Services*,
https://doi.org/10.1007/978-1-4842-4351-0_5

Software Home Checks

Sometimes, for various reasons, a DBA may come to question the integrity of a software home, such as the RDBMS installation home or the Grid Infrastructure installation itself, for example, after patching and having to roll back certain patches or after a particularly problem-ridden attempt at Grid Infrastructure upgrade/patch that requires manual intervention. It is always a good thing to be able to say that the file permissions ad user/group ownerships of all files within an Oracle software installation are correct and as they should be.

The following is an example of a call to `cluvfy` that points out a file permissions issue and specifies what the expected and observed file permissions are for the files in question to help resolve the situation:

```
[oracle@stpldb101 ~]$ cluvfy comp software -n all -d /u01/app/12.2.0.1/
grid/ -allfiles -r 12.2

Verifying Software home: /u01/app/12.2.0.1/grid/ ...FAILED (PRVG-2033)

Verification of software was unsuccessful on all the specified nodes.

Failures were encountered during execution of CVU verification request
"software".


Verifying Software home: /u01/app/12.2.0.1/grid/ ...FAILED
stpldb102: PRVG-2033 : Permissions of file
        "/u01/app/12.2.0.1/grid//bin/kfod.bin" did not match the expected
        octal value on node "stpldb102". [Expected = "751" ; Found = "0755"]
stpldb102: PRVG-2033 : Permissions of file
        "/u01/app/12.2.0.1/grid//crs/install/dropdb.pl" did not match the
        expected octal value on node "stpldb102". [Expected = "700" ; Found
        = "0755"]
stpldb102: PRVG-2033 : Permissions of file
        "/u01/app/12.2.0.1/grid//lib/acfstoolsdriver.sh" did not match the
        expected octal value on node "stpldb102". [Expected = "750" ; Found
        = "0755"]

stpldb101: PRVG-2033 : Permissions of file
        "/u01/app/12.2.0.1/grid//bin/kfod.bin" did not match the expected
```

octal value on node "stpldb101". [Expected = "751" ; Found = "0755"]
stpldb101: PRVG-2033 : Permissions of file
   "/u01/app/12.2.0.1/grid//crs/install/dropdb.pl" did not match the
   expected octal value on node "stpldb101". [Expected = "700" ; Found
   = "0755"]
stpldb101: PRVG-2033 : Permissions of file
   "/u01/app/12.2.0.1/grid//lib/acfstoolsdriver.sh" did not match the
   expected octal value on node "stpldb101". [Expected = "750" ; Found
   = "0755"]

```
CVU operation performed:     software
Date:                        Aug 19, 2017 12:23:27 PM
CVU home:                    /u01/app/12.2.0.1/grid/
User:                        oracle
[oracle@stpldb101 ~]$ echo $?
1
```

The following is an example of running cluvfy against a 12.2 RDBMS home, which came back as not having any issues:

```
[oracle@stpldb101 ~]$ cluvfy comp software -n all -d /u01/app/oracle/
product/12.2.0.1/dbhome_1 -allfiles -r 12.2

Verifying Software home: /u01/app/oracle/product/12.2.0.1/dbhome_1 ...PASSED

Verification of software was successful.

CVU operation performed:     software
Date:                        Aug 19, 2017 12:26:29 PM
CVU home:                    /u01/app/12.2.0.1/grid/
User:                        oracle
[oracle@stpldb101 ~]$ echo $?
0
```

One of the great things about the Cluster Verification Utility is that the return code of many of the commands signifies whether an issue was encountered. Because of this, it is actually easy to set up shell scripts that run cluvfy comp software and then email an administrator if an issue is found so that it can be investigated.

File System Space Checks

It is a known fact that database administrators must keep an eye on the free space available on file systems that contain Grid Infrastructure and Oracle Database software homes because of logging configurations and other various environment-specific reasons. For this reason, every database administrator likely has their own custom script to check directories or df output for space usage. However, the Cluster Verification Utility can greatly simplify these scripts, if Grid Infrastructure is installed.

Grid Infrastructure–Only Check

The following is an example of the command used to check the free space available on the file system that contains Grid Infrastructure:

```
[oracle@stpldb101 grid]$ cluvfy comp freespace -n all

Verifying '/u01/app/12.2.0.1/grid' ...FAILED (PRVG-11104)

Verification of Free Space was unsuccessful.
Checks did not pass for the following nodes:
        stpldb101

Failures were encountered during execution of CVU verification request
"Free Space".

Verifying '/u01/app/12.2.0.1/grid' ...FAILED
stpldb101: PRVG-11104 : The disk free space for file system path
        "/u01/app/12.2.0.1/grid" on node "stpldb101" is below "5.0" percent
        of total disk space. The required free space is "4960.700000000001
        MB", the available free space is "1748.0 MB" and the total disk size
        is "99214.0 MB".

CVU operation performed:      Free Space
Date:                         Aug 19, 2017 12:41:43 PM
CVU home:                     /u01/app/12.2.0.1/grid/
User:                         oracle
[oracle@stpldb101 grid]$ echo $?
0
```

While `cluvfy comp free space` is handy, it is a bit limited in what it can do. Still, it does have its uses as a quick check of whether there is any free space in the Grid Infrastructure home. It will check only whether the file system has 5 percent free space and will check only the Grid Infrastructure home. Moreover, the command does not indicate whether a space check failed with a return code, which can complicate scripting.

Generic Space Checks

There exists another type of file system free space check within the Cluster Verification Utility, and that is the one provided by `cluvfy comp space`. This type of verification is much more robust and comes with the added benefit of return codes that change depending on whether the check fails or succeeds.

To illustrate the utility of this particular verification, the output of a check on the Oracle user's home ($HOME) is shown here:

```
[oracle@stpldb101 ~]$ cluvfy comp space -n all -l /home/oracle/ -z 20G
-verbose

Verifying Available File System Space ...
  Node Name      Available                        Required                    Status
  ------------   ------------------------------   -------------------------   -------
  stpldb102      28.1875GB (2.9556736E7KB)        20GB (2.097152E7KB)         passed
  stpldb101      11.5938GB (1.2156928E7KB)        20GB (2.097152E7KB)         failed
Verifying Available File System Space ...FAILED

Verification of space availability was unsuccessful.
Checks did not pass for the following nodes:
        stpldb101

Failures were encountered during execution of CVU verification request
"space availability".

Verifying Available File System Space ...FAILED
stpldb101: Sufficient space is not available at location "/home/oracle" on node
"stpldb101" [Required space = 20GB (2.097152E7KB); available space = 11.5938GB
(1.2156928E7KB)]

CVU operation performed:      space availability
```

```
Date:                       Aug 19, 2017 4:14:49 PM
CVU home:                   /u01/app/12.2.0.1/grid/
User:                       oracle
[oracle@stpldb101 ~]$ echo $?
1
```

Cluster Verification Utility Health Checks

The Cluster Verification Utility can be used to perform health checks on three major components: databases, ASM, and clusters. We will go in depth on the health checks available for all three.

Database Health Checks

This type of check cannot be run without first performing some setup. Because CVU needs to connect to a database to run health checks and check for best-practice adherence, credentials need to be stored. Oracle uses a secure external password store also known as the *wallet*. The wallet will need to be set up for health checks to work properly for the database component. In this chapter, we will go over how to create such a wallet and how to run a health check using CVU.

CVU Wallets

Unlike the stand-alone Oracle connection wallets that can be used by regular clients, the wallet used by the Cluster Verification Utility is managed by the Grid Infrastructure software and is created, modified, and deleted via crsctl commands.

A wallet can be created by issuing the following command as the Grid Infrastructure owner. This will add a wallet entry for the user DBSNMP to the database orclcdb.

```
[oracle@stpldb101 admin]$ crsctl add wallet -name orclcdb -type CVUDB -user
DBSNMP -passwd
Enter Password:
```

In container databases, the DBSNMP user exists in the CDB$ROOT container. Ensure that the user is unlocked and has the same password that was placed into the wallet.

For example, the password database_123 is being used here; it is highly recommended to use secure passwords in a production environment.

```
SQL> alter user dbsnmp account unlock;

User altered.

SQL> alter user dbsnmp identified by "database_123";

User altered.

SQL> show con_name

CON_NAME
------------------------------
CDB$ROOT
```

Running the Health Check

The following is the expected output for the health check when it is run. This type of call to cvufy will save the output in a text file and will output only the deviations from best practices per the -deviations flag. If you require HTML output, you can use the -html flag. It is also important to note that cluvfy does not return a usable return code to decide whether deviations exist.

```
[oracle@stpldb101 admin]$ cluvfy comp healthcheck -collect database -db orclcdb -bestpractice -deviations -save -savedir /home/oracle/bestpractices

Verifying best practice for database "orclcdb"? >

*************************************************************************
        Summary of environment
*************************************************************************

Date (mm/dd/yyyy)    :  08/19/2018
Time (hh:mm:ss)      :  16:45:11
Cluster name         :  stpldb01
Clusterware version  :  12.2.0.1.0
```

```
Grid home            :  /u01/app/12.2.0.1/grid
Grid User            :  oracle
Operating system     :  Linux4.1.12-124.15.2.el6uek.x86_64
Database1            :  Database name    - orclcdb
                        Database version - 12.2.0.1.0
                        Database home    -
                        /u01/app/oracle/product/12.
                        2.0.1/dbhome_1


*************************************************************************
Database recommendation checks for "orclcdb"
*************************************************************************

Verification Check      :  Java Role Count
Verification Description :  Checks JVM roles
Verification Result     :  NOT MET
Verification Summary    :  Check for Java Role Count passed
Additional Details      :  A healthy JVM should contain six roles. If
                           there are more or less than six roles, the JVM
                           is inconsistent.

Verification Check      :  INVALID objects in the application related schemas
Verification Description :  Checks for the presence of INVALID objects in the
                           application related schemas (non SYS and SYSTEM)
Verification Result     :  NOT MET
Verification Summary    :  Check for INVALID objects in the application
                           related schemas passed
Additional Details      :  Investigate invalid objects in the application
                           related schemas (non SYS and SYSTEM).

Verification Check      :  Alert log messages indicating internal errors
                           ORA-07445
                           errors
```

Verification Description : Checks for ORA-07445 errors in alert log
Verification Result   : NOT MET
Verification Summary   : Check for Alert log messages indicating
                             internal errors ORA-07445 errors passed
Additional Details   : Recurring ORA-07445 errors may lead to
                             database block corruption or some serious
                             issue. See the trace file for more information
                             next to ORA-07445 error in alert log. If the
                             problem persists, contact Oracle Support
                             Services.

Verification Check   : FILESYSTEMIO_OPTIONS
Verification Description   : Checks FILESYSTEMIO_OPTIONS parameter
Verification Result   : NOT MET
Verification Summary   : Check for FILESYSTEMIO_OPTIONS passed
Additional Details   : FILESYSTEMIO_OPTIONS=setall supports both
                              direct I/O and asynchronus I/O which helps
                              to achieve optimal performance with database
                              data files

Complete report of this execution is saved in file "/home/oracle/
bestpractices/cvucheckreport_08192017164511.txt"

Verification of Health Check was successful.

Warnings were encountered during execution of CVU verification request
"Health Check".

Verifying Java Role Count ...WARNING
orclcdb: PRVE-2623 : The JVM roles appear to be inconsistent

Verifying INVALID objects in the application related schemas ...WARNING
orclcdb: PRVE-2563 : Application objects were found to be invalid

```
Verifying Alert log messages indicating internal errors ORA-07445 errors
...WARNING
orclcdb(orclcdb1): PRVE-2923 : ORA-07445 errors found in the alert log in alert
                   log destination
                   "/u01/app/oracle/diag/rdbms/orclcdb/orclcdb1/alert/" on node
                   "stpldb101.localdomain".

orclcdb(orclcdb2): PRVE-2923 : ORA-07445 errors found in the alert log in alert
                   log destination
                   "/u01/app/oracle/diag/rdbms/orclcdb/orclcdb2/alert/" on node
                   "stpldb102.localdomain".

Verifying FILESYSTEMIO_OPTIONS ...WARNING
orclcdb: PRVE-10138 : FILESYSTEMIO_OPTIONS is not set to the recommended value
         of setall

CVU operation performed:     Health Check
Date:                        Aug 19, 2018 4:44:59 PM
CVU home:                    /u01/app/12.2.0.1/grid/
User:                        oracle
```

A set of "mandatory" checks can also be done. If you need to save them, you can save them to a directory using the -save and -savedir flags. The following is an example of the type of checks that can be run:

```
[oracle@stpldb101 ~]$ cluvfy comp healthcheck -collect database -db orclcdb
-mandatory

Verifying mandatory requirements for database "orclcdb"

Verifying Easy Connect configuration:orclcdb ...passed
Verifying AUDIT_FILE_DEST location check ...met
Verifying Database operating system groups consistency check ...met
Verifying DB Initialization Parameters ...met
Verifying ACFS device special file ...met
Verifying /dev/shm mounted as temporary file system ...met

Verifying disk free space for Oracle Clusterware home "/u01/app/12.2.0.1/
grid"...passed
```

```
**************************************************************************
        Summary of environment
**************************************************************************

Date (mm/dd/yyyy)      :  08/19/2018
Time (hh:mm:ss)        :  16:54:57
Cluster name           :  stpldb01
Clusterware version    :  12.2.0.1.0
Grid home              :  /u01/app/12.2.0.1/grid
Grid User              :  oracle
Operating system       :  Linux4.1.12-124.15.2.el6uek.x86_64
Database1              :  Database name     -  orclcdb
                          Database version  -  12.2.0.1.0
                          Database home     -
                          /u01/app/oracle/product/12.
                          2.0.1/dbhome_1

**************************************************************************
Database requirement checks for "orclcdb"
**************************************************************************

Verification Check        :  Easy Connect configuration:orclcdb
Verification Description   :  This check ensures that the Easy Connect is
                              configured as an Oracle Net name resolution
                              method
Verification Result        :  PASSED

Node            Status     Expected Value                  Actual Value
-------------------------------------------------------------------------

stpldb102       PASSED     not applicable                  not applicable
stpldb101       PASSED     not applicable                  not applicable
_____
```

```
Verification Check         :  AUDIT_FILE_DEST location check
Verification Description    :  This task checks that AUDIT_FILE_DEST
                               parameter designates a ACFS storage location
                               that is not shared by any other instance of
                               the database
Verification Result        :  MET

Node             Status    Expected Value              Actual Value
---------------------------------------------------------------------------

orclcdb          PASSED    not applicable              not applicable
```

```
Verification Check         :  Database operating system groups consistency check
Verification Description    :  This task verifies consistency of database operating
                               system groups across nodes.
Verification Result        :  MET

Database(Instance) Status   Expected Value              Actual Value
---------------------------------------------------------------------------

orclcdb          PASSED    not applicable              not applicable
```

```
Verification Check         :  DB Initialization Parameters
Verification Description    :  This task collects DB Initialization
                               Parameters
Verification Result        :  MET

Database(Instance) Status   Expected Value              Actual Value
---------------------------------------------------------------------------

orclcdb2         Unknown   not applicable              not applicable
orclcdb1         Unknown   not applicable              not applicable
orclcdb          PASSED    not applicable              not applicable
```

```
Verification Check         :  ACFS device special file
Verification Description   :  checks the attributes for the ACFS device
                              special file
Verification Result        :  MET
Verification Summary       :  Check for ACFS device special file passed
Additional Details         :  The device special file attributes for '/dev/
                              ofsctl' must be set correctly in order for the
                              ASM instance to function correctly.
```

Node	Status	Expected Value	Actual Value
stpldb102	PASSED	not applicable	not applicable
stpldb101	PASSED	not applicable	not applicable

```
Verification Check         :  /dev/shm mounted as temporary file system
Verification Description   :  Checks whether /dev/shm is mounted correctly
                              as temporary file system
Verification Result        :  MET
Verification Summary       :  Check for /dev/shm mounted as temporary file
                              system passed
```

Node	Status	Expected Value	Actual Value
stpldb102	PASSED	true	true
stpldb101	PASSED	true	true

Verification of Health Check was unsuccessful.
Checks did not pass for the following database instances:
        orclcdb2,orclcdb1

```
CVU operation performed:    Health Check
Date:                       Aug 19, 2018 4:54:46 PM
CVU home:                   /u01/app/12.2.0.1/grid/
User:                       oracle
```

Cluster Health Checks

The Cluster Verification Utility can also perform ASM- and OS-level health checks. The
-collect cluster flag will indicate that both ASM- and OS-level checks need to be
done, although -collect asm can be used to gather only ASM-level information.

For example, the following health check found both that there are ASM disks that
do not belong to any ASM disk group (i.e., wasted space) and that jumbo frames are not
configured for the cluster interconnects, an OS-level check.

```
[oracle@stpldb101 ~]$ cluvfy comp healthcheck -collect cluster
-bestpractice -deviations

Verifying OS Best Practice

Verifying Ethernet Jumbo Frames ...not met

Verifying Clusterware Best Practice

Verifying ASM best practices


**************************************************************************
        Summary of environment
**************************************************************************

Date (mm/dd/yyyy)   :  08/19/2018
Time (hh:mm:ss)     :  17:00:37
Cluster name        :  stpldb01
Clusterware version :  12.2.0.1.0
Grid home           :  /u01/app/12.2.0.1/grid
Grid User           :  oracle
Operating system    :  Linux4.1.12-124.15.2.el6uek.x86_64
```

```
**********************************************************************
System recommendations
**********************************************************************

Verification Check       :  Ethernet Jumbo Frames
Verification Description  :  Checks if Jumbo Frames are configured on the
                            system
Verification Result      :  NOT MET
Verification Summary     :  Check for Ethernet Jumbo Frames failed
Additional Details       :  A performance improvement can be seen with
                            Jumbo Frames, check with your system and
                            network administrator first and if possible,
                            configure Jumbo Frames on interconnect.
                            See reference for more detail specific to
                            platform.
References (URLs/Notes)   :  http://docs.hp.com/en/AB290-90001/ch01s11.
                            html?jumpid=reg_R
                            1002_USEN
                            http://www.sun.com/products/networking/
                            ethernet/jumbo/
                            http://kbserver.netgear.com/kb_web_files/
                            n101539.asp
                            http://www.cisco.com/en/US/products/hw/
                            switches/ps700/produ
                            cts_configuration_example09186a008010edab.shtml
                            http://www.juniper.net/company/presscenter/
                            pr/2005/pr-05081
                            5.html
                            http://darkwing.uoregon.edu/~joe/jumbo-clean-
                            gear.html
                            http://www.dell.com/content/products/
                            productdetails.aspx/pw
                            cnt_2724?c=us&cs=04&l=en&s=bsd
                            http://www.intel.com/support/network/adapter/
                            index.htm
```

```
Node            Status    Expected Value                    Actual Value
--------------------------------------------------------------------------
stpldb102       NOT MET   eth1=9000;eth2=9000               eth1=1500;eth2=1500
stpldb101       NOT MET   eth1=9000;eth2=9000               eth1=1500;eth2=1500
```

```
**************************************************************************
ASM recommendations
**************************************************************************

Verification Check         :  Disks without disk_group
Verification Description   :  Check disks without disk group
Verification Result        :  NOT MET
Verification Summary       :  Check for Disks without disk_group passed
Additional Details         :  The GROUP_NUMBER and DISK_NUMBER columns in
                              V$ASM_DISK will only be valid if the disk
                              is part of a disk group which is currently
                              mounted by the instance. Otherwise, GROUP_
                              NUMBER will be 0, and DISK_NUMBER will be a
                              unique value with respect to the other disks
                              that also have a group number of 0.
```

```
Verification of Health Check was unsuccessful.
Checks did not pass for the following nodes:
        stpldb102,stpldb101

Failures were encountered during execution of CVU verification request
"Health Check".

Verifying Ethernet Jumbo Frames ...FAILED
stpldb102: PRVE-0293 : Jumbo Frames are not configured for interconnects
           "eth1,eth2" on node "stpldb102.localdomain".
           [Expected="eth1=9000;eth2=9000"; Found="eth1=1500;eth2=1500"]
```

```
stpldb101: PRVE-0293 : Jumbo Frames are not configured for interconnects
          "eth1,eth2" on node "stpldb101.localdomain".
          [Expected="eth1=9000;eth2=9000"; Found="eth1=1500;eth2=1500"]

Verifying Disks without disk_group ...WARNING
AFD:OCR_1C: PRVE-3073 : Disks "AFD:OCR_1C" are not part of any disk group.

AFD:OCR_1B: PRVE-3073 : Disks "AFD:OCR_1B" are not part of any disk group.

AFD:OCR_1A: PRVE-3073 : Disks "AFD:OCR_1A" are not part of any disk group.

CVU operation performed:      Health Check
Date:                         Aug 19, 2018 5:00:27 PM
CVU home:                     /u01/app/12.2.0.1/grid/
User:                         oracle
```

Cluster Verification Utility Baselines

A related feature to the health checks is the ability to create baselines and then compare them. The Cluster Verification Utility will store the contents of a health check so that it can be referenced in the future to help highlight changes in a cluster. The following example shows a way to collect best-practice information on all components on an Oracle Real Application Cluster and save them as a baseline called baseline1. The raw output is shown to help you understand the type of data that is collected by baselines.

It should be noted that if the -collect all flag is used, a baseline for best practices will be performed for any databases in the cluster. For this reason, it is recommended that you store DBSNMP passwords for all databases in the cluster.

```
[oracle@stpldb101 ~]$ cluvfy comp baseline -collect all -bestpractice -n
all -reportname baseline1

Collecting OS best practice baseline

Collecting HugePages Existence ...collected
Collecting Hardware Clock synchronization at shutdown ...collected
```

```
Collecting availability of port 8888 ...collected
Collecting Ethernet Jumbo Frames ...collected

Collecting Clusterware best practice baseline

Collecting CSS misscount parameter ...collected
Collecting CSS reboottime parameter ...collected
Collecting CSS disktimeout parameter ...collected

Collecting Database best practice baseline for database "orclcdb"

Collecting OPTIMIZER_DYNAMIC_SAMPLING ...collected
Collecting Invalid Java Objects ...collected
Collecting SYSAUX tablespace existence ...collected
Collecting JVM configuration for database ...collected
Collecting Java based user in database ...collected
Collecting Java Role Count ...collected
Collecting Invalid SYS or SYSTEM Schema Objects ...collected
Collecting INVALID objects in the application related schemas ...collected
Collecting SPFILE ...collected
Collecting Database word size(bits) ...collected
Collecting Duplicate SYS or SYSTEM Schema Objects ...collected
Collecting MAX_DUMP_FILE_SIZE ...collected
Collecting REMOTE_LISTENER ...collected
Collecting Database Datafiles in Backup Mode ...collected
Collecting Files Needing Media Recovery ...collected
Collecting In-doubt Distributed Transactions ...collected
Collecting SYS-Owned Object Tables Check ...collected
Collecting Invalid Objects in dba_registry ...collected
Collecting Materialized View Group Refresh Jobs ...collected
Collecting Materialized View Manual Group Refresh ...collected
Collecting Redo Log Size (MB) ...collected
Collecting All tablespaces are locally managed ...collected
Collecting Cluster Interconnects ...collected
Collecting Core files destination ...collected
```

```
Collecting Alert log messages indicating internal errors ORA-00600 errors
...collected
Collecting Alert log messages indicating internal errors ORA-07445 errors
...collected
Collecting Old trace files in background dump destination ...collected
Collecting Database alert log file size ...collected
Collecting Automatic segment storage management ...collected
Collecting Average GC CR Block Receive Time ...collected
Collecting Average GC Current Block Receive Time ...collected
Collecting Automatic Undo Management ...collected
Collecting FILESYSTEMIO_OPTIONS ...collected

Verifying ASM best practices

Collecting ASM_POWER_LIMIT ...collected
Collecting ASM disk I/O error ...collected
Collecting Disks without disk_group ...collected
Collecting ASM SHARED_POOL_SIZE parameter ...collected
Collecting ASM disk group free space ...collected
Collecting ASM disk rebalance operations in WAIT status ...collected

Baseline collected.
Collection report for this execution is saved in file "/u01/app/oracle/
crsdata/@global/cvu/baseline/users/baseline1.zip".

CVU operation performed:       baseline
Date:                          Aug 19, 2018 5:10:31 PM
Cluster name:                  stpldb01
Clusterware version:           12.2.0.1.0
Grid home:                     /u01/app/12.2.0.1/grid
User:                          oracle
Operating system:              Linux4.1.12-124.15.2.el6uek.x86_64
```

At a later time, a comparison can be done of stored baselines. Baselines exist as
zip files within the CVU home and should be referenced by their absolute file path in a
comparison operation. Comparisons can be made of baselines from other clusters using
the -cross_compare flag, which is not shown in this example.

```
[oracle@stpldb101 ~]$ cluvfy comp baseline -compare /u01/app/oracle/
crsdata/@global/cvu/baseline/users/baseline1.zip,/u01/app/oracle/crsdata/
@global/cvu/baseline/users/baseline2.zip

Generating Baseline Report

Preparing the report..
Comparing "System Best Practices"
Comparing "Clusterware Best Practices"
Comparing "Best Practices for database "orclcdb""
Comparing "ASM Configuration Prerequisites"

Complete report of this execution is saved in file "/u01/app/oracle/
crsdata/@global/cvu/report/html/cvucheckreport_08192017171818.html"

Opening the report in the browser..

Baseline report generation successful

Verification of baseline was successful.

CVU operation performed:      baseline
Date:                         Aug 19, 2018 5:18:16 PM
CVU home:                     /u01/app/12.2.0.1/grid/
User:                         oracle
```

Orachk

Orachk is a tool that can be used to run more comprehensive health checks and best-practice tests in an Oracle environment. Orachk comes in two flavors: Orachk and Exachk. Exachk can be used on all engineered systems other than Oracle Database Appliance, and Orachk can be used on all other commodity or engineered systems running the Oracle stack. Orachk and Exachk are similar and overlap in almost all options that are not specific to the Exadata platform (such as cell storage server checks, and so on).

Orachk is installed in the Grid Infrastructure home as well as the Oracle database software home in $ORACLE_HOME/suptools/ and can also be downloaded from Oracle directly. Each PSU that is applied to these software homes stages the latest Orachk version in the $ORACLE_HOME/suptools directory. It is recommended that you download the latest Orachk version from the Oracle web site and install that instead of using the Orachk version that is bundled with the Grid Infrastructure home.

Upgrading Orachk

Provided that the server running Orachk has access to the Internet, Orachk will prompt the user that Orachk needs upgrading if the tool determines that the version being used is older than 120 days. For this particular example, the Orachk version found within the 12.2 Oracle Database home will be used to show how the tool automatically prompts for an upgrade if it finds itself to be too old.

```
[oracle@stpldb101 orachk]$ ./orachk
This version of orachk was released on 26-May-2016 and its older than 120 days.

Latest version of orachk (ORACHK  VERSION: 12.2.0.1.3_20170719) is
available at /u01/app/oracle/product/12.2.0.1/dbhome_1/suptools/.

Do you want to upgrade to the latest version of orachk? [y/n][y]y
```

Orachk/Exachk and Oracle RESTful Data Services

The latest versions of the Orachk and Exachk tools are now able to be used via REST calls. This is made possible by the use of Oracle's ORDS feature. ORDS can be set up for Orachk only via the root user and is available only on operating systems that are compatible with Orachk daemon mode.

The following is an example of how to configure Orachk with ORDS; it enables the automatic restart of the Orachk daemon in the case of server restarts.

When the flag -ordssetup is used, it will prompt for a user password. This is the password for a new OS user called orachkords, which will be used to run the orachk daemon. The orachkords username and password must be specified in all the REST calls made to the daemon from remote hosts.

[root@stpldb101 orachk_standalone]# ./orachk -ordssetup

```
Enter a password for the user
Confirm password for the user
Oracle Rest Data Service (ORDS) URL: https://stpldb101.localdomain:7080/
ords/tfaml/orachk

Please start the daemon using following command: orachk -d start -ords or
orachk -initsetup -ords before submitting APIs
```

Oracle Rest Data Service (ORDS) started successfully

[root@stpldb101 orachk_standalone]# ./orachk -initsetup -ords

Clusterware stack is running from /u01/app/12.2.0.1/grid. Is this the correct Clusterware Home?[y/n][y] y

Checking ssh user equivalency settings on all nodes in cluster for root

Node stpldb102 is not configured for ssh user equivalency and the orachk uses ssh to execute checks on remote nodes.
Without passwordless ssh orachk can not run audit checks on the remote nodes. If necessary due to security policies the orachk can be run on each node using -localonly option.

Do you want to configure SSH for user root on stpldb102 [y/n][y] y

Enter stpldb102 root password :
Verifying root password ...

Node stpldb102 has been configured for ssh user equivalency for root

Searching for running databases . . . . .

. .
List of running databases registered in OCR

1. orclcdb
2. None of above

Select databases from list for checking best practices. For multiple databases, select 1 for All or comma separated number like 1,2 etc [1-2] [1]. 1

. . . .
. . .

Copying plug-ins

. .
. . . . . .

Setting up orachk auto restart functionality

```
oracle-orachkscheduler start/running, process 22793
Starting orachk daemon. . . . . . . . . .

orachk daemon started successfully

Daemon log file location is : /home/oracle/orachk_standalone/orachk_daemon.log
```

The ORDS setup can easily be removed by using the -ordsrmsetup flag as the root user. This will also remove the orachkords user.

```
[root@stpldb101 ~]# cd /home/oracle/orachk_standalone/
[root@stpldb101 orachk_standalone]# ./orachk -ordsrmsetup

0 collections generated by Oracle Rest Data Service (ORDS) API found at /
home/orachkords
Executing (/home/oracle/orachk_standalone/orachk -initrmsetup) to stop the
orachk daemon
orachk daemon stopped successfully (mode=init)
Oracle Rest Data Service (ORDS) user - orachkords deleted successfully
```

Recommended Settings for Orachk Daemons

There are a few settings that should be configured for the Orachk daemon to ensure that regularly scheduled health checks do not silently fail and leave a system unmonitored for best-practice usage.

Notification Emails

At a minimum, one notification email needs to be set for Orachk if automatic health checks will be run. This will ensure that any noteworthy health check failures are alerted on, even if the health check reports are not being transmitted via e-mail.

```
[root@stpldb101 orachk_standalone]# ./orachk -set "NOTIFICATION_
EMAIL=oracheckadmin@supportteam.com"
```

Retention Periods

By default, Orachk and Exachk do not purge collections within any specific retention window. Therefore, a specific retention window needs to be set if disk space is at a premium. A retention for the collection of data can be set in terms of days, per the following example:

```
[root@stpldb101 orachk_standalone]# ./orachk -get collection_retention

-------------------------------------------------------------
ID: orachk.default
-------------------------------------------------------------
-------------------------------------------------------------


[root@stpldb101 orachk_standalone]# ./orachk -set "COLLECTION_RETENTION=90"

Updated ['COLLECTION_RETENTION=90'] for Id[orachk.DEFAULT]

[root@stpldb101 orachk_standalone]# ./orachk -get collection_retention

-------------------------------------------------------------
ID: orachk.default
-------------------------------------------------------------
COLLECTION_RETENTION  =  90
-------------------------------------------------------------

[root@stpldb101 orachk_standalone]#
```

Automated Password Verification Checks

Orachk saves passwords that are used for authentication so that the daemon can run health checks without manual intervention. However, if passwords are changed, health checks will fail and not produce output. It is a best practice to set an interval at which Orachk and Exachk verify that the stored passwords are still correct. If the passwords have changed, Orachk will send an e-mail to the list of recipients in the NOTIFICATION_EMAIL setting and stop running to allow the administrator to restart the daemon and re-enter the pertinent passwords. The password verification interval is specified in terms of hours.

```
[root@stpldb101 orachk_standalone]# ./orachk -set "PASSWORD_CHECK_INTERVAL=12"

Updated ['PASSWORD_CHECK_INTERVAL=12'] for Id[orachk.DEFAULT]
```

Trace File Analyzer

Trace File Analyzer (TFA) is arguably one of the most useful tools that Oracle has released for the Oracle Database and Grid Infrastructure software in terms of enabling Oracle DBAs to react quickly and analyze all the different logfiles that the Oracle software writes errors to. Trace File Analyzer, along with the Support Tools Bundle, is extremely powerful as a troubleshooting and diagnosis tool. Most of the features related to TFA are out of scope for this book a bit, but some of the new and exciting features that can be extremely useful will be touched upon in this chapter.

Upgrading TFA to Include the Support Tools Bundle

By default, TFA is upgraded with every quarterly update patch that comes out for Grid Infrastructure and the database software (12.2 and onward). However, the version of TFA that comes shipped with PSUs is generally three months behind what is available for download from Oracle Support. Furthermore, the version of TFA that comes with quarterly patches does not include the Support Tools Bundle, which has many useful features for diagnosing problems. The Support Tools Bundle can be downloaded from TFA Collector - TFA with Database Support Tools Bundle (**Doc ID 1513912.1**). While it is perfectly acceptable to use the TFA that is bundled with a standard Grid Infrastructure installation, you should download and install the Support Tools Bundle as shown in this chapter. This will upgrade your TFA with a multitude of new and useful features.

Upgrading TFA is extremely easy and consists of unzipping the download and running the executable script contained therein. Upgrading TFA will upgrade TFA for the entire cluster.

```
[oracle@stpldb101 ~]$ unzip TFA-LINUX_v18.3.0.zip
Archive:  TFA-LINUX_v18.3.0.zip
  inflating: README.txt
  inflating: installTFA-LINUX
```

TFA must be installed/patched as the root user. This is because certain TFA files are owned by root in a Grid Infrastructure software home and because init scripts need be modified.

Some of the following output has been abridged as it is essentially the same for remote node operations:

```
[root@stpldb101 oracle]# ./installTFA-LINUX
TFA Installation Log will be written to File : /tmp/tfa_
install_5857_2018_08_20-00_27_36.log

Starting TFA installation

TFA Version: 183000 Build Date: 201808081359

TFA HOME : /u01/app/12.2.0.1/grid/tfa/stpldb101/tfa_home

Installed Build Version: 181100 Build Date: 201803280250

TFA is already installed. Patching /u01/app/12.2.0.1/grid/tfa/stpldb101/
tfa_home...
TFA patching typical install from zipfile is written to /u01/app/12.2.0.1/
grid/tfa/stpldb101/tfapatch.log

TFA will be Patched on:
stpldb101
stpldb102

Do you want to continue with patching TFA? [Y|N] [Y]: Y

Checking for ssh equivalency in stpldb102
stpldb102 is configured for ssh user equivalency for root user

Using SSH to patch TFA to remote nodes :

Applying Patch on stpldb102:

TFA_HOME: /u01/app/12.2.0.1/grid/tfa/stpldb102/tfa_home
Stopping TFA Support Tools...
Shutting down TFA
oracle-tfa stop/waiting
. . . . .
Killing TFA running with pid 23847
. . .
Successfully shutdown TFA..
Copying files from stpldb101 to stpldb102...
```

```
Current version of Berkeley DB in stpldb102 is 5 or higher, so no
DbPreUpgrade required
Running commands to fix init.tfa and tfactl in stpldb102...
Updating init.tfa in stpldb102...
Starting TFA in stpldb102...
Starting TFA..
oracle-tfa start/running, process 10467
Waiting up to 100 seconds for TFA to be started..
. . . . .
Successfully started TFA Process..
. . . . .
TFA Started and listening for commands

Enabling Access for Non-root Users on stpldb102...

.------------------------------------------------------------------.
| Host      | TFA Version | TFA Build ID         | Upgrade Status |
+-----------+-------------+----------------------+----------------+
| stpldb101 |  18.3.0.0.0 | 18300020180808135947 | UPGRADED       |
| stpldb102 |  18.3.0.0.0 | 18300020180808135947 | UPGRADED       |
'-----------+-------------+----------------------+----------------'

cleanup serializable files
```

Using Trace File Analyzer to Manage Logfiles

Old logs need to be deleted once they are no longer relevant. Every DBA knows this, and most DBAs have scripts that help to automate this task as it quickly becomes burdensome the more databases and clusters that a DBA has to manage. Up until 11g, this was a manual process that required custom shell scripts to help with the maintenance; however, in 11g Oracle came out with a concept called Automatic Diagnostic Repository (ADR). Now, the latest versions of Trace File Analyzer have become integrated with ADR, which allows for streamlined maintenance of database and Grid Infrastructure logs.

Analyzing Logfile Space Usage

TFA can be used to display the file system space used by database logs.

```
[oracle@stpldb101 ~]$ tfactl managelogs -show usage -database orclcdb
Output from host : stpldb101
------------------------------

.-------------------------------------------------------------------.
|                      Database Homes Usage                         |
+---------------------------------------------------+---------------+
| Location                                          | Size          |
+---------------------------------------------------+---------------+
| /u01/app/oracle/diag/rdbms/orclcdb/orclcdb1/alert    | 1.81 MB    |
| /u01/app/oracle/diag/rdbms/orclcdb/orclcdb1/incident | 25.68 MB   |
| /u01/app/oracle/diag/rdbms/orclcdb/orclcdb1/trace    | 119.94 MB  |
| /u01/app/oracle/diag/rdbms/orclcdb/orclcdb1/cdump    | 136.58 MB  |
| /u01/app/oracle/diag/rdbms/orclcdb/orclcdb1/hm       | 4.00 KB    |
| /u01/app/oracle/diag/rdbms/orclcdb/orclcdb1/log      | 36.00 KB   |
+---------------------------------------------------+---------------+
| Total                                             | 284.05 MB  |
'---------------------------------------------------+-----------'

Output from host : stpldb102
------------------------------

.-------------------------------------------------------------------.
|                      Database Homes Usage                         |
+---------------------------------------------------+---------------+
| Location                                          | Size          |
+---------------------------------------------------+---------------+
| /u01/app/oracle/diag/rdbms/orclcdb/orclcdb2/alert    | 1.84 MB    |
| /u01/app/oracle/diag/rdbms/orclcdb/orclcdb2/incident | 7.05 MB    |
| /u01/app/oracle/diag/rdbms/orclcdb/orclcdb2/trace    | 82.30 MB   |
| /u01/app/oracle/diag/rdbms/orclcdb/orclcdb2/cdump    | 139.87 MB  |
| /u01/app/oracle/diag/rdbms/orclcdb/orclcdb2/hm       | 4.00 KB    |
| /u01/app/oracle/diag/rdbms/orclcdb/orclcdb2/log      | 32.00 KB   |
+---------------------------------------------------+---------------+
| Total                                             | 231.09 MB  |
'---------------------------------------------------+-----------'
```

More important, Trace File Analyzer can now be used to analyze the change or variation space usage. In the following example, the Old Size shows as - because the database was newly created:

```
[oracle@stpldb101 ~]$ tfactl managelogs -show variation -older 1d -database
orclcdb


Output from host : stpldb101
-------------------------------
2018-08-20 00:42:46: INFO Checking space variation for 1 days

2018-08-20 00:42:46: INFO Space is calculated in bytes [without round off]
```

```
.------------------------------------------------------------------------------.
|                           Database Homes Variation                           |
+------------------------------------------------+----------+----------+
| Directory                                      | Old Size | New Size |
+------------------------------------------------+----------+----------+
| /u01/app/oracle/diag/rdbms/orclcdb/orclcdb1/cdump    | -        | 136.58 MB |
+------------------------------------------------+----------+----------+
| /u01/app/oracle/diag/rdbms/orclcdb/orclcdb1/alert    | -        | 1.81 MB   |
+------------------------------------------------+----------+----------+
| /u01/app/oracle/diag/rdbms/orclcdb/orclcdb1/incident | -        | 25.68 MB  |
+------------------------------------------------+----------+----------+
| /u01/app/oracle/diag/rdbms/orclcdb/orclcdb1/log      | -        | 36.00 KB  |
+------------------------------------------------+----------+----------+
| /u01/app/oracle/diag/rdbms/orclcdb/orclcdb1/trace    | -        | 119.99 MB |
+------------------------------------------------+----------+----------+
| /u01/app/oracle/diag/rdbms/orclcdb/orclcdb1/hm       | -        | 4.00 KB   |
'------------------------------------------------+----------+----------'
```

```
Output from host : stpldb102
-------------------------------
2018-08-20 00:42:54: INFO Checking space variation for 1 days

2018-08-20 00:42:54: INFO Space is calculated in bytes [without round off]
```

```
.------------------------------------------------------------------------.
|                        Database Homes Variation                        |
+------------------------------------------------+----------+----------+
| Directory                                      | Old Size | New Size |
+------------------------------------------------+----------+----------+
| /u01/app/oracle/diag/rdbms/orclcdb/orclcdb2/log      | -        | 32.00 KB |
+------------------------------------------------+----------+----------+
| /u01/app/oracle/diag/rdbms/orclcdb/orclcdb2/alert    | -        | 1.84 MB  |
+------------------------------------------------+----------+----------+
| /u01/app/oracle/diag/rdbms/orclcdb/orclcdb2/cdump    | -        | 139.87 MB|
+------------------------------------------------+----------+----------+
| /u01/app/oracle/diag/rdbms/orclcdb/orclcdb2/incident | -        | 7.05 MB  |
+------------------------------------------------+----------+----------+
| /u01/app/oracle/diag/rdbms/orclcdb/orclcdb2/hm       | -        | 4.00 KB  |
+------------------------------------------------+----------+----------+
| /u01/app/oracle/diag/rdbms/orclcdb/orclcdb2/trace    | -        | 82.35 MB |
'------------------------------------------------+----------+----------'
```

Purging Database Logfiles

By default, TFA will purge files that are older than 30 days if -purge is not specified. In the following example, all logs are purged because of the -purge 0d setting (all files older than zero days):

```
[oracle@stpldb101 ~]$ tfactl managelogs -purge -older 0d -database orclcdb

Output from host : stpldb101
-------------------------------
2018-08-20 01:00:59: INFO Purging files older than 0 days

2018-08-20 01:00:59: INFO Space is calculated in bytes [without round off]

2018-08-20 01:00:59: INFO Cleaning Database Home destinations
```

```
2018-08-20 01:01:04: INFO Purging diagnostic destination "diag/rdbms/
orclcdb/orclcdb1" for files - 2598 files deleted , 276.98 MB freed
2018-08-20 01:01:04: MESSAGE Database Home : /u01/app/oracle/product/
12.2.0.1/dbhome_1 [ Files deleted : 2598 files | Space Freed : 276.98 MB ]


.----------------------------------------------------------------.
| File System Variation : /u01/app/oracle/product/12.2.0.1/dbhome_1 |
+--------+------+----------+----------+----------+----------+-------+
| State  | Name | Size     | Used     | Free     | Capacity | Mount |
+--------+------+----------+----------+----------+----------+-------+
| Before |      | 96888540 | 76662696 | 15721604 |     83%  | /     |
| After  |      | 96888540 | 76373716 | 16010584 |     83%  | /     |
'--------+------+----------+----------+----------+----------+-------'

Output from host : stpldb102
-------------------------------

2018-08-20 01:01:06: INFO Purging files older than 0 days

2018-08-20 01:01:06: INFO Space is calculated in bytes [without round off]

2018-08-20 01:01:06: INFO Cleaning Database Home destinations

2018-08-20 01:01:08: INFO Purging diagnostic destination "diag/rdbms/
orclcdb/orclcdb2" for files - 1513 files deleted , 226.99 MB freed
2018-08-20 01:01:08: MESSAGE Database Home : /u01/app/oracle/
product/12.2.0.1/dbhome_1 [ Files deleted : 1513 files | Space Freed :
226.99 MB ]


.----------------------------------------------------------------.
| File System Variation : /u01/app/oracle/product/12.2.0.1/dbhome_1 |
+--------+------+----------+----------+----------+----------+-------+
| State  | Name | Size     | Used     | Free     | Capacity | Mount |
+--------+------+----------+----------+----------+----------+-------+
| Before |      | 96888540 | 70290896 | 22093400 |     77%  | /     |
| After  |      | 96888540 | 70055416 | 22328880 |     76%  | /     |
'--------+------+----------+----------+----------+----------+-------'
```

TFA as a Health Check Tool

Trace File Analyzer can be used to analyze logfiles on several components over a range of time for errors or warnings. This can be extremely useful as an ongoing monitoring solution for large clusters.

To show the power of this type of analysis, this example will show how all of the logfiles managed by TFA can be quickly analyzed to look for a particular type of error. In this case, the logs will be analyzed to search for any mention of swapping to check for memory pressure conditions on a particular host. All the necessary logs were analyzed within two seconds, and a report was ouput to the screen. Furthermore, tfactl changed the return code depending on the findings, which lends itself to a tfactl-centered shell script as a monitoring solution.

[oracle@stpldb101 ~]$ tfactl analyze -comp all -last 1d -type error -search "swapping" -node local
```
INFO: analyzing all (Alert and Unix System Logs) logs for the last 1440
minutes...  Please wait...
INFO: analyzing host: stpldb101

                 Report title: Analysis of Alert,System Logs
            Report date range: last ~1 day(s)
    Report (default) time zone: EST - Eastern Standard Time
           Analysis started at: 20-Aug-2018 01:13:51 AM EDT
         Elapsed analysis time: 2 second(s).
            Configuration file: /u01/app/12.2.0.1/grid/tfa/stpldb101/
                                tfa_home/ext/tnt/conf/tnt.prop
            Configuration group: all
                     Parameter: swapping
           Total message count:       18,695, from 02-Jul-2018 07:42:39 PM
                                      EDT to 20-Aug-2018 01:13:44 AM EDT
 Messages matching last ~1 day(s):      9,172, from 19-Aug-2018 01:14:00 AM
                                      EDT to 20-Aug-2018 01:13:44 AM EDT
                Matching regex: swapping
                Case sensitive: false
                   Match count: 5

[Source: /u01/app/oracle/diag/rdbms/orclcdb/orclcdb1/trace/alert_orclcdb1.
log, Line: 4847]
```

Aug 19 02:01:28 2018
WARNING: Heavy swapping observed on system in last 5 mins.
Heavy swapping can lead to timeouts, poor performance, and instance eviction.
Errors in file /u01/app/oracle/diag/rdbms/orclcdb/orclcdb1/trace/orclcdb1_
dbrm_31124.trc (incident=72122) (PDBNAME=CDB$ROOT):
ORA-00700: soft internal error, arguments: [kskvmstatact: excessive
swapping observed], [], [], [], [], [], [], [], [], [], []
Incident details in: /u01/app/oracle/diag/rdbms/orclcdb/orclcdb1/incident/
incdir_72122/orclcdb1_dbrm_31124_i72122.trc

[Source: /u01/app/oracle/diag/rdbms/_mgmtdb/-MGMTDB/trace/alert_-MGMTDB.
log, Line: 6135]
Aug 19 02:02:35 2018
WARNING: Heavy swapping observed on system in last 5 mins.
Heavy swapping can lead to timeouts, poor performance, and instance eviction.
Errors in file /u01/app/oracle/diag/rdbms/_mgmtdb/-MGMTDB/trace/-MGMTDB_
dbrm_14223.trc (incident=44115) (PDBNAME=CDB$ROOT):
ORA-00700: soft internal error, arguments: [kskvmstatact: excessive
swapping observed], [], [], [], [], [], [], [], [], [], []
Incident details in: /u01/app/oracle/diag/rdbms/_mgmtdb/-MGMTDB/incident/
incdir_44115/-MGMTDB_dbrm_14223_i44115.trc

[Source: /u01/app/oracle/diag/rdbms/orclcdb/orclcdb1/trace/alert_orclcdb1.
log, Line: 4946]
Aug 19 04:56:44 2018
WARNING: Heavy swapping observed on system in last 5 mins.
Heavy swapping can lead to timeouts, poor performance, and instance eviction.
Errors in file /u01/app/oracle/diag/rdbms/orclcdb/orclcdb1/trace/orclcdb1_
dbrm_31124.trc (incident=72123) (PDBNAME=CDB$ROOT):
ORA-00700: soft internal error, arguments: [kskvmstatact: excessive
swapping observed], [], [], [], [], [], [], [], [], [], []
Incident details in: /u01/app/oracle/diag/rdbms/orclcdb/orclcdb1/incident/
incdir_72123/orclcdb1_dbrm_31124_i72123.trc

[Source: /u01/app/oracle/diag/rdbms/orclcdb/orclcdb1/trace/alert_orclcdb1.
log, Line: 4979]
Aug 19 06:08:03 2018

```
WARNING: Heavy swapping observed on system in last 5 mins.
Heavy swapping can lead to timeouts, poor performance, and instance eviction.

[Source: /u01/app/oracle/diag/rdbms/orclcdb/orclcdb1/trace/alert_orclcdb1.
log, Line: 4982]
Aug 19 06:08:06 2018
Errors in file /u01/app/oracle/diag/rdbms/orclcdb/orclcdb1/trace/orclcdb1_
dbrm_31124.trc  (incident=72124) (PDBNAME=CDB$ROOT):
ORA-00700: soft internal error, arguments: [kskvmstatact: excessive
swapping observed], [], [], [], [], [], [], [], [], [], [], []
Incident details in: /u01/app/oracle/diag/rdbms/orclcdb/orclcdb1/incident/
incdir_72124/orclcdb1_dbrm_31124_i72124.trc
[oracle@stpldb101 ~]$ echo $?
1
```

New Health Check and Troubleshooting Features in 12.2

Oracle introduced a new health check and troubleshooting feature in 12.2 that can aid in identifying and resolving issues. Using this new feature in conjunction with the rest of the features outlined in this chapter should help to prepare a DBA for even the most vexing of performance issues.

Cluster Health Advisor

The Cluster Health Advisor is available via the chactl command and can be used to diagnose both at the cluster level and at the database level if -cluster is replaced with -db <DB_UNIQUE_NAME>.

```
[oracle@stpldb101 ~]$ chactl query diagnosis -cluster -start "2018-08-20
00:00:00" -end "2018-08-20 08:00:00"
2018-08-20 00:01:40.0  Host stpldb102  Host Memory Consumption [detected]
2018-08-20 00:01:50.0  Host stpldb101  Host Memory Consumption [detected]
2018-08-20 00:02:50.0  Host stpldb101  Host CPU Utilization [detected]
2018-08-20 00:04:35.0  Host stpldb101  Host Memory Swapping [detected]
2018-08-20 00:04:45.0  Host stpldb101  Host CPU Utilization [cleared]
```

```
2018-08-20 00:09:15.0  Host stpldb101  Host Memory Swapping [cleared]
2018-08-20 00:09:25.0  Host stpldb102  Host CPU Utilization [detected]
2018-08-20 00:16:10.0  Host stpldb102  Host CPU Utilization [cleared]
2018-08-20 00:16:10.0  Host stpldb102  Host Memory Consumption [cleared]
2018-08-20 00:18:20.0  Host stpldb102  Host Memory Consumption [detected]
2018-08-20 00:19:20.0  Host stpldb102  Host CPU Utilization [detected]
2018-08-20 00:27:05.0  Host stpldb102  Host CPU Utilization [cleared]
2018-08-20 00:30:20.0  Host stpldb102  Host CPU Utilization [detected]
2018-08-20 00:31:30.0  Host stpldb101  Host CPU Utilization [detected]
2018-08-20 00:33:50.0  Host stpldb101  Host CPU Utilization [cleared]
2018-08-20 00:34:50.0  Host stpldb102  Host CPU Utilization [cleared]
2018-08-20 02:01:05.0  Host stpldb102  Host CPU Utilization [detected]
2018-08-20 02:05:40.0  Host stpldb102  Host CPU Utilization [cleared]
2018-08-20 02:31:40.0  Host stpldb102  Host CPU Utilization [detected]
2018-08-20 02:56:55.0  Host stpldb102  Host CPU Utilization [cleared]
2018-08-20 04:00:55.0  Host stpldb102  Host CPU Utilization [detected]
2018-08-20 04:05:40.0  Host stpldb102  Host CPU Utilization [cleared]
2018-08-20 06:01:20.0  Host stpldb102  Host CPU Utilization [detected]
2018-08-20 06:05:45.0  Host stpldb102  Host CPU Utilization [cleared]
```

Problem: Host Memory Consumption

Description: CHA detected that more memory than expected is consumed on this server. The memory is not allocated by sessions of this database.

Cause: The Cluster Health Advisor (CHA) detected an increase in memory consumption by other databases or by applications not connected to a database on this node.

Action: Identify the top memory consumers by using the Cluster Health Monitor (CHM).

Problem: Host CPU Utilization

Description: CHA detected larger than expected CPU utilization on this node. The available CPU resource may not be sufficient to support application failover or relocation of databases to this node.

Cause: The Cluster Health Advisor (CHA) detected an unexpected increase in CPU utilization by databases or applications on this node.

Action: Identify CPU intensive processes and databases by reviewing Cluster Health Monitoring (CHM) data. Relocate databases to less busy machines, or limit the number of connections to databases on this node. Add nodes if more resources are required.

Problem: Host Memory Swapping
Description: CHA detected that there is not enough free memory on this server and memory swapping has started. The performance of databases on other nodes in this cluster will be affected severely. An instance eviction is likely if swapping continues.
Cause: The Cluster Health Advisor (CHA) detected that there was no more free memory because the memory requirements of processes increased.
Action: Stop database services on this server, or shut down less important database instances. Redirect the applications to the available healthy servers. Check the CHA diagnostics for the health of the other servers and databases. Add servers if more memory is required. Ensure that Huge Pages are correctly configured and used.

The Cluster Health Advisor uses data stored in the MGMTDB (Grid Management Infrastructure Repository). The amount of space used by the Grid Infrastructure Management Repository is directly correlated with the max retention (up to 168 hours) and the amount of entities/targets (up to 512) being tracked by Cluster Health Advisor.

```
[oracle@stpldb101 ~]$ chactl query repository
specified max retention time(hrs): 72
available retention time(hrs)    : 617
available number of entities     : 17
allocated number of entities     : 2
total repository size(gb)        : 15.00
allocated repository size(gb)    : 0.26
```

Summary

This chapter covered a lot of the new and old troubleshooting and health check topics in the hope of raising your awareness of the amazing options available to DBAs, especially with the new features of TFA, Orachk, and latest features in 12.2.

CHAPTER 6

Best Practices in Oracle Data Guard with Tips and Techniques

This chapter expands the book's Data Guard coverage and explains how to use many of the new features of Oracle Data Guard so you can start using them and get more use from your Oracle Data Guard databases.

Creating a Standby Database Using DBCA

In 12c R2, it is possible to create Data Guard standby databases with the Database Creation Assistant Utility (DBCA). This can be accomplished with a one-liner CLI call that is parameterized and can be used to greatly enhance and simplify attempts at creating DBaaS offerings that are developed in-house. This feature is an extension of DBCA's capabilities to duplicate databases.

Expected Error Messages per Limitations

While this feature is useful, there are a few drawbacks. For one, it is not possible to make Data Guard standby databases using DBCA when the primary database is a cluster database. The second, and probably most limiting factor, is that container databases (CDBs) are not supported. Therefore, this can be used only on single-instance noncontainer databases.

293

© Y V Ravi Kumar, Nassyam Basha, Krishna Kumar K M, Bal Mukund Sharma, Konstantin Kerekovski 2019
Y V Ravi Kumar et al., *Oracle High Availability, Disaster Recovery, and Cloud Services*,
https://doi.org/10.1007/978-1-4842-4351-0_6

As stated earlier, if the primary database is a cluster database, DBCA will fail with the following error:

```
[FATAL] [DBT-16056] Specified primary database is not a Single Instance
(SI) database.
   CAUSE: Duplicate database operation is supported only for SI databases.
```

A similar error message is also displayed if the primary database is a CDB.

```
[FATAL] [DBT-16057] Specified primary database is a container database (CDB).
   CAUSE: Duplicate database operation is supported only for non container
databases.
```

Example of a DBCA-Created Standby

Creating a simple Data Guard standby database is fairly straightforward with DBCA. The main flags that need to be passed to DBCA are -createDuplicateDB and -createAsStandby.

```
[oracle@rac501 ~]$ dbca -silent \
> -createDuplicateDB \
> -primaryDBConnectionString stpldb01-scan:1521/orcl.world \
> -gdbName orcl.world -sid orcldr \
> -createAsStandby -dbUniqueName orcldr \
> -datafileDestination +DATA/
Enter SYS user password:

[WARNING] [DBT-11203] Java pool size specified is too small.
   ACTION: Java pool size of at least (20MB) is recommended.
Listener config step
33% complete
Auxiliary instance creation
66% complete
RMAN duplicate
100% complete
Look at the log file "/u01/app/oracle/cfgtoollogs/dbca/orcldr/orcl.log" for
further details.
```

Alternative Ways to Supply the SYS Password

Whether you're using DBCA to create a Data Guard standby or a normal duplicate database, you will need to specify credentials for the SYS account in some way. There are two main ways this can be done. Credentials can be entered interactively (DBCA requests the SYS password from the standard input, as shown earlier), or credentials can be passed in I/O redirection.

I/O Redirection

Do note that the > characters are the by-product of using \ to escape newline characters and denote a continuation of a single command. In this example, the SYS password database_123 is being redirected into the command. Special care should be made to ensure that the password is not exposed in the running list of processes viewable by ps.

Here is an example of redirecting using a here-document.

```
[oracle@rac501 ~]$ dbca -silent -createDuplicateDB \
> -primaryDBConnectionString  stpldb01-scan:1521/orcl.world \
> -gdbName orcl.world -sid orcldr \
> -createAsStandby -dbUniqueName orcldr \
> -datafileDestination +DATA/ <<EOF
> database_123
> EOF
```

Here is an example of redirecting using a pipe.

```
[oracle@rac501 ~]$ echo "database_123" | dbca -silent -createDuplicateDB \
> -primaryDBConnectionString  stpldb01-scan:1521/orcl.world \
> -gdbName orcl.world -sid orcldr \
> -createAsStandby -dbUniqueName orcldr \
> -datafileDestination +DATA/
```

Diagnostic Pack on Active Data Guard

Starting with 12c R2, Oracle supports the Diagnostic Pack on an Active Data Guard instance database. As more and more people are starting to leverage this Active Data Guard feature to offload read-only workloads to Data Guard standby databases, the need for performance monitoring and tuning features provided by the Diagnostic Pack has been satisfied in 12c R2 with the Remote Management Framework.

Because ADG databases are in read-only mode, they cannot persist AWR information. Therefore, Active Workload Repository (AWR) data is transmitted to the primary database from the standby so that it can be persisted in the Active Workload Repository for later use by AWR reports. The communications between the primary database and the standby databases are mediated by database links that connect as the SYS$UMF user. In the context of the Remote Management Framework, the primary database is considered the *destination database*, and the standby database is considered the *source database*. This is because the standby database is the *source* of the AWR data in question, and the primary database is the *destination* to which the standby database sends its AWR data. The Remote Management Framework is compatible with Oracle's multitenancy feature, and RMF can be configured at the PDB or CDB level. In this chapter, RMF will be configured at the CDB level.

The SYS$UMF User

The SYS$UMF user is the user who is set up by default to have access to all of the Remote Management Framework views and is used for capturing and managing AWR data from standby databases. The SYS$UMF user is locked and expired at database creation and needs to be unlocked.

```
SQL> col username format a10
SQL> col account_status format a20
SQL> set lines 150
SQL> select username, account_status from dba_users where username = 'SYS$UMF';

USERNAME    ACCOUNT_STATUS
---------- --------------------
SYS$UMF     EXPIRED & LOCKED

SQL> show con_name

CON_NAME
--------------------------------
CDB$ROOT

SQL> alter user SYS$UMF account unlock identified by "database_123" container=ALL;
```

This changes to this user need to be made in CDB$ROOT with the containers clause. The following is an example of the type of error that will be seen if an attempt is made to modify this user within a primary database (PDB) in a CDB database:

```
SQL> show con_name

CON_NAME
------------------------------
SOMEPDB

SQL> alter user SYS$UMF account unlock identified by "database_123";
alter user SYS$UMF account unlock identified by "database_123"
*
ERROR at line 1:
ORA-65066: The specified changes must apply to all containers

User altered.
```

Creating the DB Links

The DBA can create the database links manually. Two links are needed: one database link for the primary database to connect to the standby database and one database link for the standby database to connect to the primary database.

```
SQL> show con_name

CON_NAME
------------------------------
CDB$ROOT

SQL> create public database link ORCLCDB_TO_ORCLDR connect to SYS$UMF
identified by "database_123" using 'orcldr';

Database link created.

SQL> create public database link ORCLDR_TO_ORCLCDB connect to SYS$UMF
identified by "database_123" using 'orclcdb';

Database link created.
```

Configuring the Remote Management Framework Topology

The primary and standby databases need to be configured with the DBMS_UMF package so that the Remote Management Framework can be created and used. In the following example, all of the calls to the DBMS_UMF package are called from the primary database (known as the *target* database in RMF parlance).

First, a topology will need to be created. All source and target databases belong to a *topology*.

```
SQL> exec DBMS_UMF.create_topology ('RMF_TOPOLOGY');

PL/SQL procedure successfully completed.
```

After the topology has been created, the *source* (standby) node needs to be registered, and the database links need to be specified. One particular argument to note here is the node_name argument. This argument is case sensitive and must match the db_unique_name value of the remote database.

```
SQL> BEGIN
  2          DBMS_UMF.REGISTER_NODE(
  3          topology_name       => 'RMF_TOPOLOGY'
  4          ,node_name          => 'orcldr'
  5          ,dblink_to_node     => 'ORCLCDB_TO_ORCLDR'
  6          ,dblink_from_node   => 'ORCLDR_TO_ORCLCDB'
  7          ,as_source          => 'TRUE'
  8          ,as_candidate_target => 'FALSE'
  9          );
 10   END;
 11   /
```

Once the remote node has been registered with RMF, it need to be registered as a remote database in AWR with DBMS_WORKLOAD_REPOSITORY.

```
SQL> exec DBMS_WORKLOAD_REPOSITORY.register_remote_database(node_
name=>'orcldr');

PL/SQL procedure successfully completed.
```

Viewing the Topology information

The topology information regarding which nodes are registered for remote AWR is exposed via DBA_UMF_* views. DBA_UMF_TOPOLOGY contains information about the various topologies that may exist in a *target* database. DBA_UMF_REGISTRATION contains information about all the nodes that are registered in the Remote Management Framework as well as their respective roles within the framework. DBA_UMF_SERVICE has information that shows which registered nodes have an AWR service running for remote collection (the two views can be joined on NODE_ID). The output shown next will describe the topology that the examples in this chapter created:

```
SQL> col topology_name format a15
SQL> set lines 200

SQL> select * from DBA_UMF_TOPOLOGY;


TOPOLOGY_NAME     TARGET_ID TOPOLOGY_VERSION TOPOLOGY
--------------- ---------- ---------------- --------
RMF_TOPOLOGY     554680322                4 ACTIVE

SQL> select * from DBA_UMF_REGISTRATION;


TOPOLOGY_NAME    NODE_NAME     NODE_ID NODE_TYPE AS_SO AS_CA STATE
--------------- ---------- ---------- ---------- ----- ----- ----------
RMF_TOPOLOGY     orclcdb    554680322          0 FALSE FALSE OK
RMF_TOPOLOGY     orcldr     301115545          0 TRUE  FALSE OK

SQL> select * from DBA_UMF_SERVICE;


TOPOLOGY_NAME       NODE_ID SERVICE
--------------- ---------- -------
RMF_TOPOLOGY     301115545 AWR

1 row selected.
```

Taking AWR Snapshots on ADG Databases

AWR snapshots can be created with DBMS_WORKLOAD_REPOSITORY by calling the CREATE_
REMOTE_SNAPSHOT procedure and referencing the registered node_name for the source
(standby database) as an argument.

```
exec DBMS_WORKLOAD_REPOSITORY.CREATE_REMOTE_SNAPSHOT('orcldr');
```

Creating AWR Reports for the Standby Database

It is recommended that you use the awrgrpti.sql script to pull the AWR reports because
you can use it to pull a group AWR report of all instances and it allows you to set the
DB_ID value. This value will allow the administrator to choose the ADG database's
snapshots. While it is true that a standby database actually has the same DB_ID value
as the primary database, the Remote Management Framework uses the NODE_ID value,
which is found in DBA_UMF_REGISTRATION as a substitute for the source's DB_ID value.
The AWR reports can be generated from the primary or standby database; it makes no
difference.

```
SQL> @?/rdbms/admin/awrgrpti.sql


  Specify the Report Type
  ~~~~~~~~~~~~~~~~~~~~~~~~
  AWR reports can be generated in the following formats.  Please enter the
  name of the format at the prompt. Default value is 'html'.

    'html'          HTML format (default)
    'text'          Text format
    'active-html'   Includes Performance Hub active report

Enter value for report_type: html


Type Specified: html
```

```
Instances in this Workload Repository schema
~~~~~~~~~~~~~~~~~~~~~~~~~~~~~~~~~~~~~~~~~~~~~~

  DB Id        Inst Num   DB Name     Instance     Host
------------ ---------- ---------   ----------   ------
   301115545       1     ORCLCDB     orcldr1      rac501.local
   301115545       2     ORCLCDB     orcldr2      rac502.local
 * 2756161440      1     ORCLCDB     orclcdb1     stpldb101.lo
 * 2756161440      2     ORCLCDB     orclcdb2     stpldb102.lo

Enter value for dbid: 301115545
Using 301115545 for database Id
Enter value for instance_numbers_or_all: ALL
Using instances ALL (default 'ALL')

Specify the number of days of snapshots to choose from
~~~~~~~~~~~~~~~~~~~~~~~~~~~~~~~~~~~~~~~~~~~~~~~~~~~~~~~~~

Entering the number of days (n) will result in the most recent
(n) days of snapshots being listed.  Pressing <return> without
specifying a number lists all completed snapshots.

Enter value for num_days: 1

Listing the last day's Completed Snapshots
DB Name        Snap Id        Snap Started     Snap Level
------------ ---------- ------------------- ----------

ORCLCDB             1   25 Aug 2017 18:20       1
                    2   25 Aug 2017 18:21       1

Specify the Begin and End Snapshot Ids
~~~~~~~~~~~~~~~~~~~~~~~~~~~~~~~~~~~~~~~~~

Enter value for begin_snap: 1
Begin Snapshot Id specified: 1

Enter value for end_snap: 2
End   Snapshot Id specified: 2
```

Specify the Report Name
~~~~~~~~~~~~~~~~~~~~~~~~

The default report file name is awrrpt_rac_1_2.html. To use this name,
press <return> to continue, otherwise enter an alternative.

Enter value for report_name:

Using the report name awrrpt_rac_1_2.html

SQL Tuning Advisor in ADG Databases

As of 12c R2, Active Data Guard databases can now make use of the SQL Tuning Advisor. This has been made possible by allowing DBMS_SQLTUNE.CREATE_TUNING_TASK to use database links to communicate back to the primary database for data persistence. At tuning task creation time, the argument database_link_to can be supplied with the name of a database link that points back to the primary database. In this way, the database link will be used to store data necessary to create and run tuning tasks and for any subsequent SQL plan baseline or SQL profiles that are suggested by the SQL Tuning Advisor.

Creating a Database Link for the SQL Tuning Advisor

To tune queries on an ADG instance, a database link that points to the primary database must exist. If the SQL Tuning Advisor is being called from within a PDB, the database link must connect to the PDB on the primary database. In this example, we will create a DB_LINK called PRIMARY_DB that connects as SYS$UMF to the pluggable database SOMEPDB on the primary database ORCLCDB. The database link must connect as SYS$UMF to the primary database and must be a private database link owned by the SYS user.

```
SQL> alter session set container=SOMEPDB;

Session altered.

SQL> show con_name;

CON_NAME
--------------------------------
SOMEPDB
```

```
SQL> create database link PRIMARY_DB connect to SYS$UMF identified by
"database_123" using 'stpldb01-scan:1521/somepdb.world';

Database link created.
```

Tuning a Query

In this section, you'll see an example of a query on HR.EMPLOYEES from the set of sample schemas supplied by Oracle. All the tests will be run from a PDB called SOMEPDB in the CDB ORCLDR, which is the ADG standby database for the primary database called ORCLCDB.

The Example Query

Here is the query in question:

```
SQL> select employee_id, first_name, last_name, phone_number from
hr.employees where first_name = 'Alexis';
```

EMPLOYEE_ID FIRST_NAME	LAST_NAME	PHONE_NUMBER
----------- ----------------------	---------------------------	-------------
185 Alexis	Bull	650.509.2876

```
SQL> select * from table(dbms_xplan.display_cursor());
SQL_ID  6h7jvaqfuycvj, child number 0
---------------------------------------
select employee_id, first_name, last_name, phone_number from
hr.employees where first_name = 'Alexis'

Plan hash value: 612698390
```

```
--------------------------------------------------------------------------------
| Id | Operation            | Name         | Rows | Bytes | Cost (%CPU)| Time     |
--------------------------------------------------------------------------------
|  0 | SELECT STATEMENT     |              |      |       | 2 (100) |          |
|  1 | TABLE ACCESS BY      |              |      |       |         |          |
|    | INDEX ROWID BATCHED  | EMPLOYEES    | 1    | 34    | 2  (0) | 00:00:01|
|* 2 | INDEX SKIP SCAN      | EMP_NAME_IX  | 1    |       | 1  (0) | 00:00:01|
--------------------------------------------------------------------------------
```

```
Predicate Information (identified by operation id):
---------------------------------------------------------

   2 - access("FIRST_NAME"='Alexis')
       filter("FIRST_NAME"='Alexis')

21 rows selected.
```

Creating a SQL Tuning Task

The following example will show how an SQL tuning task can be created and executed while connected to the ADG instance:

```
SQL> show con_name

CON_NAME
--------------------------------
SOMEPDB
SQL> select instance_name from v$instance;

INSTANCE_NAME
----------------
orcldr1

SQL> select open_mode from v$database;

OPEN_MODE
--------------------
READ ONLY WITH APPLY

SQL> variable STMT_TASK varchar2(2000);

SQL> EXEC :stmt_task := DBMS_SQLTUNE.CREATE_TUNING_TASK(sql_id =>
'6h7jvaqfuycvj', database_link_to => 'PRIMARY_DB.WORLD');

PL/SQL procedure successfully completed.

SQL> select :stmt_task from dual;
```

```
:STMT_TASK
----------
TASK_11
SQL> EXEC DBMS_SQLTUNE.EXECUTE_TUNING_TASK(:stmt_task);

PL/SQL procedure successfully completed.
```

You can view the SQL Tuning Task report by using the DBMS_SQLTUNE.REPORT_ TUNING_TASK function when selecting from dual and referencing the relevant task name. The following is some example output from a SQL Tuning Task Report that was run on the standby database:

```
SQL> SELECT DBMS_SQLTUNE.REPORT_TUNING_TASK(:stmt_task) from dual;

DBMS_SQLTUNE.REPORT_TUNING_TASK(:STMT_TASK)
-------------------------------------------------------------------------------
GENERAL INFORMATION SECTION
-------------------------------------------------------------------------------
Tuning Task Name    : TASK_11
Tuning Task Owner   : SYS
Workload Type       : Single SQL Statement
Scope               : COMPREHENSIVE
Time Limit(seconds): 1800
Completion Status   : COMPLETED
Started at          : 04/26/2018 12:57:06
Completed at        : 04/26/2018 12:57:08
SQL Tuning at Standby TRUE

-------------------------------------------------------------------------------
Schema Name    : SYS
Container Name: SOMEPDB
SQL ID         : 6h7jvaqfuycvj
SQL Text       : select employee_id, first_name, last_name, phone_number from
                 hr.employees where first_name = 'Alexis'

-------------------------------------------------------------------------------
There are no recommendations to improve the statement.
```

RMAN Support for NONLOGGED BLOCK recovery

In previous versions of Oracle Database, NOLOGGING operations will cause issues with Data Guard standby databases because they mark the affected database blocks as UNRECOVERABLE and any SQL statements that require reading those UNRECOVERABLE blocks on the ADG database will throw errors. For this reason, it is always recommended you keep the primary database in FORCE LOGGING mode. However, in certain cases, this may not be ideal, or the FORCE LOGGING behavior may need to be altered to expedite data loads. If this scenario ever occurs, recovering the blocks affected by NOLOGGING operations is now possible with RMAN without requiring new backups to be taken on the primary database. In this section, you'll see a thorough example of how this feature works, and all of the work will be done in the SOMEPDB PDB in the ORCLCDB CDB with the ORCLDR ADG database.

Creating a Table with the NOLOGGING Clause

A table will be created with the NOLOGGING clause, and the APPEND hint will be used to load data into the table. This will cause an unrecoverable operation because the data required to re-create the changes will not be stored in the redo logs. This will be done in a database where FORCE_LOGGING is disabled at both the CDB and PDB levels. Additionally, the NOLOGGING table will be created in the USERS tablespace, which does not have FORCE_LOGGING enabled.

```
SQL> select db_unique_name from v$database;

DB_UNIQUE_NAME
-------------------------------
Orclcdb

SQL> alter database NO FORCE LOGGING;

Database altered.

SQL> select force_logging from v$database;


FORCE_LOGGING
-----------------------------------------
NO
```

```
SQL> select force_logging from dba_pdbs where pdb_name='SOMEPDB';

FOR
---
NO

SQL> alter session set container=SOMEPDB;

Session altered.

SQL> show con_name;

CON_NAME
------------------------------
SOMEPDB

SQL> select tablespace_name, logging,force_logging from dba_tablespaces
where tablespace_name = 'USERS';

TABLESPACE_NAME                  LOGGING    FOR
------------------------------ --------- ---
USERS                            LOGGING    NO

SQL> create table HR.EMPLOYEES_NOLOG NOLOGGING TABLESPACE USERS as select *
from hr.employees where 'x'='y';

Table created.

SQL> insert /*+ APPEND */ into HR.EMPLOYEES_NOLOG select * from
hr.employees;

107 rows created.

SQL> commit;

Commit complete.
```

The previous example is intended to show a type of NOLOGGING operation. In the next two sections, the effect of the NOLOGGING operation will be shown on the standby database along with the steps necessary to recover from the situation without requiring a new full backup to be taken of the primary's datafiles for the USERS tablespace.

The Effect of NOLOGGING Operations on the Physical Standby

Once the table has been created and loaded with the APPEND hint, select statements against the table on the ADG database will error out with the ORA-26040 error.

```
SQL> select db_unique_name from v$database;

DB_UNIQUE_NAME
-------------------------------
orcldr

SQL> show con_name;

CON_NAME
-------------------------------
SOMEPDB

SQL> select * from hr.employees_nolog;
select * from hr.employees_nolog
       *
ERROR at line 1:
ORA-01578: ORACLE data block corrupted (file # 14, block # 131)
ORA-01110: data file 14:
'+DATA/ORCLDR/744827E32DAF16D5E053033AA8C089C7/DATAFILE/
users.273.985102721'
ORA-26040: Data block was loaded using the NOLOGGING option
```

Once a select statement has been run on the table, the unrecoverable blocks will be stored in the V$NONLOGGED_BLOCKS view along with some other metadata.

```
SQL> select file#, block#, blocks object# from V$NONLOGGED_BLOCK;

    FILE#     BLOCK#    OBJECT#
---------- ---------- ----------
       14        131          2
```

Because the OBJECT# value of the impacted objects is stored in the V$NONLOGGED_ BLOCK view, it can be used to determine which objects cannot be queried because of NOLOGGING operations.

```
SQL> col owner format a5
SQL> col object_name format a30
SQL> col object_type format a10
SQL> set lines 50
SQL> select owner, object_name, object_type from dba_objects where data_
object_id in (select object# from v$nonlogged_block);

OWNER OBJECT_NAME                     OBJECT_TYP
----- ------------------------------ ----------
HR    EMPLOYEES_NOLOG                TABLE
```

Fixing the Problem

As stated, in previous versions, recovering from such a scenario was complicated and
cumbersome. However, in 12c R2, this problem can be overcome with one simple RMAN
command. To run the RMAN recovery command, you need to stop managed recovery on
the standby database.

This can be done via the Broker if it is configured.

```
[oracle@rac501 ~]$ dgmgrl /
DGMGRL for Linux: Release 12.2.0.1.0

Copyright (c) 1982, 2017, Oracle and/or its affiliates.  All rights reserved.

Welcome to DGMGRL, type "help" for information.
Connected to "orcldr"
Connected as SYSDG.
DGMGRL> show database orcldr

Database - orcldr

  Role:               PHYSICAL STANDBY
  Intended State:     APPLY-ON
  Transport Lag:      0 seconds (computed 0 seconds ago)
  Apply Lag:          0 seconds (computed 0 seconds ago)
  Average Apply Rate: 59.00 KByte/s
  Real Time Query:    ON
  Instance(s):
```

```
    orcldr1
    orcldr2 (apply instance)
```

Database Status:
SUCCESS

```
DGMGRL> edit database orcldr set state='APPLY-OFF';
Succeeded.
DGMGRL>
```

Once you have stopped managed recovery, you can use RMAN to recover the required blocks on the standby database.

```
RMAN> recover database nonlogged block;

Starting recover
using target database control file instead of recovery catalog
allocated channel: ORA_DISK_1
channel ORA_DISK_1: SID=541 instance=orcldr1 device type=DISK

starting recovery of nonlogged blocks
List of Datafiles
==================
File Status Nonlogged Blocks Blocks Examined Blocks Skipped
---- ------ ---------------- --------------- --------------
1    OK     0                0               108799
3    OK     0                0               104959
4    OK     0                0               37759
5    OK     0                0               33279
6    OK     0                0               60159
7    OK     0                0               639
8    OK     0                0               12799
9    OK     0                0               3199
10   OK     0                0               34559
11   OK     0                0               66559
12   OK     0                0               12799
13   OK     0                0               12799
14   OK     0                2               637
```

Details of nonlogged blocks can be queried from v$nonlogged_block view

recovery of nonlogged blocks complete, elapsed time: 00:00:02

When the RECOVER DATABASE NONLOGGED BLOCK command is issued, the standby database will connect to the primary database and fetch the blocks from the primary datafiles. In this way, there is no requirement to take level 0 backups or copy datafiles from the primary site to the standby site as everything is handled at the block level and is automatically taken care of by the standby. In some cases, this operation may fail because the NONLOGGED blocks have not been flushed to the physical datafiles on the primary site. In such cases, you can choose to wait for the blocks to be flushed to the datafile or flush the buffer cache on the primary database. The following is an example of the type of alert log entries you may expect to see on a successful recovery of NONLOGGED blocks:

```
alter database recover datafile list clear
Completed: alter database recover datafile list clear
```

```
Started Nonlogged Block Replacement recovery on file 14 (ospid 2684 rcvid
2503064493696929793)
Data Transfer Cache defaulting to 64MB. Trying to get it from Buffer Cache
for process 2684.
2018-04-26T14:04:30.076444-04:00
Finished Nonlogged Block Replacement recovery on file 14. 0 blocks remain
  Statistics for replacement block source database (service=orclcdb)
  Blocks requested 2, blocks received 2.
```

```
Reason replacement blocks accepted or rejected            Blocks   Last block
---------------------------------------------------    ---------  ---------
Accept: SCN in range for classic non-logged block              2         132
```

Data Guard Support for Multiple Observers

As of 12c R2, Oracle Data Guard now supports up to three observers in a Data Guard Broker configuration. In this type of setup, an observer will be chosen at random to be the master observer and to be the one to initiate Fast Start Fail Over (FSFO) operations. If the master observer fails or is shut down, the surviving observer will be elected to become the master. This feature brings high availability to observers and makes FSFO configurations more reliable. In this section of the chapter, the examples will continue to use the primary database ORCLCDB and the standby database ORCLDR. There will be two observers, one on an Oracle Management Server host called oms1.localdomain and another on one of the database servers hosting the standby database rac501.localdomain.

Starting Multiple Observers

When starting observers manually, there is no special syntax that is required to enable multiple observers; this feature works seamlessly with the Oracle Data Guard Broker.

- OMS1.LOCALDOMAIN

```
DGMGRL> connect sys@orclcdb
Password:
Connected to "orclcdb"
Connected as SYSDBA.
DGMGRL> start observer logfile is '/home/oracle/oms1_orclcdb_observer.log';
```

- RAC501.LOCALDOMAIN

```
DGMGRL> connect sys/database_123@orclcdb
Connected to "orclcdb"
Connected as SYSDBA.
DGMGRL> start observer logfile is '/home/oracle/rac501_orclcdb_observer.log'
```

Determining the Master Observer

You can determine which observer is the master observer via DGMGRL.

The master observer will have an asterisk next to the hostname in the Observers list displayed by show fast_start failover.

```
DGMGRL> show fast_start failover;

Fast-Start Failover: ENABLED

  Threshold:          45 seconds
  Target:             orcldr
  Observers:      (*) oms1.localdomain
                      rac501.localdomain
```

```
Lag Limit:            30 seconds
Shutdown Primary:     TRUE
Auto-reinstate:       TRUE
Observer Reconnect:   (none)
Observer Override:    FALSE

Configurable Failover Conditions
  Health Conditions:
    Corrupted Controlfile         YES
    Corrupted Dictionary          YES
    Inaccessible Logfile          NO
    Stuck Archiver                NO
    Datafile Write Errors         YES

  Oracle Error Conditions:
    (none)
```

Additionally, the command show observer will expose the master/backup relationship directly.

```
DGMGRL> show observer

Configuration - orclcdb

  Primary:            orclcdb
  Target:             orcldr

Observer "oms1.localdomain" - Master

  Host Name:                    oms1.localdomain
  Last Ping to Primary:         1 second ago
  Last Ping to Target:          3 seconds ago

Observer "rac501.localdomain" - Backup

  Host Name:                    rac501.localdomain
  Last Ping to Primary:         2 seconds ago
  Last Ping to Target:          2 seconds ago
```

Manually Changing the Master Observer

If the automatically defined master observer is not desired, the master observer role can be assigned to a different observer via DGMGRL.

```
DGMGRL> set masterobserver to rac501.localdomain;
Sent the proposed master observer to the data guard broker configuration.
Please run SHOW OBSERVER to see if master observer switch actually happens.

DGMGRL> show observer;

Configuration - orclcdb

  Primary:           orclcdb
  Target:            orcldr

Observer "rac501.localdomain" - Master

  Host Name:                   rac501.localdomain
  Last Ping to Primary:        2 seconds ago
  Last Ping to Target:         2 seconds ago

Observer "oms1.localdomain" - Backup

  Host Name:                   oms1.localdomain
  Last Ping to Primary:        0 seconds ago
  Last Ping to Target:         0 seconds ago
```

Data Guard Multi-instance Apply

With 12c R2, Oracle Data Guard now supports multi-instance redo apply (MIRA) on physical standby databases. By default, a physical standby database will not apply redo using multiple instances, but this can be changed via DGMGRL by modifying the applyinstances property of the Broker configuration member for the physical standby database.

Broker Example

In this example, all instances of the ORCLDR database will be used to apply redo. There is an alter database command that can be used if a Broker configuration does not exist.

```
DGMGRL> edit database orcldr set state='APPLY-OFF';
Succeeded.
```

```
DGMGRL> edit database orcldr set property applyinstances='ALL';
Property "applyinstances" updated
```

```
DGMGRL> edit database orcldr set state='APPLY-ON';
Succeeded.
```

SQLPLUS Example

The INSTANCES clause has been added to the ALTER DATABASE RECOVER MANAGED STANDBY DATABASE command to specify which instances should participate in redo apply.

```
SQL> ALTER DATABASE RECOVER MANAGED STANDBY DATABASE DISCONNECT INSTANCES
ALL NODELAY;
```

Selectively Applying Redo for PDBs in Data Guard

It is now possible to selectively enable redo apply for pluggable databases using the ENABLED_PDBS_ON_STANDBY initialization parameter on the physical standby database. In this example, the primary ORCLCDB and the standby ORCLDR will be used to show how this new parameter works. This parameter is valid only on a standby database and is ignored on primary databases. A new PDB TESTPDB has been created to showcase this functionality. The parameter is used to specify which PDBs are eligible to have their redo applied on a standby database. If the parameter is not set, the default of * denoting that all PDBs should have their redo applied is used. The parameter essentially acts a whitelist of PDBs that the managed recovery process will apply redo for in the standby database.

```
SQL> show parameter ENABLED_PDBS_ON_STANDBY

NAME                                     TYPE        VALUE
---------------------------------------- ----------- ----------------------
enabled_PDBs_on_standby                  string      *

SQL> show spparameter ENABLED_PDBS_ON_STANDBY

SID      NAME                            TYPE        VALUE
-------- ------------------------------- ----------- --------------------
*        enabled_PDBs_on_standby         string
```

When the new database PDB called TESTPDB was created on the primary, it was automatically created on the standby database because the ENABLED_PDBS_ON_STANDBY parameter had a default value of *.

```
SQL> col name format a30
SQL> set lines 200
SQL> select name, recovery_status from v$pdbs;

NAME                             RECOVERY
-------------------------------- --------
PDB$SEED                         ENABLED
SOMEPDB                          ENABLED
TESTPDB                          ENABLED
```

Effects of the ENABLED_PDBS_ON_STANDBY Parameter

The parameter can be modified on a running instance, but it must have the same value on all RAC instances. Furthermore, the parameter is evaluated only at PDB creation time; therefore, it cannot be used to disable recovery for an existing PDB, as shown next. The RECOVERY_STATUS column for the TESTPDB does not change despite the PDB not being in the list specified by ENABLED_PDBS_ON_STANDBY.

```
SQL> alter system set ENABLED_PDBS_ON_STANDBY='SOMEPDB' scope=BOTH sid='*';

System altered.

SQL> col name format a30
SQL> set lines 200
SQL> select name, recovery_status from v$pdbs;
```

```
NAME                             RECOVERY
------------------------------   --------
PDB$SEED                         ENABLED
SOMEPDB                          ENABLED
TESTPDB                          ENABLED
```

Creating a NEWPDB Pluggable Database on the Primary

Now observe what happens when a PDB is created on the primary database after this
ENABLED_PDBS_ON_STANDBY value has been changed on the standby.

```
SQL> select db_unique_name from v$database;

DB_UNIQUE_NAME
------------------------------
orclcdb

SQL> CREATE PLUGGABLE DATABASE NEWPDB ADMIN USER pdbadmin IDENTIFIED BY
"database_123" ROLES=(CONNECT)  file_name_convert=NONE  STORAGE ( MAXSIZE
UNLIMITED MAX_SHARED_TEMP_SIZE UNLIMITED);

Pluggable database created.

SQL> alter pluggable database NEWPDB open read write instances=ALL;

Pluggable database altered.
```

Alert Log Entries on Standby Database

The PDB is added to the controlfile of the standby database, but its datafiles are not
created.

```
Recovery created pluggable database NEWPDB
NEWPDB(5):File #23 added to control file as 'UNNAMED00023'. Originally
created as:
NEWPDB(5):'+DATA/ORCLCDB/745FE299A29B5954E053023AA8C0C85F/DATAFILE/
system.460.985202561'
NEWPDB(5):because the pluggable database was created with nostandby
NEWPDB(5):or the tablespace belonging to the pluggable database is
NEWPDB(5):offline.
```

```
NEWPDB(5):File #24 added to control file as 'UNNAMED00024'. Originally
created as:
NEWPDB(5):'+DATA/ORCLCDB/745FE299A29B5954E053023AA8C0C85F/DATAFILE/
sysaux.461.985202561'
NEWPDB(5):because the pluggable database was created with nostandby
NEWPDB(5):or the tablespace belonging to the pluggable database is
NEWPDB(5):offline.
NEWPDB(5):File #25 added to control file as 'UNNAMED00025'. Originally
created as:
NEWPDB(5):'+DATA/ORCLCDB/745FE299A29B5954E053023AA8C0C85F/DATAFILE/
undotbs1.459.985202561'
NEWPDB(5):because the pluggable database was created with nostandby
NEWPDB(5):or the tablespace belonging to the pluggable database is
NEWPDB(5):offline.
(5):File #26 added to control file as 'UNNAMED00026'. Originally created as:
(5):'+DATA/ORCLCDB/745FE299A29B5954E053023AA8C0C85F/DATAFILE/
undo_2.463.985202649'
(5):because the pluggable database was created with nostandby
(5):or the tablespace belonging to the pluggable database is
(5):offline.
```

Recovery Status of the NEWPDB Pluggable Database

The NEWPDB database is not configured to be recovered, and no redo will be applied for this pluggable database.

```
SQL> col name format a30
SQL> set lines 200
SQL> select name, recovery_status from v$pdbs;

NAME                              RECOVERY
------------------------------    --------
PDB$SEED                          ENABLED
SOMEPDB                           ENABLED
TESTPDB                           ENABLED
NEWPDB                            DISABLED
```

Disabling Redo Apply for an Existing PDB

If it is desired to disable redo apply for an already existing PDB, this can be accomplished through an ALTER PLUGGABLE DATABASE command. In this example, the PDB TESTPDB will be altered. This can be done only after managed recovery has been stopped; otherwise, an ORA-01156 error will be thrown. Additionally, the PDB needs to be closed on all instances, or an ORA-65025 error will be thrown.

```
SQL> alter session set container=TESTPDB;

Session altered.

SQL> alter pluggable database TESTPDB close immediate instances=ALL;

Pluggable database altered.

SQL> alter pluggable database TESTPDB disable recovery;

Pluggable database altered.

SQL> select name, recovery_status from v$pdbs;

NAME                            RECOVERY
------------------------------- --------
TESTPDB                         DISABLED
```

Data Guard Database Compare

In 12c R2, it is now possible to detect lost writes and NONLOGGED blocks without using the DB_LOST_WRITE_PROTECT parameter. This is possible with the DBMS_DBCOMP package. Currently, DBMS_DBCOMP has only one procedure, called DBCOMP, which can be used to compare datafiles between a primary database and a standby database. It can be called from the standby or the primary database and works only for physical standby databases because it does a block for block comparison between the primary and standby databases.

```
SQL> desc DBMS_DBCOMP
PROCEDURE DBCOMP
 Argument Name                          Type                      In/Out Default?
 ------------------------------         ----------------------    ------ --------
 DATAFILE                               VARCHAR2                   IN
 OUTPUTFILE                             VARCHAR2                   IN
 BLOCK_DUMP                             BOOLEAN                    IN     DEFAULT
```

The output file can be specified either with an absolute path or with a relative filename. By default, the output is placed in $ORACLE_HOME/dbs. The default value for BLOCK_DUMP is false, so it is recommended to explicitly set the argument to TRUE so that information about blocks that differ between the primary database and the standby database are dumped.

Using DBMS_DBCOMP to Detect Nologging Operations

To borrow an example from a previous section in this chapter, a NOLOGGING table will be created and then detected via DBMS_DBCOMP.

```
SQL> alter session set container=SOMEPDB;

Session altered.

SQL> create table HR.EMPLOYEES_NOLOG NOLOGGING TABLESPACE USERS as select *
from hr.employees where 'x'='y';

Table created.

SQL> insert /*+ APPEND */ into HR.EMPLOYEES_NOLOG select * from hr.employees;

107 rows created.

SQL> commit;

Commit complete.
```

The comparison details will be dumped into a file called /home/oracle/dbcomp.txt.

```
SQL> exec DBMS_DBCOMP.DBCOMP(datafile =>'ALL', outputfile => '/home/oracle/
dbcomp.txt',block_dump =>TRUE);

PL/SQL procedure successfully completed.
```

Contents of the dbcomp.txt File

Because of the NOLOGGING operation that was performed, there are two corrupted blocks. In a healthy database, corrupted database blocks should not be present. The number of corrupted database blocks found during a comparison operation are written into the third CORR column. In this example, there are two corrupted database blocks where ID=6 (transactional data):

```
[oracle@stpldb101 ~]$ cat /home/oracle/dbcomp.txt
Client is connected to database: orclcdb. Role: primary database.
Remote database orcldr.remote db role: physical standby

Slave Id  0
Summary:
****************************************************************************
                     TOTAL: total no. of blocks found
                       |
    +--------+------------+-------+---------+---------+
    |        |            |       |         |         |
    |     DIFFV:          LOST_WRITE  |     CORR: corrupted blocks
  SAMEV    diff ver       |        SKIPPED:
    |       block pairs    +--+--+    direct load, empty blocks,
+--+--+--+                 |  |  |    RMAN optimized blocks,
| | | | | |                |  |  |    flashback optimized blocks
| | | | SAMEV&C:           |  |  |
| | | | same ver &         |  LWLOC: lost writes at local db
| | | | same checksum &  LWRMT: lost writes at remote db
| | | | same contents
| | | |
|   | SAMEV_NO_CHKSUM: same ver & same contents but diff checksum
|   |             (checksum can be diff but identical contents)
|   |
| DIFFPAIR: same ver but differrent contents (data inconsistency)
|
ENCERR: undecided block pairs due to encryption related issue
        (e.g. when Wallet is not open)
```

ID	TOTAL	CORR	SKIPPED	DIFFV	SAMEV	SAMEV&C	ENCERR	LWLOC	LWRMT	DIFFPAIR
00	0017131	0000	0017131	0000000	0000000	0000000	0000000	000000	000000	0000000
02	0000118	0000	0000000	0000011	0000107	0000107	0000000	000000	000000	0000000
06	0066357	**0002**	0036590	0000079	0029686	0029686	0000000	000000	000000	0000000
14	0000001	0000	0000000	0000000	0000001	0000001	0000000	000000	000000	0000000
16	0000764	0000	0000000	0000000	0000764	0000764	0000000	000000	000000	0000000
23	0000061	0000	0000000	0000000	0000061	0000061	0000000	000000	000000	0000000
25	0000061	0000	0000000	0000000	0000061	0000061	0000000	000000	000000	0000000
26	0000009	0000	0000000	0000000	0000009	0000009	0000000	000000	000000	0000000
27	0000798	0000	0000000	0000000	0000798	0000798	0000000	000000	000000	0000000
29	0000005	0000	0000000	0000001	0000004	0000004	0000000	000000	000000	0000000
30	0000625	0000	0000000	0000001	0000624	0000624	0000000	000000	000000	0000000
32	0001296	0000	0000000	0000004	0001292	0001292	0000000	000000	000000	0000000
33	0001158	0000	0000000	0000001	0001157	0001157	0000000	000000	000000	0000000
35	0001158	0000	0000000	0000000	0001158	0001158	0000000	000000	000000	0000000
38	0000020	0000	0000000	0000011	0000009	0000009	0000000	000000	000000	0000000
58	0026594	0000	0026591	0000003	0000000	0000000	0000000	000000	000000	0000000
61	0003078	0000	0000000	0000000	0003078	0003078	0000000	000000	000000	0000000
62	0000160	0000	0000000	0000000	0000160	0000160	0000000	000000	000000	0000000
63	0000341	0000	0000000	0000000	0000341	0000341	0000000	000000	000000	0000000
64	0000950	0000	0000000	0000000	0000950	0000950	0000000	000000	000000	0000000
69	0000521	0000	0000000	0000000	0000521	0000521	0000000	000000	000000	0000000
70	0005632	0000	0005627	0000005	0000000	0000000	0000000	000000	000000	0000000
80	0000128	0000	0000000	0000001	0000127	0000127	0000000	000000	000000	0000000
81	0000001	0000	0000000	0000000	0000001	0000001	0000000	000000	000000	0000000
82	0000128	0000	0000000	0000000	0000128	0000128	0000000	000000	000000	0000000
83	0000128	0000	0000000	0000000	0000128	0000128	0000000	000000	000000	0000000
84	0000127	0000	0000000	0000000	0000127	0000127	0000000	000000	000000	0000000

```
Short description for each block type:
*********************************************************************************
02: KTU UNDO BLOCK
06: trans data
14: KTU UNDO HEADER W/UNLIMITED EXTENTS
16: DATA SEGMENT HEADER - UNLIMITED
23: BITMAPPED DATA SEGMENT HEADER
```

```
25: BITMAP INDEX BLOCK
26: BITMAP BLOCK
27: LOB BLOCK
29: KTFB Bitmapped File Space Header
30: KTFB Bitmapped File Space Bitmap
32: FIRST LEVEL BITMAP BLOCK
33: SECOND LEVEL BITMAP BLOCK
35: PAGETABLE SEGMENT HEADER
38: KTU SMU HEADER BLOCK
58: block type 58
61: NGLOB: Hash Bucket
62: NGLOB: Committed Free Space
63: NGLOB: Segment Header
64: NGLOB: Persistent Undo
69: NGLOB: Lob Extent Header
70: block type 70
80: KTFBN File Space Property Map
81: Stats Segment Header
82: Stats Map
83: Stats Map Summary
84: Stats bitmap
```

Password File Change Synchronization

Oracle Data Guard has become easier to manage in 12c R2 because of a change that stores information in the redo logs regarding the Oracle password file changes. This makes things much easier to manage because SYS passwords can be changed on a primary database without having take explicit steps to modify the standby database password files. In previous releases, the Oracle Data Guard Transport service would break down if the primary database's SYS password in the password file was changed to a different value than what the standby database's password file had. This new feature will be shown with a simple check of checksums before and after changing SYS passwords.

Checksums Prior to the SYS Password Change

In the following example, it is shown that both the primary and standby password files have a checksum of 2468345953.

```
[oracle@stpldb101 old_backup]$ srvctl config database -d orclcdb |grep -i
password
Password file: +DATA/orclcdb/pwdorclcdb.ora
```

```
[oracle@stpldb101 ~]$ asmcmd cp +DATA/orclcdb/pwdorclcdb.ora /home/oracle/
prim_pw_before_change.ora
```

```
[oracle@stpldb101 ~]$ cksum /home/oracle/prim_pw_before_change.ora
2468345953 3584 /home/oracle/prim_pw_before_change.ora
```

```
[oracle@rac501 ~]$ srvctl config database -d orcldr |grep -i password
Password file: +DATA/DB_UNKNOWN/PASSWORD/pwddb_unknown.277.985101591
```

```
[oracle@rac501 ~]$ asmcmd cp +DATA/DB_UNKNOWN/PASSWORD/pwddb_
unknown.277.985101591 /home/oracle/stby_before_change.ora
```

```
[oracle@rac501 ~]$ cksum /home/oracle/stby_before_change.ora
2468345953 3584 /home/oracle/stby_before_change.ora
```

Changing the Password

The password can simply be changed with an ALTER USER command on the primary database.

```
SQL> alter user sys identified by "somenew_password";
```

```
User altered.
```

Checksums After to the SYS Password Change

The checksum has changed from 2468345953 to 2291626709 on both the primary and the standby password files without any manual intervention on the standby database. In previous releases of the Oracle Database, this would have required stopping transport services and manually changing the password file values, which can leave databases vulnerable to data loss if an unfortunate catastrophic failure renders the primary database inoperable before it can send archived log files to the standby database.

```
[oracle@stpldb101 ~]$ asmcmd cp +DATA/orclcdb/pwdorclcdb.ora /home/oracle/
prim_pw_after_change.ora

[oracle@stpldb101 ~]$ cksum /home/oracle/prim_pw_after_change.ora
2291626709 3584 /home/oracle/prim_pw_after_change.ora

[oracle@rac501 ~]$ asmcmd cp +DATA/DB_UNKNOWN/PASSWORD/pwddb_
unknown.277.985101591 /home/oracle/stby_after_change.ora

[oracle@rac501 ~]$ cksum /home/oracle/stby_after_change.ora
2291626709 3584 /home/oracle/stby_after_change.ora
```

In-Memory Columnar Store for ADG Instances

Active Data Guard databases can now leverage the powerful in-memory columnar store to improve the performance of reporting queries and other read-only workloads that are being offloaded to Active Data Guard databases.

Enabling this feature is controlled by a new parameter called INMEMORY_ADG_ENABLED that has a default value of TRUE. With this parameter, an INMEMORY_SIZE value can be specified for an ADG instance to enable the use of the in-memory columnar store. However, this feature comes with a few limitations in this version. ADG INMEMORY is not compatible with multi-instance redo apply, and all INMEMORY expressions are evaluated from the primary database. Additionally, INMEMORY join groups and FSFO are not supported as of version 12.2.0.1.

```
SQL> show parameter inmemory_adg_enabled

NAME                                 TYPE         VALUE
------------------------------------ ------------ ------------------------
inmemory_adg_enabled                 boolean      TRUE

SQL> show spparameter inmemory_adg_enabled

SID      NAME                        TYPE         VALUE
-------- --------------------------- ------------ ---------------------
*        inmemory_adg_enabled        boolean
```

Role Transition Connection Preservation

In 12c R2, it is now possible to preserve connections in a standby database as it undergoes a role change. This can be particularly useful in applications that maintain two connections pools, one to the primary database and another to a designated standby database. In this way, a role transition from standby to primary does not require connections to be recycled and re-established, effectively allowing a zero-downtime transition from an application's perspective.

This new parameter is controlled through the STANDBY_DB_PRESERVE_STATES parameter, which has a default value of NONE and can be set to either NONE, ALL, or SESSION to control which types of sessions are preserved during a role transition. Changing the parameter requires a bounce of the standby database.

```
SQL> show parameter STANDBY_DB_PRESERVE_STATES

NAME                                         TYPE         VALUE
-------------------------------------------- ------------ -----------------------
standby_db_preserve_states                   string       NONE

SQL> show spparameter STANDBY_DB_PRESERVE_STATES

SID      NAME                                TYPE         VALUE
-------- ----------------------------------- ------------ --------------------
*        standby_db_preserve_states          string
```

In this example, the parameter will be set to a value of ALL, and a test will be done via SQLPlus. A connection will be made to the PDB SOMEPDB on the ORCLDR CDB ADG database while it is in the database role of PHYSICAL STANDBY. After the connection is made, a role transition will be initiated from a separate session from the Broker.

Establishing the Connection

No special connection-specific details have to be set for this to work; it even works for basic EZCONNECT sessions.

```
[oracle@stpldb101 ~]$ sqlplus hr/test_123@//rac5-scan:1521/somepdb.world

SQL*Plus: Release 12.2.0.1.0 Production
```

Copyright (c) 1982, 2016, Oracle. All rights reserved.

Connected to:
Oracle Database 12c Enterprise Edition Release 12.2.0.1.0 - 64bit Production

SQL> select db_unique_name, database_role from v$database;

DB_UNIQUE_NAME   DATABASE_ROLE
------------------------------   -----------------
orcldr   PHYSICAL STANDBY

SQL> show con_name

CON_NAME

SOMEPDB

Performing the Role Transition

Here is the command:

```
DGMGRL> switchover to orcldr;
Performing switchover NOW, please wait...
Operation requires a connection to database "orcldr"
Connecting ...
Connected to "orcldr"
Connected as SYSDBA.
New primary database "orcldr" is opening...
Oracle Clusterware is restarting database "orclcdb" ...
Connected to "orclcdb"
Connected to "orclcdb"
Switchover succeeded, new primary is "orcldr"
```

Checking the Existing Session

Finally, here's the check:

SQL> select db_unique_name, database_role from v$database;

```
DB_UNIQUE_NAME                    DATABASE_ROLE
------------------------------    ----------------
orcldr                            PRIMARY

SQL> show con_name

CON_NAME
------------------------------
SOMEPDB
```

PDB Migrate

It is possible to migrate pluggable databases from one container to another using DGMGRL. This functionality makes it easy to migrate pluggable databases using just one command. A pluggable database can be migrated from its primary container CDB to another read-write CDB, generally on the same primary host, or it can be migrated from its standby CDB to another read-write CDB, generally on the same standby host. The latter scenario is known as a *PDB failover* and can be used to migrate one PDB out of a container in the case that the primary PDB has failed, but performing a failover operation at the CDB level is undesirable because of the downtime requirements of the rest of the tenants in the primary CDB. The chief restriction that exists with PDB migrations is that the target CDB needs to have direct access to the XML manifest file that the source CDB creates during the migration process, either via NFS or through a shared local filesystem if both CDBs are on the same host. Additionally, the PDBs datafiles need to be directly accessible to both the source CDB and the target CDB. Lastly, both the source and the target CDBs of the migration need to be part of their own respective Broker configurations, even if both Broker configurations consist of just primary databases with no standby databases.

In this section, the PDB SOMEPDB will be migrated from its primary CDB, ORCLDB, to an alternate CDB called ALTCDB, which has been created on the same cluster as ORCLCDB. This type of operation is called a *PDB migration* as opposed to a PDB failover, which is initiated from a standby CDB.

ALTCDB Broker Configuration

The Data Guard command-line interface (DGMGRL) enables you to manage a Data Guard Broker configuration and its databases directly from the command line.

```
DGMGRL> show configuration;

Configuration - altcdb

  Protection Mode: MaxPerformance
  Members:
  altcdb - Primary database

Fast-Start Failover: DISABLED

Configuration Status:
SUCCESS    (status updated 14 seconds ago)

SQL> select db_unique_name from v$database;


DB_UNIQUE_NAME
-------------------------------
altcdb

SQL> show pdbs;

    CON_ID CON_NAME                         OPEN MODE  RESTRICTED
---------- ------------------------------ ---------- ----------
         2 PDB$SEED                         READ ONLY  NO
```

Broker Configuration

Check the Broker configuration for the orclcdb database using DGMGRL.

```
DGMGRL> show configuration;

Configuration - orclcdb

  Protection Mode: MaxPerformance
  Members:
  orclcdb - Primary database
```

```
    orcldr  - Physical standby database

Fast-Start Failover: DISABLED

Configuration Status:
SUCCESS    (status updated 50 seconds ago)

SQL> select db_unique_name from v$database;

DB_UNIQUE_NAME
-------------------------------
orclcdb

SQL> show pdbs;

    CON_ID CON_NAME                        OPEN MODE  RESTRICTED
---------- ------------------------------ ---------- ----------
         2 PDB$SEED                        READ ONLY  NO
         3 SOMEPDB                         READ WRITE NO
```

The Migration

The pluggable database can be migrated by using the MIGRATE PLUGGABLE DATABASE
command while connected to the source CDB through the Broker. The operation
is extremely fast and in most cases will complete in about one minute of runtime
regardless of database size. This is because the pluggable database is migrated into the
target CDB by internally using the NOCOPY clause of the CREATE PLUGGABLE DATABASE
command.

```
DGMGRL> connect sys/database_123@orclcdb
Connected to "orclcdb"
Connected as SYSDBA.
DGMGRL> migrate pluggable database somepdb to container altcdb using
'/home/oracle/somepdb.xml' connect as sys/database_123@altcdb
Connected to "altcdb"
Connected as SYSDBA.
```

```
Beginning migration of pluggable database SOMEPDB.
Source multitenant container database is orclcdb.
Destination multitenant container database is altcdb.

Closing pluggable database SOMEPDB on all instances of multitenant
container database orclcdb.
Unplugging pluggable database SOMEPDB from multitenant container database
orclcdb.
Pluggable database description will be written to /home/oracle/somepdb.xml.
Dropping pluggable database SOMEPDB from multitenant container database orclcdb.
Creating pluggable database SOMEPDB on multitenant container database altcdb.
Opening pluggable database SOMEPDB on all instances of multitenant
container database altcdb.
Migration of pluggable database SOMEPDB completed.
Succeeded.
```

Source Database Alert Log Entry

Internally, the pluggable database is unplugged into an XML manifest file, and the datafiles are kept in place.

```
Completed: alter pluggable database SOMEPDB unplug into '/home/oracle/
somepdb.xml'
drop pluggable database SOMEPDB keep datafiles
```

Target Database Alert Log Entry

On the target database, a pluggable database is plugged in with the NOCOPY clause, which is why this operation is performed so quickly.

```
Completed: create pluggable database SOMEPDB using '/home/oracle/somepdb.xml'
nocopy standbys=none tempfile reuse
alter pluggable database SOMEPDB open instances=all
```

State of ALTCDB Post-Migration

At the end of the operation, the pluggable database SOMEPDB will be in the ALTCDB container database with its datafiles unmoved. For this reason, it is recommended that the source and destination container databases of a PDB migrate operation share the same ASM storage or the same faster NFS storage.

```
SQL> select db_unique_name from v$database;

DB_UNIQUE_NAME
------------------------------
Altcdb

SQL> show pdbs;

    CON_ID CON_NAME                        OPEN MODE  RESTRICTED
---------- ------------------------------ ---------- ----------
         2 PDB$SEED                        READ ONLY  NO
         3 SOMEPDB                         READ WRITE NO

SQL> select con_id,name from v$datafile order by con_id;

    CON_ID NAME
---------- ------------------------------------------------------------------
         1 +DATA/ALTCDB/DATAFILE/undotbs2.524.985217387
         1 +DATA/ALTCDB/DATAFILE/users.512.985217191
         1 +DATA/ALTCDB/DATAFILE/undotbs1.511.985217189
         1 +DATA/ALTCDB/DATAFILE/system.509.985217119
         1 +DATA/ALTCDB/DATAFILE/sysaux.510.985217165
         2 +DATA/ALTCDB/4700A987085B3DFAE05387E5E50A8C7B/DATAFILE/
           sysaux.520.985217263
         2 +DATA/ALTCDB/4700A987085B3DFAE05387E5E50A8C7B/DATAFILE/
           system.521.985217263
         2 +DATA/ALTCDB/4700A987085B3DFAE05387E5E50A8C7B/DATAFILE/
           undotbs1.522.985217263
```

```
3 +DATA/ORCLCDB/744827E32DAF16D5E053033AA8C089C7/DATAFILE/
    system.289.985198351
3 +DATA/ORCLCDB/744827E32DAF16D5E053033AA8C089C7/DATAFILE/
    sysaux.392.985198355
3 +DATA/ORCLCDB/744827E32DAF16D5E053033AA8C089C7/DATAFILE/
    undotbs1.393.985198359
3 +DATA/ORCLCDB/744827E32DAF16D5E053033AA8C089C7/DATAFILE/
    undo_2.377.985198359
3 +DATA/ORCLCDB/744827E32DAF16D5E053033AA8C089C7/DATAFILE/
    users.390.985198361
```

Summary

With each new release, Oracle is enhancing Oracle Data Guard and increasingly making it a feature that serves not only as a good disaster recovery solution but also as a feature that can be used to offload read-only workloads. After reading this chapter, you should have a good understanding of many of the new features of Data Guard in 12c R2 that help make maintaining and tuning ADG databases much easier.

CHAPTER 7

Oracle Sharding

Oracle Database 12c introduced a popular feature called *sharding*. Unlike RAC, this requires an application change to implement. Sharding applications must be designed correspondingly to be able to fully use the benefits of sharding.

Compared with RAC, an Oracle sharded database (SDB) does not share hardware or software between servers. Each shard is an independent server and uses its local storage, memory, CPU, and so on. The failure of one shard does not impact the transactions that are running on other shards.

One of the benefits of sharding is that each shard can run a different release of Oracle Database if the application supports it. Oracle sharding does not require shared storage components or Clusterware components.

The sharded database architecture can elastically scale up without downtime. You can add any platform and any version of SDBs. Currently, you can scale up to 1,000 shards (version 12.2).

Oracle sharding means that you are horizontally partitioning data across up to 1,000 independent Oracle Databases (shards), and partitioning splits a database table across shards so that each shard contains the table with the same columns but a different subset of rows.

You can compare it to the regular partition technology that is used with traditional Oracle Databases. The difference between sharded and nonsharded database partitioning, though, is that each partition of a sharded table resides in a separate tablespace, and each tablespace is associated with a specific shard instead of being in the same physical database.

Figure 7-1 shows that in the sharded architecture, a table will be created in the sharded catalog database and will contain only the table structure/metadata without any rows. The sharded databases will contain the table metadata and rows. Each shard contains a different set of rows, and data is evenly distributed between them. You also see this when you make a test load in SDBs.

© Y V Ravi Kumar, Nassyam Basha, Krishna Kumar K M, Bal Mukund Sharma, Konstantin Kerekovski 2019
Y V Ravi Kumar et al., *Oracle High Availability, Disaster Recovery, and Cloud Services*,
https://doi.org/10.1007/978-1-4842-4351-0_7

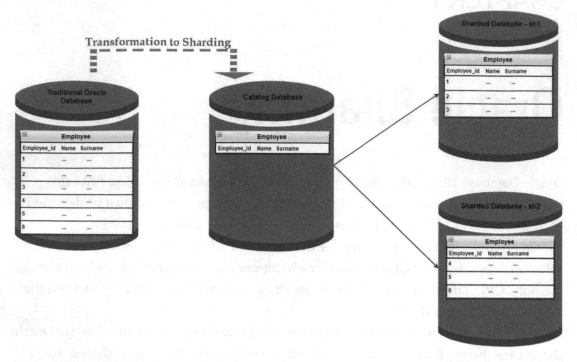

Figure 7-1. *Oracle sharding architecture*

The following are the minimum prerequisites for Oracle sharding:

- Oracle Enterprise Edition is a prerequisite.

- There's no separate license for Oracle partitioning in the Oracle sharding architecture.

- Oracle sharding requires a minimum release of Oracle Database v12.2.0.1 and Oracle Client v12.2.0.1.

- The initial release of Oracle sharding v12.2.0.1 does not support Oracle multitenant. This limitation will be lifted in future releases.

- For the first release of Oracle sharding, Oracle recommends using the same operating system (OS) for all the shards.

Components of the Sharding Architecture

Figure 7-2 shows the components of the Oracle sharding architecture.

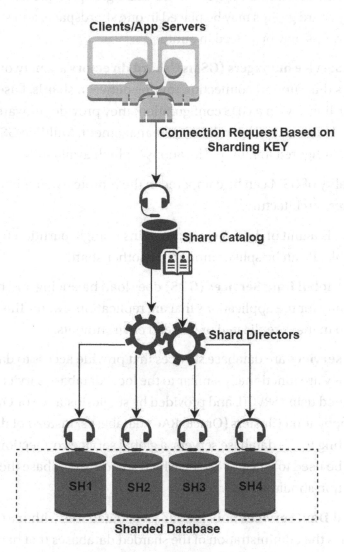

Clients/App Servers

Connection Request Based on Sharding KEY

Shard Catalog

Shard Directors

SH1   SH2   SH3   SH4

Sharded Database

Figure 7-2. *Components of Oracle sharding architecture*

- A **shard** is an individual physical server that is a subset of a sharded database.

- A **sharded database (SDB)** is a logical database that is distributed between several shards.

- A **shard group** is a grouping of one or more shards such as the primary and standby shard groups.

- A **shardspace** consists of one or more shard groups. For example, primary shard groups may be placed in one shardspace, and standby shard groups may be placed in another.

- **Global service managers (GSMs)/shard directors** are network listeners that support connection routing between shards, based on the sharding key. In a GDS configuration, they provide software-level failover, load balancing, and central management. Multiple GSMs can be configured in multiple locations for high availability.

The functionality of GSM can be compared to the remote listener in an Oracle Real Application Clusters architecture.

- A **chunk** is a unit of data. A chunk contains a single partition from each table. It can be split or moved to another shard.

- **Oracle Global Data Services (GDS)** does load balancing and high availability for the applications that are replication-aware. This makes easier to manage replicated or sharded environments.

- **Global services** are database services that provide access to data in SDB. They are functionally similar to the local database services that are created using SRVCTL and provided by single-instance or Oracle Real Application Clusters (Oracle RAC) databases. Instead of directly connecting to the database servers, a global service connection should be used to let GSM decide which sharding database the connection should be redirected to.

- A **Global Data Services pool** is a subset of databases within a GDS. It simplifies the administration of the sharded databases that have many shards. A database can belong to only a single Global Data Services pool.

- A **Global Data Services region** typically corresponds to a local area network (LAN) or metropolitan area network (MAN). It is also a subset of a database within a GDS based on the database location in a specific region.

- The **Global Data Services catalog/sharded catalog** is associated with only one GDS configuration, which must be in Oracle Database 12c or later. A Global Data Services catalog is a repository that stores configuration data for a Global Data Services configuration and all global services provided by that configuration. It is a repository database, and it can be cohosted with RMAN or EM catalogs. Because it is a critical component, Oracle strongly recommends using HA technologies such as Oracle Data Guard or Real Application Clusters.

- **GDSCTL** is a command-line utility that is used to manage SDBs.

Methods of Sharding

There are several methods of sharding in Oracle 12c R2.

- **System-managed sharding** is considered the simplest method because data is automatically maintained and does not require database administrator intervention to map data to specific shards. The partitioning algorithm evenly and randomly distributes data across the shards. This method is based on the consistent hash algorithm.

- **Composite sharding** makes data to be sharded by range or list for the first time and later by consistent hash. In this method, you need to manually maintain a balanced data distribution.

- **User-defined sharding** requires high DBA intervention to maintain the balance between shards. Users must map the data to individual shards. This method can be considered to be error-prone and relies on a DBA's own implementation. So, this method is not recommended until explicitly required. Moreover, this method requires two sharding keys (the super sharding key and the sharding key).

CREATE TABLE Syntax in SDB

In normal, nonsharded databases, you can create tables using the CREATE TABLE command. Sharded databases introduce new syntaxes: CREATE SHARDED TABLE and CREATE DUPLICATED TABLE.

SQL syntax for Sharded table:

```
CREATE SHARDED TABLE customers
( cust_id      NUMBER NOT NULL
, name         VARCHAR2(50)
, address      VARCHAR2(250)
, registered   DATE
,CONSTRAINT cust_pk PRIMARY KEY(cust_id))
PARTITION BY CONSISTENT HASH(cust_id)
PARTITIONS AUTO
TABLESPACE SET mytbsset;
```

In addition to sharded tables, SDBs can contain tables that are duplicated on all shards called DUPLICATED TABLES. This feature is useful when a table is quite small and frequently accessed. Read operations can become faster if they are distributed between shards that contain the same data.

Synchronization happens using materialized view replication. A duplicated table is a read-only materialized view. The master table is located in the shard catalog database. The following syntax automatically creates a materialized view, master table, and other objects necessary for a materialized view:

Here is the SQL syntax for a duplicated table:

```
CREATE DUPLICATED TABLE customers_dup(
cust_id      NUMBER NOT NULL PRIMARY KEY
, name          VARCHAR2(50)
, address       VARCHAR2(250)
, registered   DATE)
TABLESPACE mytbs;
```

Figure 7-3 illustrates that sharded tables are horizontally partitioned across shards and that duplicated tables are replicated to all shards.

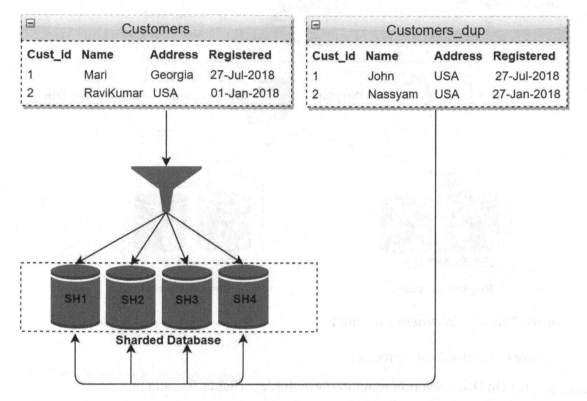

Figure 7-3. *Difference between sharded tables and duplicated tables*

Installation and Configuration

Here is the environment summary (see Figure 7-4):

- **Shard database servers**:

  - *Primary*: shdb1 and shdb2 in the region us-west

  - *Standby*: shdb3 and shdb4 in the region us-east

- **GSM and shard catalog server**: shcat in the region us-north

- **Shard catalog database name**: SHRCAT

Install Oracle DB 12cR2 on all five nodes with the following options

> Install DB software only
> Single Instance Database Installation with Data Guard
> Enterprise Edition

Software:

* Oracle DB 12cR2
* Oracle 12cR2 Global Service Manager (GSM/GDS)
5 hosts:

Catalog: SHCAT
Primary: SHDB1, SHDB2
Standby: SHDB3, SHDB4

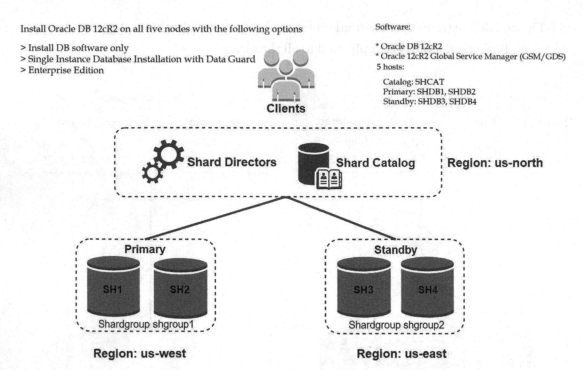

Figure 7-4. Environment summary

Here is the installation process:

1. On DNS servers or temporarily in the /etc/hosts file, add the entries about each server.

2. Create logical volumes for storing database files on the shard and catalog nodes, if not using ASM.

3. Calculate the size of /dev/shm.

4. Disable iptables and firewalls on all hosts.

5. Disable IPv6.

6. Install an Oracle RDBMS pre-installation RPM on all hosts.

7. Create the necessary directories on each sharded database (shdb1 and shdb2) and catalog/GSM nodes (shcat).

8. Install the Oracle Database 12c R2 software only on the shard and catalog nodes.

9. Create the non-container database SHRCAT using DBCA on the catalog/GSM node.

10. On the catalog/GSM node, install the GSM software in a different home.

11. Prepare the SHRCAT database.

12. Using GSDCTL create the shard catalog.

13. Register shard nodes to the SHRCAT database.

14. Create the shard group, director, and shards.

15. Deploy shards using GSDCTL.

16. Create a global service.

17. Disable the Fast-Start Failover (FSFO) Observer (optional).

18. Create the tablespaces, schemas, and tables.

Add the DNS or Hosts File Entries

Add the DNS or hosts file entries on each database and catalog/GSM nodes. Here's an example:

```
# cat /etc/hosts

10.0.2.6        shdb1.localdomain        shdb1
10.0.2.7        shdb2.localdomain        shdb2
10.0.2.8        shdb3.localdomain        shdb3
10.0.2.9        shdb4.localdomain        shdb4
10.0.2.10       shcat.localdomain        shcat
```

Add a Disk for Database Storage, Create LVM on It, and Mount It

Do the following on each database and catalog/GSM node:

```
# pvcreate /dev/sdb
Physical volume "/dev/sdb" successfully created.

# vgcreate dbstorage /dev/sdb
Volume group "dbstorage" successfully created
```

343

```
# lvcreate -l 100%FREE -n oradata dbstorage
Logical volume "oradata" created.

# mkdir /u01
# mkfs -t ext4 /dev/dbstorage/oradata

# echo "/dev/dbstorage/oradata /u01 ext4 defaults 0 0" >> /etc/fstab

# mount /u01
```

Calculate the Size of /dev/shm

Let's calculate the size.

1. Calculate the size of /dev/shm using the following formula for each database and catalog/GSM node:

   Take 80 percent of the total memory in gigabytes for each system and round it up to the next available integer (ceil):

```
v_OracleMemory = ceil( cat /proc/meminfo |grep MemTotal|awk '{print $2}'
/1024/1024 * 0.8)
```

2. Indicate the value of v_OracleMemory as a size of /dev/shm.

```
# echo "tmpfs /dev/shm tmpfs size=v_OracleMemoryG 0 0" >> /etc/fstab
```

For example:

```
# echo "tmpfs /dev/shm tmpfs size=2G 0 0" >> /etc/fstab
# mount -o remount tmpfs
```

In case you already have the entry in fstab, just modify it according to the previous rules.

Disable iptables and Firewalls on All Hosts

Here are the commands to do this:

```
# systemctl stop iptables
# systemctl disable iptables
# systemctl stop firewalld
# chkconfig iptables off
# systemctl disable firewalld
```

Disable IPv6

Not disabling IPv6 makes trouble when some services are started. The service may choose to start on IPv6. Do the following on all hosts:

1. Add the following at the bottom of /etc/sysctl.conf:

```
net.ipv6.conf.all.disable_ipv6 = 1
net.ipv6.conf.default.disable_ipv6 = 1
net.ipv6.conf.lo.disable_ipv6 = 1
```

2. Reboot the server.

```
# reboot
```

Install the Oracle RDBMS Pre-installation RPM on All Hosts

Here's the command:

```
# yum install oracle-database-server-12cR2-preinstall* -y
```

Create the Necessary Directories on Each Sharded Database (shdb1 and shdb2) and Catalog/GSM Nodes (shcat)

Do the following on all hosts:

```
# mkdir -p /u01/app/oracle/product/12.2.0/dbhome_1
# mkdir -p /u01/app/oraInventory
# mkdir -p /u01/app/oracle/oradata
# mkdir -p /u01/app/oracle/fast_recovery_area/
# mkdir -p /u01/install
# chown -R oracle:oinstall /u01
# chmod 755 -R /u01
```

Create a GSM home directory on the catalog/GSM server only (shcat).

```
# mkdir -p /u01/app/gsm/12.2.0/
```

Install the Database Software in Silent Mode on Each Sharded Database (shdb[1-4]) and Catalog/GSM Node (shcat)

Here are the steps:

1. Modify the following values in the response file:

```
oracle.install.responseFileVersion=
/oracle/install/rspfmt_dbinstall_response_schema_v12.2.0
oracle.install.option=INSTALL_DB_SWONLY
UNIX_GROUP_NAME=oinstall
INVENTORY_LOCATION=/u01/app/oraInventory
ORACLE_HOME=/u01/app/oracle/product/12.2.0/dbhome_1
ORACLE_BASE=/u01/app/oracle
oracle.install.db.InstallEdition=EE
oracle.install.db.OSDBA_GROUP=dba
oracle.install.db.OSOPER_GROUP=dba
oracle.install.db.OSBACKUPDBA_GROUP=dba
oracle.install.db.OSDGDBA_GROUP=dba
oracle.install.db.OSKMDBA_GROUP=dba
oracle.install.db.OSRACDBA_GROUP=dba
SECURITY_UPDATES_VIA_MYORACLESUPPORT=false
DECLINE_SECURITY_UPDATES=true
```

2. From the oracle user, run the installation using the modified response file.

```
$ cd /u01/install/database

$ ./runInstaller -silent -responseFile /u01/install/database/response/
db_install.rsp

Starting Oracle Universal Installer...
Checking Temp space: must be greater than 500 MB.   Actual 49101 MB    Passed
Checking swap space: must be greater than 150 MB.   Actual 2047 MB     Passed
```

Preparing to launch Oracle Universal Installer from /tmp/OraInstall2018-07-31_01-55-55AM. Please wait ...[oracle@shdb1 database]$ You can find the log of this install session at:
/u01/app/oraInventory/logs/installActions2018-07-31_01-55-55AM.log
The installation of Oracle Database 12c was successful.
Please check '/u01/app/oraInventory/logs/silentInstall2018-07-31_01-55-55AM.log' for more details.

   3.   As a root user, execute the following scripts:

```
# /u01/app/oraInventory/orainstRoot.sh
# /u01/app/oracle/product/12.2.0/dbhome_1/root.sh
```

   4.   Run these scripts as a root user:

```
# /u01/app/oraInventory/orainstRoot.sh
# /u01/app/oracle/product/12.2.0/dbhome_1/root.sh
```

Create a Noncontainer Database Using DBCA and a Local Listener Using NETCA on the Catalog/GSM Node Only

Follow these steps:

   1.   Run this as the oracle user:

```
$ cd /u01/app/oracle/product/12.2.0/dbhome_1/bin
$ ./dbca -silent \
-createDatabase \
-templateName General_Purpose.dbc \
-gdbName SHRCAT \
-sid SHRCAT \
-SysPassword oracle \
-SystemPassword oracle \
-emConfiguration NONE \
-redoLogFileSize 500  \
-recoveryAreaDestination /u01/app/oracle/fast_recovery_area \
-datafileDestination /u01/app/oracle/oradata \
-storageType FS \
```

```
-characterSet UTF8 \
-nationalCharacterSet UTF8 \
-automaticMemoryManagement true \
-databaseType MULTIPURPOSE \
-memoryPercentage 80
    ...
Copying database files
1% complete
2% complete
18% complete
33% complete
Creating and starting Oracle instance
35% complete
40% complete
44% complete
49% complete
50% complete
53% complete
55% complete
Completing Database Creation
56% complete
57% complete
58% complete
62% complete
65% complete
66% complete
Executing Post Configuration Actions
100% complete
Look at the log file "/u01/app/oracle/cfgtoollogs/dbca/SHRCAT/SHRCAT1.log"
for further details
```

2.   Here's a sample of the listener response file called /u01/app/
      oracle/product/12.2.0/dbhome_1/assistants/netca/netca.rsp:

```
[GENERAL]
RESPONSEFILE_VERSION="12.2"
CREATE_TYPE="CUSTOM"
[oracle.net.ca]
INSTALLED_COMPONENTS={"server","net8","javavm"}
INSTALL_TYPE=""typical""
LISTENER_NUMBER=1
LISTENER_NAMES={"LISTENER"}
LISTENER_PROTOCOLS={"TCP;1521"}
LISTENER_START=""LISTENER""
NAMING_METHODS={"TNSNAMES","ONAMES","HOSTNAME"}
NSN_NUMBER=1
NSN_NAMES={"EXTPROC_CONNECTION_DATA"}
NSN_SERVICE={"PLSExtProc"}
NSN_PROTOCOLS={"TCP; shcat;1521"}
```

3.   As the oracle user, run NETCA and indicate the modified response
      file, as shown here:

```
$ cd /u01/app/oracle/product/12.2.0/dbhome_1/bin

$ ./netca -silent -responseFile /u01/app/oracle/product/12.2.0/dbhome_1/
assistants/netca/netca.rsp
Parsing command line arguments:
Parameter "silent" = true
Parameter "responsefile" = /tmp/netca.rsp
Done parsing command line arguments.
Oracle Net Services Configuration:
Profile configuration complete.
Oracle Net Listener Startup:
Running Listener Control:

/u01/app/oracle/product/12.2.0/dbhome_1/bin/lsnrctl start LISTENER
Listener Control complete.
Listener started successfully.
```

```
Listener configuration complete.
Oracle Net Services configuration successful.
The exit code is 0
```

4. If you have a large amount of memory, you should use hugepages and Automatic Shared Memory Management (ASMM) and we can expand Automatic Memory Management (AMM) instead of 'AMM'.

5. Identify the correct value for LOCAL_LISTENER.

```
$ export ORACLE_HOME=/u01/app/oracle/product/12.2.0/dbhome_1
$ export ORACLE_BASE=/u01/app/oracle
$ export PATH=$ORACLE_HOME/bin:$PATH
```

$ lsnrctl status

```
LSNRCTL for Linux: Version 12.2.0.1.0 - Production on 31-JUL-2018 10:40:12

Copyright (c) 1991, 2016, Oracle.  All rights reserved.

Connecting to (DESCRIPTION=(ADDRESS=(PROTOCOL=TCP)(HOST=shcat.localdomain)
(PORT=1521)))
STATUS of the LISTENER
------------------------
Alias                     LISTENER
Version                   TNSLSNR for Linux: Version 12.2.0.1.0 - Production
Start Date                31-JUL-2018 10:39:54
Uptime                    0 days 0 hr. 0 min. 19 sec
Trace Level               off
Security                  ON: Local OS Authentication
SNMP                      OFF
Listener Parameter File   /u01/app/oracle/product/12.2.0/dbhome_1/network/
                            admin/listener.ora
Listener Log File         /u01/app/oracle/diag/tnslsnr/shcat/listener/
                            alert/log.xml
Listening Endpoints Summary...
  (DESCRIPTION=(ADDRESS=(PROTOCOL=tcp)(HOST=shcat.localdomain)(PORT=1521)))
  (DESCRIPTION=(ADDRESS=(PROTOCOL=ipc)(KEY=EXTPROC1521)))
The listener supports no services
The command completed successfully
```

6.   Set the LOCAL_LISTENER parameter for the catalog database.

```
$ . oraenv
ORACLE_SID = [oracle] ? SHRCAT
The Oracle base has been set to /u01/app/oracle
```

$ sqlplus / as sysdba
```
SQL*Plus: Release 12.2.0.1.0 Production on Tue Jul 31 10:44:13 2018
Copyright (c) 1982, 2016, Oracle.  All rights reserved.
Connected to:
Oracle Database 12c Enterprise Edition Release 12.2.0.1.0 - 64bit Production

SQL> alter system set local_listener='(DESCRIPTION=(ADDRESS=(PROTOCOL=tcp)
(HOST=shcat.localdomain)(PORT=1521)))';
System altered.

SQL> alter system register;
System altered.
```

7.   Check the status of the listener again to be sure that the database
     is registered.

$ lsnrctl status
```
LSNRCTL for Linux: Version 12.2.0.1.0 - Production on 31-JUL-2018 10:44:41
Copyright (c) 1991, 2016, Oracle.  All rights reserved.
Connecting to (DESCRIPTION=(ADDRESS=(PROTOCOL=TCP)(HOST=shcat.localdomain)
(PORT=1521)))
STATUS of the LISTENER
------------------------
Alias                     LISTENER
Version                   TNSLSNR for Linux: Version 12.2.0.1.0 -
Production
Start Date                31-JUL-2018 10:39:54
Uptime                    0 days 0 hr. 4 min. 48 sec
Trace Level               off
Security                  ON: Local OS Authentication
SNMP                      OFF
```

```
Listener Parameter File    /u01/app/oracle/product/12.2.0/dbhome_1/network/
                           admin/listener.ora
Listener Log File          /u01/app/oracle/diag/tnslsnr/shcat/listener/
                           alert/log.xml
Listening Endpoints Summary...
  (DESCRIPTION=(ADDRESS=(PROTOCOL=tcp)(HOST=shcat.localdomain)(PORT=1521)))
  (DESCRIPTION=(ADDRESS=(PROTOCOL=ipc)(KEY=EXTPROC1521)))
Services Summary...
Service "SHRCAT" has 1 instance(s).
  Instance "SHRCAT", status READY, has 1 handler(s) for this service...
Service "SHRCATXDB" has 1 instance(s).
  Instance "SHRCAT", status READY, has 1 handler(s) for this service...
The command completed successfully
```

Install the GSM Software on the Catalog/GSM Node (shcat)

Follow these steps:

1. Download the Oracle Database 12c Release 2 Global
   Service Manager (GSM/GDS) (12.2.0.1.0) for Linux x86-64
   (linuxx64_12201_gsm.zip).

2. Install the software silently in a separate home at /u01/app/
   gsm/12.2.0.

2.1. Here's a sample of the response file /u01/install/gsm/response/
   gsm_install.rsp:

```
oracle.install.responseFileVersion=/oracle/install/rspfmt_gsminstall_
response_schema_v12.2.0
UNIX_GROUP_NAME=oinstall
INVENTORY_LOCATION=/u01/app/oraInventory
ORACLE_HOME=/u01/app/gsm/12.2.0
ORACLE_BASE=/u01/app/gsm
```

2.2   As the oracle user, run the following:

$ **./runInstaller -silent -responseFile /u01/install/gsm/response/gsm_**
install.rsp
Starting Oracle Universal Installer...
Checking Temp space: must be greater than 551 MB.   Actual 27403 MB   Passed
Preparing to launch Oracle Universal Installer from /tmp/OraInstall2018-
07-31_10-53-40AM. Please wcat gsm]$ You can find the log of this install
session at:
/u01/app/oraInventory/logs/installActions2018-07-31_10-53-40AM.log As a
root user, execute the following script(s):
1. /u01/app/gsm/12.2.0/root.sh
Successfully Setup Software.

2.3   Run the root.sh file.

/u01/app/gsm/12.2.0/root.sh

Performing root user operation.

The following environment variables are set as:
    ORACLE_OWNER= oracle
    ORACLE_HOME= /u01/app/gsm/12.2.0
    Copying dbhome to /usr/local/bin ...
    Copying oraenv to /usr/local/bin ...
    Copying coraenv to /usr/local/bin ...

Entries will be added to the /etc/oratab file as needed by
Database Configuration Assistant when a database is created
Finished running generic part of root script.
Now product-specific root actions will be performed.

If you prefer to install GSM in GUI mode, please do the following:

1.   As the root user, install the necessary RPMs for VNC.

yum install -y tigervnc-*
yum install -y xterm

2.   Switch to the oracle user and set the password for VNC.

```
# su - oracle
$ vncpasswd
Password:
Verify:
Would you like to enter a view-only password (y/n)? n
A view-only password is not used
```

3.   Run VNC.

```
$ vncserver -geometry 1024x1024
xauth:  file /home/oracle/.Xauthority does not exist
New 'shcat:1 (oracle)' desktop is shcat:1
Creating default startup script /home/oracle/.vnc/xstartup
Creating default config /home/oracle/.vnc/config
Starting applications specified in /home/oracle/.vnc/xstartup
Log file is /home/oracle/.vnc/shcat:1.log
```

4.   Ensure that the TCP/5901 port is open from your computer to the catalog/GSM server to be able to connect via vncviewer.

5.   Connect to the catalog/GSM server using vncviewer and run the GSM installation from the terminal.

```
$ /u01/install/gsm/runInstaller
Starting Oracle Universal Installer...
Checking Temp space: must be greater than 551 MB.   Actual 38234 MB
Passed
Checking monitor: must be configured to display at least 256
colors.   Actual 16777216   Passed
Preparing to launch Oracle Universal Installer from /tmp/OraInstall2018-07-
31_06-58-51PM. Please wait ...[oracle@shcat ~]$
```

After running runInstaller, the window in Figure 7-5 appears. Enter paths for the Oracle base and software location.

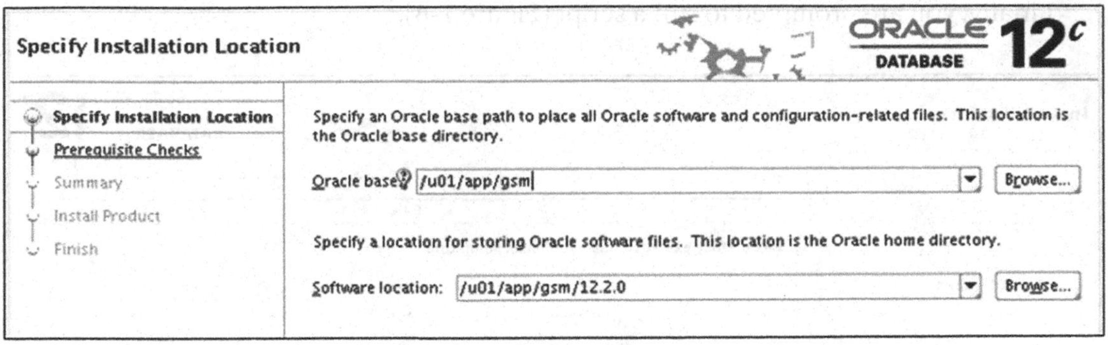

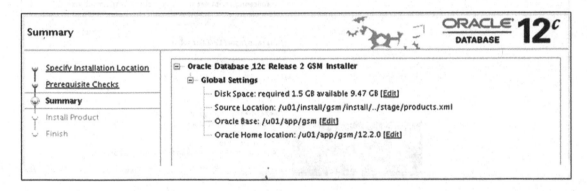

Figure 7-5. *Specifying the base and software location for GSM*

After reviewing the summary, click the OK button in the window shown in Figure 7-6.

Figure 7-6. *Installation summary of GSM*

The installation starts (Figure 7-7).

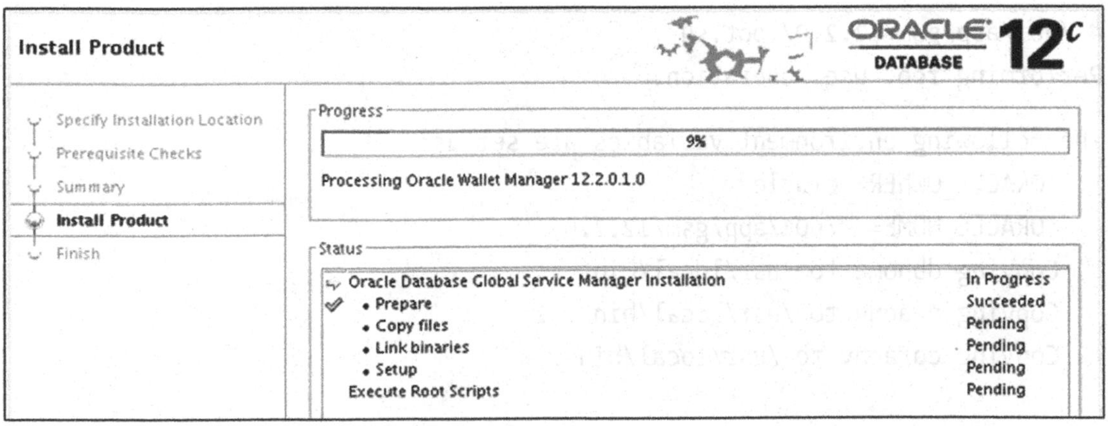

Figure 7-7. *Installation process of GSM*

Finally, you are prompted to run a script (Figure 7-8).

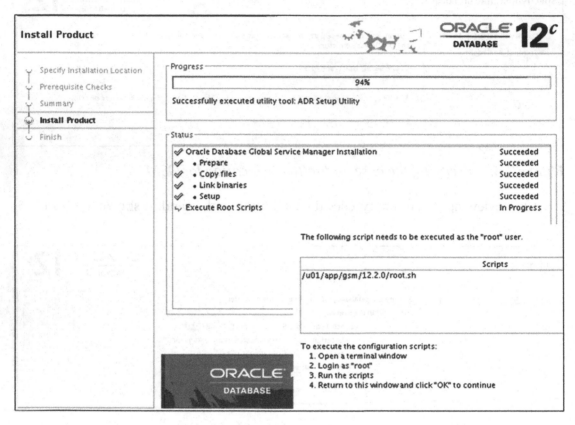

Figure 7-8. *Execute root.sh to complete the installation process of GSM*

6.   Run the root.sh script.

```
# /u01/app/gsm/12.2.0/root.sh
Performing root user operation.

The following environment variables are set as:
    ORACLE_OWNER= oracle
    ORACLE_HOME=  /u01/app/gsm/12.2.0
  Copying dbhome to /usr/local/bin ...
  Copying oraenv to /usr/local/bin ...
  Copying coraenv to /usr/local/bin ...
```

Entries will be added to the /etc/oratab file as needed by
Database Configuration Assistant when a database is created
Finished running generic part of root script.
Now product-specific root actions will be performed.

7. Click the OK button in the GUI.

Create a Shard Catalog Schema in the SHRCAT Database in the SHCAT Node

Follow these steps:

1. Connect to the SHRCAT database as a SYS and do the following
    steps:

```
$ . oraenv
ORACLE_SID = [oracle] ? SHRCAT
The Oracle base has been set to /u01/app/oracle

$ sqlplus / as sysdba
```

2. Set the db_create_file_dest parameter.

```
SQL> alter system set db_create_file_dest='/u01/app/oracle/oradata';
System altered.
```

3. The gsmcatuser schema is used by the shard director while
    connecting to the shard catalog database. Unlock the schema and
    set the password.

```
SQL> alter user gsmcatuser account unlock;
User altered.

SQL> alter user gsmcatuser identified by oracle;
User altered.
```

4. Create the administrator schema and grant the necessary
    permissions.

```
SQL> create user gsmadmin identified by oracle;
User created.
SQL> grant connect, create session, gsmadmin_role to gsmadmin;
Grant succeeded.
```

5. Change the following values in the spfile.

```
SQL> alter system set open_links=16 scope=spfile;
System altered.
SQL> alter system set open_links_per_instance=16 scope=spfile;
System altered.
```

6. Restart the SHRCAT database for the changes to take effect.

```
SQL> shutdown immediate
Database closed.
Database dismounted.
ORACLE instance shut down.
SQL> startup
ORACLE instance started.
Total System Global Area       1677721600 bytes
Fixed Size                        8621424 bytes
Variable Size                  1073742480 bytes
Database Buffers                587202560 bytes
Redo Buffers                      8155136 bytes
Database mounted.
Database opened.
```

7. Shards are created by the DBMS_SCHEDULER package that is
    executed on the shard catalog (SHRCAT). It communicates with the
    scheduler agents on shard hosts (shdb1 and shdb2).

Agents that are running on shard servers are invoking the DBCA and NETCA tools to
create database and local listeners.

For configuring a scheduler agent, run the following commands on the SHRCAT database:

```
SQL> execute dbms_xdb.sethttpport(8080);
PL/SQL procedure successfully completed.

SQL> commit;
Commit complete.
SQL> @?/rdbms/admin/prvtrsch.plb
PL/SQL procedure successfully completed.
Session altered.
PL/SQL procedure successfully completed.
PL/SQL procedure successfully completed.
Session altered.
Session altered.
Package created.
No errors.
Grant succeeded.
Session altered.
Session altered.
Package body created.
No errors.
Session altered.
Session altered.
Procedure created.
No errors.
Function created.
No errors.
Procedure created.
No errors.
Procedure created.
No errors.
Procedure created.
No errors.
Procedure created.
No errors.
```

```
Procedure created.
No errors.
Procedure created.
No errors.
Procedure created.
No errors.
Procedure created.
No errors.
Procedure created.
No errors.
Procedure created.
No errors.
Audit policy altered.
1 row updated.
Commit complete.
Session altered.
PL/SQL procedure successfully completed.
```

8. Set the password for the agent.

```
SQL> exec DBMS_SCHEDULER.SET_AGENT_REGISTRATION_PASS('oracle');
PL/SQL procedure successfully completed.
```

Start the Scheduler Agents on Sharding Nodes

Scheduler agents come with the database 12c R2 software, so there's no need to install additional software.

Please consider that port 8080 must be accessible from the sharding nodes to the catalog/GSM node.

1. Connect as the oracle user and register the hosts with the agent.
    Then run the following command on each DB node:

```
$ export ORACLE_HOME=/u01/app/oracle/product/12.2.0/dbhome_1
$ export ORACLE_BASE=/u01/app/oracle
$ export PATH=$PATH:$ORACLE_HOME/bin
```

```
$ schagent -registerdatabase shcat 8080
Agent Registration Password ? ******* <<<Enter the password here, in our
case it is oracle
Oracle Scheduler Agent Registration for 12.2.0.1.2 Agent
Agent Registration Successful!
```

2. Start the agent and check the status on each database node.

2.1. Connect to the sharded database (shdb1).

```
[oracle@shdb1 ~]$ schagent -start
Scheduler agent started using port 44064

[oracle@shdb1 ~]$ schagent -status
Agent running with PID 3332

Agent_version:12.2.0.1.2
Running_time:00:00:18
Total_jobs_run:0
Running_jobs:0
Platform:Linux
ORACLE_HOME:/u01/app/oracle/product/12.2.0/dbhome_1
ORACLE_BASE:/u01/app/oracle
Port:44064
Host:shdb1.localdomain
```

2.2. Connect to the sharded database (shdb2).

```
[oracle@shdb2 ~]$ schagent -start
Scheduler agent started using port 22847

[oracle@shdb2 ~]$ schagent -status
Agent running with PID 2951

Agent_version:12.2.0.1.2
Running_time:00:00:18
Total_jobs_run:0
Running_jobs:0
Platform:Linux
```

```
ORACLE_HOME:/u01/app/oracle/product/12.2.0/dbhome_1
ORACLE_BASE:/u01/app/oracle
Port:22847
Host:shdb2.localdomain
```

2.3.   Connect to the sharded database (shdb3).

```
[oracle@shdb3 ~]$ schagent -start
Scheduler agent started using port 20265
[oracle@shdb3 ~]$ schagent -status
Agent running with PID 2952
Agent_version:12.2.0.1.2
Running_time:00:00:18
Total_jobs_run:0
Running_jobs:0
Platform:Linux
ORACLE_HOME:/u01/app/oracle/product/12.2.0/dbhome_1
ORACLE_BASE:/u01/app/oracle
Port:20265
Host:shdb3.localdomain
```

2.4.   Connect to the sharded database (shdb4).

```
[oracle@shdb4 ~]$ schagent -start
Scheduler agent started using port 40482

[oracle@shdb4 ~]$ schagent -status
Agent running with PID 2980
Agent_version:12.2.0.1.2
Running_time:00:00:18
Total_jobs_run:0
Running_jobs:0
Platform:Linux
ORACLE_HOME:/u01/app/oracle/product/12.2.0/dbhome_1
ORACLE_BASE:/u01/app/oracle
Port:40482
Host:shdb4.localdomain
```

Using GSDCTL to Create the Shard Catalog

Follow these steps:

1. Connect to the catalog database using GSDCTL and run the following commands.

   Run this as the oracle user:

```
$ export ORACLE_HOME=/u01/app/gsm/12.2.0/
$ export ORACLE_BASE=/u01/app/gsm
$ export PATH=$ORACLE_HOME/bin:$PATH

$ gdsctl

GDSCTL: Version 12.2.0.1.0 - Production on Tue Jul 31 11:09:21 EDT 2018
Copyright (c) 2011, 2016, Oracle.  All rights reserved.
Welcome to GDSCTL, type "help" for information.
Warning: current GSM name is not set automatically because gsm.ora contains
zero or several GSM entries. Use "set  gsm" command to set GSM for the session.
Current GSM is set to GSMORA

GDSCTL> create shardcatalog -database shcat:1521:SHRCAT -user gsmadmin/
oracle -chunks 12 -sdb SHRCAT -region us-west,us-east,us-north

Catalog is created
```

2. Create and start the shard director; you will need to indicate the free port number. In the password field, you need to write the password for the gsmcatuser user.

```
GDSCTL>add gsm -gsm mysharddirector -listener 1522 -pwd oracle -catalog
shcat:1521:SHRCAT -region us-north
GSM successfully added

GDSCTL>start gsm -gsm mysharddirector
GSM is started successfully
```

3. Check the status of gsm.

```
GDSCTL> status gsm
Alias                     MYSHARDDIRECTOR
Version                   12.2.0.1.0
Start Date                31-JUL-2018 11:12:05
Trace Level               off
Listener Log File         /u01/app/gsm/diag/gsm/shcat/mysharddirector/
                          alert/log.xml
Listener Trace File       /u01/app/gsm/diag/gsm/shcat/mysharddirector/
                          trace/ora_8412_140134614061440.trc
Endpoint summary          (ADDRESS=(HOST=shcat.localdomain)(PORT=1522)
                          (PROTOCOL=tcp))
GSMOCI Version            2.2.1
Mastership                Y
Connected to GDS catalog  Y
Process Id                8415
Number of reconnections   0
Pending tasks.     Total  0
Tasks in  process. Total  0
Regional Mastership       TRUE
Total messages published  0
Time Zone                 -04:00
Orphaned Buddy Regions:
    None
GDS region                us-north
```

4. If the oracle user does not have a password, set it now on all sharding nodes. For simplicity, use the same password for each shard.

```
# passwd oracle
Changing password for user oracle.
New password:
BAD PASSWORD: The password is shorter than 8 characters
Retype new password:
passwd: all authentication tokens updated successfully.
```

```
GDSCTL>add credential -credential os_oracle_cred -osaccount oracle
-ospassword oracle
The operation completed successfully
```

Create the Shard Group, Director, and Shards

Follow these steps:

1. Connect to the catalog database using GDSCTL.

```
GDSCTL>set gsm -gsm mysharddirector
GDSCTL>connect gsmadmin/oracle
Catalog connection is established
```

2. Add the shard groups.

```
GDSCTL>add shardgroup -shardgroup shgroup1 -deploy_as primary -region us-west
The operation completed successfully

GDSCTL>add shardgroup -shardgroup shgroup2 -deploy_as active_standby
-region us-east
The operation completed successfully
```

3. Because we used nondefault character sets when creating the catalog database using DBCA (-nationalCharacterSet UTF8, -characterSet UTF8), we must create a parameter file with the following values on the catalog server via the oracle user:

    Place the values in one line.

```
$ cat /tmp/dbcaparams
-nationalCharacterSet UTF8 -characterSet UTF8

$ chmod 777 /tmp/dbcaparams
```

   Otherwise, you will get the following error when running the shard addition command:

```
GSM-45029: SQL error
ORA-03719: Shard character set does not match catalog character set.
```

```
ORA-06512: at "GSMADMIN_INTERNAL.DBMS_GSM_POOLADMIN", line 7469
ORA-06512: at "SYS.DBMS_SYS_ERROR", line 79
ORA-06512: at "GSMADMIN_INTERNAL.DBMS_GSM_POOLADMIN", line 5770
ORA-06512: at line 1
```

   4. Add shards for each shdb[1-4].

```
GDSCTL> add invitednode shdb1 -group shgroup1
GDSCTL> create shard -shardgroup shgroup1 -destination shdb1 -credential
os_oracle_cred -dbparamfile /tmp/dbcaparams -sys_password oracle
The operation completed successfully
DB Unique Name: sh1

GDSCTL> add invitednode shdb2 -group shgroup1
GDSCTL> create shard -shardgroup shgroup1 -destination shdb2 -credential
os_oracle_cred -dbparamfile /tmp/dbcaparams -sys_password oracle
The operation completed successfully
DB Unique Name: sh2

GDSCTL> add invitednode shdb3 -group shgroup2
GDSCTL> create shard -shardgroup shgroup2 -destination shdb3 -credential
os_oracle_cred -dbparamfile /tmp/dbcaparams -sys_password oracle
The operation completed successfully
DB Unique Name: sh3

GDSCTL> add invitednode shdb4 -group shgroup2
GDSCTL> create shard -shardgroup shgroup2 -destination shdb4 -credential
os_oracle_cred -dbparamfile /tmp/dbcaparams -sys_password oracle
The operation completed successfully
DB Unique Name: sh4
```

> You have created four shards: sh1 and sh2 in primary shard group
> called shgroup1 and sh3 and sh4 in the standby shard group
> called shgroup2.

5. After adding shards, check the configuration.

```
GDSCTL>config

Regions
-----------------------
us-east
us-north
us-west

GSMs
-----------------------
mysharddirector

Sharded Database
-----------------------
shrcat

Databases
-----------------------
sh1
sh2
sh3
sh4

Shard Groups
-----------------------
shgroup1
shgroup2

Shard spaces
-----------------------
shardspaceora

Services
-----------------------

GDSCTL pending requests
-----------------------
```

```
Command                          Object                      Status
-------                          ------                      ------

Global properties
-----------------------
Name: oradbcloud
Master GSM: mysharddirector
DDL sequence #: 0
```

GDSCTL>**config shard**

```
Name    Shard Group    Status    State    Region    Availability
----    -----------    ------    -----    ------    ------------
sh1     shgroup1       U         none     us-west   -
sh2     shgroup1       U         none     us-west   -
sh3     shgroup2       U         none     us-east   -
sh4     shgroup2       U         none     us-east   -
```

GDSCTL> **config shardspace**

```
Shard space                 Chunks
------------                ------
shardspaceora               12
```

Deploy Shards Using GSDCTL

Follow these steps:

1. To create databases on the shdb1 and shdb2 servers, you just
   need to run the DEPLOY command from GSDCTL. It will take care
   of creating the database using DBCA and create listeners using
   NETCA.

   Be patient; it needs time.

```
GDSCTL>deploy
deploy: examining configuration...
deploy: deploying primary shard 'sh1' ...
deploy: network listener configuration successful at destination 'shdb1'
```

```
deploy: starting DBCA at destination 'shdb1' to create primary shard 'sh1' ...
deploy: deploying primary shard 'sh2' ...
deploy: network listener configuration successful at destination 'shdb2'
deploy: starting DBCA at destination 'shdb2' to create primary shard 'sh2' ...
deploy: waiting for 2 DBCA primary creation job(s) to complete...
deploy: waiting for 2 DBCA primary creation job(s) to complete...
deploy: waiting for 2 DBCA primary creation job(s) to complete...
deploy: waiting for 2 DBCA primary creation job(s) to complete...
deploy: waiting for 2 DBCA primary creation job(s) to complete...
deploy: waiting for 2 DBCA primary creation job(s) to complete...
deploy: waiting for 2 DBCA primary creation job(s) to complete...
deploy: waiting for 2 DBCA primary creation job(s) to complete...
deploy: waiting for 2 DBCA primary creation job(s) to complete...
deploy: DBCA primary creation job succeeded at destination 'shdb1' for shard 'sh1'
deploy: deploying standby shard 'sh3' ...
deploy: network listener configuration successful at destination 'shdb3'
deploy: starting DBCA at destination 'shdb3' to create standby shard 'sh3' ...
deploy: DBCA primary creation job succeeded at destination 'shdb2' for shard 'sh2'
deploy: deploying standby shard 'sh4' ...
deploy: network listener configuration successful at destination 'shdb4'
deploy: starting DBCA at destination 'shdb4' to create standby shard 'sh4' ...
deploy: waiting for 2 DBCA standby creation job(s) to complete...
deploy: waiting for 2 DBCA standby creation job(s) to complete...
deploy: waiting for 2 DBCA standby creation job(s) to complete...
deploy: DBCA standby creation job succeeded at destination 'shdb3' for shard 'sh3'
deploy: DBCA standby creation job succeeded at destination 'shdb4' for shard 'sh4'
deploy: requesting Data Guard configuration on shards via GSM
deploy: shards configured successfully
The operation completed successfully
```

2. Check the configuration.

```
GDSCTL>config shard
```

Name	Shard Group	Status	State	Region	Availability
sh1	shgroup1	Ok	Deployed	us-west	ONLINE
sh2	shgroup1	Ok	Deployed	us-west	ONLINE
sh3	shgroup2	Ok	Deployed	us-east	READ ONLY
sh4	shgroup2	Ok	Deployed	us-east	READ ONLY

```
GDSCTL>databases
Database: "sh1" Registered: Y State: Ok ONS: N. Role: PRIMARY Instances:
1 Region: us-west
Alert: Data Guard observer is not running.
   Registered instances:
     shrcat%1
Database: "sh2" Registered: Y State: Ok ONS: N. Role: PRIMARY Instances:
1 Region: us-west
Alert: Data Guard observer is not running.
   Registered instances:
     shrcat%11
Database: "sh3" Registered: Y State: Ok ONS: N. Role: PH_STNDBY Instances:
1 Region: us-east
   Registered instances:
     shrcat%21
Database: "sh4" Registered: Y State: Ok ONS: N. Role: PH_STNDBY Instances:
1 Region: us-east
   Registered instances:
     shrcat%31

GDSCTL>config shard -shard sh1
Name: sh1
Shard Group: shgroup1
Status: Ok
State: Deployed
Region: us-west
Connection string: shdb1.localdomain:1521/sh1.localdomain:dedicated
SCAN address:
```

ONS remote port: 0
Disk Threshold, ms: 20
CPU Threshold, %: 75
Version: 12.2.0.0
Failed DDL:
DDL Error: ---
Failed DDL id:
Availability: ONLINE
Rack:
Supported services

Name   Preferred Status

----   ---------- ------

GDSCTL> **config shard -shard sh2**
Name: sh2
Shard Group: shgroup1
Status: Ok
State: Deployed
Region: us-west
Connection string: shdb2.localdomain:1521/sh2.localdomain:dedicated
SCAN address:
ONS remote port: 0
Disk Threshold, ms: 20
CPU Threshold, %: 75
Version: 12.2.0.0
Failed DDL:
DDL Error: ---
Failed DDL id:
Availability: ONLINE
Rack:
Supported services

Name Preferred Status

---- ---------- ------

```
GDSCTL>config shard -shard sh3
Name: sh3
Shard Group: shgroup2
Status: Ok
State: Deployed
Region: us-east
Connection string: shdb3.localdomain:1521/sh3.localdomain:dedicated
SCAN address:
ONS remote port: 0
Disk Threshold, ms: 20
CPU Threshold, %: 75
Version: 12.2.0.0
Failed DDL:
DDL Error: ---
Failed DDL id:
Availability: READ ONLY
Rack:
Supported services
------------------------
Name Preferred Status
---- --------- ------
GDSCTL>config shard -shard sh4
Name: sh4
Shard Group: shgroup2
Status: Ok
State: Deployed
Region: us-east
Connection string: shdb4.localdomain:1521/sh4.localdomain:dedicated
SCAN address:
ONS remote port: 0
Disk Threshold, ms: 20
CPU Threshold, %: 75
Version: 12.2.0.0
```

```
Failed DDL:
DDL Error: ---
Failed DDL id:
Availability: READ ONLY
Rack:
Supported services
----------------------
Name Preferred Status
---- --------- ------
GDSCTL>config chunks
Chunks
----------------------
Database                From      To
--------                ----      --
sh1                     1         6
sh2                     7         12
sh3                     1         6
sh4                     7         12
```

Create the Global Service

Follow these steps:

1. On the catalog server, run the following command from the GDSCTL interface:

```
GDSCTL>add service -service PRIMDB -preferred_all -role primary

The operation completed successfully

GDSCTL>add service -service STANDB -preferred_all -role physical_standby

The operation completed successfully
GDSCTL>config service
   Name     Network name          Pool      Started Preferred all
   ----     ------------          ----      ------- -------------
   primdb   primdb.shrcat.oradbcloud   shrcat   No      Yes
   standb   standb.shrcat.oradbcloud   shrcat   No      Yes
```

```
GDSCTL> start service -service PRIMDB, STANDB
The operation completed successfully
GDSCTL>status service
Service "primdb.shrcat.oradbcloud" has 2 instance(s). Affinity: ANYWHERE
   Instance "shrcat%1", name: "sh1", db: "sh1", region: "us-west", status: ready.
   Instance "shrcat%11", name: "sh2", db: "sh2", region: "us-west", status: ready.
Service "standb.shrcat.oradbcloud" has 2 instance(s). Affinity: ANYWHERE
   Instance "shrcat%21", name: "sh3", db: "sh3", region: "us-east", status: ready.
   Instance "shrcat%31", name: "sh4", db: "sh4", region: "us-east", status: ready
```

Disable the FSFO-Observer (Optional)

The Deploy command enables Fast Start Failover (FSFO) with a Data Guard Broker configuration.

   Even on nonsharded environments, most DBAs choose to disable it and assume they will do a failover manually, whenever it is necessary.

   1.   Disable FSFO on shdb1.

```
[oracle@shdb1 ~]$ . oraenv
ORACLE_SID = [oracle] ? sh1

[oracle@shdb1 ~]$ dgmgrl /
DGMGRL for Linux: Release 12.2.0.1.0 - Production on Tue Jul 31 12:21:46 2018
Copyright (c) 1982, 2017, Oracle and/or its affiliates.All rights reserved.
Welcome to DGMGRL, type "help" for information.
Connected to "sh1"
Connected as SYSDG.

DGMGRL> show fast_start failover

Fast-Start Failover: ENABLED

Threshold:            30 seconds
Target:               sh3
Observer:             (none)
Lag Limit:            30 seconds
Shutdown Primary:     TRUE
Auto-reinstate:       TRUE
```

```
Observer Reconnect: (none)
Observer Override:  FALSE

Configurable Failover Conditions
Health Conditions:
Corrupted Controlfile           YES
Corrupted Dictionary            YES
Inaccessible Logfile             NO
Stuck Archiver                   NO
Datafile Write Errors           YES

Oracle Error Conditions:
  (none)
```

DGMGRL> **disable fast_start failover**
```
Disabled.
```
DGMGRL> **show fast_start failover**

```
Fast-Start Failover: DISABLED

Threshold:          30 seconds
Target:             (none)
Observer:           (none)
Lag Limit:          30 seconds
Shutdown Primary:   TRUE
Auto-reinstate:     TRUE
Observer Reconnect: (none)
Observer Override:  FALSE

Configurable Failover Conditions
Health Conditions:
Corrupted Controlfile           YES
Corrupted Dictionary            YES
Inaccessible Logfile             NO
Stuck Archiver                   NO
Datafile Write Errors           YES

Oracle Error Conditions:
  (none)
```

```
DGMGRL> show configuration;

Configuration - sh1

Protection Mode: MaxPerformance
Members:
sh1 - Primary database
sh3 - Physical standby database

Fast-Start Failover: DISABLED

Configuration Status:
SUCCESS    (status updated 24 seconds ago)
```

2.   Do the same for another database from the shdb2 database server.

```
[oracle@shdb2 ~]$ . oraenv
ORACLE_SID = [oracle] ? sh2
The Oracle base has been set to /u01/app/oracle

[oracle@shdb2 ~]$ dgmgrl /
DGMGRL for Linux: Release 12.2.0.1.0 - Production on Tue Jul 31 12:29:12 2018

Copyright (c) 1982, 2017, Oracle and/or its affiliates.  All rights reserved.

Welcome to DGMGRL, type "help" for information.
Connected to "sh2"
Connected as SYSDG.

DGMGRL> show fast_start failover

Fast-Start Failover: ENABLED

Threshold:          30 seconds
Target:             sh4
Observer:           (none)
Lag Limit:          30 seconds
Shutdown Primary:   TRUE
Auto-reinstate:     TRUE
Observer Reconnect: (none)
Observer Override:  FALSE
```

```
Configurable Failover Conditions
Health Conditions:
Corrupted Controlfile          YES
Corrupted Dictionary           YES
Inaccessible Logfile            NO
Stuck Archiver                  NO
Datafile Write Errors          YES
Oracle Error Conditions:
    (none)
```

DGMGRL> **disable fast_start failover**
Disabled.

DGMGRL> **show fast_start failover**

Fast-Start Failover: DISABLED

```
Threshold:         30 seconds
Target:            (none)
Observer:          (none)
Lag Limit:         30 seconds
Shutdown Primary:  TRUE
Auto-reinstate:    TRUE
Observer Reconnect: (none)
Observer Override: FALSE
```

```
Configurable Failover Conditions
Health Conditions:
Corrupted Controlfile          YES
Corrupted Dictionary           YES
Inaccessible Logfile            NO
Stuck Archiver                  NO
Datafile Write Errors          YES

Oracle Error Conditions:
    (none)
```

DGMGRL> **show configuration;**

Configuration - sh2

Protection Mode: MaxPerformance
Members:
sh2 - Primary database
  sh4 - Physical standby database

Fast-Start Failover: DISABLED

Configuration Status:
SUCCESS   (status updated 3 seconds ago)

Create Tablespaces, Schemas, and Tables

The table creation syntax has changed for a sharding database. The shard table
definition will be created in the sharding catalog database, and the actual data will be
distributed across the shard databases at the tablespace level.

   Please note that for each session you must enable the shard DDL before running the
SQL statements.

   1. Connect to the shard catalog database, create the user, and grant
       the necessary privileges.

```
$ . oraenv
ORACLE_SID = [oracle] ? SHRCAT
The Oracle base has been set to /u01/app/oracle

[oracle@shcat ~]$ sqlplus / as sysdba
SQL*Plus: Release 12.2.0.1.0 Production on Jul 31 12:33:59 2018 2018
Copyright (c) 1982, 2016, Oracle.  All rights reserved.
Connected to:
Oracle Database 12c Enterprise Edition Release 12.2.0.1.0 - 64bit Production

SQL> alter session enable shard ddl;
Session altered.

SQL> create user appuser identified by oracle;
User created.

SQL> grant connect, resource to appuser;
Grant succeeded.
```

```
SQL> grant select_catalog_role to appuser;
Grant succeeded.

SQL> grant all privileges to appuser;
Grant succeeded.

SQL> grant execute on dbms_crypto to appuser;
Grant succeeded.

SQL> grant gsmadmin_role to appuser;
Grant succeeded.

SQL> grant execute on dbms_crypto to appuser;
Grant succeeded.

SQL> grant dba to appuser;
Grant succeeded.
```

> Please note that if you exit this session and reconnect, or connect
> from another session, you must enable the shard DDL again.

2. Create the tablespace set and tablespace.

```
SQL> create tablespace set mytbsset
using template (datafile size 100m autoextend on next 5M maxsize unlimited
extent management local segment space management auto );

Tablespace created.
SQL> create tablespace mytbs
datafile size 100m autoextend on next 5m maxsize unlimited
extent management local uniform size 1m;

Tablespace created
```

3. Create the shard table.

3.1. Connect to the application schema (appuser) and create a table
called books.

```
SQL> connect appuser/oracle
Connected.
```

```
SQL> alter session enable shard ddl;
Session altered.

SQL> create sharded table books (
    bookid number,
    title varchar2(50) not null,
    auth_fname varchar2(30) not null,
    auth_lname varchar2(50),
    constraint books_pk primary key (bookid))
    tablespace set mytbsset
    partition by consistent hash (bookid) partitions auto;
  2    3    4    5    6    7    8    9
 Table created.
```

3.2.   Fill the table with sample data using a loop.

```
SQL> begin
for i in 1..200 loop
insert into BOOKS values(i, 'My Book', 'MyName', 'MySurname');
end loop;
end;
/  2    3    4    5    6
PL/SQL procedure successfully completed.
SQL> commit;
Commit complete.
```

In the shard catalog database (shrcat), there is only created table structure, and real data is distributed between shard databases (sh1 and sh2) and using Oracle Data Guard functionality data will be replicated to standby shard databases (sh3 and sh4).

4.   Check the dba_segments view on each database.

On the catalog database SHRCAT, run this:

```
$ . oraenv
ORACLE_SID = [SHRCAT] ?
The Oracle base remains unchanged with value /u01/app/oracle
$ sqlplus appuser/oracle
SQL> select segment_type
```

```
from dba_segments
where segment_name='BOOKS'
and owner='APPUSER';   2    3    4
no rows selected
```

5. Check dba_objects for the catalog database.

```
SQL> select object_type
    from dba_objects
    where object_name='BOOKS';  2   3   4
OBJECT_TYPE
-----------------------
TABLE PARTITION
TABLE
```

> The previous output shows that the catalog database has only the table metadata. Since there is no data in the table, there are no segments created for that table.

6. Connect to the sharded database (sh1).

```
$ . oraenv
ORACLE_SID = [sh1] ?
The Oracle base remains unchanged with value /u01/app/oracle
$ sqlplus appuser/oracle

SQL> select segment_type
    from dba_segments
    where segment_name='BOOKS'
    and owner='APPUSER';   2   3   4
SEGMENT_TYPE
------------------
TABLE PARTITION
TABLE PARTITION
TABLE PARTITION
TABLE PARTITION
TABLE PARTITION
TABLE PARTITION

6 rows selected.
```

7. From the same database, check the number of rows in the appuser.books table.

```
SQL> select count(*)
     from appuser.books;
COUNT(*)
----------
104
```

8. Connect to the sharded database (sh2).

```
SQL> select segment_type
from dba_segments
where segment_name='BOOKS'
and owner='APPUSER'; 2    3    4
SEGMENT_TYPE
------------------
TABLE PARTITION
TABLE PARTITION
TABLE PARTITION
TABLE PARTITION
TABLE PARTITION
TABLE PARTITION

6 rows selected.
```

9. From the same database, check the number of rows in the appuser.books table.

```
SQL> select count(*)
  from appuser.books;

COUNT(*)
----------
      96
```

This means that data was evenly distributed between the sh1 and sh2 shard database servers.

10. Other object structures are also created on the catalog database and later propagated to shards.

```
SQL> CREATE OR REPLACE FUNCTION PasswCreate(PASSW IN RAW)
 RETURN RAW
IS
 Salt RAW(8);
BEGIN
 Salt := DBMS_CRYPTO.RANDOMBYTES(8);
 RETURN UTL_RAW.CONCAT(Salt, DBMS_CRYPTO.HASH(UTL_RAW.CONCAT(Salt,PASSW),
DBMS_CRYPTO.HASH_SH256));
END;
/  2    3    4    5    6    7    8    9

Function created.

SQL> CREATE OR REPLACE FUNCTION PasswCheck
(PASSW IN RAW, PHASH IN RAW)

RETURN INTEGER IS
BEGIN
RETURN UTL_RAW.COMPARE( DBMS_CRYPTO.HASH(UTL_RAW.CONCAT(UTL_RAW.SUBSTR
(PHASH, 1, 8),PASSW), DBMS_CRYPTO.HASH_SH256), UTL_RAW.SUBSTR(PHASH, 9));
END;
/  2    3    4    5    6    7    8
Function created.
```

Testing the Methodology

Follow these steps:

1. Check the objects in the current schema on the catalog database.

```
$ sqlplus appuser/oracle

SQL*Plus: Release 12.2.0.1.0 Production on Thu Jul 26 00:09:09 2018
Copyright (c) 1982, 2016, Oracle.  All rights reserved.
Last Successful login time: Thu Jul 26 2018 00:02:18 +04:00
```

```
Connected to:
Oracle Database 12c Enterprise Edition Release 12.2.0.1.0 - 64bit Production

SQL>  select object_name,
      object_type
      from user_objects;  2    3

OBJECT_NAME                                   OBJECT_TYPE
-------------------------------------------- --------------------
BOOKS                                        TABLE PARTITION
BOOKS                                        TABLE
BOOKS_PK                                     INDEX PARTITION
BOOKS_PK                                     INDEX
PASSWCHECK                                   FUNCTION
BOOKID_SEQ                                   SEQUENCE
PASSWCREATE                                  FUNCTION
ORA_SHARD_POOL@ORA_MULTI_TARGET              DATABASE LINK

8 rows selected.
```

     2.   Connect as the SYS user.

```
SQL> connect / as sysdba
Connected.

SQL> show user
USER is "SYS"
```

     3.   Check the partition information.

```
SQL> select table_name,
  2  partition_name,
  3  tablespace_name
  4  from dba_tab_partitions
  5  where tablespace_name like '%SET%';

TABLE_NAME      PARTITION_NAME  TABLESPACE_NAME
-------------   --------------- --------------------
BOOKS           BOOKS_P1    MYTBSSET
```

4. Check the chunk distribution.

```
SQL> select a.name shard,
        count(b.chunk_number) chunks
from gsmadmin_internal.database a,
     gsmadmin_internal.chunk_loc b
where a.database_num=b.database_num
group by a.name;  2    3    4    5    6

SHARD                          CHUNKS
--------------------- ----------
sh1                               6
sh2                               6
sh3                               6
sh4                               6
```

5. From the shard catalog database server, run GDSCTL and observe that there were no failures.

```
$ export ORACLE_HOME=/u01/app/gsm/12.2.0/
$ export ORACLE_BASE=/u01/app/gsm
$ export PATH=$ORACLE_HOME/bin:$PATH
$ gdsctl
GDSCTL: Version 12.2.0.1.0 - Production on Tue Jul 31 12:42:11 EDT 2018
Copyright (c) 2011, 2016, Oracle.  All rights reserved.
Welcome to GDSCTL, type "help" for information.
Current GSM is set to MYSHARDDIRECTOR

GDSCTL>show ddl
Catalog connection is established
id      DDL Text                                Failed shards
--      --------                                -------------
2       grant connect, resource to appuser
3       grant select_catalog_role to appuser
4       grant all privileges to appuser
5       grant execute on dbms_crypto to appuser
6       grant gsmadmin_role to appuser
7       grant execute on dbms_crypto to appuser
8       grant dba to appuser
```

```
9       create tablespace set mytbsset using ...
10      create tablespace mytbs datafile size...
11      create sharded table books (     booki...
```

6. Run the following for each shard to be sure that there were no DDL errors:

```
GDSCTL>config shard -shard sh1
Name: sh1
Shard Group: shgroup1
Status: Ok
State: Deployed
Region: us-west
Connection string: shdb1.localdomain:1521/sh1.localdomain:dedicated
SCAN address:
ONS remote port: 0
Disk Threshold, ms: 20
CPU Threshold, %: 75
Version: 12.2.0.0
Failed DDL:
DDL Error: ---
Failed DDL id:
Availability: ONLINE
Rack:
Supported services
------------------------
Name Preferred Status
---- --------- ------
primdb Yes     Enabled
standb Yes     Enabled
```

7. Do the same for the second shard.

```
GDSCTL>config shard -shard sh2
Name: sh2
Shard Group: shgroup1
Status: Ok
```

```
State: Deployed
Region: us-west
Connection string: shdb2.localdomain:1521/sh2.localdomain:dedicated
SCAN address:
ONS remote port: 0
Disk Threshold, ms: 20
CPU Threshold, %: 75
Version: 12.2.0.0
```

Failed DDL:

DDL Error: ---

Failed DDL id:

```
Availability: ONLINE
Rack:
Supported services
------------------------
Name    Preferred Status
----    --------- ------

primdb Yes       Enabled
standb Yes       Enabled
```

8. Check the chunk distribution between shards from the GDSCTL command-line interface.

GDSCTL>**config chunks**

```
Chunks
------------------------
Database                    From    To
--------                    ----    --
sh1                         1       6
sh2                         7       12
sh3                         1       6
sh4                         7       12
```

9. Verify that tablespaces are created on the sh1 and sh2 databases.

9.1. Run the following on the shard database (sh1):

```
$ . oraenv
ORACLE_SID = [oracle] ? sh1
The Oracle base has been set to /u01/app/oracle
$ sqlplus / as sysdba
SQL> set pagesize 800
SQL> select tablespace_name,bytes/1024/1024 mb
   from sys.dba_data_files
   order by tablespace_name;  2    3    4

TABLESPACE_NAME                    MB
------------------------------ ----------
C001MYTBSSET                      100
C002MYTBSSET                      100
C003MYTBSSET                      100
C004MYTBSSET                      100
C005MYTBSSET                      100
C006MYTBSSET                      100
MYTBS                             100
MYTBSSET                          100
SYSAUX                            490
SYSTEM                            800
UNDOTBS1                               70
USERS                                   5
12 rows selected.
```

9.2.   Run the following on the shard database (sh2):

```
$ . oraenv
ORACLE_SID = [oracle] ? sh2
The Oracle base has been set to /u01/app/oracle
[oracle@shdb2 ~]$ sqlplus / as sysdba

SQL> set pagesize 800
SQL>  select tablespace_name, bytes/1024/1024 mb
   from sys.dba_data_files
   order by tablespace_name;  2    3    4
```

TABLESPACE_NAME	MB
C007MYTBSSET	**100**
C008MYTBSSET	**100**
C009MYTBSSET	**100**
C00AMYTBSSET	**100**
C00BMYTBSSET	**100**
C00CMYTBSSET	**100**
MYTBS	**100**
MYTBSSET	**100**
SYSAUX	490
SYSTEM	800
UNDOTBS1	70
USERS	5

12 rows selected.

10. Move the chunk operation in a sharded database.

GDSCTL>**config shard**

Name	Shard Group	Status	State	Region	Availability
sh1	shgroup1	Ok	Deployed	us-west	ONLINE
sh2	shgroup1	Ok	Deployed	us-west	ONLINE
sh3	shgroup2	Ok	Deployed	us-east	READ ONLY
sh4	shgroup2	Ok	Deployed	us-east	READ ONLY

11. Note the current chunk layout with the following command:

GDSCTL>**config chunks -show_reshard**
Chunks

Database	From	To
sh1	1	6
sh2	7	12

```
sh3                     1           6
sh4                     7           12
Ongoing chunk movement
------------------------
Chunk     Source     Target    status
-----     ------     ------    ------
```

12. Execute move chunk from one sharded database to another sharded database.

```
GDSCTL>move chunk -chunk 7 -source sh2 -target sh1
The operation completed successfully
```

13. Observe that chunk 7 moved from shard 2 to shard 1, and the corresponding chunks also moved accordingly.

```
GDSCTL>config chunks -show_reshard
Chunks
------------------------
Database          From      To
--------          ----      --
sh1               1         7
sh2               8         12
sh3               1         7
sh4               8         12
Ongoing chunk movement
------------------------
Chunk     Source     Target    status
-----     ------     ------    ------
```

14. Now you can check the transactions between the primary shard databases (shdb1 and shdb2) and the standby shard database (shdb3 and shdb4).

14.1. Check the existing data on the shard databases (shdb1 and shdb2). Run this from the shdb1 database:

```
[oracle@shdb1 ~]$ sqlplus appuser/oracle
SQL> select * from books order by bookid;
...
197 My Book          MyName              MySurname
199 My Book          MyName              MySurname
200 My Book          MyName              MySurname
124 rows selected.
```

Run this from the shdb2 database:

```
  [oracle@shd2 ~]$ sqlplus appuser/oracle
SQL> select * from books order by bookid;
...
193 My Book          MyName              MySurname
194 My Book          MyName              MySurname
198 My Book          MyName              MySurname
76 rows selected.
```

14.2.   Connect to the shard catalog database (shcat) and insert data.

```
[oracle@shcat ~]$ sqlplus appuser/oracle
SQL> insert into books values(201, 'Your Book', 'YourName', 'YourSurname');
1 row created.
SQL> commit;
Commit complete.
```

14.3.   Check both shards to see where the data was inserted.

Run this from the shdb1 database:

```
[oracle@shdb1 ~]$ sqlplus appuser/oracle

...
199 My Book          MyName              MySurname
200 My Book          MyName              MySurname
124 rows selected.
```

Run this from the shdb2 database:

```
[oracle@shdb2 ~]$ sqlplus appuser/oracle
SQL> select * from books order by bookid;
...
```

| 198 My Book | MyName | MySurname |
| *201 Your Book* | *YourName* | *YourSurname* |

```
77 rows selected.
```

15. As you can see, the row was sent to the second shard. Now let's check its standby database.

```
Run this from the shdb4 database:
[oracle@shdb4 ~]$ sqlplus appuser/oracle
SQL>  select * from books order by bookid;
...
198 My Book        MyName        MySurname
201 Your Book      YourName      YourSurname

77 rows selected.
```

As expected, the change was reflected on the standby database.

16. Repeat the steps and insert another row.
    From shcat:

```
[oracle@shcat ~]$ sqlplus appuser/oracle
SQL> insert into books values(202, 'Your Book', 'YourName', 'YourSurname');
1 row created.
SQL> commit;
Commit complete.
```

17. Check both shards.
    Run this from the shdb1 database:

```
[oracle@shdb1 ~]$ sqlplus appuser/oracle
SQL>  select * from books order by bookid;
...
```

```
199 My Book          MyName               MySurname
200 My Book          MyName               MySurname
202 Your Book             YourName             YourSurname
125 rows selected.
```

Run this from the **shdb2** database:

```
[oracle@shdb2 ~]$ sqlplus appuser/oracle
SQL>  select * from books order by bookid;
...
194 My Book          MyName               MySurname
198 My Book          MyName               MySurname
201 Your Book        YourName             YourSurname
77 rows selected.
```

The row was inserted on the first shard.

18. Let's check its standby database.

```
[oracle@shdb3 ~]$ sqlplus appuser/oracle
SQL>  select * from books order by bookid;
...
199 My Book     MyName          MySurname
200 My Book     MyName          MySurname
202 Your Book      YourName        YourSurname
125 rows selected.
```

The second change was also reflected on the corresponding standby.

Troubleshooting

When there is a problem, it is important to start troubleshooting from the right place. You have already gone through the steps to check the configuration, but in case something happens after the initial configuration, you need to know where to search the additional information.

To find the shard director listener log and trace file locations, follow these steps on the catalog database server:

1. Connect as the oracle user.

```
$ export ORACLE_HOME=/u01/app/gsm/12.2.0/
$ export ORACLE_BASE=/u01/app/gsm
$ export PATH=$ORACLE_HOME/bin:$PATH
$ gdsctl
GDSCTL: Version 12.2.0.1.0 - Production on Tue Jul 31 12:55:21 EDT 2018
Copyright (c) 2011, 2016, Oracle.  All rights reserved.
Welcome to GDSCTL, type "help" for information.
Current GSM is set to MYSHARDDIRECTOR
GDSCTL> status
Alias                    MYSHARDDIRECTOR
Version                  12.2.0.1.0
Start Date               31-JUL-2018 11:12:05
Trace Level              off
Listener Log File        /u01/app/gsm/diag/gsm/shcat/mysharddirector/
                           alert/log.xml
Listener Trace File      /u01/app/gsm/diag/gsm/shcat/mysharddirector/
                           trace/ora_8412_140134614061440.trc
Endpoint summary         (ADDRESS=(HOST=shcat.localdomain)(PORT=1522)
                         (PROTOCOL=tcp))
GSMOCI Version           2.2.1
Mastership               Y
Connected to GDS catalog Y
Process Id               8415
Number of reconnections  0
Pending tasks.    Total  0
Tasks in  process. Total 0
Regional Mastership      TRUE
Total messages published 182
Time Zone                -04:00
```

```
Orphaned Buddy Regions:
    None
GDS region                    us-north
```

The shard director alert logfile location is $GSM_BASE/diag/
gsm/<node-name>/<director-name>/trace/alert_*.log.

```
# ll /u01/app/gsm/diag/gsm/shcat/mysharddirector/trace/alert_gsm.log
-rw-r-----. 1 oracle oinstall 481257 Jul 26 05:09 /u01/app/gsm/diag/gsm/
shcat/mysharddirector/trace/alert_gsm.log
```

2. Before validating shards, alter the password for gsmuser on each
   shard node.

Run this on the shard database (sh1):

```
$ . oraenv
ORACLE_SID = [sh1] ?
The Oracle base remains unchanged with value /u01/app/oracle
$ sqlplus / as sysdba

SQL> alter user gsmuser identified by oracle;
User altered.

SQL> alter user gsmuser account unlock;
User altered.
```

Run this on the shard database (sh2):

```
$ . oraenv
ORACLE_SID = [oracle] ? sh2
The Oracle base remains unchanged with value /u01/app/oracle
$ sqlplus / as sysdba

SQL> alter user gsmuser identified by oracle;
User altered.
SQL> alter user gsmuser account unlock;
User altered.
```

3. On the shard catalog database, from GDSCTL, run the following to modify the password for each shard:

```
GDSCTL> modify shard -shard sh1 -pwd oracle
GDSCTL> modify shard -shard sh2 -pwd oracle

GDSCTL> modify shard -shard sh3 -pwd oracle
GDSCTL> modify shard -shard sh4 -pwd oracle
```

4. The GDSCTL tool gives you an ability to validate the whole configuration using the VALIDATE command.

```
GDSCTL>validate catalog -catpwd oracle -dbpwd oracle -database sh1
Validation results:
Total errors: 0.

GDSCTL>validate catalog -catpwd oracle -dbpwd oracle -database sh2
Validation results:
Total errors: 0.

GDSCTL>validate catalog -catpwd oracle -dbpwd oracle -database sh3
Validation results:
Total errors: 0.

GDSCTL>validate catalog -catpwd oracle -dbpwd oracle -database sh4
Validation results:
Total errors: 0.
```

High Availability with Oracle Sharded Databases

Shards can be replicated between one or more data centers using well-known Oracle technologies such as Oracle Data Guard, Oracle GoldenGate, and Oracle Streams Replication.

Optionally, you can use single shard as an Oracle RAC cluster to create a more reliable system.

Note that placing shards in different data centers is not recommended because a network delay may affect queries that require several shards to be accessed. If you have many such queries, then you should consider creating high network connectivity between the catalog and shard servers. See Figure 7-9.

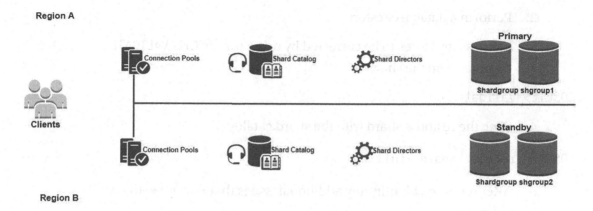

Figure 7-9. *Oracle sharding architecture with HA capability*

Backup and Recovery for SDBs

In general, existing backup and recovery best practices apply for sharded databases also. But there are some limitations that you must consider, especially when you are doing point-in-time recovery or there is a chunk movement.

- Prevent backups from occurring during chunk movement. Chunk movement occurs automatically when a shard is added or manually by user. To determine whether chunk movement is occurring or is scheduled, use GDSCTL CONFIG CHUNKS and suspend it so that a backup can be taken; otherwise, you will have an incorrect layout of data.

To suspend chunk movement, use the following commands from GDSCTL:

```
GDSCTL> alter move –suspend –chunk 11,12

GDSCTL> alter move –resume –chunk 11,12
```

- A *point-in-time recovery* of a shard database may lead to incorrect chunk layout and missing Data Definition Language (DDL) operations. To avoid this, run the GDSCTL VALIDATE and RECOVER SHARD commands f4e shard that was just restored.

Follow these steps to do a correct point-in-time recovery (PITR):

1. Disable the global service for the shard to be restored and recovered.

2. Perform a database restore.

3. Identify any issues to be corrected by using the GDSCTL VALIDATE command on the shard.

```
GDSCTL> validate
```

4. Sync the restored shard with the shard catalog.

```
GDSCTL> recover shard -full
```

5. After recovery, identify any additional issues that may need to be corrected.

```
GDSCTL> validate
```

6. Enable the global service when everything is corrected.

Summary

In this chapter, you learned about the Oracle sharding technology that was introduced in Oracle Database 12 R2. We described its main components and terminology.

The Oracle sharding architecture supports rolling upgrades, linear scalability, fault isolation, and horizontal partitioning.

We compared sharding to other Oracle high-level technology like Oracle Real Application Clusters. Data Guard, Oracle Golden Gate, and Oracle Streams Replication can be used with sharding to achieve the maximum high availability architecture. Implementing Oracle RAC will also make shard servers more reliable and node fault tolerant.

We described backup and recovery best practices for sharded databases and the shard catalog.

We explained the step-by-step installation procedures of sharding. Every single aspect that must be done before and during the installation was described to make sure that the process of setting up sharding will go smoothly for you.

CHAPTER 8

Oracle Engineered Systems for High Availability

Oracle Corporation offers two engineered database systems with major innovations for database solutions. In 2008, Oracle Exadata Database Machine was introduced for high performance and is fully available at an affordable cost with intelligence for storage and networking. In 2011, Oracle introduced Oracle Database Appliance as a family of engineered systems with reduced storage, CPU, and memory resources to fulfill the needs of medium and low-scaled customers.

This chapter is fully dedicated to Oracle Engineered Systems (Oracle Exadata and Oracle Database Appliance). We'll start with the architecture, then cover the underlying hardware of ODA, and finally explain how to manage ODA and its various features. Oracle Database Appliance was initially for database systems, but in later releases (starting with 2.5), ODA is available on bare metal and also in the format of an Oracle VM. With an Oracle VM, the great advantage is that you can manage both the database and applications in a single box by designating virtual machines. The Oracle VM reduces your costs and requires less infrastructure maintenance.

Oracle Exadata Database Machine is available in four formats: Eighth Rack (two compute nodes and three storage servers), Quarter Rack (two compute nodes and three storage servers), Half Rack (four compute nodes and seven storage servers), and Full Rack (eight compute nodes and fourteen storage servers).

The difference between the Oracle Exadata Eighth Rack and Quarter Rack is that half of the cores per server will be disabled in the compute nodes and half of the storage cores per rack, SSDs/SASs per server, and flash cache cards per server will be disabled in each storage server. (Extreme flash storage servers are SSD based, and the high-capacity storage servers are SAS based.)

In addition to these formats, Oracle Exadata is available in two specific formats for Half Rack (x7-8) and Full Rack (x7-8). The difference between the x7-2 (HR and FR) and x7-8 (HR and FR) models is the basically the number of compute nodes, the server model, and the total cores per server.

Oracle Exadata (x7-8, Half Rack) consists of two physical servers (192 cores per server, with 384 total cores per rack) and three storage servers. Oracle Exadata (x7-8, Full Rack) consists of two (up to three) physical servers (192 cores per server, with 384 total cores per rack, up to 576 total cores per rack) and 14 storage servers.

The server model for both Oracle Exadata (x7-8, Half Rack) and Oracle Exadata (x7-8, Full Rack) is Oracle x7-8 (5U).

The major advantage of Oracle Exadata Database Machine is that you can run new software releases on earlier Oracle Exadata systems.

The initial Oracle Database Appliance release had a two-node cluster and also attached shared storage as a single box. Based on the generation of the appliances, the resources such as cores, memory, and network configuration will be increased to achieve the best performance to handle the heavy data loads.

The hardware of ODA is named x3-2, x4-2, x5-2, x6-2, and so on. The latest ODA version is available in three formats: ODA x7-2S, x7-2M, x7-2-HA. Each hardware version contains a different number of cores and amount of memory, functionality changes such as redundancy, different costs, and different resources.

Oracle Database Appliances works on Oracle Linux with a default two-node Grid Infrastructure. Regarding the licensing of ODA, Oracle lets you pay as you go. The great flexibility is there is no need to pay for all the CPUs. Instead, you can pay for only two CPUs depending on your business requirement. In the recent models of ODA, Oracle offers a Standard Edition as well as Enterprise Edition. In addition to the Oracle Linux and Oracle RDBMS, ODA uses Oracle Appliance Kit (via OAKCLI) to manage the entire stack of ODA. OAKCLI and ODACLI simplified the environment by using simple commands to streamline administration such as database creation, patching, management, and support.

Figure 8-1 shows the front view of some Oracle Database Appliance x5-2 hardware.

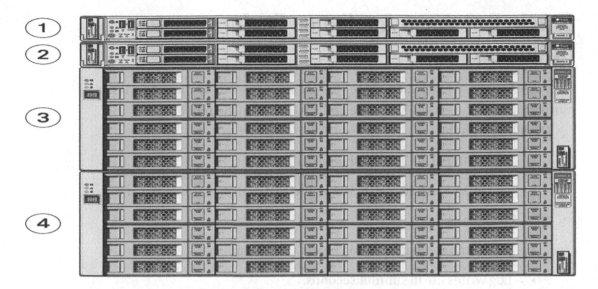

Figure 8-1. *Oracle Database Appliance hardware front view*

Here's the technical specification:

- In Figure 8-1, the numbers 1 and 2 denote Server Node 1 and Server Node 0.

- Two servers, each with 36 Intel Xeon CPU cores.

- 256 GB memory, expandable to 768 GB memory.

- Redundant InfiniBand Interconnect.

- 10 GB Ethernet public network.

Here's the storage specification:

- In Figure 8-1, the numbers 3 and 4 denote the storage shelf and the optional storage expansion shelf.

- 800 GB flash log storage.

- 1.6 TB flash cache storage.

- 64 TB hard disk drives (HDDs).

Oracle Database Appliance Performance Optimization

In Oracle Database Appliance, there are various components that boost the high performance of the Oracle Database and also increase the reliability.

ODA Flash Cache

- The ODA Flash Cache is shared across nodes.

- The ODA Flash Cache increases the cache hit ratio for applications.

ODA Flash Logs

- The database writes to redo logs to ODA flash.

- Log writes are in submilliseconds.

- There is flexibility to create redo logs with a 4KB block size.

ODA Flash Files

- Flash files store filesystem metadata in ODA flash.

- Overall This improves filesystem reads and writes.

- You get native file system performance for snapshots.

Technical Specifications of the ODA x7-2 Family

Oracle has developed various models such as Entry, Performance, Consolidation, and High Availability from ODA x6-2 and x7-2 onward. The customer should aware of the various hardware available with ODA x7-2. Based on the requirements and the cost of the appliance, the customer may prefer any of the models. The models in Figure 8-2 will give you a high level of understanding.

Oracle Database Appliance X7-2S	Oracle Database Appliance X7-2M	Oracle Database Appliance X7-2-HA
• Single-instance SE/SE1/SE2 or EE Database • 10 Core Intel® Xeon® Silver 4114 processor • 192GB (expandable to 384GB) • 2 x 10 GbE ports (RJ45) OR 2 x 10/25 GbE ports (SFP28) • 10GbE SFP+ Public Network • 12.8 TB (2 X 6.4TB NVMe) • 480 GB M.2 SATA SSD (Boot Disk) • Bare Metal with optional KVM Virtualization (Deployment Option)	• Single-instance SE/SE1/SE2 or EE Database • 36 cores Intel® Xeon® Gold 6140 Processors • 384GB (expandable to 768GB) • 2 x 10 GbE ports (RJ45) OR 2 x 10/25 GbE ports (SFP28) • 12.8 TB (2 X 6.4TB NVMe) • 480 GB M.2 SATA SSD (Boot Disk) • Bare Metal with optional KVM Virtualization (Deployment Option)	• Database SE/EE • Two Servers, 2 x 18 core Intel® Xeon® Gold 6140 Processors 2.3 GHz • 384 GB (12 x 32 GB) • 2 x 480 GB M.2 SATA SSD • Network e. 2 x 10 GbE ports (RJ45) OR 2 x 10/25 GbE ports (SFP28) • Ethernet 25GB (Interconnect) • Bare Metal or Virtualization

Figure 8-2. *Oracle Database Appliance (ODA) models*

Oracle Database Appliance x7-2-HA Architecture and Storage Specifications

Oracle Database Appliance x7-2-HA has the following features:

- Two compute nodes (physical servers) and one storage shelf per system.

- An optional second storage shelf may be added for storage expansion.

- Two internal 480 GB M.2 SATA SSDs (mirrored) per compute node for placing the operating system, KVM libraries, logfiles, and Oracle Database software.

- Base system storage shelf contains four solid-state drives (SSDs) for REDO. So total raw capacity is 3.2TB (4 x 800GB). Exclusive ASM disk group +REDO with high redundancy. This space will be used for redo logs.

- Base system storage shelf contains another set of five solid-state drives (SSDs) for FLASH/DATA. So total raw capacity is 16TB (5 x 3.2TB).

- This space will be used for databases.

- ODA includes SSDs to enhance the performance of certain operations. SSDs are used for accelerating redo log writes, caching database data, and improving I/O performance for database files.

Figure 8-3 gives a high-level view of storage capacity and how much this machine can support.

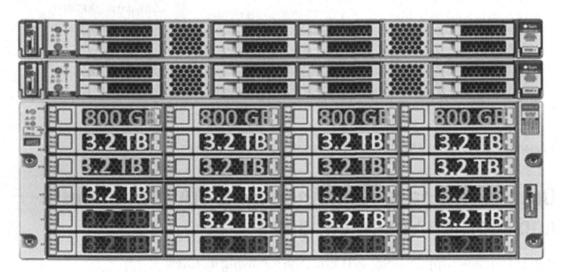

Figure 8-3. *Storage architecture (redo, data/flash)*

The following are the hardware options available for ODA X7-2-HA machines.

- **ODA X7-2-HA High Performance (HP) Hardware**

  - *M2 drives*: Operating system, KVM libraries, Oracle home software, log files

  - *Filesystems*: Database files, redo logs, backups, VM disk and images

- *ASM disk groups and contents*

  - +DATA (database files)

  - +RECO (archive logs, backups)

  - +REDO (database redo log files)

- **ODA X7-2-HA High Capacity (HC) Hardware**

  - *M2 drives*: Operating system, KVM libraries, Oracle Home
    software, log files

  - *File systems*: Database files, redo logs, backups, VM disk and
    images

  - *ASM disk groups and contents*

    - +DATA (database files)

    - +RECO (archive logs, backups)

    - +REDO (database redo log files)

    - +FLASH (HDD metadata file, database files, database buffer
      cache)

Storage expansion (optional):

- 384 GB (12 times 32 GB) per compute node for a total of 768 GB each.
  Both servers must contain the same amount of memory.

- Solid-state drive (SSD), 3.2 TB, five pack (16 TB).

- Expansion shelf (HP), up to 4 x 800 GB + 20 x 3.2 TB

- HDD 10TB, 15 pack (150 TB)

- Expansion shelf (HC), 4 x 800 GB + 5 x 3.2 TB + 15 x 10 TB

Figure 8-4 shows the storage expansion shelf.

Figure 8-4. *Storage expansion shelf*

ODA Deployment Models

Oracle has two different deployment models from x6 onward. One is bare metal, and the other is a virtualized deployment model. In bare-metal deployments, you will have preloaded "images" of the Oracle Linux operating system, hardware drivers, ILOM, and appliance manager. In this deployment model, you will have two Oracle Enterprise Linux systems that are directly using all the available hardware resources for Oracle Database instances.

ODA Bare-Metal Components

ODA does not ship with any Oracle Grid Infrastructure or Oracle Database binaries preinstalled. They were always installed by deploying the end-user bundle for bare-metal system deployments. The end-user bundle will need to be copied onto the ODA system into a temporary directory. In bare metal, the components are ODA Manager, Oracle Linux operating system, Grid Infrastructure (ACFS filesystem, ASM, and Clusterware), and Oracle Database. Figure 8-5 shows the components.

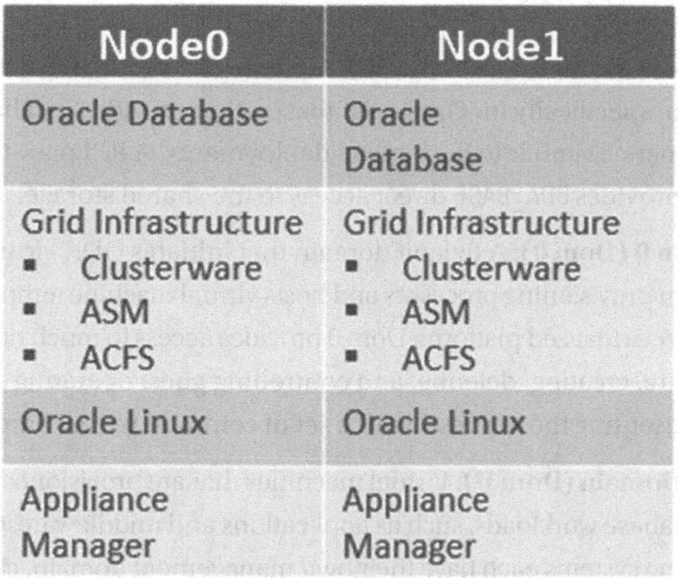

Node0	Node1
Oracle Database	Oracle Database
Grid Infrastructure - Clusterware - ASM - ACFS	Grid Infrastructure - Clusterware - ASM - ACFS
Oracle Linux	Oracle Linux
Appliance Manager	Appliance Manager

Figure 8-5. *Components of ODA bare-metal deployments*

ODA Virtualized Components

In ODA virtualized deployments, Oracle Database runs in the ODA base domain to provide native disk performance. Domains and CPU pools provide application isolation. Appliance Manager provides VM template and domain management. In this deployment model, an Oracle VM virtualization environment is used with an additional domain called ODA_BASE with the dedicated database resources associated. Figure 8-6 shows the components.

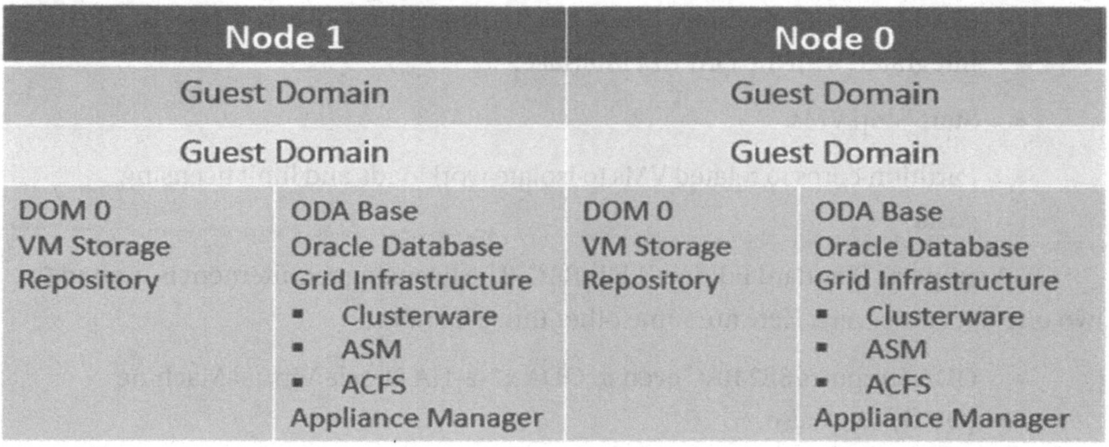

Node 1		Node 0	
Guest Domain		Guest Domain	
Guest Domain		Guest Domain	
DOM 0 VM Storage Repository	ODA Base Oracle Database Grid Infrastructure - Clusterware - ASM - ACFS Appliance Manager	DOM 0 VM Storage Repository	ODA Base Oracle Database Grid Infrastructure - Clusterware - ASM - ACFS Appliance Manager

Figure 8-6. *Components of ODA virtualized deployments*

Here are descriptions of the components in Figure 8-6:

- **ODA Base Domain (ODA_BASE)**: A privileged virtual machine domain, specifically for Oracle databases, that provides database performance similar to bare-metal deployments. A PCI pass-through driver provides ODA_BASE direct access to the shared storage.

- **Domain 0 (Dom 0)**: A default domain that initiates ODA virtualized platform provisioning processes and hosts virtual machine templates. In the ODA virtualized platform, Dom 0 provides access to much of the system hardware, creating, deleting, and controlling guest operating systems and presenting those guests with a set of common virtual hardware.

- **Guest Domain (Dom U)**: Virtual machines that are provisioned to host nondatabase workloads, such as applications and middleware. Guest operating systems each have their own management domain, called a *user domain* (Domain U). These domains are unprivileged domains that have no direct access to the hardware or to the device drivers. Each Domain U starts after Dom 0 is running on the ODA virtualized platform.

- High availability of guest VMs with automatic restart and failover. The virtual machine automatically restarts after a hardware or software failure or whenever your database host computer restarts. Deploy the guest VM using either the `virt-install` command-line tool or the KVM graphical user interface (GUI) tool called `virt-manager`.

- VDisk Management allows the dynamic addition of storage to an existing virtual machine. This VDisk management tool is completely integrated with the OAKCLI interface.

- Start/stop VMs.

- Partition cores to related VMs to isolate workloads and limit licensing costs.

ODA supports Standard Edition (SE2) RAC. The licensing requirement is limited to two one-socket servers. Here are some other things to note:

- ODA supports SE2 RAC even in ODA x7-2-HA Oracle Virtual Machine (OVM) stack also.

- The ODA SE RAC licensing requirements have no socket restrictions.

- You can provision SE and SE2 RAC databases, but you are limited to using the OVM virtualization on ODA x7-2-HA and following the SE2 socket restrictions.

- An ODA bare-metal deployment uses the ODACLI software stack. If it is Oracle Database Appliance Virtualized, x[67]-2-HA will be using the OAKCLI software stack.

- For the latest update on ODA software versions, see MOS Doc 888888.1.

- For the latest on the minimum supported Appliance Manager versions, see MOS Doc 2228502.1.

- In Normal Redundancy configuration, usable database storage will be between 3.9TB and 17.2TB.

- The performance of ODA is based on NVM express SSDs compared to conventional SSDs. In conventional SSDs, flash data is first transformed to the SAS protocol and then bandwidth to each SSD is limited to SAS-3 bandwidth. NVM express SSDs eliminates the protocol transformation to SAS and interfaces with the root complex over a four-lane PCIe Gen3 interface.

Options for ODA Virtualized Environments

You can also use a kernel-based virtual machine (KVM)/Oracle VM on ODA.

- **Features/Options Supported by KVM**

    - It consolidates the database and applications on a single box (solution in a box).

    - It has the ability to patch database and application layers independently.

    - It won't support Oracle Databases running in VMs.

    - It will support only Linux as supported guests.

    - You can use virt-manager and virsh as a management tools. (virt-manager, also known as Virtual Machine Manager, provides a graphical tool for administering virtual machines in ODA. It uses the libvirt library as the management API.)

- **Features/Options Supported by an Oracle VM**

  - It consolidates the database and applications in a single box
    (solution in a box).

  - It has the ability to patch the database and application layers
    independently.

  - It will support Oracle Databases running in VMs.

  - It will support Windows, Linux, and Solaris for the x86 platform
    as supported guests.

  - You can use `virt-manager` and `virsh` as management tools.

Deployment in ODA

Deployment and management in ODA are simplified based on the Entry, Performance,
Consolidated, and High Availability systems from x6 and x7, and you can use either the
command line or the web console.

- The ODACLI command-line and web console for ODA for x6-2S/x6-
  2M/x6-2L and x7-2-HA (bare-metal platform)

- OAKCLI command-line and GUI configurator for ODA for x6-2-HA
  and x7-2-HA (virtualized platform).

If you did not create an external ODA configuration file by using the stand-alone
Oracle Appliance Manager Configurator, you can deploy in real time by running the
Oracle Appliance Manager without specifying a configuration file. You will need to
start the X Window system and possibly set your `DISPLAY` variable depending on your
environment.

A valid IP address needs to be configured for Integrated Lights Out Management
(ILOM) by using either the DHCP or BIOS approach to start the bare-metal restore
procedure. Connect to Oracle ILOM from a client machine by using a browser and log in
as the root user. See Figure 8-7.

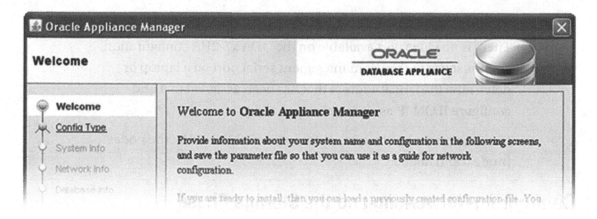

Figure 8-7. *ODA Appliance Manager*

The Flow of Deployment in ODA

Here are the configuration steps:

1. Download the latest ODA software bundle.

2. Gather the configuration information through a wizard.

3. Deploy ODA with a single instance in less than a hour and with Oracle RAC in less than 90 minutes.

Here are the advantages:

- There is no need to install or configure the OS on cluster nodes.

- There is no knowledge required to install the Oracle Clusterware stack, Oracle RAC, and databases.

- The configuration and deployment of ODA are completely tested and validated by Oracle.

ODA Deployment in a Bare-Metal Environment

Figure 8-8 shows the deployment flow.

Figure 8-8. *Deployment flow in ODA*

Here are the prerequisites:

- There is no video port available on the ODA x7-2HA configuration. You must use the server management serial port on a laptop or determine the DHCP address that has been assigned to it and configure ILOM IP using serial connectivity.

- Push the power button on the storage shelf followed by the nodes (node 0 and node 1).

Configuring Networking and the Storage Phase

In the configuring network phase, connect to ODA via a web browser using the IP address that either DHCP or you assigned to the ODA ILOM. To access ODA, you will need to configure the ILOM IP address. This is done through the serial management port on the back of the ODA machine connected to your laptop. Make sure to connect the laptop's serial port to the SerMgt connector on the back of node 0.

Once logged into ILOM as the root user, check the following and verify the connections and network:

- Make sure your storage is connected correctly and you are on the right node, node 0.

```
# /opt/oracle/dcs/bin/odacli validate-storagetopology
```

- Validate the interconnect networking using ethtool and look at "link detected =yes".

```
# ethtool p1p1
# ethtool p1p2
```

Note   p1p1 and p1p2 are interconnect ports for high availability IP (HAIP) addresses for ODA.

- Check the version of the ODA software installed using the following command:

```
# /opt/oracle/dcs/bin/odacli describe-component -v
```

- Configure the IP address for btbond1. You can do this for *both* nodes.

```
# /opt/oracle/oak/bin/configure-firstnet
```

(Specify a public IP address for node 0.)

Log in to node 1 and enter the node 1 public IP address.

```
# ssh <IP address for Node 1>
# /opt/oracle/oak/bin/configure-firstnet
# exit
```

Create and Configure the Cluster Phase

You can use a USB stick mounted on ODA with your files on it; plug it into the USB slot and copy the files to the /opt directory or use the FTP tool to copy them to ODA in the /opt directory. Use the following command to mount:

```
# mount /dev/sdb1 /mnt
# cd /mnt
```

Next copy all the files you need, upload the Grid Infrastructure, database, and other files to the /opt directory on both nodes:

- p27119393_1221X0_Linux-x86-64.zip (GI)

- p27119402_1221X0_Linux-x86-64.zip (12.2)

Note   Here, X denotes the version of the software based on your environment.

Now unzip any files you copied to both nodes in the /opt directory.

- Node 0

```
# unzip /opt/p27119393_1221X0_Linux-x86-64.zip
# unzip /opt/<any database files>
# exit
```

- Node 1

```
# unzip /opt/p27119393_1221X0_Linux-x86-64.zip
# unzip /opt/<any database files>
# exit
```

Updating the 12.2 Version of Grid Infrastructure

You need to do this on the nodes:

- Node 0:

```
# /opt/oracle/dcs/bin/odacli update-repository -f /opt/oda-sm-12.2.1.X.0-
XXXXXX-GI-12.2.0.2.zip; sleep 120
```

Make sure the previous process completed successfully with the following command:

```
# /opt/oracle/dcs/bin/odacli list-jobs
```

- Node 1:

```
# /opt/oracle/dcs/bin/odacli update-repository -f /opt/oda-sm-12.2.1.X.0-
XXXXXX-GI-12.2.0.2.zip; sleep 120
```

Make sure the previous process completed successfully with the following command:

```
# /opt/oracle/dcs/bin/odacli list-jobs
```

Updating the 12.2 Version of Oracle Database

Copy the files and unzip them in the /opt directory; then execute the following commands on both nodes, in other words, node 0 and node 1. You will have options to run Oracle Database versions 12.1, 12.2, and 11g on ODA.

- **Node 0**:

```
# /opt/oracle/dcs/bin/odacli update-repository -f /opt/oda-sm-12.2.1.X.0-
XXXXXX-DB-12.1.0.2.zip; sleep 120
```

Make sure the previous process completed successfully with the following command:

```
# /opt/oracle/dcs/bin/odacli list-jobs
```

- **Node 1**:

```
# ssh <Node1>
# /opt/oracle/dcs/bin/odacli update-repository -f /opt/oda-sm-12.2.1.X.0-
XXXXXX-DB-12.1.0.2.zip; sleep 120
```

Make sure the previous process completed successfully with the following command:

```
# /opt/oracle/dcs/bin/odacli list-jobs
```

Creating and Configuring the Appliance

Once you have copied the GI and database-related files to the /opt directory, you can configure the appliance using the following steps:

1. Log in to the web console on node 0:

```
https://<public-ip-address>:7093/mgmt/index.html
```

If you can't use a web console, you can also use the command line.

```
# odacli create-appliance
```

2. After logging in, click the Create Appliance link and enter the configuration information.

3. You can watch the jobs run by using the following command:

```
# /opt/oracle/dcs/bin/odacli describe-job -i <job id>
```

4. You can verify ODA has been successfully deployed by running the following command:

```
# /opt/oracle/dcs/bin/odacli describe-appliance
```

5. If you have any issues installing/deploying ODA, check the following logfile:

```
# tail -f /opt/oracle/dcs/log/dcs-agent.log
```

415

Configuring the CPU Core Count on ODA

Check the current core count using the following command:

```
# /opt/oracle/dcs/bin/odacli describe-cpucore
```

Note   You can check the core count using the web console by selecting the Appliance tab.

Set the core count based on the licenses for ODA.

```
# /opt/oracle/dcs/bin/odacli update-cpucore - -cores <numberOfCores>
```

Once you set the core count using the following command, you can check the current core count:

```
# /opt/oracle/dcs/bin/odacli list-cpucores Or
# /opt/oracle/dcs/bin/odacli describe-cpucore
```

Additional Information for Creating Databases

For more details about creating a database using OAKCLI, see in section 12.1. Do not use the Oracle Database Configuration Assistant (DBCA) to create databases on ODA. Only use the Oracle Appliance Manager for database configuration on ODA. When deploying Oracle Database instances either in Small, Medium, Large, and High Availability models, the Oracle Appliance Manager ensures that these Oracle Databases are properly configured, optimized, and supported on ODA.

Creating and Configuring ASR

ASR can be configured during the initial deployment of ODA for both internal and external ASR Manager servers.

To configure internal ASR, you need the following information about the environment:

- Proxy server
- Proxy server port
- Proxy username and password

- My Oracle Support account with administrator privileges

- Simple Network Management Protocol (SNMP) version information

To configure external ASR, you need the following information from the environment:

- ASR Manager IP address/hostname

- ASR Manager port

- SNMP version information

ASR can be configured or modified after the initial deployment of ODA using OAKCLI commands. It is simple to convert from an internal ASR to the external ASR configuration.

To display ASR configuration details with the show command, use this command:

```
# oakcli show asr [-h]
```

To configure ASR using an interactive script, use this command:

```
# oakcli configure asr [-h]
```

To validate the ASR component with the validate command, use this command:

```
# oakcli validate -c asr
```

To test the ASR configuration, use this command:

```
# oakcli test asr [-h]
```

CleanupDeploy on ODA to Reset ODA

Optionally, you can run the cleanup.pl script to reset ODA to re-deploy if you need to do so (without removing the database software) and run the web Appliance Manager again. Please note that this will wipe out all your configuration information and any database and you must re-deploy.

```
# perl /opt/oracle/oak/onecmd/cleanup.pl (This "cleanup.pl" command takes
about 5 to 10 minutes)
```

For debugging all issues, please collect the logs from the following path:

`/opt/oracle/dcs/log/*.log`

Note that the `cleanup.pl` command does not remove any public/private IP addresses.

ODA Deployment in a Virtualized Environment

Here are the prerequisites:

- There is no video port available on the ODA x7-2HA configuration. You must use the Server Management serial port on a laptop or determine the DHCP address that has been assigned to it and configure ILOM IP using serial connectivity.

- Push the power button on the storage shelf followed by on the nodes (node 0 and node 1).

Logging In and Configuring the Network

First check the version of ODA with the following command:

`# odacli describe-component`

Configure the IP address for `btbond1` on node 0 and followed by node 1. Please specify the public IP address.

`# /opt/oracle/oak/bin/configure-firstnet`

Reimaging with VM Both Nodes and Installing the ODA Base Phase

You will need the following files for the VM ISO Image and `ODA_BASE`:

- `p16186163_12xxx0_Linux-x86-64.zip` (VM ISO Image)

- `16186172_12xxx0_Linuxx86-64_1of2.zip`

- `p16186172_12xxx0_Linux-x86-64_2of2.zip` (ODA_BASE) on your laptop/desktop

First unzip the `p16186163_12xxx0_Linux-x86-64.zip` ISO image.

Log in as a root user and connect to node 0's ILOM from the browser, which will guide you on the basic steps to configure ODA.

Launch a window to ODA by clicking the Launch Remote Console link.

Running the FIRSTNET Phase

Assign IP addresses to Dom 0 on both nodes by running the following command

```
# oakcli configure firstnet
```

Installing the ODA_BASE Phase

First you need to copy to node 0 the ODA_BASE file and unzip both the files.

```
Ex: p16186172_28xxx_Linux-x86-64_1of2.zip and
    p16186172_28xxx_Linux-x86-64_2of2.zip
```

Run the following command; this will create two files, `oda_base_2.xx.tar.gz00` and `oda_base_2.xx.tar.gz01`.

```
# unzip p16186172_28xxx_Linux-x86-64_1of2.zip
# unzip p16186172_28xxx_Linux-x86-64_2of2.zip
```

After that, you need to concatenate the two files using the `cat` command.

```
# cat oda_base_12.xx.gz01 oda_base_12.xx.gz02 > oda_base_12.xx.tar.gz
```

Finally, you will deploy ODA_BASE using the following command:

```
# oakcli deploy oda_base
```

There will be templates based on the database class (odb-01s, odb-1, and so on), matching database templates to core count and RAM size on Oracle database appliance virtualized platform and you will prompt for the option to set up a VLAN to ODA_BASE during deployment.

Finally, ODA_BASE should now be up and running. You can check it by running the following command:

```
# oakcli show oda_base
```

Note   There will be matching database templates for the core count and physical RAM size on the ODA virtualized platform.

The template looks like the following:

```
Enter the template location: <absolute path of file>
Core Licensing Options:
1. 2 CPU Cores
2. 4 CPU Cores
3. 6 CPU Cores
4. 8 CPU Cores
5. 10 CPU Cores
6. 12 CPU Cores
7. 14 CPU Cores
8. 16 CPU Cores
9. 18 CPU Cores
10. 20 CPU cores
11. 22 CPU cores
12. 24 CPU Cores
13. 26 CPU Cores
14. 28 CPU Cores
15. 30 CPU Cores
16. 32 CPU Cores
17. 34 CPU Cores
18. 36 CPU Cores
Selection[1...18] :
```

Note   Enter the line number of the number of cores you need, not the actual number of cores.

ODA base domain memory in GB (min 16, max 362) default 288]:

After selecting the line, you need to set up a VLAN to ODA_BASE during deployment and after that check the ODA_BASE status by running the following command:

```
# oakcli show oda_base
```

Deployment End-User Bundle Software Phase

Log into oda_base via the private IP from Dom 0 or through the console <ssh IP Address>.

Run firstnet to configure oda_base.

```
# oakcli configure firstnet
```

Start a VNC server in oda_base and use the VNC viewer and connect to < ODA_BASE IP address>:1.

Deploy software on ODA_BASE using the following command:

```
# oakcli deploy
```

To validate the installation, run the following command from ODA_BASE:

```
# oakcli show version -detail
```

Check the current enabled cores with the following command:

```
# oakcli describe-cpucore
```

Change the core count from node 0 with the following command:

```
# oakcli update-cpucore -cores <number of cores>
```

Note   You can increase the core count once it's set. The command sets the cores on node 0 and node 1.

Patching (OAKCLI Stack) Phase

Download the three-part patch files and copy all three patch files to ODA_BASE on node 0 and node 1.

```
p27119652_122xxx_Linux-x86-64_1of3.zip
p27119652_122xxx_Linux-x86-64_2of3.zip
p27119652_122xxx_Linux-x86-64_3of3.zip
```

Unpack all three patch files on node 0 and node 1.

```
# oakcli unpack –package /<specified dir>/p27119652_122xxx_Linux-x86-
64_1of3.zip
# oakcli unpack –package /<specified dir>/p27119652_122xxx_Linux-x86-
64_2of3.zip
# oakcli unpack –package /<specified dir>/p27119652_122xxx_Linux-x86-
64_3of3.zip
```

Verify the components getting patched with the following command:

```
# oakcli update -patch 12.2.x.x.x --verify
# oakcli update -patch 12.2.x.x.x --server
```

Update the shared storage firmware; the nodes might reboot with the following command:

```
# oakcli update -patch 12.2.x.x.x --storage
```

After the nodes (node 0 and node 1) reboot, check that the cluster is running with the following command:

```
# /u01/app/12.2.0.1/grid/bin/crsctl check crs
```

CleanupOdaBase Phase

If you need to reinstall ODA_BASE, run the command from Dom 0 (this removes ODA_BASE, which means re-installing ODA_BASE and redeploying).

```
# /opt/oracle/oak/tools/cleanOdabase.py
```

Or, you can run from ODA_BASE (restores the servers to their predeployment state but does not remove the VMs, Dom 0, ODA_BASE, or database or Grid software):

```
# /opt/oracle/oak/onecmd/cleanupDeploy.pl
```

You can get a list of configuration parameters using the following command:

```
# /opt/oracle/oak/onecmd/onecommand.params (in ODA_BASE if virtualized)
```

ORACHK can be used to check all items within the ODA stack (OS, GI, DB, and CRS).

```
# /opt/oracle/oak/ORACHK/ORACHK –a –o verbose (run from ODA_BASE if
virtualized)
```

Purging LOGs in ODA

Using the purgeODALog tool, you can clean up the trace and log files. With a single command, all the logs are managed in ODA. if no arguments are passed with purgeODALog then all the logs older than 30 days will be deleted. Please refer for more details "Cleanup trace and log files Using purgeODALog Tool (Doc ID 2081655.1)". You can purge files related to audits, listeners, the trace file analyzer, databases, the operating system watcher, and so on.

```
$ ./purgeODALog help
Invalid extra options passed: help
```
Usage:
```
purgeODALog [ -days <days> [ -aud ] [ -lsnr ] ]
                [ -orcl <days> [ -aud ] [ -lsnr ] ] |
                [ -tfa <days> ] |
                [ -osw <days> ] |
                [ -oak <days> ] |
                [ -extra '<folder>':<days> | [, '<folder>':<days>] ]
                [ -dryrun ]
```

purgeODALog OPTIONS

```
-days  <days>       Purge orcl,tfa,osw,oak components logs & traces older
                    then # days
-orcl  <days>       Purge only GI/RDBMS logs & traces (Default 30 days)
-tfa   <days>       Purge only TFA repository older then # days (Default
                    30 days)
-osw   <days>       Purge only OSW archives older then # days (Default 30
                    days)
-oak   <days>       Purge only OAK logs and trace older then # days
                    (Default 30 days)
-extra '<folder>':<days> Purge only files in user specified folders
                    (Default 30 days)
-aud                Purge Audit logs based on '-orcl <days>' option
-lsnr               It will force the cleanup of listeners log
                    independently by the age
-dryrun             It will show the purge commands w/o execute them
-h                  Display this help and exit
```

Log in to the putty session as the root user. Use the commands in Figure 8-9 to purge the logs.

PurgeODALog	Description
./purgeODALog –osw 25 –oak 25	To clean OSWatcher archive logs and OAK logs use below command. This command will clear OSWatcher and OAK logs older than 25 days.
./purgeODALog –orcl 25 –lsnr	To clean listener logs use below command. This command will clear listener logs older than 25 days.
./purgeODALog –tfa 25	To clean listener logs use below command. This command will clear listener logs older than 25 days.
./purgeODALog –orcl 15	All the logs generated by RDBMS and Grid infrastructure can be cleaned by using '-orcl' parameter with purgeODALog. As a root user issue below command to cleanup all logs generated older than 15 days.
./purgeODALog –orcl 15 –aud	To clean audit logs use below command. This command will clear audit files older than 15 days.
./purgeODALog	Purge all logs older than 'x' number of days. By default purge tool will delete all logs older than 30 days. If we want to delete all files older than 'X' number days. '-days' parameter can be used with days.

Figure 8-9. *purgeODALog utility with options*

Management and Diagnostics of ODA

Let's cover some management and diagnostics.

Auto Service Request (ASR)

The ASR monitors and creates automatic service requests on any hardware component failure with Oracle Support.

ODA ORACHK

Similar to the EXACHK tool available in Exadata systems to monitor the health of the system and identify problems, a handy validation tool called ORACHK is available on ODA machines. You can find it at /opt/oracle/oak/orachk. ORACHK was formerly called ODACHK. ORACHK is integrated with the Oracle database appliance command-line interface OAKCLI.

The ORACHK configuration tool validates important configuration settings such as database standards and undocumented parameter settings, ASM, Grid Infrastructure and RDBMS settings, operating system kernel parameters and packages, and shared memory configurations. ORACHK also checks for best practices.

OEM ODA Plug-In

With the ODA plug-in, you can monitor ODA targets using Oracle Enterprise Manager Cloud Control (OEMCC) 12c/13c. The ODA plug-in provides configuration and monitoring information about any ODA target running Appliance Manager 12.1.x.x or higher. ODA components (database, ILOM, host, virtual machines, hypervisor, ASM, and Oracle Appliance Manager) are grouped and can be monitored under a target. This will support both bare-metal and virtualized platform deployments and is for all ODA hardware versions.

Diagnostics Collection

The Oracle Appliance Manager diagnostics and validation tool is managed with Oracle Appliance Manager oakcli validate commands. Some of the commands are given in this section.

Using the following command, you can list and describe all validation command options:

```
# oakcli validate -l
```

The following command runs all system checks:

```
# oakcli validate -a
```

The following command performs a system check for disk calibration:

```
# oakcli validate -c DiskCalibration
```

odaadmcli manage diagcollect

The odaadmcli manage diagcollect command gathers all relevant logs from the hardware and software components and produces a single bundle for support.

System Check for ODA Environments

ORACHK validates the hardware and software components of ODA. ORACHK quickly identifies any anomaly or violation of best-practice compliance in the complete stack of ODA.

ODA ORACHK applies to the following:

- ODA software, all versions

- x3-2, all versions

- x4-2, all versions

- x5-2, all versions

- ODA x6-2 hardware, all versions

- ODA x7-2 hardware, all versions

Executing ODACHK has a few prerequisites.

- The server login should be root.

- Log in to the putty session of the ODA machine (i.e., DBServer01) as the root user. Use oakcli orachk.

- Execute ORACHK using oakcli.

```
$ oakcli orachk
Checking for prompts on dbserver01 for grid user...
Checking ssh user equivalency settings on all nodes in cluster
Node dbserver02 is configured for ssh user equivalency for root user
Checking for prompts for grid user on all nodes...
Searching for running databases . . . . .
. . . . . . . . . . . . . . . . . . . . . . . . . . . . . . . . .
List of running databases registered in OCR

1. test01db
2. test02db
3. test03db
4. All of above
5. None of above
```

Select databases from list for checking best practices. For multiple databases, select 4 for All or comma separated number like 1,2 etc [1-5][4]. **4**
Searching out ORACLE_HOME for selected databases.
. .
Checking for prompts for oracle user on all nodes...
. . . .
Checking Status of Oracle Software Stack - Clusterware, ASM, RDBMS

                                                    Oracle Stack Status
----
Host Name CRS Installed RDBMS Installed CRS UP   ASM UP   RDBMS UP DB
Instance Name
----
dbserver01
Yes   Yes   Yes   Yes   Yes   test01db1
test02db1 test03db1
dbserver02
Yes   Yes   Yes   Yes   Yes   test01db2
test02db2 test03db2

*** Checking Best Practice Recommendations (PASS/WARNING/FAIL) ***
Collections and audit checks log file is
/opt/oracle/oak/orachk/orachk_dbserver01_032218_094259/log/orachk.log
Checking for prompts in /root/.bash_profile on dbserver01 for root user...
Checking for prompts in /root/.bash_profile on dbserver02 for root user...
Starting to run orachk in background on dbserver02
==
                     Node name - dbserver01
==
Collecting - ASM Diskgroup Attributes
Collecting - ASM initialization parameters
Collecting - Database Parameters for test01db database
Collecting - Database Parameters for test02db database
Collecting - Database Parameters for test03db database
Collecting - Database Undocumented Parameters for test01db database

Collecting - Database Undocumented Parameters for test02db database
Collecting - Database Undocumented Parameters for test03db database
Collecting - RDBMS Feature Usage for test01db database
Collecting - RDBMS Feature Usage for test02db database
Collecting - RDBMS Feature Usage for test03db database
Collecting - Kernel parameters
Collecting - Maximum number of semaphore sets on system
Collecting - Maximum number of semaphores on system
Collecting - Maximum number of semaphores per semaphore set
Collecting - OS Packages
Collecting - Patches for Grid Infrastructure
Collecting - Patches for RDBMS Home
Collecting - number of semaphore operations per semop system call
Collecting - CRS user limits configuration
Collecting - Firmware and software versions
Collecting - Network and Bonding Interfaces Status
Collecting - OS Disk Storage Status
Collecting - System Component Status
Collecting - Validate Shared storage
Data collections completed. Checking best practices on dbserver01.

... output deleted for brevity ...
Detailed report (html) - /opt/oracle/oak/orachk/orachk_
dbserver01_032218_094259/orachk_dbserver01_032218_094259.html

UPLOAD (if required) - /opt/oracle/oak/orachk/orachk_
dbserver01_032218_094259.zip
Once Orachk is complete, a html file (orachk_dbserver01_032218_094259.html)
and .zip file (orachk_dbserver01_032218_094259.zip) is created in '/opt/
oracle/oak/orachk' directory. Html file generated with orachk is Oracle
Database Appliance Assessment Report.

Details of the ODA Assessment Report

The detailed report will have the following information. OAKCLI will generate HTML as well as zip files after the orachk command.

- Cluster summary

- Database server

- Patch recommendation

- Cluster-wide checks

- PeopleSoft checks

- Top ten time-consuming checks

ODA Patching

ORACHK was formerly known as ODACHK. ORACHK is integrated with the OAKCLI interface and should be run as the root user. ORACHK is typically used to validate the ODA configuration regularly after each upgrade or patch, or every three months, and so on. The ORACHK script tool included in ODA helps the environment by checking and validating the configuration, best practices, and patches on the system.

The patch process is similar for bare-metal and virtualized platform deployments. The OAKCLI interface will take care of the complete patch cycle. You do not need to research the required patches of firmware for Oracle Database; the automated patching process does the work for you.

The following components have to be patched in Oracle Database Appliance:

- All system firmware

- Operating system

- System management software (ASR)

- Appliance Manager

- Grid Infrastructure

- Oracle Database

Figure 8-10 shows the flow of ODA patching.

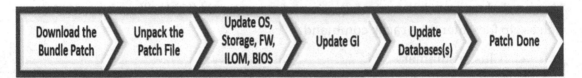

***Figure 8-10.** Patch cycle of Oracle Database Appliance*

Figure 8-11 shows examples of the OAKCLI interface for patching the ODA stack.

OAKCLI Interface	Examples Of OAKCLI Interface
Updates all firmware, OS, ILOM, Appliance Manager, and ASR	oakcli update –patch 12.1.x.x –-infra
Updates Grid Infrastructure	oakcli update –patch 12.1.x.x –-gi
Patch databases	oakcli update –patch 12.1.x.x –-database
Create new 12.1.0.2 Oracle Home	oakcli create dbhome –version 12.1.0.x
Upgrade the database to the newly created 12.1.0.x home	oakcli upgrade database –db <dbname> –to <dest_home>

***Figure 8-11.** Usage of the oakcli command*

Figure 8-12 shows the levels and order of patches.

Patches	Commands
Server Patch	$ oakcli update -patch 12.1.2.10.0 --server <--local>
Storage Patch	$ oakcli update -patch 12.1.2.10.0 –storage
Database Patch	$ oakcli update -patch 12.1.2.10.0 --database <--local>

***Figure 8-12.** Levels of patches and usage of the oakcli command*

Prerequisites

Patch 12.1.2.10.0 can be applied on ODA systems that are running 12.1.2.6.0 or higher. Check the space in the following directories and make sure to have enough space:

- /u01
- /tmp
- /boot

Applying the 12.1.2.10.0 Patch

Follow these steps:

1. Download the patch bundle from Oracle Support. The patch bundle contains two zip files.

p25499210_1212100_Linux-x86-64_1of2.zip
p25499210_1212100_Linux-x86-64_2of2.zip

Copy the patch files to all the ODA nodes in /tmp or any other location.

2. Log in to each node as the root and unpack the patch bundles in both nodes.

Log in to DBServer01.

```
[root@dbserver01: Wed Apr 05, 03:52 PM : /tmp/patches/ODA ]
$ /opt/oracle/oak/bin/oakcli unpack -package /tmp/patches/ODA/
p25499210_1212100_Linux-x86-64_1of2.zip

Unpacking will take some time, Please wait...
Successfully unpacked the files to repository.
[ root@dbserver01 : Wed Apr 05, 03:55 PM : /tmp/patches/ODA ]

$ /opt/oracle/oak/bin/oakcli unpack -package /tmp/patches/ODA/
p25499210_1212100_Linux-x86-64_2of2.zip

Unpacking will take some time, Please wait...
Successfully unpacked the files to repository.
[ root@dbserver01: Wed Apr 05, 03:56 PM : /tmp/patches/ODA ]
```

Log in to DBServer02:

```
[root@dbserver02 : Wed Apr 05, 03:58 PM : /root ]
```

```
$ /opt/oracle/oak/bin/oakcli unpack -package /tmp/patches/ODA/
p25499210_1212100_Linux-x86-64_1of2.zip
```

```
Unpacking will take some time, Please wait...
Successfully unpacked the files to repository.
[ root@dbserver02 : Wed Apr 05, 03:58 PM : /root ]
```

```
Unpacking will take some time, Please wait...
```

***$ /opt/oracle/oak/bin/oakcli unpack -package /tmp/patches/ODA/
p25499210_1212100_Linux-x86-64_2of2.zip***

```
Successfully unpacked the files to repository.
```

3. In each node, verify the components getting patched using the command verify.

```
$ /opt/oracle/oak/bin/oakcli update -patch  12.1.2.10.0 --verify
```

```
INFO: 2017-04-05 18:52:25: Reading the metadata file now...
```

Component Name	Installed Version	Proposed Patch Version
Controller_INT	4.230.40-3739	Up-to-date
Controller_EXT	09.00.00.00	10.00.00.00
Expander	0018	Up-to-date
SSD_SHARED {		
[c2d20,c2d21,c2d22, c2d23,c2d44,c2d45,c2 d46,c2d47]	A29A	Up-to-date
[c2d16,c2d17,c2d18, c2d19,c2d40,c2d41,c2 d42,c2d43]	A29A	Up-to-date
}		
HDD_LOCAL	A72A	Up-to-date

```
HDD_SHARED {
[ c2d24,c2d25,c2d26,         P9E2                    PAG1
c2d27,c2d28,c2d29,c2
d30,c2d31,c2d32,c2d3
3,c2d34,c2d35,c2d36,
c2d37,c2d38,c2d39 ]
[ c2d0,c2d1,c2d2,c2d         A3A0                    Up-to-date
3,c2d4,c2d5,c2d6,c2d
7,c2d8,c2d9,c2d10,c2
d11,c2d12,c2d13,c2d1
4,c2d15 ]
}
ILOM                         3.2.7.26.a r112579      3.2.8.24 r114580
BIOS                         30090200                30100400
IPMI                         1.8.12.4                Up-to-date
HMP                          2.3.5.2.5               2.3.5.2.8
OAK                          12.1.2.9.0              12.1.2.10.0
OL                           6.8                     Up-to-date
GI_HOME                      12.1.0.2.161018(2400    12.1.0.2.170117(2473
                             6101,23854735)          2082,24828633)

DB_HOME {
[ OraDb11204_home1 ]         11.2.0.4.161018(2400    Up-to-date
                             6111,23054319)
[ OraDb12102_home1 ]         12.1.0.2.161018(2400    12.1.0.2.170117(2473
                             6101,23854735)          2082,24828633)
}
ASR                          5.5.1                   Up-to-date
```

4. Apply the patch for server components.

Issue the following command to patch the server components. The -`local` option
can be used to patch each node separately. If the -`local` option is not used, both nodes
will be patched.

```
$ oakcli update -patch  12.1.2.10.0 -server <-local>
$ oakcli update -patch  12.1.2.10.0 --server
```

```
********************************************************************************

*****   For all X5-2 customers with 8TB disks, please make sure to    *****
*****    run storage patch ASAP to update the disk firmware to "PAG1". *****
********************************************************************************
INFO: DB, ASM, Clusterware may be stopped during the patch if required
INFO: Both Nodes may get rebooted automatically during the patch if
required
Do you want to continue: [Y/N]?: Y
INFO: User has confirmed for the reboot
INFO: Patch bundle must be unpacked on the second Node also before applying
the patch
Did you unpack the patch bundle on the second Node? : [Y/N]? : Y
INFO: Running pre-install scripts
INFO: Running  prepatching on node 0
INFO: Running prepatching on node 1
INFO: Completed pre-install scripts
INFO: Patching server component (rolling)
INFO: Patching the server on node: dbserver02
INFO: it may take upto 60 minutes. Please wait
INFO: Running postpatch on node dbserver02...
INFO: Infrastructure patching summary on node: dbserver01
INFO: Infrastructure patching summary on node: dbserver02
SUCCESS: 2017-04-05 20:21:15:  Successfully upgraded the HMP
SUCCESS: 2017-04-05 20:21:15:  Successfully updated the OAK
SUCCESS: 2017-04-05 20:21:15:  Successfully updated the JDK
INFO: 2017-04-05 20:21:15:  IPMI is already upgraded
SUCCESS: 2017-04-05 20:21:15:  Successfully upgraded the OS
SUCCESS: 2017-04-05 20:21:15:  Successfully updated the ILOM & BIOS
INFO: 2017-04-05 20:21:15:  Storage patching summary
SUCCESS: 2017-04-05 20:21:15:  There are no failures found during Storage
upgrade
SUCCESS: 2017-04-05 20:21:15:  Successfully applied the patch on the Home /
u01/app/12.1.0.2/grid
INFO: 2017-04-05 20:21:15: Some of the components patched on node
<dbserver02>
```

```
INFO: 2017-04-05 20:21:15: require node reboot. Rebooting the node
INFO: 2017-04-05 20:21:16: rebooting dbserver02 via /tmp/pending_actions...
INFO: 2017-04-05 20:26:46: dbserver02 is rebooting...
INFO: 2017-04-05 20:26:46: Waiting for dbserver02 to reboot...
INFO: 2017-04-05 20:34:46: dbserver02 has rebooted...
INFO: 2017-04-05 20:34:46: Waiting for processes on dbserver02 to start...
INFO: Patching server component on node: dbserver01
INFO: 2017-04-05 20:36:50: Patching Server Components (including Grid
software)
INFO: 2017-04-05 20:36:51: --------------Patching HMP--------------------
SUCCESS: 2017-04-05 20:37:01: Successfully upgraded the HMP
INFO: 2017-04-05 20:37:02: /usr/lib64/sun-ssm already exists.
INFO: 2017-04-05 20:37:02: --------------Patching OAK--------------------
SUCCESS: 2017-04-05 20:37:35: Successfully upgraded OAK
INFO: 2017-04-05 20:37:39: --------------Patching JDK--------------------
SUCCESS: 2017-04-05 20:37:44: Successfully upgraded JDK
INFO: 2017-04-05 20:37:45: --------------Patching IPMI--------------------
INFO: 2017-04-05 20:37:45: IPMI is already upgraded or running with the
latest version
INFO: 2017-04-05 20:37:45: --------------Patching OS--------------------
INFO: 2017-04-05 20:37:57: Clusterware is running on local node
INFO: 2017-04-05 20:37:57: Attempting to stop clusterware and its resources
locally
SUCCESS: 2017-04-05 20:41:11: Successfully stopped the clusterware on local
node
INFO: 2017-04-05 20:41:53: Trying to recreate /boot/initramfs-2.6.39-
400.290.1.el6uek.x86_64.img
INFO: 2017-04-05 20:42:24: Successfully recreated /boot/initramfs-2.6.39-
400.290.1.el6uek.x86_64.img
```

Some output has been deleted for brevity. Also, note that the machine will be restarted after the server patch. Verify all Grid infrastructure services are up and running once the machine is back online.

```
$crsctl check crs
CRS-4638: Oracle High Availability Services is online
CRS-4537: Cluster Ready Services is online
```

CRS-4529: Cluster Synchronization Services is online

CRS-4533: Event Manager is online

After a server patch is successful, apply the storage patch. There is no <-local> option for the storage patch. Node 1 is patched first and then node 2. Issue the following command to perform the storage patch:

```
[ root@dbserver01 : Wed Apr 05, 09:47 PM : /tmp/patches/ODA ]
$ oakcli update -patch  12.1.2.10.0 --storage
INFO: DB, ASM, Clusterware may be stopped during the patch if required
INFO: Both Nodes may get rebooted automatically during the patch if
required
Do you want to continue: [Y/N]?: Y
INFO: User has confirmed for the reboot
INFO: Running pre-install scripts
INFO: Running  prepatching on node 0
INFO: Running  prepatching on node 1
INFO: Completed pre-install scripts
INFO: Shared Storage components need to be patched
INFO: Stopping OAKD on both nodes...
INFO: Stopped Oakd
INFO: Attempting to shutdown clusterware (if required)..
INFO: 2017-04-05 21:49:23: Clusterware is running on one or more nodes of
the cluster
INFO: 2017-04-05 21:49:23: Attempting to stop clusterware and its resources
across the cluster
SUCCESS: 2017-04-05 21:50:05: Successfully stopped the clusterware
INFO: Patching storage on node dbserver02
INFO: Patching storage on node dbserver01
INFO: 2017-04-05 22:13:02: ----------------Patching Storage----------------
INFO: 2017-04-05 22:13:02: ...................Patching SSDs..............
INFO: 2017-04-05 22:13:02: Disk : d16  is already running with :
HSCAC2DA4SUN400G A29A
INFO: 2017-04-05 22:13:02: Disk : d17  is already running with :
HSCAC2DA4SUN400G A29A
INFO: 2017-04-05 22:13:02: Disk : d18  is already running with :
HSCAC2DA4SUN400G A29A
```

```
INFO: 2017-04-05 22:13:02: Disk : d19  is already running with :
HSCAC2DA4SUN400G A29A
INFO: 2017-04-05 22:13:02: Disk : d20  is already running with :
HSCAC2DA6SUN200G A29A
INFO: 2017-04-05 22:13:03: Disk : d21  is already running with :
HSCAC2DA6SUN200G A29A
INFO: 2017-04-05 22:13:03: Disk : d22  is already running with :
HSCAC2DA6SUN200G A29A
INFO: 2017-04-05 22:13:03: Disk : d23  is already running with :
HSCAC2DA6SUN200G A29A
INFO: 2017-04-05 22:13:03: Disk : d40  is already running with :
HSCAC2DA4SUN400G A29A
INFO: 2017-04-05 22:13:03: Disk : d41  is already running with :
HSCAC2DA4SUN400G A29A
INFO: 2017-04-05 22:13:03: Disk : d42  is already running with :
HSCAC2DA4SUN400G A29A
INFO: 2017-04-05 22:13:04: Disk : d43  is already running with :
HSCAC2DA4SUN400G A29A
INFO: 2017-04-05 22:13:04: Disk : d44  is already running with :
HSCAC2DA6SUN200G A29A
INFO: 2017-04-05 22:13:04: Disk : d45  is already running with :
HSCAC2DA6SUN200G A29A
INFO: 2017-04-05 22:13:04: Disk : d46  is already running with :
HSCAC2DA6SUN200G A29A
INFO: 2017-04-05 22:13:04: Disk : d47  is already running with :
HSCAC2DA6SUN200G A29A
INFO: 2017-04-05 22:13:04: ...........Patching Shared HDDs..............
INFO: 2017-04-05 22:13:04: Disk : d0  is already running with :
H7280A520SUN8.0T PAG1
INFO: 2017-04-05 22:13:05: Disk : d1  is already running with :
H7280A520SUN8.0T PAG1
INFO: 2017-04-05 22:13:05: Disk : d2  is already running with :
H7280A520SUN8.0T PAG1
INFO: 2017-04-05 22:13:05: Disk : d3  is already running with :
H7280A520SUN8.0T PAG1
```

```
INFO: 2017-04-05 22:13:05: Disk : d4  is already running with :
H7280A520SUN8.0T PAG1
INFO: 2017-04-05 22:13:05: Disk : d5  is already running with :
H7280A520SUN8.0T PAG1
INFO: 2017-04-05 22:13:05: Disk : d6  is already running with :
H7280A520SUN8.0T PAG1
INFO: 2017-04-05 22:13:06: Disk : d7  is already running with :
H7280A520SUN8.0T PAG1
INFO: 2017-04-05 22:13:06: Disk : d8  is already running with :
H7280A520SUN8.0T PAG1
INFO: 2017-04-05 22:13:06: Disk : d9  is already running with :
H7280A520SUN8.0T PAG1
INFO: 2017-04-05 22:13:06: Disk : d10  is already running with :
H7280A520SUN8.0T PAG1
INFO: 2017-04-05 22:13:06: Disk : d11  is already running with :
H7280A520SUN8.0T PAG1
INFO: 2017-04-05 22:13:06: Disk : d12  is already running with :
H7280A520SUN8.0T PAG1
INFO: 2017-04-05 22:13:07: Disk : d13  is already running with :
H7280A520SUN8.0T PAG1
INFO: 2017-04-05 22:13:07: Disk : d14  is already running with :
H7280A520SUN8.0T PAG1
INFO: 2017-04-05 22:13:07: Disk : d15  is already running with :
H7280A520SUN8.0T PAG1
INFO: 2017-04-05 22:13:07: Disk : d24  is already running with :
H7240AS60SUN4.0T A3A0
INFO: 2017-04-05 22:13:07: Disk : d25  is already running with :
H7240AS60SUN4.0T A3A0
INFO: 2017-04-05 22:13:07: Disk : d26  is already running with :
H7240AS60SUN4.0T A3A0
INFO: 2017-04-05 22:13:08: Disk : d27  is already running with :
H7240AS60SUN4.0T A3A0
INFO: 2017-04-05 22:13:08: Disk : d28  is already running with :
H7240AS60SUN4.0T A3A0
INFO: 2017-04-05 22:13:08: Disk : d29  is already running with :
H7240AS60SUN4.0T A3A0
```

```
INFO: 2017-04-05 22:13:08: Disk : d30  is already running with :
H7240AS60SUN4.0T A3A0
INFO: 2017-04-05 22:13:08: Disk : d31  is already running with :
H7240AS60SUN4.0T A3A0
INFO: 2017-04-05 22:13:08: Disk : d32  is already running with :
H7240AS60SUN4.0T A3A0
INFO: 2017-04-05 22:13:09: Disk : d33  is already running with :
H7240AS60SUN4.0T A3A0
INFO: 2017-04-05 22:13:09: Disk : d34  is already running with :
H7240AS60SUN4.0T A3A0
INFO: 2017-04-05 22:13:09: Disk : d35  is already running with :
H7240AS60SUN4.0T A3A0
INFO: 2017-04-05 22:13:09: Disk : d36  is already running with :
H7240AS60SUN4.0T A3A0
INFO: 2017-04-05 22:13:09: Disk : d37  is already running with :
H7240AS60SUN4.0T A3A0
INFO: 2017-04-05 22:13:09: Disk : d38  is already running with :
H7240AS60SUN4.0T A3A0
INFO: 2017-04-05 22:13:10: Disk : d39  is already running with :
H7240AS60SUN4.0T A3A0
INFO: 2017-04-05 22:13:10: ...................Patching Expanders.........
INFO: 2017-04-05 22:13:10: Expander : c1x0  is already running with : DE2-
24C 0018
INFO: 2017-04-05 22:13:10: Expander : c1x1  is already running with : DE2-
24C 0018
INFO: 2017-04-05 22:13:10: Expander : c2x0  is already running with : DE2-
24C 0018
INFO: 2017-04-05 22:13:10: Expander : c2x1  is already running with : DE2-
24C 0018
INFO: 2017-04-05 22:13:10: .............Patching Shared Controllers.......
INFO: 2017-04-05 22:13:10: Updating the  Controller : c1 with the Firmware
: 0x0097 10.00.00.00
SUCCESS: 2017-04-05 22:15:32: Successfully updated the Firmware
on  Controller : c1 to 0x0097 10.00.00.00
... output deleted for brevity ...
```

Note   After the storage patch, both nodes will be rebooted. Log in to the
dbserver01 and dbserver02 nodes and verify the ODA storage update using
oakcli. Issue the following command to verify the storage update:

$ oakcli update -patch 12.1.2.10 --verify

See Figure 8-13.

```
$ oakcli update -patch 12.1.2.10 --verify
INFO: 2017-04-18 13:14:11: Reading the metadata file now...
            Component Name              Installed Version          Proposed Patch Version
            --------------              -----------------          ----------------------
            Controller_INT              4.230.40-3739              Up-to-date
            Controller_EXT              10.00.00.00                Up-to-date
            Expander                    0018                       Up-to-date
            SSD_SHARED {
            [ c2d20,c2d21,c2d22,        A29A                       Up-to-date
            c2d23 ]
            [ c2d16,c2d17,c2d18,        A29A                       Up-to-date
            c2d19 ]
                            }
            HDD_LOCAL                   A72A                       Up-to-date
            HDD_SHARED                  PAG1                       Up-to-date
            ILOM                        3.2.8.24 r114580           Up-to-date
            BIOS                        30100400                   Up-to-date
            IPMI                        1.8.12.4                   Up-to-date
            HMP                         2.3.5.2.8                  Up-to-date
            OAK                         12.1.2.10.0                Up-to-date
            OL                          6.8                        Up-to-date
            GI_HOME                     12.1.0.2.170117(2473       Up-to-date
                                        2082,24828633)
            DB_HOME {
            [ OraDb11204_home2,O        11.2.0.4.161018(2400       Up-to-date
            raDb11204_home1 ]           6111,23054319)
            [ OraDb12102_home2,O        12.1.0.2.170117(2473       Up-to-date
            raDb12102_home1 ]           2082,24828633)
                            }
            ASR                         5.5.1                      Up-to-date
```

Figure 8-13. *Components version after patch*

5.   Apply the database patch.

The database patch can be applied using the `-local` option. If the `-local` option is
not used, the database patch is applied in a rolling fashion. Node 1 is patched first and
then node 2. Issue the following command to apply the database patch:

```
$ oakcli update -patch  12.1.2.10.0  --database <--local>
$ /opt/oracle/oak/bin/oakcli update -patch  12.1.2.10.0  --database
INFO: 2017-04-05 22:25:35: Clusterware is not running on one or more nodes
of the cluster
INFO: 2017-04-05 22:25:35: Attempting to start clusterware and its
resources across the cluster
```

INFO: 2017-04-05 22:25:36: Sleeping for 30 seconds waiting for clusterware to start
SUCCESS: 2017-04-05 22:26:06: Successfully started the clusterware
INFO: Running pre-install scripts
INFO: Running prepatching on node 0
INFO: Running prepatching on node 1
INFO: Completed pre-install scripts
INFO: 2017-04-05 22:26:41: ------------------Patching DB------------------
INFO: 2017-04-05 22:26:41: Getting all the possible Database Homes for patching
INFO: 2017-04-05 22:27:00: Patching 11.2.0.4 Database Homes on the Node dbserver01
Found the following 11.2.0.4 homes possible for patching:

HOME_NAME	HOME_LOCATION
OraDb11204_home1	/u01/app/oracle/product/11.2.0.4/dbhome_1

[Please note that few of the above Database Homes may be already up-to-date. They will be automatically ignored]

Would you like to patch all the above homes: Y | N ? : **Y**
INFO: 2017-04-05 22:27:09: Updating OPATCH
Verifying Opatch version for home:</u01/app/oracle/product/11.2.0.4/dbhome_1>.
Expecting version:<11.2.0.3.15>
Opatch version on node <dbserver01> is <11.2.0.3.15>
Opatch version on node <dbserver02> is <11.2.0.3.15>
INFO: 2017-04-05 22:28:02: Performing the conflict checks...
SUCCESS: 2017-04-05 22:28:10: Conflict checks passed for all the Homes
INFO: 2017-04-05 22:28:10: Checking if the patch is already applied on any of the Homes
INFO: 2017-04-05 22:28:14: Following Homes are already Up-to-date
/u01/app/oracle/product/11.2.0.4/dbhome_1
INFO: 2017-04-05 22:28:14: Patching 11.2.0.4 Database Homes on the Node dbserver02

INFO: 2017-04-05 22:29:13: Patching 12.1.0.2 Database Homes on the Node dbserver01
Found the following 12.1.0.2 homes possible for patching:

HOME_NAME	HOME_LOCATION
OraDb12102_home1	/u01/app/oracle/product/12.1.0.2/dbhome_1

[Please note that few of the above Database Homes may be already up-to-date. They will be automatically ignored]
Would you like to patch all the above homes: Y | N ? : Y
INFO: 2017-04-05 22:29:21: Updating OPATCH
Verifying Opatch version for home:</u01/app/oracle/product/12.1.0.2/dbhome_1>.
Expecting version:<12.2.0.1.8>
Opatch version on node <dbserver01> is <12.2.0.1.8>
Opatch version on node <dbserver02> is <12.2.0.1.8>
INFO: 2017-04-05 22:30:55: Performing the conflict checks...
SUCCESS: 2017-04-05 22:31:04: Conflict checks passed for all the Homes
INFO: 2017-04-05 22:31:04: Checking if the patch is already applied on any of the Homes
INFO: 2017-04-05 22:31:08: Home is not Up-to-date
SUCCESS: 2017-04-05 22:31:31: Successfully stopped the Database consoles
SUCCESS: 2017-04-05 22:31:58: Successfully stopped the EM agents
INFO: 2017-04-05 22:32:03: Applying patch on /u01/app/oracle/product/12.1.0.2/dbhome_1 Homes
INFO: 2017-04-05 22:32:03: It may take upto 15 mins. Please wait...
SUCCESS: 2017-04-05 22:37:29: Successfully applied the patch on the Home : /u01/app/oracle/product/12.1.0.2/dbhome_1
SUCCESS: 2017-04-05 22:37:29: Successfully started the Database consoles
SUCCESS: 2017-04-05 22:37:56: Successfully started the EM Agents
INFO: 2017-04-05 22:38:10: Patching 12.1.0.2 Database Homes on the Node dbserver02
INFO: DB patching summary on node: dbserver01
INFO: 2017-04-05 22:45:41: The Homes /u01/app/oracle/product/11.2.0.4/dbhome_1 are already Up-to-date

SUCCESS: 2017-04-05 22:45:41: Successfully applied the patch on the Home /u01/app/oracle/product/12.1.0.2/dbhome_1

INFO: DB patching summary on node: dbserver02

INFO: 2017-04-05 22:45:41: The Homes /u01/app/oracle/product/11.2.0.4/ dbhome_1 are already Up-to-date

SUCCESS: 2017-04-05 22:45:41: Successfully applied the patch on the Home /u01/app/oracle/product/12.1.0.2/dbhome_1

INFO: Executing /tmp/pending_actions on both nodes

The oakcli show command is used to verify whether patches are applied. Issue the following command to verify patches. Log in as root to each node and issue the following command (see Figure 8-14):

```
$ oakcli show version -detail
```

```
$ oakcli show version -detail
Reading the metadata. It takes a while...
System Version   Component Name          Installed Version      Supported Version
--------------   --------------          -----------------      -----------------
12.1.2.10.0
                 Controller_INT          4.230.40-3739          Up-to-date
                 Controller_EXT          10.00.00.00            Up-to-date
                 Expander                0018                   Up-to-date
                 SSD_SHARED {
                 [ c2d20,c2d21,c2d22,    A29A                   Up-to-date
                 c2d23 ]
                 [ c2d16,c2d17,c2d18,    A29A                   Up-to-date
                 c2d19 ]
                               }
                 HDD_LOCAL               A72A                   Up-to-date
                 HDD_SHARED              PAG1                   Up-to-date
                 ILOM                    3.2.8.24 r114580       Up-to-date
                 BIOS                    30100400               Up-to-date
                 IPMI                    1.8.12.4               Up-to-date
                 HMP                     2.3.5.2.8              Up-to-date
                 OAK                     12.1.2.10.0            Up-to-date
                 OL                      6.8                    Up-to-date
                 GI_HOME                 12.1.0.2.170117(2473   Up-to-date
                                         2082,24828633)
                 DB_HOME {
                 [ OraDb11204_home2,O    11.2.0.4.161018(2400   Up-to-date
                 raDb11204_home1 ]       6111,23054319)
                 [ OraDb12102_home2,O    12.1.0.2.170117(2473   Up-to-date
                 raDb12102_home1 ]       2082,24828633)
                               }
                 ASR                     5.5.1                  Up-to-date
```

Figure 8-14. *Components version before patch*

You have upgraded to the latest version, so now you can check that it worked (see Figure 8-15):

```
oakcli show version -detail
```

```
$ oakcli show version -detail
Reading the metadata. It takes a while...
System Version   Component Name            Installed Version        Supported Version
--------------   ---------------           -----------------        -----------------
12.2.1.2.0
                 Controller_INT            4.650.00-7176            Up-to-date
                 Controller_EXT            13.00.00.00              Up-to-date
                 Expander                  0018                     Up-to-date
                 SSD_SHARED {
                 [ c2d20,c2d21,c2d22,      A29A                     Up-to-date
                 c2d23 ]
                 [ c2d16,c2d17,c2d18,      A29A                     Up-to-date
                 c2d19 ]
                          }
                 HDD_LOCAL                 A7E0                     Up-to-date
                 HDD_SHARED                PAG1                     Up-to-date
                 ILOM                      3.2.9.23 r116695         Up-to-date
                 BIOS                      30110000                 Up-to-date
                 IPMI                      1.8.12.4                 Up-to-date
                 HMP                       2.4.1.0.6                Up-to-date
                 OAK                       12.2.1.2.0               Up-to-date
                 OL                        6.8                      Up-to-date
                 GI_HOME                   12.2.0.1.171017(2671     Up-to-date
                                           0464,27020386)
                 DB_HOME {
                 [ OraDb12102_home1 ]      12.1.0.2.171017(2671     12.1.0.2.171017(2671
                                           7470,25942196)          7470,26914423)
                 [ OraDb11204_home2,O      11.2.0.4.171017(2639     Up-to-date
                 raDb11204_home1 ]         2168,26609929)
                 [ OraDb12102_home2 ]      12.1.0.2.170418(2517     12.1.0.2.171017(2671
                                           1037,25942196)          7470,26914423)
                          }
                 ASR                       5.7.7                    5.7.6
```

Figure 8-15. *Components version after patch*

Using ODACLI Commands to Patch a System and Upgrade Databases

You can use the ODACLI and ODAADMCLI command-line interfaces as well as the web console to patch systems, create databases, delete databases, view database homes, upgrade databases, and so on, after ODA x5-2 generation.

Uploading a Patch to Oracle Database Appliance

ODA does not ship with the Grid Infrastructure and Oracle Database software preloaded. You must download the GI and Oracle database software prior to deployment.

- oda-sm-12.2.1.2.0-171124-GI-12.2.0.1.zip (Grid Infrastructure clone files)

- oda-sm-12.2.1.2.0-171124-DB-12.2.0.1.zip (Oracle Database 12.2 clone files)

- oda-sm-12.2.1.3.0-180116-server.zip (ODA patch bundle)

After downloading the following files, you must update the ODA repository using the `odacli update-repository` command. If it is ODA HA configuration, you need to do this on both the nodes.

```
$ sudo odacli update-repository -f /home/user02/oda-sm-12.2.1.2.0-171124-
DB-12.2.0.1.zip
```

```
$ sudo odacli update-repository -f /home/user02/oda-sm-12.2.1.2.0-171124-
GI-12.2.0.1.zip
```

```
$ sudo odacli update-repository -f /home/user02/oda-sm-12.2.1.3.0-180116-
server.zip
```

Once you update the repository in both the nodes using the previous commands, the clone files are all loaded into the repository, and also you can update the DCS agent on both the nodes through the web console before actually updating the server. The purpose of the DCS agent is that provides intelligent and automation. Once the DCS agent is updated, you will be disconnected from the web console, and you need to log back in so you can check for the updated version of DCS agent. Finally, you are ready to deploy the appliance followed by creating the database.

Updating the System Infrastructure

The following command will update Grid Infrastructure, the operating system, ILOM, Appliance Manager, ASR, and the firmware. If it is an ODA HA configuration, you need to do this on both nodes.

```
odacli update-server -v 12.2.1.2
```

Updating the Repository of Grid Infrastructure and Databases Using the ODACLI Command

Let's look at the commands:

```
[user01@c965a4 ~]$ sudo odacli update-repository -f /home/user01/oda-sm-
12.2.1.2.0-171124-DB-12.2.0.1.zip
{
    "jobId" : "e665e178-c170-401c-a619-572b34a376d7",
    "status" : "Running",
    "message" : "Submitted the job for update repository",
    "reports" : [ {
      "taskId" : "TaskSequential_UR1",
      "taskName" : "Checking for user validity and permissions",
      "taskResult" : "User permissions looks fine!",
      "startTime" : "June 13, 2018 15:58:26 PM UTC",
      "endTime" : "June 13, 2018 15:58:26 PM UTC",
      "status" : "Scheduled",
      "taskDescription" : "Checking for user permissions",
      "parentTaskId" : "",
      "jobId" : "",
      "tags" : [ "UpdRepo1", "updRepo2" ],
      "reportLevel" : "Info",
      "updatedTime" : "June 13, 2018 15:58:26 PM UTC"
    }, {
      "taskId" : "TaskSequential_UR2",
      "taskName" : "Creating the repository location",
      "taskResult" : "Creation of repository location looks fine!",
      "startTime" : "June 13, 2018 15:58:26 PM UTC",
      "endTime" : null,
      "status" : "Scheduled",
      "taskDescription" : "Creating the repository location",
      "parentTaskId" : "",
      "jobId" : "",
      "tags" : [ "UpdRepo1", "updRepo2" ],
      "reportLevel" : "Info",
```

```
    "updatedTime" : "June 13, 2018 15:58:26 PM UTC"
  }, {
    "taskId" : "TaskSequential_UR3",
    "taskName" : "Copying the patch binaries",
    "taskResult" : "Copying of the patch binaries looks fine!",
    "startTime" : "June 13, 2018 15:58:26 PM UTC",
    "endTime" : "June 13, 2018 15:58:26 PM UTC",
    "status" : "Scheduled",
    "taskDescription" : "Copying the patch binaries",
    "parentTaskId" : "",
    "jobId" : "",
    "tags" : [ "UpdRepo1", "updRepo2" ],
    "reportLevel" : "Info",
    "updatedTime" : "June 13, 2018 15:58:26 PM UTC"
  } ],
  "createTimestamp" : "June 13, 2018 15:58:26 PM UTC",
  "resourceList" : null,
  "description" : "Repository Update",
  "updatedTime" : "June 13, 2018 15:58:26 PM UTC"
}
```

```
[user01@c965a4 ~]$ sudo odacli update-repository -f /home/user01/oda-sm-
12.2.1.2.0-171124-GI-12.2.0.1.zip
```

```
{
  "jobId" : "c0199b15-e792-4fbd-a23a-890812ef295d",
  "status" : "Running",
  "message" : "Submitted the job for update repository",
  "reports" : [ {
    "taskId" : "TaskSequential_UR1",
    "taskName" : "Checking for user validity and permissions",
    "taskResult" : "User permissions looks fine!",
    "startTime" : "June 13, 2018 15:55:51 PM UTC",
    "endTime" : "June 13, 2018 15:55:51 PM UTC",
    "status" : "Scheduled",
    "taskDescription" : "Checking for user permissions",
    "parentTaskId" : "",
```

```
    "jobId" : "",
    "tags" : [ "UpdRepo1", "updRepo2" ],
    "reportLevel" : "Info",
    "updatedTime" : "June 13, 2018 15:55:51 PM UTC"
  }, {
    "taskId" : "TaskSequential_UR2",
    "taskName" : "Creating the repository location",
    "taskResult" : "Creation of repository location looks fine!",
    "startTime" : "June 13, 2018 15:55:51 PM UTC",
    "endTime" : null,
    "status" : "Scheduled",
    "taskDescription" : "Creating the repository location",
    "parentTaskId" : "",
    "jobId" : "",
    "tags" : [ "UpdRepo1", "updRepo2" ],
    "reportLevel" : "Info",
    "updatedTime" : "June 13, 2018 15:55:51 PM UTC"
  }, {
    "taskId" : "TaskSequential_UR3",
    "taskName" : "Copying the patch binaries",
    "taskResult" : "Copying of the patch binaries looks fine!",
    "startTime" : "June 13, 2018 15:55:51 PM UTC",
    "endTime" : "June 13, 2018 15:55:51 PM UTC",
    "status" : "Scheduled",
    "taskDescription" : "Copying the patch binaries",
    "parentTaskId" : "",
    "jobId" : "",
    "tags" : [ "UpdRepo1", "updRepo2" ],
    "reportLevel" : "Info",
    "updatedTime" : "June 13, 2018 15:55:51 PM UTC"
  } ],
  "createTimestamp" : "June 13, 2018 15:55:51 PM UTC",
  "resourceList" : null,
  "description" : "Repository Update",
  "updatedTime" : "June 13, 2018 15:55:51 PM UTC"
}
```

```
$ sudo odacli update-repository -f /home/user01/oda-sm-12.2.1.3.0-180116-
server.zip
{
  "jobId" : "0b2f-49ca-8639-48dfca59f24f",
  "status" : "Running",
  "message" : "Submitted the job for update repository",
  "reports" : [ {
    "taskId" : "TaskSequential_UR1",
    "taskName" : "Checking for user validity and permissions",
    "taskResult" : "User permissions looks fine!",
    "startTime" : "February 26, 2018 19:13:08 PM PST",
    "endTime" : "February 26, 2018 19:13:08 PM PST",
    "status" : "Scheduled",

... output deleted for brevity ...
```

Updating the Databases to the Latest PSU

The odacli list-databases command will display each database including its ID and
its database home ID. You have to pass the database home ID as an argument to the
odacli update-dbhome command to update the patch for that database home ID.

```
$ sudo odacli update-dbhome -i 3b645d-ec7d-40c3-928f-9bb9906a85 -v
12.2.1.3.0
{
  "jobId" : "c8c0-4fec-9ca4-21c5f382ec08",
  "status" : "Running",
  "message" : "Submitted Update-DBHome Job",
  "reports" : [ {
    "taskId" : "TaskSequential_34",
    "taskName" : "Check the existence of DBHome Location",
    "taskResult" : "DBHome is valid!",
    "startTime" : "March 22, 2018 22:15:01 PM UTC",
    "endTime" : null,
    "status" : "Scheduled",

... output deleted for brevity ...
```

You can check the job status using the following command:

```
$ sudo odacli describe-job -i c8c0-4fec-9ca4-21c5f382ec08

Job details
----------------------------------------------------------------
ID:  c8c0-4fec-9ca4-21c5f382ec08
Description:  Update DBHome
Status:  Success
Created:  March 22, 2018 10:15:01 PM UTC
Message:  Submitted Update-DBHome Job

Task Name                                Start Time
------------------------------------     ------------------------------
End Time                         Status
------------------------------   -------
Check the existence of DBHome Location  March 22, 2018 10:15:01 PM UTC
March 22, 2018 10:15:09 PM UTC  Success
Checking for update permissions         March 22, 2018 10:15:01 PM UTC
March 22, 2018 10:15:10 PM UTC  Success
Updating the database binaries          March 22, 2018 10:15:01 PM UTC
March 22, 2018 10:15:11 PM UTC  Success
```

Upgrading Database Patchsets or to Major Releases

There are two commands to look at here. The following command will create a new version of 12.2.x Oracle Home.

```
odacli create-dbhome -v 12.2.x
```

The next command will upgrade the database to the newly created version of 12.2.x Oracle Home. You have to pass the source database home ID as well as the destination database home ID.

```
odacli upgrade-database -i <database-id> -from <source-db-home-id> -to
<destination-db-home-id>
```

ODACLI Commands

Figure 8-16 shows the commands for the database, database storage, and CPUs.

Feature	Command
Appliance	create-appliance describe-appliance
CPUCore	describe-cpucore list-cpucores update-cpucore
Database	create-database delete-database describe-database list-databases register-database upgrade-database
DB Home	create-dbhome delete-dbhome describe-dbhome list-dbhomes update-dbhome
DBStorage	create-dbstorage delete-dbstorage describe-dbstorage list-dbstorages

Figure 8-16. *List of odacli commands*

Commands for Creating Databases

You can run the following to create a database:

```
$ sudo odacli create-database -h
$ sudo odacli create-database -m -n db3 -v 12.1.0.2
```

Appliance Commands

To deploy ODA in silent mode using the JSON file, use this:

```
odacli create-appliance
```

To display appliance details, use this:

```
odacli describe-appliance
```

CPU Core Commands

The following displays details about cores:

```
odacli describe-cpucore
```

The following lists the current cores enabled:

```
odacli list-cpucores
```

The following changes the number of enabled cores in multiples of 2:

```
odacli update-cpucore -c <core_number>
```

Database Commands

To create additional databases, use this:

```
odacli create-database
```

To delete a database, use this:

```
odacli delete-database
```

To display the database details, use this:

```
odacli describe-database -I <dbID>
```

To display information about the databases, use this:

```
odacli list-databases
```

To register a migrated database with the appliance, use this:

```
odacli register-database
```

To upgrade a database, for example, from 11g to 12c, use this:

```
odacli upgrade-database
```

To restore a database from one system to other system, use this:

```
odacli recover-database -iDatabase Resource ID
```

DB Home Commands

To create a new database home, use this:

```
odacli create-dbhome
```

To delete a database home, use this:

```
odacli delete-dbhome -i <ID>
```

To display information about the database homes, use this:

```
odacli describe-dbhome –i <home id>
```

To list the current database homes, use this:

```
odacli list-dbhomes
```

To update a specific RDBMS home to the latest patch bundle version, use this:

```
odacli update-dbhome
```

DB Storage Commands

To create the file system for database migrations, use this:

```
odacli create-dbstorage
```

To delete database storage, use this:

```
odacli delete-dbstorage
```

To display the storage configuration details, use this:

```
odacli describe-dbstorage
```

To display a list of all the database storage configured in the appliance, use this:

```
odacli list-dbstorages
```

ODAADMCLI Commands

You can one more additional command-line interface, odaadmcli, for appliance maintenance.

Storage Commands

To display the status of a single disk or of all disks, use this:

```
sudo odaadmcli show disk
```

To display the details of the controller, use this:

```
sudo odaadmcli show controller (0/1)
```

To show the storage controllers, expanders, and disks, use this:

```
sudo odaadmcli show storage
```

To list the configured disk groups, use this:

```
sudo odaadmcli show diskgroup
```

Hardware Monitoring

To display the server details, use this:

```
sudo odaadmcli show server
```

To display the memory details, use this:

```
sudo odaadmcli show memory
```

To display the processor details, use this:

```
sudo odaadmcli show processor
```

To display the power supply details, use this:

```
sudo odaadmcli show power
```

To show the cooling details, use this:

```
sudo odaadmcli show cooling
```

To show the network details, use this:

```
sudo odaadmcli show network
```

To display the RAID SYNC status, use this:

```
sudo odaadmcli show raidsyncstatus
```

To display the filesystem details, use this:

```
sudo odaadmcli show fs
```

When listing ASM disk groups that have been configured by Appliance Manager on ODA's storage, you should understand the following:

- DATA is where the database data files are stored.

- FLASH is where the hot files or small databases can be placed to improve performance.

- RECO is where the database's backups, archive logs, and redo logs are stored.

- REDO is where the database's redo logs are stored.

Resize the ACFS File System in ODA

You can use either the OAKCLI utility or the acfs utility or ASMCA utility login as a Grid user to resize the acfs filesystem in ODA. If you configure alerts through EM Cloud Control with threshold values, you will get alerts through EM Cloud Control.

Depending on which ACFS file system you are going to resize on ODA, you have to use different commands because in ODA you have nondatabase volumes as well as database volumes. The database volumes are data, redo, reco, and flash, and the nondatabase volumes are /cloudfs, and so on.

Nondatabase Volumes

Log in as the root user to node 1 of the ODA through the Putty SSH and execute the resize command:

```
/sbin/acfsutil size <new size>  <file system mount>
```

Here's an example:

```
/sbin/acfsutil size 800G /cloudfs
```

Database Volumes

Log in as the root user to node 1 of ODA through the Putty SSH and issue the following command:

```
oakcli resize dbstorage <storage type> <new storage size in GB>
```

Here's an example:

```
oakcli resize dbstorage -data 500
```

The complete options are shown here for the `oakcli resize` command:

```
$oakcli resize dbstorage -h
Usage:
oakcli resize dbstorage  [-data <size>] [-reco <size>] [-redo <size>]
                                        [-flash <size>] [-cdb  <db_name>]
where:
      data  - extendable size in GB for the DATA volume
      redo  - extendable size in GB for the REDO volume
      reco  - extendable size in GB for the RECO volume
      flash - extendable size in GB for the FLASH volume (available from
              x5-2 hardware)
      db_name      - volumes created for this 'cdb' database get extended.
```

Alert Received from EM Cloud Control

Figure 8-17 shows that we have received an alert from the OEM regarding filesystem space and saying we should add more space to that filesystem.

```
Host=█████████.com
Target type=Asm Proxy
Target name=+APX1 ██████-c
Categories=Capacity
Message=The ASM Cluster File System using volume device /dev/asm/█████████-415 is 97.082% full. Resize the file system to add more space.
Severity=Critical
Event reported time=Aug 8, 2018 7:20:04 AM EDT
Target Lifecycle Status=Staging
Line of Business=Database Admin
```

***Figure 8-17.** Alert received from Enterprise Manager Cloud Control on filesystem*

Note   You can check the available space using the df command.

Method 1:

Here's how to resize the mount point (500 GB) using the OAKCLI utility:

```
$ oakcli resize dbstorage -data 500 -cdb cdbdata
INFO: 2018-08-08 08:22:07: Please look at the log file '/opt/oracle/oak/
log/server01/tools/12.2.1.2.0/resizedbstorage_38976.log' for more details
Recommended extension size for RECO volume is :  397
Recommended extension size for REDO volume is :  4
Do you want to extend RECO REDO volumes with the recommended values : [Y|N] ?N
INFO: 2018-08-08 08:23:17: Resizing the data volume mounted at /u02/app/
oracle/oradata/datcdbdata by +500 GB
SUCCESS: 2018-08-08 08:23:35: Successfully extended the volume mounted at
/u02/app/oracle/oradata/datcdbdata
```

Check the new size for the mountpoint after adding space.

```
$ df -h /u02/app/oracle/oradata/datcdbdata
```

Filesystem	Size	Used	Avail	Use%	Mounted on
/dev/asm/ datcdbdata-415	6.3T	5.7T	674G	90%	/u02/app/oracle/ oradata/datcdbdata

Method 2:

Use the `acfsutil` utility to reduce the size of the ACFS volume that is mounted on the RECO disk group.

```
[root@dbserver01  ~]# acfsutil size -1T /u01/app/oracle/fast_recovery_area/
datastore
```

Method 3:

Using the ASM Configuration Assistant (ASMCA), follow these steps:

- Connect as the `grid` user.

- Run the ASM Configuration Assistant (ASMCA) utility.

- Choose the ASM Cluster File System tab.

- Select the `cloudfs` to be resized and right-click.

- Change the size and then click the OK button.

- Get confirmation of the new size.

Using the OAKCLI Command Utility with Databases

To create a database in ODA, you can use the `oakcli` command utility with arguments such as the database name and database home. You can use the options to create a single instance, a Real Application Clusters instance, and a RAC one-node instance, You can also specify whether the database is for online transaction processing (OLTP) or is for decision support system (DSS).

Using the `oakcli` command, you can do the following:

- Create a single-instance database

- Create a RAC database

- Upgrade the database from Oracle 11g R2 (11.2.0.4.0) to Oracle 12cR 2 (12.1.0.2.0)

- Create a snapshot database

- Drop a snapshot database

Creating a Single-Instance Database

Let's get started:

```
$ oakcli create database -db entestdv -oh OraDb11204_home1
INFO: 2018-04-09 17:06:54: Please check the logfile '/opt/oracle/oak/log/
dbserver01/tools/12.2.1.2.0/createdb_entestdv_85010.log' for more details
INFO: 2018-04-09 17:06:56: Database parameter file is not provided. Will be
using default parameters for DB creation
INFO: 2018-04-09 17:07:01:
Database will be created on ACFS volume
Please enter the 'SYSASM'  password : (During deployment we set the SYSASM
password to 'welcome1'):
Please re-enter the 'SYSASM' password:
Database home edition is : Enterprise Edition
Please select one of the following for Database type  [1 .. 2] :
1     => OLTP
2     => DSS
1
The selected value is : OLTP
Please select one of the following for Database Deployment  [1 .. 3] :
1     => SI : Single Instance
2     => RACONE
3     => RAC
1
The selected value is : SI
Please select one of the following for Node Number  [1 .. 2] :
1     => dbserver01
2     => dbserver02
1

The selected value is : dbserver01
Specify the  Database Class (1. odb-01 '1 core, 8 GB memory'   2. Others)
[1] : 1
The selected value is : odb-01 '1 core, 8 GB memory'
INFO   : Logging all actions in the file /opt/oracle/oak/log/dbserver01/
patch/12.2.1.2.0/dbserver01-20180409170929.log and traces in  the file
```

```
/opt/oracle/oak/log/dbserver01/patch/12.2.1.2.0/dbserver01-20180409170929.
trc
INFO    : Loading the configuration file /opt/oracle/oak/onecmd/create_
database.params...
INFO    : Creating the node list files...
INFO    : Setting up ssh for root...
INFO    : Setting up SSH across the Private Network...
...INFO    : Running as root: /usr/bin/ssh -l root 192.168.16.24 /root/
DoAllcmds.sh
INFO    : Running as root: /usr/bin/ssh -l root 192.168.16.25 /root/
DoAllcmds.sh
INFO    : Background process 3530 (node: 192.168.16.24) gets done with the
exit code 0
INFO    : Background process 3599 (node: 192.168.16.25) gets done with the
exit code 0
INFO    : Setting up SSH completed successfully
INFO    : Running the command /usr/bin/rsync -tarqvz /opt/oracle/oak/onecmd/
INFO: 2018-04-09 17:19:18: Successfully unlocked the DBSNMP user

... output deleted for brevity ...

SUCCESS: 2018-04-09 17:19:23: Successfully created the Database : entestdv
[ root@dbserver01 : Mon Apr 09, 05:19 PM : /root ]
```

Creating a RAC Database

Now here's the RAC version:

```
$  oakcli create database  -db ctrans -oh OraDb12102_home1 -cdb

INFO: 2018-06-29 12:12:16: Please check the logfile  '/opt/oracle/oak/log/
dbserver01/tools/12.2.1.2.0/createdb_ctrans_40768.log' for more details
INFO: 2018-06-29 12:12:18: Database parameter file is not provided. Will be
using default parameters for DB creation
INFO: 2018-06-29 12:12:29:
Database will be created on ASM volume
```

Please enter the 'SYSASM' password : (During deployment we set the SYSASM password to 'welcome1'):

Please re-enter the 'SYSASM' password:

INFO: 2018-06-29 12:12:46: CDB creation may take long time as it installs more components. Please monitor dbca log for Database creation...

Database home edition is : Enterprise Edition

Please select one of the following for Database type [1 .. 3] :

```
1    => OLTP
2    => DSS
3    => In-Memory
1
```

The selected value is : OLTP

Please select one of the following for Database Deployment [1 .. 3] :

```
1    => SI : Single Instance
2    => RACONE
3    => RAC
3
```

The selected value is : RAC

Specify the Database Class (1. odb-01 '1 core, 8 GB memory'   2. Others) [1] : 2

Please select one of the following for Database Class [1 .. 7] :

```
1    => odb-01s  (    1 cores ,     4 GB memory)
2    =>  odb-01  (    1 cores ,     8 GB memory)
3    =>  odb-02  (    2 cores ,    16 GB memory)
4    =>  odb-04  (    4 cores ,    32 GB memory)
5    =>  odb-06  (    6 cores ,    48 GB memory)
6    =>  odb-12  (   12 cores ,    96 GB memory)
7    =>  odb-16  (   16 cores ,   128 GB memory)
2
```

The selected value is : odb-01 (1 cores ,   8 GB memory)

Default datafile size for the Database Class 'odb-01' is : 100 GB

Please enter Y to continue with the default DB size or enter the required size in GB : Y

```
INFO    : Logging all actions in the file /opt/oracle/oak/log/dbserver01/
patch/12.2.1.2.0/dbserver01-20180629121314.log and traces in  the file
/opt/oracle/oak/log/dbserver01/patch/12.2.1.2.0/dbserver01-20180629121314.trc
INFO    : Loading the configuration file /opt/oracle/oak/onecmd/create_
database.params...
INFO    : Creating the node list files...
INFO    : Setting up ssh for root...
INFO    : Setting up SSH across the Private Network...
...INFO    : Running as root: /usr/bin/ssh -l root 192.168.16.24 /root/
          DoAllcmds.sh
INFO    : Running as root: /usr/bin/ssh -l root 192.168.16.25 /root/
          DoAllcmds.sh
INFO    : Background process 49556 (node: 192.168.16.24) gets done with the
          exit code 0
INFO    : Background process 49608 (node: 192.168.16.25) gets done with the
          exit code 0
INFO    : Setting up SSH completed successfully

--Output truncated --------------------
```

Upgrading the Database from Oracle 11g R2 (11.2.0.4.0) to Oracle 12c R2 (12.1.0.2.0)

Here is the upgrade command:

```
$ oakcli upgrade database -db entestdv -from OraDb11204_home1 -to
OraDb12102_home1
INFO: 2018-04-09 18:06:06: Look at the log file '/opt/oracle/oak/log/
loris01dblxa/tools/12.2.1.2.0/dbupgrade_2855.log' for more details
Please enter the 'SYS'  password :
Please re-enter the 'SYS' password:
INFO: 2018-04-09 18:06:48: Upgrading the database entestdv. It will take
few minutes. Please wait...
SUCCESS: 2018-04-09 18:21:57: Successfully upgraded the database entestdv
[ root@loris01dblxa : Mon Apr 09, 06:21 PM : /u01/app/oracle/oradata/
datastore/entestdv/ENTESTDV ]
```

Creating a Snapshot Database

You can create snapshot databases from any Oracle Database that is stored on an Oracle ASM Cluster File System (ACFS) on ODA using the oakcli command.

Creating snapshot databases has the following restrictions:

- Must not be a standby or container database

- Must not be in read-only mode, restricted mode, or online backup mode

- Must be in ARCHIVELOG mode

- Must have all defined datafiles available and in online mode

- Must be Oracle 11g R2 (11.2.0.4) or later

```
[oracle@dbserver01 ~]$ . oraenv
ORACLE_SID = [entestdv] ? entestdv
The Oracle base remains unchanged with value /u01/app/oracle

$ oakcli create snapshotdb -db ensnapdv -from entestdv
INFO: 2018-04-10 11:33:34: Please check the logfile  '/opt/oracle/oak/log/
dbserver01/tools/12.2.1.2.0/createdb_ensnapdv_23319.log' for more details
Please enter the 'SYS' password for the Database entestdv:
Please re-enter the 'SYS' password:
Please select one of the following for EE Database Node  [1 .. 2] :
1    => dbserver01
2    => dbserver02
1
The selected value is : dbserver01
Specify the  Database Class (1. odb-01 '1 core, 8 GB memory'   2. Others)
[1] : 1
The selected value is : odb-01 '1 core, 8 GB memory'
SUCCESS: All nodes in /opt/oracle/oak/temp_clunodes.txt are pingable and
alive.
SUCCESS: All nodes in /opt/oracle/oak/temp_clunodes.txt are pingable and
alive.
INFO: 2018-04-10 11:37:17: Creating the SNAP Database 'ensnapdv' from the
source Database 'entestdv'
```

```
INFO: 2018-04-10 11:37:29: Do not perform any Structural change to Database
'entestdv' till SNAP Database 'ensnapdv' is created
INFO: 2018-04-10 11:38:03: Taking SNAP of the Database 'entestdv'
INFO: 2018-04-10 11:38:06: Successfully took  the SNAP of database:
entestdv
INFO: 2018-04-10 11:39:33: Creating controlfile for database: ensnapdv
INFO: 2018-04-10 11:39:48: Successfully created the control file for the
database : ensnapdv
INFO: 2018-04-10 11:39:52: Recovering the database: ensnapdv,  snapshot
time : '2018-04-10:11:38:04' , until time : '2018-04-10:11:38:33'
INFO: 2018-04-10 11:39:54: Successfully recovered the database
INFO: 2018-04-10 11:39:54: Opening the database with resetlogs
INFO: 2018-04-10 11:40:06: Successfully opened the database after recovery
INFO: 2018-04-10 11:40:09: Setting the temporary tablespace for database :
ensnapdv
INFO: 2018-04-10 11:40:11: Successfully set the temporary tablespace for
the database : ensnapdv
INFO: 2018-04-10 11:40:57: Successfully changed the Database ID
INFO: 2018-04-10 11:42:03: Adding the Database resource to the clusterware
INFO: 2018-04-10 11:42:38: Successfully started the database
INFO: 2018-04-10 11:42:38: Updating the TNS entries for the database
ensnapdv
INFO: 2018-04-10 11:43:24: Successfully set the RMAN SNAPSHOT control file
INFO: 2018-04-10 11:43:41: Disabling the external references in the
database 'ensnapdv' inherited from 'entestdv'
INFO: 2018-04-10 11:43:42: Successfully disabled the external references
INFO: 2018-04-10 11:44:18: Run the SQL script '/u01/app/oracle/
product/12.1.0.2/dbhome_1/enable_external_refs_ensnapdv_QbNK.sql' on the
database 'ensnapdv' to enable these external references
Also need to restart the database after running the SQL script
SUCCESS: 2018-04-10 11:44:57: Successfully created the Database 'ensnapdv'
from 'entestdv'
[ root@dbserver01 : Tue Apr 10, 11:44 AM : /root ]
```

Dropping a Snapshot Database

Here is how to drop the snapshot database:

[oracle@dbserver01 ~]$. oraenv
```
ORACLE_SID = [esnapdv] ? ensnapdv
The Oracle base remains unchanged with value /u01/app/oracle
```

$ oakcli delete database -db ensnapdv
```
INFO: 2018-04-10 11:57:39: Look at the log file '/opt/oracle/oak/log/
dbserver01/tools/12.2.1.2.0/deletedatabase_ensnapdv_65317.log' for more
details
Please enter the 'SYS' password :
Please re-enter the 'SYS' password:
INFO: 2018-04-10 11:58:22: Setting up SSH
SUCCESS: Ran /usr/bin/rsync -tarqvz /opt/oracle/oak/onecmd/
root@192.168.16.25:/opt/oracle/oak/onecmd --exclude=*zip --exclude=*gz
--exclude=*log --exclude=*trc --exclude=*rpm and it returned:
RC=0
SUCCESS: All nodes in /opt/oracle/oak/onecmd/tmp/db_nodes are pingable and
alive.
INFO: 2018-04-10 11:59:24: SSH has been successfully established
INFO: 2018-04-10 12:00:30: Successfully deleted the database 'ensnapdv'
INFO: 2018-04-10 12:00:35: Attempting to cleanup the SNAP entries for the
database: ensnapdv
INFO: 2018-04-10 12:00:35: Successfully deleted the SNAP entries
[ root@dbserver01 : Tue Apr 10, 12:00 PM : /root ]
```

Dropping a Database

Here is how to drop a database:

```
$ oakcli delete database -db entestdv
INFO: 2018-04-10 12:03:31: Look at the log file '/opt/oracle/oak/log/
dbserver01/tools/12.2.1.2.0/deletedatabase_entestdv_98481.log' for more
details
Please enter the 'SYS' password :
```

```
Please re-enter the 'SYS' password:
INFO: 2018-04-10 12:04:24: Setting up SSH
...SUCCESS: Ran /usr/bin/rsync -tarqvz /opt/oracle/oak/onecmd/
root@192.168.16.25:/opt/oracle/oak/onecmd --exclude=*zip --exclude=*gz
--exclude=*log --exclude=*trc --exclude=*rpm and it returned: RC=0
SUCCESS: All nodes in /opt/oracle/oak/onecmd/tmp/db_nodes are pingable and
alive.
INFO: 2018-04-10 12:05:25: SSH has been successfully established
INFO: 2018-04-10 12:06:32: Successfully deleted the database 'entestdv'
INFO: 2018-04-10 12:06:37: Attempting to cleanup the SNAP entries for the
database: entestdv
INFO: 2018-04-10 12:06:38: Successfully deleted the SNAP entries
[ root@dbserver01 : Tue Apr 10, 12:06 PM : /root ]
```

Dismounting an ACFS Filesystem

To reinstall the ACFS/ADVM modules on a clustered database on ODA, you need to
dismount the ACFS filesystem first. Before that, you need to check which applications
are accessing the ACFS filesystem.

```
$ df -m /cloudfs/
Filesystem            1M-blocks    Used     Available    Use%    Mounted on
/dev/asm/acfsvol-336  332800       51101    281700       16%     /cloudfs
```

This ACFS filesystem is not being used or accessed, as confirmed by the following
two commands:

```
[root@dbserver01 ~]# lsof /cloudfs
[root@dbserver01 ~]# fuser /cloudfs
```

You are able to see that Oracle GoldenGate is accessing the /cloudfs folder.

```
$ lsof /cloudfs/ | grep -e extract -e mgr -e replicat

replicat   5832 oracle  cwd     DIR 250,172035     16384         46
/cloudfs/goldengate/product/12.1.2/gghome_11
replicat   5832 oracle  txt     REG 250,172035  43672639         2402
/cloudfs/goldengate/product/12.1.2/gghome_11/replicat
```

```
replicat   5832 oracle   mem     REG 250,172035    1567440      2397 /cloudfs/
goldengate/product/12.1.2/gghome_11/ggMessage.dat
replicat   5832 oracle   mem     REG 250,172035    6489865      2370 /cloudfs/
goldengate/product/12.1.2/gghome_11/libggnnzitp.so
extract    8276 oracle   cwd     DIR 250,172035      16384        46 /
cloudfs/goldengate/product/12.1.2/gghome_11
extract    8276 oracle   txt     REG 250,172035   50972514      2404 /
cloudfs/goldengate/product/12.1.2/gghome_11/extract
extract    8276 oracle   mem     REG 250,172035    1567440      2397 /cloudfs/
goldengate/product/12.1.2/gghome_11/ggMessage.dat
extract    8276 oracle   mem     REG 250,172035    6489865      2370 /cloudfs/
goldengate/product/12.1.2/gghome_11/libggnnzitp.so
extract    8276 oracle   mem     REG 250,172035    1738887      2407 /cloudfs/
goldengate/product/12.1.2/gghome_11/libggperf.so
extract    8276 oracle   mem     REG 250,172035    1805316      2430 /cloudfs/
goldengate/product/12.1.2/gghome_11/libdb-5.2.so
extract    8276 oracle   mem     REG 250,172035    2479263      2420 /cloudfs/
goldengate/product/12.1.2/gghome_11/libggrepo.so
extract    8276 oracle    4w     REG 250,172035  179488151   4104755 /
cloudfs/goldengate/product/12.1.2/gghome_11/ggserr.log
mgr       14459 oracle   cwd     DIR 250,172035      16384        46 /
cloudfs/goldengate/product/12.1.2/gghome_11
mgr       14459 oracle   txt     REG 250,172035   14889321      2387 /
cloudfs/goldengate/product/12.1.2/gghome_11/mgr
mgr       14459 oracle   mem     REG 250,172035    1567440      2397 /cloudfs/
goldengate/product/12.1.2/gghome_11/ggMessage.dat
mgr       14459 oracle   mem     REG 250,172035    6489865      2370 /cloudfs/
goldengate/product/12.1.2/gghome_11/libggnnzitp.so
mgr       14459 oracle   mem     REG 250,172035    5323241      2368 /cloudfs/
goldengate/product/12.1.2/gghome_11/libxerces-c.so.28
```

The ACFS filesystem needs to be dismounted using the srvctl stop filesystem -d /dev/asm/<volume name> -f command as follows:

```
[root@dbserver01 ~]# srvctl stop filesystem -d /dev/asm/acfsvol-336
```

Or you can use this:

```
[root@dbserver01 ~]# srvctl stop filesystem -d /dev/asm/acfsvol-336 -f
```

If the srvctl stop filesystem -d command still fails when dismounting the ACFS filesystem, then the filesystem can be dismounted using the umount -l + umount -f (forced manner) option as follows:

```
[root@dbserver01 ~]# umount -l /cloudfs
[root@dbserver01 ~]# umount -f /cloudfs
```

For ACFS issues after database patching in ODA, check the database status using the ps command.

```
[oracle@Dbserver01 ~]$ ps -ef | grep pmon
grid        79903      1    0      05:34 ?           00:00:00 asm_pmon_+ASM2
oracle      80547  80518       0   09:54 pts/4   00:00:00 grep pmon
```

Here you can check the drivers for acfs:

```
$ lsmod | grep oracle
[ root@Dbserver01 : Thu Apr 19, 10:43 AM : /u01/app/12.1.0.2/grid/bin ]

$ ./acfsdriverstate loaded
ACFS-9204: false
```

Here it tried to start, but we got the following error:

```
[ root@Dbserver01 : Thu Apr 19, 10:43 AM : /u01/app/12.1.0.2/grid/bin ]
$ ./acfsload start
ACFS-9391: Checking for existing ADVM/ACFS installation.
ACFS-9392: Validating ADVM/ACFS installation files for operating system.
ACFS-9393: Verifying ASM Administrator setup.
ACFS-9308: Loading installed ADVM/ACFS drivers.
ACFS-9154: Loading 'oracleoks.ko' driver.
FATAL: Module oracleoks not found.
ACFS-9109: oracleoks.ko driver failed to load.
ACFS-9127: Not all ADVM/ACFS drivers have been loaded.
```

$ /u01/app/12.2.0.1/grid/bin/acfsload start -s
FATAL: Module oracleoks not found. <<<<<<<<<<<<
ACFS-9109: oracleoks.ko driver failed to load.
ACFS-9127: Not all ADVM/ACFS drivers have been loaded.

Check the installed drivers for acfs.

```
$ /u01/app/12.2.0.1/grid/bin/acfsroot install
ACFS-9300: ADVM/ACFS distribution files found.
ACFS-9314: Removing previous ADVM/ACFS installation.
ACFS-9315: Previous ADVM/ACFS components successfully removed.
ACFS-9307: Installing requested ADVM/ACFS software.
ACFS-9308: Loading installed ADVM/ACFS drivers.
ACFS-9321: Creating udev for ADVM/ACFS.
ACFS-9323: Creating module dependencies - this may take some time.
ACFS-9154: Loading 'oracleoks.ko' driver.
ACFS-9154: Loading 'oracleadvm.ko' driver.
ACFS-9154: Loading 'oracleacfs.ko' driver.
ACFS-9327: Verifying ADVM/ACFS devices.
ACFS-9156: Detecting control device '/dev/asm/.asm_ctl_spec'.
ACFS-9156: Detecting control device '/dev/ofsctl'.
ACFS-9309: ADVM/ACFS installation correctness verified.
```

Check the installed drivers information for acfs.

```
$ ./acfsdriverstate supported
ACFS-9200: Supported
[ root@Dbserver01 : Thu Apr 19, 10:46 AM : /u01/app/12.1.0.2/grid/bin ]

$ ./acfsdriverstate installed
ACFS-9203: true
[ root@Dbserver01 : Thu Apr 19, 10:47 AM : /u01/app/12.1.0.2/grid/bin ]
```

Stop the Cluster Ready Services (CRS) in Dbserver01 with this:

```
$ /u01/app/12.2.0.1/grid/bin/crsctl stop crs
CRS-2791: Starting shutdown of Oracle High Availability Services-managed
resources on 'Dbserver01'
CRS-2673: Attempting to stop 'ora.crsd' on 'Dbserver01'
```

```
CRS-2790: Starting shutdown of Cluster Ready Services-managed resources on
server 'Dbserver01'
CRS-2673: Attempting to stop 'ora.LISTENER_SCAN2.lsnr' on 'Dbserver01'
CRS-2673: Attempting to stop 'ora.FLASH.dg' on 'Dbserver01'
CRS-2673: Attempting to stop 'ora.DATA.dg' on 'Dbserver01'
CRS-2673: Attempting to stop 'ora.RECO.dg' on 'Dbserver01'
CRS-2673: Attempting to stop 'ora.REDO.dg' on 'Dbserver01'
CRS-2673: Attempting to stop 'ora.LISTENER.lsnr' on 'Dbserver01'
CRS-2677: Stop of 'ora.REDO.dg' on 'Dbserver01' succeeded
CRS-2677: Stop of 'ora.FLASH.dg' on 'Dbserver01' succeeded
CRS-2677: Stop of 'ora.DATA.dg' on 'Dbserver01' succeeded
CRS-2677: Stop of 'ora.RECO.dg' on 'Dbserver01' succeeded
-------------------------------- Output Truncated ------------------------
CRS-4133: Oracle High Availability Services has been stopped.
```

Start Cluster Ready Services (CRS) in Dbserver01.

```
$ /u01/app/12.2.0.1/grid/bin/crsctl start crs
CRS-4123: Oracle High Availability Services has been started.
```

Verify the ACFS/ADVM modules were loaded and are present in memory using the lsmod command.

```
$ lsmod | grep oracle
```

```
oracleacfs              4595712        14
oracleadvm              806912         25
oracleoks               659456         2 oracleacfs,oracleadvm
```

Check the module information.

```
$ modinfo oracleacfs
filename:               /lib/modules/4.1.12-94.4.1.el6uek.x86_64/weak-updates/
usm/oracleacfs.ko
description:            Oracle ASM Cluster File System (ACFS)
author:                 Oracle Corporation
license:                Proprietary
srcversion:             BEF3E32DC51BDE9AA817A8B
depends:                oracleoks
vermagic:               4.1.12-32.el6uek.x86_64 SMP mod_unload modversions
```

Check the following after reloading the ACFS drivers:

- Check the volume status using the df command.

- Check the database instances' status.

gDBClone Package for Oracle Engineered Systems

The gDBClone package is a simple tool that provides methods to clone a database for testing or development environments, including engineered systems (Exadata and Oracle Database Appliance). The Automatic Storage Management Cluster File System is a filesystem provided by Oracle on various operating systems that are truly integrated with Automatic Storage Management (ASM).

- You can create a database clone using Recovery Manager (RMAN) backup sets.

- You can create a snapshot RAC database from a standby database.

- You can do a database upgrade using Transient Logical Standby (TLS).

- You can clone a database from a Recovery Manager (RMAN) full backup to ACFS as a standby database.

- You can clone a database encrypted with Transparent Data Encryption (TDE).

- You can convert a single-instance database, RACONE node database to a RAC database.

- You can clone a remote/local database to ACFS.

- You can convert a non-CDB database to a pluggable database (PDB) of a given container database (CDB) and much more.

gDBClone Package RPM Installation

gDBClone can be installed using the Red Hat Package Manager (RPM). The gDBClone package also requires the RPM perl-XML-Simple.

- perl-XML-Simple-2.18-6.el6.noarch.rpm

- gDBClone-3-0.2.noarch.rpm

```
# rpm -ivh perl-XML-Simple-2.18-6.el6.noarch.rpm
warning: perl-XML-Simple-2.18-6.el6.noarch.rpm: Header V4 DSA/SHA1
Signature, key ID 192a7d7d: NOKEY
Preparing...              ########################################### [100%]
   1:perl-XML-Simple      ########################################### [100%]

# rpm -ivh gDBClone-3-0.2.noarch.rpm
warning: gDBClone-3-0.2.noarch.rpm: Header V4 RSA/SHA1 Signature, key ID
e7004b4d: NOKEY
Preparing...              ########################################### [100%]
   1:gDBClone             ########################################### [100%]
gDBClone has been installed on /opt/gDBClone succesfully!
```

Check the installed gDBClone package in the /opt/gDBClone directory.

```
$ cd /opt/gDBClone/
$ ls -lrth
-rwxr-xr-x 1 root root  46K May 29 14:20 gDBClone
drwxr-xr-x 2 root root 4.0K Jun 28 22:18 lib
```

Here are the complete options from the gDBClone package:

```
# ./gDBClone
Usage:
    gDBClone clone -sdbname <source DB name>
                    -sdbscan <source DB Host SCAN name> | -sbckloc '<backup
                    location path>'
                    -tdbname <Target Database Name> -tdbhome <Target
                    Database Home Name>
                  { -dataacfs <acfs mount point> [ -redoacfs <acfs mount
                    point> ] [ -recoacfs <acfs mount point> ] } |
                  { -datadg <asm data diskgroup> [ -redodg <asm redo
                    diskgroup> ] [ -recodg <asm reco diskgroup> ] }
                  [ -sga_max_size <size Mb> ] [ -sga_target <size Mb> ]
                  [ -sdbport <Source DB SCAN Listener Port> ] [ -tdbport
                    <Target DB SCAN Listener Port> ]
                  [ -standby [-pmode maxperf|maxavail|maxprot] [-activedg]
                    [-rtapply] ]
```

```
            [ -racmod <db type> ]
            [ -opc ]
            [ -syspwf <sys password file>]
   gDBClone snap  -sdbname <source DB name> -tdbname <Target Database
            Name>
            [ -tdbhome <Target Database Home Name> ]
            [ -sga_max_size <size Mb> ] [ -sga_target <size Mb> ]
            [ -standby [-pmode maxperf|maxavail|maxprot] [-activedg]
               [-rtapply] ]
            [ -sdbport <SCAN Listener Port> ]
            [ -racmod <db type> ]

gDBClone convert -sdbname <source noCDB name>
                 -racmod <1|2> | -tdbname <target CDB name> [-check]
                 {[-copy] [-path <path>]}
                 [ -syspwf <sys password file>] [ -tsyspwf <sys password
                    file>]

gDBClone listhomes [ -verbose ]
gDBClone listdbs [ -tree ] | [ -verbose ]
gDBClone deldb  -tdbname <database name> [ -force ]
gDBClone listsnaps -dataacfs <acfs_mount_point> [ -tree ]
gDBClone delsnap  -snapname <snapshot name> -dataacfs <acfs_mount_
                   point>
gDBClone syspwf -syspwf <SYS encrypted password file path>

gDBClone OPTIONS
-sdbname      Source Database Name
-sdbscan      Source DB Host SCAN Name
-sdbport      Source SCAN Listener Port (default 1521)
-sbckloc      Source RMAN Full Backup Location
-tdbname      Target Database Name
-tdbhome      Target Database Home Name
-tdbport      Target SCAN Listener Port (default 1521)
-standby      The clone/snap will be a physical standby database
-pmode        Standby option: maxperf/maxavail/maxprot (default maxperf)
-activedg     Enable Active Dataguard
```

```
-rtapply      Enable real time apply
-racmod       0/1/2 == SINGLE/RACONE/RAC (default 0)
-dataacfs     Database datafiles target ACFS storage
-redoacfs     Database redologs target ACFS storage (default dataacfs)
-recoacfs     Database recovery target ACFS storage (default dataacfs)
-datadg       Database datafiles target ASM diskgroup (default +DATA)
-redodg       Database redologs target ASM diskgroup (default +REDO)
-recodg       Database recovery target ASM diskgroup (default +RECO)
-sga_max_size SGA Max Size (Mb)
-sga_target   SGA Target (Mb)
-opc          Required option on RACDBaaS environment
-syspwf       SYS encrypted password file
-tsyspwf      SYS encrypted password file
-check        Will perform a CDB to PDB conversion pre-check
-copy         Will copy the source noCDB datafiles to CDB location
              (default: nocopy)
-path         Path where to copy the dbfiles (default CDB system dbf
              path)
-tree         With listdb will show the Parent/Snapshot tree
-verbose      Display OH & version on listdb
-force        With deldb will unregister the db
```

Using gDBClone

Here's how to create the cloned database mproddb for the proddb database:

```
# ./gDBClone clone -sdbname proddb -sdbscan rac-scan -tdbhome OraDB12Home1
-tdbname mproddb -dataacfs /vol1 -racmod 2
```

Here's how to create the physical standby database sproddb for the proddb database:

```
./gDBClone clone -sdbname proddb -sdbscan rac-scan -tdbname sproddb
-tdbhome OraDB12Home1 -dataacfs /vol1 -racmod 2 -standby
```

Here's how to create Active Data Guard database with real-time apply using gDBClone:

```
# ./gDBClone clone -sdbname proddb -sdbscan rac-scan -tdbname pstandby
-tdbhome OraDB12Home1 -dataacfs /vol1 -racmod 2 -standby -activedg –rtapply
```

Here's how to create a cloned Active Data Guard database with real-time apply using gDBClone:

```
# ./gDBClone clone -sdbname proddb -sdbscan rac-scan -tdbname pstandby
-tdbhome OraDB12Home1 -dataacfs /vol1 -racmod 2 -standby -activedg –rtapply
```

Please refer to the following for more details:

- "gDBClone Database Clone /Snapshot Management Script" (Doc ID 2099214.1)

- https://www.oracle.com/technetwork/pt/articles/database-performance/gdbclone-em-rac-5023304-ptb.html

Oracle Exadata Database Machine

An Oracle Exadata Database Machine will handle tough availability problems for mission-critical environments. Oracle's latest-generation machine is Oracle Exadata Database Machine x7-2 with High Capacity Storage Server (HC) and Extreme Flash Storage Server (EF) options.

- Redundant database, storage, and network tier hardware components

- Highly available code in the database, storage, and network tiers

- Rolling patch support for database, storage, and network tiers

- Highly available cell bootup configuration

- Highly available operating system configuration

- Highly available network configuration (InfiniBand and Client Access Network)

- Enhanced connectivity (now it supports client systems connecting to over 25 Gigabit Ethernet)

Oracle Exadata Hardware Generation Advances from v1 to X7

Figure 8-18 summaries the models.

Oracle Exadata Model	Processor	Storage (TB)	Flash Cache (TB)	CPU (Cores)	Physical Memory (GB) - Max	Ethernet (Gb/s)
Exadata V1	Xeon E5430	168 TB (1 TB Size)	0	64	256 GB	8
Exadata V2	Xeon E5540	336 TB (2 TB Size)	5.3 TB	64	576 GB	24
Exadata X2	Xeon E5670	504 TB (3 TB Size)	5.3 TB	128	1152 GB	184
Exadata X3	Xeon E5-2690	504 TB	22.4 TB	128	2048	400
Exadata X4	Xeon E5-697v2	672 TB (4 TB Size)	44.8 TB	192	4096	400
Exadata X5	Xeon E5-2699 v3	1344 TB (8 TB Size)	89.6 TB	288	6144	400
Exadata X6	Xeon E5-2699 v4	1344 TB	179.2 TB	352	6144	400
Exadata X7	Xeon 8160	1680 TB (10 TB Size)	358.4 TB	384	12000	800

Figure 8-18. *Various models of Oracle Exadata with technical specifications*

Oracle Exadata Database Machine x7-2 Component Specifications

Figure 8-19 shows the components, which are explained afterward.

Scale-Out Database Servers
- 2 Socket Xeon Processors
- 48 Cores per Server
- 384 GB - 1.5 TB DRAM

Fastest Internal Fabric
- 40 Gb/s InfiniBand Internal Network
- 25/10/1 GigE External Network

Scale-Out Intelligent Storage
- 120 TB Disk Capacity (10 TB Helium Disks)
- 25.6 TB PCI NVMe Flash
- 20 Cores for SQL Offload
- 51.2 TB PCI NVMe Flash
- 20 Cores for SQL Offload

Storage Options
- High-Capacity Storage Server
- Extreme Flash Storage Server

Figure 8-19. *Core components of Oracle Exadata database machine*

Here are the configurations for Oracle Exadata X7-2 database servers:

- 48 cores, two 24-core Intel Xeon 8160 processors for each compute node

- 384 GB (12 × 32 GB), expandable to 1.5 TB DRAM

- 25 GB Ethernet for client connectivity

Here are the configurations for Oracle Exadata x7-8 database servers:

- 192 cores, eight 24-core Intel Xeon 8160 processors for each compute node

- 3 TB (48 × 64 GB), expandable to 6 TB

- 25 GB Ethernet for client connectivity

- 2 × 6.4 TB 2.5-inch flash accelerator F640 PCIe drives (hot-pluggable)

- No hard drives

Here are the configurations for the Oracle Exadata x7-2 Extreme Flash (EF) storage server:

- Two 10-core Intel Xeon 4114 processors, with 192 GB DRAM for each storage server

- Hot plug 8 × 6.4 TB PCIe rear-mounted flash cards

- Capacity increases to 51.2 TB

- 2× 150 GB M.2dDrives performing boot and rescue functions

- A new feature called Do-Not-Service LED

Here are the configurations for the Oracle Exadata x7-2 High Capacity (HC) storage server:

- Two 10-core Intel Xeon 4114 processors, with 192 GB DRAM for each storage server

- Hot plug 4 × 6.4TB PCIe rear-mounted flash cards

- 12 × 10 TB 7.2K RPM HC SAS (hot-swap), 3.5-inch disk size

- 2× 150 GB M.2 drives performing boot and rescue functions

- A new feature called Do-Not-Service LED

Oracle Exadata Unique Smart Database Software Features

Here is a list of features.

Exadata Smart Analytics

- It will move queries to storage servers, not storage to queries.

- It will automatically offload and parallelize queries across all Exadata storage servers.

- It will offload all index fast full scans in Exadata storage servers.

Exadata Smart Storage

- Exadata Hybrid Columnar Compression (EHCC) reduces space usage by 10×. You can choose either Warehouse Compression or Online Archival Compression based on the application requirements.

- Database-aware flash caching gives the speed of flash with a capacity of the disk.

- Storage indexes eliminate the unnecessary I/O between storage servers and compute nodes.

Exadata Smart OLTP

- A special InfiniBand protocol enables 3× faster OLTP messaging.

- There is instant detection of node failure and I/O issues.

- Active Automatic Workload Repository (AWR) includes all storage statistics for end-to-end monitoring.

Exadata Smart Consolidation

- Critical database messages jump to the head of the queue for ultrafast latency.

- CPU, I/O, and network resources are prioritized for end-to-end quality of service.

Enhancements and Features of Oracle Exadata x7-2

Oracle Exadata x7-2 comes with Exadata Storage Software version 18.1.*x*. You can check the cell version in the following ways.

Check using the cell version `cellcli` and pass `cellVersion` as an argument.

```
[celladmin@CellServer01 ~]$ cellcli -e list cell detail | grep cellVersion
        cellVersion:            OSS_18.1.4.0.0_LINUX.X64_180125.3
```

Log in into the Oracle Exadata Storage Server using `cellcli`.

```
[celladmin@CellServer01 ~]$ cellcli
CellCLI: Release 18.1.4.0.0 - Production on Thu Aug 09 18:20:43 EDT 2018
Copyright (c) 2007, 2016, Oracle and/or its affiliates. All rights reserved.
CellCLI>
```

Oracle Exadata x7 High vs. Normal Redundancy

For critical production databases, you should configure the DATA disk group with high redundancy and the RECO disk group with normal redundancy. There is no DBFS disk group from the Oracle Exadata x7 generation (see Figure 8-20).

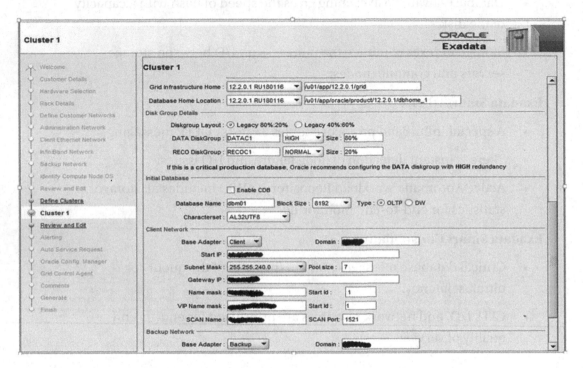

Figure 8-20. *Disk groups with redundancy with size with OEDA tool*

Oracle Exadata Deployment Assistant

The Oracle Exadata Deployment Assistant (OEDA) tool is used to configure the Exadata software stack based on information from the configuration files. Log in as the root user on the first Oracle Exadata database server.

So, you won't find the DBFS disk group from Oracle Exadata X7-2 onward.

```
ASMCMD> lsdg
State          Type      Rebal    Sector      Voting_files      Name
-----------    -------   -------   --------    --------------    ----------
MOUNTED        HIGH      N         512         Y                 DATAC1/
MOUNTED        NORMAL    N         512         N                 RECOC1/
ASMCMD>
```

M.2 Hot-Swappable Boot Drives from Oracle Exadata x7-2

Here are some tips:

- Previous generations of Oracle Exadata Database Machine use portions of two disks at slot 0 and slot 1 as system partitions in the Oracle Exadata Storage Server where the operating system and Exadata Storage Software are installed. Starting with Oracle Exadata x7, there are two M.2 disks dedicated for system partitions in every Exadata Storage Server. Apart from these two M.2 disks, all other hard disks on High Capacity Storage Server and all flash disks on Extreme Flash Storage Server are dedicated to data storage only. Oracle Exadata Storage Server x7 comes with two M.2 SSDs.

- M.2 SSDs serve as dedicated system disks, and they are hot pluggable.

- System/software partitions no longer share the disks at slots 0 and 1 with data either with space or I/O.

```
[celladmin@CellServer01 ~]$ cellcli
CellCLI: Release 18.1.4.0.0 - Production on Thu Aug 09 18:27:57 EDT 2018
Copyright (c) 2007, 2016, Oracle and/or its affiliates. All rights
reserved.
```

```
CellCLI> list physicaldisk
        252:0              ROWB6K                          normal
        252:1              ROXESK                          normal
        252:2              ROXN9K                          normal
        252:3              ROY11K                          normal
        252:4              ROYEPK                          normal
        252:5              ROYVGK                          normal
        FLASH_10_1         PHLE730300GV6P4BGN-1    normal
        FLASH_10_2         PHLE730300GV6P4BGN-2    normal
        FLASH_5_1          PHLE730100A56P4BGN-1    normal
        FLASH_5_2          PHLE730100A56P4BGN-2    normal
        M2_SYS_0               PHDW7291009N150A         normal
        M2_SYS_1               PHDW7291016Q150A         normal
CellCLI>
```

Finding the Model of the Oracle Exadata

Oracle Exadata comes in Eighth, Quarter, Half, and Full Rack versions. You can find out the Eighth Rack configuration through the CELLCLI property eighthRack is TRUE, and also you can the find the model and other information from Oracle Exadata compute nodes using different methods.

```
[celladmin@CellServer01 ~]$ cellcli -e list cell detail | grep -e
cellVersion -e eighthRack -e makeModel -e releaseVersion -e rpmVersion
        cellVersion:               OSS_18.1.4.0.0_LINUX.X64_180125.3
        eighthRack:                TRUE
        makeModel:                 Oracle Corporation ORACLE SERVER
                                   X7-2L High Capacity
        releaseVersion:            18.1.4.0.0.180125.3
        rpmVersion:                cell-18.1.4.0.0_LINUX.X64_180125.3-
                                   1.x86_64

[celladmin@CellServer01 ~]$
```

Information on Oracle Exadata Database Machine Models

Here is how to get the information from the Oracle Exadata compute nodes:

```
$ grep -i MACHINETYPES /opt/oracle.SupportTools/onecommad/databasemachine.xml
                <MACHINETYPES>X4-2 Eighth Rack HC 4TB</MACHINETYPES>
```

You can get the information from view v$asm_disk. Just log in as the oracle user and execute the following command on the Oracle Exadata compute node:

```
SQL> select failgroup, count(*) from v$asm_disk group by failgroup;
14 rows
```

Note   Fourteen rows means it's Oracle Exadata Full Rack.

Get the information from the ipmitool method. Log in as the root user and execute the following command from the Oracle Exadata compute node.

```
$ ipmitool sunoem cli "show /SP system_identifier"
```

Improved Oracle Database Deployment Assistant

You can see the models like Eighth Rack, Quarter Rack, Half Rack and Full Rack with storage options of High Capacity (HC) and Extreme Flash (EF) with different sizes of disk. The Oracle engineered system with a disk capacity of 10 TB.

We have two storage options in Oracle Exadata (Eighth Rack, Quarter Rack, Half Rack and Full Rack) like High Capacity (HC) and Extreme Flash (EF) with different sizes. Based on Oracle Exadata model (x2-2 to x7-2), you can check harddisk and flashdisk sizes.

```
CellCLI> list physicaldisk attributes name,physicalsize where disktype=harddisk
CellCLI> list physicaldisk attributes name,physicalsize where disktype=flashdisk
```

Oracle Exadata x7: Unique Fault-Tolerant In-Memory Databases

This feature is available only on Oracle Engineered Systems. Traditional in-memory databases can reduce database availability because a server crash makes memory inaccessible until after the data is reloaded.

On Oracle Engineered Systems, an in-memory Oracle Database uniquely duplicates in-memory columns on another server. The database downtime will be eliminated by automatically switching to duplicate after failure.

Quorum Disks in Oracle Exadata

Quorum disks are configured and placed additionally in compute nodes. The advantage of storing voting disks in multiple locations is that it protects the Grid Infrastructure (GI) in the event of a double partner storage failure or an event involving the Exadata Storage Server being offline.

- At least one high redundancy disk group exists.

- Quorum disks on compute nodes are implemented when there are fewer than five storage cells in the high redundancy disk group.

- All high redundancy disk groups contain quorum disks.

- If the number of Exadata Storage Servers is greater than or equal to 5, all the voting files are in the Exadata Storage Servers.

- This configuration is especially crucial for the Eighth Rack version of Oracle Exadata.

To verify the quorum disks configuration, use crsctl query css votedisk.

```
[grid@exadm01 ~]$ crsctl query css votedisk
##      STATE         File Universal Id
--      ------        ---------------------------------

File Name                                                                    Disk group
---------------------------------------------------------------            ----------

1.      ONLINE        2086ab2a2c7c4f4bbfa0c20bb0d943a2
(o/192.168.10.24;192.168.10.25/DATAC1_CD_03_CellServer01)                  [DATAC1]

2.      ONLINE        3642a309f3f24f9fbf6d365f9d2b904a
(o/192.168.10.28;192.168.10.29/DATAC1_CD_02_CellServer03)                  [DATAC1]

3.      ONLINE        a16febb909e34f72bf864c9cc95b4bcc
(o/192.168.10.26;192.168.10.27/DATAC1_CD_02_CellServer02)                  [DATAC1]

4.      ONLINE        2125a519032a4f75bf240e53c8bf9d32
(/dev/exadata_quorum/QD_DATAC1_EXADM01)                                     [DATAC1]
```

5.   ONLINE   6234b334f5454fd5bf9a328ff8566dcb
(/dev/exadata_quorum/QD_DATAC1_EXADM02)   *[DATAC1]*

Located 5 voting disk(s).
[grid@exadm01 ~]$

Checking the Volumes (/ and /u01) in All Oracle Exadata Compute Nodes

By default, in Oracle Exadata compute nodes, the volumes (/ and /u01) will be created as 30 GB and 99 GB (standard configuration). You need to increase the volumes for any upgrade activities, logs, and so on. This space may not be sufficient to store trace files, logfiles, and diagnostic files for multiple databases in a database consolidation environment. Before increasing the space, check the available space in volume groups.

You can extend the /u01 volume in Oracle Exadata compute nodes to do the following:

- To store trace files, log files, diagnostic file, and other files for multiple databases

- To install multiple Oracle RDBMS homes

- When upgrading Grid Infrastructure (GI), to keep space for the old GI home for downgrading purpose for some reason

$ df -h /
```
Filesystem              Size        Used    Avail  Use%  Mounted on
/dev/mapper/VGExaDb-LVDbSys1
                        30G          17G     12G    58%   /
```
$ df -h /u01
```
Filesystem              Size        Used    Avail  Use%  Mounted on
/dev/mapper/VGExaDb-LVDbOra1
                        99G          82G     12G    88%    /u01
```

```
$ vgdisplay -s
  "VGExaDb"  1.63 TiB  [185.00 GiB used / 1.45 TiB free]
$ vgdisplay VGExaDb | grep Free
  Free                 PE / Size         380948      / 1.45 TiB
```

Note   Plan to increase these two volumes in the initial setup of the Oracle Exadata Database Machine because it will create fewer monitoring activities. If not, you have shut down any running databases, CRS, and so on, for safety measures before increasing these volumes.

Here are the steps to increase the volumes:

```
df -h /
df- h /u01
tune2fs -l /dev/mapper/VGExaDb-LVDbSys1 | grep resize_inode
vgdisplay -s
lvdisplay /dev/VGExaDb/LVDbSys1
lvdisplay /dev/VGExaDb/LVDbSys2
lvdisplay /dev/VGExaDb/LVDbOra1
lvextend -L +150G /dev/VGExaDb/LVDbSys1
resize2fs /dev/VGExaDb/LVDbSys1
e2fsck -f /dev/VGExaDb/LVDbSys1
lvextend -L +150G /dev/VGExaDb/LVDbSys2
resize2fs /dev/VGExaDb/LVDbSys2
e2fsck -f /dev/VGExaDb/LVDbSys2
lvm lvextend -L +150G --verbose /dev/VGExaDb/LVDbOra1
resize2fs -f /dev/VGExaDb/LVDbOra1
e2fsck -f /dev/VGExaDb/LVDbOra1
df -h /
df -h /u01
```

Here's an example:

```
[grid@exadm01 ~]$ df -h /
Filesystem                  Size         Used  Avail  Use%  Mounted on
/dev/mapper/VGExaDb-LVDbSys1
                            178G   16G           154G  10%    /
[grid@exadm01 ~]$
```

```
[grid@exadm01 ~]$ df -h /u01
Filesystem                  Size         Used   Avail  Use%  Mounted on
/dev/mapper/VGExaDb-LVDbOra1
                            246G   84G          152G        36%       /u01
[grid@exadm01 ~]$
```

Configuring Hugepages in Oracle Exadata

One of the best practices for Oracle Exadata is to use Hugepages. You can allocate additional memory to the SGA buffer cache. Do not exceed 50 percent of the physical RAM if you expect a large connection load or large PGA usage.

Check the parameter to ensure Hugepages is being used. Hugepages is particularly important when PageTables in /proc/meminfo exceeds 2 percent of the physical memory. You need to create a user called orarom for this setting.

```
[grid@exadm01 ~]$ cat /etc/security/limits.conf |grep orarom
orarom       soft     memlock    476038080
orarom       hard    memlock    476038080
[grid@exadm01 ~]$
```

```
[grid@exadm01 ~]$ cat /etc/sysctl.conf | grep hugepages
vm.nr_overcommit_hugepages=13
vm.nr_hugepages=133941
[grid@exadm01 ~]$
```

Generating Cell Events on Exadata Storage Server

You can generate cell events on the Oracle Exadata Storage Server to find the errors and utilization of cells. When you get errors in Oracle Exadata like ORA-27626, ORA-27603 and Exadata error: 201 (Generic I/O error) it will be stored in alertlog and trace files of the Oracle Exadata Storage Servers.

$ cat alert_proddb1.log | grep ORA-276
```
ORA-27603: Cell storage I/O error, I/O failed on disk
o/192.168.20.118;192.168.20.119/DATAC1_CD_04_Exa2cel06 at offset
451971907584 for data length 1048576
ORA-27626: Exadata error: 201 (Generic I/O error)
ORA-27603: Cell storage I/O error, I/O failed on disk
o/192.168.20.118;192.168.20.119/DATAC1_CD_04_Exa2cel06 at offset
451971907584 for data length 1048576
ORA-27626: Exadata error: 201 (Generic I/O error)
ORA-27603: Cell storage I/O error, I/O failed on disk
o/192.168.20.108;192.168.20.109/DATAC1_CD_01_Exa2cel01 at offset
458141728768 for data length 1048576
```

Log in to the Exadata Storage Server and set trace with the following commands:

```
[celladmin@<cell name> ~]$ cellcli
CellCLI: Release 12.2.1.1.3 - Production on Thu Apr 05 17:37:04 EDT 2018
Copyright (c) 2007, 2016, Oracle and/or its affiliates. All rights
reserved.

CellCLI> alter cell events = 'trace[cellsrv_cache_layer.*] memory=high,
disk=high';
CellCLI> alter cell events = 'trace[cellsrv_disk_layer.*] memory=high,
disk=high';
CellCLI> alter cell events = 'trace[CELLSRV_Flash_Cache_Layer.*] disk=high,
memory=high';
CellCLI> alter cell events = 'trace[CELLSRV_IO_Layer.*]
disk=high,memory=high'
```

See Figure 8-21.

```
CellCLI> list cell detail
        name:                  ████████████
        accessLevelPerm:       remoteLoginEnabled
        bbuStatus:             normal
        cellVersion:           OSS_12.2.1.1.3_LINUX.X64_171017
        cpuCount:              40/40
        diagHistoryDays:       7
        events:                trace [CELLSRV.CELLSRV_CACHE_LAYER] memory=high, disk=high
                               trace [CELLSRV.CELLSRV_IO_LAYER] disk=high,memory=high
                               trace [CELLSRV.CELLSRV_FLASH_CACHE_LAYER] disk=high, memory=high
                               trace [CELLSRV.CELLSRV_DISK_LAYER] memory=high, disk=high
        fanCount:              8/8
        fanStatus:             normal
        flashCacheMode:        WriteBack
```

Figure 8-21. *Enabling trace events for the storage server*

You can generate state dump information for Oracle Exadata storage with the following command:

```
[celladmin@CellServer01 ~]$ cellcli
CellCLI: Release 12.2.1.1.3 - Production on Fri Apr 06 10:54:34 EDT 2018
Copyright (c) 2007, 2016, Oracle and/or its affiliates. All rights
reserved.

CellCLI> alter cell events = "immediate cellsrv.cellsrv_statedump(2,0)"
Dump sequence #1 has been written to /opt/oracle/cell/log/diag/asm/cell/
CellServer01/trace/svtrc_22097_82.trc
Cell Cellserver01 successfully altered

CellCLI> exit
```

Once you have collected trace files and state dump information, you can trace off after generating the trace files and state dump from Exadata storage servers with the following commands:

```
[celladmin@<cell name> ~]$ cellcli
CellCLI: Release 12.2.1.1.3 - Production on Thu Apr 05 20:47:04 EDT 2018
Copyright (c) 2007, 2016, Oracle and/or its affiliates. All rights reserved.

CellCLI> alter cell events = 'trace[CELLSRV_IO_Layer.*] off;'
Cell CellServer01 successfully altered

CellCLI> alter cell events = 'trace[CELLSRV_Flash_Cache_Layer.*] off;'
Cell CellServer01 successfully altered
```

```
CellCLI> alter cell events = 'trace[cellsrv_disk_layer.*] off';
Cell CellServer01 successfully altered

CellCLI> alter cell events = 'trace[cellsrv_cache_layer.*] off';
Cell CellServer01 successfully altered
```

Provide the following trace files and state dump for Oracle Support:

```
tar -cvfz /tmp/celloflsrv-`hostname -s`.tar.gz /opt/oracle/cell/log/diag/
asm/cell/SYS_*
tar -cvfz /tmp/cell-`hostname -s`.tar.gz $CELLTRACE/../
tar -cvfz /tmp/deploy-`hostname -s`.tar.gz /var/log/oracle/deploy
```

Configuring SSH Equivalence from Oracle Exadata Compute Nodes to All Exadata Storage Servers and IB Nodes for the Root User

When you execute the EXACHK report from one of the Exadata compute nodes, it will collect the information from all the components of the Oracle Exadata Database Machine. While executing the EXACHK report, it has to get into other Exadata components using root user privileges.

Executing EXACHK Without SSH Equivalence

The EXACHK report prompts for root passwords for the Exadata compute nodes, Exadata storage servers, and IB nodes.

Create a file called all_group with all the Exadata compute nodes, Exadata storage servers, and IB nodes. Create SSH equivalence with the root user.

```
$ ssh-keygen -t dsa
Generating public/private dsa key pair.
Enter file in which to save the key (/root/.ssh/id_dsa):
/root/.ssh/id_dsa already exists.
Overwrite (y/n)? n
[ root@exadb01node01 : Tue May 08, 02:03 PM : /root ]

$ ssh-keygen -t rsa
Generating public/private rsa key pair.
```

```
Enter file in which to save the key (/root/.ssh/id_rsa):
/root/.ssh/id_rsa already exists.
Overwrite (y/n)? n
[ root@exadb01node01 : Tue May 08, 02:03 PM : /root ]
```

> **Note**   If public/private key already exists, just leave it. If not, let it create new keys using the above commands.

Distributing the Key to All Servers

This will distribute the key to Exadata compute nodes, Exadata storage servers, and IB nodes:

$ dcli -g ./all_group -l root -k -s '-o StrictHostKeyChecking=no'

```
root@exadb01node01's password:
root@exacelnode01's password:
root@exacelnode02's password:
root@exacelnode03's password:
Password:
Password:
exadb01node01: ssh key added
exadb01node02: ssh key already exists
exacelnode01: ssh key added
exacelnode02: ssh key added
exacelnode03: ssh key added
exaibnode01: ssh key added
exaibnode02: ssh key added
[ root@exadb01node01 : Tue May 08, 02:04 PM : /root ]
$
```

- The -t option tells DCLI to first print out names of all compute nodes on which it will run, which is useful for double-checking that you are getting connected and hitting the correct compute nodes.

- The -g command provides the name of the file that contains the list of nodes to operate on (in this case, nodelist in the current directory).

491

Here's how to check the results:

```
$ dcli -g all_group -l root hostname
exadb01node01: exadb01node01
exadb01node02: exadb01node02
exacelnode01: exacelnode01
exacelnode02: exacelnode02
exacelnode03: exacelnode03
exaibnode01: exaibnode01
exaibnode02: exaibnode02
[ root@exadb01node01 : Tue May 08, 02:04 PM : /root ]
```

Note   Repeat steps 1 through 4 on the other Exadata compute nodes if you'd like to set up the SSH equivalence for the other Exadata compute nodes.

Disk Scrubbing Feature for Oracle Exadata Storage Server

Disk scrubbing is a new feature introduced in Oracle 11.2.0.4 and Oracle Exadata 11.2.3.3.0 Storage Server versions. Disk scrubbing is used to periodically validate the integrity of the mirrored ASM extents and thus eliminate latent corruption. Disk scrubbing is designed to be scheduled on production servers when the average I/O utilization is minimal because disk scrubbing can cause spikes in disk utilization and latency and adversely affect database performance. By default, the hard disk scrub runs every two weeks.

The following parameters control the disk scrubbing:

- hardDiskScrubInterval

This command sets the interval for proactive resilvering of latent bad sectors. Valid options are daily, weekly, biweekly, and none.

- hardDiskScrubStartTime

This command sets the start time for proactive resilvering of latent bad sectors. Valid options are a date/time combination or now.

These schedules are available to enable hard disk scrub activity:

- hardDiskScrubInterval=daily

- hardDiskScrubInterval=weekly

- hardDiskScrubInterval=biweekly

Ways to Check the Alert Log on the Oracle Exadata Storage Server

You can use the following:

- ADRCI

- CELLTRACE

Here's where to look in Oracle Exadata Storage Servers:

- Exadata Storage Server 1: CellServer01

```
[celladmin@CellServer01 ~]$ cd $CELLTRACE
[celladmin@CellServer01 trace]$ pwd
/opt/oracle/cell12.1.2.3.3_LINUX.X64_161109/log/diag/asm/cell/CellServer01/
trace
[celladmin@CellServer01 trace]$ ls -l alert*
-rw-rw---- 1 root celladmin 254890 Mar 11 05:03 alert.log
[celladmin@CellServer01 trace]$
```

   (OR)

```
[celladmin@CellServer01 ~]$ adrci
ADRCI: Release 12.1.0.2.0 - Production on Mon Mar 13 12:49:12 2017
Copyright (c) 1982, 2016, Oracle and/or its affiliates.  All rights
reserved.
ADR base = "/opt/oracle/cell12.1.2.3.3_LINUX.X64_161109/log"

adrci> show alert

Choose the home from which to view the alert log:

1: diag/asm/user_root/host_136421473_80
2: diag/asm/user_root/host_136421473_82
3: diag/asm/cell/CellServer01
```

```
4: diag/asm/cell/SYS_121233_161109
5: diag/asm/cell/SYS_112331_151006
Q: to quit
```

Please select option 3, as shown here:

```
Output the results to file: /tmp/alert_35417_1399_CellServer01_1.ado

Begin scrubbing CellDisk:CD_03_CellServer01.
Begin scrubbing CellDisk:CD_04_CellServer01.
Begin scrubbing CellDisk:CD_07_CellServer01.

---Output truncated

2017-02-24 10:55:08.976000 -05:00
Finished scrubbing CellDisk:CD_01_CellServer01, scrubbed blocks
(1MB):7465024, found bad blocks:0
2017-02-24 12:19:33.389000 -05:00
Finished scrubbing CellDisk:CD_00_CellServer01, scrubbed blocks
(1MB):7465024, found bad blocks:0
2017-02-24 17:40:33.013000 -05:00
Finished scrubbing CellDisk:CD_05_CellServer01, scrubbed blocks
(1MB):7499632, found bad blocks:0
2017-02-24 17:44:36.352000 -05:00

---Output truncated
```

- Exadata Storage Server 2: CellServer02

```
[celladmin@CellServer02 ~]$ cd $CELLTRACE
[celladmin@CellServer02 trace]$ pwd
/opt/oracle/cell12.1.2.3.3_LINUX.X64_161109/log/diag/asm/cell/CellServer02/
trace

[celladmin@CellServer02 trace]$ ls -lrth alert*
-rw-rw---- 1 root celladmin 4.2M Mar 11 02:57 alert.log
[celladmin@CellServer02 trace]$
```

Or you can do this:

```
[celladmin@CellServer02 ~]$ adrci
ADRCI: Release 12.1.0.2.0 - Production on Mon Mar 13 13:32:42 2017
Copyright (c) 1982, 2016, Oracle and/or its affiliates.  All rights reserved.

ADR base = "/opt/oracle/cell12.1.2.3.3_LINUX.X64_161109/log"
adrci> show alert

Choose the home from which to view the alert log:

1: diag/asm/user_root/host_1634209856_80
2: diag/asm/user_root/host_1634209856_82
3: diag/asm/cell/CellServer02
4: diag/asm/cell/SYS_112331_151006
5: diag/asm/cell/SYS_121233_161109
Q: to quit
```

Please select option 3, as shown here:

```
Output the results to file: /tmp/alert_5413_14027_CellServer02_1.ado

Begin scrubbing CellDisk:CD_02_CellServer02.
Begin scrubbing CellDisk:CD_00_CellServer02.
Begin scrubbing CellDisk:CD_11_CellServer02.
Begin scrubbing CellDisk:CD_10_CellServer02.
```

---*Output truncated*

```
2017-02-24 11:32:04.092000 -05:00
Finished scrubbing CellDisk:CD_01_CellServer02, scrubbed blocks
(1MB):7465024, found bad blocks:0
2017-02-24 12:47:37.032000 -05:00
```

---*Output truncated*

- Exadata Storage Server 3: CellServer03

```
[celladmin@CellServer03 ~]$ adrci
ADRCI: Release 12.1.0.2.0 - Production on Tue Mar 14 14:48:47 2017
Copyright (c) 1982, 2016, Oracle and/or its affiliates.  All rights reserved.
```

```
ADR base = "/opt/oracle/cell12.1.2.3.3_LINUX.X64_161109/log"
adrci> show alert
```

Choose the home from which to view the alert log:

1: diag/asm/user_root/host_4214962514_80

2: diag/asm/user_root/host_4214962514_82

3: diag/asm/cell/SYS_112331_151006

4: diag/asm/cell/SYS_121233_161109

5: diag/asm/cell/CellServer03

Q: to quit

Please select option 5, as shown here:

```
Output the results to file: /tmp/alert_37829_1402_CellServer03_1.ado

Begin scrubbing CellDisk:CD_02_CellServer03.
Begin scrubbing CellDisk:CD_07_CellServer03.
Begin scrubbing CellDisk:CD_10_CellServer03.
```

---Output truncated

```
2017-02-24 12:26:46.102000 -05:00
Finished scrubbing CellDisk:CD_00_CellServer03, scrubbed blocks
(1MB):7465024, found bad blocks:0
2017-02-24 13:31:16.168000 -05:00
Finished scrubbing CellDisk:CD_01_CellServer03, scrubbed blocks
(1MB):7465024, found bad blocks:0
2017-02-24 18:02:35.900000 -05:00
```

---Output truncated

Note   You can do the same process based on an Oracle Exadata Database
Machine model (Eighth Rack, Quarter Rack, Half Rack, and Full Rack).

Here's the command to verify the hard disk scrub activity enabled on Oracle Exadata:

```
[celladmin@CellServer01 ~]$ cellcli -e list cell attributes
name,hardDiskScrubInterval
        CellServer01     weekly
```

```
[celladmin@CellServer02 ~]$ cellcli -e list cell attributes name,
hardDiskScrubInterval
        CellServer02    weekly
```

```
[celladmin@CellServer03 ~]$ cellcli -e list cell attributes
name,hardDiskScrubInterval
        CellServer03    weekly
```

Here's the command to stop the hard disk scrub activity enabled on Oracle Exadata:

```
[celladmin@CellServer01 ~]$ cellcli -e alter cell hardDiskScrubInterval=none
[celladmin@CellServer02 ~]$ cellcli -e alter cell hardDiskScrubInterval=none
[celladmin@CellServer03 ~]$ cellcli -e alter cell hardDiskScrubInterval=none
```

When to Schedule

Disk scrubbing will take I/O when it is running on the storage servers, so there will be small load in the Oracle Database. Before disk scrubbing, check the idle window for mission-critical production databases. Check the following steps to schedule a time.

Stop disk scrubbing and reschedule it for nonpeak hours.

```
CellCLI> ALTER CELL hardDiskScrubInterval=none
```

Set hardDiskScrubStartTime to start over the weekend or nonpeak hours.

```
CellCLI> ALTER CELL hardDiskScrubStartTime='<Specify the Time>'
```

Change the interval to biweekly if the previous action was implemented to stop the disk scrub.

```
CellCLI> ALTER CELL hardDiskScrubInterval=biweekly
```

```
[oracle@exadm01 ~]$ dcli -g celllist.txt cellcli -e list cell attributes
name,hardDiskScrubInterval
10.110.12.63: CellServer01    biweekly
10.110.12.64: CellServer02    biweekly
10.110.12.65: CellServer03    biweekly
[oracle@exadm01 ~]$
```

```
[oracle@exadm01 ~]$ dcli -g celllist.txt cellcli -e list cell attributes
name,harddiskscrubstarttime
10.110.12.63: CellServer01        2018-03-17T08:00:00-04:00
10.110.12.64: CellServer02        2018-03-17T08:00:00-04:00
10.110.12.65: CellServer03        2018-03-17T08:00:00-04:00
[oracle@exadm01 ~]$
```

Deleting Trace Files from Oracle Exadata Storage Servers

You have to schedule maintenance tasks in Oracle Exadata Storage Servers. Using the
DCLI command-line utility, you can check metrics across all the Oracle Exadata Storage
Servers from the Exadata compute nodes.

```
$ dcli -g celllist.txt cellcli -e list cell attributes metricHistoryDays
10.1.1.105: 7
10.1.1.106: 7
10.1.1.107: 7
10.1.1.108: 7
10.1.1.109: 7
10.1.1.110: 7
10.1.1.111: 7

$ dcli -l root -g cell_group 'du -sm /opt/oracle/cell/cellsrv/deploy/
config/metrics'
CellServer01: 139        /opt/oracle/cell/cellsrv/deploy/config/metrics
CellServer02: 140        /opt/oracle/cell/cellsrv/deploy/config/metrics
CellServer03: 140        /opt/oracle/cell/cellsrv/deploy/config/metrics
CellServer04: 140        /opt/oracle/cell/cellsrv/deploy/config/metrics
CellServer05: 139        /opt/oracle/cell/cellsrv/deploy/config/metrics
CellServer06: 139        /opt/oracle/cell/cellsrv/deploy/config/metrics
CellServer07: 139        /opt/oracle/cell/cellsrv/deploy/config/metrics

$ dcli -c CellServer01 'du -sm /opt/oracle/cell/log/diag/asm/cell/
CellServer01/trace'
CellServer01: 276        /opt/oracle/cell/log/diag/asm/cell/CellServer01/
trace
[ oracle@exadm01.rjf.com : Tue Dec 05, 11:48 AM : /home/oracle ]
```

```
$ dcli -c CellServer02 'du -sm /opt/oracle/cell/log/diag/asm/cell/
CellServer02/trace'
CellServer02: 588          /opt/oracle/cell/log/diag/asm/cell/CellServer02/
trace
[ oracle@exadm01.rjf.com : Tue Dec 05, 11:49 AM : /home/oracle ]
```

```
$ dcli -c CellServer03 'du -sm /opt/oracle/cell/log/diag/asm/cell/
CellServer03/trace'
CellServer03: 284          /opt/oracle/cell/log/diag/asm/cell/CellServer03/
trace
[ oracle@exadm01.rjf.com : Tue Dec 05, 11:49 AM : /home/oracle ]
```

Change the retention for this metric with the following command to avoid high filesystem utilization on storage servers:

```
cellcli>alter cell metricHistoryDays=<<RetentionDays>>
```

Here is an example:

```
cellcli>alter cell metricHistoryDays=3
```

Once this is done, verify the changes with the following command:

```
cellci> list cell attributes metricHistoryDays
exit

find /opt/oracle/cell/log/diag/asm/cell/CellServer01/trace -name "*.trm"
-ctime +14
find /opt/oracle/cell/log/diag/asm/cell/CellServer01/trace -name "*.trc"
-ctime +14

# Grooming Trace files
01 01 * * * $HOME/groomfiles.sh >/dev/null 2>&1
```

Or you can do this:

```
[root@ CellServer02 ~]# crontab -l
##################################################
# GROOM DIRECTORIES
##################################################
01 01 1,15 * * /opt/oracle/groomfiles.sh >/dev/null 2>&1
```

Note   Every month 1st day and 15th day this will execute. Create the schedule based on your environment requirements.

```
$ cat groomfiles.sh
export adate=`date +"%Y-%m-%d"`
export HOST=`hostname -s`
export TRACE_DIR=/opt/oracle/cell/log/diag/asm/cell/CellServer01/trace
export LOG=/home/oracle/logs/groomfiles.log
export PURGE_TRACE_DAYS=14
echo "Below trace files will be deleted from trace directory" >> $LOG
find ${ALERT_DIR} -type f -name '*.trc' -o -name '*.trm' -mtime +${PURGE_
TRACE_DAYS} -exec ls -l '{}' \; >> $LOG
echo "Purge process will be started on `$adate`" >> $LOG
find ${ALERT_DIR} -type f -name '*.trc' -o -name '*.trm' -mtime +${PURGE_
TRACE_DAYS} -exec rm -f '{}' \; >> $LOG
echo "Purge process is finished on `$adate`" >> $LOG
```

Note   Please refer for more details here:

- "File System /opt/oracle has Exceeded 90% in Exadata Cell node" (Doc ID 2137561.1)

- "Exadata Storage server /opt/oracle Filesystem Utilization is high" (Doc ID 2254412.1)

Oracle Exadata x7-2: Do-Not-Service LED Property

Powering off an Oracle Exadata Storage Server in a cluster environment with reduced redundancy may cause the Oracle ASM disk group to force dismount and compromise data availability. To prevent human errors such as mistakenly powering off the wrong Oracle Exadata Storage Server, Exadata Storage Servers on Exadata Database Machine x7 come with a new LED called Do-Not-Service.

Oracle Exadata x7 High Capacity (HC) and Extreme Flash (EF) storage servers come with a new LED, 'Do-Not-Service LED,' that indicates whether it is safe to power off the cell for services. See Figure 8-22.

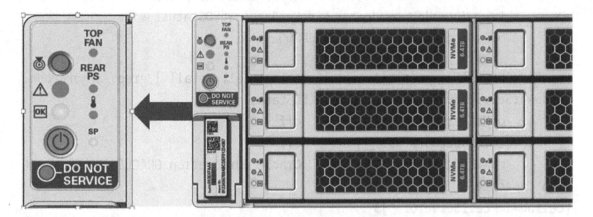

Figure 8-22. *Do-Not-Service property of Exadata x7*

The Oracle Exadata software checks whether it is safe to power down a cell when the power button is pressed.

- If it is safe, continue to power off the cell.

- Otherwise, alert users and abort the power off.

Here are the minimum requirements for the Do-Not-Service LED:

- Oracle Exadata Storage Server Software release 18.1.0.0.0

- Oracle Exadata Storage Server x7

- Oracle Grid Infrastructure:

  - Release 12.1.0.2 July 2017 BP with ARU 21405133

  - Release 12.1.0.2 October 2017 BP or later

  - Release 12.2.0.1 July 2017 BP with ARU 21405125

  - Release 12.2.0.1 October 2017 BP or later

To check the attribute, log into Exadata Storage Server:

- List cell attributes: doNotServiceLEDStatus

    If 'doNotServiceLEDStatus' is 'on' you should not power
    down the cell for services and 'doNotServiceLEDStatus' is
    'off' you can power down the cell for services.

```
[celladmin@CellServer01 ~]$ cellcli -e list cell detail | grep -e makeModel
-e doNotServiceLEDStatus -e locatorLEDStatus
        doNotServiceLEDStatus:        off
        locatorLEDStatus:             off
        makeModel:                    Oracle Corporation ORACLE SERVER X7-2L
High Capacity
[celladmin@CellServer01 ~]$
```

Online Flash Disk Replacement in Oracle Exadata x7

Management Server (MS) in Oracle Exadata Storage Server monitors flash disk health
and auto prepares it for replacement if a flash disk has a bad health.

To proactively replace a perfectly normal flash disk in Exadata Storage Server, use the
following command after logging in to the Storage Server using the CELLCLI command
line.

```
CellCLI> ALTER PHYSICALDISK <disk_id> DROP FOR REPLACEMENT
```

For Oracle Exadata x7-2 HC and Oracle Exadata x7-2 EF, the Storage Server
procedure is the same. See Figure 8-23.

Exadata X7-2 High Capacity (HC) OR Exadata X7-2 Extreme Flash (EF)	Exadata X7-8 High Capacity (HC) OR Exadata x7-8 Extreme Flash (EF)
Removal Card • PCI lane turned off • Power LED off • Remove the card	*Removal Card* • PCI lane turned off • Power LED off • Remove dual PCIe card carrier (DPCC) and remove the card
Insert Card • PCI lane turn On • Online upgrade firmware	*Insert Card* • Insert Card in DPCC and push back DPCC • Press ATTN button to power on • Online upgrade firmware

Figure 8-23. *Flash disk replacement for Exadata x7-2 and x7-8*

RAID 0 on Flash Disks in Oracle Exadata x7

You want to create a RAID disk on top of flash disks from the same flash card in Exadata x7. The Management Server automatically does the following:

- Creates a software RAID0 after discovering new flash cards.

- Re-assembles the software RAID after the flash card pull/push or power cycle

- Re-assembles the software RAID upon system reboot if necessary

Until Oracle Exadata x7, the relationship between physical disks, LUNs, cell disks, and grid disks has always been 1-1-1-N. See Figure 8-24.

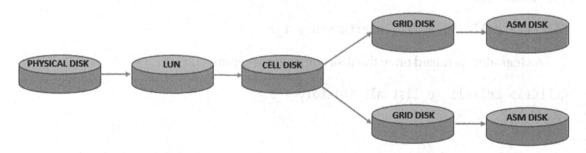

Figure 8-24. *1-1-1-N relation*

From Oracle Exadata x7, with RAID 0 on flash disks, the relationship between physical disks, LUNs, cell disks, and grid disks supports M-1-1-N. See Figure 8-25.

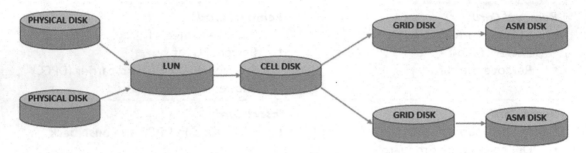

Figure 8-25. *M-1-1-N relation*

Oracle Exadata x7: Disk Controller CacheVault Flash Module Monitoring

Normally writes are much faster when they go to the DRAM cache first, and then the disk controller writes it back to the actual storage. If the cache mode is Write Back, you should back up the cache in case of an AC power failure.

The MS on the Exadata Storage Server has always been managing and monitoring the power module in the CacheVault. There was no way to monitor the flash module previously.

Oracle Exadata x7 provides the capability to monitor the flash module.

The MS in 18.1 version or later included this new capability and monitors the flash module health.

A critical alert is raised if the flash module fails, and you can check this through `alerthistory`.

```
CELLCLI> cellcli -e list alerthistory 1_1
```

A clear alert is raised once the disk controller is replaced.

```
CELLCLI> cellcli -e list alerthistory 1_2
```

Exafusion Parameter on the Oracle Exadata Database Machine

The Exafusion Direct-to-Wire Protocol parameter allows database processes to read and send Oracle RAC messages directly over the InfiniBand network, bypassing the overhead of entering the operating system (OS) kernel and running the normal networking software stack. Exafusion improves the response time and scalability of the Oracle RAC environment on the Oracle Exadata Database Machine. This feature is available in the Oracle Exadata Linux environment only. Exafusion especially improves the performance in online transaction processing (OLTP) environments.

Here are the prerequisites for the Exafusion parameter on Oracle Exadata:

- Oracle Exadata Storage Server Software release 12.1.2.1.1 or later

- Oracle Database Release 12.1.0.2.0 BP11 or later

- Mellanox ConnectX-2 and ConnectX-3 host channel adapters (HCAs) are required

- Oracle Enterprise Kernel 2 Quarterly Update 5 (UEK2QU5) kernels (2.6.39-400.2nn) or later required

Here's how to enable the Exafusion parameter:

- Exafusion is disabled by default.

- Enable Exafusion and set the EXAFUSION_ENABLED initialization parameter to 1.

- Disable Exafusion and set the EXAFUSION_ENABLED initialization parameter to 0.

- The Exafusion parameter cannot be set dynamically. It must be set before instance startup.

- All the instances in an Oracle RAC cluster must enable this parameter, or all of the instances in an Oracle RAC cluster must disable the parameter.

Note   You need the orarom user for the Exafusion parameter settings.

Here's the errors alert log:

```
ORA-00600: internal error code, arguments: [ipc_create_que_1], [1], [0],
[], [], [], [], [], [], [], []
Incident details in: /u01/app/oracle/diag/rdbms/dbm/dbm1/incident/
incdir_181263/dbm1_ora_319306_i181263.trc
Dumping diagnostic data in directory=[cdmp_20171215121403], requested by
(instance=2, osid=37555), summary=[incident=133253].
Use ADRCI or Support Workbench to package the incident.
See Note 411.1 at My Oracle Support for error and packaging details.
```

Here is the solution:

1. Add the orarom user in /etc/security/limits.conf on both nodes.

2. As a workaround, add memlock privileges to individual users in /etc/security/limits.conf, and every user who wants to connect to the database with Exafusion needs to have memlock privileges.

```
##### BEGIN. DO NOT REMOVE. ADDED BY ORACLE EXADATA DEPLOYMENT ASSISTANT
#####
grid        soft        core    unlimited
grid        hard        core    unlimited
grid        soft        nproc   400000
grid        hard        nproc   400000
grid        soft        nofile  400000
grid        hard        nofile  400000
grid        soft        memlock 476038080
grid        hard        memlock 476038080

oracle    soft      core    unlimited
oracle    hard      core    unlimited
oracle    soft      nproc   400000
oracle    hard      nproc   400000
oracle    soft      nofile      400000
oracle    hard      nofile      400000
oracle    soft      memlock 476038080
```

```
oracle    hard       memlock 476038080
##### END. DO NOT REMOVE. ADDED BY ORACLE EXADATA DEPLOYMENT ASSISTANT
#####

##################################################
orarom       soft      memlock       476038080
orarom       hard      memlock       476038080
##################################################
```

See Figure 8-26.

```
SQL> show parameter exafusion

NAME                                        TYPE                                     VALUE
-------------------------------------- --------------------------------------- ---------
exafusion_enabled                           integer                                  1
SQL>
SQL> select inst_id,name,display_value from gv$spparameter
  2  where name like '%exafusion_enabled%' order by 1;

INST_ID NAME                     DISPLAY_VALUE
------- --------------------     --------------------
      1 exafusion_enabled        1
      2 exafusion_enabled        1

SQL> show spparameter exafusion

SID     NAME                     TYPE                                     VALUE
------- --------------------     --------------------------------------- ------
*       exafusion_enabled        integer                                  1
SQL>
```

Figure 8-26. *Checking the Exafusion parameter*

Note   For more details, refer to this MOS note: "ORA-00600: [ipc_create_que_1] in Exafusion enabled environment like database version 12.2" (Doc ID 2282831.1).

Oracle Exadata: Flash Cache Compression

Starting from Oracle Exadata x5, you can't use the flash cache compression feature on Exadata Storage Servers. See Figure 8-27.

Smart Flash Cache Expected Size Table

System Description	Common Name	Cache Size with Smart Flash Log	Cache Size without Smart Flash Log	Cache Size with flashCacheCompression and Smart Flash Log	Cache Size with flashCacheCompression and no Smart Flash Log
X4275	X2-2(4170)	0.356201171875T 364.75G	0.356689453125T 365.25G	FCC not available on this hardware	FCC not available on this hardware
X4270 M2	X2-2, X2-8	0.356201171875T 364.75G	0.356689453125T 365.25G	FCC not available on this hardware	FCC not available on this hardware
X4270 M3	X3-2, X3-8	1.453857421875T 1488.75G	1.454345703125T 1489.25G	2.908935546875T 2978.75G	2.909423828125T 2979.25G
X4270 M3	EIGHTH	0.7266845703125T 744.125G	0.7271728515625T 744.625G	1.4542236328125T 1489.125G	1.4547119140625T 1489.625G
X4-2L	X4-2	2.908935546875T 2978.75G	2.909423828125T 2979.25G	5.8193359375T 5959G	5.81982421875T 5959.5G
X4-2L	EIGHTH	1.4542236328125T 1489.125G	1.4547119140625T 1489.625G	2.909423828125T 2979.25G	2.909912109375T 2979.75G
X5-2L	X5-2	5.82122802734375T	5.82171630859375T	FCC not available on this hardware	FCC not available on this hardware
X5-2L	EIGHTH	2.910369873046875T	2.910858154296875T	FCC not available on this hardware	FCC not available on this hardware
X6-2L	X6-2, X6-8	11.64312744140625T	11.64361572265625T	FCC not available on this hardware	FCC not available on this hardware
X6-2L	EIGHTH	5.8213195800781250T	5.821807861328125T	FCC not available on this hardware	FCC not available on this hardware
X7-2L	X7-2	23.28692626953125T	23.28741455078125T	FCC-NA	FCC-NA
X7-2L (all flash)	X7-2	2.3287353515625T	2.3287353515625T	FCC-NA	FCC-NA

Figure 8-27. *Status of flash cache compression in various models of Exadata*

Here's some information about flash cache compression:

- Oracle Exadata x5, x6, and x7 don't support flash cache compression.

- Oracle Exadata x7 supports only cell version starting from 18.1.0.0.0.

- Oracle Exadata v2 to x4 will support flash cache compression provided you have to take an Oracle Advanced Compression (ACO) license.

- Based on the Oracle Exadata model, flash cache compression will support not based on cell version.

Note   For more information, see this MOS Note: "EXADATA Flash Cache Compression - FAQ" (Doc ID 1664257.1).

Flash Card Changes in Oracle Exadata x4-2/x6-2

When performing maintenance on Exadata Storage Servers, it may be necessary to power down or reboot the Exadata Storage Server. If a storage server is to be shut down when one or more databases are running, then verify that taking the storage server offline will not impact Oracle ASM disk group and database availability.

For example, if you want to change the flash disk in one of the Exadata Storage Servers, then log in to Exadata Storage Server as the celladmin user.

```
[celladmin@CellServer03 ~]$ cellcli
CellCLI: Release 12.1.2.3.4 - Production on Tue Jul 18 17:26:30 EDT 2017
Copyright (c) 2007, 2016, Oracle.  All rights reserved.
```

Check the status of the Cellsrv, MS, and RS processes.

```
CellCLI> list cell detail
```

Next you need to check whether ASM will be OK if the grid disks go offline. The following command should return Yes for the grid disks being listed:

```
CellCLI> list griddisk attributes name,asmmodestatus,asmdeactivationoutcome
```

Note   If one or more disks does not return the status of the parameter 'asmdea ctivationoutcome'='Yes', you should check the respective disk group and restore the data redundancy for that disk group.

Here is the command to inactivate all grid disks on the cell you want to power down/reboot:

```
CellCLI> alter griddisk all inactive
```

Note   This action could take 10 or 15 minutes or longer depending on activity. It is important to make sure you were able to offline all the disks successfully before shutting down the cell services.

Confirm that the grid disks are now offline by performing the following series of commands:

```
CellCLI> list griddisk attributes name,asmmodestatus,asmdeactivationoutcome
CellCLI> list griddisk
```

Note   Oracle Exadata Storage Servers are powered off and rebooted by the Oracle Support/Unix team. Wait for their confirmation. Once they have confirmed or completed the activity, proceed with the following steps.

Check the status of processes: `Cellsrv`, `MS`, and `RS` processes.

```
CellCLI> list cell detail
```

Once the cell comes back online, you will need to reactive the grid disks. Before that, check the following commands:

```
CellCLI> list griddisk attributes name,asmmodestatus,asmdeactivationoutcome
CellCLI> list griddisk
CellCLI> alter griddisk all active
```

Verify all grid disks have been successfully put online using the following command:

```
CellCLI> list griddisk attributes name,asmmodestatus,asmdeactivationoutcome
```

Note   Oracle ASM synchronization is complete only when all grid disks show `asmmodestatus=ONLINE`.

This operation uses the Fast Mirror Resync operation, which does not trigger an ASM rebalance.

Wait until `asmmodestatus` is `ONLINE` for all grid disks. Each disk will go to a `SYNCING` state first followed by a status of `ONLINE`.

Verify all grid disks have been successfully put online using the following command:

```
CellCLI> list griddisk
```

Note   You will receive alerts through Oracle Exadata Alerts in each stage (Example, Flash disk failed, Flash disk was removed and Flash disk was replaced) from Oracle Exadata Storage Server.

- **Maintenance: Hardware Alert**: The flash disk failed. (You will get this alert when the flash disk failed on the Oracle Exadata Storage Server.)

- **Maintenance: Hardware Alert**: The flash disk was removed. (You will get this alert when changes are happening on the Oracle Exadata Storage Server.)

- **Maintenance: Hardware Alert**: The flash disk was replaced. (Figure 8-28 shows what you will get after the flash disk was replaced on the Oracle Exadata Storage Server.)

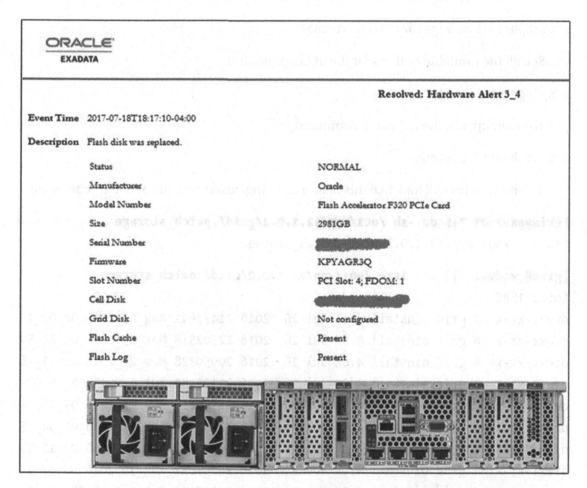

Figure 8-28. *Alert message from Enterprise Manager after flash disk replacement*

Please refer to "Steps to shut down or reboot an Exadata storage cell without affecting ASM" (Doc ID 1188080.1).

Oracle Exadata: Patch Backups Taking Up a Lot of Disk Space

When applying interim patches or critical patch update (CPU) patches, OPatch takes a big amount of disk space under $ORACLE_HOME/.patch_storage to store a backup of the affected libraries and modules that have been updated.

The following directory will have all these files in Exadata compute nodes:

/u01/app/12.1.0.2/grid/.patch_storage

See all the available options for the util command:

$ opatch util -help

To clean up, use the following command:

$ opatch util cleanup

The directories will look like this before cleaning based on your patched schedules:

```
[grid@exadm01 ~]$ du -sh /u01/app/12.1.0.2/grid/.patch_storage
21G     /u01/app/12.1.0.2/grid/.patch_storage

[grid@exadm01 ~]$ ls -lrth /u01/app/12.1.0.2/grid/.patch_storage
total 188K
drwxr-xr-x  4 grid oinstall 4.0K Jul 26  2016 21436941_Aug_13_2015_04_00_40
drwxr-xr-x  4 grid oinstall 4.0K Jul 26  2016 22502518_Mar_29_2016_02_24_50
drwxr-xr-x  4 grid oinstall 4.0K Jul 26  2016 20950328_May_22_2015_03_33_26
drwxr-xr-x  4 grid oinstall 4.0K Jul 26  2016 21125181_Jul_1_2015_06_36_02
drwxr-xr-x  4 grid oinstall 4.0K Jul 26  2016 21949015_Jan_18_2016_03_16_24
drwxr-xr-x  4 grid oinstall 4.0K Jul 26  2016 22806133_Apr_13_2016_06_04_25
drwxr-xr-x  4 grid oinstall 4.0K Jul 26  2016 23006522_Apr_15_2016_02_11_55
drwxr-xr-x  4 grid oinstall 4.0K Nov 24  2016 24007012_Aug_30_2016_00_17_17
drwxr-xr-x  4 grid oinstall 4.0K Nov 24  2016 24340679_Oct_3_2016_08_45_59
drwxr-xr-x  4 grid oinstall 4.0K Nov 24  2016 23144544_Jul_15_2016_00_38_23
drwxr-xr-x  4 grid oinstall 4.0K Nov 24  2016 24846605_Oct_14_2016_04_57_57
```

```
drwxr-xr-x  4 grid oinstall 4.0K Apr 15   2017 25101514_Dec_26_2016_00_59_28
drwxr-xr-x  4 grid oinstall 4.0K Apr 15   2017 24732088_Jan_12_2017_06_25_43
drwxr-xr-x  4 grid oinstall 4.0K Apr 15   2017 24828643_Jan_2_2017_23_59_16
drwxr-xr-x  4 grid oinstall 4.0K Sep 23   2017 26112084_May_21_2017_01_11_04
drwxr-xr-x  4 grid oinstall 4.0K Sep 23   2017 25397136_Mar_28_2017_02_34_07
drwxr-xr-x  4 grid oinstall 4.0K Sep 23   2017 25481150_Mar_7_2017_23_57_51
drwxr-xr-x  4 grid oinstall 4.0K Sep 23   2017 23727148_Jul_15_2016_08_43_29
drwxr-xr-x  4 grid oinstall 4.0K Sep 23   2017 25363750_Feb_2_2017_23_57_22
drwxr-xr-x 20 grid oinstall 4.0K Dec  9   2017 NApply
-rw-r--r--  1 grid oinstall  21K Dec  9   2017 record_inventory.txt
-rw-r--r--  1 grid oinstall  29K Dec  9   2017 interim_inventory.txt
-rw-r--r--  1 grid oinstall   92 Dec  9   2017 LatestOPatchSession.
properties
[grid@exadm01 ~]$
```

Snap Clone Feature in Oracle Exadata

In Oracle Exadata Database Machine, using snapshot databases, space-efficient database snapshots can be quickly provisioned for test and development environments. Snapshot databases support all Oracle Exadata features, such as Exadata Smart Scan and Exadata Smart Flash Cache. Snapshots start with a shared read-only copy of a database. As changes are made, each snapshot writes changed blocks to a sparse disk group. To create a sparse grid disk and sparse disk groups, use the following commands.

Oracle Exadata database snapshots are integrated with the container database (CDB) option so that you can create pluggable databases (PDBs).

Here are the characteristics for sparse disk groups:

- Sparse files can be created only in a sparse disk group.

- cell.sparse_dg is a new attribute that must be set to all sparse for a sparse disk group.

- They must have compatible.asm and compatible.rdbms set to 12.1.0.2.

- Uses 16× extent size for 4M AU; each extent is 64M.

- Sparse disk groups use virtually allocated metadata.

Creating Sparse Grid Disks

Creating sparse grid disks and a sparse disk group through the Cell Control command-line interface (CellCLI). The CellCLI utility is the command-line administration tool for Oracle Exadata.

CellCLI runs on each cell to enable you to manage an individual Oracle Exadata Storage Server.

Log in to the cell server/Oracle Exadata Storage Server as the celladmin user.

```
login as: celladmin
celladmin@192.168.2.xx's password:
[celladmin@cell11 ~]$ cellcli
CellCLI> create griddisk all harddisk prefix=SPARSE_DG, size=250G,
virtualsize=2000G
```

Creating a Sparse Disk Group

Before creating a sparse disk group, you have to create sparse disks with a virtual size as well as a physical size.

```
SQL> Create diskgroup SPARSE_DG
normal redundancy
disk 'o/*/SPARSE_DG*'
attribute
'compatible.asm' = '12.1.0.2','compatible.rdbms' = '12.1.0.2',
'cell.smart_scan_capable' = 'true','cell.sparse_dg' = 'allsparse',
'au_size' = '4M';
```

Creating a PDB Using the Snapshot Copy Method

After creating sparse grid disks and sparse disk group, create a snapshot PDB based on a pluggable database (PDB) using the following command:

```
SQL> CREATE PLUGGABLE DATABASE <snapshot name>
FROM <source pluggable database (pdb)>
CREATE_FILE_DEST='+SPARSE_DG'
SNAPSHOT COPY;
```

Summary

Oracle Engineered Systems come bundled with software, compute, networking, and storage to work together seamlessly. Oracle Engineered Systems are preconfigured, pretested systems for all database applications. They handle all types of database workloads, including OLTP, data warehousing, and in-memory analytics as well as a consolidation of mixed workloads. There's no redundancy at all layers, so there are no performance bottlenecks and no single point of failure can affect the complete engineered systems.

CHAPTER 9

Oracle Cloud Overview

As a CXO, you are looking for a cloud-based solution that should be able to store data efficiently, manage it with ease, and transact huge quantities of data, whether it is transactional data, a data warehouse, or from MIS, in a highly secure, performant, and cost-effective manner.

There are essentially three major deployment models that you as a customer have from Oracle. First is the traditional on-premise model where you manage, own, and build your own data centers, infrastructure, networking, and storage, as well as the software licenses.

The second option is that other cloud providers can host your services. In this option, they provide compute as a service so you no longer have to manage your data center, but you still have to procure and manage your Oracle software. Basically, you're dealing with two different vendors for your workload on cloud.

If you are looking for Infrastructure-Compute, storage, Networking etc and you simply want to get out of the data center business, then you can opt for Oracle's infrastructure as a service platform. If you're looking to build out your applications by leveraging Oracle's database and middleware services, then you have the ability to be able to leverage these through the platform as a service offering built on Oracle Cloud Infrastructure.

The *Oracle public cloud* is technically all of the Oracle technology and software available in the cloud.

Note   Oracle provides three distinct deployment models for customers: traditional on-premise, cloud as a customer, and the public cloud. From these three offerings for deployment, the Oracle public cloud offerings can be further classified into three broad categories: software as a service (SaaS), platform as a service (PaaS), and infrastructure as a service (IaaS). We will discuss these three offerings in more detail, but our focus will be mainly on Oracle database management services and the related infrastructure available on the Oracle public cloud.

General Cloud Concepts: What Is a Private Cloud?

A *private cloud* is all about automating the lifecycle of a service deployment. It simplifies the administrative tasks involved on a day-to-day basis and is typically delivered to end users via a self-service portal. Common deployments normally provide infrastructure as a service, database as a service, and middleware as a service.

This kind of deployment is widely used when data residency and security are concerns. A higher level of security and privacy is achieved using corporate policies and security implementations. Normally this kind of deployment is handled by an internal IT department along with a service integrator responsible for running and maintaining the environment.

Some of the challenges of this approach is that all management, maintenance, and updating of data centers is the responsibility of the company, and they have the risks associated with aging servers, data center expenses, power, cooling, floor space, and making sure service level agreements are meet.

There are tools available that help set up a private cloud such as Enterprise Manager Cloud Control to implement and provide infrastructure, database, and middleware as a service.

A typical deployment of a private cloud focuses on increasing the quality of service, enabling faster provisioning of services, providing required elasticity for services, and providing accountability in terms of metering and chargeback.

What Is a Public Cloud?

A *public cloud* is a computing environment that is offered by a cloud vendor and hosting provider across data center regions and consumed by customers over the Internet through various networking options such as an IPSec VPN or dedicated Internet Direct Connect options like Oracle's Fast Connect or AWS Direct Connect, depending on the service provider and location. The public cloud provider is responsible for services such as infrastructure, platform, and software as a service, and so on, and for the desired service level agreements. It eliminates the need for an expensive data center, and customers can do digital transformations through various cloud capabilities.

Mostly these kinds of offerings are through subscriptions such as monthly or hourly, and they provide customers with the flexibility to subscribe to these services based on the use cases. Customers are charged based on their consumption of the services, which is different than a traditional licensing model, which involves up-front commitment and capex. Another advantage of this model is that customers do not pay for hardware and software support costs, which is a significant operational cost associated with the on-premise licensing model, and they do not need to size the environment for peak workloads because the public cloud provides them with elasticity on demand.

In this kind of service model, the cloud service provider is responsible for all the management and maintenance of the system and shares responsibilities with the customer. The benefits of a public cloud are faster service provisioning, elasticity, and resource bursting capabilities. Public clouds now are capable of providing required advanced networking and security, depending on the implementation and architecture the customer uses.

The main differentiator between public and private clouds is that you are responsible only for operational aspects in a public cloud and not for any of the management of a public cloud hosting solution. Your data is stored in the provider's data center, and the provider is responsible for the management and maintenance of the data center. This type of cloud environment is a great ease to many companies because it reduces lead times in testing and deploying new products and has a faster time to market. However, many companies feel security could be lacking with a public cloud, but in reality it is equally important for the public cloud vendor to protect a customer's data.

What Is a Hybrid Cloud?

A *hybrid cloud* is a computing environment that is a combination of both public clouds and private clouds, and it allows data and applications to be shared between these environments. A typical hybrid cloud environment example is running your all production workload on-premise within your data centers and having the disaster recovery environment hosted with a public cloud vendor.

What Is a Community Cloud?

A *community cloud* is normally run by a third-party organization or cross-company team of providers and is shared across multiple organizations.

Now since you know various kinds of cloud environments, we will cover what Oracle provides in terms of public cloud offerings.

What Is the Oracle Public Cloud?

The Oracle public cloud can be classified into SaaS, PaaS, and IaaS. This way, Oracle is able to offer its customer a complete cloud portfolio for various kinds of use cases.

What Is Oracle's Software as a Service?

As part of Oracle's software as a service layer, Oracle offers a complete cloud suite of SaaS applications you need to run your business, from CX to ERP to HCM to EPM to supply chain management. This enables customers to modernize their business using the latest technologies such as artificial intelligence and machine learning.

Customers like running SaaS-based applications in the public cloud because Oracle, as the cloud provider, does all the work. It provides all the required updates and latest features and does all the required patching.

What Is Oracle's Platform as a Service?

Oracle's platform as a service is a comprehensive, standards-based combination of Oracle technologies and open source technologies that enable you to more efficiently build, deploy, integrate, secure, and manage your enterprise applications. You get the required infrastructure, storage, and all the characteristics of cloud computing along with these platform services, and it is all managed by Oracle. As a customer, you are responsible for developing applications on top of this platform. Oracle has a lot of PaaS products that it offers to the customers, such as the Database Cloud Service, the Java Cloud Service (which is the WebLogic application server on the cloud), the Oracle Mobile Cloud, the Business Intelligence Cloud Service, the Process Cloud, and the Integration Cloud. Each of these PaaS products caters to different use cases. Whether the customer is choosing a public cloud or a private cloud scenario, the underlying PaaS platform and the infrastructure platform are one in the same.

In addition, Oracle provides autonomous PaaS solutions that are self-driving, self-securing, and self-repairing, helping you innovate faster, make smarter decisions, and deliver exceptional customer experience. These platforms leverage deep artificial intelligence, machine learning, and analytic capabilities, which makes the platform autonomous in nature.

For organizations with strict data residency, compliance, or latency requirements, the Oracle Cloud Platform can be deployed within a customer's data center, commonly known as *cloud at the customer*, and this is fully managed by Oracle has an advantage of the agility, innovation, and subscription-based pricing of the Oracle Cloud Platform even for on-premise and private cloud deployments.

The platform as a service can be further classified under these topics: data management, application development, integration, business analytics, security, system management, content, and experience. Our goal for the chapter is to cover mostly Oracle data management portfolio. For more PaaS information, please refer to the Oracle documentation at `https://cloud.oracle.com/en_US/paas`.

What Is Oracle's Infrastructure as a Service?

IaaS, which is infrastructure as a service, is the cloud computing layer where you get compute, storage, networking, virtualization, and so on. Oracle public cloud's foundation is Oracle's Cloud Infrastructure (OCI) architecture, which is optimized to run Oracle Database applications. It is considered as a broad ecosystem that supports third-party apps, tools, and frameworks. Customers who want to run these same services behind a corporate firewall can leverage cloud at the customer services, which are available in the form of Oracle cloud machine (OCM) as well Exadata Cloud at the customer (ExaCC).

Oracle's infrastructure as a service layer offers the highest performance, most cost-effective IaaS. It enables customers to run their application workloads in the Oracle public cloud. Under this offering, Oracle provides a computing portfolio, which includes everything from bare-metal compute to elastic compute to a container service to help you manage your data. It also offers the ability to help migrate your data and applications through products like Ravelo. It is a complete storage offering, including local NVME flash, block-based storage, object-based storage, archive storage, backup services, networking, and connectivity services. Customers can also get their own dedicated environments with dedicated compute to eliminate noisy neighbors. For a complete list of cloud services offered under IaaS, please visit `https://cloud.oracle.com/en_US/iaas`.

Oracle Infrastructure as a Service (IaaS)

Now let's take a look at the various services Oracle offers for its platform today.

- The Identity and Access Management (IAM) service helps you set up administrators, users, and groups and specify their permissions.

- The audit service helps you track the user activity within your cloud environment.

- The networking service helps you set up software-defined versions of traditional physical networks. As part of this, customers get edge DNS,VPN, FastConnect, and email services.

- The compute service helps you provision and manage compute instances. Service offerings consist of VMs, bare-metal, and GPU shapes.

- The storage service consists of NVME, block storage, object storage, archive storage, and file services for use cases. The block storage service helps you dynamically provision and manage block storage volumes for your workloads.

- The object storage service helps you manage data as objects that are accessed through the application over the Internet through the REST API or cloud interfaces.

- The load balancing service helps you create a load balancer within your virtual cloud network.

- The database service helps you provision and manage Oracle databases and is available on VMs, bare-metal, and Exadata systems. We will cover Exadata more later in the chapter.

The Oracle Cloud Infrastructure provides high-performance servers as a compute option, high-performance storage like SSD and NVME-based flash supporting millions of IOPS. Platform services such as databases that can run on the same systems provided by OCI and engineered systems make a compelling case for running critical enterprise workload.

Oracle Cloud Infrastructure Concepts

It is important to understand a few of the concepts behind Oracle Cloud Infrastructure so you can build a robust solution architecture for your database deployments.

OCI operates in regions, which is basically a metropolitan area available in a city. Regions serve different geographies and provide disaster recovery capabilities. If you look at regions closely, you will see there are various availability domains spanning multiple data centers within the same region. Oracle provides three availability domains in each regions. These availability domains (ADs) are isolated from each other, and all your resources such as compute and database go inside an AD. ADs are wired together over private dark fiber, and there is very little latency between Ads, making them a perfect fit for a high availability primitive and for the replication of data within a multiple availability domains (OCI AD's). Oracle provides a dedicated backbone connecting these ADs. The backbone plugs into the edge or peering points of presence where customers can get direct connections into your network from their infrastructure or data centers. See Figure 9-1.

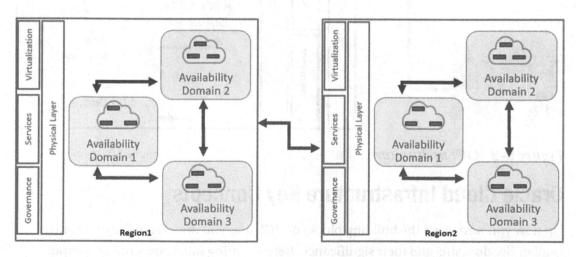

Figure 9-1. *Regions and availability domains within Oracle Cloud Infrastructure*

Since each region has multiple availability domains, you have a great foundation for high availability and disaster protection using Oracle technologies.

Inside of these ADs, a high-performance physical network is designed to provide the lowest latency and no resource contention. It runs on a highly scalable back end oracle cloud architecture to the degree of one million network peer connections per AD. It is never oversubscribed, so you get tremendously good latency with support of 25 Gbps of network bandwidth between hosts.

A virtual network with off-box virtualization to optimize I/O performance and offer unique services such as bare-metal servers on-demand integrated compute, storage, database, networking, and platform services to migrate existing apps without change, and build optimal new apps connectivity and edge services to connect different Oracle regions and your data center, as well as optimize end user experience. It also offers, simplified yet powerful abilities to segment, secure, and offer resources in complex organizations. See Figure 9-2.

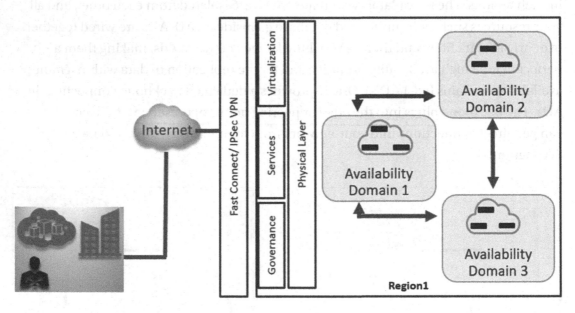

Figure 9-2. *OCI architecture*

Oracle Cloud Infrastructure Key Concepts

Up now you have seen the building blocks of OCI, and you understand regions and availability domains and their significance. Before getting into provisioning compute and database services in OCI, it is important to understand a few more key concepts.

Identity and Access Management Service

The IAM service is critical for any customer; it allows you to control who can access your OCI account, what services they can use, and how they can use these resources. In Oracle Cloud Infrastructure, a cloud resource can be considered as an object that you create such as compute instances, databases, block volumes, and so on. There are five important concepts you need to know to better understand IAM: principals, users, groups, policies, and compartments.

Principals

A *principal* is an IAM entity that is allowed to interact with OCI resources. For example, say you want an instance within your compartment to make API calls to other services within OCI. OCI has three types of principals: root users, IAM users, and instance principals.

Root User

When customers sign up for an OCI account, the first IAM user is called the *root user*. The root user is persistent, having complete administrative access to all OCI resources within their tenancy.

IAM Users/Groups

Users are persistent identities set up through the IAM service to represent individual people or applications; it also enforces the principle of least privilege. You need to add users to one or more groups to provide permission on resources. Normally *groups* are defined with at least one policy with permission to tenancy or a compartment.

A group is a collection of users who all need the same type of access to a particular set of resources; one user can belong to multiple groups.

Instance principals can make API calls against other OCI services without storing credentials in a configuration file and are implemented in OCI with dynamic groups.

Membership in the dynamic group is determined by a set of matching rules. When you set up a dynamic group, you also define the rules for membership in the group. Resources that match the rule criteria are members of the dynamic group. Dynamic groups also need policies to access OCI resources.

Tenancy

This is equivalent to an account that contains all of your OCI resources provisioned with a single, top-level compartment called the *root compartment*.

Compartments

Compartments help you organize resources to provide flexibility and makes it easier for the end user to control access to resources (such as an instance, cloud network, storage volume, database, and so on) within them. When you sign up for a cloud trial, your root compartment is created for you by Oracle when your tenancy is provisioned on Oracle Cloud Infrastructure, as shown in Figure 9-3. Anyone with administrator privileges can create more compartments in the root compartment and then add the access rules for the users to control which users can take action for resources. You can consider compartments as a logical container used to organize and isolate cloud resources.

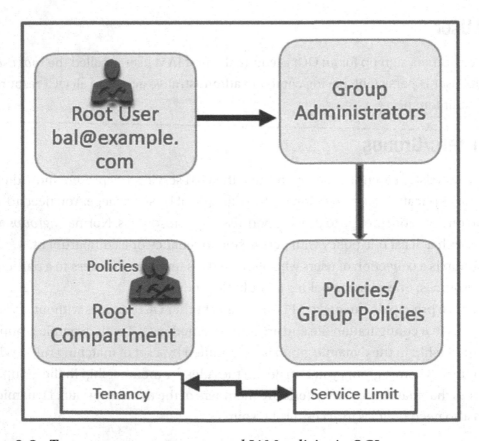

Figure 9-3. *Tenancy, compartments, and IAM policies in OCI*

The Oracle Cloud Console displays only the resources in that compartment for the region you are assigned in. To see resources in another compartment, you must switch to that compartment and need to have access to it.

Tip   Once a compartment is created with resources required underneath, you cannot move them across another compartment.

Note   Once you sign up for Oracle Cloud Infrastructure, a set of service limits are configured for your tenancy, as depicted in Figure 9-3. This is the quota set on a resource. For example, you can set the maximum number of compute instances per availability domain within tenancy.

The root user(s), administrator group, and root compartment are created at the time of provisioning.

The root compartment holds all the cloud resources. As a best practice, you should create dedicated compartments for different users, projects, and use cases.

A policy allows a group administrator to manage all resources within tenancy in OCI. Refer to Figure 9-4, which shows a policy statement to allow the group administrator to manage all resources in tenancy.

Tenant Admin Policy

| Update Version Date | Delete | Apply Tag(s) |

| Policy Information | Tags |

OCID: ...pia7ea Show Copy
Version Date: Keep Policy current
Compartment: cloudarchana

Description: Tenant Admin Policy
Created: Thu, 22 Feb 2018 22:37:01 GMT

Statements   Displaying 1 Statements

| Add Policy Statement |

ALLOW GROUP Administrators to manage all-resources IN TENANCY   Delete

Figure 9-4. *Policy statement to allow resources in the Tenant Admin Policy within OCI*

Everything is a resource in the cloud; every resource gets a unique ID, called an OCID. The tenancy OCID is always located at the bottom of every console page.

Now let's talk about the steps an end user has to take to access the Oracle cloud.

Signing Up for Oracle Cloud Infrastructure Services

You can sign up for Oracle Cloud Infrastructure services in three ways: by contacting your Oracle sales representative, by visiting `https://shop.oracle.com` and signing up for Oracle Cloud Infrastructure services, and by signing up for a free trial at `http://cloud.oracle.com/tryit`.

Oracle provides a $300 credit for trials valid for 30 days. Please refer to Figure 9-5 to understand the flow for getting started with Oracle Cloud Infrastructure.

Figure 9-5. *Options to get started with OCI*

When a user signs up for a cloud trial, the user will get an e-mail within five to ten minutes, as depicted in Figure 9-6. The access credential for cloud services is needed to log in and use the Oracle cloud and is provided with the welcome e-mail after a successful cloud trial sign-up.

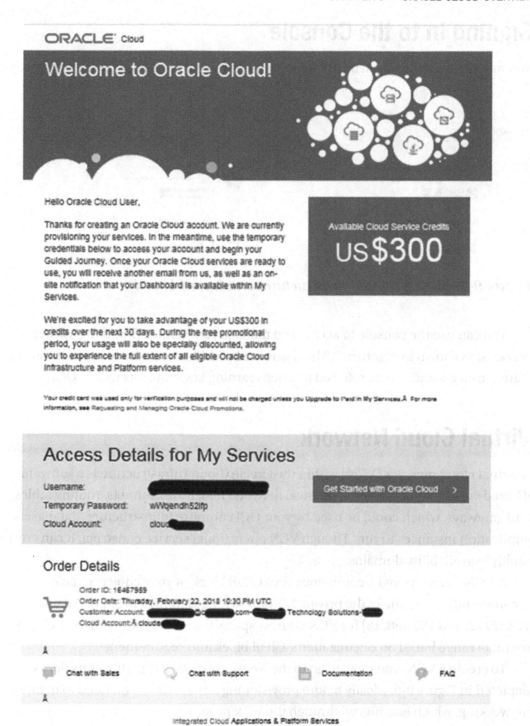

Figure 9-6. *Welcome e-mail after signing up for an Oracle cloud trial*

Signing In to the Console

You might get a region-based URL for the web-based console, as depicted in Figure 9-7.

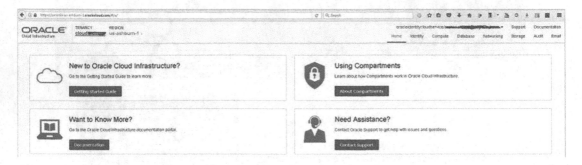

Figure 9-7. *Oracle Cloud Infrastructure console dashboard*

You can use the console to access and manage your Oracle Cloud Infrastructure services, as shown in Figure 9-7. The dashboard provides you with an opportunity to get started quickly and can be referred to when learning key concepts within OCI.

Virtual Cloud Network

A virtual cloud network (VCN) within the Oracle Cloud Infrastructure is a software-defined version of a traditional physical network. It includes subnets, routing tables, and gateways, which could be used by your OCI compute infrastructure, database, or application instances to run. Though VCN is a regional service construct, it can cross multiple availability domains.

A VCN covers a single, contiguous IPv4 CIDR block of your choice. Oracle recommends using one of the private IP address ranges in RFC 1918 (10.0.0.0/8, 172.16/12, and 192.168/16) for VCN address space. However, you can use a publicly routable range based on organizations' CIDR block and requirements.

To create a VCN, you need to go to the Networking tab within the console, as depicted in Figure 9-8. Ideally before provisioning any services, you need to define your networking, which is achieved through the VCN page.

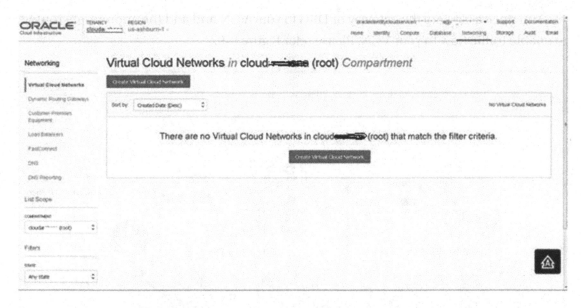

Figure 9-8. *Virtual Cloud Networks page on Oracle Cloud Infrastructure console dashboard*

Subnet

Each VCN network is subdivided into subnets, and each subnet is contained within a single availability domain. You can have more than one subnet in an AD for a given VCN.

Each subnet has a contiguous range of IPs, described in CIDR notation. Subnet IP ranges may not overlap. Subnets can be designated as either public or private and OCI instances draw their internal IP address and network configuration from their subnet.

Internet Gateway

An Internet gateway provides a path for network traffic between your VCN and the Internet. You need to add a route for the gateway in the VCN's route table to enable traffic flow after creating an Internet gateway (IG).

Dynamic Routing Gateway

DRG is a virtual router that provides a point of entry for remote networks coming into the VCN. You can establish a connection directly with your DRG instances either via FastConnect or via an IPSec VPN.

You must associate the gateway or DRG to your VCN and add the appropriate routes to enable traffic flow to your VCN. Please refer Figure 9-9.

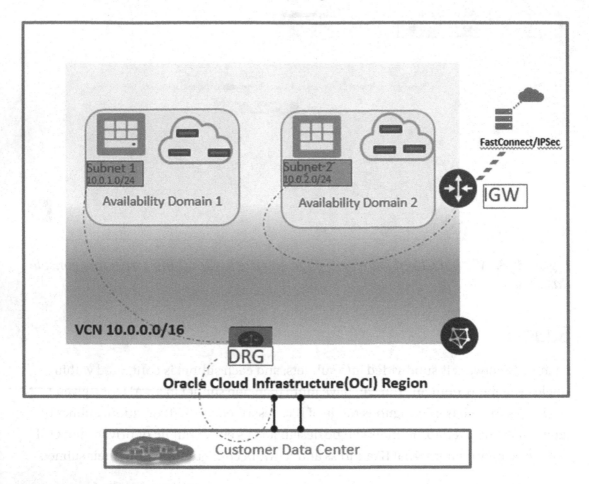

Figure 9-9. *Virtual cloud networks with network components DRG and IGW*

Security List

A security list is a common set of firewall rules associated with a subnet and applied to all instances launched inside the subnet. Security lists provide ingress and egress rules that specify the types of traffic allowed in and out of the instances, and while creating rules, you can choose whether a given rule is stateful or stateless.

Route Table

A route table is set of route rules that provide a mapping for the traffic from subnets via gateways to destinations outside the VCN.

Once you go to the Oracle Cloud Infrastructure dashboard and select Networking ➤ Virtual Cloud Networks from the menu, you have the opportunity to create a VCN, which you can utilize for your resources such as compute and databases. Figure 9-10 shows inputs required for a VCN creation. A compartment is preselected based on your selection on the OCI dashboard. You need to specify a name for the VCN and the way you need this to be created. The default is a VCN with all required resources such as a subnet, DNS, Internet gateway, and security list. For simplicity, select Create Virtual Cloud Network Plus Related Resources.

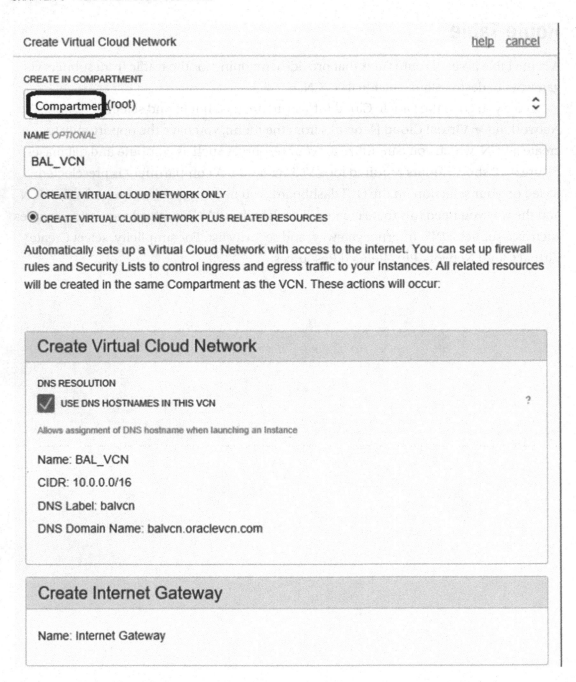

Figure 9-10. *Virtual Cloud Networks page on Oracle Cloud Infrastructure console dashboard*

Update Default Route Table

Add Route Rule: 0.0.0.0/0 - Internet Gateway

Create Subnet

Name: Public Subnet IGRK:US-ASHBURN-AD-1

Security List: Default Security List

DHCP Options: Default DHCP Options

CIDR: 10.0.0.0/24; 10.0.0.0 - 10.0.0.255 (256 IP addresses)

Route Table: Default Route Table

DNS Label: Auto-generated

Create Subnet

Name: Public Subnet IGRK:US-ASHBURN-AD-2

Security List: Default Security List

DHCP Options: Default DHCP Options

CIDR: 10.0.1.0/24; 10.0.1.0 - 10.0.1.255 (256 IP addresses)

Route Table: Default Route Table

DNS Label: Auto-generated

Create Subnet

Name: Public Subnet IGRK:US-ASHBURN-AD-3

Security List: Default Security List

DHCP Options: Default DHCP Options

CIDR: 10.0.2.0/24; 10.0.2.0 - 10.0.2.255 (256 IP addresses)

Route Table: Default Route Table

DNS Label: Auto-generated

☑ View detail page after this resource is created

Create Virtual Cloud Network

Figure 9-10. (*continued*)

After confirming your inputs, your network resources will be created, as confirmed with Figure 9-11.

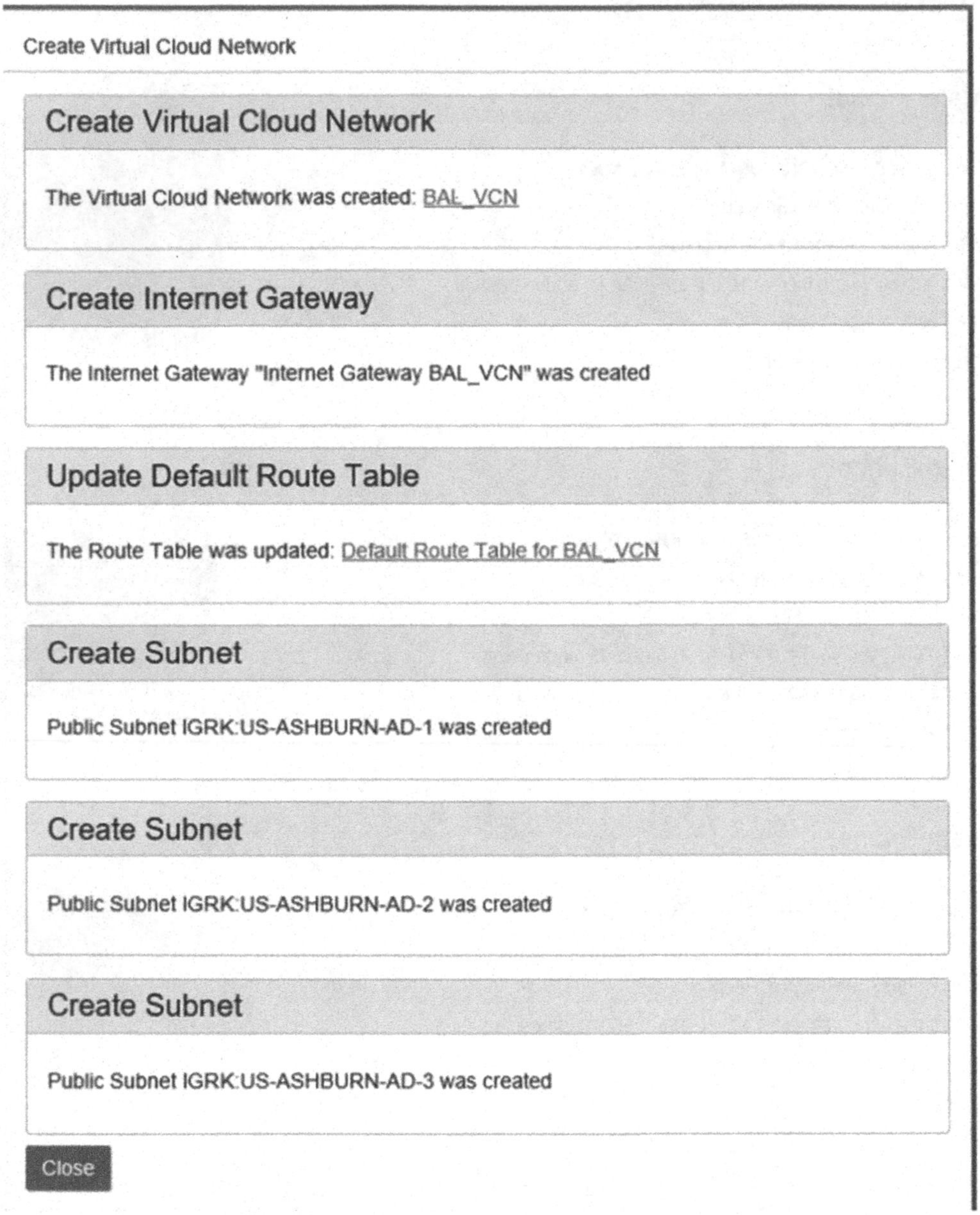

Figure 9-11. *Virtual Cloud Networks page VCN resource creation*

Once you have created a VCN, it will appear on the cloud dashboard within the Virtual Cloud Networks page, as shown in Figure 9-12.

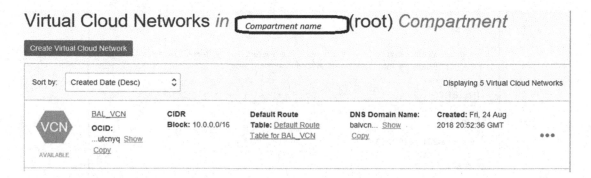

Figure 9-12. *Virtual Cloud Networks page available within a compartment on Oracle Cloud Infrastructure console dashboard*

Creating a Compute Instance in the Public Cloud

To create a compute instance, navigate to the OCI dashboard and go to the Compute ➤ Instances page. Click Create Instance, as shown in Figure 9-13. Select the compartment where you need to create this compute resource.

Figure 9-13. *Compute creation on Oracle Cloud Infrastructure*

Once you are at the Instances page, click Create Instance, which will provide another page requiring certain inputs such as instance name, availability domain, boot volume, operating system, shape of instance in terms of number of OCPU's and the public key that you would like to use for the instance provisioning. Figure 9-14 and Figure 9-15 show these options.

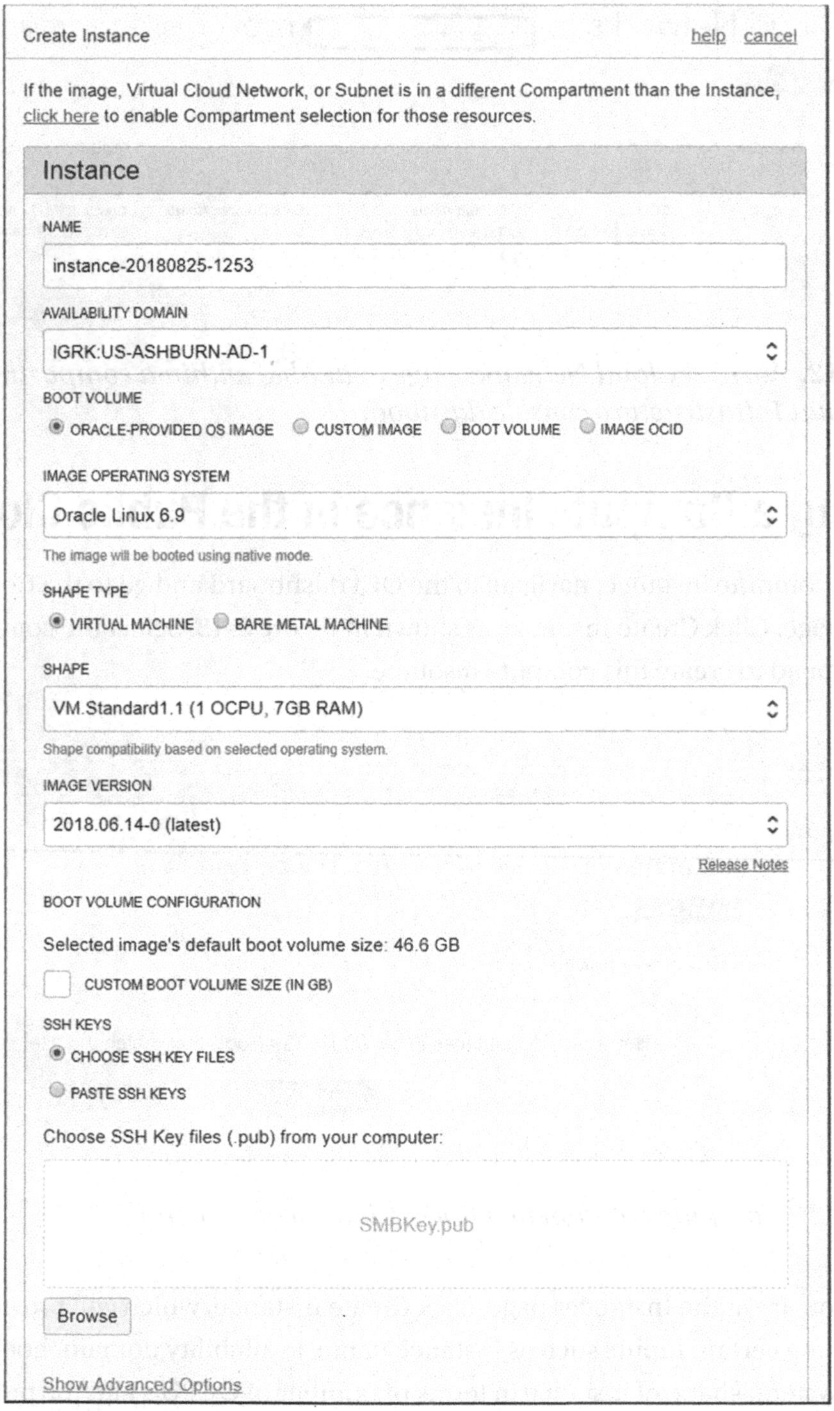

Figure 9-14. *Compute instance creation on OCI*

Note   You need to have a public and private key pair created to use them during instance creation. Depending on whether you are working on a Windows OS or Linux machine, there are ways to use tools available on these platforms to do it.

Now look at Networking section where you need to select the VCN created earlier as well select the associated subnet. Keep in mind subnets are availability domain-specific resources. Refer to Figure 9-15, where you specify these and complete the instance creation.

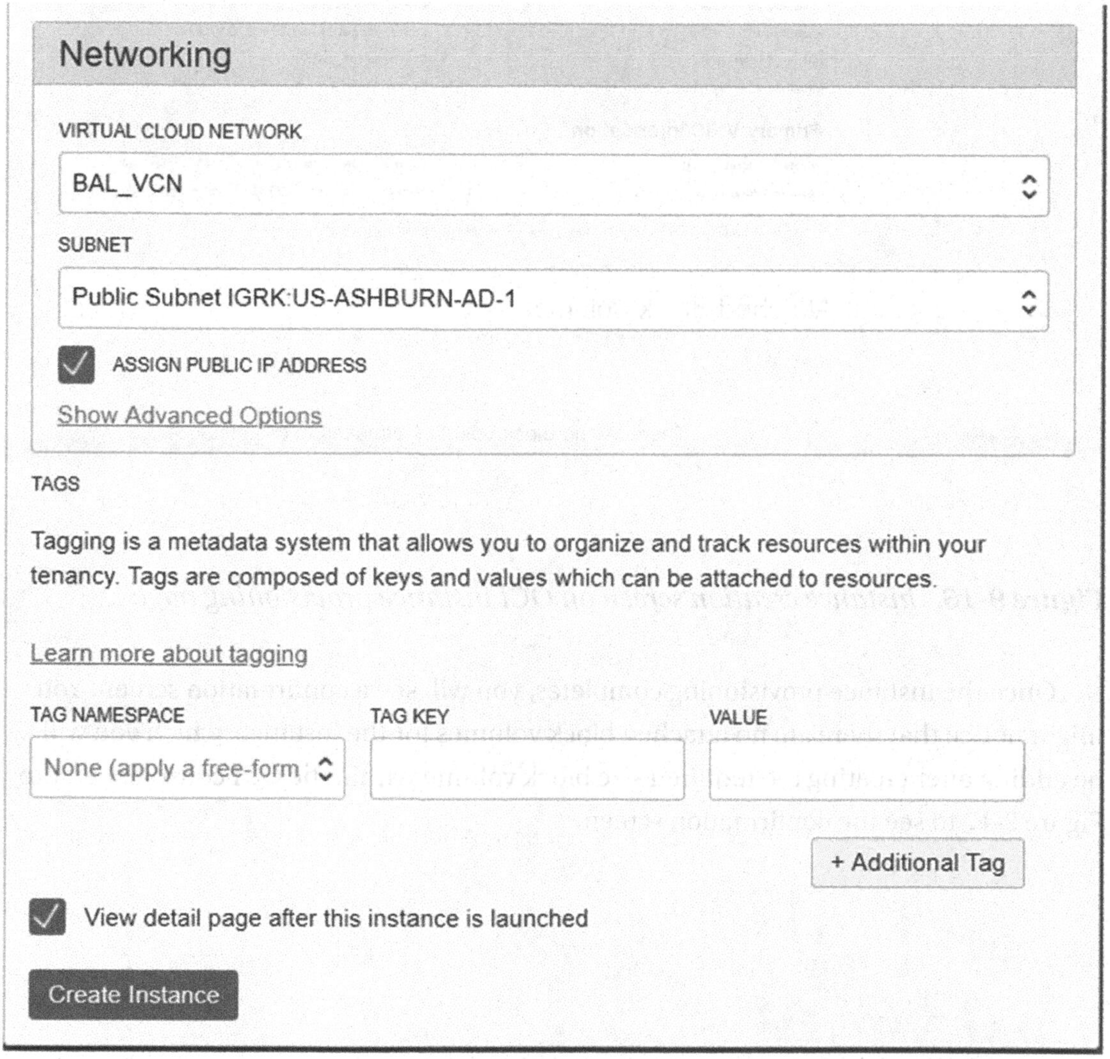

Figure 9-15. *VCN and availability domain selection on instance creation page*

After confirming the details depending on your selections, a compute instance will be provisioned within a minute. Figure 9-16 shows the instance creation status.

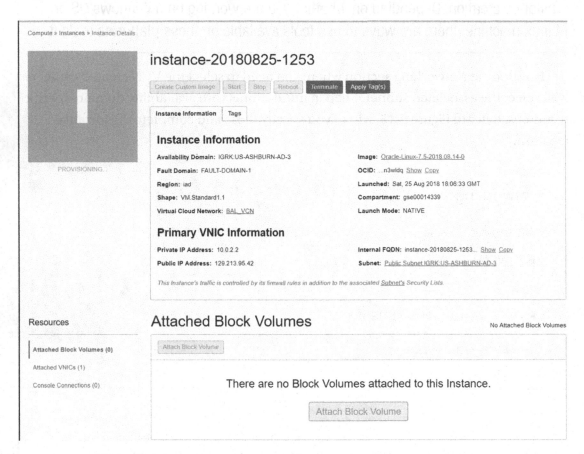

Figure 9-16. *Instance creation screen on OCI instance provisioning page*

Once the instance provisioning completes, you will see a confirmation screen. You might notice that there are no attached block volumes for the instance, which you will be adding after creating the required size block volume within the OCI console. Refer to Figure 9-17 to see the confirmation screen.

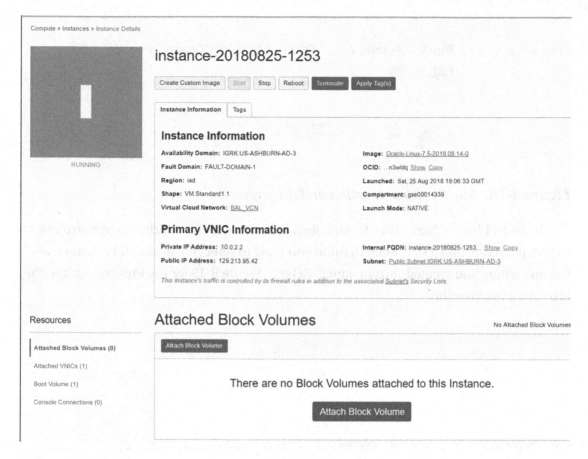

Figure 9-17. *Instance creation completed phase*

The status page shows an instance is running and its associated private and public IP addresses. You will use the public IP address shown in Figure 9-17 to connect to the instance using a private key and SSH client like Putty.

To create a block volume, you need to navigate to the Block Storage menu in the OCI console, which provides an option to create the desired block volume for use with the compute instance. Refer to Figure 9-18 to create the block volume.

Figure 9-18. *Block volume creation on OCI page*

To add a block volume, click Create Block Volume, which provides an opportunity to give it a name and a size. Keep in mind you need to select the availability domain as the one where you created your instance. Refer to Figure 9-19 for the inputs required for block volume creation.

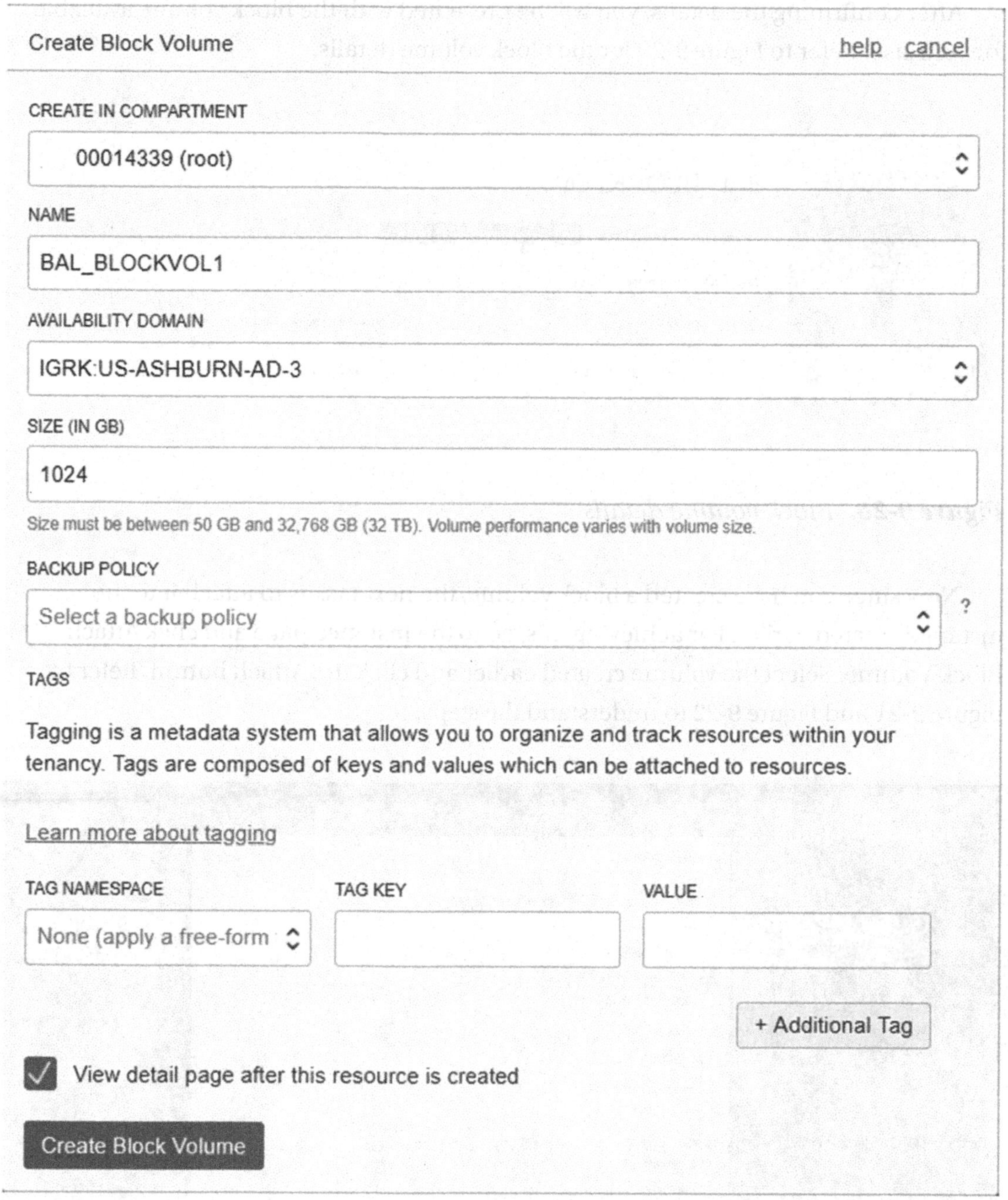

Create Block Volume   help cancel

CREATE IN COMPARTMENT

00014339 (root)   ⬍

NAME

BAL_BLOCKVOL1

AVAILABILITY DOMAIN

IGRK:US-ASHBURN-AD-3   ⬍

SIZE (IN GB)

1024

Size must be between 50 GB and 32,768 GB (32 TB). Volume performance varies with volume size.

BACKUP POLICY

Select a backup policy   ⬍   ?

TAGS

Tagging is a metadata system that allows you to organize and track resources within your
tenancy. Tags are composed of keys and values which can be attached to resources.

Learn more about tagging

TAG NAMESPACE   TAG KEY   VALUE

None (apply a free-form ⬍

                                                        + Additional Tag

☑ View detail page after this resource is created

Create Block Volume

Figure 9-19. *Block volume creation on OCI dashboard*

After confirming the details, you will be presented with the block volume available for your use. Refer to Figure 9-20 for the block volume details.

Figure 9-20. *Block volume details*

Now since you have created a block volume, the next task is to attach it to the instance created earlier. For achieving this, go to the instance page and click Attach Block Volume. Select the volume created earlier and click the Attach button. Refer to Figure 9-21 and Figure 9-22 to understand the steps.

Figure 9-21. *Block volume attachment to instance*

Upon confirmation, it will provide the required actions to be completed for adding the block volume to the compute instance. Refer to Figure 9-22 for the instruction.

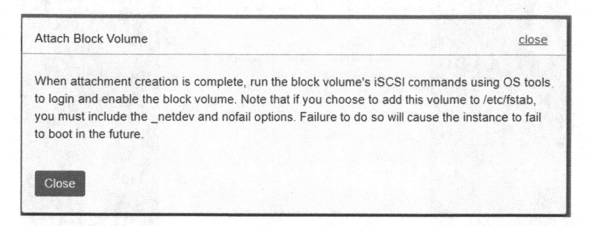

Figure 9-22. *Instructions for attaching a block volume through OS commands*

For the next steps, go to the instance home page. At the bottom under the Attached Block Volumes section, expand the dots to find the iSCSI command details. Refer to Figure 9-23 to find the details for the next steps.

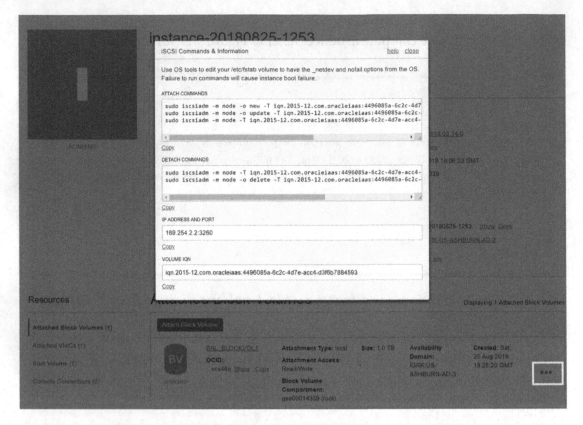

Figure 9-23. *iSCSI commands and information for attaching a block volume to instance*

Copy the commands available on the screen for attaching a block volume to the compute instance and open an SSH client session to perform the activities. For connecting to an instance, you need to have an SSH session with a public IP address, and a private key needs to be configured on the Auth tab, as depicted in Figure 9-24.

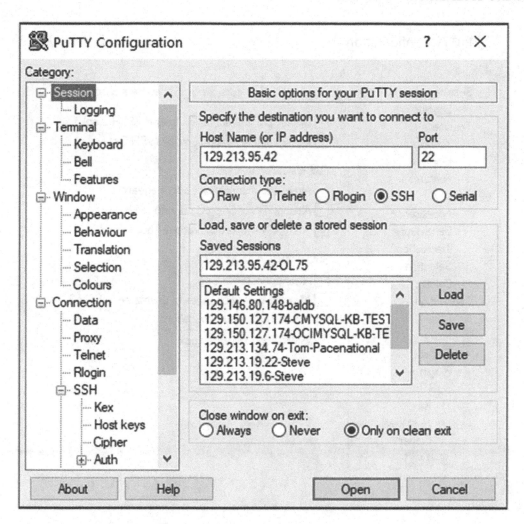

Figure 9-24. *Connection details for compute instance*

Once you have provided the public IP address in the Host Name field, go to the SSH section and expand the Auth tab to provide the private keys to make the connection. Refer to Figure 9-25 through 9-27 for the steps.

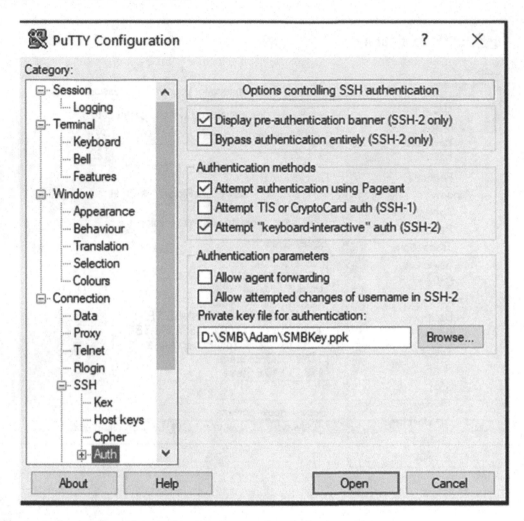

Figure 9-25. *Private key selection on Auth tab for connection*

Once you have provided these options, you can click Open and accept the warning; it prompts for your username and any passphrase if you have provided one for protecting these keys. Use **opc** as the user and provide the passphrase to get the session established. Refer to Figure 9-26, which shows you are connected to the cloud instance via the opc user.

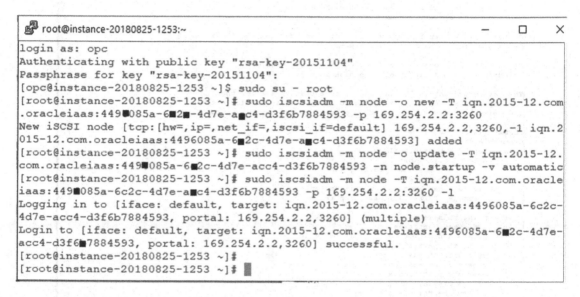

Figure 9-26. *The session for the OCI cloud compute instance*

Once a session is established, you can switch to the root user to run the iSCSI commands and mount the block volume. See Figure 9-27.

```
login as: opc
Authenticating with public key "rsa-key-20151104"
Passphrase for key "rsa-key-20151104":
[opc@instance-20180825-1253 ~]$ sudo su - root
[root@instance-20180825-1253 ~]# sudo iscsiadm -m node -o new -T iqn.2015-12.com
.oracleiaas:449█085a-6█2█-4d7e-a█c4-d3f6b7884593 -p 169.254.2.2:3260
New iSCSI node [tcp:[hw=,ip=,net_if=,iscsi_if=default] 169.254.2.2,3260,-1 iqn.2
015-12.com.oracleiaas:4496085a-6█2c-4d7e-a█c4-d3f6b7884593] added
[root@instance-20180825-1253 ~]# sudo iscsiadm -m node -o update -T iqn.2015-12.
com.oracleiaas:449█085a-6█2c-4d7e-acc4-d3f6b7884593 -n node.startup -v automatic
[root@instance-20180825-1253 ~]# sudo iscsiadm -m node -T iqn.2015-12.com.oracle
iaas:449█085a-6c2c-4d7e-a█c4-d3f6b7884593 -p 169.254.2.2:3260 -l
Logging in to [iface: default, target: iqn.2015-12.com.oracleiaas:4496085a-6c2c-
4d7e-acc4-d3f6b7884593, portal: 169.254.2.2,3260] (multiple)
Login to [iface: default, target: iqn.2015-12.com.oracleiaas:4496085a-6█2c-4d7e-
acc4-d3f6█7884593, portal: 169.254.2.2,3260] successful.
[root@instance-20180825-1253 ~]#
[root@instance-20180825-1253 ~]#
```

Figure 9-27. *The iSCSI commands' output on the OCI cloud compute instance*

After running the iSCSI commands to attach the block volume, now there is a little housekeeping work, such as to create and partition the volume, create a file system, and attach it to the instance. See Figure 9-28 for how to create a new partition on the compute instance using the Linux command FDISK.

```
[root@instance-20180825-1253 ~]# fdisk -l
WARNING: fdisk GPT support is currently new, and therefore in an experimental ph
ase. Use at your own discretion.

Disk /dev/sda: 50.0 GB, 50010783744 bytes, 97677312 sectors
Units = sectors of 1 * 512 = 512 bytes
Sector size (logical/physical): 512 bytes / 4096 bytes
I/O size (minimum/optimal): 4096 bytes / 1048576 bytes
Disk label type: gpt
Disk identifier: C733C3EF-0667-41D3-B1B8-D6EDEE52A064


#         Start            End    Size  Type               Name
1          2048         411647    200M  EFI System         EFI System Partition
2        411648       17188863      8G  Linux swap
3      17188864       97675263   38.4G  Microsoft basic

Disk /dev/sdb: 1099.5 GB, 1099511627776 bytes, 2147483648 sectors
Units = sectors of 1 * 512 = 512 bytes
Sector size (logical/physical): 512 bytes / 4096 bytes
I/O size (minimum/optimal): 4096 bytes / 1048576 bytes

[root@instance-20180825-1253 ~]# fdisk /dev/sdb
Welcome to fdisk (util-linux 2.23.2).

Changes will remain in memory only, until you decide to write them.
Be careful before using the write command.

Device does not contain a recognized partition table
Building a new DOS disklabel with disk identifier 0xcd01272f.

The device presents a logical sector size that is smaller than
the physical sector size. Aligning to a physical sector (or optimal
I/O) size boundary is recommended, or performance may be impacted.

Command (m for help): m
Command action
   a   toggle a bootable flag
   b   edit bsd disklabel
   c   toggle the dos compatibility flag
   d   delete a partition
   g   create a new empty GPT partition table
   G   create an IRIX (SGI) partition table
   l   list known partition types
   m   print this menu
   n   add a new partition
   o   create a new empty DOS partition table
   p   print the partition table
   q   quit without saving changes
   s   create a new empty Sun disklabel
   t   change a partition's system id
   u   change display/entry units
   v   verify the partition table
   w   write table to disk and exit
   x   extra functionality (experts only)

Command (m for help): n
Partition type:
   p   primary (0 primary, 0 extended, 4 free)
   e   extended
Select (default p): p
Partition number (1-4, default 1):
First sector (2048-2147483647, default 2048):
Using default value 2048
Last sector, +sectors or +size{K,M,G} (2048-2147483647, default 2147483647):
Using default value 2147483647
Partition 1 of type Linux and of size 1024 GiB is set

Command (m for help): w
The partition table has been altered!

Calling ioctl() to re-read partition table.
Syncing disks.
[root@instance-20180825-1253 ~]# 
```

Figure 9-28. *The FDISK commands to create a new partition on the OCI cloud compute instance*

Once a new partition is created as shown in Figure 9-28, you can format the disk and attach it to the instance, as depicted in Figure 9-29. This shows `fdisk -l` listing the partition; in our case, it is /dev/sdb1. You can use `mkfs.ext4` or any other command based on the requirements to format the newly created partition. Once the formatting is created, you can mount the partition under a mountpoint; in our case, we created /u01 as a mountpoint and mounted the formatted volume.

```
[root@instance-20180825-1253 ~]# fdisk -l
WARNING: fdisk GPT support is currently new, and therefore in an experimental phase. Use at
 your own discretion.

Disk /dev/sda: 50.0 GB, 50010783744 bytes, 97677312 sectors
Units = sectors of 1 * 512 = 512 bytes
Sector size (logical/physical): 512 bytes / 4096 bytes
I/O size (minimum/optimal): 4096 bytes / 1048576 bytes
Disk label type: gpt
Disk identifier: C733C3EF-0667-41D3-B1B8-D6EDEE52A064


#         Start          End    Size  Type             Name
 1         2048       411647    200M  EFI System       EFI System Partition
 2       411648     17188863      8G  Linux swap
 3     17188864     97675263   38.4G  Microsoft basic

Disk /dev/sdb: 1099.5 GB, 1099511627776 bytes, 2147483648 sectors
Units = sectors of 1 * 512 = 512 bytes
Sector size (logical/physical): 512 bytes / 4096 bytes
I/O size (minimum/optimal): 4096 bytes / 1048576 bytes
Disk label type: dos
Disk identifier: 0xcd01272f

   Device Boot      Start         End      Blocks   Id  System
/dev/sdb1            2048  2147483647  1073740800   83  Linux
[root@instance-20180825-1253 ~]# mkfs
mkfs          mkfs.cramfs  mkfs.ext3    mkfs.fat     mkfs.msdos   mkfs.xfs
mkfs.btrfs    mkfs.ext2    mkfs.ext4    mkfs.minix   mkfs.vfat
[root@instance-20180825-1253 ~]# mkfs.ext4 /dev/sdb1
mke2fs 1.42.9 (28-Dec-2013)
Filesystem label=
OS type: Linux
Block size=4096 (log=2)
Fragment size=4096 (log=2)
Stride=0 blocks, Stripe width=256 blocks
67108864 inodes, 268435200 blocks
13421760 blocks (5.00%) reserved for the super user
First data block=0
Maximum filesystem blocks=2415919104
8192 block groups
32768 blocks per group, 32768 fragments per group
8192 inodes per group
Superblock backups stored on blocks:
        32768, 98304, 163840, 229376, 294912, 819200, 884736, 1605632, 2654208,
        4096000, 7962624, 11239424, 20480000, 23887872, 71663616, 78675968,
        102400000, 214990848

Allocating group tables: done
Writing inode tables: done
Creating journal (32768 blocks): done
Writing superblocks and filesystem accounting information: done

[root@instance-20180825-1253 ~]# mkdir /u01
[root@instance-20180825-1253 ~]# mount /dev/sdb1 /u01
[root@instance-20180825-1253 ~]# df -h
Filesystem      Size  Used Avail Use% Mounted on
devtmpfs        3.3G     0  3.3G   0% /dev
tmpfs           3.3G     0  3.3G   0% /dev/shm
tmpfs           3.3G   17M  3.3G   1% /run
tmpfs           3.3G     0  3.3G   0% /sys/fs/cgroup
/dev/sda3        39G  1.8G   37G   5% /
/dev/sda1       200M  9.8M  191M   5% /boot/efi
tmpfs           672M     0  672M   0% /run/user/0
tmpfs           672M     0  672M   0% /run/user/1000
/dev/sdb1      1008G   77M  957G   1% /u01
[root@instance-20180825-1253 ~]#
```

Figure 9-29. *Creating the file system and adding it to OCI compute instance*

To make sure the volume is available after a reboot, you need to add it under /etc/ fstab with the required options, as depicted in Figure 9-21 earlier.

Congratulations, your compute instance is ready to be used for the workload you are planning! There are several other things that can be explored such as security rules and networking capabilities provided by OCI.

To summarize, Oracle Cloud Infrastructure provides various deployment options to meet the service level agreements required for critical workloads. Oracle's software-defined network design provides you with both virtual-machine and bare-metal compute instances, all available on the same network and accessible through the same portal and API set.

Plus, bare-metal compute servers provide the same level of control as a physical server in your own data center. You can use these instances through the serial console access as well. Oracle Cloud Infrastructure does not virtualize I/O through hypervisors. Oracle Cloud Infrastructure does it in the network, which provides better encapsulation and isolation, as well as supporting unique compute options.

Oracle provides Oracle Database on Exadata and RAC in the cloud, supporting millions of transactions per second, databases that scale to hundreds of terabytes, and the highest levels of availability, and it differentiates Oracle from other cloud vendors.

Now that you understand how to get started with Oracle Cloud Infrastructure and core concepts such as virtual cloud networks, availability domains, subnets, identity management, security rules, and so on, you will learn the different architectural considerations needed for production deployments in terms of high availability, disaster recovery, backup consideration, and so on.

In the next few sections, you will focus on the database deployment options available in OCI.

Oracle Database Cloud Service Options

Oracle's public database cloud offerings include database as a service (DBaaS).

The Oracle Database Cloud Service provides several offerings that give you options for running a virtual machine with a fully configured CDB and PDB, running an Oracle Database instance in Elastic Compute, running a fully configured CDB, and running an Oracle Database instance on Oracle Cloud Infrastructure (formerly known as bare-metal servers). The Database Cloud Service offers elastic database services for application development, test, and production deployment. The service delivers an easy-to-use web console user interface and a RESTful API to provision and administer Oracle Database on Oracle Cloud Infrastructure offerings.

The services that are available in the Oracle public cloud can be categorized into four distinct offerings, covered next.

Database Standard Edition

This offering includes Database STandard Edition 2, so you get a full database instance in a Virtual Machine. While provisioning a Database Standard Edition you can decide on your backup needs, It provides you option as "Local Backup", a "Cloud Backup" or both, which are based on Recovery Manager (RMAN). If you need a cloud backup, you need to have access to Object Storage bucket or container depending on where you want to launch database service -Oracle Cloud Infrastructure (OCI) or Oracle Cloud Infrastructure Classic (OCI-C) respectively. Databases on OCI-C can use a backup cloud service, which is a platform as a service offering for Oracle backups and it uses a storage container.

One thing to note here is Oracle Transparent Data Encryption (TDE) is included for all database offerings including Standard Edition, which helps you secure data at rest.

Database Enterprise Edition

As part of this offering, customers get the Enterprise Edition of the database and a few additional Enterprise Manager packs including Diagnostic Pack, Tuning Pack, and Real Application Testing, Data Masking, and Subsetting. This is optimal where you need to have a disaster recovery site in addition to your primary database as it comes default with Data Guard technologies.

Database Enterprise Edition High Performance

This offering extends Enterprise Edition with additional database options such as Multitenant, Advanced Compression, Advanced Security, Label Security, Partitioning, Database Vault, OLAP, Advance Analytics, Enterprise Manager Database Lifecycle Management Pack, and Enterprise Manager Cloud Management Pack.

So, this offering can be considered if your workload demands these options.

Database Enterprise Edition Extreme Performance

This option extends the High Performance package with Database In-Memory, Active Data Guard, and Real Application Clusters (you need to factor at least two VMs with two OCPUs as a minimum). The Oracle Exadata Cloud service as well as Exadata Express cloud services come by default with the Extreme Performance package.

You now understand that Oracle provides various options for building out databases for different use cases such as production, disaster recovery, Test and Development, and so on. You now will explore architectural considerations for deploying different use cases.

Database Cloud Deployment Scenarios

Oracle provides a maximum availability architecture for various deployment scenarios and can be categorized broadly into four categories.

Bronze Category

This category is more suitable for single-instance databases for noncritical workloads such as test and development kinds of workloads. Along with a single-instance database, you can choose local backups or backups to the Oracle cloud. It will have a higher recovery time objective (RTO).

Databases falling into this category can select a database option of either Oracle Cloud Infrastructure Classic (OCI-C) or OCI Databases, meaning Standard Edition 2, Enterprise Edition, High Performance, Database Backup Cloud Service available on OCI, OCI Object Storage, and so on.

Enterprise Edition has advantages over Standard Edition 2 in terms of a few key features such as corruption protection, flashback technologies, online maintenance activities such as datafile move, and online objects reorganization/redefinition, which increases the availability. On the other hand, Enterprise Manager Pack, which is available with Enterprise Edition Diagnostic & Tuning and Real Application Testing, helps to do proactive database performance management.

Silver Category

This category can be chosen when you need to run critical workloads where instance availability is important. Real Application Clusters (RAC) can achieve this goal. Optionally you can also configure a local Data Guard copy within the same Oracle Cloud Infrastructure region in a different availability domain for high availability purposes. Of course, you need to configure a cloud backup using either RMAN on object storage or locally.

You can select OCI/OCI-C, DBCS on VMs/dedicated environments like bare metal, ExaCS, ExaCC, or OCM. Oracle RAC is available only with the Extreme Performance edition of Oracle Cloud DBaaS Service. By following maximum availability architecture design principles, you can achieve a goal of 0 RPO and second-to-minutes RTO.

Gold Category

This category can use Oracle cloud databases with RAC for the primary and a Data Guard configuration within the same region for high availability purposes for achieving fast failovers. Disaster recovery should be planned in a different geographic region using Active Data Guard technology available on the Oracle public cloud. Backups are stored either locally or using a cloud backup on object storage.

You can achieve zero data loss as well fast failovers using technologies such as Active Data Guard/Far Sync and RAC. These options can provide a 0 RTO as well as 0 RPO in most failure scenarios.

Platinum Category

If your objective is to have zero data loss and RPO capabilities across any distance along with application continuity, you can architect your deployment using RAC, Active Data Guard, local/cloud backup, local high availability using Data Guard, and Golden Gate on the cloud platform.

This is suitable for mission-critical databases. You will design the production database with Real Application Clusters in the OCI region across availability domains, with local standby databases and backups. GoldenGate can be utilized for replication and application upgrades, and edition-based redefinition technologies can provide the highest level of data availability.

Options available on the Oracle public cloud are Database Extreme Performance, Exadata Cloud Service, Exadata Cloud Machine, and GoldenGate Cloud Service/Data Integration Platform Cloud Service.

Now that we've discussed various categories for design consideration, it is important to understand the maximum availability architecture for the cloud.

Significance of a Maximum Availability Architecture

You want to design an architecture to avoid a single point of failure, prevent data loss, reduce downtime cost, and reduce the revenue impact for planned and unplanned outages. At certain times you need to have a disaster recovery and data protection methods for compliance and regulatory purposes as well.

The purpose of a maximum availability architecture is to eliminate a single point of failure so that applications and data remain available when an outage occurs with the database system. There could be several factors causing outages such as human error, hardware faults, software bugs, cyberattacks, or even catastrophic events that can cause an entire data center to fail.

There are several considerations an organization needs to think about when implementing high availability. It needs to be cost effective, be easy to manage, and provide a high return on investment. Additionally, it needs to be comprehensive, addressing both unexpected outages and planned downtime to the extent required to meet service level expectations. You often need to consider RPO and RTO objectives clearly and design the required high availability architecture.

We will discuss how you can handle the requirements in terms of building a highly available system. To start, let's look at some of the practical considerations when it comes to implementing a disaster recovery solution, which is a key component of maximum availability architecture.

- Complex architecture and deployment for disaster recovery site consideration

- Longer time to provision a disaster recovery site

- Data inconsistency and corruption issue handling

- Higher capex and management cost associated with solution

- Required elasticity to support capacity on demand and bursting capabilities over capex

- Data security/compliance concerns

Now that you understand the various challenges as well as the options available and design considerations, you will look at a few deployment scenario. The Oracle public cloud addresses these challenges through a flexible deployment model.

Disaster Recovery Deployments with the Oracle Public Cloud

Oracle provides a simple deployment model with the Oracle Cloud Infrastructure providing several options for database deployment including Active Data Guard, Real Application Clusters on its platform as a service offering (license including PaaS), or bring your own license (BYOL) to the Oracle Cloud Infrastructure.

The Oracle public cloud provides great alternatives in terms of cloud bursting capability and on-demand elasticity, with no data inconsistency or corruption because of continuous validation, which solves a major issue around data corruption. Users might want to consider the Oracle public cloud as a disaster recovery solution for their on-prem databases, or they might be interested in creating a DR solution for a database they have already on the Oracle public cloud. Oracle cloud tools provide options to select the kind of deployment you need during the provisioning process. There are various possibilities such as single-instance, single-instance with disaster recovery, or maybe a RAC clustered database with a clustered DR. Let's look at a typical database deployment.

Within each region there are several data centers with separate racks, power, cooling, and high-speed networks to support the enterprise workloads available. For example, you can consider Chicago & Ashburn as the data center within the United States. In EMEA, use Slough & Amsterdam. Oracle provisioning provides the opportunity to select the region you want to have your resources, In EMEA, use Region "Slough & Amsterdam" when you are initially creating your VCN in Oracle OCI Console.

Earlier in the chapter you saw how a region is defined within the Oracle Cloud Infrastructure and how each region has availability domains across distinct data centers connected over high-speed network infrastructure, which provides a great options for users to design their data protection and high availability.

557

Note   High availability is considered as having both the primary and standby in the same data center in the case of OPC Classic or in the same region with different availability domains in the case of OCI.

Disaster recovery, on the other hand, means the primary and standby are in different data centers (OPC) or across regions in the case of OCI (previously known as a bare-metal cloud).

Let's see an example how you can deploy a disaster recovery setup in the Oracle public cloud on OCI-C. You will see how databases can be created on OCI in the next chapters.

Log in with the cloud credentials you received from your cloud administrator or Oracle subscription.

1.   Navigate to the Oracle Database Cloud Service console, and click Create Services. Refer to Figure 9-30.

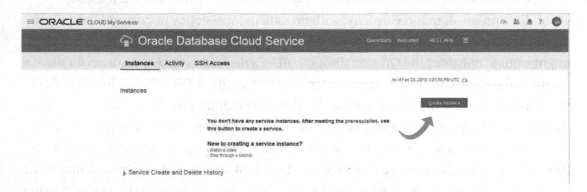

Figure 9-30.   *The database cloud service creation service console*

2.   Once you click Create Service, you will see the screen as shown in Figure 9-31. Carefully select the software release, software edition, and database type.

For example, if you create a Data Guard environment in high availability node, two VMs are created in two separate availability domains in the same data center region, which is good for a local standby database running in SYNC mode Redo Log Transport and serves local high availability requirements.

But if your business continuity requirements are to have a Disaster
Recovery site with a Physical Standby Database running in
Maximum Performance Mode in a different region, this needs
to be selected under the appropriate category shown on cloud
database provisioning page.

Note that the option to create a Data Guard Configuration is only
available in Extreme Performance Package bundle. All other
choices- Enterprise and High Performance versions in oracle cloud,
does not include Data Guard Configuration during deployment time.

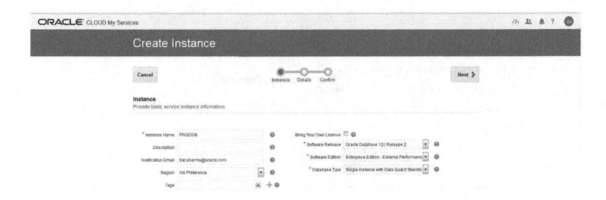

Figure 9-31. *The database cloud service creation with the high availability option*

3.   In this example, in Figure 9-31 I have selected a single instance
     with Data Guard along with the Extreme Performance edition. You
     will see the standby configuration option on the next screen. Fill
     out the options as they are easy to understand. One thing to note
     here is the selection of HA versus DR; the difference is that if you
     select HA, the services are created in the same data center. DR
     creates the services across different data center locations.

Once you are done with your selection, you can go to the next screen and fill out
details in terms of the database configuration, backup configuration, and advanced
settings required.

In Figure 9-32, you need to provide the database name and PDB name because
all instances on the Enterprise Edition follow the CDB/PDB architecture. You need to
provide a complex password and specify database size estimates. You need to pick up
the right shape to start with as well as the SSH public key.

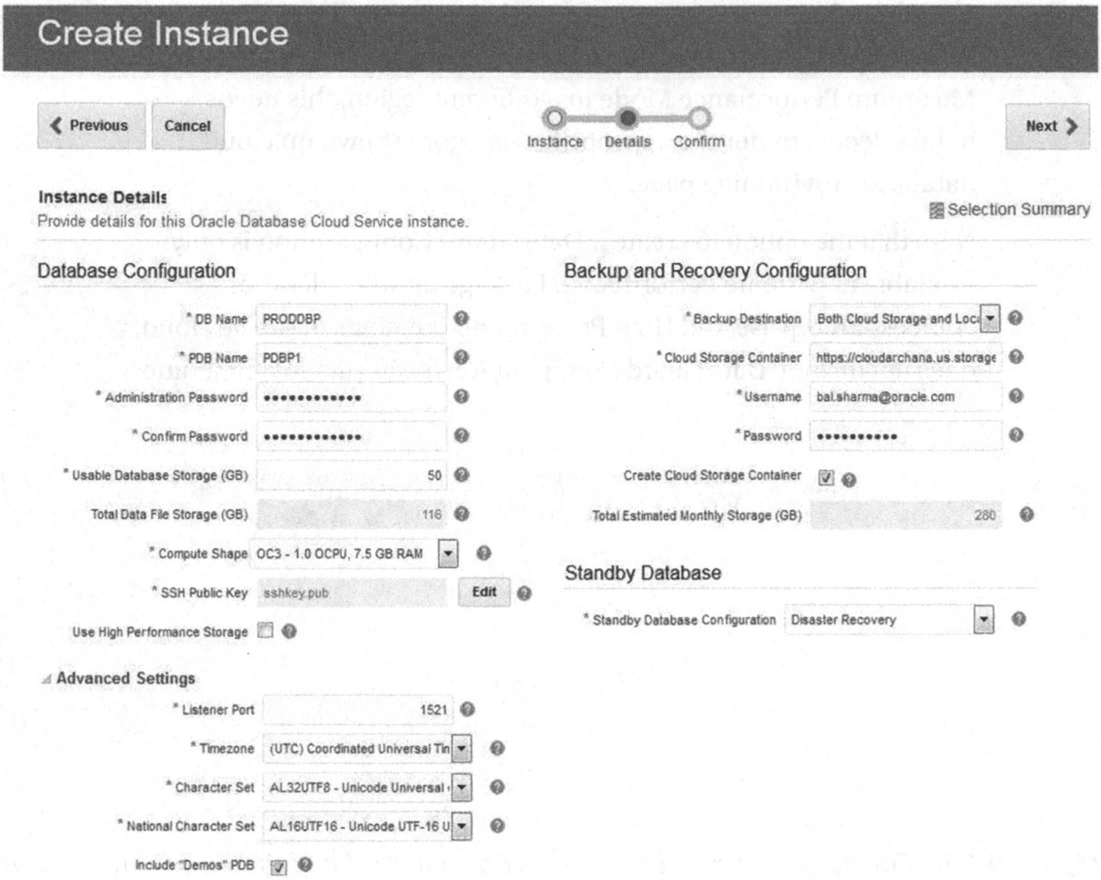

Create Instance

Figure 9-32. *The database cloud service creation, details page*

You additionally have the option to select storage between oracle block (or) high-performance SSD storage during storage provisioning during instance creation.

You can select the required backup configuration at the time of deployment or later and also define advanced settings such as the listener port, time zone, character set, and so on, on this page.

Once this information is filled in, you next move to the backup configuration section, as shown in Figure 9-33. You need to have the cloud storage container information as well credentials available to fill in here. If a container does not exist, you can click Create Container during the process for it to be created automatically. The storage container holds the backup for databases.

Create Instance

< Previous   Cancel

○——●——○
Instance Details Confirm

Next >

Instance Details
Provide details for this Oracle Database Cloud Service instance.

⊞ Selection Summary

Database Configuration

* DB Name	PRODDBP
* PDB Name	PDBP1
* Administration Password	••••••
* Confirm Password	••••••
* Usable Database Storage (GB)	50
Total Data File Storage (GB)	116
* Compute Shape	OC3 - 1.0 OCPU, 7.5 GB RAM ▼
* SSH Public Key	sshkey.pub Edit
Use High Performance Storage	☐

◢ **Advanced Settings**

* Listener Port	1521
* Timezone	(UTC) Coordinated Universal Tin ▼
* Character Set	AL32UTF8 - Unicode Universal ▼
* National Character Set	AL16UTF16 - Unicode UTF-16 U ▼
Include "Demos" PDB	☑

Backup and Recovery Configuration

* Backup Destination	Both Cloud Storage and Loc ▼
* Cloud Storage Container	https://cloudarchana.us.storage
* Username	bal.sharma@oracle.com
* Password	••••••••••
Create Cloud Storage Container	☐
Total Estimated Monthly Storage (GB)	280

Standby Database

* Standby Database Configuration	Disaster Recovery ▼

Figure 9-33. *The database cloud service creation, Backup Configuration option*

You can select the required backup configuration at the time of deployment or later. If you don't have the backup cloud details, you can proceed without providing them, as shown in Figure 9-34, and configure them later.

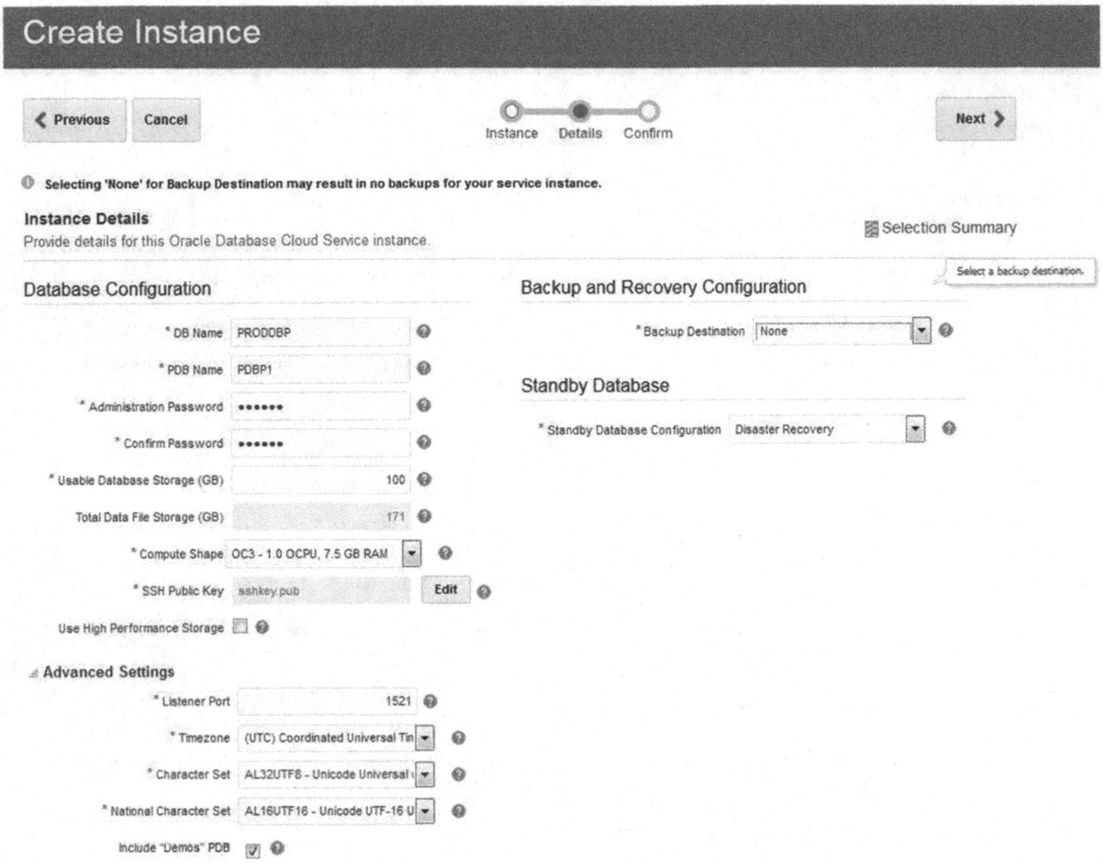

Create Instance

Figure 9-34. The database cloud service creation, without backup configuration

Once the backup section is taken care of, you can proceed with the section Standby Database and select appropriately either Disaster Recovery or High Availability. Next comes the confirmation screen, as shown in Figure 9-35. This is the page where you will review all the options selected earlier and modify any if changes are required.

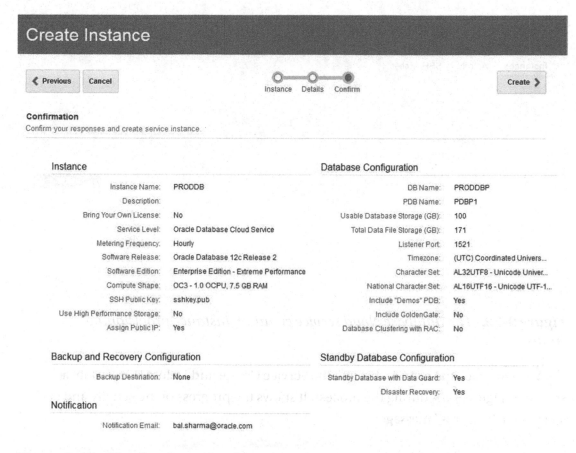

Figure 9-35. *The database cloud service creation, input confirmation screen*

Upon confirmation, you will see the instance is getting provisioned, as shown in Figure 9-36. This is the first database instance, which is the primary database getting created and will be followed with the disaster recovery instance creation.

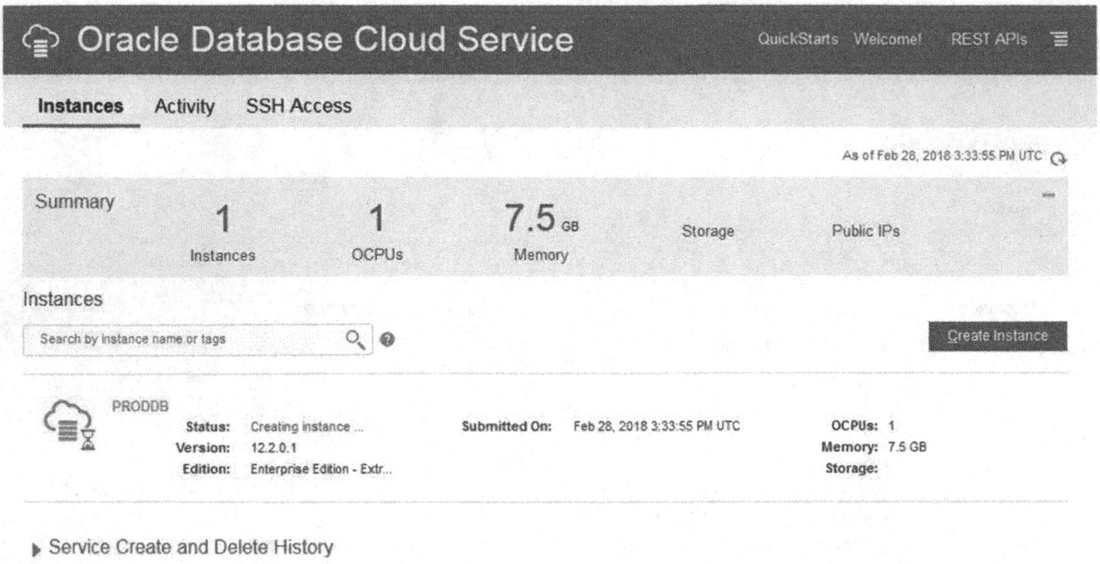

Figure 9-36. *The database cloud service creation, instance provisioning status*

You can track the activity through the Service Create and Delete History tab, as shown in Figure 9-37, during the process. It shows the progress of the activity and each step with a "Success" message.

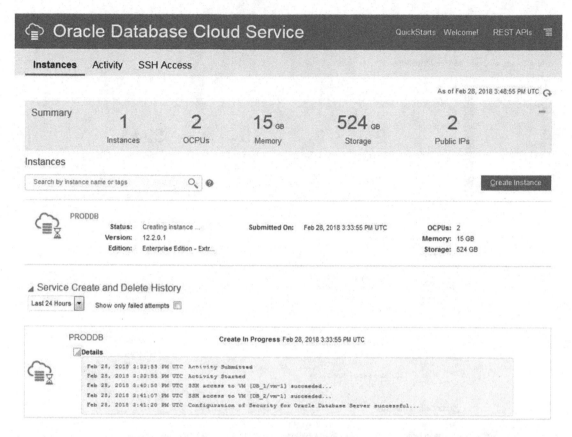

Figure 9-37. *The database cloud service instance provisioning status screen under DBaaS*

Once the activity progresses, the dashboard shows the status on the Instance Overview page. An important thing on this page is that each instance now has a public IP address, which you might want to use for connecting to the database instance just created. This page also displays the database host, SID, associated resources, connection string, and so on. See Figure 9-38.

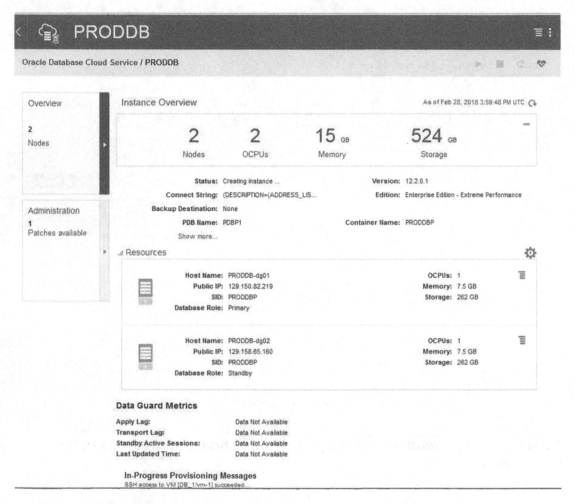

Figure 9-38. *The database cloud service creation, instance provisioning progress*

Once provisioning completes, you will see details for both the VMs in the cloud console, as shown in Figure 9-39, with their database roles. Additionally, you can see the details on the page showing two different data centers across regions. The details on the page are self-explanatory. You can click each of these service and see details on the instance as well the cloud tooling available for them.

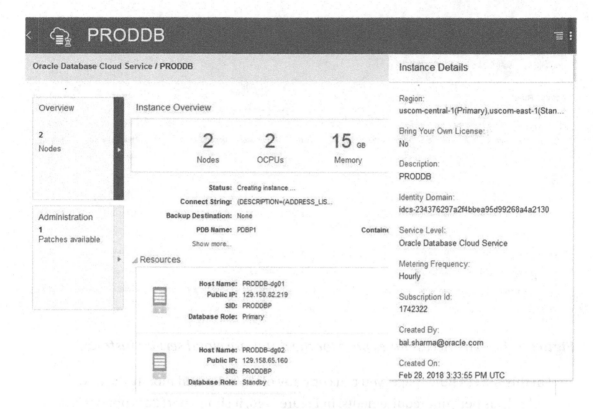

Figure 9-39. *The database cloud service creation, completed status*

You are provided with the tooling available in the dashboard, allowing you to do a switchover or failover operations depending on your needs. Once the cloud instances are provisioned, you can look at the Access Rules tab and enable or disable the rules for various kinds of tools/network requirements. These kinds of changes are required for allowing tools such as Enterprise Manager, SQL Developer, or any third-party tools you need to connect to a database instance. See Figure 9-40 for the configuration options.

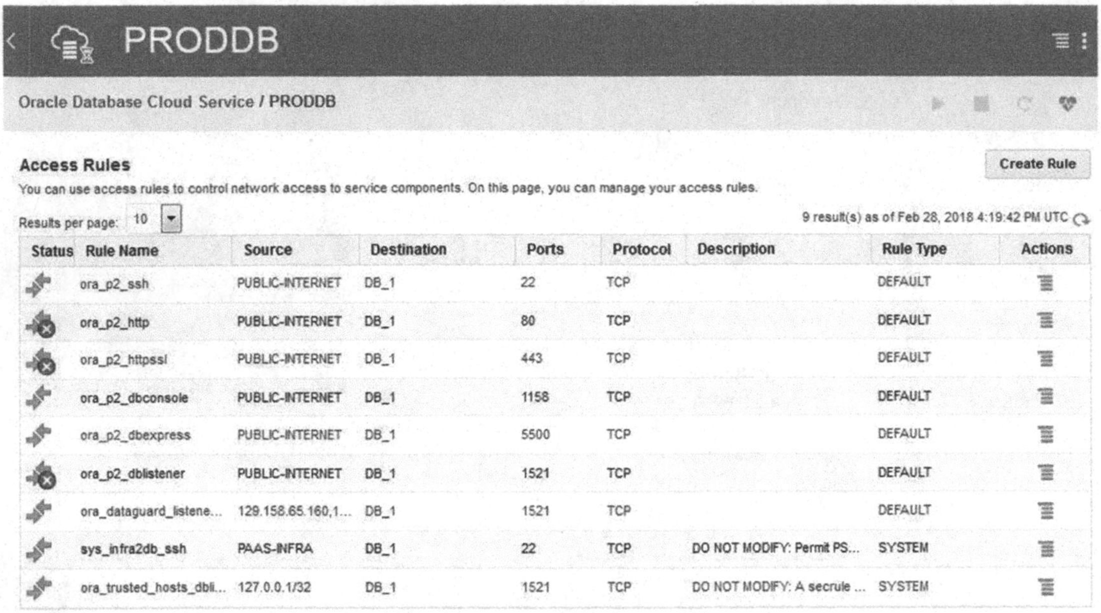

Figure 9-40. *The Access Rules page for the database cloud service instance*

On this Access Rules page, you can copy any of the rules and modify the newly created rule as per your requirements. In Figure 9-40, it shows port 22 is open with TCP as it is required for you to access the instance through the SSH client. Ports 1158, 5500, 1521, and so on, are for cloud tools and could be associated with the DBaaS console, Application Express, Enterprise Manager Console, and database listener ports depending on the configuration you perform.

You can explore additional options available on the Oracle public cloud databases by navigating through the dashboard. On the Resources tab, you can see options to control the service instances such as Start, Stop, Restart, Scale and Up/Down. You can also see Data Guard options such as Switch Over, Failover, Reinstiantiate, and so on. See Figure 9-41 for the options.

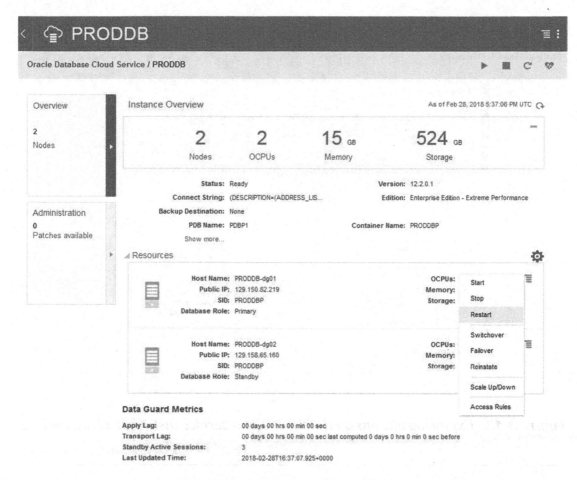

Figure 9-41. *Exploring options via database cloud service instance dashboard*

For using additional tooling such as the DbaaS Monitor, EM Console, and Application Express, console access is provided, and access rules and ports are enabled as discussed before. On the dashboard under the Administration menu, you can explore Backup, Snapshots, and Patch Scheduling options under this Oracle Database Cloud Service/<Your Database Instance Name> See Figure 9-42 for details.

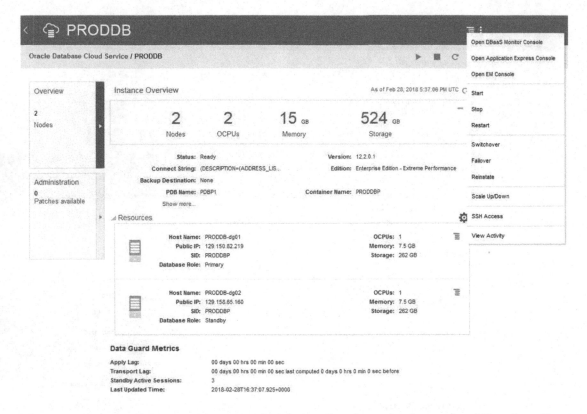

Figure 9-42. Exploring options on database cloud service instances, cloud tooling

---

Note   You can use the API `dbaascli` to manage Data Guard operations as well.

Now you have seen how you can provision a database instance along with Data Guard configuration. The Oracle cloud also provides you with a Real Application Clusters instance with its Extreme Performance bundle, as discussed earlier. As a user, you need to select it during your cloud service creation. See Figure 9-43.

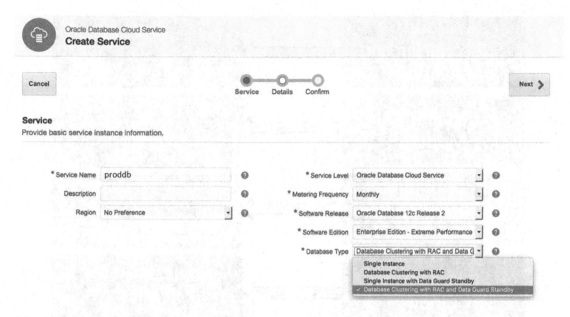

Figure 9-43. *Provisioning Real Application Clusters database through the cloud service console*

You can select Extreme Performance for any combination of RAC you want to deploy on OCI-C or OCI.

Moving an On-Premise Database to the Oracle Database Cloud Service

There are multiple ways to move databases to the Oracle Database Cloud Service whether on OCI-C or OCI. It also depends on factors such as the database version, platform, availability, or downtime requirements as well the use case you are looking at. You will look at an easy way using the backup cloud service to move to the DBCS platform.

Databases can be instantiated in the cloud using a preexisting cloud backup. The backup cloud can be used for on-premises databases or any other cloud databases such as DBCS/ExaCS/ExaCC. Once backups are available, you can restore from the backup on the Oracle cloud. During the instantiation, DBCS chooses the last backup, and by selecting it, you can create an Oracle cloud instance. See Figure 9-44 to understand the steps involved in setting up a backup cloud service.

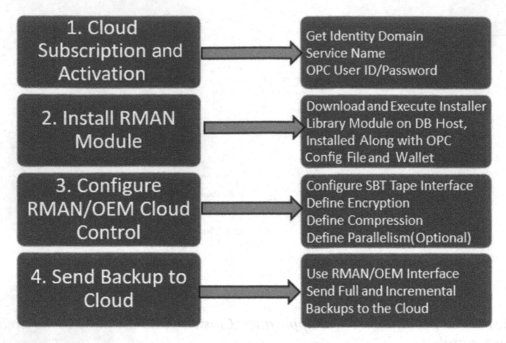

Figure 9-44. *Backup cloud service configuration flow*

You can take advantage of the Oracle backup cloud service for instantiating the database in the cloud. For each of on-premise databases you want to migrate to the cloud, you can configure the Oracle cloud as the backup destination and plan to restore from there. You can either use API or use Enterprise Manager Cloud Control, which has support for configuring a backup to the Oracle public cloud. For getting started with the backup cloud service, you need to follow these steps:

1. Sign up for either a Oracle Public Cloud Trial (30 days/$300; Oracle Database Backup Cloud Service) or Paid version (Oracle Database Backup/Public Cloud Service).

Note   Trial and paid subscriptions to the Oracle Database Backup Cloud Service appear as the Oracle Storage Cloud service.

---

2. Activate, verify the service activation, and select Datacenter and Replication Policy. Optionally create user accounts and assign them the roles of Storage Administrator and Database Backup Administrator.

To get started with the backup cloud service, follow these steps:

1. Create an Oracle OTN user if you don't have one for login to download the backup module from the Oracle web site.

```
http://www.oracle.com/technetwork/database/availability/oracle-cloud-
backup-2162729.html
```

2. Install the backup module.

```
~]$ unzip opc_installer.zip
~]$ mkdir -p OPC/wallet OPC/lib
~]$ java -jar opc_install.jar -serviceName <cloud service> -identityDomain
<domain ID> -opcId <cloudUser> -opcPass '<pwd>' -walletDir /home/oracle/
OPC/wallet -libDir /home/oracle/OPC/lib
where
serviceName => Oracle Database Backup Cloud Service name. Default is
Storage (case-sensitive)
identityDoman => domain ID of the Backup Cloud Service
opcID       => Backup cloud service user id
opcPass  =>  Backup cloud service user password
walletDir => directory to store the backup cloud service credential (eg. ~/
OPC/wallet
libDir  => directory to store the backup cloud service library (libopc.so
in Unix and oraopc.dll in Windows)
                eg. ~/OPC/lib
Post installation, the backup module creates a configuration file by name
opcSID.ora under $ORACLE_HOME/dbs directory. It contains backup cloud
service container url and wallet location. SID is the oracle instance name.
Note: opcSID.ora must be defined for each instance that you want to backup
to oracle database backup cloud service
```

3. Configure the SBT channels to the Oracle database backup cloud service and optionally configure parallelism.

```
CONFIGURE CHANNEL DEVICE TYPE sbt PARMS 'SBT_LIBRARY=${OPCLIB}/libopc.so,
SBT_PARMS=(OPC_PFILE=${ORACLE_HOME}/dbs/opc${ORACLE_SID}.ora)';
where OPCLIB is the path to OPC library
```

```
Set the encryption Key for backup
        SET ENCRYPTION ON IDENTIFIED BY 'oracle123' only;
Configure Compression algorithm
        CONFIGURE COMPRESSION ALGORITHM 'MEDIUM';
Configure Parallelism
 CONFIGURE DEVICE TYPE 'SBT_TAPE' PARALLELISM 4 BACKUP TYPE TO BACKUPSET;
```

   4. Perform RMAN backups.

```
RMAN> SET ENCRYPTION ON IDENTIFIED BY 'abc123' ONLY;
RMAN> BACKUP DEVICE TYPE SBT AS COMPRESSED BACKUPSET DATABASE PLUS
ARCHIVELOG FORMAT '%d_%U';
You can use usual RMAN commands to manage the backup taken to backup cloud.
```

Now you are ready to instantiate the databases using the backup available on the cloud. The backup available on the Oracle public cloud can be utilized for creating database instances for test/dev, for disaster recovery for migration from on-premise to the Oracle cloud, and so on.

Summary

In this chapter, you got an overview of the cloud as well as the Oracle Cloud Infrastructure, which is important for understanding your options for database-related deployments. A few examples were shown from the Oracle public cloud classic interface. We focused on understanding different components of the Oracle Cloud Infrastructure and the deployment options. The Oracle public cloud service is continuously evolving, and new services and features are getting added with each release. For complete details, you can refer to cloud.oracle.com or the Oracle documentation.

CHAPTER 10

Exadata Cloud Provisioning

This chapter will focus on deploying Exadata Cloud Service (ExaCS). At the end of this chapter, you will learn how to activate an instance of ExaCS. You will start with understanding the necessary components such as networking, backups, and subnets, and so on, to make the deployment steps easier.

Oracle Exadata Engineered Systems have been around for years and are known as proven platforms for running critical database workloads and as great Oracle Database consolidation platforms. Several organizations are taking advantage of the engineering done in the hardware supporting Exadata as well the software that powers the platform. Exadata Cloud Service enables an enterprise to run and operate from the same engineered system platform as the Oracle public cloud. The advantage is that it comes with all the Oracle Database options (advanced security options, Database Vault, Database In-Memory, multitenancy, Real Application Clusters, and advanced compression, to name a few) as well all the Enterprise Manager pack options (Diagnostic Pack, Tuning Pack, Real Application Testing Pack, Cloud Management Pack, Database Lifecycle Management Pack, Data Masking & Subsetting Management Pack) by default.

Oracle Exadata Cloud Service delivers all the advanced features of Exadata including smart scan, storage indexes, query offloading, hybrid columnar compression, and so on, in the Oracle public cloud. At the same time, it provides flexibility through subscription models where customers can use CPU bursting to scale the workload as and when needed through increasing OCPUs (Oracle CPUs).

As part of this cloud service, Oracle provides an easy deployment method; maintains datacenter networking, storage, firmware, and Exadata storage software; and shares several responsibilities with the end user. Typically speaking, DBAs and organizations spend a significant time on these tasks.

© Y V Ravi Kumar, Nassyam Basha, Krishna Kumar K M, Bal Mukund Sharma, Konstantin Kerekovski 2019
Y V Ravi Kumar et al., *Oracle High Availability, Disaster Recovery, and Cloud Services*,
https://doi.org/10.1007/978-1-4842-4351-0_10

Another thing to note here is that Exadata Cloud Service is a dedicated service for customers with no over-provisioning of hardware, which means a predictable response time and throughput for running critical workloads and for scaling on demand. With the cloud model now, Exadata can be experienced by customers who have not explored the capabilities of the machine for their workloads because of the cost. Customers can set up a hybrid cloud environment with their existing Exadata to the Oracle public cloud without worrying about capex.

Note   The Oracle Exadata Cloud Service is available in two distinct models: in the Oracle public cloud commonly known as ExaCS and as an Exadata cloud at customer. We will discuss ExaCS in more detail in the chapter. ExaCC is an Oracle public cloud offering that is delivered securely on-premise in your datacenter behind your firewall. With Oracle Exadata cloud at customer, you can combine Oracle's powerful database platform with the simplicity, agility, and elasticity of cloud deployment. Oracle Exadata can be consumed through a flexible subscription model and managed in your datacenter by a team of Oracle Cloud experts. The ExaCC offering takes precedence if data residency is a primary concern for customers.

Exadata Cloud Service on Oracle Cloud Infrastructure

Oracle Exadata uses a virtual cloud network (VCN) and private subnets from network service components provided on Oracle Cloud Infrastructure. An Internet gateway is used for routing between VCN and the Internet. The Dynamic Routing Gateway provides private routing between VCN and the on-premise network in case you want to establish a dedicated network link through the Oracle Fast Connect option for backup purpose to factor in the object storage cloud service, which is an offering on Oracle Cloud Infrastructure as a service.

The Identity and Access Management service is a key foundation to the ExaCS in the Oracle cloud environment. It provides strong authentication and authorization access to all resources needed in the OCI environment. You require credentials to access the OCI cloud console. An API signing key is needed for access to manage resources; in addition, sending an API request requires keys in the PEM format. Access to the operating system within ExaCS is through SSH keys.

Tenancy is the equivalent of an account that contains all of your OCI resources, provisioned with a single, top-level in OCI console access hierarchy called the *root compartment*. Please refer to Chapter 9 for a better understanding of these concepts.

When tenancy is created, the default root compartment can contain all the resources created by users such as VCN resources, block storage, routing resources, and so on, as well as ExaCS resources as part of the deployment.

We have discussed tenancy, compartments, IAM policies, VCN, and so on, in the previous chapter. Please refer to Chapter 9 for a better understanding of the terms used here.

Exadata Cloud Service: Provisioning

Let's start with ExaCS provisioning. Follow these steps to get started:

1. Log in to your cloud console by providing your tenancy ID, username, and password. Click Continue after providing the tenant ID on the login screen. See Figure 10-1 for reference. You need to provide the cloud tenant ID to get started. The URL for signing in is provided in your cloud subscription e-mail.

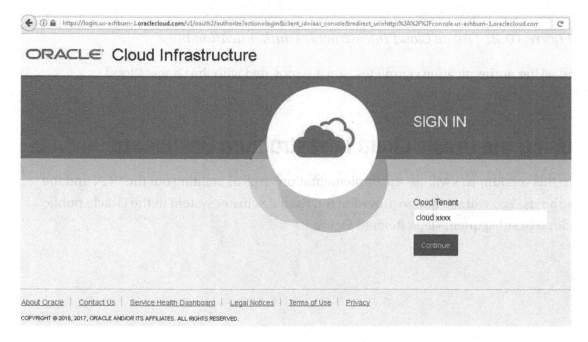

Figure 10-1. *Oracle Cloud Infrastructure login page*

2. After you provide your tenancy ID, click the Continue button and
    provide the username and password to authenticate yourself
    to the Oracle public cloud. Refer to Figure 10-2. After you do
    this, click the Sign In button to get on the Oracle public cloud
    dashboard.

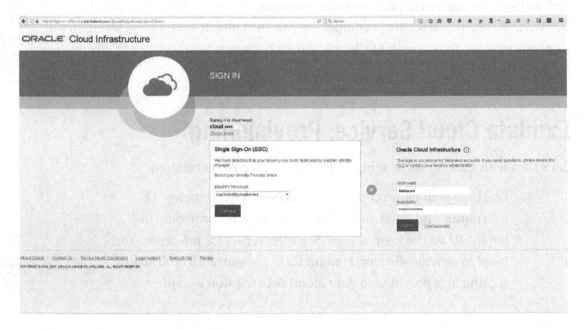

Figure 10-2. *Oracle Cloud Infrastructure authentication page*

After authentication completes, you are provided with the Oracle Cloud
Infrastructure dashboard.

Using the Oracle Cloud Infrastructure Dashboard

In this section, you will see the implementation steps of building out the VCN and the
subnets. You will see how to provision the Exadata cluster system in the Oracle public
cloud in subsequent steps. Refer to Figure 10-3.

Figure 10-3. Oracle Cloud Infrastructure dashboard

1. You need to provision the virtual cloud network (VCN), which
    will be used later for ExaCS. This is the most important step on
    Oracle Cloud Infrastructure, so click the Networking tab and select
    VCN. This will take you to your VCN console. See Figure 10-4.

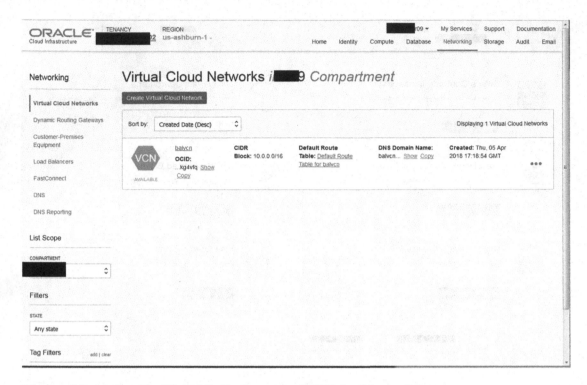

Figure 10-4. *Oracle Cloud Infrastructure VCN dashboard*

2. You'll now create that virtual cloud network. Click the Create
    Virtual Cloud Network button and fill in some information to get
    started. First give this VCN a name. You do not want any extra
    public subnets, so you will need to create subnets explicitly. Refer
    to Figure 10-5 to see how it is done.

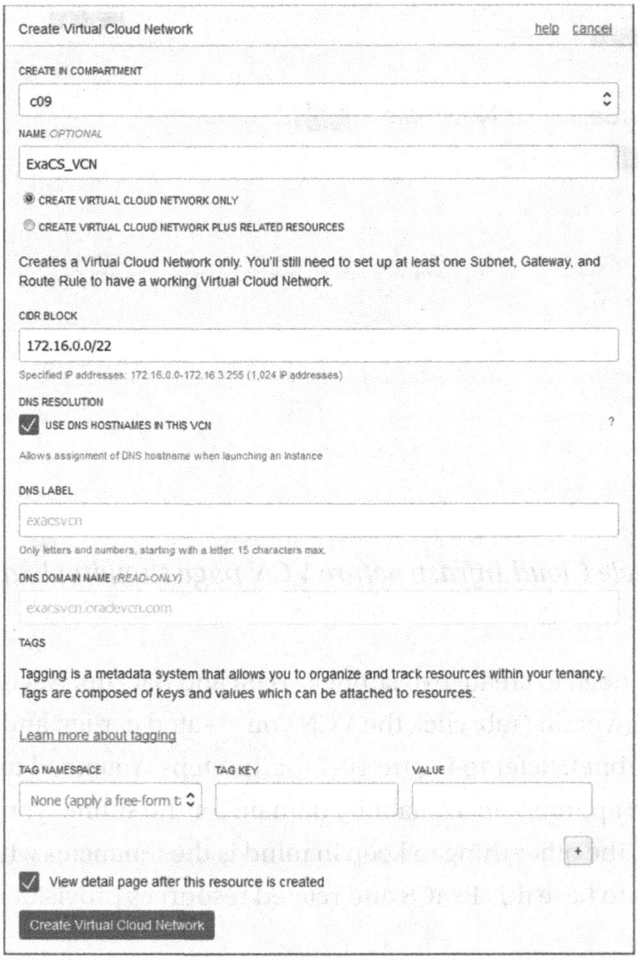

Figure 10-5. *Oracle Cloud Infrastructure VCN creation page*

3. In the pop-up, give the VCN a name. In our case, the name is
    ExaCS_VCN. Assign a CIDR. In this case, use the 172.16/22 IP space
    for the CIDR range. The CIDR range must fall between 10.0.0.0/8,
    172.16.0.0/12, and 192.168.0.0/16, as defined by RFC 1918. As shown
    in Figure 10-5, with this notation, the CIDR range provides range of
    IP's reserved for VNC up to 1,024 IP address within the VCN so that
    you can use them for additional subnets. Leave the DNS Resolution
    checkbox selected. The purpose of DNS resolution is to allow the
    VCN resolver with DNS resolution inside the VCN you are creating
    and later with hostname resolution within VCN. With all the above
    steps been completed, creation of a new VCN is ready for the
    Exadata Cloud Service provisioning. See Figure 10-6.

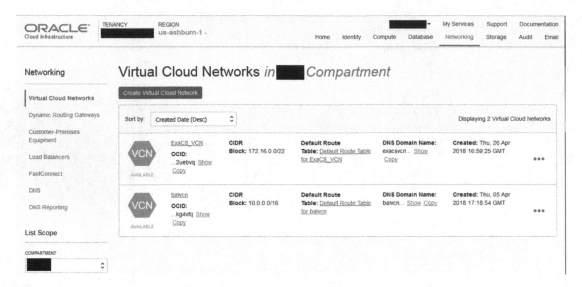

Figure 10-6. *Oracle Cloud Infrastructure VCN page showing ExaCS_VCN created earlier*

4. Now you need to create two subnets: data and backup. Navigate
    to the Networking tab, click the VCN you created earlier, and click
    Create Subnet. Refer to Figure 10-7 for the steps. You need to
    select the appropriate availability domain for the subnet you are
    creating. The other thing to keep in mind is the tenancies where
    you want to have this ExaCS and related resources provisioned.

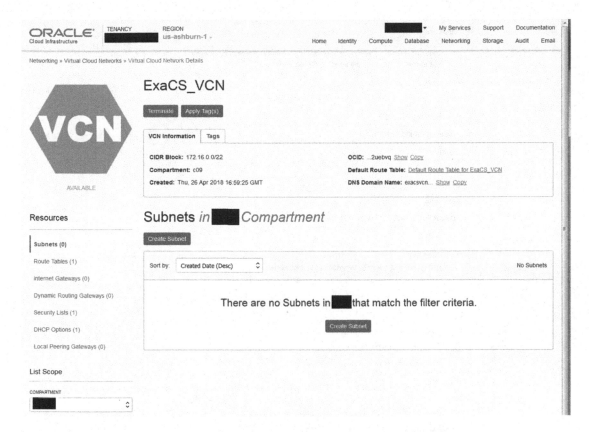

***Figure 10-7.** Oracle Cloud Infrastructure VCN page showing VCN with subnet creation page*

5. Once the Subnet Creation page appears, provide the name of the subnet: data. This will be used for the client network within the ExaCS deployment. Select an appropriate availability domain. CIDR blocks should be created as a subset of the VCN created earlier. In this case, let's go with 172.16.1.0/24. This will provide 256 address subnets in the VCN range 172.16.0.0/22. Choose the default route table that was created as part of your VCN. You can select Default DHCP Options, and if you created a custom DHCP option earlier, you can use it if needed. Once you click Create with these inputs, your data subnet is ready to be used for the client network. Refer to Figure 10-8 for details.

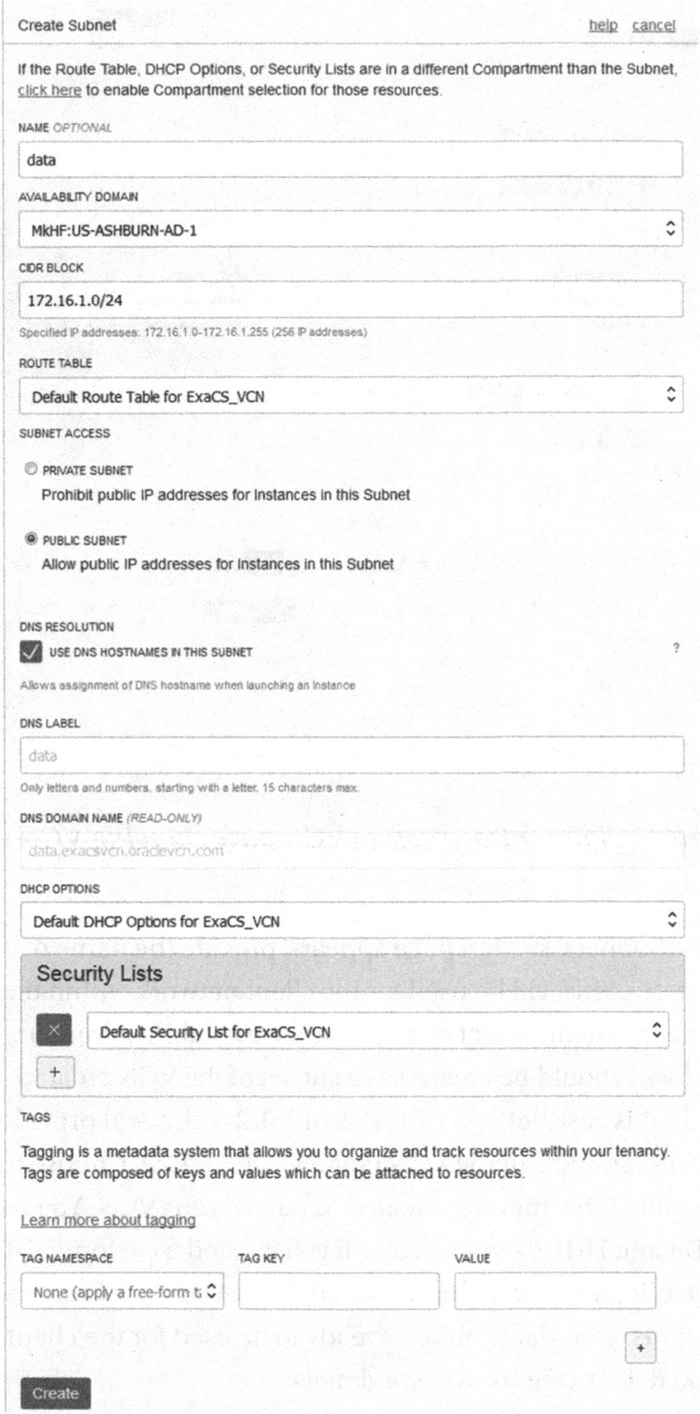

Figure 10-8. *Oracle Cloud Infrastructure subnet page showing public subnet creation*

Note   You should not use a subnet that overlaps with 192.168.16.16/28 for both the client subnet and the backup subnet since it is used by the Oracle Clusterware private interconnect on the database instance. Specifying an overlapping subnet will cause the private interconnect to not function as expected. See Figure 10-9.

Figure 10-9. *Oracle Cloud Infrastructure VCN page showing data subnet*

6. Follow the same process to create the backup subnet, but instead of 172.16.1, use 172.16.2.0/24 for your CIDR block. Also, make sure to use the same availability domain where you created the data subnet. See Figure 10-10.

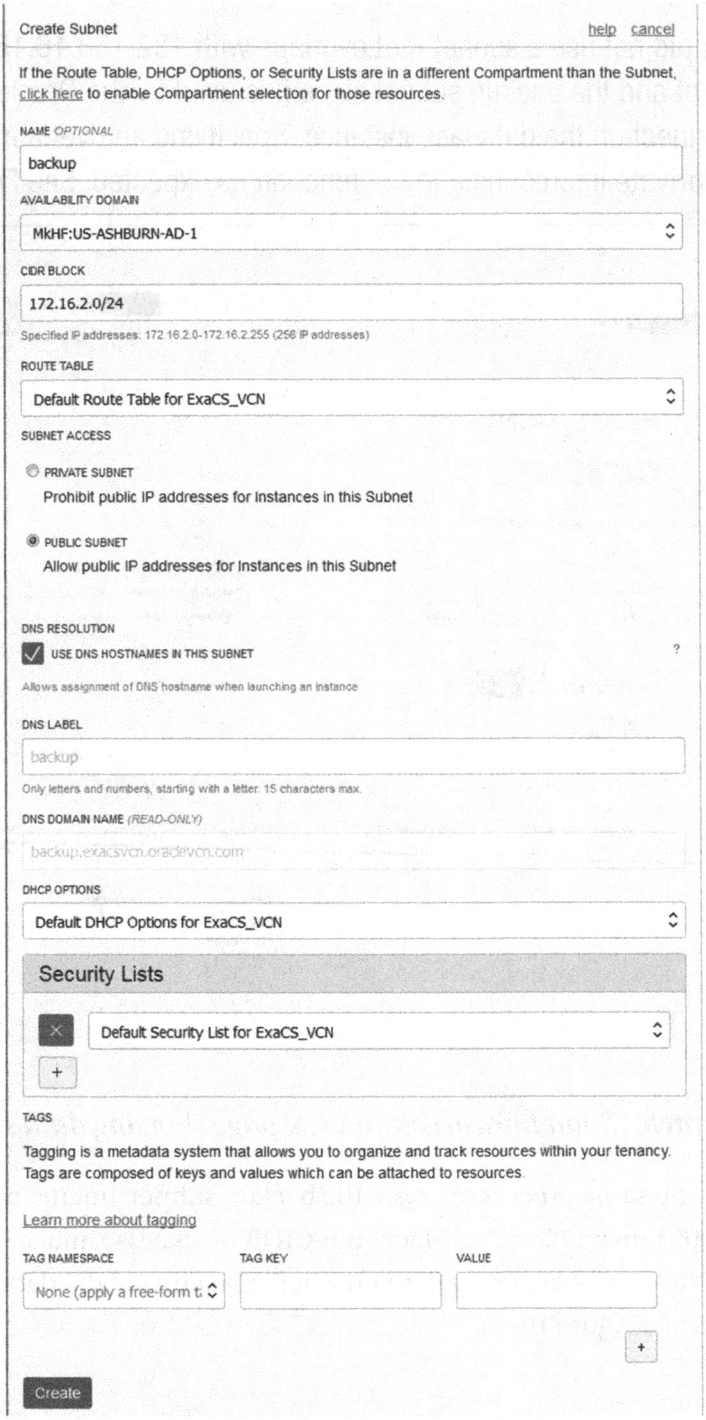

Figure 10-10. *Oracle Cloud Infrastructure VCN page showing backup subnet creation*

Now you have two subnets. Figure 10-11 shows both subnets—one for data and one for your backup—so it's time to move forward with the next steps.

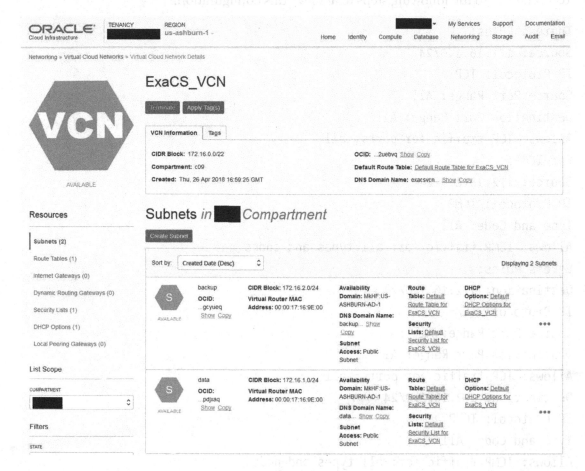

Figure 10-11. *Oracle Cloud Infrastructure VCN page showing data and backup subnets*

You need to additionally configure the security list ingress and egress rules for the subnets. The client subnet (data) must allow TCP and ICMP traffic between all nodes and all ports in the respective subnet across the ExaCS configuration. If the TCP connectivity fails across the nodes, the Exadata database system fails to provision.

For example, in our case, the client subnet is using the source CIDR 172.16.1.0/24 (10.0.5.0/24). Create the rules as shown in the following example.

Recommended Configuration for Security Rules

You can refer to the following steps to achieve this configuration:

```
Ingress Rules:
Source: 172.16.1.0/24
IP Protocol: TCP
Source Port Range: All
Destination Port Range: All
Allows: TCP traffic for ports: all
For ICMP:
Source: 172.16.1.0/24
IP Protocol: ICMP
Type and Code: All
Allows: ICMP traffic for: all types and codes
Egress Rules:
Destination: 172.16.1.0/24
IP Protocol: TCP
Source Port Range: All
Destination Port Range: All
Allows: TCP traffic for ports: all
Destination: 172.16.1.0/24
IP Protocol: ICMP
Type and Code: All
Allows: ICMP traffic for: all types and nodes
```

If you don't do these steps and later you click to create the configuration, you would get this error:

> *"InvalidParameter - Request is rejected as ingress TCP ports are not open. Make sure the security list ingress and egress rules for client subnet is configured to allow TCP and ICMP traffic between all nodes and all ports in the respective subnet. The Exadata DB System will fail to provision if TCP connectivity fails across nodes."*

Navigate to Network ➤ Virtual Cloud Network ➤ Subnet. Click Default Security List for ExaCS_VCN under the data subnet. Refer to Figure 10-12 for details.

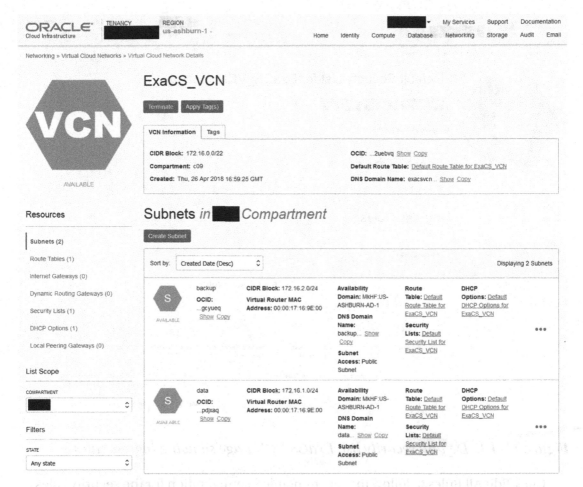

Figure 10-12. *ExaCS VCN page showing the security list to be edited*

Click the highlighted section Default Security List for ExaCS_VCN to navigate to the default security list page. See Figure 10-13.

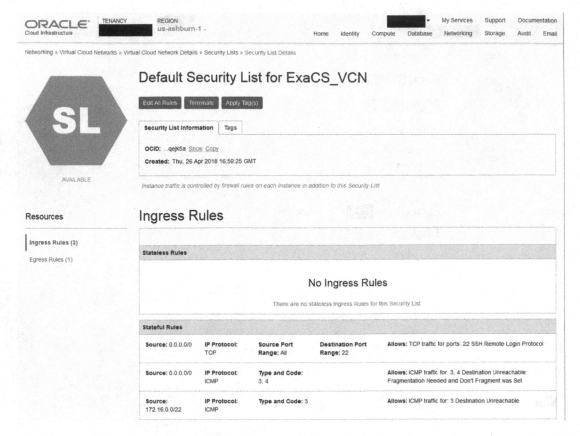

Figure 10-13. *Default security list, ExaCS VCN page showing ingress rules*

Click Edit All Rules to follow the recommended configuration for the security rules discussed earlier. The initial page looks like the one in Figure 10-14.

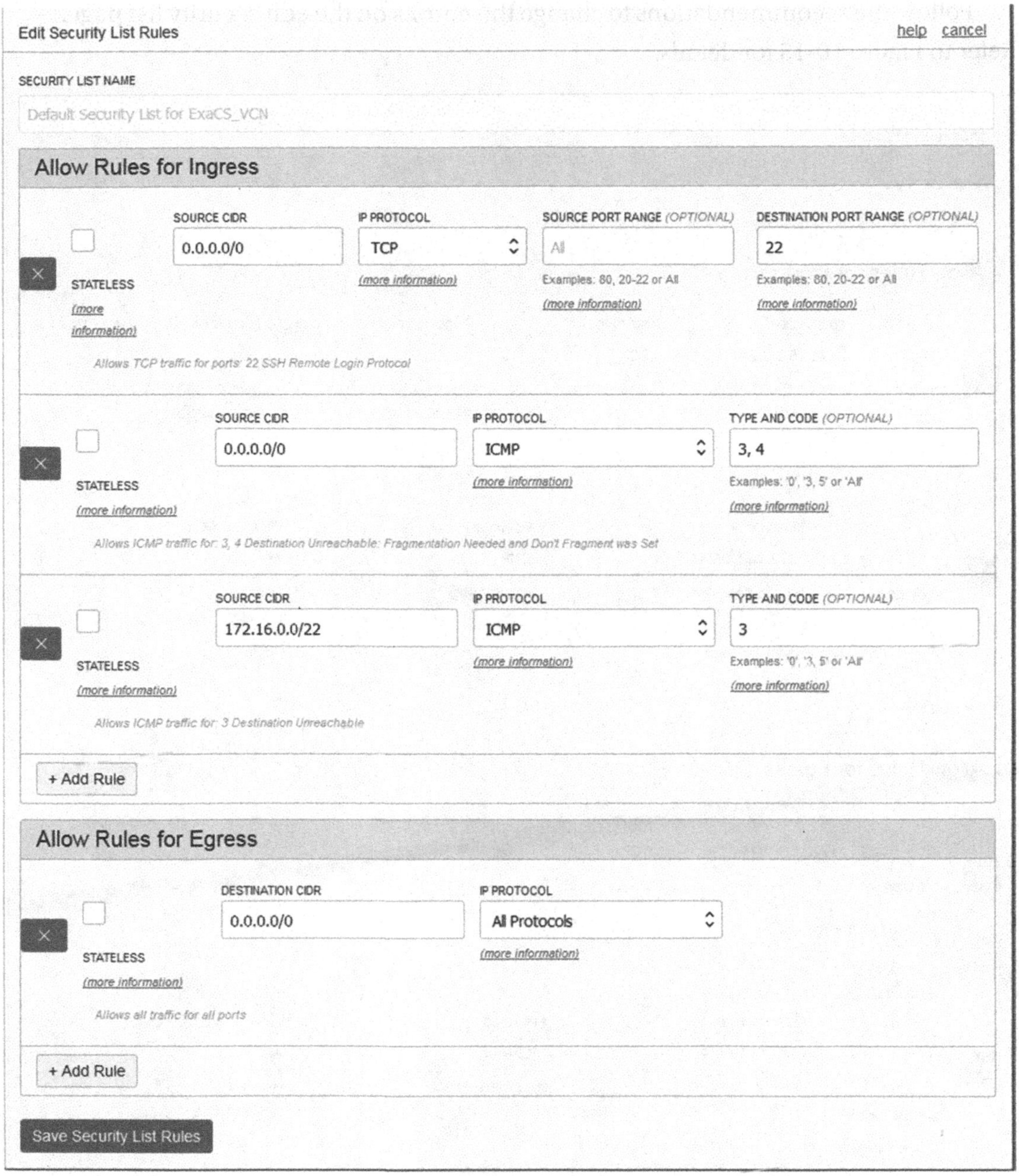

Figure 10-14.   Edit security list, ExaCS VCN page showing default rules

Follow the recommendations to change the entries on the edit security list page. Refer to Figure 10-15 for details.

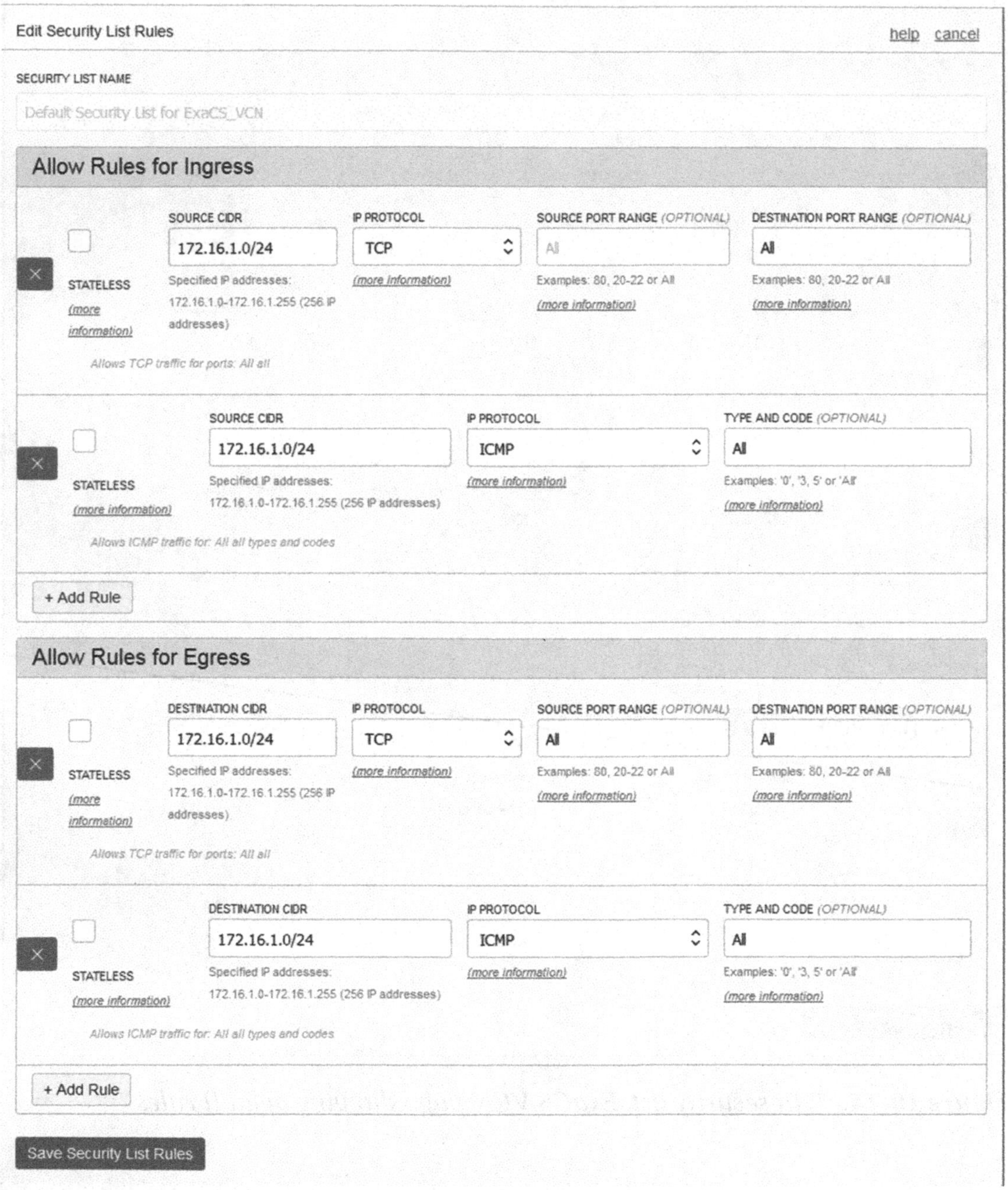

Figure 10-15. *Edit security list page, ExaCS_VCN ingress and egress rules*

Once you save the security list rules, the security list ingress and egress rules for the client subnet will be configured to allow TCP and ICMP traffic between all nodes and all ports in the respective subnet, which is a prerequisite for configuration. Figure 10-16 shows the changes just implemented.

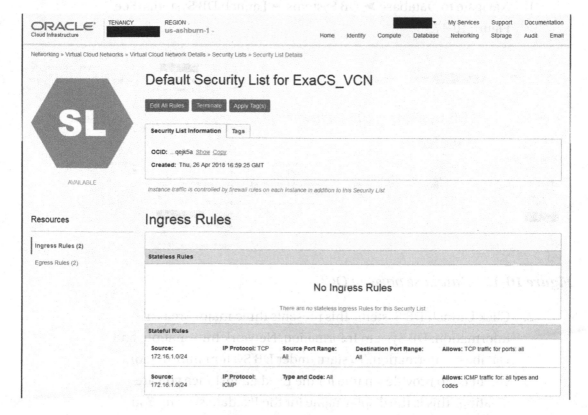

Figure 10-16. Default security list page, ExaCS_VCN showing stateful rules

This completes the requirements for provisioning the ExaCS instance.

Creating the Exadata Database System

Now you can proceed to create the Exadata database system and database instances on Oracle Cloud Infrastructure.

1. Navigate to Database ➤ DB Systems ➤ Launch DB Systems. See Figure 10-17.

Figure 10-17. *Database page on OCI*

2. Click Launch DB System. This presents three major areas of information: DB System Information, Network Information, and Database Information. To start, under DB System Information, you need to provide a name for the Exadata Instance you are creating. This is the display name for the Exadata system. You need to select the availability domain where you created the two subnets earlier.

3. Next, pick the Exadata shape. Depending on your subscription, you can select Quarter/Half or Full. For this example, we will go ahead and select Quarter, which starts with 22 OCPUs with the ability to scale all the way up to 84 total OCPUs. Notice that when you select a specific shape, by default the minimum CPU count will be selected for the configuration. Let's give this cluster a name—something unique that will provide an identification to the environment. With 22 OCPUs, you can scale up later, or you can add more now and scale up to 84 in a Quarter configuration later. You can specify the name of the RAC cluster here under Cluster Name.

4. Select you license type, which can be license included (LiPaaS) or bring your own license (BYOL).

5. Attach an SSH key. This key is for connecting the ExaCS instance remotely via SSH to the underlying database host. This allows you to further configure or further customize your Exadata implementation as needed.

6. Within Advanced Options in this section, you can decide how your data storage percentage will be created and how ASM is configured. You have a choice of either 40 percent or 80 percent; 40 percent is going to isolate that much storage for data, leaving the other 60 percent for recovery purposes such as FRA, redo logs, backups, and so on. If you select the 80 percent option, only 20 percent of the data is reserved for recovery options. This lends itself to more of an off-instance backup strategy like Oracle Cloud Backup, which utilizes object storage for backup store on OCI. The advantage is that you get twice as much usable storage from a database perspective.

In terms of disk redundancy, Exadata Cloud Service sets it to high with three mirrored copies. Few shapes provide an option between choosing two-way or three-way mirroring. Depending on the setting, you will end up having one or two disks in a failure group. As a suggested approach, three-way mirroring is best for data protection. Refer to Figure 10-18 to see the options just discussed.

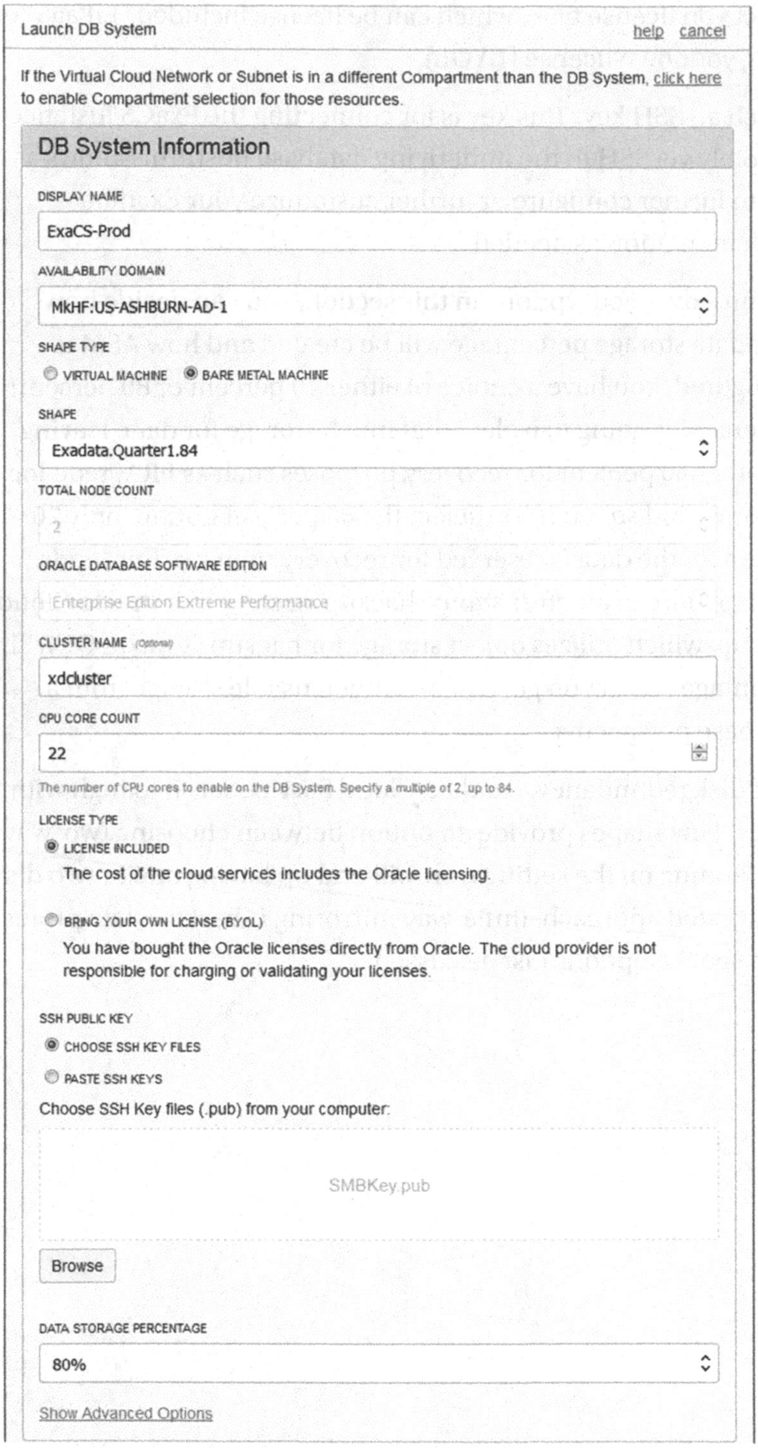

Launch DB System   help   cancel

If the Virtual Cloud Network or Subnet is in a different Compartment than the DB System, click here
to enable Compartment selection for those resources.

DB System Information

DISPLAY NAME

ExaCS-Prod

AVAILABILITY DOMAIN

MkHF:US-ASHBURN-AD-1

SHAPE TYPE

○ VIRTUAL MACHINE   ● BARE METAL MACHINE

SHAPE

Exadata.Quarter1.84

TOTAL NODE COUNT

2

ORACLE DATABASE SOFTWARE EDITION

Enterprise Edition Extreme Performance

CLUSTER NAME *(Optional)*

xdcluster

CPU CORE COUNT

22

The number of CPU cores to enable on the DB System. Specify a multiple of 2, up to 84.

LICENSE TYPE

● LICENSE INCLUDED
    The cost of the cloud services includes the Oracle licensing.

○ BRING YOUR OWN LICENSE (BYOL)
    You have bought the Oracle licenses directly from Oracle. The cloud provider is not
    responsible for charging or validating your licenses.

SSH PUBLIC KEY

● CHOOSE SSH KEY FILES

○ PASTE SSH KEYS

Choose SSH Key files (.pub) from your computer:

SMBKey.pub

Browse

DATA STORAGE PERCENTAGE

80%

Show Advanced Options

Figure 10-18.   Launch database instance creation page on OCI

7. Next comes the Network Information section. Choose the virtual
    network that you created earlier. You need to pick the data subnet
    for the client subnet and the backup subnet for the corresponding
    backup subnet in this section. Specify a hostname prefix, and
    all the nodes in the cluster will be prefixed with this prefix. Note
    that this hostname gets entered into DNS within the VCN DNS
    resolver, which we discussed previously. It allows you to connect
    to your ExaCS instance using that hostname within your VCN. See
    Figure 10-19.

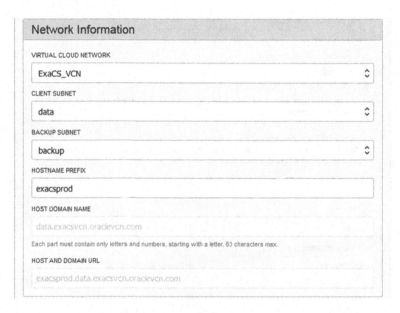

Figure 10-19. *Launch database instance creation page on OCI, Network
Information section*

8. Fill in the Database section, including the database name, version,
    whether you're using a pluggable database, the database admin
    password, and the automated backup selection. Additional
    options under the Advanced Options allow you to choose the
    character set if you need to change that. Finally, click the button
    Launch Database System to get the ExaCS instance created along
    with the database. See Figure 10-20.

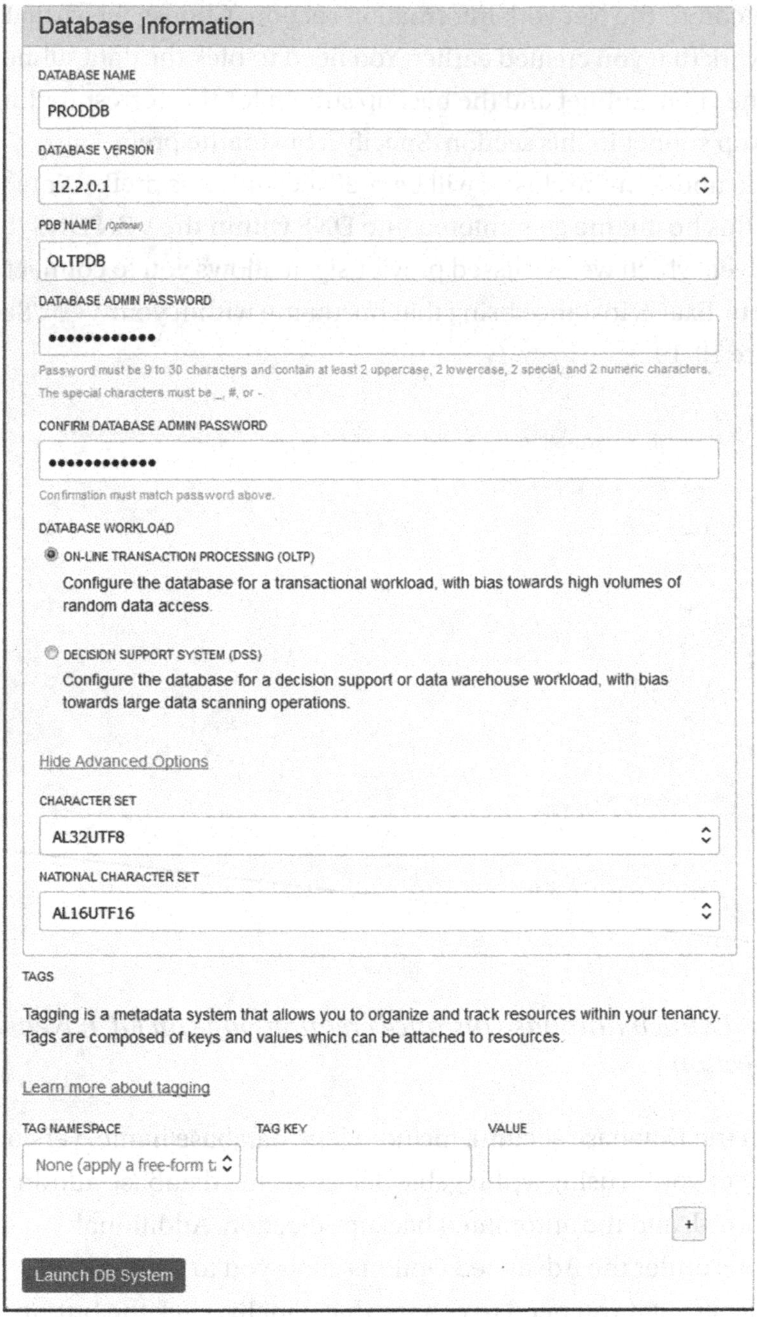

Figure 10-20. Database Information section

It will take a little while to provision this instance. You'll see a yellow icon, and when it turns from yellow to green, it is available and ready for use. See Figure 10-21.

Figure 10-21. *A successful provision*

Congratulations, you have provisioned ExaCS in the Oracle public cloud.

Summary

In this chapter, you learned how to configure required networking elements such as a VCN, different subnets, security rules, database shape, options, and so on, along with factors affecting instance provisioning. You might notice that it is much easier to create a database system without worrying about the complexity of networking, data center constructs, and so on. Once an ExaCS instance is created along with your database, you can further create other databases as per you needs. You can utilize Enterprise Manager Cloud Control or SQL Developer tools to connect to the provisioned instances for manageability.

CHAPTER 11

Migrating Databases to Exadata Cloud Service Using DIPC

In previous chapters, you saw how to provision databases on Oracle Cloud Infrastructure. In this chapter, we will discuss on how you can move, or *migrate*, to a database service on DBCS or ExaCS. We will refer to your target database on the cloud as the *DBCS instance* because the process for data replication remains the same. This chapter contains a high-level representation of how you can migrate your data to DBCS. Replication works between the on-premise and DBCS databases using the Data Integration Platform Cloud Service (DIPC).

This chapter provides the steps involved to set up the real-time data capture and real-time data replication capabilities of Oracle GoldenGate present in DIPC from the on-premise database to the cloud database.

Oracle GoldenGate is deployed on the same host server as the on-premise database to capture (integrated) changes locally and pump the changes to the remote DIPC VM. DIPC is deployed on a separate VM than the DBCS database VM and performs remote integrated delivery to the DBCS database.

This chapter covers how to create DIPC services and configure the environment for unidirectional replication from the on-premise Oracle database to the DBCS database. See Figure 11-1.

© Y V Ravi Kumar, Nassyam Basha, Krishna Kumar K M, Bal Mukund Sharma, Konstantin Kerekovski 2019
Y V Ravi Kumar et al., *Oracle High Availability, Disaster Recovery, and Cloud Services*,
https://doi.org/10.1007/978-1-4842-4351-0_11

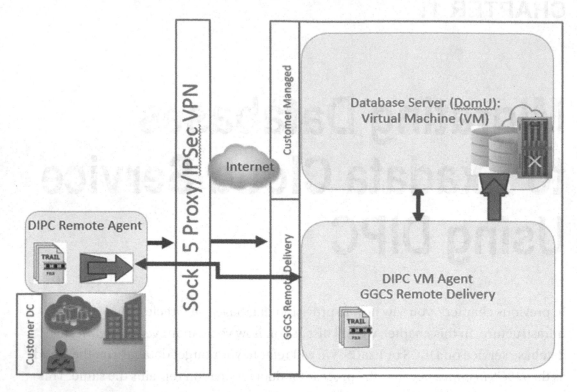

Figure 11-1. *Data integration platform with Oracle Cloud Infrastructure Database*

DIPC Enterprise Edition provides you with the capability to replicate your current DMLs happening on your on-premises database to databases on DBCS or ExaCS. This is achieved by deploying and running DIPC agents inside the DIPC VM. DIPC also gives you the option to deploy DIPC agents in your on-premises environment for golden gate capture process (recommended) and ship trail files to the DIPC VM. The agents running in each environment configure Oracle GoldenGate instances that are responsible for capture, pump, and replication. Trail files ship from the on-premises VM to the DIPC VM over the SOCKS5 proxy, providing security in the transfer process over the network.

DIPC also provides the capability to do an initial data synchronization. Hence, the initial data synchronization is always carried out by initial data loading techniques as per MOS Note 1311707.1. The oracle database utility data pump can be used to export data a huge volume of Oracle data. You can limit the scope to GGCS replication only for specific use cases for uni direction replication during data migrations.

As part of the environment, you will be using a VM that is configured with the DB12.2 database. The DIPC agent configuration steps are covered later in this same chapter.

The following sections contain the steps to perform the required configuration and capture the results.

Creating a DBCS Service

Before provisioning a DIPC instance, you need to create a DBCS instance that you can provide as an input during the DIPC service provisioning. The provisioning steps of DBCS uses database classic option for the DIPC deployment.

Note   You must choose cloud and local storage while provisioning the DBCS instance; otherwise, this service will not be listed for selection while provisioning the DIPC service.

To provision the database, log in to Oracle Cloud Infrastructure, as shown in Figure 11-2. You need to provide the user credentials; just make sure you have the identity domain correctly displayed, as shown in the figure.

Figure 11-2. *Login screen for Oracle Cloud Infrastructure environment*

After logging in to the OCI dashboard, you need to navigate to the database creation page. Make sure you select Database Classic from the menu in the dashboard to create this database. See Figure 11-3, which shows the database creation page.

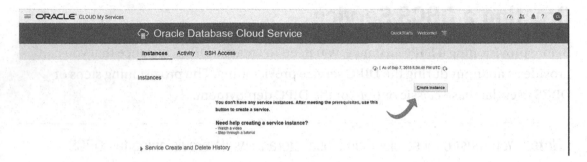

Figure 11-3. *Database creation page on OPC classic interface*

The screen is self-explanatory; click "Create services" for a new database instance, as shown in Figure 11-4. You can provide an instance name, which will appear as the service name; we have used the name DBCS-DIPC. Also, you need to select a few more details such as the database version, edition, and so on, as shown in Figure 11-4.

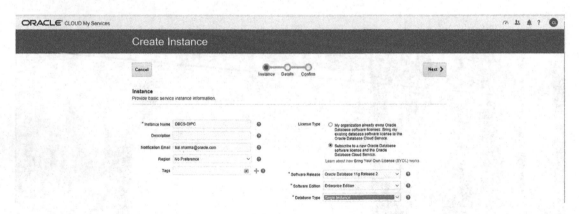

Figure 11-4. *Database creation page, instance details*

After providing these details, proceed to the next page by clicking Next. On this new page, you need to provide the storage container details, which will be used for database backups, and so on. You will create a storage container, as shown in Figure 11-5, before proceeding to use it in the next window. You can navigate to the storage from the cloud dashboard and create a container to be used.

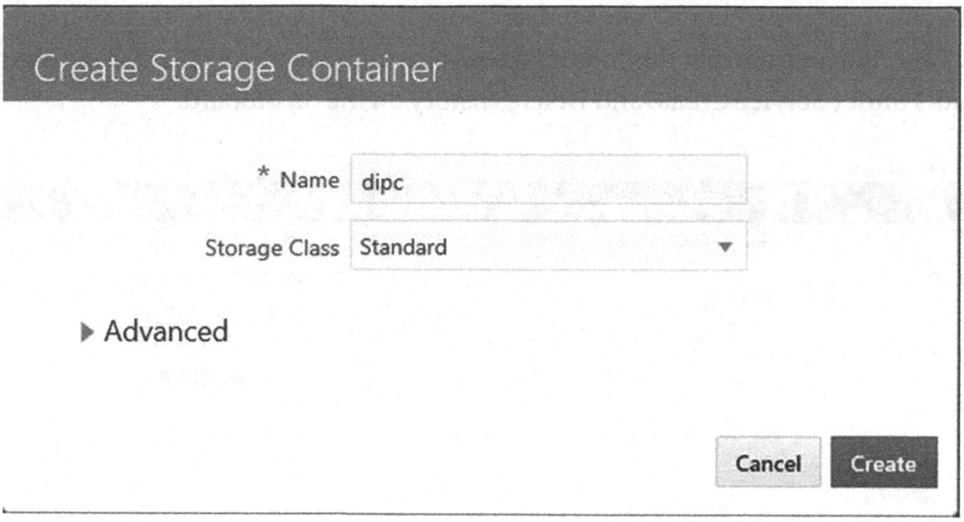

Figure 11-5. *Storage container creation window*

Once you have the storage container created, you can complete all the inputs for database creation, as shown in Figure 11-6. Important parameters used here are the shape of the database, the SSH key to access the database VM, the character set, the database name, the PDB name, and so on.

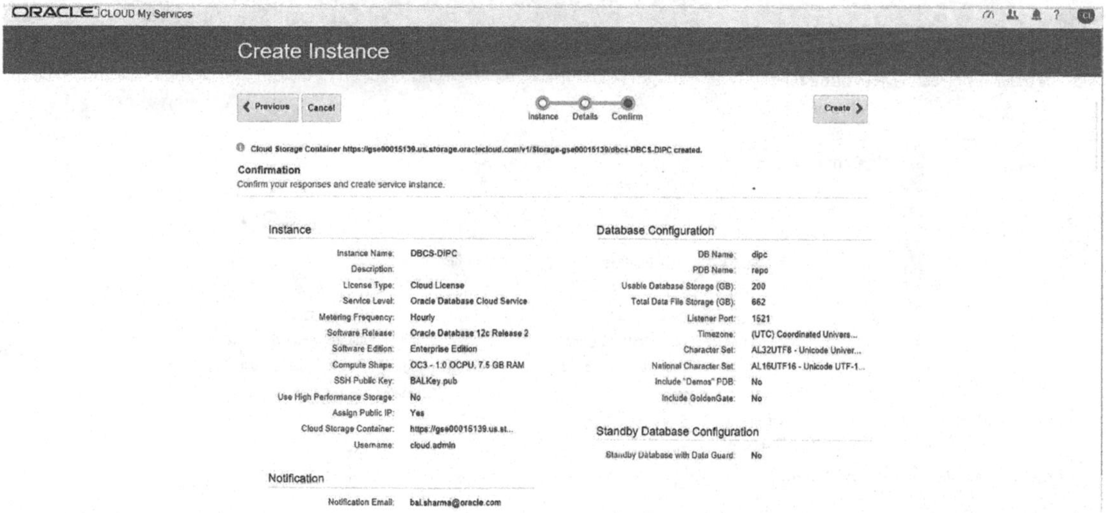

Figure 11-6. *Database creation input confirmation page*

After all the inputs, click Create, and the database creation starts, as shown in Figure 11-7. Please note that this might take several minutes to complete. You can track the status under Service Create and Delete History on the dashboard.

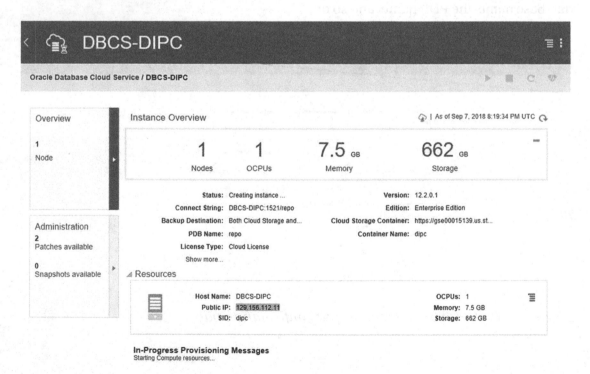

Figure 11-7. *Database creation, status dashboard*

Click DBCS-DIPC to get VM details such as the public IP, service name, PDB name, SID name, and so on, which you will be needing later while creating the DIPC service. See Figure 11-8 for these details.

Figure 11-8. *Database instance details*

You can track the detailed activity of instance creation, as shown in Figure 11-9.

Figure 11-9. *Database instance creation, detailed activities*

Once the database creation is complete, enable the service access rules, as shown in Figure 11-10. These are required in order to be accessible from DIPC.

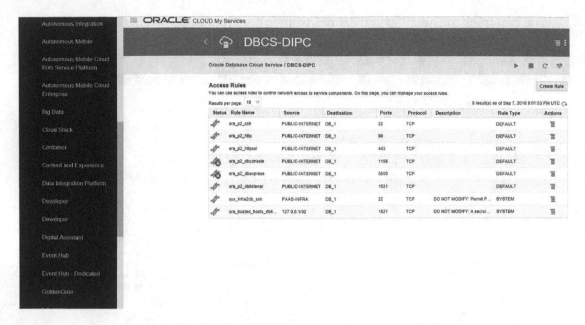

Figure 11-10. *Access rules for the database*

Once the database-side configuration is completed, you are ready to deploy the DIPC cloud service.

Creating a DIPC Service (18.x.x)

From your console dashboard, click Open Service Console in the Data Integration Platform Cloud menu. See Figure 11-11.

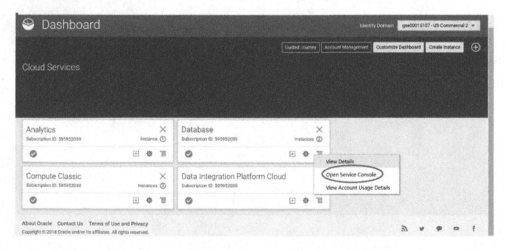

Figure 11-11. *Dashboard to open the service console for DIPC*

Click Create Instance in the instances dashboard, as shown in Figure 11-12. On this page, you need to click create instance to start DIPC provisioning.

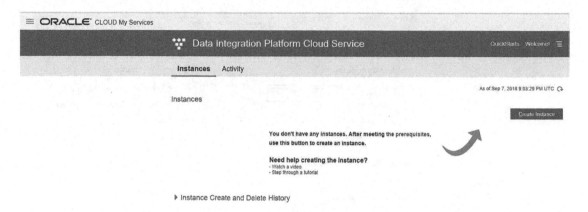

Figure 11-12. *Instance dashboard to create DIPC instance*

Provide a name for the cloud service name; here, it's BALDIPC with a cluster size of 1. Choose Enterprise Edition, which includes GGCS along with Oracle Data Integrator (ODICS). Provide basic information about the instance name, service edition, and so on. Refer to Figure 11-13.

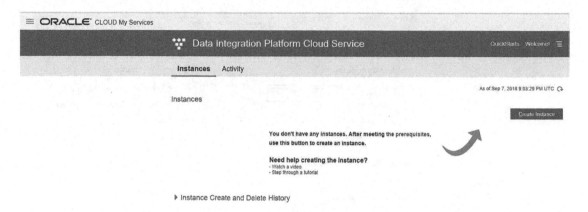

Figure 11-13. *Create Instance page, with instance information for the DIPC instance*

Click Next to go to the details page and choose the database service DBCS-DIPC from the drop-down, along with the PDB name "repo." Provide the login credentials for the database user. This page has three sections: Database Configuration, Backup and Recovery Configuration, and WebLogic Service Configurations. Refer to Figure 11-14.

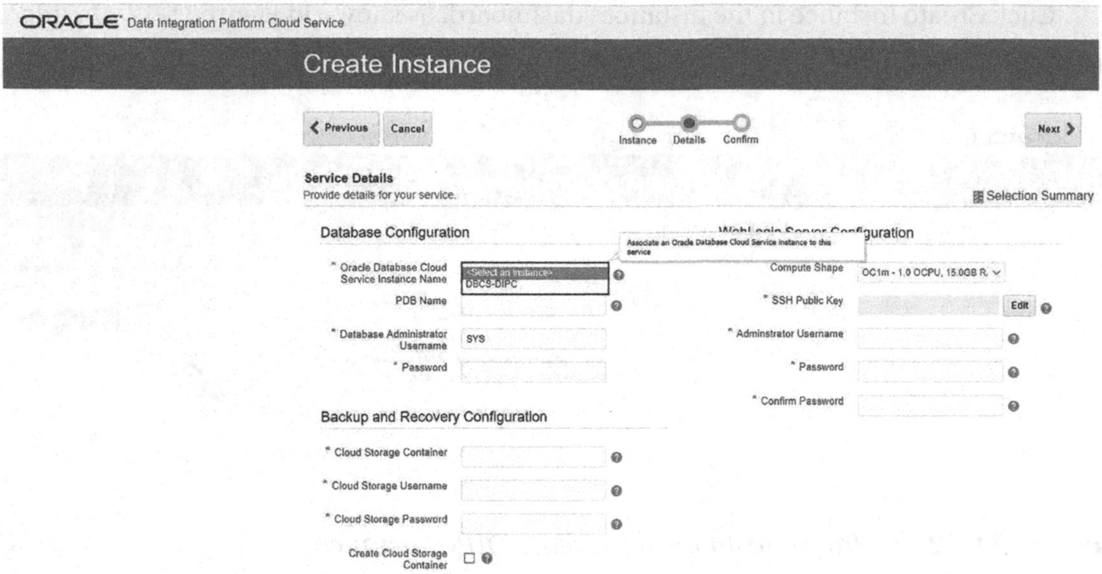

Figure 11-14. *Create Instance details page, with detail information on database, backup, and WebLogic for the DIPC instance*

Once you are done with the database configuration details, click Next and provide the cloud storage container and the credentials. You can use the same container (DIPC) that you provided while provisioning the DBCS service. Refer to Figure 11-15 for details.

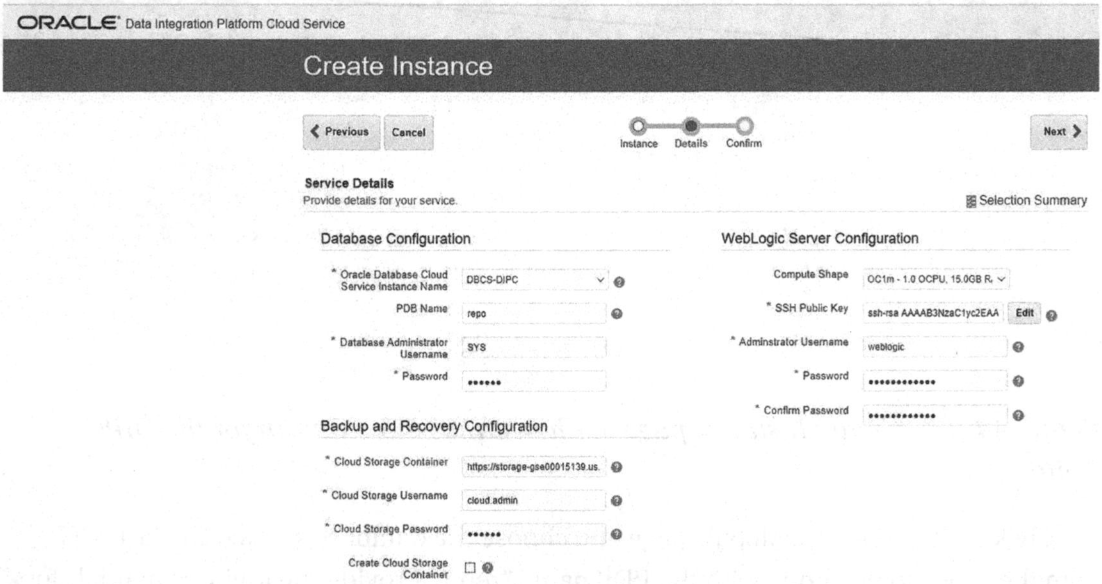

Figure 11-15. *Create Instance details page, with detail information on backup configuration and WebLogic for the DIPC instance*

For the WebLogic configuration, choose a compute shape and provide your SSH key file. See the following section for the steps. Depending on the operating system environment, you can use tools like Putty KeyGen on Windows or ssh-keygen on Linux.

Generating a Secure Shell (SSH) Public/Private Key Pair on Linux

To generate an SSH key pair on the Unix or Linux platform using the ssh-keygen utility, follow the instructions in this section.

Navigate to your home directory.

```
$ cd /home/oracle
```

Run the ssh-keygen utility, providing your choice of file name for the private key.

```
$ ssh-keygen -b 2048 -t rsa -f filename
```

The ssh-keygen utility prompts you for a passphrase for the private key. You can enter a passphrase for the private key or simply press Enter to create a private key without a passphrase.

```
Enter passphrase (empty for no passphrase): passphrase
```

Note   Passphrases are specified as a security measure to protect the private key from unauthorized access. When you specify a passphrase, you must enter the passphrase every time the private key is used with any program such as Putty, SSH clients, file transfer utilities, and so on.

The ssh-keygen utility prompts you to enter the passphrase again.

Enter the passphrase again, or press Enter to continue creating a private key without a passphrase.

```
Enter the same passphrase again: passphrase
```

The ssh-keygen utility will display a message indicating that the private key has been saved as the file name provided earlier and the public key has been saved as filename. pub. It also displays information about the key fingerprint with a random art image.

See the following example:

```
$ ssh-keygen -t rsa -N "password" -b "2048" -C "RSA Key for DIPC" -f /tmp/
id_rsa
Generating public/private rsa key pair.
Your identification has been saved in /tmp/id_rsa.
Your public key has been saved in /tmp/id_rsa.pub.
The key fingerprint is:
SHA256:WwwMgJa3FclT466a9zeXXAHnKwlXAo6AsVEFtyiEfIg RSA Key for DIPC
The key's randomart image is:
+---[RSA 2048]----+
| o ==***= ..     |
|E B.+o=B =  o o  |
| . ooo..*. . *   |
|    .. . o.. o   |
|       S oo . o  |
|      .o o o     |
|      .. . +     |
|     o.  o +     |
|     o. ... o    |
+----[SHA256]-----+
```

Generate SSH Key Pair on Windows Using the PuTTYgen Program

To generate an SSH key pair on Windows using the PuTTYgen program, follow the instructions in this section.

Download from `https://www.puttygen.com/` and install both PuTTY or PuTTYgen. Run Puttygen for generating a public-private key pair and Putty to accessing respective instance.

Set the "Type of key to generate" option to SSH-2 RSA.

Enter **2048** in the "Number of bits in a generated key" box.

Click Generate to generate a public/private key pair.

As the key is being generated, you need to move the mouse around the blank area as directed. Refer to Figure 11-16 for the options available with the putty key generator.

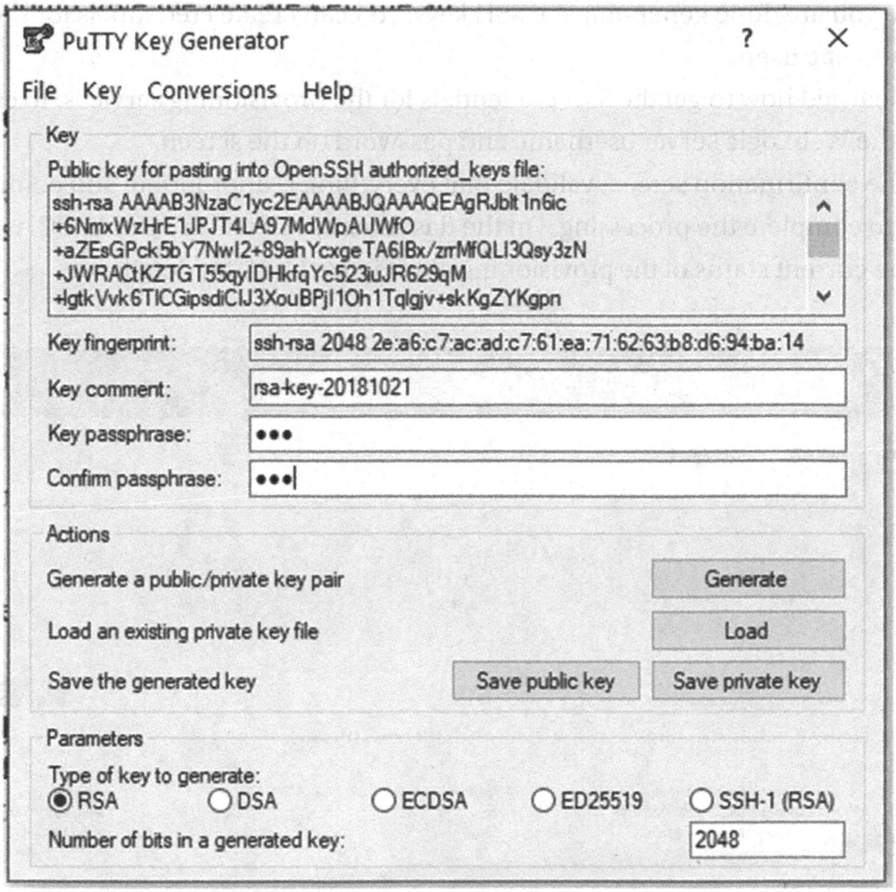

Figure 11-16. *Putty key generator screen for generating keys*

Enter a passphrase optionally for the private key in the "Key passphrase" box and "Confirm passphrase" box.

Click "Save private key" to save the private key to a file. You should give the private key file an extension of .ppk (PuTTY private key).

Select all the characters in the public key for pasting into the OpenSSH authorized_keys file box, and save it with the extension .pub for public keys.

If you are going to use an SSH client that requires the OpenSSH format for private keys to connect from the linux host using SSH, export the private key using conversions menu from puttygen tool, choose Export OpenSSH Key.

Save the private key in the OpenSSH format in the folder where you saved the private and public keys, using an extension such as .openssh to indicate the file's content.

Once you are done generating the SSH keys, you can create credentials for the oracle and opc users.

You learned how to get the SSH credentials for the provisioning services; to continue, provide the WebLogic server username and password on the screen.

On the confirmation screen, validate that everything is appropriate and confirm in order to complete the processing. On the dashboard, you will see BALDIPC, which shows the current status of the provisioning. See Figure 11-17 for details.

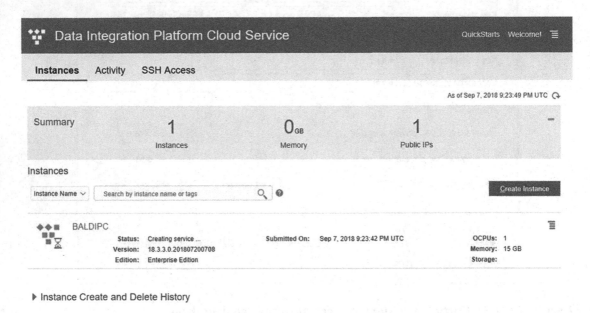

Figure 11-17. *Provisioning status*

A load balancer is also created. Click Associations to see the DBCS associated with the DIPC service. Figure 11-18 shows the association.

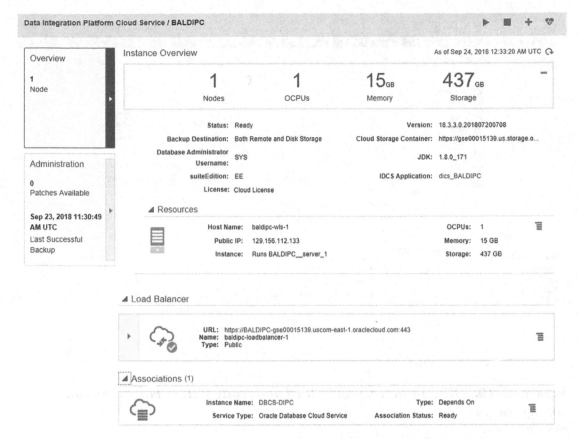

Figure 11-18. *Load balancer and database association*

Provisioning is complete when you see a status of Ready. The DIPC version is 18.3.3, as depicted by Figure 11-19.

Figure 11-19. *DIPC instance, provisioned and ready status, with details on configuration*

DIPC Remote Agent Deployment

While replicating data from an on-premise database, it is more efficient to deploy an agent local to the server than configure a remote capture from the DIPC VM to the on-premise server. Follow the instructions in this section to download and configure the remote agent on the on-premise server.

You can download the DIPC agent either in your on-premises server or in the DIPC VM (via VNC). Downloading in the DIPC VM is a faster option, and you can use scp to transfer the zip file to the on-premises server.

Log into your cloud account and from the DIPC instance (here BALDIPC) overview page, click the hamburger icon. From the drop-down, click Data Integration Platform Console. This opens a new browser tab for the DIPC home. Click the link on the left to download the agent for the on-premises VM. See Figure 11-20.

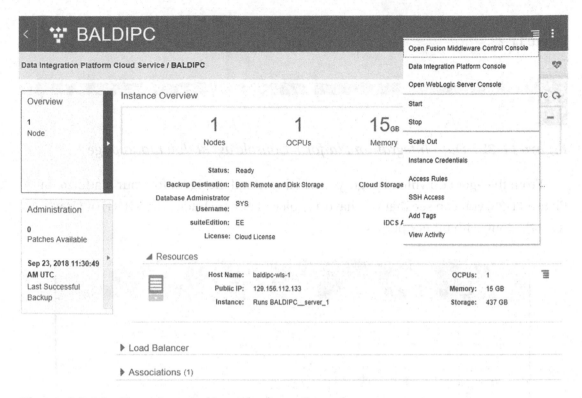

Figure 11-20. *Data Integration Platform Console*

Once you are at the Data Integration Platform Console, you can manage and download agents for your platform as well see the overall status of services. See Figure 11-21.

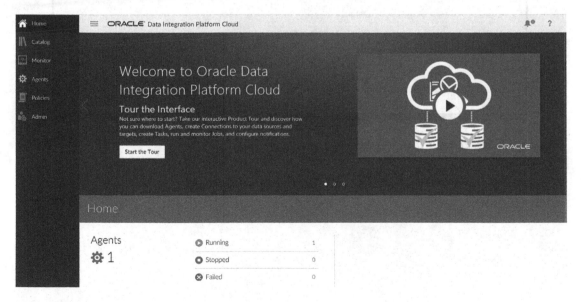

Figure 11-21. *Data Integration Platform Console dashboard*

From the left pane, click Agents ➤ Download Installer ➤ Linux 64-bit (400 MB). See Figure 11-22.

Figure 11-22. *Data Integration Platform Console agent download page*

From the agent download page, you can download the agent for your platform. In Figure 11-23, you can see that you have a choice of either Oracle 11g (OGG) or Oracle 12c (OGG), along with other options.

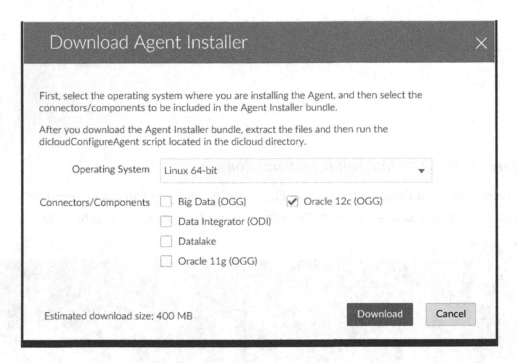

Figure 11-23. *Download Agent Installer window*

This can be downloaded to the ~oracle/Downloads directory or saved to a location when prompted.

Configuring a Remote Agent for the On-Premise Host

In this example, the on-premise hostname is `baldemo`. Your on-premise platform should have a certified version of Java because DIPC is certified with Java 1.8 and greater. Execute `java -version` from your on-premise host to check the version. Upgrade to this version if it's lower than 1.8. To verify the version, connect to the server using the terminal and issue the following command. The output may be different depending on your OS platform.

```
Java -version
Java Version "1.8.0_181"
Java(TM) SE Runtime Environment (build 1.8.0_181-b13)
Java HotSpot(TM) 64-bit Server VM (build 25.181-b13. mixed mode)
```

Unzip the binary. First create the directory to hold the DIPC binary and transfer the downloaded agent zip to extract the file from there. We created a directory called `Dipc` and then copied the agent binary. Then we unzipped it, as shown in Figure 11-24.

```
[oracle@baldemo Dipc]$ chmod 755 agent-linux.64.bit.zip
[oracle@baldemo Dipc]$ ls
agent-linux.64.bit.zip
[oracle@baldemo Dipc]$ unzip agent-linux.64.bit.zip
Archive:  agent-linux.64.bit.zip
   creating: dicloud/
   creating: dicloud/agent/
```

Figure 11-24. *Agent installer steps*

You will also notice upon extraction that there is a directory called `dicloud` that gets created that has other subdirectories along with additional scripts that you will be using later. Refer to Figure 11-25 to see the directory structure.

```
[oracle@baldemo dicloud]$ pwd
/home/oracle/Dipc/dicloud
[oracle@baldemo dicloud]$ ls -lrtha
total 28K
drwxr-xr-x. 10 oracle oinstall 4.0K Jun 13 06:26 oci
drwxr-xr-x. 29 oracle oinstall 4.0K Jun 13 06:31 gghome
-rwxr-x---.  1 oracle oinstall  358 Jul 20 03:40 dicloudUpgradeAgent.sh
-rwxr-x---.  1 oracle oinstall 1001 Jul 20 03:40 dicloudConfigureAgent.sh
drwxr-xr-x.  5 oracle oinstall 4.0K Jul 20 03:40 .
drwxr-xr-x.  3 oracle oinstall 4.0K Jul 20 03:51 agent
drwxr-xr-x.  4 oracle oinstall 4.0K Sep 24 04:13 ..
```

Figure 11-25. *Agent installer directories and files*

Note on the directories created:

gghome contains the 12c OGG binaries.

gghome11g contains the 11g OGG binaries.

dicloudConfigureAgent.sh is the file to configure the remote DIPC agent in the on-premises environment.

agent is the directory where the remote DIPC agent binaries are present.

Edit the file dicloudConfigureAgent.sh for the following values:

```
cd /home/oracle/Dipc/dicloud
./dicloudConfigureAgent.sh <agentInstanceDirectory> -recreate -debug
-dipchost=<dipc.example.host.com> -dipcport=<port> -user=<diuser>
-password=<dipassword> -authType=<BASIC/OAUTH2> -idcsServerUrl=<idcs server
url> -agentIdcsScope=<agent IDCS Client Scope> -agentClientId=<Agent IDCS
clientID> -agentClientSecret=<Agent IDCS clientSecret>
```

Here are the parameter values:

- agentInstanceDirectory

  - **Description**: This is the agent instance base directory. This is optional, and in absence of any value, a default directory named dipcagent001 is created under <unzipped directory>/dicloud/ agent.

  - **Value**: The default is /home/oracle/Dipc/dicloud/agent/ dipcagent001.

- dipchost

  - **Description**: This is the DIPC VM load balancer hostname/ public IP for your DIPC service.

  - **Value**: This is fetched from the cloud console for the DIPC service (BALDIPC in your case). Here it is BALDIPC-gse00015139.uscom-east-1.oraclecloud.com. It will vary in your case depending on your cloud environment details. See Figure 11-26.

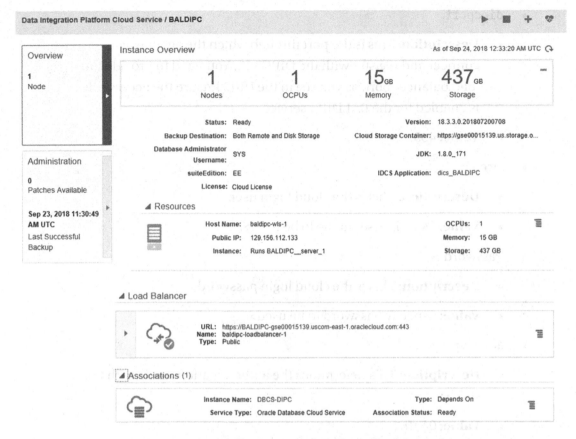

Figure 11-26. *DIPC Agent installer option details in dashboard*

Pick the hostname, as shown in Figure 11-27, by expanding the load balancer link on the dashboard.

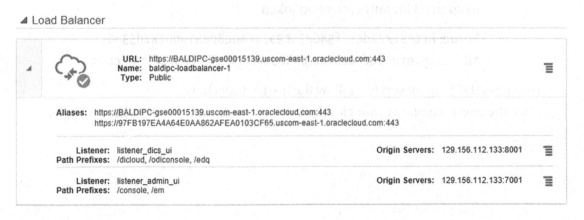

Figure 11-27. *DIPC load balancer URL and port for agent installer option*

- `dipcport`

  - **Description**: This is the port through which the agent will connect and register with the DIPC VM. You need to provide the load balancer port, as you see in the URL. Ensure the access rule is enabled for the BALDIPC service.

  - **Value**: 433.

- User

  - **Description**: This is the cloud login user.

  - **Value**: <specify user name to be used>.

- Password

  - **Description**: This is the cloud login password.

  - **Value**: <specify password to be used>.

- authType

  - **Description**: This determines the authentication mode with the server.

  - **Value**: OAUTH2.

- idcsServerUrl

  - **Description**: This is applicable for authentication mode OAUTH2. This is IDCS URL that will be used by the remote agent to connect for authentication tokens.

  - **Value**: `https://idcs-f546a35c9a744adc8d881abb782d536b.identity.oraclecloud.com`. This will be different in your case.

To access IDCS Agent service, follow the instructions here.

Click the users icon from your cloud service console page. Refer to Figure 11-28.

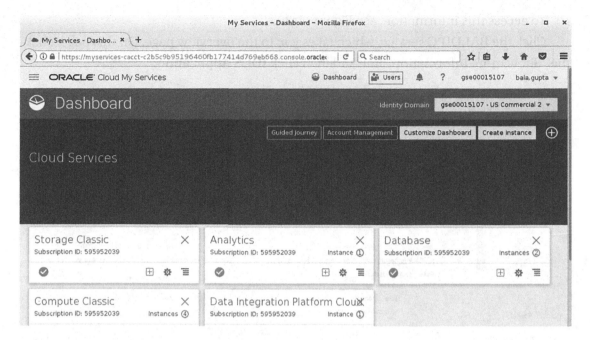

Figure 11-28. *Users link in dashboard*

Click Identity Console and copy the URL, which is opened to `https://idcs-d6cee7e` `439a24b6986f9a9cca08e6bd1.identity.oraclecloud.com`.

Above provisioned URL would be used for the parameter `idcsServerUrl`. See Figure 11-29.

Figure 11-29. *Users Management link in dashboard*

`https://idcs-d6cee7e439a24b6986f9a9cca08e6bd1.identity.oraclecloud.com`

- `agentIdcsScope`

    - **Description**: For authentication mode OAUTH2, provide the client scope of this agent from the IDCS server.

    - **Value**: `https://97FB197EA4A64E0AA862AFEA0103CF65.uscom-` `east-1.oraclecloud.com:443external`. This will differ in your case.

To access this information, see Figure 11-30.

Click the BALDIPC service, which takes you to the overview page. On this page, click the "Show more information" link and then click IDCS Application.

Figure 11-30. *DIPC instance overview in the dashboard*

This opens a new browser window, as shown in Figure 11-31. Notice the various tabs on this page.

Figure 11-31. *DIPC application details page*

Click the Configuration and Expand Resources tab. Refer to Figure 11-32 and Figure 11-33 for details. Copy the text in the Primary Audience box and add **external** after port value 443 from above screen.

- **Copied**: https://97FB197EA4A64E0AA862AFEA0103CF65.uscom-east-1.oraclecloud.com:443

- **Added**: https://97FB197EA4A64E0AA862AFEA0103CF65.uscom-east-1.oraclecloud.com:443external

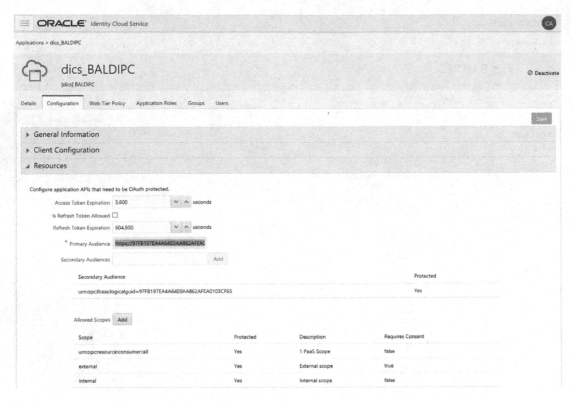

Figure 11-32. *DIPC application details page*

Figure 11-33. *DIPC application configuration details page*

- agentClientId

  - **Description:** For authentication mode OAUTH2, provide the IDCS Apps client ID of this agent, obtained from the same admin console as per Figure 11-33. DIPC application configuration details page.

  - **Value:** 97FB197EA4A64E0AA862AFEA0103CF65_APPID. This will vary in your case.

Refer to Figure 11-34 for details.

Figure 11-34. *DIPC application configuration, client ID*

- agentClientSecret

  - **Description:** For authentication mode OAUTH2, this is the agent client secret for the DIPC apps within IDCS.

  - **Value:** bf8b8a26-7c7b-4abd-b5e5-48d19ed269a0.

To access DIPC application configuration, click Show Secret in the same admin console; refer to Figure 11-35.

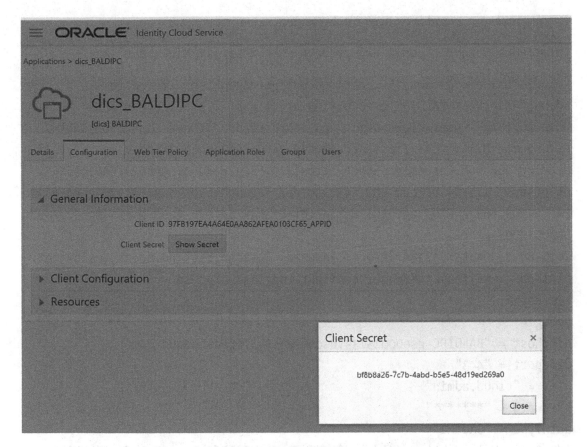

Figure 11-35. *DIPC application configuration, client secret value*

Once you have the values for all the variables, you can execute this command in the guestvm (databasevm) to configure the remote agent in the on-premises VM.

```
[oracle@databasevm dicloud]$ pwd
/home/oracle/Dipc/dicloud
[oracle@databasevm dicloud]$ export JAVA_HOME=/usr/java/jdk1.8.0_121

[oracle@databasevm dicloud]$ ./dicloudConfigureAgent.sh  -recreate
-debug -dipchost=BALDIPC-gse00015139.uscom-east-1.oraclecloud.com
-dipcport=443 -user=xyz@oracle.com -password=XXXXXXX -authType=OAUTH2
-idcsServerUrl=https://idcs-d6cee7e439a24b6986f9a9cca08e6bd1.identity.
oraclecloud.com -agentIdcsScope=https://97FB197EA4A64E0AA862AFEA0103CF65.
uscom-east-1.oraclecloud.com:443external -agentClientId=97FB197EA4A64E0AA86
2AFEA0103CF65_APPID -agentClientSecret=bf8b8a26-7c7b-4abd-b5e5-48d19ed269a0
```

You will see several messages on the screen.

```
[oracle@baldemo dicloud]$ export JAVA_HOME=/usr/java/jdk1.8.0_181

[oracle@baldemo dicloud]$ ./dicloudConfigureAgent.sh  -recreate
-debug -dipchost=BALDIPC-gse00015139.uscom-east-1.oraclecloud.com
-dipcport=443 -user=cloud.admin -password=cOlorEd@1Week -authType=OAUTH2
-idcsServerUrl=https://idcs-d6cee7e439a24b6986f9a9cca08e6bd1.identity.
oraclecloud.com -agentIdcsScope=https://97FB197EA4A64E0AA862AFEA0103CF65.
uscom-east-1.oraclecloud.com:443external -agentClientId=97FB197EA4A64E0AA86
2AFEA0103CF65_APPID -agentClientSecret=bf8b8a26-7c7b-4abd-b5e5-48d19ed269a0
DEBUG MODE
2018-09-24 04:35:53.786 INFO    [global] (oracle.dicloud.agent.deployment.
DICloudAgentLifeCycleManager configureLogging) dipcOsp = "Linux"
recreate = ""
debug = ""
dipchost = "BALDIPC-gse00015139.uscom-east-1.oraclecloud.com"
dipcport = "443"
user = "cloud.admin"
password = "*******"
authType = "OAUTH2"
idcsServerUrl = "https://idcs-d6cee7e439a24b6986f9a9cca08e6bd1.identity.
oraclecloud.com"
agentIdcsScope = "https://97FB197EA4A64E0AA862AFEA0103CF65.uscom-east-1.
oraclecloud.com:443external"
agentClientId = "97FB197EA4A64E0AA862AFEA0103CF65_APPID"
agentClientSecret = "bf8b8a26-7c7b-4abd-b5e5-48d19ed269a0"

2018-09-24 04:35:53.878 INFO    [oracle.dicloud.agent.core.
GGCCAgentInstallation] (oracle.dicloud.agent.core.GGCCAgentInstallation
handleCreateInstance) Creating agent instance home at :/home/oracle/Dipc/
dicloud/agent/dipcagent001
2018-09-24 04:35:53.883 INFO    [oracle.dicloud.agent.core.
GGCCAgentInstallation] (oracle.dicloud.agent.core.GGCCAgentInstallation
handleCreateInstance) Agent instance home created successfully at :/home/
oracle/Dipc/dicloud/agent/dipcagent001
```

2018-09-24 04:35:54.038 INFO   [global] (oracle.dicloud.agent.deployment.
AgentDeployer getOdiHome) odiPluginHome : /home/oracle/Dipc/dicloud/agent/
oracle/plugins/odi doesn't exist
2018-09-24 04:35:55.037 INFO   [oracle.jps.common] (oracle.security.jps.
JpsStartup start) Jps initializing.
2018-09-24 04:35:55.606 INFO   [oracle.jps.common] (oracle.security.jps.
JpsStartup start) Jps started.
2018-09-24 04:35:55.983 INFO   [global] (oracle.dicloud.agent.deployment.
AgentDeployer buildAgentPropertiesFromTemplate) SSL is configured with
default JDK Trust store here : /usr/java/jdk1.8.0_181/jre/lib/security/
cacerts
2018-09-24 04:35:55.995 INFO   [global] (oracle.dicloud.agent.deployment.
AgentDeployer buildAgentPropertiesFromTemplate) Default Trust-store was
configured using default trust store unlock password.
2018-09-24 04:35:55.998 INFO   [global] (oracle.dicloud.agent.
deployment.AgentDeployer buildAgentPropertiesFromTemplate) Need to change
'agentTrustStorePath' property in agent.properties for using a different
Trust-store
2018-09-24 04:35:56.006 INFO   [global] (oracle.dicloud.agent.
deployment.AgentDeployer buildAgentPropertiesFromTemplate) Use
updateTrustStoreUnlockPassword.sh/bat utility to add the Trust-store unlock
password to agent wallet.
2018-09-24 04:35:56.143 INFO   [global] (oracle.dicloud.agent.deployment.
AgentDeployer getOdiHome) odiPluginHome : /home/oracle/Dipc/dicloud/agent/
oracle/plugins/odi doesn't exist
2018-09-24 04:35:56.169 INFO   [global] (oracle.dicloud.agent.deployment.
DICloudAgentLifeCycleManager main) Agent Instance successfully created at :
/home/oracle/Dipc/dicloud/agent/dipcagent001
2018-09-24 04:35:56.175 INFO   [global] (oracle.dicloud.agent.
deployment.DICloudAgentLifeCycleManager main) Start the agent using this
startAgentInstance(.sh/.bat) script in : /home/oracle/Dipc/dicloud/agent/
dipcagent001/bin
2018-09-24 04:35:56.177 INFO   [global] (oracle.dicloud.agent.
deployment.DICloudAgentLifeCycleManager main) Stop the agent using this
stopAgentInstance (.sh/.bat) script in : /home/oracle/Dipc/dicloud/agent/
dipcagent001/bin

2018-09-24 04:35:56.178 INFO   [global] (oracle.dicloud.agent.deployment.
DICloudAgentLifeCycleManager main) Agent configuration properties file is
available at : /home/oracle/Dipc/dicloud/agent/dipcagent001/conf/agent.
properties
2018-09-24 04:35:56.181 INFO   [global] (oracle.dicloud.agent.deployment.
DICloudAgentLifeCycleManager main) Refer the configuration file for more
information on agent configuration.
2018-09-24 04:35:56.185 INFO   [global] (oracle.dicloud.agent.deployment.
DICloudAgentLifeCycleManager main) If agent properties are edited then
restart the agent for changes to take affect.

The agent configuration process creates a config properties file on-premises that
can be found at /home/oracle/Dipc/dicloud/agent/dipcagent001/conf/agent.
properties.

Starting the Agent

You can start the remote agent on the on-premise server by following the steps shown in
Figure 11-36.

```
cd /home/oracle/Dipc/dicloud/agent/dipcagent001/bin
```

```
[oracle@baldemo bin]$ pwd
/home/oracle/Dipc/dicloud/agent/dipcagent001/bin
[oracle@baldemo bin]$ ls
addAgentIdcsClientDetails.sh        startAgentInstance.sh           updateServerCred.sh
createIDStoreUnlockPassword.sh      stopAgentInstance.sh            updateTrustStoreUnlockPassword.sh
createProxyCred.sh                  updateAgentIdcsClientDetails.sh viewAgentIdcsClientDetails.sh
createServerCred.sh                 updateIDStoreUnlockPassword.sh  viewProxyCred.sh
createTrustStoreUnlockPassword.sh   updateProxyCred.sh             viewServerCred.sh
[oracle@baldemo bin]$ ./startAgentInstance.sh
AGENT_HOME : /home/oracle/Dipc/dicloud/agent/dipcagent001/bin/../../oracle
```

Figure 11-36. *Depicting agent startup*

2018-09-24 04:42:43.996 NOTIFICATION Agent Registration status : REGISTERED
2018-09-24 04:42:43.999 NOTIFICATION AgentIdentification ...
Done. agentID: 421636be-f70e-4fd5-9b83-5aac90be1072
2018-09-24 04:42:44.183 NOTIFICATION Successfully registered this agent for
message subscription
2018-09-24 04:42:44.452 ERROR DIPC-AGNT-0002: ERROR : Agent request to
GoldenGate failed. Check if GoldenGate Performance Metrics Server is

running on the connected GoldenGate instance : java.net.ConnectException: Connection refused (Connection refused)

2018-09-24 04:42:44.456 NOTIFICATION GoldenGate Manager is not running or configured ....

2018-09-24 04:42:44.457 NOTIFICATION Configuring GoldenGate Manager ..

2018-09-24 04:42:44.531 NOTIFICATION GoldenGate is using the LD_LIBRARY_PATH = /home/oracle/Dipc/dicloud/oci

2018-09-24 04:42:52.899 NOTIFICATION Done. GoldenGate Manager is configured now.

Once the agent is been started, check the status in DIPC console, it should as "Running", as shown in Figure 11-37. You can notice both the cloud agent as well the agent for on-premise that you just installed.

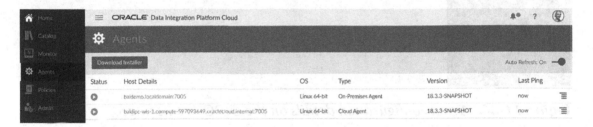

Figure 11-37. *Agent status on the DIPC Agents page*

You can see more details in the console by clicking the agent link. You can additionally click the configurations of the agent installed. Refer to Figure 11-38 for configuration details.

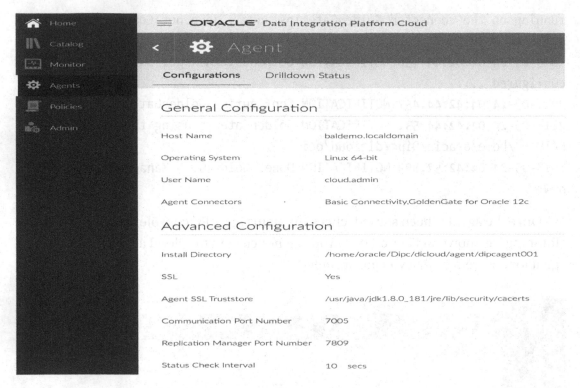

Figure 11-38. Agent configuration details on the DIPC Agents page

Additionally, you can check the agent drill-down status, as shown in Figure 11-39. A green status for all the components means that the agent is running fine and is functional.

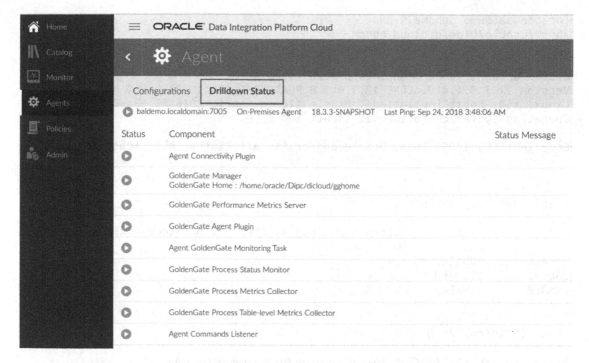

Figure 11-39. *Agent drill-down status details under the DIPC Agents page*

Now check from gghome on the on-premises VM that the manager process is running and check the port at which it is running. Refer to Figure 1-40. You can navigate to the GoldenGate home and use the ggsci command.

```
[oracle@baldemo gghome]$ pwd
/home/oracle/Dipc/dicloud/gghome
[oracle@baldemo gghome]$ ./ggsci

Oracle GoldenGate Command Interpreter for Oracle
Version 12.3.0.1.4 OGGCORE_12.3.0.1.0_PLATFORMS_180415.0359_FBO
Linux, x64, 64bit (optimized), Oracle 12c on Apr 16 2018 00:53:30
Operating system character set identified as UTF-8.

Copyright (C) 1995, 2018, Oracle and/or its affiliates. All rights reserved.



GGSCI (baldemo) 1> info all

Program       Status        Group        Lag at Chkpt  Time Since Chkpt

MANAGER       RUNNING
JAGENT        STOPPED
PMSRVR        RUNNING


GGSCI (baldemo) 2> █
```

Figure 11-40. *GoldenGate process status for on-premise VM*

You can additionally check the status of individual components. Refer to Figure 11-41.

```
GGSCI (baldemo) 2> info mgr

Manager is running (IP port baldemo.7809, Process ID 27432).

GGSCI (baldemo) 3> █
```

Figure 11-41. *GoldenGate Manager process status for on-premise VM*

Now you can go ahead and configure the on-premises GoldenGate parameter files for capture from the source. Stop the agent to perform the next steps.

Stopping the Agent

You can stop the agent from another terminal, as shown in Figure 11-42.

/home/oracle/Dipc/dicloud/agent/dipcagent001/bin/stopAgentInstance.sh

```
[oracle@baldemo bin]$ export JAVA_HOME=/usr/java/jdk1.8.0_181
[oracle@baldemo bin]$ pwd
/home/oracle/Dipc/dicloud/agent/dipcagent001/bin
[oracle@baldemo bin]$ ls
addAgentIdcsClientDetails.sh      startAgentInstance.sh          updateServerCred.sh
createIDStoreUnlockPassword.sh    stopAgentInstance.sh           updateTrustStoreUnlockPassword.sh
createProxyCred.sh                updateAgentIdcsClientDetails.sh viewAgentIdcsClientDetails.sh
createServerCred.sh               updateIDStoreUnlockPassword.sh viewProxyCred.sh
createTrustStoreUnlockPassword.sh updateProxyCred.sh             viewServerCred.sh
[oracle@baldemo bin]$ ./stopAgentInstance.sh
AGENT_HOME : /home/oracle/Dipc/dicloud/agent/dipcagent001/bin/../../oracle
```

Figure 11-42. *Stopping the agent for the on-premise VM*

You can check the step log in the other window where you started the agent.

2018-09-24 04:58:58.444 NOTIFICATION msgProcessorPool is being shutdown

2018-09-24 04:58:58.445 NOTIFICATION msgProcessorPool is being shutdown ... done

2018-09-24 04:58:58.455 NOTIFICATION Stopping Plugins(2) ...
Issuing stop command for Performance Metrics Server ...

2018-09-24 04:59:06.476 NOTIFICATION Stopping Plugins(2) ... Done.

2018-09-24 04:59:07.985:INFO:oejs.AbstractConnector:Thread-17: Stopped ServerConnector@37672cbd{HTTP/1.1,[http/1.1]}{localhost:7005}

2018-09-24 04:59:07.994:INFO:oejsh.ContextHandler:Thread-17: Stopped o.e.j.s.ServletContextHandler@bef2d72{/dicloud,null,UNAVAILABLE}
[oracle@baldemo bin]$

[
2018-04-11 12:40:21.589 ERROR javax.ws.rs.ProcessingException: org.apache.http.NoHttpResponseException: BALDIPC-gse00015139.uscom-east-1.oraclecloud.com:443 failed to respond

2018-04-11 12:42:36.472 ERROR javax.ws.rs.ProcessingException: org.apache.http.conn.HttpHostConnectException: Connect to BALDIPC-gse00015139.uscom-east-1.oraclecloud.com:443 [BALDIPC-gse00015139.uscom-east-1.oraclecloud.com/129.158.66.68, BALDIPC-gse00015139.uscom-east-1.oraclecloud.com/129.158.66.91] failed: Connection refused (Connection refused)

2018-04-11 12:42:36.521 WARNING MessageRetriever.run() getMessage(). agentId=f7f9573d-60e8-475b-9fda-a14d1230573c.f7f9573d-60e8-475b-9fda-a14d1230573c: DIPC-AGTMED-0002 : Error during Agent Mediator service operation. Error: org.apache.http.conn.HttpHostConnectException: Connect to BALDIPC-gse00015139.uscom-east-1.oraclecloud.com:443 [BALDIPC-gse00015139.uscom-east-1.oraclecloud.com/129.158.66.68, BALDIPC-

```
gse00015139.uscom-east-1.oraclecloud.com/129.158.66.91] failed: Connection
refused (Connection refused)
2018-04-11 12:44:51.038 ERROR javax.ws.rs.ProcessingException: org.apache.
http.NoHttpResponseException: BALDIPC-gse00015139.uscom-east-1.oraclecloud.
com:443 failed to respond
2018-04-11 12:47:10.775 NOTIFICATION msgProcessorPool is being shutdown
2018-04-11 12:47:10.776 NOTIFICATION msgProcessorPool is being shutdown ...
done
Stopping Plugins... : 2 : {ggmon=Entry [id=ggmon, pc=[name=Oracle
GoldenGate Monitor, id=ggmon, className=oracle.dicloud.agent.goldengate.
plugin.GGPlugIn, version=1.0.0, pluginDirectory=/home/oracle/Dipc/
dicloud/agent/oracle/plugins/ggmon], t=Thread[Thread-2,5,], ap=oracle.
dicloud.agent.goldengate.plugin.GGPlugIn@61afb5], odi=Entry [id=odi,
pc=[name=Oracle Data Integrator, id=odi, className=oracle.dicloud.agent.
odi.plugin.ODIPlugIn, version=1.0.0, pluginDirectory=/home/oracle/Dipc/
dicloud/agent/oracle/plugins/odi], t=Thread[Thread-3,5,], ap=oracle.
dicloud.agent.odi.plugin.ODIPlugIn@43ff740d]}
Stopping ... ggmon
Issuing stop command for Performance Metrics Server ...
Stopping ... ggmon ... Done
Stopping ... odi
Stopping ... odi ... Done
2018-04-11 12:47:26.970:INFO:oejs.AbstractConnector:Thread-16: Stopped
ServerConnector@4b5a5ed1{HTTP/1.1,[http/1.1]}{localhost:7005}
2018-04-11 12:47:26.976:INFO:oejsh.ContextHandler:Thread-16: Stopped o.e.j.
s.ServletContextHandler@78aab498{/dicloud,null,UNAVAILABLE}
Clean up calling :
Stopping Plugins... : 2 : {ggmon=Entry [id=ggmon, pc=[name=Oracle
GoldenGate Monitor, id=ggmon, className=oracle.dicloud.agent.goldengate.
plugin.GGPlugIn, version=1.0.0, pluginDirectory=/home/oracle/Dipc/
dicloud/agent/oracle/plugins/ggmon], t=Thread[Thread-2,5,], ap=oracle.
dicloud.agent.goldengate.plugin.GGPlugIn@61afb5], odi=Entry [id=odi,
pc=[name=Oracle Data Integrator, id=odi, className=oracle.dicloud.agent.
odi.plugin.ODIPlugIn, version=1.0.0, pluginDirectory=/home/oracle/Dipc/
dicloud/agent/oracle/plugins/odi], t=Thread[Thread-3,5,], ap=oracle.
dicloud.agent.odi.plugin.ODIPlugIn@43ff740d]}
```

```
Stopping ... ggmon
Issuing stop command for Performance Metrics Server ...
Stopping ... ggmon ... Done
Stopping ... odi
Stopping ... odi ... Done
[oracle@databasevm bin]$
]
```

You will also see the stop status in the console on the home screen, as shown in
Figure 11-43.

Earlier the Agents Running status had a value of 2, and now it's 1.

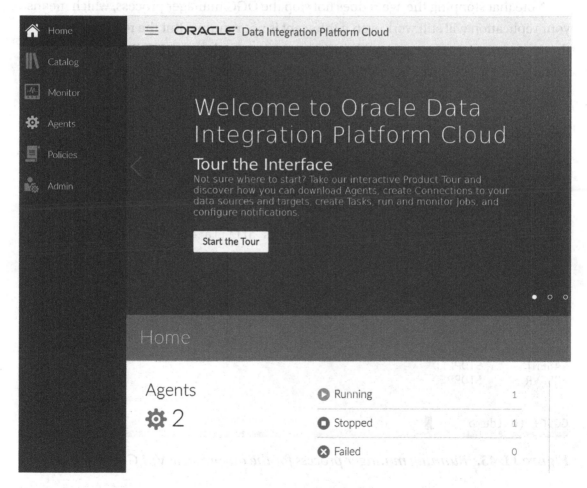

Figure 11-43. Stopped agent for on-premise VM in the console

Click the Agent link in the left panel; this will list all the configured agents and status, as shown in Figure 11-44. You can see that the on-premise agent is stopped.

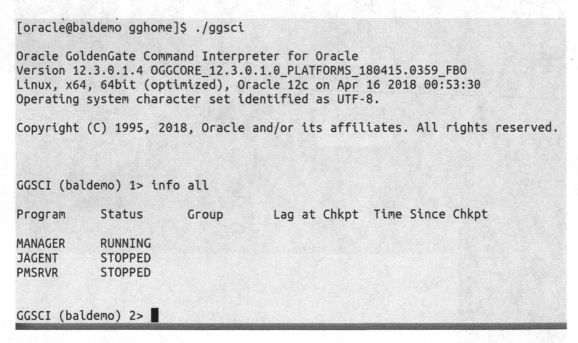

Figure 11-44. *All agents' status in console*

Note that stopping the agent does not stop the OGG manager process, which means your replication will still work even if the agent is not running. But the registration of the on-premises remote agent with DIPC is mandatory when using DIPC for your data replication solution to be in compliance with the licensing policy. It helps the customer in monitoring the process as well. See Figure 11-45.

```
[oracle@baldemo gghome]$ ./ggsci

Oracle GoldenGate Command Interpreter for Oracle
Version 12.3.0.1.4 OGGCORE_12.3.0.1.0_PLATFORMS_180415.0359_FBO
Linux, x64, 64bit (optimized), Oracle 12c on Apr 16 2018 00:53:30
Operating system character set identified as UTF-8.

Copyright (C) 1995, 2018, Oracle and/or its affiliates. All rights reserved.


GGSCI (baldemo) 1> info all

Program     Status        Group        Lag at Chkpt  Time Since Chkpt

MANAGER     RUNNING
JAGENT      STOPPED
PMSRVR      STOPPED


GGSCI (baldemo) 2> █
```

Figure 11-45. *Running manager process for the on-premise VM GoldenGate*

Configuration On-Premise

Here is the environment configuration:

- **Database name**: opmcdb (on-premise master class container database)

- **Release**: 12.2.0.1

- **Listener port**: 1521

- **PDB**: opdwh (on-premise data warehouse)

- **Schema**: dipcsrc

- **Tablespace**: USERS

- **Tables**: CUSTOMERS, ORDERS, and so on

- **Scripts directory**: /home/oracle/Dipc/scripts

Now here is the target information:

- **Database type**: Oracle

- **Deployment**: Database Cloud Service (Enterprise Edition Extreme Performance)

- **Database release**: 12.2.0.1

- **Option**: Multitenant

- **Database name (cdb)**: EXADB

- **PDB name**: prodb

- **GoldenGate version**: 12.2.0.1

- **Target schema**: dipctgt

- **OGG admin user**: oggtgt

Preparing the Scripts

Here are the database prerequisites for OGG configuration:

vi /home/oracle/Dipc/scripts/srcdbcfg.sql

```
set echo on pages 100 lines 120
spool srcdbcfg.log
select log_mode,supplemental_log_data_min,force_logging from v$database
/
alter database force logging
/
alter database add supplemental log data
/
alter system switch logfile
/
select log_mode,supplemental_log_data_min,force_logging from v$database
/
alter system set enable_goldengate_replication=true scope=both
/
show parameter enable_goldengate_replication
create user c##oggsrc identified by oggsrc
/
grant dba to c##oggsrc container=all
/
exec dbms_goldengate_auth.grant_admin_privilege('C##OGGSRC',
container=>'all')
/
Exit
```

Creating the Capture Parameter File

Here's the capture parameter file:

```
export GGHOME=/home/oracle/Dipc/dicloud/gghome
cd $GGHOME/dirprm
vi edwh.prm

    extract edwh
    UseridAlias oggsrc
    TranLogOptions IntegratedParams (max_sga_size 1024)
    LogAllSupCols
    UpdateRecordFormat Compact
```

```
ExtTrail ./dirdat/ed
ReportCount Every 2 Minutes, Rate
Table opdwh.dipcsrc.*;
```

Creating the PUMP Parameter File

Now here's the PUMP parameter file:

```
cd $GGHOME/dirprm
vi pdwh.prm

    extract pdwh
    UseridAlias oggsrc
    RmtHost 129.156.112.133, MgrPort 7704, socksproxy 127.0.0.1:9000
    RmtTrail ./dirdat/rd
    ReportCount Every 2 Minutes, Rate
    PassThru
    Table opdwh.dipcsrc.*;
```

Note   IP against `RmtHost` is the DIPC VM's public IP, and `MgrPort` is the port on which the manager process is running on the DIPC VM. This includes the SOCKS5PROXY parameter to transfer golden gate trail files over a secure tunnel.

Preparing the OGG OBEY Files

Secure credentials format sample for the OBEY file:

```
cd $GGHOME/dirprm
vi sec_cred.oby
create wallet
add credentialstore
alter credentialstore add user c##oggsrc password oggsrc alias oggsrc
info credentialstore
dblogin useridalias oggsrc
add schematrandata opdwh.dipcsrc
info schematrandata opdwh.dipcsrc
```

Here is the OGG process for the format of OBEY files for adding processes:

```
cd $GGHOME/dirprm
vi add_procs.oby

start mgr
dblogin useridalias oggsrc
register extract edwh, database container (opdwh);
add extract edwh, integrated tranlog, begin now
add ExtTrail ./dirdat/ed, extract edwh
add extract pdwh, ExtTrailSource ./dirdat/ed
add RmtTrail ./dirdat/rd,extract pdwh
info all
```

Executing the Scripts

Let's run them:

```
cd /home/oracle/Dipc/scripts
sqlplus system/oracle@opdwh @srcdbcfg.sql

cd $GGHOME
ggsci> obey sec_cred.oby
ggsci> obey add_procs.oby
```

The source environment is not undergoing any data changes, and data in the DBCS schema has already been kept in sync using the initial database synchronization method.

Initial Source Data Dump

Here's how to check the current source database:

```
sqlplus system/oracle@opdwh
sqlplus > Select to_char(current_scn) from v$database;   --value to be
use for flashback_scn parameter of datapump and starting scn from where
replicat should start

expdp system/oracle@opdwh dumpfile=dipcsrc.dmp logfile=expdp_dipcsrc.log
directory=dp parallel=4 flasback_scn=nnnnn
```

Use oci cli to copy the dump files to oci object store that you can import to **DBCS** for initial data sync

]

Start extract process
ggsci> start edwh

Starting the DIPC Remote Agent

From your on-premises VM desktop, you can start the DIPC remote agent from a terminal.

export JAVA_HOME=/usr/java/jdk1.8.0_121
cd /home/oracle/Dipc/dicloud/agent/dipcagent001/bin/
./startAgentInstance.sh

Setting Up and Starting the SOCKS5 Proxy Tunnel for the PUMP Process

From your on-premises VM desktop, you can set up and start the SOCKS5 proxy tunnel from a terminal.

The agent binary includes a script to run the SOCKS5 proxy in your on-premises server as follows:

/home/oracle/Dipc/dicloud/gghome/SSH_SOCK5_SETUP.sh

Copy the privateKey file of your DIPC VM to the on-premises server where the DIPC agent is running into the directory /home/oracle/Dipc/dicloud/gghome and change the permission to 600.

cd /home/oracle/Dipc/dicloud/gghome
chmod 600 privateKey
cp SSH_SOCK5_SETUP.sh SSH_SOCK5_SETUP.sh.bkp

Edit the SSH_SOCK5_SETUP.sh file to replace with your DIPC VM public IP and the complete path of your private key

For example, in our configuration, the following change was made to SSH_SOCK5_SETUP.sh:

```
ssh -i /home/oracle/Dipc/dicloud/gghome/privateKey -v -N -f -D
127.0.0.1:9000 opc@129.156.112.133 >./dirrpt/ggcs_socksproxy.log 2>&1
```

To start the proxy tunnel, run the following from the shell prompt:

```
./SSH_SOCK5_SETUP.sh
```

Steps to Access DIPC VM and DBCS/EXACS

The DIPC agent has been downloaded and configured on your VM. Access the DIPC VM from your host machine directly using putty tool or VNC viewer (https://www.realvnc.com/en/connect/download/viewer/) utility.

Insert a DIPC VM public IP of **129.156.112.113** and name it **DIPCVM**, as shown in Figure 11-46.

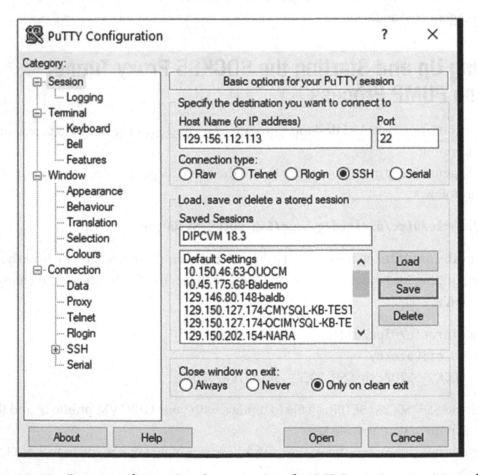

Figure 11-46. *Putty configuration for accessing the DIPC service provisioned VM*

Click Data and enter **opc** for the auto-login username. The default user on the Oracle public cloud is opc, which has all the sudo rights to other users. See Figure 11-47.

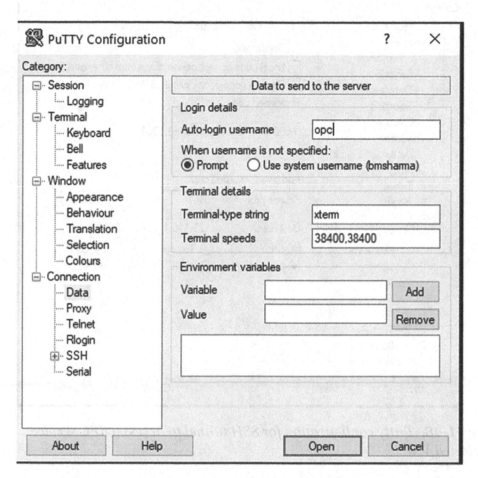

Figure 11-47. *Putty configuration for auto-login for the opc user to login the DIPC VM*

Click SSH ➤ Tunnels.

For Source Port, enter **5901**.

For Destination, enter **129.156.112.113:5901** and click Add. See Figure 11-48.

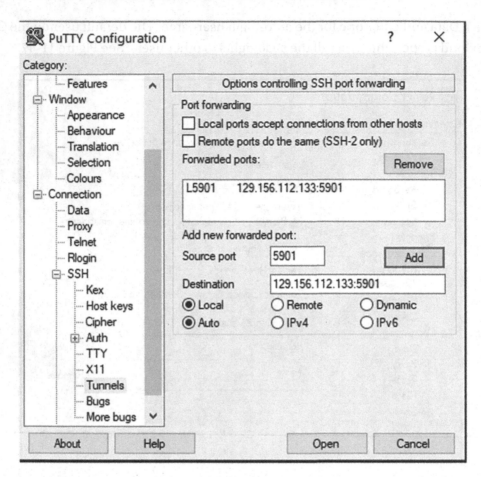

Figure 11-48. *Putty configuration for SSH tunnel to access DIPC service provisioned VM*

Click Auth and provide the location of the private key file. Refer to the SSH key generation step mentioned earlier. Browse to the private key for the SSH session and save the configuration for later use. See Figure 11-49.

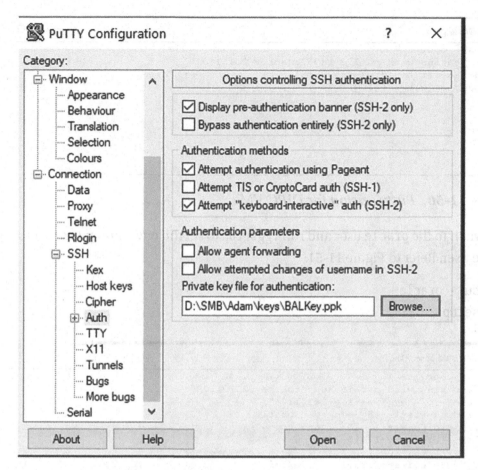

Figure 11-49. *Putty configuration for the SSH private key under Auth for the DIPC VM*

Click Session ➤ Save.

To connect using putty, click Open to log into the DIPC VM putty session using the opc user. Provide any passphrase you have been given during key generation. You will be login to the DIPC VM using Putty. Refer to Figure 11-50.

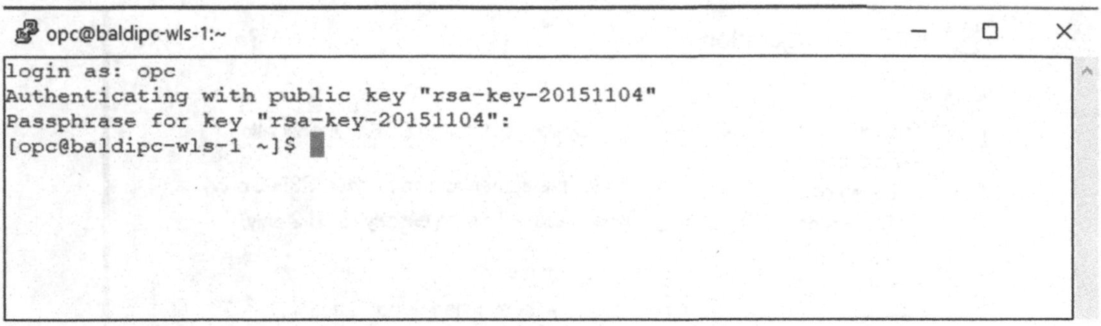

```
opc@baldipc-wls-1:~                                                    —    □    ×

login as: opc
Authenticating with public key "rsa-key-20151104"
Passphrase for key "rsa-key-20151104":
[opc@baldipc-wls-1 ~]$ █
```

Figure 11-50. *Putty session for DIPC VM*

Switch to the oracle user and run .ggsetup to set the environment variables for the oracle user. Refer to Figure 11-51.

```
sudo su - oracle
. .ggsetup
```

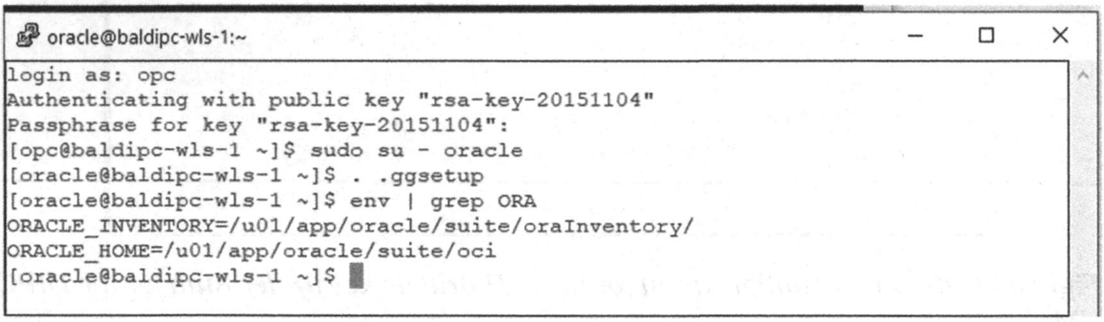

```
oracle@baldipc-wls-1:~                                                 —    □    ×

login as: opc
Authenticating with public key "rsa-key-20151104"
Passphrase for key "rsa-key-20151104":
[opc@baldipc-wls-1 ~]$ sudo su - oracle
[oracle@baldipc-wls-1 ~]$ . .ggsetup
[oracle@baldipc-wls-1 ~]$ env | grep ORA
ORACLE_INVENTORY=/u01/app/oracle/suite/oraInventory/
ORACLE_HOME=/u01/app/oracle/suite/oci
[oracle@baldipc-wls-1 ~]$ █
```

Figure 11-51. *Setting up GoldenGate variables on the DIPC VM*

Connecting to the DIPC VM via VNC

To log in to VNC, use the TigerVNC Viewer application.

1. Open the putty session to DICPVM (if not started in the previous step) to start an SSH tunnel.

2. Run the TigerVNC Viewer application and enter **localhost: 5901**. See Figure 11-52.

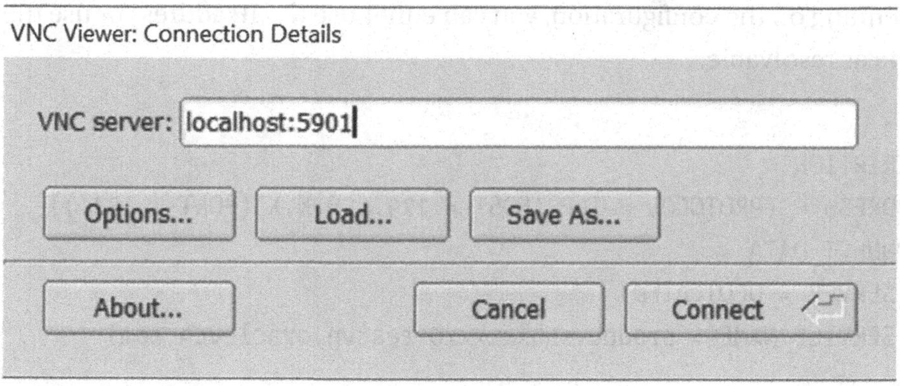

VNC Viewer: Connection Details

VNC server: localhost:5901|

Options...   Load...   Save As...

About...   Cancel   Connect

Figure 11-52. VNC connectivity to the DIPC VM

The password is dipcvnc.

This will open the DIPCVM desktop.

3. After logging in, open a terminal and switch to the oracle user.

Steps to connect to DBCS/EXACS from the DIPC VM

Gather the DBCS/EXACS database credentials and tnsnames configuration and add it to the tnsnames.ora file on the DIPC VM. Check for hostname resolution; otherwise, replace the hostname with an IP address for testing.

```
PRODDB =
  (DESCRIPTION =
    (ADDRESS = (PROTOCOL = TCP)(HOST = exanode1.subxxxxxx50.testvn.
    oraclxxxn.com)(PORT = 1521))
    (CONNECT_DATA =
      (SERVER = DEDICATED)
      (SERVICE_NAME = proddb.sub0xxxxxx50.testvn.oraclevcn.com)
    )
  )
```

Copy the connection string for the target database where you want to replicate. In our case, this is proddb from the earlier tnsnames.ora file obtained from the target. Add the entry to the following:

/u01/app/oracle/suite/oci/network/admin/tnsnames.ora

vi /u01/app/oracle/suite/oci/network/admin/tnsnames.ora

Depending on the configuration, you can either use the IP address or use the hostname as resolvable.

```
PRODDB =
  (DESCRIPTION =
    (ADDRESS = (PROTOCOL = TCP)(HOST = 129.156.X.X)(PORT = 1521))
    (CONNECT_DATA =
      (SERVER = DEDICATED)
      (SERVICE_NAME = proddb.subxxxxxx0.testvn.oraclevcn.com)
    )
  )
```

Now you can test the connection with the following:

```
sqlplus bal/xxxxxxxxx@proddb
```

Configuring the DIPC VM

Follow the next steps to configure the DIPC VM to apply the on-premises changes remotely to DBCS.

Creating a Target

The DIPCCLOUD user will be the target database schema in DBCS/EXACS to be used for the replication of the on-premises data.

Connect to DBCS/EXACS using sqlplus and run the following commands:

```
create user dipccloud identified by NotAllowed#_ default tablespace users;
alter user dipccloud quota unlimited on users;
grant create session, resource to dipccloud;
conn dipccloud/NotAllowed#_@proddb alter user ggadmin
```

Creating the GoldenGate User on the Cloud Target Database

You need to create and define a GoldenGate replication user for the target environment. This can be done either by using the DIPC VM or logging in to the target database. The SQLPlus binary is already present in the DIPC VM.

```
~/.ggsetup
```

This sets the path for TNS_ADMIN and an instant client (/u01/app/oracle/suite/oci/sqlplus):

```
which sqlplus
sqlplus -version

sqlplus sys/xxxxxxx@EXADB as sysdba
set echo on pages 100 lines 120
spool tgtdbcfg.log
select log_mode,supplemental_log_data_min,force_logging from v$database
/
alter database force logging
/
alter database add supplemental log data
/
alter system switch logfile
/
select log_mode,supplemental_log_data_min,force_logging from v$database
/
alter system set enable_goldengate_replication=true scope=both
/
show parameter enable_goldengate_replication
create user c##oggtgt identified by NotAllowed#_
/
grant dba to c##oggtgt container=all
/
exec dbms_goldengate_auth.grant_admin_privilege('C##OGGTGT',
container=>'all')
/
Exit
```

Validate the connection from SQLPlus, as shown in Figure 11-53.

Note In the DBCS environment, the parameter `sec_case_sensitive_logon` is set to TRUE. Hence, remember to enter the password in same case as provided during creation of the account else you get invalid username/password error. Or else try resetting the password to lowercase for simplicity.

You need to establish connectivity to the remote database (DBCS/ExaCS) from the DIPC VM for the remote delivery of data.

```
[oracle@baldipc-wls-1 ~]$ . .ggsetup
[oracle@baldipc-wls-1 ~]$ env | grep ORA
ORACLE_INVENTORY=/u01/app/oracle/suite/oraInventory/
ORACLE_HOME=/u01/app/oracle/suite/oci
[oracle@baldipc-wls-1 ~]$ which sqlplus
/u01/app/oracle/suite/oci/sqlplus
[oracle@baldipc-wls-1 ~]$ sqlplus

SQL*Plus: Release 12.1.0.2.0 Production on Fri Sep 28 23:57:40 2018

Copyright (c) 1982, 2014, Oracle.  All rights reserved.

Enter user-name: bal@proddb
Enter password:
Last Successful login time: Fri Sep 28 2018 23:15:28 +00:00

Connected to:
Oracle Database 12c EE Extreme Perf Release 12.2.0.1.0 - 64bit Production

SQL>
```

Figure 11-53. *Remote target database connectivity from the DIPC VM*

Once you are able to connect to the remote database, check for the GoldenGate-specific parameters and run the required statements. See Figure 11-54.

```
ExitSQL>    2
LOG_MODE       SUPPLEME FORCE_LOGGING
------------  -------- ----------------------------------------
ARCHIVELOG    NO       YES

SQL>   2   alter database force logging
*
ERROR at line 1:
ORA-12920: database is already in force logging mode


SQL>   2
Database altered.

SQL>   2
System altered.

SQL>   2
LOG_MODE       SUPPLEME FORCE_LOGGING
------------  -------- ----------------------------------------
ARCHIVELOG    YES      YES

SQL>   2
System altered.

SQL>
NAME                                           TYPE         VALUE
---------------------------------------------- -----------  --------------------------------
enable_goldengate_replication                  boolean      TRUE
SQL>   2
User created.

SQL>   2
Grant succeeded.

SQL>

PL/SQL procedure successfully completed.

SQL>
Grant succeeded.

SQL> Disconnected from Oracle Database 12c EE Extreme Perf Release 12.2.0.1.0 - 64bit Production
[oracle@exanode1 ~]$
[oracle@exanode1 ~]$ ■
```

Figure 11-54. *Remote target database preparation for the GoldenGate replication*

OGG Process Configuration

Open a putty session to the DIPC VM and follow these steps:

```
sudo su - oracle
. .ggsetup    ➤ this step will set up the environment variables for your OGG 12
environment
cd $GGHOME
./ggsci
ggsci> info all
```

Refer to Figure 11-55 for the command output.

```
[opc@baldipc-wls-1 ~]$ sudo su - oracle
[oracle@baldipc-wls-1 ~]$ . .ggsetup
[oracle@baldipc-wls-1 ~]$ cd $GGHOME
[oracle@baldipc-wls-1 gghome]$ ./ggsci

Oracle GoldenGate Command Interpreter for Oracle
Version 12.3.0.1.4 OGGCORE_12.3.0.1.0_PLATFORMS_180415.0359_FBO
Linux, x64, 64bit (optimized), Oracle 12c on Apr 16 2018 00:53:30
Operating system character set identified as UTF-8.

Copyright (C) 1995, 2018, Oracle and/or its affiliates. All rights reserved.


GGSCI (baldipc-wls-1) 1> info all;
ERROR: Invalid command.

GGSCI (baldipc-wls-1) 2> info all

Program     Status       Group        Lag at Chkpt   Time Since Chkpt

MANAGER     RUNNING
JAGENT      STOPPED
PMSRVR      RUNNING
```

Figure 11-55. *Manager process for GoldenGate replication*

```
ggsci> stop mgr
ggsci> edit param mgr

PORT 7704
DynamicPortList 7704-7760
AccessRule,Prog collector,IpAddr 129.156.112.113,Allow
PurgeOldExtracts ./dirdat/* UseCheckPoints, MinKeepHours 2
AutoRestart Replicat *,Retries 3,WaitMinutes 2,ResetMinutes 120

ggsci > start mgr
```

This manager process should be first started on the DIPC VM before the pump process can be started on the on-premise server.

Prepare the obey files.

```
cd $GGHOME
```

Create the secure credentials obey file.

```
vi dirprm/sec_creds_tgt.oby
start mgr
create wallet
add credentialstore
alter credentialstore add user c##oggtgt@proddb password NotAllowed#_ alias
ggadmintgt
info credentialstore
dblogin useridalias ggadmintgt
Create replicate parameter file:
vi $GGHOME/dirprm/rdwh.prm
```

```
replicat rdwh
useridalias ggadmintgt
reportcount every 2 minutes, rate
assumetargetdefs
map opdwh.dipcsrc.*, target dipctgt.*;
```

See Figure 11-56 and Figure 11-57 to execute the OBEY files and add the replicat process.

```
cd $GGHOME
ggsci> obey dirprm/sec_creds_tgt.oby
ggsci> add replicat rdwh,ExtTrail ./dirdat/rd, nodbcheckpoint
```

```
GGSCI (baldipc-wls-1) 1> obey dirprm/sec_creds_tgt.oby

GGSCI (baldipc-wls-1) 2> start mgr

MGR is already running.


GGSCI (baldipc-wls-1) 3> create wallet


Created wallet.

Opened wallet.

GGSCI (baldipc-wls-1) 4> add credentialstore


A credential store already exists.

ERROR: Unable to create a new credential store.

GGSCI (baldipc-wls-1) 5> alter credentialstore add user c##oggtgt@proddb passwor
d NOtAll0wed#_ alias ggadmintgt


Credential store altered.

GGSCI (baldipc-wls-1) 6> info credentialstore


Reading from credential store:

Default domain: OracleGoldenGate

  Alias: ggadmintgt
  Userid: c##oggtgt@proddb

GGSCI (baldipc-wls-1) 7> dblogin useridalias ggadmintgt

Successfully logged into database PRODDB.

GGSCI (baldipc-wls-1 as c##oggtgt@exadb/PRODDB) 8>

GGSCI (baldipc-wls-1 as c##oggtgt@exadb/PRODDB) 8>
```

Figure 11-56. *Obey files and adding the replicat process for GoldenGate*
replication

```
GGSCI (baldipc-wls-1 as c##oggtgt@exadb/PRODDB) 8> add replicat rdwh,ExtTrail ./
dirdat/rd, nodbcheckpoint
REPLICAT added.

GGSCI (baldipc-wls-1 as c##oggtgt@exadb/PRODDB) 9>
```

Figure 11-57. *Steps to add replicate*

NODBCHECKPOINT forces replicat to use a checkpointing file mechanism.

INITIAL DATA SYNCHRONIZATION

Since the source and target databases are both Oracle, the initial data synchronization to the DIPCTGT schema in DBCS is done using a data pump.

For the demo, you have taken a dump of the source data, which is not undergoing any change. In this case you need to take a new export dump SCN based on the data change time on the target.

The dump files are uploaded to either the DBCS instance or the OCI object store (using oci cli). The data is then imported into dipctgt in DBCS using an import dump.

impdp admin/Welcome_123#@proddb directory=data_pump_dir credential=DIPC_ IMPDeP_USE logfile=impdp_dipcsrc_tables.log dumpfile= SCHEMA_TABLE.DMP remap_ schema=dipcsrc:dipctgt remap_tablespace=USERS:DATA

Please note that the DBMS_CLOUD package is not available in the release 12.2.0.1 OCI DBaaS, so it could not create the credentials to use the swift URL for the data pump. Rather, use the dump file on either block storage or file storage for DBCS on OCI until the API becomes available. Currently, the API is available on autonomous data warehouse and autonomous OLTP cloud services, and the following statement can be used as an example to load the data from object storage:

impdp admin/Welcome_123#@proddb directory=data_pump_dir credential=DIPC_ IMPDeP_USE logfile=impdp_dipcsrc_tables.log dumpfile=https:// swiftobjectstorage.us-ashburn-1.oraclecloud.com/v1/baldemo/bucket_tenantXX/ SCHEMA_TABLE.DMP remap_schema=dipcsrc:dipctgt remap_tablespace=USERS:DATA

Starting the OGG Pump and Replicate Process

You have the DIPC remote agent started on the on-premises VM. The SSH proxy tunnel has been started between the on-premises and the DIPC VM, the manager process on the DIPC VM is up and running, and data on the target has already been imported.

Note   The OGG capture process does not have a dependency on the SOCKS5 proxy. This is the pump process that requires you to establish a secure connection with the DIPC VM before transferring any data. Hence, it is required that the SSH tunnel is first started along with manager process running on the DIPC VM.

Now you can start the pump process on the on-premises server and the replicate process on the DIPC VM and validate some replication scenarios like insert, update, and delete.

Here's the code for on-premises:

```
cd $GGHOME
ggsci> start pdwh
```

Here's the code for the DIPC VM:

```
cd $GGHOME
ggsci> start rdwh
```

Validating

In a real-world scenario, you have a data source on both the source and the target, so it's easy to verify the replication. For our purposes, you can create table structures both on the source and on the target and perform some DMLs and validate by querying the target and also checking the stats.

```
create table lineorder (cust_id number, ord_id number, ord_qty number, ord_
date date, status varchar2(10), primary key (ord_id));
```

Execute the following on the on-premises `dipcsrc` schema and query that table on the target (`dipctgt@proddb`) to see that the data has been replicated.

```
insert into lineorder values (1001, 3000005, 1000, sysdate,'CNF');
commit;
--check in target

update lineorder set ord_qty=1000 where ord_id=3000005;
commit;
--check in target

delete lineorder where ord_id=3000005;
commit;
--check in target
```

Gathering Stats

You can run the following commands to the check the stats of the OGG processes.

Here's the code for on-premises:

```
cd $GGHOME
ggsci> dblogin useridalias oggsrc
ggsci> lag edwh
ggsci> stats edwh,total,hourly,latest,reset, table opdwh.dipcsrc.lineorder
ggsci> stats edwh reportrate min table opdwh.dipcsrc.lineorder
ggsci> lag pdwh
ggsci> stats pdwh,total,hourly,latest,reset, table opdwh.dipcsrc.lineorder
ggsci> stats pdwh reportrate min, table opdwh.dipcsrc.lineorder
ggsci> view report, edwh
ggsci> view report, pdwh
```

Here's the code for the DIPC VM:

```
cd $GGHOME
ggsci>stats rdwh,total,hourly,latest,reset ,table exadb.dipctgt.LINEORDER
ggsci>stats rdwh reportrate min, table exadb.dipctgt.LINEORDER
ggsci>view report, rdwh
```

Summary

In this chapter, you learned how to configure your data replication with DIPC from on-premises to an Oracle cloud database on DBCS/ExaCS. This approach is particularly useful when you are dealing with different database versions, different cloud environments, and different database editions and want to migrate to Oracle public cloud databases. DIPC also supports an initial data synchronization through an elevated task known as the *data synchronization task*. You need to have a VPN connection from the remote agent to the DIPC host because the initial load task is done through the ODI function on the DIPC host. In the example, we used the SOCK5 proxy, so you handled the initial load separately to make both the source and the target consistent, and replication started from a specific system change number (SCN).

CHAPTER 12

Managing Exadata Cloud Service

This chapter will focus on managing the Exadata Cloud Service environment you provisioned earlier. At the end of this chapter, you will learn your responsibilities on the Oracle public cloud in terms of managing the environment of ExaCS. Oracle Enterprise Manager (OEM) is used across organizations for managing the database and related IT resources and provides a complete database cloud lifecycle management solution. In the case of the Oracle Exadata Cloud Service, OEM provides support for monitoring and managing customer-visible targets. This is because of the separation of roles and responsibilities between the customer and Oracle. The customer can have Exadata Cloud Service deployments accessed in two possible ways: one with VPN and the other without VPN configuration. Accordingly, an OEM Cloud Control deployment needs to consider these scenarios.

With ExaCS, Oracle does all the updates and patches all the components of the Exadata system that you don't have access to. This includes Exadata Storage Server, Integrated Light Out Management (ILOM), power distribution units (PDUs), network switches, and physical database servers (Dom 0).

As a customer, you are responsible for patching and updating database servers (Dom U), operating systems, Grid Infrastructure software, and Oracle RDBMS software when you are notified about the availability of these in your dashboards. Oracle pushes updates regularly. You can schedule these patches in a rolling fashion wherever applicable to ensure service availability.

Look at Figure 12-1 for an understanding of the Oracle versus customer responsibilities for Exadata Cloud Service (ExaCS).

© Y V Ravi Kumar, Nassyam Basha, Krishna Kumar K M, Bal Mukund Sharma, Konstantin Kerekovski 2019
Y V Ravi Kumar et al., *Oracle High Availability, Disaster Recovery, and Cloud Services*,
https://doi.org/10.1007/978-1-4842-4351-0_12

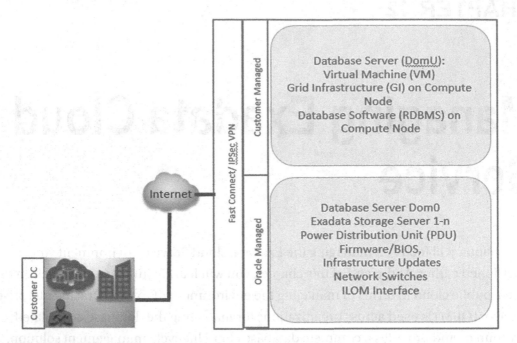

Figure 12-1. Oracle versus customer responsibilities in Exadata Cloud Service environment

Managing patches and updates to Dom U environments can be done using standard Exadata tools and techniques as applicable to on-premise environments. As a best practice, you can open up a proactive service request with Oracle before applying these updates.

Now that you understand what customers can manage, you can use Enterprise Manager Cloud Control to monitor and manage Exadata Cloud components.

You need to install EM agents on the Exadata Cloud Compute nodes and then discover the Grid Infrastructure, cluster databases, and other associated targets like listeners etc on Exadata Cloud Service.

In reality, the process is no different than discovering these database and ASM cluster targets on any database on-premise or on the cloud on the Exadata machine; the exception is with discovering infrastructure components, which Oracle manages are not discoverable such as Storage cells, Infiniband, PDU, Switch etc. This is the reason we do not follow same process of discovering Exadata Target on Exadata Cloud Service.

Make sure the network ports required for the Enterprise Manager Cloud Control agent are open through a firewall or through an SSH tunnel or IPsec VPN. The default port is 3872 used for communication.

Keep in mind that Oracle provides cloud tooling for managing several aspects of its platform. A customer has to know what tooling to use when. For certain tasks, the cloud tooling has to be used from the cloud dashboard. To summarize, the following tasks can be performed through cloud automation:

- Controlling database start, stop, restart on database nodes

- Managing SSH access to the nodes

- Database creation and deletion operations

- Database backups and restore operations

- Database snapshot creation and deletion tasks

- Database patching

- ASM disk group operations

Enterprise Manager can be used to perform the following tasks:

- Monitoring and managing ASM storage

- Database jobs creation and scheduling

- Resource management

- Database feature uses and compliance tracking

- Database schema operation

- Database performance management using diagnostic, tuning, and Real Application Testing (RAT)

- Database In-Memory configuration and operation

Agent Deployment on Exadata Cloud Service

Depending on the deployment model agent, the deployment process might differ. Ideally, there could be two distinct models; a customer can choose to install an agent on ExaCS, namely, a hybrid cloud agent installation without a VPN to the cloud service. Another implementation is an agent deployment with a VPN in place. Enterprise Manager can reside in an on-premise datacenter at the customer's location and can choose to deploy agents on compute VMs on Exadata Cloud either through a hybrid cloud agent or through standard installation with a VPN.

There are several issues to consider for deployment. OMS should be able to resolve the fully qualified domain name (FQDN) of compute instances. This can be achieved by adding the FQDN of compute nodes in the /etc/hosts file on the OMS server. It is better to include the OMS server's FQDN/IP address to cloud VM instances as well to avoid name resolution. Additionally, SSH public and private keys would be needed on the EM console host from where you are going to discover the cloud instances.

In addition, you need to get the passwords for ASM, SCAN name, and a database account (ideally DBSNMP with required privileges); these are needed for target discovery, additionally make sure you have an open port for agent communication. For details please refer to Oracle Enterprise Manager Agent requirements for adding database and host targets.

You need to make sure there is sufficient disk space on the compute VMs. Normally it takes around 1 GB space for the agent deployment, and you should check the prerequisites in the documentation. You need to identify the mountpoint that will hold the binaries as well the permissions on this directory.

Once you have these details, you can create named credentials for the Exadata cloud compute nodes. OMS uses private SSH keys to access compute nodes and gives the opc and oracle users a passwordless authentication.

Please refer to Chapter 11 for steps to create a SSH public,private key pair using key-gen utilities.

Once you are done with the SSH key generation, you can create credentials for the oracle and opc users.

Creating the Credentials

This section lists the steps for creating credentials for the oracle and opc users.

Here's how to create a named credential for the user oracle:

1. Navigate to Setup ➤ Security ➤ Named Credentials.

2. Click Create and provide a name for it.

3. Make sure Authenticating Target Type is set to Host.

4. For the credential type, select the SSH key.

5. Set Scope to global.

6. Select the SSH private key for the VM by browsing and uploading it from the saved location and open it.

7. Do not specify any run privilege.

8. Save the configuration and ignore the warning that the host is not discovered.

To create the credentials for the user opc, all the steps are the same except you need to select Sudo for the run privilege as well enter **root** for Run as. The reason is that the opc user has sudo access root as well as oracle, grid OS accounts on any cloud compute VM's provisioned in OCI.

Deploying the Oracle Enterprise Manager Cloud Control Agent

Once the prerequisite steps are done, you can deploy OEM Cloud Control agents on ExaCS compute nodes.

Standard Agent Deployment on ExaCS with a VPN

You need to make sure the ports for OMS and agent communication are open and enabled through security rules. Name resolution to and from OMS to the ExaCS compute instance should be working before attempting to deploy the agent. The steps needed to deploy the agents are as follows:

1. Navigate to Setup ➤ Add Target ➤ Add Target Manually.

2. Select the install agent on the host and click Add.

3. Enter the FQDN or IP address of the compute node on ExaCS, and select Linux x86_64 for the platform. We assume that your OMS is installed on a Linux host, so it will have an agent for Linux x86_64 in place. If your OMS is running on another operating system, make sure you have the required agent binaries in place before attempting the deployment. Click Next.

4. Specify the installation directory and select the named credential for `oracle` as well the root credential. The root credential will use the `opc` user as configured earlier.

5. Select the port for deployment and click Next.

After reviewing all the inputs, click Deploy Agent. It might take 15 to 30 minutes to get deployed, and you can review the progress from the OEM console.

Summary

In this chapter, you learned how to deploy agents on ExaCS database VMs. You can manage clusters, ASM, database performance management, and more from OEM Cloud Control.

Index

A

ACFS creation
  ASM, source cluster, 194, 196
  standby
    clusterware resource, 197
    GI home owner, 197
ACFS file system
  database volumes, 456
  EM cloud control, 457–458
  nondatabase volumes, 456
  ODA, 455
  reinstallation, 466
ACFS replication
  primary initiation, 204
  standby node
    ADVM compatibility
      attribute, 202–203
    initiation command, 202
    standby filesystems, 203
  testing, 205, 207
Active automatic workload repository
    (AWR), 296, 479
  reports, 300–302
  snapshots, 300
Agent base, 92
agentClientId, 628
Agent deployment, ExaCS, 666–667
Agent home, 92
agentIdcsScope, 623

Agent instance, 92
agentInstanceDirectory, 620
ALTCDB broker configuration, 329
ALTCDB Post-Migration, 332–333
ALTER DISKGROUP command, 237, 239
apt-get command, 140
ASM configuration assistant
    (ASMCA), 233, 458
ASM_DISKSTRING parameter, 189, 193
ASM filter driver (AFD)
  configuration, 188
  manual configuration, 189–193
  Oracle 12c R2 (12.2) Grid
    Infrastructure, 187
Automatic approach, hybrid DR
  DG readiness check, 57, 59–60
  NOLOGGING class, 54
  Oracle DBaaS, 54
  Oracle Storage Cloud Service, 56
  RPM installation, 57
  storage container, 61
  storage creation, 55
Automatic diagnostic
    repository (ADR), 283
Automatic storage
    management (ASM), 471
Automatic teller machines (ATMs), 1
Auto service request (ASR), 424
Availability domains (ADs), 523

© Y V Ravi Kumar, Nassyam Basha, Krishna Kumar K M, Bal Mukund Sharma, Konstantin Kerekovski 2019
Y V Ravi Kumar et al., *Oracle High Availability, Disaster Recovery, and Cloud Services*,
https://doi.org/10.1007/978-1-4842-4351-0

S